IN STEP WITH GOD'S WORD

INTERPRETING THE NEW TESTAMENT WITH GOD'S PEOPLE

IN STEP WITH GOD'S WORD

INTERPRETING THE NEW TESTAMENT WITH GOD'S PEOPLE

FREDRICK J. LONG

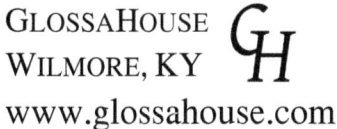

GlossaHouse
Wilmore, KY
www.glossahouse.com

IN STEP WITH GOD'S WORD
INTERPRETING THE NEW TESTAMENT WITH GOD'S PEOPLE

© 2017 by GlossaHouse

All rights reserved. No part of this work may be reproduced or transmitted in any form or by any means, electronic or mechanical, including photocopying and recording, or by means of any information storage or retrieval system, except as may be expressly permitted by the 1976 Copyright Act or in writing from the publisher. Requests for permission should be addressed in writing to:

GlossaHouse, LLC
110 Callis Circle Wilmore,
KY 40390

Publisher's Cataloging-in-Publication Data

Long, Fredrick J., 1966-

In step with God's word : interpreting the New Testament with God's people / Fredrick J. Long. – Wilmore, KY : GlossaHouse, ©2017.

xiv, 479 pages : illustrations ; 28 cm–(GlossaHouse hermeneutics & translation series ; vol. 1)

Includes bibliographical references and indexes.
ISBN 9781942697299 (hardback)
ISBN 9781942697183 (paperback)

1. Bible. New Testament --Hermeneutics. 2. Bible. New Testament—Criticism, interpretation, etc. I. Title. II. Series.

Library of Congress Control Number: 2017932173
BS2331.L663 2017   225.6

Scripture quotations identified by NASB are from the NEW AMERICAN STANDARD Bible, © Copyright The Lockman Foundation 1960, 1962, 1963, 1968, 1971, 1972, 1973, 1975, 1977, 1995. Used by permission. Quotations identified by NIV (and NIV84) are from THE HOLY Bible: NEW INTERNATIONAL VERSION © 1973, 1978, 1984, 2011 by International Bible Society. Used by permission of Zondervan Publishing House. All rights reserved. Scripture quotations identified by ESV are from The Holy Bible, English Standard Version®, © 2001 by Crossway Bibles, a division of Good News Publishers. Used by permission. All rights reserved. Scripture quotations identified by NLT are taken from the *Holy Bible* New Living Translation, © 1996, 2004, 2007. Used by permission of Tyndale House Publishers, Carol Stream, Illinois 60188. All rights reserved. Scripture quotations identified by NET are taken from the NET Bible First Editions © 1996–2005 Biblical Studies Press. Used by permission. All rights reserved. Scripture quotations identified by HCSB are taken from *The Holy Bible: Hol-man Christian Standard Version* © 2002, 2003, 2009 Holman Bible Publishers. Used by permission. All rights reserved. Scrip-ture quotations identified as RSV and NRSV are from the Revised Standard Version and the New Revised Standard Version Bible, copyright © 1971 and 1989, respectively, Division of Christian Education of the National Council of the Churches of Christ in the U.S.A., and are used by permission. All rights reserved. Scripture quotations identified by NA and UBS are copy-righted 1993, 1994, 1998, 2000, 2012, 2014 by the German Bible Society. All rights reserved. Scripture quotations identified by SBLGNT are copyrighted 2010 by Lexham Press and the Society of Biblical Literature.

The fonts used to create this work are available from www.linguistsoftware.com/lgku.htm.
Book Design and Typesetting by Fredrick J. Long (printing version 4, March 2018).
Cover Design by T. Michael W. Halcomb.

For my Mentors and Students

I dedicate *In Step with God's Word* to two groups of people.

First, I am thoroughly indebted to those who have mentored me in method at each stage of my journey in graduate and post-graduate education:

- David R. Bauer (Inductive Bible Study) during seminary at Asbury Theological Seminary
- A. Ross Scaife, in fond memory (Classical Greek Literature) during my masters work at the University of Kentucky who oversaw my application of discourse analysis to the Tyrannicides Discourse in Thucydides
- Julian V. Hills (Historical-Criticism, especially Form Criticism) during my doctoral studies at Marquette University
- Carol Kern Stockhausen, my Doktormutter (Intertextuality and Rhetorical Criticism) at Marquette University
- Vernon K. Robbins (Socio-Rhetorical Interpretation) in my postdoctoral research with the Rhetoric of Religious Antiquities study group

Many thanks to each of you! I have been so enriched by your pedagogy, your concern for proper methodology, and your example of excellence in Biblical and Classical Studies. My apologies for any inadequacies and deficiencies in my methodological and hermeneutical reflections.

Second, I dedicate this work to my many students in various settings and levels of formal educa-tion: Sunday school, adult education, undergraduate programs, graduate studies, and postgraduate research. You have been my "experimental subjects" willingly (and at times unwillingly) endur-ing my high expectations, many assignments, and poor hand-writing in marking your papers. I have learned so much with you and from you. In the context of our learning together, many in-sights have emerged that otherwise would not have. In this regard I must also acknowledge the Lord who has helped all of us greatly to comprehend the truth of His Word. This manual of Bible interpretation incorporates much material that I have developed for our study of God's Word in our classes together; it is a culmination of the inspiration that you all have given me.

Thank you!

GlossaHouse Hermeneutics & Translation Series

Volume 1

Contents

Acknowledgements   x
List of Charts, Graphics, and Illustrations   xi

Part I: Foundations for Walking in Step with God's Word

How to Use this Book   3
Chapter Alpha: A Foundation for Interpreting Scripture   9
    I. God the Father's and Jesus's Interpretive Community   9
    II. Communal Exegesis   26
    III. The Holy Spirit's Role in Scriptural Interpretation   29

    IV. The Nature of the Subject of Our Devotion and Study   33
    V. Priorities and Pursuits of Scriptural Study   37
    VI. Principles of Scriptural Study   40
    VII. Core Interpretive Areas, Tasks, and Skills   42

Part II: Walking Inside and Around the Word

Step 1: Contextual Location   49
    I. Primary Survey   50
       Primary Interpretive Procedures   63
    II. Secondary Study   63
       Secondary Interpretive Procedures   67
    III. Tertiary Research   68
       Tertiary Interpretive Procedures   71
    IV. Bibliography   71

Step 2: Textual Comparisons   73
    I. Primary Survey   74
       Primary Interpretive Procedures   82
    II. Secondary Study   82
       Secondary Interpretive Procedures   96
    III. Tertiary Research   96
       Tertiary Interpretive Procedures   101
    IV. Bibliography   102

Step 3: Grammatical Study   105
    I. Primary Survey   106
       Primary Interpretive Procedures   117

II. SECONDARY STUDY	117
SECONDARY INTERPRETIVE PROCEDURES	138
III. TERTIARY RESEARCH	139
TERTIARY INTERPRETIVE PROCEDURES	147
IV. BIBLIOGRAPHY	147

STEP 4: SEMANTIC ANALYSIS — 150

I. PRIMARY SURVEY	151
PRIMARY INTERPRETIVE PROCEDURES	166
II. SECONDARY STUDY & III. TERTIARY RESEARCH	166
SECONDARY AND TERTIARY INTERPRETIVE PROCEDURES	172
IV. BIBLIOGRAPHY	172

PART III: EXPLORING AROUND AND OUTSIDE THE WORD

STEP 5: LEXICAL RESEARCH — 175

I. PRIMARY SURVEY	176
PRIMARY INTERPRETIVE PROCEDURES	186
II. SECONDARY STUDY	188
SECONDARY INTERPRETIVE PROCEDURES	191
III. TERTIARY RESEARCH	193
TERTIARY INTERPRETIVE PROCEDURES	210
IV. BIBLIOGRAPHY	213

STEP 6: LITERARY FORMS — 215

I. PRIMARY SURVEY	216
PRIMARY INTERPRETIVE PROCEDURES	229
II. SECONDARY STUDY	230
SECONDARY INTERPRETIVE PROCEDURES	241
III. TERTIARY RESEARCH	242
TERTIARY INTERPRETIVE PROCEDURES	251
IV. BIBLIOGRAPHY	252

STEP 7: HISTORICAL CONTEXT — 253

I. PRIMARY SURVEY	252
PRIMARY INTERPRETIVE PROCEDURES	267
II. SECONDARY STUDY	267
SECONDARY INTERPRETIVE PROCEDURES	272
III. TERTIARY RESEARCH	272
TERTIARY INTERPRETIVE PROCEDURES	287
IV. BIBLIOGRAPHY	288

Step 8: Scriptural Correlations — 293
- I. Primary Survey — 294
  - Primary Interpretive Procedures — 309
- II. Secondary Study — 309
  - Secondary Interpretive Procedures — 318
- III. Tertiary Research — 319
  - Tertiary Interpretive Procedures — 334
- IV. Bibliography — 334

Part IV: Moving Towards Appropriating the Word

Step 9: Interpretive Decisions — 339
- I. Primary Survey & II. Secondary Study — 340
  - Primary and Secondary Interpretive Procedures — 359
- III. Tertiary Research — 362
  - Tertiary Procedure: Structural Notes for Writing an Academic Paper — 367
- IV. Bibliography — 369

Step 10: Biblical Theology — 370
- I. Primary Survey — 371
  - Primary Interpretive Procedures — 381
- II. Secondary Study & III. Tertiary Research — 382
  - Secondary and Tertiary Interpretive Procedures — 391
- IV. Bibliography — 392

Step 11: Evaluated Applications — 397
- I. Primary Survey — 398
  - Primary Interpretive Procedures — 418
- II. Secondary Study — 421
  - Secondary Interpretive Procedures — 425
- III. Tertiary Research — 428
- IV. Bibliography — 430

Step 12: Presentation Brainstorm — 431
- Perspectives on Stories, Analogies, and Illustrations — 432
- Presentation Brainstorm Procedures — 444

Part V: Embodying and Awaiting the Word

Chapter Omega: A Postlude on Embodiment & An Eschatology for the Future — 447

Indices
- Author — 449
- Subject — 454
- Chart, Diagram, & Illustration Index — 463
- Scripture & Other Ancient Texts and Artifacts — 466

Acknowledgements

Many people have helped proofread and correct mistakes in this book, too many to name and some I have forgotten (my apologies). I want especially to thank Doug Phillips, Ryan Giffin, Kevin Southerland, Kei Hiramatsu, Shawn Craigmiles, Benson Goh, Nathan Rickard, and Lindsay Rickard for working through one or more of these chapters. Any mistakes that remain are entirely my fault and do not reflect poorly on their fine and much appreciated efforts.

List of Charts, Graphics, and Illustrations

How to Use this Book
The Interpretive Journey	4
Biblical Book Abbreviations	7
Common Abbreviations	8

Chapter Alpha: A Foundation for Interpreting Scripture
OT Scripture in the Book of Acts	24
Matrix of our Critical-Literary Approach to Scripture	27
The Word of God Permeating the Community of God's People	28
The Family of Interpretive Principles	41
How to Study the Bible (graphic by Wilbert Webster White)	44
The Interpretive Journey ("you are here")	45

Step 1: Contextual Location
Levels of Context	50
Hebrew Bible or *TaNaK (Torah, Nebi'im, Kethubim)* or Old Testament	51
The New Testament in Canonical Order	52
The Protestant Old Testament = 39 Books	53
Historical Factors in NT Canon Formation	56
Standard Abbreviations of Books and Bibles according to the Society of Biblical Literature (SBL)	58
Abbreviations for Common English Translations	58
Common Abbreviations	59
Major Semantic Relationships	68
Supporting Semantic Relationships that Help Convey MSRs	69

Step 2: Textual Comparisons
"Extra" Verses: A Comparison of English Versions	75
"Missing" Verses in the NIV with Explanation in Footnotes	76
Paleography of New Testament Manuscripts	78
Extant Manuscripts of the NT	79
Early Church Fathers' Quotations of the NT	79
Comparison of Classical Texts and the NT	80
Papyrus 52	82, 97
Commonly Confused Uncial Letters	85
Depiction of Text Distribution through Locales	87
NA^{27} Textual Variants in 1 Cor 2:1–5	91
UBS^4 Textual Variants and Apparati in 1 Cor 2:1–5	92
Comparison of Textual Variant Entries for 2 Cor 3:9 in Textual and Other Commentaries	94

Textual Variants of Rom 12:1–2 in the NA²⁷	98
Important *Sigla* of GNT Critical Editions	98
Manuscripts Identified by Text-Type Location	99

Step 3: Grammatical Study

The Parts of Speech	108
Important Characteristics of Verbs	110
Types of Clausal Connections	113
Types of Phrasal Meanings	113
Basic Observations for Narratives or Stories	114
English Grammar and Constituent Marking	115
Sophy Hollington's Artwork ("Hope" in Greek Study)	117
Greek Grammar and Constituent Marking	118
"Semantics" of Coordinating & Subordinating Conjunctions	120
Processing Constraints of Coordinating Connectors	122
Processing Constraints of Subordinating Connectors	124
Phrasal Modifying Relations	126
Greek Pronouns (with occurrence in the GNT)	127
Common Verbal Aspect and *Aktionsart* "Categories"	129
Verbal Aspect and Pragmatic Functions of Tenses in Narratives	130
Frequency of Greek Verb Tenses and Moods	132
Word Order Variations and Prominence	141
Emphatic and Pragmatic Constructions Indicating Prominence	145

Step 4: Semantic Analysis

Major Semantic Relationships	152
Supporting Semantic Relationships to Help Convey MSRs	152
Zones (of Semantic Diagramming)	156–59
Types of Modifiers	159
Semantic Analysis of Rom 5:10–11	164
Types of Greek Modifiers	167
Types of Modifiers and Zones	168

Step 5: Lexical Research

Levels of Context	176
Greek Synonyms of "Body" in the NT	184
LXX Usage Graphic for Περιπατέω	190
Chiastic Structure of Eph 5:22–24	205
Σωτήρ and Close Cognates in the NT	206
Σωτήρ and Close Cognates before the Second-Century AD	207
Artifacts of the Emperor and Roma Cult	210

STEP 6: LITERARY FORMS

MAJOR BIBLICAL GENRES	217
FEATURES OF BIBLICAL LISTS	220
A CATALOG OF NT LISTS	224
TEACHING FORMS OF JESUS	225
AUGUSTINE'S ALLEGORICAL INTERPRETATION OF GOOD SAMARITAN PARABLE	227
BLOMBERG'S DESCRIPTION OF COMMON PARABLES STRUCTURES	227
GRECO-ROMAN PERSONAL *DOCUMENTARY* LETTER FORMS	233
PAULINE EPISTOLARY AND RHETORICAL FORMS	234
MODES OF PERSUASION	236
SMITH'S OBJECTIVE CRITERIA TO EVALUATE CHIASMS	238
TYPES OF LITERARY FORMS IN THE NT	239
GUIDANCE FOR IDENTIFYING THE PRESENCE OF LITERARY FORMS	240
BLENDED SPACES & LOCATIONS IN EARLY CHRISTIAN RHETOROLECTS	243
"ARENAS" OF ANCIENT RHETORICAL INVENTION	244
"AREAS" FOR INVESTIGATING NT RHETORIC	245
CHIASM OF EPHESIANS 2:11–22	249

STEP 7: HISTORICAL CONTEXT

IMPORTANT OT DATES (WITH *BIBLICAL SOURCES*)	254
IMPORTANT INTERTESTAMENTAL DATES	255
IMPORTANT NT DATES (WITH *BIBLICAL SOURCES*)	255
IMPORTANT POST-NEW TESTAMENT DATES (WITH *SOURCES*)	255
A MORE-DETAILED NT CHRONOLOGY	256
CRITICAL-REALISM AND HISTORICAL INQUIRY	259
WARNING INSCRIPTION OF FOREIGNERS ENTERING THE JEWISH TEMPLE AREA	265
WOMEN'S HEAD COVERINGS	271
SOCIAL, CULTURAL, AND IDEOLOGICAL TOPOI IN EPH 2:10	276
IMAGE OF A DENARIUS COIN MINTED UNDER TIBERIUS	277
STRUCTURAL DEPICTION OF EPH 5:22–27	279
SUMMARY OF KEY OBSERVATIONS AND QUESTIONS FOR EPH 5:22–33	280
SEARCH RESULTS FROM THE PHI SEARCHABLE INSCRIPTIONAL DATABASE	281
TWO SAMPLE INSCRIPTIONS OF THE ROMAN IMPERIAL PERIOD WITH ἔνδοξος	281

STEP 8: SCRIPTURAL CORRELATIONS

RELATIONSHIPS BETWEEN THE SYNOPTIC GOSPELS	295
A "PROPHECY" OF NOSTRADAMUS	300
SCRIPTURE QUOTATION AND CITATION IN MATTHEW	302
MAJOR TYPES OF THE NT'S USE OF THE OT	306

COMPARISON OF FOOTNOTES OF SELECT MODERN ENGLISH TRANSLATIONS	307
FIRST-CENTURY MEDITERRANEAN EDUCATIONAL SYSTEMS	313
THE SEVEN RULES OF HILLEL	316
TEXT-TYPES AND COMMUNAL EXEGETICAL TRADITIONS	321
VALIDATION CRITERIA FOR INTERTEXTUAL ALLUSIONS OR ECHOES	323
EXPLICITNESS AND ELABORATION OF OT QUOTATIONS	325

STEP 9: INTERPRETIVE DECISIONS

ANALYTICAL INTERPRETIVE WORKFLOW	344
INTERPRETATION OF MATT 5:19	347
ESSENTIAL ELEMENTS OF A RESEARCH PROJECT	362
CONSTRUCTION OF AN ARGUMENT PLAN	363

STEP 10: BIBLICAL THEOLOGY

MAJOR THEOLOGICAL TOPICS	372
THEOLOGICAL SOURCES → TAKEN TO EXTREMES	375
NINE THESES OF THEOLOGICAL INTERPRETATION	378
GOD'S HISTORY OF REVELATION AND MAJOR THEOLOGICAL CATEGORIES	382
INTERRELATION OF THE MAJOR BRANCHES OF THEOLOGY	386
RÉSUMÉ OF THEOLOGICAL THEMES FROM PAUL'S QUOTATION OF SCRIPTURE	389
INDEX OF THEOLOGICAL TOPICS FROM PAUL'S QUOTATION OF SCRIPTURE	389

STEP 11: EVALUATED APPLICATIONS

CONTINUUM OF PARTICULARITY AND TRANSCENDENCE	399
THE CYCLE OF VALUES	403
LITERALISM VS. SKEPTICISM	405
THE PRINCIPLIZING BRIDGE	407
THE SEVEN FOCAL LENSES OF SCRIPTURE	411
THE CONTEXTS OF THEOLOGICAL EXEGESIS	415
HOW TO BEST INTERPRET THE OT LAW: SOME "DOS" AND "DON'TS"	416
PRINCIPLES OF BIBLICAL ETHICS	421
MAIN TYPES OF BIBLICAL DISCOURSE	423

STEP 12: PRESENTATION BRAINSTORM

LIFE DOMAINS AS METAPHORS IN THE PAULINE EPISTLES	434
THE AGORA AND ENVIRONS OF ROMAN CORINTH	439
INFOGRAPHICS FOR PHILIPPIANS	440
DOS AND DON'TS WHEN USING STORIES AND ANALOGIES	441

Part I:

Foundations for Walking in Step with God's Word

How to Use this Book

As much as we might wish that Scripture were a direct pipeline of truth to us today, in fact, the Bible is firmly rooted in time and space, cultures and languages that are quite different from our own. Although our various translations help mediate what is communicated divinely to us, each translation represents an interpretation; translations typically are unable to communicate all that is present and sometimes, even worse, they too often obscure important facets of the content.

This book presents an incremental approach to Bible study involving PRIMARY SURVEY, SECONDARY STUDY, and TERTIARY RESEARCH of the New Testament (NT) from a procedural perspective of twelve interpretive "areas" or "places" of investigation that are described as STEPS. By using STEPS, I am deliberately using a spatial metaphor of walking since the STEPS are incremental, progressive, directional, and purposeful. The STEPS reflect a movement and journey through and around the biblical text and its world to our modern contexts and world. It is certainly possible to jump around from step to step, or to play hopscotch, so to speak. However, the progressive STEPS are what might be considered "best practices" of biblical interpretation. So, to the extent that we are able to move with Scripture itself, to the world around it, and to its unfolding story and then merge it into our own story in the world, the more likely we will have maintained the integrity of Scripture, ourselves, and our understanding of God as we esteem each accordingly and properly.

These STEPS include foundational perspectives on the nature of Scripture in order to offer understanding of distinct interpretive areas. The STEPS foster the development of critical skill sets with specific interpretive procedures and are often enabled or enhanced by utilizing strategic resources. Importantly, this book conjoins traditional exegetical approaches (such as textual criticism, grammatical analysis, lexical research, historical context), the hermeneutics and methodology of inductive biblical study (such as book surveys, detailed semantic analysis, interpretation, evaluation, appropriation), and the transmodern perspective of socio-rhetorical interpretation (such as intertexture, social-cultural texture, rhetorolects, and sensory-aesthetic texture).[1] Also, since proper interpretation entails human development in that interpreters seek to progress in their relationship with God, self, others, and all of creation, the interpretive journey encourages growth in observing, asking, researching, interpreting, evaluating, applying, appropriating, and proclaiming biblical truth within the context of God's people who are called to give testimony in word and deed to God's presence in the world.

Each exegetical area is introduced in full as a distinct STEP that is described first in principle, then illustrated with examples and practiced with in-text exercises, and finally operationalized in a list of procedures. A depiction of the Journey through the STEPS is given on the next page. The

---

[1] For Inductive Bible Study see the works of David R. Bauer and Robert A. Traina; for socio-rhetorical interpretation, see the works of Vernon K. Robbins.

STEPS traverse around the Alpha and Omega progressively from top left down to top right. They may be understood in groups of four. The first four STEPS (1–4) entail *walking around inside the biblical passage*; the next four STEPS (5–8) involve *walking from within to outside the passage*. The final four STEPS (9–12) move us towards *hearing and appropriating the passage today*. As depicted, a central focus is on STEP 9: INTERPRETIVE DECISIONS since this STEP marks a critical moment where data as evidence are gathered from the prior STEPS and then weighed as we make decisions—even as tentative and provisional as they may (need to) be at times—regarding the meaning of particularly difficult questions arising from the passage under investigation.

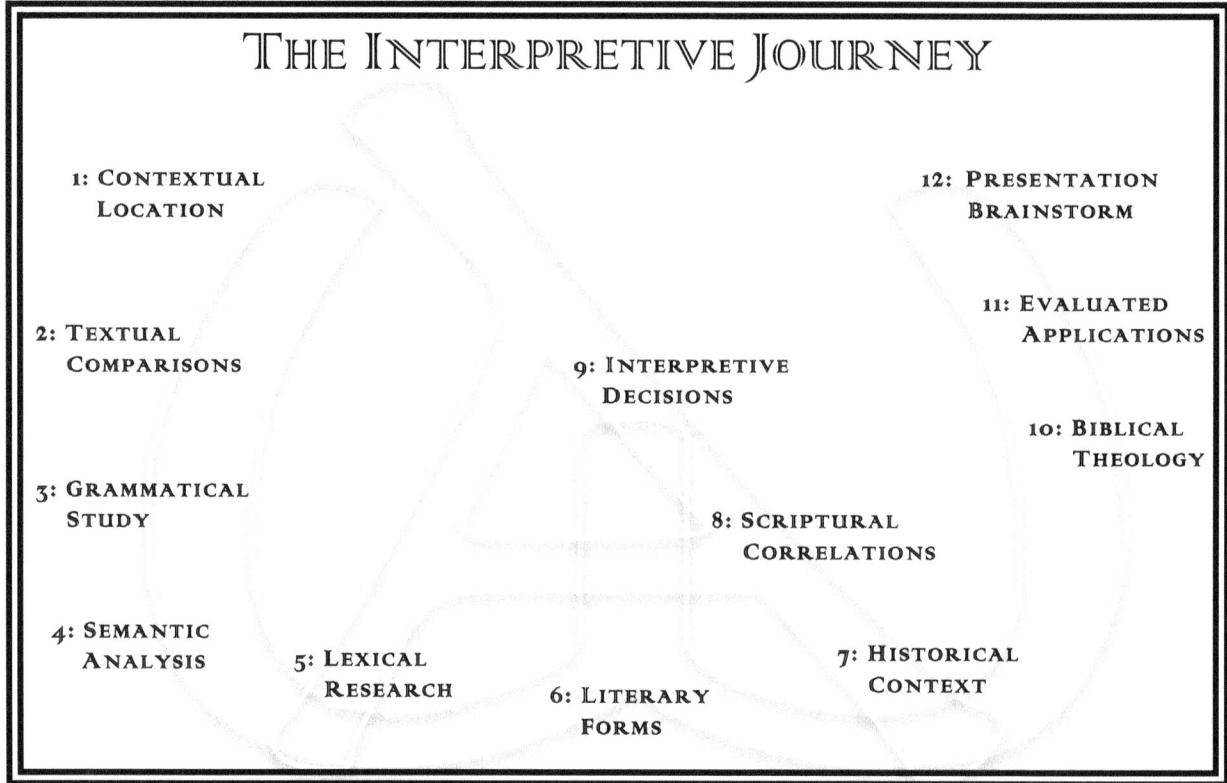

I have added an incremental dimension when describing most of the STEPS of interpretation. Thus, I will present interpretive perspectives, examples, skills, and procedures at primary, secondary, and tertiary levels—depending on one's ability to access Greek and academic resources. These levels reflect respectively what I might consider to be an average good goal for educated laity (PRIMARY SURVEY), pastors (SECONDARY STUDY), and postgraduate/doctoral students (TERTIARY RESEARCH). Hence, *In Step with God's Word* could function as an instruction manual of biblical interpretation for willing and able lay persons, for graduate students and pastors/teachers, and for postgraduate students doing advanced research in the field of Biblical Studies. With time, effort, training, and practice, people are able incrementally to develop and advance in their interpretive skills under each of the twelve exegetical areas, thus growing into the next level of study from PRIMARY SURVEY to SECONDARY STUDY and finally to TERTIARY RESEARCH.

For example, within STEP 2: TEXTUAL COMPARISONS the interpretive task is presented incrementally as follows: At the PRIMARY level of SURVEY (laity) after discussing where our New Testament texts come from and how manuscripts were copied and transmitted, a person learns to access Bible notes in English translations that discuss different manuscript readings or what are called "variants"; likewise, someone understands how and why to compare English translations. At the SECONDARY level of STUDY (pastors), I provide a discussion of critical editions of the Greek NT and explain how to best utilize the United Bible Society's Greek NT critical editions (=UBS$^{3/4/5}$) and as well as other helpful resources like Roger L. Omanson and Bruce M. Metzger, *A Textual Guide to the Greek New Testament: An Adaptation of Bruce M. Metzger's Textual Commentary for the Needs of Translators* (Stuttgart: Deutsche Bibelgesellschaft, 2006). A pastor would also be able to evaluate whether or not to mention and comment on any significant textual variants in the biblical passage depending on the preaching or teaching setting. Lastly, at a TERTIARY level of RESEARCH (postgraduate), I offer a more complete understanding of text-critical methodology and research for accessing and engaging the critical edition of the Greek NT of Nestle-Aland 27th/28th editions (NA$^{27/28}$) as well as other advanced resources such as the *Editio Critica Maior* (ECM) prepared by the University of Muenster and the University of Birmingham that have interactive databases available online.[2] It is incumbent for doctoral students to address the most significant textual variants in their exegetical research and writing for any given passage; sometimes even the less significant variants need attention depending on the research question.

Throughout *In Step with God's Word*, I have used several ways to identify important information. First, I have typically organized each STEP and its chapter as follows: STEP identified, STEP icon, quotable quote(s), brief introduction, and then incremental discussions with interpretive procedures concluding with a bibliography. Altogether this looks for STEP 3 as follows:

STEP 3: GRAMMATICAL STUDY
    STEP Icon & Quotable Quote(s)
    Introduction
    I. PRIMARY SURVEY
        PRIMARY INTERPRETIVE PROCEDURES
    II. SECONDARY STUDY
        SECONDARY INTERPRETIVE PROCEDURES
    III. TERTIARY RESEARCH
        TERTIARY INTERPRETIVE PROCEDURES
    IV. BIBLIOGRAPHY

> Textboxes function as "metacomments" to help draw attention to important points of the discussion.

Second, I have used italics to stress important points that sometimes are placed within textboxes to give them even more prominence. *You should think of these textboxes as "metacomments" to help draw your attention to important points of the discussion.*

---

[2] http://egora.uni-muenster.de/intf/index_en.shtml.

Third, throughout each interpretive STEP are found in-text **EXERCISES** that are marked in CAPS, **bold underline**, and placed within grey highlighting. These exercises will give readers a chance to continue thinking about some aspect of interpretation and how to apply it in principle and practice with a variety of issues from various NT texts. Occasionally, in the immediately following discussion I will provide *some* guidance or perspective for completing these in-text exercises; but typically, you are on your own. It is conceivable that a supplemental book will be developed that offers outlines of suitable answers for these in-text exercises. (We'll see!)

Fourth, concluding each major incremental section of PRIMARY SURVEY, SECONDARY STUDY, and TERTIARY RESEARCH are sections called **PRIMARY INTERPRETIVE PROCEDURES**, **SECONDARY INTERPRETIVE PROCEDURES**, and **TERTIARY INTERPRETIVE PROCEDURES** that provide **specific procedures placed in bold type** sometimes with additional explanations. These procedures offer "best interpretive practices" that represent a sound and incrementally appropriate interpretive workflow. After gaining proficiency in the procedures, one may combine or abbreviate them; however, in general I encourage people to follow the procedures in the order given. Students may accomplish these procedures in the context of writing an "Interpretive Report" for that STEP. In the reports I encourage clarity, accuracy, proper citation, completeness, conciseness, and creativity. When conducting your research and creating your interpretive reports, try to implement the following characteristics:

1. *clarity of what you are saying* so that others can follow and understand your work;
2. *proper citing of sources* so that someone could verify and retrieve that same data;
3. *completeness* and *thoroughness* of gathering information for *all* verses treated; but also
4. *selectivity*, *conciseness*, and *creativity* of gathering and presenting information; and
5. *relevance of your interpretive work* for the proclamation of the truth of the gospel and the ongoing mission of God's people in the world.

In a forthcoming follow up book (mostly written already!), I will provide "model" SAMPLE STEPS that perform the interpretive procedures sequentially at each incremental level on Romans 12:1–8, which is among my favorite NT passages and in many ways foundational for Christian living.

Finally, throughout I will generally follow the practices of citing, abbreviating, and referring to biblical and other materials as found in the *Society of Biblical Literature (SBL) Handbook of Style*, 2nd ed. (Atlanta: SBL Press, 2014). For abbreviations to journals and volumes in this book, please consult this *Handbook*. To begin summarizing the essentials, at §8.2 this specifies:

> Books of the Bible cited without chapter (or chapter and verse) should ordinarily be spelled out in the main text. Books of the Bible cited with chapter are more commonly abbreviated unless they come at the beginning of the sentence. [from 1st ed: "All occurrences of biblical books in parentheses and footnotes should be abbreviated."] Authors citing more than one translation of the Bible must indicate which translation is used in a particular citation. When this citation is in parentheses, a comma is not needed between the reference and the abbreviation of the translation, as is indicated in the fourth example below.

Correct:	The passage in 1 Cor 5 is often considered crucial.	
	The passage, 1 Cor 5:6, is often considered crucial.	
	First Corinthians 5:6 is a crucial text.	
	"Do you not know that a little yeast leavens the whole batch of dough?" (1 Cor 5:6 NRSV).	
Incorrect:	1 Cor 5:6 is a crucial text.	
	1 Corinthians 5:6 is a crucial text.	

Below are common biblical books and their abbreviations. Notice that no period is added to the abbreviations. Also, 1–4 Kgdms refers to the books 1–2 Samuel and 1–2 Kings as are found in the Septuagint (LXX), a Greek translation of the OT.

BIBLICAL BOOK ABBREVIATIONS

OT= Old Testament				NT= New Testament		
Gen	Isa	Nah	Ruth	Matt	Phil	1-2-3 John
Exod	Jer	Hab	Song [Cant]	Mark	Col	Jude
Lev	Ezek	Zeph	Eccl [Qoh]	Luke	1-2 Thess	Rev
Num	Hos	Hag	Lam	John	1-2 Tim	
Deut	Joel	Zech	Esth	Acts	Titus	
Josh	Amos	Mal	Dan	Rom	Phlm	
Judg	Obad	Ps (Pss)	Ezra	1-2 Cor	Heb	
1-2 Sam	Jonah	Job	Neh	Gal	Jas	
1-2 Kgs	Mic	Prov	1-2 Chr	Eph	1-2 Pet	
1-4 Kgdms [in LXX]						

Just as important as using correct abbreviations is the proper use of punctuation. Below is a summary of the most common situations:

- A **colon** separates chapter numbers from verse numbers (e.g., Num 10:1).
- An **en dash** signifies a span verses or chapters (e.g., Exod 1:10–30; Zech 1:1–3:4).
- Use **commas** to separate verses from within the same chapter (e.g., Rom 1:1, 3, 5, 7, 9).
- Use **semicolons** to separate verses from different chapters of the same source or between sources (e.g., Matt 1:15, 19; 6:16–20; 9:10–11:2; Luke 1:2–5).
- When citing only **book chapters**, use the abbreviated book title: Rom 9–11 or 1 Cor 5.
- Write out the complete book number at the beginning of a sentence: "Second Corinthians is Paul's most argumentative letter" **rather than** "2 Corinthians is argumentative."
- To indicate parallel passages, use **double lines** //; e.g., Matt 11:2–6//Luke 7:18–23.

As much as possible one should use common abbreviations like OT, HB, NT, etc. as well as the proper abbreviations for dating. Further abbreviations are found in the *SBL Handbook of Style*, §8.1.2–3.

COMMON ABBREVIATIONS

AD = A*nno Domini* means "in the year of our Lord X" and thus is placed before the date.
BC = *Before Christ*
CE = Common Era; this has been increasingly used instead of AD.
BCE = Before the Common Era; this has been increasingly used instead of BC.
OT = Old Testament
HB = Hebrew Bible
LXX = Greek translation of the OT
MT = Masoretic Text. The Masoretic Jewish Scribes (sixth- to tenth-centuries CE) transmitted the HB and developed the vowel pointing, accents, and punctuation systems.

Some other common abbreviations include the following:

b. = born	**ibid.** = *ibidem* = in the same place
c. = century	**idem** = the same
ca. = *circa* = approximately (in dating)	**i.e.** = *id est* = that is,
cf. = *confere* = "compare with"	**κτλ.** = καὶ τὰ λοιπά = and the rest, etc.
ch. = chapter (*avoid ambiguity*)	**loc. cit.** = *loco citato* = in the place cited
chs. = chapters (*avoid ambiguity*)	**n.d.** = no date
cj. = conjecture	**n.p.** = no page or no place
d. = died	**op. cit.** = *opera citato* = in the work cited
e.g.= *exempli gratia* = "for example"	**q.v.** = *quod vide* = which see
ex. = example	**s.v.** = *sub verbo* = under the word (just referred to)
et al. = *et alia* = "and others"	**s.v.** = *sub verso* = under the verse (in question)
f. = the following verse	**v.** = verse (*avoid ambiguity*)
ff. = the following two verses	**vv.** = verses (*avoid ambiguity*)
fl. = *floruit* = he/she lived at this time	**viz.** = *videlicet* = namely

Although one may at times use v. and vv. and ch. and chs. when referring to verses and chapters, it is usually best to use chapter number and colon as in 5:4; never would one write this: ch. 5 v. 4. Also, one should not use f. and ff.; instead, one should give the exact verse range as in 5:4–5.

In the end, the goal of this book is to encourage laity and pastors, preachers and teachers to delve deeply into God's Word and to best appropriate and proclaim it in the world today. Scripture is best interpreted within the community of God's people who have both an opportunity to be enriched by the Word and a calling to be a blessing to all people. I hope that *In Step with God's Word* will help you align with the nature of Scripture as God's sufficient self-revelation culminating with Jesus himself who is truly a treasure-trove to be searched for, discovered, and shared.

—Fredrick J. Long
Ordinary Time 2017

Chapter Alpha

A Foundation for Interpreting Scripture

I. God the Father's and Jesus's Interpretive Community

Let me ask you to consider this question:

> What is *the most significant thing* that Jesus "did" or "said" after his resurrection and before his ascension *for the ongoing fruitful life and ministry of his followers*?

I earnestly believe that this question is the single most pressing one facing the global church today. At stake is our understanding of what Jesus has provided for his followers in order to continue his ministry on earth. This assumes that Jesus intended for his followers to continue his mission, but such a view is already justified by Jesus's repeated injunction, "If anyone wants to come after Me, let them deny themselves, take up their cross, and follow Me" (Matt 16:24; cf. Matt 10:38//Luke 14:27).[1] Then, too, the Great Commission in Matt 28:18–20 is given to Jesus's followers after his resurrection. Although not everyone in the church assembly is a missionary or an evangelist (cf. Eph 4:11), nevertheless everyone either prayerfully and/or financially supports one.

To answer the question above, then, first we should determine where in the NT Jesus's actions and speech between his resurrection and ascension are recorded. Let me offer these places along with a basic summary of the passage.

Matt 28:1–15 Resurrection of Jesus and the reports of the guards
Matt 28:16–20 Jesus gives the Great Commission
Mark 16:1–8 Two Marys and Salome at the tomb

---

[1] Unless otherwise noted, English translations are my own.

Luke 24:1–12 The Resurrection of Jesus
Luke 24:13–35 The walk to Emmaus
Luke 24:36–49 Jesus appears to his disciples
Luke 24:50–53 The ascension of Jesus
John 20:14–18 Jesus's first resurrection appearance
John 20:19–29 Jesus's next appearance to the disciples
John 21 Jesus's third resurrection appearance to the disciples
Acts 1:1–8 Prologue, resurrection appearance, and commission of Jesus
Acts 1:9–11 Ascension of Jesus and the comments of the two angels
1 Cor 15:1–8 Christ's Death and Resurrection according to the Scriptures and witnesses to Jesus's resurrection

Other passages that may possibly describe aspects of Jesus's actions or speech after his resurrection include the following:

Eph 4:8–9 Jesus "descended into the lower parts of the earth," which may (or may not) describe a place where Jesus went, such as Sheol/Hades (a "holding tank" for the dead) before ascending and being exalted to God's right hand; compare with 1 Pet 3:18–4:6 below.
1 Pet 3:18–22; 4:6 After "having died for sins once and for all… to bring us to God," Jesus preached to the spirits in prison, which may have occurred between his resurrection and ascension to the right hand of God.
Heb 1:3 Jesus "made purification of sins" before sitting at God's right hand.
Rev 5:5–6 Jesus "has conquered so as to open the book," i.e., Jesus gained a victory through his death.

These latter passages are difficult to interpret. However, these texts contribute to the question by affirming the aftermath of Jesus's resurrection and what this resurrection confirms about various aspects of Jesus's mission: he descended to the lower parts of the earth for a time (possibly "Hades"); he came to save people and purify them from their sins; he preached to imprisoned "spirits"; and generally, he conquered death.

Based especially on the former passages from the Gospels and Acts, let's now consider some viable answers to the question, "What is *the most significant thing* that Jesus 'did' after his resurrection and before his ascension *for the ongoing fruitful life and ministry of his followers?*" I've asked this question in every NT Introduction class I've taught. Here is list of the most common answers students have given:

- ❖ Jesus showed himself alive to the disciples.
- ❖ Jesus provided many signs that he was alive.
- ❖ Jesus breathed the Holy Spirit on the disciples.
- ❖ Jesus promised that the Holy Spirit would come with power for witnessing.
- ❖ Jesus restored Peter to his leadership position.

- ❖ Jesus issued the Great Commission.
- ❖ Jesus revealed himself in the breaking of the bread.

These are all great answers! We don't have to reject any of them and, in fact, we would do well to reflect on each of them. However, nestled among the accounts of the resurrection appearances and what Jesus said and did, Luke's Gospel preserves a recurring activity of Jesus after his resurrection: *He explains the Hebrew Scriptures to his disciples.* Jesus's explanation first occurs on the road to Emmaus. Poor Cleopas and his companion who were walking with Jesus in ignorance! Yet, how blessed they were! They walked from Jerusalem to Emmaus a distance of about eight miles—with the resurrected Jesus. With an average walking pace of 15 minutes per mile, this journey would have lasted about two hours. Imagine walking with the recently resurrected Jesus for two hours (assuming Jesus joined them very near to the start). We are told that their eyes were not opened to recognize him initially (presumably by God)—but why? *It would seem that the disciples' state of grief and puzzlement was allowed by God in order for them to be more attentive to what Jesus was explaining to them.*

> God allowed the disciples' state of grief and puzzlement in order for them to become more attentive to what the resurrected Jesus was explaining to them.

What was Jesus speaking to them about? Notice in 24:32 what Luke records just after Jesus finally reveals himself to them at the breaking of the bread: "They said to one another, 'Were not our hearts burning within us while He was speaking to us on the road while He was explaining the Scriptures to us?'" Their hearts were burning as Jesus had been explaining the Scriptures to them. Right away these two companions returned to Jerusalem to the eleven disciples and testified to Jesus's resurrection (24:33–34). Immediately, they began explaining to the other disciples about "the matters on the road" [i.e., Jesus's explaining the Scriptures to them] and how they recognized him at the breaking of the bread (24:35). At this very moment when Cleopas and his companion are relating their encounter, Jesus shows up in their midst! Imagine the shock; imagine the timing—right as they were explaining about their journey listening to Jesus's explanation about the Messiah from God's Word and how he was revealed at the breaking of the bread at the table, Jesus appears.

Next, after the disciples confirmed Jesus's identity and watched him eat some fish, Luke records Jesus saying this: "These are my words which I spoke to you while still being with you, that it is necessary that all that is written in the Law of Moses and the Prophets and the Psalms concerning me would be fulfilled" (24:44). *Right here Jesus promotes a Christocentric reading of the OT*—i.e, viewing the Hebrew Bible as concerned about the eventual coming of the Jewish Messiah. Moreover, he connects his explanation to what he had previously explained to the disciples before he died and was raised about the Scriptures. *There is continuity between Jesus's teaching of Scripture <u>before</u> he died and <u>after</u> he was resurrected.* Furthermore, Luke immediately explains what Jesus was doing for the disciples at this very moment (24:45–49a):

⁴⁵ At that time he opened their minds to understand the Scriptures ⁴⁶ and said this to them: 'Thus it has been written that the Messiah would suffer and be raised from the dead on the

third day [47] and repentance for the forgiveness of sins would be preached in his name into all the Nations. And beginning from Jerusalem, [48] you yourselves are witnesses of these things. [49a] And I myself will send the promise of my Father to you...'

How did Jesus open up their minds to understand the Scriptures? Well, simply, *he explained the Scriptures to them*. It is that simple. Moreover, we must remember that Jesus connected his opening of their minds to speaking to them earlier during his earthly ministry; he said, "These are my words which I spoke to you while I was still with you" (24:44). So, Jesus links together his earthly teaching with his resurrection teaching in 24:44–49.

> There is continuity between Jesus's teaching of Scripture <u>before</u> he died and then <u>after</u> he was resurrected.

<u>**JESUS'S EARTHLY TEACHING**</u>   correlates with   <u>**JESUS'S RESURRECTION TEACHING**</u>
WORDS WITH DISCIPLES BEFORE HIS DEATH   =   "THESE WORDS" JESUS SPEAKS TO HIS DISCIPLES AFTER HIS RESURRECTION

To understand the equation, we need to recognize *how Jesus had been opening their minds all along during his earthly ministry by living out and speaking Scripture to them*. When did this start? We must go to the very beginning of Jesus's ministry with the Father's affirmation of Jesus.[2]

Now, perhaps it should not be surprising that Jesus's ministry began with the heavenly Father commissioning him by speaking from Hebrew Scripture:

"You are my beloved Son, in whom I am well-pleased." (Mark 1:11)

This affirmation is so important that God repeats it again at Jesus's transfiguration into glorious form just as he was traveling to Jerusalem to face his imminent death (Mark 9:7//Matt 17:5//Luke 9:35; cf. 2 Pet 1:17–18). What is the meaning of this affirmation? As acknowledged by Bible translations and interpreters, the Father's statement is actually a combination of three texts of Hebrew Scripture: Ps 2:7, Isa 42:1, and Gen 22.[3] How important is the Father's statement? Very important. In fact, these OT passages are a key to understanding Jesus's ministry and the passing of this ministry to his followers.

---

[2] In Luke's account we are taken even further back to the very beginning of Jesus's life when Mary speaks Scripture as prayer with Jesus in the womb (1:50) and at eight days after being born when Joseph and Mary faithfully obeyed when to circumcise and name Jesus according to the Law (Luke 2:21–23, 39) as well as faithfully attended the Feast of Passover every year (2:41–42).

[3] For example, the NASB translation provides these references: Ps 2:7; Isa 42:1; Matt 3:17; 12:18; Mark 9:7; Luke 3:22. The passages from Matt 3:17//Luke 3:22 are parallel passages. Matthew 12:18–21 is where Isaiah 42:1–3 is quoted at length. Finally, Mark 9:7 is where the Father speaks the same word to Jesus after he has predicted the death and resurrection of the Son of Man (8:31). As for Genesis 22, see for example Larry W. Hurtado who summarizes: "A son **whom I love** echoes Genesis 22:2, where God addresses Abraham, telling him to offer his son ("your only son, Isaac, whom you love") (*Mark*, Understanding the Bible Commentary Series [Grand Rapids: Bakers, 2011], 19–20, emphasis original).

First, the Father's statement at Jesus's baptism is a commissioning statement, a vocational calling to Jesus, a plan for mission in the world. Larry W. Hurtado has aptly summarized the rationale for this view:

> This vision and the accompanying voice from heaven are similar to the OT accounts of prophets who were called by God to speak to Israel. Isaiah (6:1–13) and Ezekiel (1:1–2:10) give extended descriptions of such experiences, but such visions and accompanying experiences of being called by God seem to have prompted the ministry of several other prophets as well (e.g. Amos 7:1–9:1). Certainly Mark saw Jesus as more than a prophet, but this account seems to describe the beginning of Jesus's ministry as provoked by a prophetic calling experience. It is worth noting that Jesus elsewhere likens himself to a prophet (6:4) and that some people so regarded him (6:15; 8:28). But though the form of the calling here is like that of OT prophets, the substance of the call is to serve as God's chosen Son![4]

Indeed, to see Hebrew Scripture woven together here has tremendous implications.

Second, these texts do not represent just any passages of Scripture; they represent three rather important moments, if not arguably the highest moments, in Hebrew Scripture. Each text is integrally related to God's saving history with Israel by referring to the blessing to Abraham (Gen 22), Israel's King (Ps 2), and the mysterious Suffering Servant (Isa 42).

Third, these passages have the broader world in view, that is, "the nations" beyond the singular nation of Israel. We would do well to carefully consider these verses and how Jesus viewed his ministry purpose in light of them. Below are the Father's words to Jesus, their Hebrew Scriptural references, and an outline of important aspects of each passage in context.

1. *"You are my ... Son"* is from **Ps 2:7**.
   a. This is the King of Israel's Enthronement Psalm—it is Messianic in expectation.
   b. The Nations belong to the King to rule (Ps 2:8).

2. *"You are my Beloved Son"* (ἀγαπητός).
   a. The "beloved son" (ἀγαπητός, LXX) is Isaac in **Gen 22:2, 12, 16**
   b. At stake are Abraham's faith and the blessing of God extending to the Nations.
   c. In the Gospel tradition Jesus understood himself to be the "beloved son" (ἀγαπητός) in the parable of the tenants of the vineyard (see Luke 20:13).

3. *"With you I am well-pleased"* is from **Isa 42:1**; one should read the fuller context of Isaiah, especially the following seven verses.
   a. This passage describes the Suffering Servant and is quoted at length in Matt 12:15–21.
   b. This Servant will bring justice/righteousness to the nations (Isa 42:1).
   c. As in Isaiah, Jesus receives the Spirit at his baptism (Luke 4:18; Isa 42:1).
   d. The Suffering Servant will become "a covenant for the people"; such covenants will naturally involve blood sacrifice (Isa 42:6).

---

[4] Hurtado, *Mark*, 20. I have been teaching this to my students my entire career.

In the end, the Heavenly Father combined these verses together as a commissioning statement for Jesus to ponder at the giving of the Holy Spirit just like the Suffering Servant was to receive (Isa 42:1). Notice too how, after Jesus's baptism, the Spirit immediately drove him into the desert to face temptations before beginning his ministry. How much time did Jesus have to pray about and reflect on his commission from the Father? Forty days. During this time Jesus must have pondered and prayed about what the Father's mission meant for him. Jesus needed to interpret the significance of this combination of Scripture and how he would fulfill it by being Israel's Messiah King ruling the nations, God's beloved Son fulfilling the Abrahamic blessing for the nations, and the sacrificial Suffering Servant becoming a covenant for the people and enlightening the nations. Furthermore, we must consider that Jesus did not have the content and knowledge of Scripture entered *supernaturally* into his mind—he needed to learn it just like everyone else needs to—hearing, reading, and embodying it obediently. Before being baptized, it is likely that Jesus attended synagogue meetings where Hebrew Scripture was regularly read aloud, heard, and discussed. But, having heard the Father's commission while being in the desert now, he had forty days to reflect and during this time (perhaps at the very end), Satan came to test him precisely on the matter of Jesus's identity: "If you are the Son of God, do this ... and do that ...!"

In response Jesus quoted three scriptural texts from Deut 6–8, a passage that describes the wilderness failings of the fledgling nation of Israel. This is of paramount importance for this whole discussion because it reveals that *Jesus understood Scripture contextually and typologically*. His quotation of this passage shows that *Jesus was thinking scripturally about himself and God's purposes for him as being analogous to the temptations and failings of the nation of Israel*. For this reason interpreters are correct to conclude that Jesus understood himself as fulfilling Israel's vocation/calling and purposes. In fact, these purposes are at the very heart of Isaiah's prophecy about the Suffering Servant—a restatement of hope for how God would come to his people to bring justice, proclaim the good news to the outcasts, and establish "a covenant for the people and a light to the nations" (42:6). Jesus is the One to fulfill this mission.

Let's pause here a moment to consider this question: How did Jesus receive "information" from God at his baptism? He received a statement infused with Scripture that encapsulated high points of God's salvation plan as a call on his life. Was God speaking through the Spirit? Or, was God speaking through the previously written Hebrew Scripture? Well, "yes": God spoke through both the Spirit and the Word. So, at Jesus's baptism the Father gave Jesus scriptural material to ponder, live out, and proclaim. In fact, as our survey of Jesus's ministry continues below, we will see that *Jesus continued to think, speak, and act scripturally* even as he preached the gospel, showed compassion in profound ways, taught in parables, predicted his coming death and resurrection, and quoted Scripture while confronting the religious leaders. The question for us is this: *Are we any different than Jesus? As his followers, should we do things differently or rather like Jesus did them?* God speaks to us through the Spirit in concert with his revealed Word.

> After receiving God the Father's scriptural call, Jesus continued to think, speak, and act scripturally.

Scripture was the continuing focus of Jesus's life and ministry. Jesus's scripture-infused life actually began with his conception, birth, and early formative years. His godly parents modeled this for him, who themselves obeyed and enacted Scripture. For example, Mary's *Magnificat* in Luke 1:46–55, which is named for the first word of the Latin translation meaning "exalts," is full of scriptural allusion and even an explicit quotation of Ps 103:17 at Luke 1:50. Moreover, Mary and Joseph circumcised him and named "Jesus" on the eighth day and offered the suitable sacrifice, all in accordance with the Mosaic Law (Luke 2:21–24, 39). Furthermore, they pilgrimaged yearly to Jerusalem for Passover according to the custom (Luke 2:41–43).

So then, even after Jesus's baptism and commissioning and his temptation and response by quoting Scripture, *Jesus's whole ministry was shaped by and infused with Scripture*. In what follows, I will demonstrate this by looking broadly at Jesus's ministry activities of proclamation, compassion and healing, teaching in general and telling parables in particular, his final fateful journey to Jerusalem, his confrontation with the religious leaders, and his messianic self-understanding. Let's look at these in turn.

First, consider Jesus's ***essential message and proclamation***. Mark 1:2–3 provides a critical framework for the whole narrative by quoting and combining Isa 40:3 and Mal 3:1. The point is to explain how John the Baptist fulfills a role to prepare for the coming of the Lord. Scripture is unfolding in the events of the Gospel. Then, after Jesus was baptized and received his commissioning from the Father, he immediately proclaimed the message, "The time is fulfilled: God's Kingdom has arrived; be repenting and trusting in the good news!" (Mark 1:15). So important is this message that John the Baptist is recorded in Matthew's Gospel as proclaiming the exact same message that Jesus proclaimed: "Be repenting, for God's Kingdom has arrived!" (3:2; 4:17). This unified proclamation of John and Jesus originated from the Hebrew prophetic expectation of God's coming reign and the need for God's covenant people to prepare and repent, as Isa 56:7 announced:

> Jesus's whole ministry was shaped by and infused with Scripture.

> How lovely on the mountains
> Are the feet of him who brings good news,
> Who announces peace
> And brings good news of happiness,
> Who announces salvation,
> *And* says to Zion, "Your God reigns!" (NASB)

Thus, the central proclamation of John and Jesus, "Repent, for God's Kingdom has arrived!" essentially encapsulates the Jewish expectation as expressed in Scripture in the prophets.

Second, consider Jesus's ***healing and compassion for the poor and outcasts***. At the start of his ministry, Jesus is shown reading Scripture about the Jubilee Year from Isa 61. After opening the scroll and finding the passage, Jesus read and concluded by saying, "Today this scripture is fulfilled in your hearing" (Luke 4:21). In fact, Luke's Gospel intimately associates Jesus's preaching and ministry with Isa 61. Indeed, Jesus understood his own ministry as fulfilling Isaiah's vision.

After Jesus read Isaiah and indicated its present fulfillment, Luke showed subsequently how he fulfilled Isaiah's vision of the Jubilee year since the Gospel is preached to the poor, the lame are healed, and the captives are released. Notice how often the poor, crippled, lame, and the blind are identified in Luke; the **bolded verses** identify where these vulnerable people are listed altogether:

a. the poor (πτωχός) occurs at **4:18**; 6:20; **7:22**; **14:21**; 16:20, 22; 18:22; 19:8; 21:3
b. the crippled (ἀνάπειρος) occurs at **14:21**
c. the lame (χωλός) occurs at **7:22**; **14:21**
d. the blind (τυφλός) occurs at **4:18**; 6:39; **7:21–22**; **14:21**; 18:35

The notes on 4:18 from the Oxford New American Bible summarize this point well:

> [M]ore than any other gospel writer Luke is concerned with Jesus's attitude toward the economically and socially poor (see Luke 6:20,24; 12:16–21; 14:12–14; 16:19–26; 19:8). At times, the poor in Luke's gospel are associated with the downtrodden, the oppressed and afflicted, the forgotten and the neglected (Luke 4:18; 6:20–22; 7:22; 14:12–14), and it is they who accept Jesus's message of salvation.

In addition to Jesus's reading of Isaiah in 4:16–21, two other passages show how Jesus brings fulfillment to the Isaianic vision: 7:17–23 and 14:21. In this first passage, John the Baptist is wondering whether Jesus is the "Expected One" (i.e., Messiah) or not; in reply, at 7:22 Jesus weaves in material from Isaiah (these portions are indicated by SMALL CAPS): "And He answered and said to them, 'Go and report to John what you have seen and heard: *the* BLIND RECEIVE SIGHT, *the* lame walk, *the* lepers are cleansed, and *the* deaf hear, *the* dead are raised up, *the* POOR HAVE THE GOSPEL PREACHED TO THEM'" (NASB). John's response to Jesus's reply in Luke 7:27 was to quote Mal 3:1. In the second passage of Luke 14:21, Jesus, while challenging the self-serving attitude of some Pharisees at banquets held for each other, tells a parable in which "the poor, the crippled, the blind, and the lame" should be invited to share in such festive dinners.

Third, consider the focus and basis of Jesus's *teaching*. In the Sermon of Mount, Jesus announces his purpose: "to fulfill the Law and the Prophets" (Matt 5:17). By the end of the Sermon, Jesus can indicate of the Golden Rule ("to be doing to others just as you yourselves would want them to be doing to you") that "This is the Law and the Prophets" (7:12). In essence, Jesus has shown how he and his teaching are fulfilling the Law and the Prophets.

Fourth, consider Jesus's *parables*. Jesus understood his teaching the people in parables as a fulfillment of Isaiah (Matt 13:14). Matthew the Gospel writer also describes it as fulfilling the Psalmist's prerogative to so speak by quoting Ps 78:2 at Matt 13:35. Matthew 13:10–17 records the disciples' asking Jesus why he spoke in parables to the people and his response, in which he differentiates the disciples who are entrusted with the knowledge from the people who are not:

Matt 13:14–15 "In their case the prophecy of Isaiah is being fulfilled, which says,
'YOU WILL KEEP ON HEARING, BUT WILL NOT UNDERSTAND;

YOU WILL KEEP ON SEEING, BUT WILL NOT PERCEIVE;
¹⁵ FOR THE HEART OF THIS PEOPLE HAS BECOME DULL,
WITH THEIR EARS THEY SCARCELY HEAR,
AND THEY HAVE CLOSED THEIR EYES,
OTHERWISE THEY WOULD SEE WITH THEIR EYES,
HEAR WITH THEIR EARS,
AND UNDERSTAND WITH THEIR HEART AND RETURN,
AND I WOULD HEAL THEM.' " (NASB)

> Jesus spoke in parables both as a sign of their dullness of heart and as the best way to reach the people.

Most troubling for us is the explanation following the word "otherwise." It would appear that Jesus did not want the people to truly understand and return to the Lord to be healed. *Yet, how can this be correct?* Students of Scripture struggle with this teaching. However, we must realize that Jesus understood Isaiah's time as parallel to his own: It was a time of impending judgment because of the people's waywardness from God. This coming judgment was what motivated John's proclamation and his baptizing of people in order to help prepare them to avoid the "wrath to come" (Luke 3:8), which was the impending fall of Jerusalem in AD 70 (Luke 21:23).[5] *Jesus spoke in parables because it was the best way to explain the nature of God's Kingdom; at the same time, his speaking in parables was due to the people's dullness of heart.* Parables are merciful and grave at the same time. People were given a chance to understand. What distinguished disciples (literally "learners") from non-learners was approaching Jesus to ask him to explain the parables. This is what Jesus's disciples did and were thus blessed to hear and understand Jesus's explanation (Matt 13:10, 16). So, Jesus here expected his followers to probe, to consider, and to ask him questions, and this would distinguish them from the general populace following him, wanting miracles and handouts of food, yet not truly understanding his purposes and the coming Kingdom of God. In all, then, Jesus's ministry of teaching in parables was motivated by his understanding of Scripture and the imminent time of judgment, not unlike the time of Isaiah as found in Scripture.

Fifth, Jesus understood **his fateful journey to Jerusalem** along with his death and resurrection in view of Scripture. As Jesus traveled to Jerusalem in Luke 18:31-33, he explained to the disciples the significance of his impending death by making reference to the OT prophets:

> 31 Then He took the twelve aside and said to them, 'Behold, we are going up to Jerusalem, and **all things which are written through the prophets about the Son of Man will be accomplished**. 32 For He will be handed over to the Gentiles, and will be mocked and mistreated and spit upon, 33 and after they have scourged Him, they will kill Him; and the third day He will rise again.' (*emphasis* added to my translation)

This passage illustrates also that when Jesus predicted his death and resurrection, he preferred to

---

[5] The word for "wrath" (ὀργή) occurs only twice in Luke's Gospel: here in the verse explaining the context of John's message (3:8) and then at Jesus's prediction of the fall of Jerusalem (21:23). Sadly, Jesus arrived at the brink of this national disaster and wept about it; he worked to avert it, but recognized the nation's blindness (19:41–44).

refer to himself as "the Son of Humanity," traditionally translated as "the Son of Man" (Mark 8:31; 9:30; 10:33–34).[6] But what does this phrase mean and why would Jesus refer to himself in such a way? The source for his self-identification is most likely Dan 7 where Daniel wrote down his dreams and visions.[7] He says there,

> "The Son of Man" is Jesus's most common self-designation. It occurs in Mark's Gospel at 2:10, 28; 8:31, 38; 9:9, 12, 31; 10:33, 45; 13:26; 14:21, 41, 62.

Dan 7:13–14 "I kept looking in the night visions,
And behold, with the clouds of heaven
One like a Son of Man was coming,
And He came up to the Ancient of Days
And was presented before Him.
[14] And to Him was given dominion,
Glory and a kingdom,
That all the peoples, nations and *men of every* language
Might serve Him.
His dominion is an everlasting dominion
Which will not pass away;
And His kingdom is one
Which will not be destroyed." (NASB)

Although the interpretation of the imagery is debated, the Son of Humanity in Dan 7 would appear to be (a) representative of the persecuted people of Israel who are vindicated and exalted to a status of ruling presence next to the Ancient of Days, namely, God.[8] *Critically, the Son of Humanity is the most common designation that Jesus uses of himself.*[9] This has tremendous implications for re-

---

[6] The recent Common English Bible (CEB) has chosen to translate this phrase "the Human One." My decision here to use "the Son of Humanity" reflects a decision to maintain a word-for-word translation that helps convey that the phrase is a title and should be understood as such; I follow here T. Michael W. Halcomb and Fredrick J. Long, *Mark: GlossaHouse Illustrated Greek-English New Testament*, Accessible Greek Resources and Online Studies (Wilmore, KY: GlossaHouse, 2014) and *John: GlossaHouse Illustrated Greek-English New Testament*, Accessible Greek Resources and Online Studies (Wilmore, KY: GlossaHouse, 2017, *forthcoming*).

[7] Another fairly viable option is that "the Son of Man" comes from Ezekiel and how the Lord addressed the prophet throughout (see, e.g., Ezek 2:1, 3, 6, 8). Certainly, Jesus acts like a prophet like Ezekiel. However, when Jesus is pushed to explain whether he is the Messiah or not, he quotes from Dan 7:13 and Ps 110:1, clearly co-identifying himself with the Son of Man of Daniel, who would be exalted to sit at God's right hand (Ps 110:1).

[8] For a recent discussion of the various interpretive options for the identity of the "son of man" in Dan 7, see Jim Edlin, *Daniel: A Commentary in the Wesleyan Tradition*, NBBC (Kansas City: Beacon Hill, 2009), 179–80.

[9] In the Gospels and Acts, there are eighty-five occurrences, many of which are parallels to one another: Matt 8:20; 9:6; 10:23; 11:19; 12:8, 32, 40; 13:37, 41; 16:13, 27, 28; 17:9, 12, 22; 18:11; 19:28; 20:18, 28; 24:27, 30, 37, 39, 44; 25:31; 26:2, 24, 45, 64; Mark 2:10, 28; 8:31, 38; 9:9, 12, 31; 10:33, 45; 13:26; 14:21, 41, 62; Luke 5:24; 6:5, 22; 7:34; 9:22, 26, 44, 56, 58; 11:30; 12:8, 10, 40; 17:22, 24, 26, 30; 18:8, 31; 19:10; 21:27, 36; 22:22, 48, 69; 24:7; John 1:51; 3:13, 14; 5:27; 6:27, 53, 62; 8:28; 9:35; 12:23, 34; 13:31; Acts 7:56. Among these references are several quota-

covering Jesus's self-understanding as Messiah and the early Christians' understanding of Jesus. For example, the Book of Revelation features Jesus as "the Son of Man" in the first vision of 1:9–20 that provides a framework for the book. Additionally, I would argue that Rev 5 depicts Jesus as the slain Lamb approaching God, the One sitting on the throne, and standing at God's right hand to receive the sealed book (5:6–7) and "to receive power and riches and wisdom and might and honor and glory and blessing" (5:12) corresponding to the Son of Humanity of Dan 7:13–14.

Sixth, we ought to consider Jesus's confrontation with the *religious leaders*. When Jesus finally arrived at Jerusalem, we see him entering the temple and teaching Scripture. In fact, Mark sequences events in his Gospel so that we focus on Jesus's teaching in 11:17.[10] Such a presentation is called a "chiasm."

> A Curse of fig tree is spoken (vv.12–14)
>   B Jesus and the disciples *enter Jerusalem* and enter the temple (v.15a)
>   C Jesus *acts* adversatively toward the buyers-sellers (vv.15b–16)
>   **D Jesus *teaches* adversatively concerning the buyers-sellers (v.17—see below)**
>   C' The chief priests and scribes *act* adversatively toward Jesus (v.18)
>   B' Jesus and the disciples *leave the city* (v.19)
> A' Curse of fig tree is realized (vv.20–25).

Several things are significant about 11:17. First, Jesus is going on the "offensive" by asking a rhetorical question of the religious authorities: "Hasn't it been written…? [Yes it has.]" Second, Jesus combines two prophetic passages of Scripture (Isa 56:7 with Jer 7:11) in order to condemn the practices of the religious leaders and predict the temple's falling (see the context of Jer 7). Third, Mark 11:17 is itself chiastic in arrangement in order to stress the contrast between the religious leaders and those adversely affected by their actions of allowing buying and selling in the temple, namely, "all the nations."

> A ὁ οἶκός μου   My House
>   B οἶκος προσευχῆς   a house of prayer
>   C κληθήσεται   will be called
>   D πᾶσιν τοῖς ἔθνεσιν;   for all the nations
>   D' ὑμεῖς δὲ   But you
>   C' πεποιήκατε   have made
>   B' αὐτὸν   it
> A' σπήλαιον λῃστῶν   a den of robbers!

---

tions of Dan 7:13: Matt 24:30//Mark 13:26//Luke 21:27 and Matt 26:64//Mark 14:62. Moreover, Dan 7:13 is alluded to in Rev 1:7, 13; 14:14. Additionally, Dan 7:14 is alluded to in Matt 24:30//Mark 13:26; Matt 28:18; Luke 1:33; John 12:34; Rev 10:11; 11:15; 19:6; cf. the other uses of Dan 7 in Revelation.

[10] What follows here is a summary of Mark A. Awabdy and Fredrick J. Long, "Mark's Inclusion of 'For All Nations' in 11:17d and the International Vision of Isaiah," *The Journal of Inductive Biblical Studies* 1.2 (2014): 224–55 available as a PDF download at http://place.asburyseminary.edu/jibs/vol1/iss2/5/.

Mark 11:17 is a powerful moment; so powerful in fact that the religious leaders are reported as immediately conspiring to destroy Jesus (11:18)! Death was sometimes the price for speaking Scripture prophetically to God's rebellious people. Jesus made one momentous trip to Jerusalem knowing that he would need to confront the "establishment" and that this would cost him his life.[11]

If space permitted, I would systematically walk through Mark 11–12 and demonstrate how thoroughly Jesus was thinking, confronting, and speaking Scripture (see esp. 12:1, 11–12, 24–26, 29–31, 35–37). Fortunately, Benson Goh has already done so and I heartily recommend his article.[12] These two chapters are the great showdown between Jesus and the religious leaders that leaves them speechless such that "no one would dare to ask him any more questions" (12:34). Significantly, the showdown ends with Jesus getting the last word. Quoting from Ps 110:1, Jesus asked a final question to the religious authorities:

> **Mark 12:35–37** And Jesus, answering back, was speaking as he was teaching in the temple, "How are the scribes saying that the Christ is the son of David? [36] David himself said in the Holy Spirit, 'THE LORD SAID TO MY LORD, "SIT AT MY RIGHT HAND, UNTIL I PUT YOUR ENEMIES BENEATH YOUR FEET."' [Ps 110:1] [37] David himself calls Him 'Lord'; so in what way is He his son?" And the large crowd was gladly listening to Him.

Jesus's point was that the Christ that David himself foretold is also superior to David because he is not simply a descendent but is elevated to God's right hand. The full significance of Jesus's interpretation comes later in Mark's Gospel when Jesus was asked whether or not he himself was the Messiah (14:61–62). In response, Jesus replied, "I am," and then quoted Ps 110:1 combined with Dan 7:13, thus interpreting both verses in light of each other.

Seventh, Jesus's ***understanding of Messiahship*** involved his own appropriation of these two key OT passages at pivotal moments in the narrative. At Mark 12:35–37, as I have just explained, Jesus quoted Ps 110:1 while asking a question concerning the identity of the mysterious Lord who is able to attain to the position of God's right hand. Shortly after this when under trial in Mark 14:61–62, Jesus, when questioned about whether he was the Messiah, answered, "I am" and then quoted and combined Dan 7:13 with Ps 110:1. Here are these verses given in full (NASB):

> **Psalm 110:1** A Psalm of David. The LORD says to my Lord: 'Sit at My right hand Until I make Your enemies a footstool for Your feet.'

> **Daniel 7:13** I kept looking in the night visions, And behold, with the clouds of heaven One like a Son of Man was coming, And He came up to the Ancient of Days And was presented before Him.

---

[11] See, e.g., N. T. Wright, *Jesus and the Victory of God* (Minneapolis: Fortress, 1996), 540–653.

[12] Benson Goh, "The Charge of Being Deluded Interpreters of Scripture: A Reassessment of the Importance of Chiasms in Mark 11–12," *The Journal of Inductive Biblical Studies* 2.1 (2015): 30–61 available as a PDF download at http://place.asburyseminary.edu/jibs/vol2/iss1/4/.

In the first passage, Mark 12:35, Jesus quoted Ps 110:1 in a question that is unanswered by his opponents, the religious authorities. But why did Jesus ask this question in this way? Jesus advanced the idea that *the Messiah is more than the son of David* and must not remain on earth, but ascend to the right hand of God where he exercises authoritative rule over his enemies. Jesus's view here was contrary to the very popular view that the Messiah would rule from earth as a geo-political ruler. As I have pondered this matter, it occurs to me that what Jesus offered was not a geo-political kingdom, but a celestial-ethical one, that is, a kingdom overseen by him on the throne at God's right hand in heaven where God's will would be done as it would be on earth. In the NT the Heavenly Jerusalem is understood as coming down from heaven to earth (Gal 4:26; Heb 12:22; Rev 3:12; 21:2, 10). Jesus commissioned his followers to continue his mission from his place of exaltation having all authority in heaven and on earth (Matt 28:18–20).

In the second passage, Mark 14:61–62, Jesus more directly connected his identity as Messiah to the Son of Humanity (Dan 7:13) who would be exalted to God's right hand into a position of authority over his enemies (Ps 110:1). Importantly, Jesus here further disclosed what it meant for him to be the Messiah exactly when he was asked whether he was the Messiah or not. Here is the passage in context (NASB, underlining added):

> Psalm 110 and Dan 7:13 are the most widely quoted or alluded to verses across the entire NT. The source for this is none other than Jesus.

> **Mark 14:61–64** But He kept silent and did not answer. Again the high priest was questioning Him, and saying to Him, "Are You the Christ, the Son of the Blessed One?" ⁶² And Jesus said, "I am; and you shall see THE SON OF MAN SITTING AT THE RIGHT HAND OF POWER, and COMING WITH THE CLOUDS OF HEAVEN." ⁶³ Tearing his clothes, the high priest said, "What further need do we have of witnesses? ⁶⁴ "You have heard the blasphemy; how does it seem to you?" And they all condemned Him to be deserving of death.

Notice how Jesus interwove these two OT passages beginning and ending with Dan 7:13 (underlined). These OT passages did not exhaust the totality of Jesus's own self-understanding as the Messiah, yet they provided scriptural testimony recognizable to these scriptural experts. What was their response? They charged Jesus with blasphemy because he was co-identifying himself as the Son of Man of Dan 7:13 and as the Messiah as Lord ascending to God's right hand of Ps 110:1.

In light of all this, perhaps it should come as no surprise that *both scriptural passages are the most widely quoted or alluded to across the entire NT.*[13] So important are these verses that I

---

[13] The next closest in frequency, significantly, is Lev 19:18 ("love your neighbor as yourself") quoted in Matt 5:43; 19:19//Luke 10:27; 22:39//Mark 12:31, 33); Rom 13:9; Gal 5:14; Jas 2:8 and alluded to in Rom 12:19. After this, the next closest in frequency is Isa 6:9–10 quoted in Matt 13:14–15//Mark 4:12//Luke 8:10 and John 12:39–41; Acts 28:26–27; Rom 11:8. Compare also the single longest quotations from Scripture: Joel 2:28–32 in Acts 2:17–21; Ps 34:12–16 in 1 Pet 3:10–12; and Jer 31:31–34 in Heb 8:8–12.

will provide them in full below (NASB **bold** added). Quotations of Ps 110:1 in the Gospels are found in Matt 22:44//Mark 12:36//Luke 20:42–43 and Matt 26:64//Mark 14:62//Luke 22:69 (quoted above); and also in Acts 2:33–36; Heb 1:13. (Psalm 110:4 is also quoted in Heb 5:6; 7:17, 21.)

> **Acts 2:33–36** Therefore having been exalted to the right hand of God, and having received from the Father the promise of the Holy Spirit, He has poured forth this which you both see and hear. ³⁴ "For it was not David who ascended into heaven, but he himself says: "THE LORD SAID TO MY LORD, 'SIT AT MY RIGHT HAND, ³⁵ UNTIL I MAKE YOUR ENEMIES A FOOTSTOOL FOR YOUR FEET.'" ³⁶ Therefore let all the house of Israel know for certain that God has made Him both Lord and Christ—this Jesus whom you crucified.

> **Heb 1:13** But to which of the angels has He ever said, "SIT AT MY RIGHT HAND, UNTIL I MAKE YOUR ENEMIES A FOOTSTOOL FOR YOUR FEET"?

Allusions and verbal parallels to Ps 110:1 are found in 1 Cor 15:25; Rom 8:34; Eph 1:20; 2:6; Col 3:1; Heb 1:3; 8:1; 10:12, 13; 12:2; cf. Mark 16:19. (Psalm 110:4 is alluded to in John 12:34; Heb 5:10; 6:20; 7:3.)

> **1 Cor 15:23–25** But each in his own order: Christ the first fruits, after that those who are Christ's at His coming, ²⁴ then *comes* the end, when He hands over the kingdom to the God and Father, when He has abolished all rule and all authority and power. ²⁵ For He must reign **until He has put all His enemies under His feet**.

> **Rom 8:34** who is the one who condemns? Christ Jesus is He who died, yes, rather who was raised, who is **at the right hand of God**, who also intercedes for us.

> **Eph 1:18–23** *I pray that* the eyes of your heart may be enlightened, so that you will know what is the hope of His calling, what are the riches of the glory of His inheritance in the saints, ¹⁹ and what is the surpassing greatness of His power toward us who believe. *These are* in accordance with the working of the strength of His might ²⁰ which He brought about in Christ, when He raised Him from the dead and **seated Him at His right hand** in the heavenly *places*, ²¹ far above all rule and authority and power and dominion, and every name that is named, not only in this age but also in the one to come. ²² And He put all things in subjection **under His feet,** and gave Him as head over all things to the church, ²³ which is His body, the fullness of Him who fills all in all.

> **Eph 2:4–7** But God, being rich in mercy, because of His great love with which He loved us, ⁵ even when we were dead in our transgressions, made us alive together with Christ (by grace you have been saved), ⁶ and raised us up with Him, and **seated us with Him** in the heavenly *places* in Christ Jesus, ⁷ so that in the ages to come He might show the surpassing riches of His grace in kindness toward us in Christ Jesus.

Col 3:1–4 Therefore if you have been raised up with Christ, keep seeking the things above, where Christ is, **seated at the right hand of God**. ² Set your mind on the things above, not on the things that are on earth. ³ For you have died and your life is hidden with Christ in God. ⁴ When Christ, who is our life, is revealed, then you also will be revealed with Him in glory.

Heb 1:3 And He is the radiance of His glory and the exact representation of His nature, and upholds all things by the word of His power. When He had made purification of sins, **He sat down at the right hand of the Majesty** on high,

Heb 8:1–2 Now the main point in what has been said *is this*: we have such a high priest, who has taken His seat at the right hand of the throne of the Majesty in the heavens, ² a minister in the sanctuary and in the true tabernacle, which the Lord pitched, not man.

Heb 10:11–12 Every priest stands daily ministering and offering time after time the same sacrifices, which can never take away sins; ¹² but He, having offered one sacrifice for sins for all time, **SAT DOWN AT THE RIGHT HAND OF GOD**, ¹³ waiting from that time onward **UNTIL HIS ENEMIES BE MADE A FOOTSTOOL FOR HIS FEET**.

Heb 12:1 Therefore, since we have so great a cloud of witnesses surrounding us, let us also lay aside every encumbrance and the sin which so easily entangles us, and let us run with endurance the race that is set before us, ² fixing our eyes on Jesus, the author and perfecter of faith, who for the joy set before Him endured the cross, despising the shame, and **has sat down at the right hand of the throne of God**.

Daniel 7:13 is quoted in Matt 24:30//Mark 13:26//Luke 21:27 and Matt 26:64//Mark 14:62 (given above) and alluded to in Rev 1:7, 13; 14:14. Daniel 7:14 is alluded to in Matt 24:30//Mark 13:26; Matt 28:18; Luke 1:33; John 12:34; Rev 10:11; 11:15; 19:6; cf. uses of Dan 7 in Revelation.

Finally, we should consider that Jesus's last words "My God, my God, why have you forsaken me?" in Mark 15:34//Matt 27:46 are from Ps 22:1 that begins sadly but ends in hope (22:24)—a hope that Jesus had.

This concludes our survey of Jesus's knowledge and use of Scripture. Once again, what is the most significant thing that Jesus "did" after his resurrection and before his ascension for the ongoing fruitful life and ministry of his followers? Quite simply, he opened their minds to understand the Scriptures by explaining his life and ministry in light of Scripture. This survey shows that *Jesus's post-resurrection focus on Scripture corresponds to his pre-resurrection ministry*. Jesus reflects the great extent to

> Jesus's post-resurrection focus on Scripture corresponds to his pre-resurrection ministry.

which he himself was informed and formed by Scripture and then also his desire to inform and form his followers with Scripture. We must conclude that knowing Scripture in light of Christ is important for the ongoing life and ministry of the church.

Luke, the author of the Gospel and the Acts of the Apostles, understood this. *In Acts, Luke is careful to show how the apostles are a community dedicated to enumerating the Scriptures in light of the revelation of Christ as they continue the ministry of Jesus.* Such can be seen how and where Luke shows the apostles and the early Christians preaching, teaching, and being a part of the spread of the Word of God. This chart displays this critical theme:

> In Acts the apostles are a community dedicated to enumerating the Scriptures in light of the revelation of Christ as they continue the ministry of Jesus.

OT Scripture in the Book of Acts

Acts	OT Scripture	Summary
1:20	Ps 69:25 Ps 109:8	as justification for selecting a replacement for Judas
2:17–21	Joel 2:28–32	to explain the gift of the Holy Spirit
2:25–28	Ps 16:8–11	to explain the resurrection of Jesus
2:34–35	Ps 110:1	to explain the ascension of Jesus to God's right hand
3:22–23	Deut 18:15, 18, 19	Jesus is the Prophet that Moses foretold
3:24	broad sweep	all the Prophets starting from Samuel foretold these days
3:25	Gen 22:18	blessing will come to the peoples of the earth
4:11	Ps 118:22	explain that Jesus, though rejected, is the capstone
7:3 7:7 7:27–28 7:32 7:34 7:37 7:40 7:42–43 7:48–50	Gen 12:1 Gen 15:13–14 Exod 2:14 Exod 3:6 Exod 3:5, 7, 8, 10 Deut 18:15 Exod 32:1 Amos 5:25–27 Isa 66:1–2	Stephen's speech here in Acts 7 is a survey of the history of Israel particularly with respect to their disobedience.
8:32–35	Isa 53:7–8	Philip explains Isa 53 to the eunuch
13:33	Ps 2:7	resurrection of Jesus as King
13:34	Isa 55:3	resurrection of Jesus
13:35	Ps 16:10	resurrection of Jesus
13:41	Hab 1:5	warning not to hear and still disbelieve the gospel
13:47	Isa 49:6	justification for preaching to the Gentiles

15:15–18	Amos 9:11–12	justification for accepting the Gentiles as co-believers
23:5	Exod 22:28	Paul apologizing for not obeying Scripture due to ignorance
24:14	Law and Prophets	Paul's affirmation of them, esp. as relates to resurrection
28:25–27	Isa 6:9–10	Paul's warning that the Jews would ever hear but not understand; therefore, he goes to the gentiles
ACCUSATIONS AGAINST THE CHRISTIANS		
6:13	accusations against Stephen that he speaks against the Law	
18:13	Paul accused: "This man persuades men to worship God contrary to the **Law**."	
21:21, 24, 28; 22:3; 24:6	Paul facing a crowd who believes he was "teaching all the Jews who are among the Gentiles to forsake Moses, telling them not to circumcise their children nor to walk according to the customs."	
GENERAL REFERENCES TO "SCRIPTURE"		
1:16	to explain the betrayal of Judas	
17:2–3	Paul's custom of reasoning from the Scripture the suffering and resurrection of the Christ	
17:11	the Bereans' careful investigation of Paul's teaching through the Scriptures	
18:24	Apollos is described as being "mighty in the Scriptures"	
18:28	Apollos in Achaia "powerfully refuted the Jews in public, demonstrating by the **Scriptures** that Jesus was the Christ."	
GENERAL REFERENCE TO THE "LAW" (AND "PROPHETS")		
13:39	Paul generalizes about the Law and its relation to not prevent sin	
15:15	argument that Gentiles need to be circumcised accord. to the Law (by Judiazers)	
22:12	Ananias, a man who was devout by the standard of the Law	
24:14	Paul believes everything in accordance with the Law and the Prophets	
25:8	Paul defends himself against the claim of disregarding the Law	
26:22, 27	Paul testifies by "stating nothing but what the **Prophets** and Moses said was going to take place."	
28:23	Paul taught the Law and Prophets to visiting Jews	
GENERAL REFERENCE TO THE "PROPHETS"		
3:18, 21, 24, 25	Peter mentioning the fulfillment of the Prophets	
10:43	Peter explaining the testimony of all the Prophets about Jesus	
13:27	Paul explains the death of Jesus according to the Prophets and fulfilled by rulers	

What I would posit is that *Jesus was intending all along to inform and to form an "exegetical community"*—i.e., an interpretive community that is dedicated to reading and expositing the holy

Scriptures as the revelation of God and God's will. These followers would be committed to live according to Scripture and to experience, proclaim, and await God's salvation for humanity and all of creation. *But, what does an exegetical, interpretive community look like?*

II. COMMUNAL EXEGESIS

Many years ago I visited a good friend of mine from my seminary days. In addition to fishing for catfish and bass (great fun!), we worked together on a biblical passage for his next sermon. We were surprised by what we learned from each other and what perspectives we each brought to the passage. Why hadn't we done this before?! Since that time, I have wondered how often this sort of thing happened in church settings. Do pastors prepare sermons alone or in tandem with others? I have pleasantly learned that some of the very best preachers in fact rely on others to help them study and craft the message. The sermon is a communal effort.

Scripture reveals and church history attests that biblical interpretation is a corporate endeavor. Consider Nehemiah 8: The ***rediscovery*** of the Law was for men and women (8:2–3); it involved corporate teaching (with a podium) and explanation/interpretation (8:4–5, 7–8); it resulted in worship (8:6), mourning (8:9), and celebration with evangelism (8:10); and it was disseminated from the scribe Ezra to the fathers of all the households (8:13). Consider also the Qumran community (very possibly the Essenes) and their focus on scriptural interpretation (150 BC to AD 70); thanks to them we have the earliest documents of the Hebrew Scriptures and the first preserved commentaries on the Bible. Finally, Jesus himself as a twelve year old benefited from the community of Jewish interpreters and also surprised the teachers with his questions and insights (Luke 2:46–47). As we have seen, Jesus's ministry focused upon teaching, and especially teaching material from the Word of God (e.g., Mark 1:21–22; 2:13; 4:1–2; 6:6, 34; 8:31; 10:1; 12:35–40).

The evangelical Protestant heritage rightly celebrates *sola Scriptura,* that is, Scripture alone as our authority. However, in western cultural contexts like North America so much emphasis is placed on individual or personal salvation that *the typical scriptural experience is in the context of private devotions* or a preached word "for me." Moreover, devotional books and other media often offer not only poor interpretations of Scripture but misguided interpretive assumptions and approaches (i.e., a wrong hermeneutics) that involve proof-texting, allegorical interpretation, and the spiritualization of Scripture. The study of Scripture is typically understood as a personal matter. Furthermore, unfortunately too often the study of Scripture is not methodical, critical, rigorous, or informed with sound interpretive principles, if even "study" is undertaken at all.

People are confused about how best to study Scripture while being hungry for Scripture. The essential problem is *one's approach to Scripture*; this is called "hermeneutics." Brian D. McClaren has stated, "Many people think there are only two ways to read the Bible: their way and the wrong way. But there are many approaches to the Bible, as this [following] matrix shows."[14]

---

[14] Image adapted from Brian D. McLaren, "Author's Commentary to *We Make the Road by Walking: A Year-Long Quest for Spiritual Formation, Reorientation, and Activation* (New York: Jericho Books, 2015)," p. 9.

MATRIX OF OUR CRITICAL-LITERARY APPROACH TO SCRIPTURE

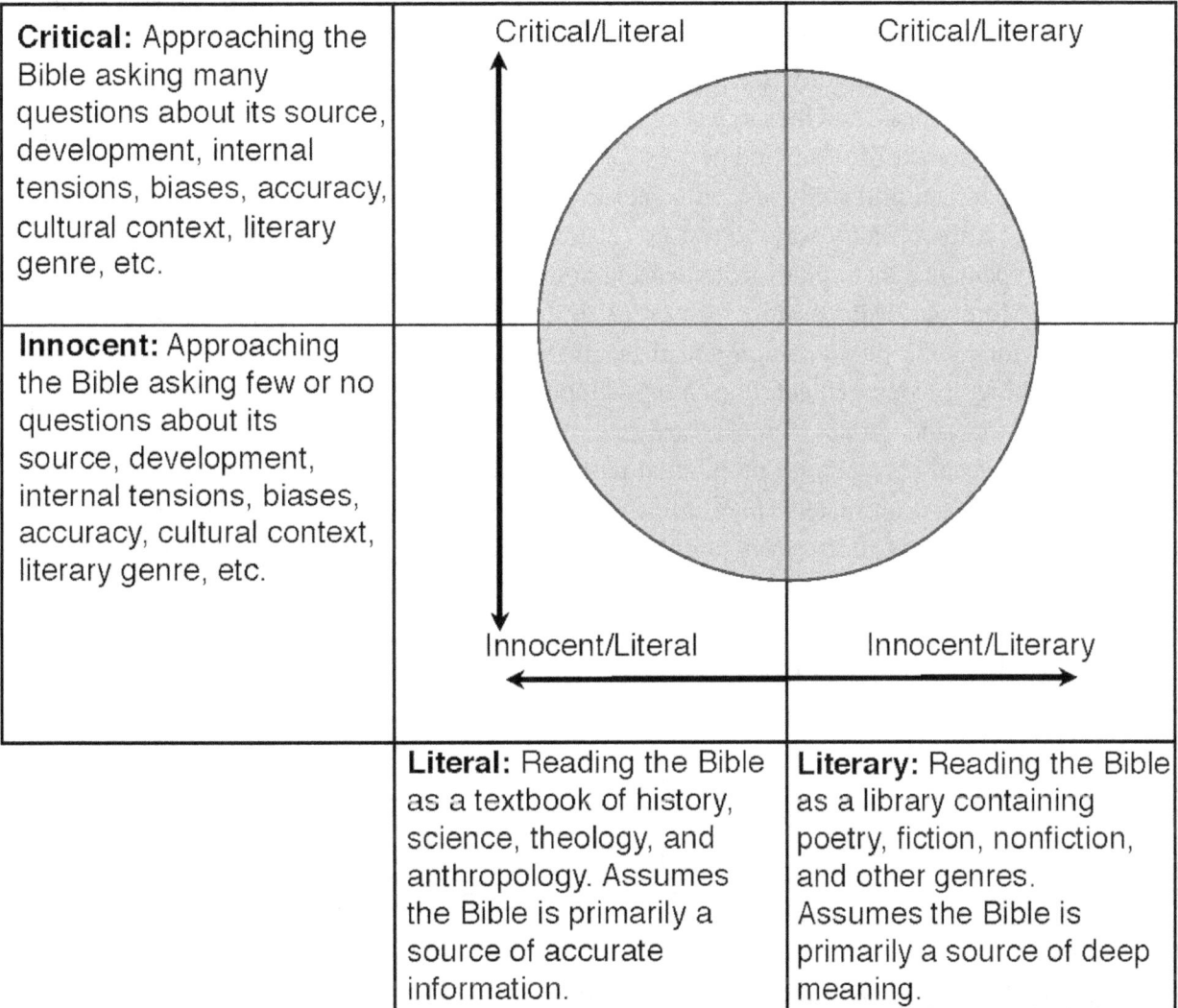

McLaren presents this matrix to allow us to see where we may be located along the axes of "critical" vs. "innocent" and "literal" vs. "literary." Many faithful believers hold an innocent literal view; "the Bible says it and I believe it." Often with such a stance, however, is an unreflective assumption that *how I view Scripture is what Scripture actually says: What I already understand in Scripture is what I read back out of Scripture.* However, Jesus shows us how to read Scripture in a literary and contextual way, in a way that is discerning (even critical) and meaningful.

Within the past two decades, we observe significant movements of scriptural study that help people move past the "innocent literal" approach; e.g., Kay Arthur's Precept Ministries International and Bible Study Fellowship (BSF). These groups reflect a continued interest to learn and teach Scripture. But, we still wonder, why aren't more Christ-followers committed to the careful study of Scripture as Jesus obviously demonstrated? It would seem that in large part Christians are influenced by current philosophical values in Western culture that are opposed to biblical values. The rise of post-modernism and its bedfellows—personal freedom vs. normative authority; the relativity of truth ("It's true for me"); the pursuit of "egoistical self expression" over against meaningful and consistent community life; the confusion over the meaning of central biblical ideas like love, mercy, and holiness; and the neglect of considering long-term consequences—all these subtly undermine the abundant life that God desires for His people. This life would be nourished by careful, contextual, and faithful study of God's Word.

One way, the primary way, to restore relationship with God is for a full-orbed community response of repentance that comes from hearing anew the Word of God through corporate care in Bible study. Moreover, it is possible for pastors to have a group of interpreters assist in the study of Scripture for public proclamation and dissemination. These may be called STEP-UP groups (Study, Teaching, Encouragement, Preaching—Upbuilding Persons). The benefits of such an experience for pastors and group members are that they may experience accountability, may gain broadened beneficial perspectives on biblical passages, may be mutually sharpened by honing interpretative skills, and ultimately, may offer better and more substantive food for the sheep. The diagram below indicates many ways that the Word of God could be disseminated in order to directly impact people's lives through forming a STEP-UP group in a church fellowship setting.

THE WORD OF GOD PERMEATING THE COMMUNITY OF GOD'S PEOPLE

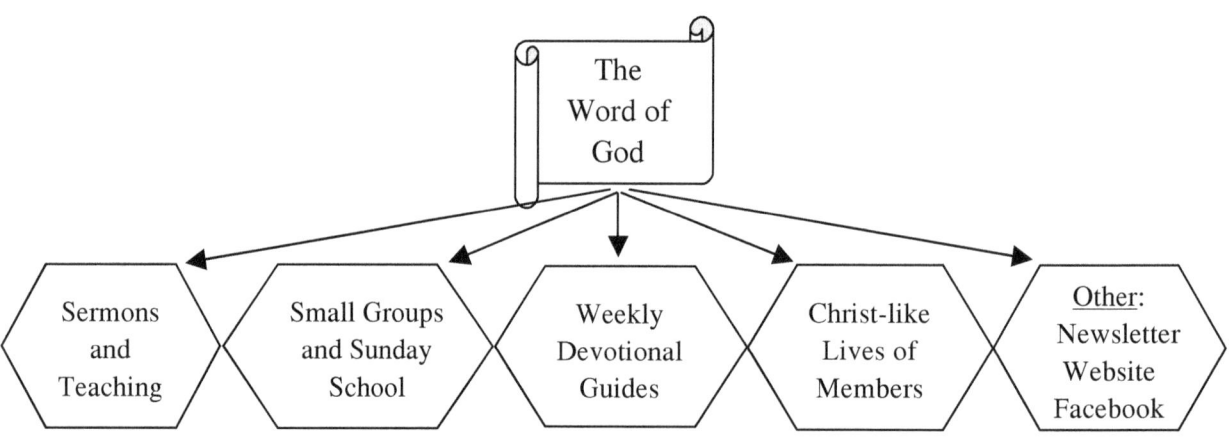

Essentially, then, the purpose of the corporate study of Scripture is to have God as Father, Son, and Holy Spirit become the primary influence upon our souls in matters of the heart (moral transformation), relationships (mimesis "imitation"), communal life (music, fellowship, and ministry), outreach (mission), and all of creation (creation care). God in Christ through the Spirit affects moral transformation through mimesis in a divine choreography that involves worship, music, ministry, mission, and stewardship. The Holy Spirit aids us in these endeavors, and especially interpretation … but how?

III. THE HOLY SPIRIT'S ROLE IN SCRIPTURAL INTERPRETATION[15]

John 14:26a "But the Helper, the Holy Spirit, ... He will teach you all things...."

John 16:13 "Moreover, when he, the Spirit of truth, comes, he will guide you in all the truth; for he will not speak on his own initiative, but whatever he hears, he will speak and he will report to you the things that are coming."

I have often heard it said, "If such verses are true, then why do I need to study Scripture since I have the Spirit of God dwelling within me?" I believe that these verses are true, but more importantly that they need to be interpreted properly in context. *Both verses are spoken when Jesus is preparing to leave his disciples after his death, resurrection, and ascension.* He offers a "Farewell Discourse" (John 13–17). It was a sad and distressing time for both Jesus and his disciples. What he promises here is the sending of the Holy Spirit who will encourage, guide, and teach the truth to his closest followers. Importantly, the "you" in these verses is plural referring to the addressees of his farewell address, namely, the disciples with him at the time. So, *it is immediately problematic to apply these verses to each one of us as "private" individuals* as if Jesus were speaking these words to us in this moment. Moreover, we need to consider how and in what circumstances the Spirit mediated "all truth" to the disciples in John's Gospel. Let's take a closer look.

Regarding 14:26a, the Spirit is active in teaching "all things" to these disciples of Jesus, but the second half of the verse (14:26b) is not often quoted: "and bring to your remembrance all that I said to you." The Spirit will teach and assist the first disciples in remembering what Jesus had already done and said. Why would this be important for them? Because John's Gospel itself serves here as the end product of the Spirit's further teaching and bringing to remembrance Jesus's words and actions. So, in 14:26 Jesus was speaking about a very specific situation: His closest disciples would be assisted in knowing the truth and remembering Jesus's words that would become John's Gospel, written Scripture. John 21:24–25 ends by testifying to the communal composition of John's Gospel that has an individual speaking ("I") within a community setting ("we").

Regarding 16:13, once again the wording and the context are critical. First, the Greek verb "guide" (ὁδηγέω) involves a metaphor of "journeying" and "traveling"—the verb entails giving "assistance" and thus the Spirit is not the sole means or agency to reach the truth.[16] In other words, the disciples also retain their agency and role in walking along the journey. What this verse affirms is that the Spirit works with whatever is already in existence and helps the disciples to arrive at that destination. Second, the last portion of the verse provides support for the first half; that's what is signaled by the conjunction "for" in the supporting sentence, "for he will not speak on his own ini-

---

[15] See the recent volume on this topic by Craig S. Keener, *Spirit Hermeneutics: Reading Scripture in Light of Pentecost* (Grand Rapids: Eerdmans, 2016).

[16] The standard Greek Lexicon provides these two definitions each beginning with "assist": "to assist in reaching a desired destination ... to assist someone in acquiring information or knowledge" (BDAG 690).

tiative but whatever he hears, he will speak and he will report/announce to you the things that are coming." Once again, we see that the Spirit takes what is already spoken and reports it to the disciples. In this regard, the Spirit continues doing what was already happening with Jesus's ministry: Jesus was hearing from the Father and speaking it to the world (e.g., 3:32–35; 7:16–18; 8:26–29, 42–43; 12:47–50). Thus, the Spirit also hears and relates it to the disciples for the ongoing mission of the church. For example, in Acts 8:29–40 the Spirit told Philip to go to the chariot as the Ethiopian Eunuch was reading Isaiah in order to explain it to him and the eunuch was baptized.

Furthermore, "the things that are coming" (in Greek, τὰ ἐρχόμενα) need not refer only or primarily to things in the "far" future, although the Spirit does at times announce things coming in the future (Acts 20:23; 21:11; 1 Tim 4:1). However, in John's Gospel "the things that are coming" (τὰ ἐρχόμενα) may refer simply to the events befalling Jesus in the "near" future as he was arrested in the garden, given the mock trial, and then executed. The exact same phrase occurs again as Jesus was betrayed in the garden in 18:4: he "was knowing all the things that are coming upon him" and then he was arrested.[17]

In sum, both 14:26 and 16:13 affirm the Spirit's role in aiding the disciples of Jesus at a critical transition of Jesus's departure and the events that would be transpiring: The Spirit will help them recall and give them insight into the events of Jesus's life and death, taking what was already spoken and what the Spirit "hears" for the composition of John's Gospel. Does the Spirit have a broader function than this? Certainly. The Book of Acts and the rest of the NT attest to this. The apostle Paul in 1 Cor 12–14 provides the fullest and most systematic description of the Spirit's role in the manifestation of gifts for building up the body of Christ and the ongoing witness of the church to the world (cf. Heb 2:4).

There is an intimate relationship between the Holy Spirit and the Word of God—by hearing the Word we may have the opportunity to be hearing and learning truth from the Spirit of God. The Spirit is intimately connected to the truth (John 14:17; 15:26; 1 John 4:6). In fact, John says, "the Spirit is the Truth" (1 John 5:6). Since Scripture is God-inspired, it is true and is thus permeated with the Spirit. However, hearing Scripture and learning the truth is not automatic.

It certainly is possible to approach Scripture from a contrary spirit, and not discern or hear the truth that is contained within it. To see the truth of Scripture, one must submit to God as God is self-revealed in the Scripture. Of course, the Spirit of God is working "outside" the Scriptures among all people; one way that the Spirit works is to help people not be deceived and to see (and to want to see) what is the actual sobering and marvelous truth about our human condition, our truest needs, and the singular remedy, Christ in His fullness. Yet, this "external" work of the Spirit is never forced on someone, and usually this is an incremental process, a wooing. God respects the freewill of individuals. But certainly, a person can begin to read Scripture with good benefit when he or she submits to the Spirit with a responsive and submissive heart. The Spirit will assist them

---

[17] Another possibility held by a number of interpreters is that "the things that are coming" (τὰ ἐρχόμενα) that the Spirit will announce refers to the Book of Revelation itself, i.e., that which has become Scripture; for those holding such a view, see George R. Beasley-Murray, *John*, WBC 36 (Dallas: Word, 2002), 284.

to experience truth in their perceptions of themselves and world around them and with what God has said in Scripture. When this external testimony of the Spirit corresponds with what they are able to read and apprehend in the Scripture, they experience the truth about themselves, the world, and God in Christ.

Importantly, the NT connects notions of "spirit" with reading/learning/cognition. Paul in 1 Corinthians attempts to redirect the Corinthians' zealousness for "spirits" by urging them to pursue the gift of prophecy in 14:12: "Since you are zealous for spirits, seek in order to abound for the edification of the church." Then in 1 John, believers are warned about teachings from "spirits" that may mislead and are false (4:1–6). As believers, however, we have an "anointing" that is sufficient, and teaches us the Truth—in John's view, the Holy Spirit is an anointing poured out on believers (2:27). Then, too, Paul says to Timothy: "But the Spirit explicitly says that in later times some will fall away from the faith, paying attention to deceitful spirits and doctrines of demons" (1 Tim 4:1). We also see the Holy Spirit speaking to believers about events in the future (Acts 20:23; 21:11; 1 Cor 2:10–11), particularly here warning against false spirits.

What I am hoping to establish here is that the Holy Spirit, truth, and Scripture belong together and that scriptural truth is as much cognitive as it is spiritual in nature. We should not dichotomize and partition spirit and mind, supernatural and natural. The fact that many believers separate the natural world from supernatural reality is the result of Enlightenment thinking: "We can really only know what is physical/natural; what ever else is there is supernatural." But, I take very seriously Paul's injunction to "be renewed in the spirit of your mind" (Eph 4:23). Is this a big "S" (Holy Spirit) or little "s" (human spirit, or disposition)? Or, is it both—our minds are powerfully spiritual, and this spirituality is cognitive and combines rationality and relationality. Thus, our minds are powerful places of the Holy Spirit's influence. This is a good revelation for us all because we tend to emotionalize the Holy Spirit as a feeling, and by doing so we greatly restrict his work in our life. This Spirit conveys not only God's relational love, but also teaches us the cognitive truth in Scripture and in the world, and seeks to make us holy by convicting us of sin.

So, with regard to Scripture the Holy Spirit guides us with what has already been spoken by the Father and by Jesus as we study and attend to it. In general, the Spirit is aligned with God's Word and strives to align us to Scripture. At this point let me summarize several positive aspects of the Spirit's work pertaining to the interpretation and appropriation of Scripture. I have been influenced by multiple sources here generally,[18] but the progression presented below occurs to me now as most logical:

1. The Holy Spirit, who is completely in concert with God's reality and love and desire of relationship with people, will help people acquire a basic pre-understanding of essential truths for interpreting Scripture (Acts 26:18; 2 Cor 4:6; Heb 6:4; Eph 1:17–21; 3:16–19;

---

[18] See, e.g., the very fine summary in Ch.12 "The Role of the Holy Spirit" by J. Scott Duvall and J. Daniel Hays, *Grasping God's Word: A Hands-on Approach to Reading, Interpreting, and Applying the Bible*, 2nd ed. (Grand Rapids: Zondervan, 2005); also see see David R. Bauer and Robert A. Traina, *Inductive Bible Study: A Comprehensive Guide to the Practice of Hermeneutics* (Grand Rapids: Baker, 2010), 10, 25–26, 36–41 et passim.

Col 1:9–12). This pre-understanding would include God's love for all creation and people, God's mission to save us from sins, and God's formation of a people who walk in the light, who perform "good deeds" in the world, and who participate in God's mission in the world (e.g., Matt 5:3–16; Gal 6:9–10; Eph 2:10; 1 Tim 2:1–7; Titus 2:11–14).

2. The Holy Spirit will foster in us a receptive disposition or yearning for Scripture, like newborn infants longing to be fed by a mother's milk (1 Pet 2:1–3). This may be experienced as motivation, especially in an attitude of love, which seeks to respect, value, and understand "the other," i.e., that which is different, other, and strange to us. *Scripture is precisely such a stranger to us, coming to us in different languages, times, cultures, and literary forms.* Our cozy familiarity with Scripture may very well breed contempt—we need to respect its being different from us.

> Scripture is a stranger to us, coming to us in different languages, times, cultures, and literary forms.

3. The Holy Spirit will work for the total salvation of our hearts, minds, souls, communities, and all of creation. How? The Spirit will convict us of our sin and unbelief (John 16:8–9). The Spirit is grieved as we live sinfully (Eph 4:30). At the same time, the Holy Spirit encourages our faithful, loving obedience to the Word of God. In this regard the Holy Spirit will prompt faithful living in our respective situations and settings (Eph 5:17–22). The Spirit's primary role is to sanctify us as vessels of God's love within creation.

4. The Holy Spirit helps us to be aware of Scripture and brings to our remembrance scriptural notions and words so that we may correlate scriptural ideas. In this sense the Spirit may "guide" us to ponder particular words and verses as pieces of evidence to help us interpret Scripture. As a testimony, I have often experienced the Spirit's help to be more efficient in research and thus finding something that I remembered or that I need in a timely manner when I am actively conducting research prayerfully and attentively. J. Scott Duvall and J. Daniel Hays also rightly state, "[T]he Spirit's role is not to author a new Bible (i.e., revealing new meaning through personal experience or community tradition), but to bring home to us the meaning of the Scripture he has already authored."[19]

5. The Holy Spirit sustains and supports the human capacities to comprehend the truth of Scripture. Paul described a "renewing of one's mind" (Titus 3:5; Rom 12:1–2; Eph 4:23). Such renewing of the mind can be restorative of proper discernment and rationality (Heb 5:12–14). In this regard David R. Bauer and Robert A. Traina helpfully state, "The Spirit often works through the human mind and certainly seeks to work through the mind, especially as the rational faculties, limited by our creatureliness and infirmed by our sinfulness, have been healed or empowered by the Spirit of God to function in a truly effective way."[20]

6. Even further, the Holy Spirit may indeed broaden one's "spiritual insight" into the nature of God, Scripture, human relationships, and life more generally. Such insight may manifest

---

[19] *Grasping God's Word* (2nd ed.), 206.
[20] *Inductive Bible Study*, 40.

itself in creative, sympathetic, and probing reflections when interpreting Scripture. Again, Bauer and Traina comment on this aspect,

> So important is the spiritual factor that one sometimes finds individuals who, though deficient in the skills of interpretation, far surpass in insight those who have had the best training in exegetical procedures. Nevertheless, even as technical expertise is not a substitute for spiritual experience in the pursuit of the fullest and most penetrating interpretation, so also spiritual experience cannot be a substitute for technical and methodological expertise.[21]

Finally, let me pass along this anecdote or "chreia."[22] I have heard my colleague Ben Witherington III tell this on several occasions and he kindly relayed this to me in an email:

> A student is complaining about all this language training and studying history and he says 'I don't know why I need all this information. Why, I can just get up in the pulpit and the Spirit will give me utterance.' My reply was 'its a shame you're not giving the Spirit more to work with. Don't use the Holy Spirit as a labor saving device.'

Indeed, let's give the Holy Spirit something to work with by committing ourselves to the task of studying Scripture; this is not simply for our own benefit, but for the benefit of all around us.

IV. THE NATURE OF THE SUBJECT OF OUR DEVOTION AND STUDY

Before we can describe how best to study Scripture, we must understand what Scripture is because *our study of something should correspond materially to what it is in its essence* (see the axiom below). For example, what is the best way to study a tiger? We would not want to go to the zoo, would we? If we did and thought this was the best way, we would likely arrive at wrong conclusions: Tigers have a tendency to be methodical creatures pacing back and forth on the same path; they often stare blankly at nothing; they are unbothered by humans who might walk right in front of them. No, if we really wanted to study tigers, we would go to their natural habitats and camp there for some time, as unobtrusively as possible, carefully making observations and asking probing questions and seeking answers to those questions. In fact, the more we *misunderstand* the tiger's native habitat and context, the more we miss seeing the tiger for what it really is.

What is Scripture most primarily about? Most fundamentally, Scripture contains God's self-disclosure, that is, God's revelation about God's own nature as Father, Son, and Spirit. This is what Scripture is whether one agrees with this or not. Moreover, God's Word is understood as "infallible," because it is trustworthy and reliable; it is true in what it affirms in all matters of salva-

---

[21] *Inductive Bible Study*, 36.

[22] A chreia is brief piece of spoken or enacted wisdom from a teacher when confronted with a situation or question. The composition of a chreia was part of ancient rhetorical education before and during in the NT era. A chreia is a literary form that commonly occurs in the Gospels and Acts; see STEP 6: LITERARY FORMS.

tion, faith, history, theology, practice, and whatever else. This is logically consequential if Scripture is God's self-disclosure.[23] The key question however is, *what does Scripture affirm? What is it that Scripture would have us believe as true?* To answer these questions is one of the primary purposes of Bible Study.[24] Therefore, the most important enterprise is our careful engagement and handling of God's Word.

There are at least five further features of God's self-disclosed Word that should inform our efforts in interpretation. God's self-disclosure is:

1. *Progressive* in theological revelation; i.e., God's nature and will is revealed somewhat progressively through Scripture in their historical testimony of God's historical involvement with God's people;
2. *Incarnational* in literary, human conventions culminating in Jesus of Nazareth as the Christ, i.e., God's revelation in Scripture is fully divine yet fully involves human involvement;
3. *Salvific* in its historical purposes, i.e., bringing complete salvation involving the granting of forgiveness, justification, restoration, sanctification, holiness, love, and glorification;
4. *Perspicacious* in its communication, i.e., clear in its central affirmations for the faithful interpreter; and yet also,
5. *Constrained* or *limited* in its theological, literary, and historical disclosure, i.e., Scripture does not disclose all knowledge, but only that knowledge necessary and helpful for eternal relationship with God, oneself, others, and creation.

One could argue for other core features. However, these five must always be kept in mind and are foundational for considering how best to approach and interpret Scripture.

---

[23] Many, including myself, will make a further affirmation, namely, that God's Word is "inerrant"— "without error or fault in all its teaching" in its autographs (original documents). This position is partially "faith-based," since we do not have access to the original documents; but through textual criticism, we seek to arrive at what they likely contained. For an explanation of what the doctrine of inerrancy affirms and denies, see "The Chicago Statement of Biblical Inerrancy" online at http://www.bible-researcher.com/chicago1.html with bibliography there for locations of the statement in print. It needs to be said that the affirmation of inerrancy takes into account scriptural definitions of what is true and is not negated by phenomena encountered in Scripture such as "a lack of modern technical precision, irregularities of grammar or spelling, observational descriptions of nature, the reporting of falsehoods, the use of hyperbole and round numbers, the topical arrangement of material, variant selections of material in parallel accounts, or the use of free citations" (from Article XIII). These qualifications are critical in a proper understanding of inerrancy.

[24] Presupposed in these questions is that "what is true" or "what is truth" can be known. This is a matter of epistemology (theory of knowledge). To delve into this area is beyond the scope of this book. What is presupposed here is a critical-realism epistemology; see Paul G. Hiebert, "Epistemological Foundations for Science and Theology," *Theological Students Fellowship Bulletin* 8.4 (March 1, 1985): 5–10. As developed by N. T. Wright in *The New Testament and the People of God* ([Minneapolis: Fortress, 1992], 32–37), critical realism proceeds from observation, hypotheses, critical reflection, conclusion of falsification or verification (as summarized in and discussed by Grant R. Osborne, *The Hermeneutical Spiral: A Comprehensive Introduction to Biblical Interpretation*, 2nd ed. [Downers Grove, IL: IVP, 2006], 512). For the very similar inductive methodological underpinnings of biblical study, see Bauer and Traina, *Inductive Bible Study*. For the popular establishment of "truth" as viable existential commitment, see Chad V. Meister, *Building Belief: Constructing Faith from the Ground Up* (Grand Rapids: Baker, 2006), ch.1.

At this point, in conjunction with the general **axiom** restated from above, I will add a particular **premise**, and argue that both lead to a specific **conclusion** about a proper methodological foundation for interpreting Scripture.

1. **Axiom**: Our careful study of anything should be suited to the *nature* of the material under investigation in its appropriate *environment* as much as possible.[25] This axiom can be stated in a more succinct form: *The nature of our study of Scripture should correspond to the nature of Scripture itself*; or, put another way, *Scripture's nature must govern the nature of our scriptural study*.

   > The nature of our study of Scripture should correspond to the nature of Scripture itself.

2. **Premise**: Arguably, the nature and environment of the biblical materials may well be described in ten attributes:

   - *theological*—God revealing
   - *literary*—humanly communicated
   - *historical*—located in time and space
   - *truthful*—infallible in what it affirms[26]
   - *canonical*—authority recognizing
   - *ecclesial*—community [in]forming
   - *moral-formative*—people sanctifying
   - *apologetic*—ideologically engaging
   - *experiential*—experientially empowering
   - *missional-evangelical*—gospel of Christ proclaiming and people saving

   At the core, these are what Scripture is; it is more certainly, but it is certainly not less.

3. **Conclusion**: We should, therefore, study the biblical materials according to their nature and environment as essentially theological, literary, historical, truthful, canonical, ecclesial, moral-formative, apologetic, experiential, evangelical, and missional.

Let me offer three considerations before discussing the methodological implications of this conclusion. First, while it is certainly possible to prioritize these ten attributes as to their importance (e.g., some would probably rightly say that Scripture is first and foremost "theological" in nature), this may prematurely limit our scriptural interpretation to "find" *only* what is *theological*. In reality the theological nature of Scripture is integrally linked to the larger complexity of what the Scripture is in essence, and this complexity understood more completely would greatly enrich our understanding of God. So, for instance, the missional-evangelical dimension of Scripture pro-

---

[25] As stated in Traina, "If, then, a particular approach to the Scriptures is to be valid, it must bear a substantial likeness to the Scriptures themselves" (*Methodical Bible Study* [Wilmore, KY: Robert A. Traina, 1952], 7).

[26] I use the term synonymously with inerrant but I want to avoid the fundamentalism associated with inerrant.

foundly arises out of God's creational and covenantal relation to the world and his people within that world. Likewise, the truthful and apologetic nature of Scripture is seen in the ideological confrontation of the world and its philosophies that suppress true knowledge, true freedom from sinfulness, and true worship of God. So, if we begin by focusing on only one scriptural attribute, this will likely lead us to under-appreciate other equally valid dimensions of Scripture. So, let me urge us to understand Scripture fully since this will help us understand God in God's fullness.

Second, I would postulate that the nature of Scripture reflects the essential nature of humanity made in God's image, yet now estranged from God's creational and covenantal purposes. Scripture comes to us the way it does because we are what we are as humans currently, both as part of God's good creation and as fallen creatures. The implication of this is that for us to properly understand Scripture is to properly understand humanity in our current complex reality.

Third, we learn who we are by studying Scripture: The more fully Scripture is studied and understood, the more fully both God and humanity are understood. There is something completely "humanizing" for us as we study Scripture; we become more complete and appreciative of the human experience. We will gain a realistic, God-intended sense of what God wants humanity to be. We will discover that God's Word is embodied in Jesus, the Messiah King, the perfect human.

In the end, we approach Scripture openly and without our agendas that would delimit us and constrain us from seeing Scripture as it really is. The great linguist Eugene A. Nida has said of Scripture, "We are not as realistic about the Bible as the Bible is. Why shouldn't we be taking it for what it says, instead of trying to dress it up and say, 'Oh yes, but the folks who wrote it didn't really mean that.'"[27] So then, *the goal of our study is not to presume upon Scripture our understanding, but to let Scripture speak realistically and soberly to us about ours.* What will we discover in Scripture if we dare to do so honestly and openly?

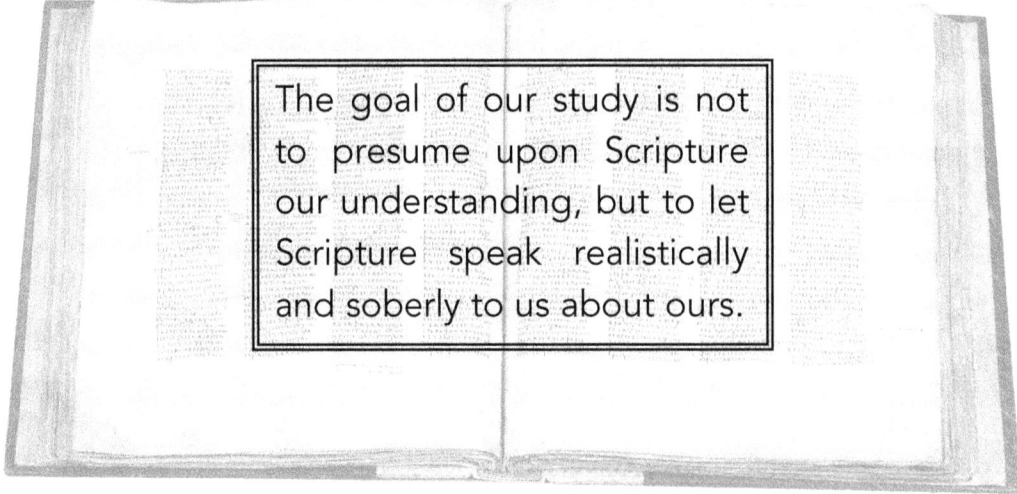

---

[27] From his message "How to Reach Out" at the 1989 Kingdom Conference Asbury Theological Seminary, Call Number BV4070.A882 K5 1989 no.5. In context Nida talks about the realism of Ecclesiastes, the celebration of sex in the Song of Solomon, how much of a "stinker" David was, and how much of an absolute failure David was as a family man, etc.

V. PRIORITIES AND PURSUITS OF SCRIPTURAL STUDY

A. **Priorities of Scriptural Study**: Given the ten attributes of God's Word as described above, we can further reflect on what implications they have for our interpretation of Scripture as follows:

If Scripture is **Theological**, **Ecclesial**, and **Moral-Formative** in nature, then as we study Scripture we are obliged *especially* to consider…

1. God's self-disclosed nature;
2. God's calling forth of an ecclesial community;
3. God's moral will and formative purposes for this ecclesial community within humanity;
4. God's relationship with his ecclesial community and how God empowers them for life; and
5. Furthermore, we should consider the theological and moral-formative traditions of the ecclesial communities that have devoted themselves to the study of the Scripture; this involves the study of church history and the history of scriptural interpretation.

Complicating factors to our theological, ecclesial, and moral-formative study of Scripture include the following: We have theological and ecclesial "baggage" and moral failures that cause us to resist interpretative conclusions about God, God's will, the nature of God's people, and God's formation within us. Also, we have limited exposure to alternative ecclesial traditions and limited time to study properly these traditions well. So, in this light how are we to learn about God, God's people, and God's will?

a. We will need God's strength, convicting presence, and insight from Scripture itself; it would seem that God's Spirit of truth is God's gift to assist us; but this does not remove our need for diligence and devotion in our *study*.
b. We will thus need to study Scripture through literary and historical means to ascertain the truth about the theological, ecclesial, and moral-formative affirmations contained therein and to evaluate which theological, ecclesial, and moral-formative traditions merit our focus and attention; all this effort is assisted by the work and presence of the Holy Spirit.

If Scripture is **Literary** in nature, then as we study Scripture we are obliged *especially* to study and consider…

1. the original languages (Hebrew, Aramaic, Greek), if at all possible, or have access to and have respect for people who do;
2. the genres and literary forms in Scripture as is informed by comparative studies;
3. methodological studies treating original language, genres, comparative studies, and their interpretation;
4. interpretations and interpreters who study Scripture through original languages, informed methodological perspectives, and accurate knowledge of literary genres and forms; and
5. the history of interpretation relating to the literary interpretation of Scripture.

Complicating factors to our literary interpretation of Scripture include our epistemological and hermeneutical "baggage," limited time, conflicting commitments, restricted access to the fullness of language/genre/literary studies, and our lack of concrete statements of authorial intention or intended audiences, all of which will result in presuppositional, investigative, and procedural deficiencies. So, in this light how are we to learn to study Scripture literarily according to its original languages, literary genres, literary forms, and history of interpretation?

    a. We will strive to access the original languages necessary to study Scripture, if possible.
    b. We will learn discerningly to rely on others who show particular expertise and competency in these respective areas where we are deficient.
    c. We will be cautious about ascribing authorial intent and assuming intended audiences.
    d. We will trust in God's direction of our studies to focus on those aspects of literary interpretation that God may deem our area of specialization as a contribution to the interpretation of Scripture for the benefit of all others.
    e. We will learn research strategies to access the history of interpretation in this area.

If Scripture is **Historical**, **Truthful**, and **Canonical** in nature, then as we study Scripture we are obliged *especially* to study and consider…

    1. the history surrounding the events described in Scripture and the apparent and relative truth claims in Scripture made about them;
    2. the history of the formation of the texts of Scripture and the history of their transmission and of their canonization;
    3. methodological studies treating the history surrounding the biblical texts and the canonical formation of Scripture;
    4. the history of interpretation with respect to the history of the events, the transmission of texts, and the formation of the canon; and
    5. the canonical interrelation of texts to one another and the history of interpretation of canonical interrelations.

Complicating factors to our historical and canonical interpretation of Scripture include our epistemological and hermeneutical "baggage" about history, truth, and canon, our uncertainty about particular historical interpretations in relation to others, our limited time, and our limited access to the recovery of historical events, all of which will result in presuppositional, heuristic, and procedural deficiencies. So, in this light how should we to learn to study Scripture historically, truthfully, and canonically?

    a. We will strive to learn all we can with regard to ancient history in relation to Scripture.
    b. We will learn discerningly to rely on others who show particular expertise and competency in these respective areas where we are deficient.
    c. We will trust in God's direction of our studies to focus on those aspects of history, truth claims, and canon formation that God may deem our area of specialization as a contribu-

tion to the interpretation of Scripture for the benefit of all others.

d. We will learn research strategies to access the history of interpretation in these areas.

If Scripture is **Apologetic**, **Experiential**, and **Missional-Evangelistic** in nature, then as we study Scripture we are obliged *especially* to study and consider…

1. the apologetic-ideological nature of Scripture to empower persons and communities to confront falsehood and injustice in and around us;
2. the centrality of the missional-evangelistic nature of Scripture "to proclaim the good news of Jesus Christ as Lord" and "to seek and to save what was lost";
3. those argumentative and powerfully experiential means that Scripture deems as legitimate in order to engage and evangelize the world of fallen humanity;
4. how best to proclaim the truth of Scripture to the contemporary church calling it to faithfulness and fruitfulness in its mission; and
5. how best to engage contemporary societies and the broader world at all human levels (e.g., intellectual, ideological, social) drawing deeply from the fruit of our study in conversation with other fields of knowledge and experience.

Complicating factors include the fact that we are located within fallen structures and ideologies that promote self-interest and preservation at the expense of outreach to others. We have blind spots to our own presuppositions and baggage that causes us inadvertently or intentionally to work against one another; we push our own agendas onto the biblical materials; we employ oppressive means and uncompassionate manners in our discipleship and in our own dysfunctional mission to the world; we lack compassion and we are insensitive and arrogant. So, in this light how are we to interpret Scripture apologetically, experientially, evangelistically, and missionally?

a. We confess our sin, inadequacies, propensity to be self-oriented to the neglect of others, and our participation in perpetuating injustice; and we repent of these things.
b. We ask God to fill us with his Spirit to convict and empower us to persist in holy acts of love, justice, and the proclamation of the gospel of Christ.
c. We act boldly and compassionately at the stirring of God's voice for prayerful action.
d. We, as peacemakers, actively seek reconciliation between injured parties.
e. We pray for and actively support the church's mission to save that which was lost.

B. **Pursuits of Scriptural Study**: Since Scripture is essentially *theological* (God revealing), *canonical* (authority recognizing), *ecclesial* (community [in]forming), *moral-formative* (people sanctifying), *literary* (humanly communicated), *historical* (temporally and spatially located), *truthful* (inerrant in what it affirms), *apologetic* (ideologically engaging), *experiential* (experientially empowering), *missional-evangelical* (gospel proclaiming and people saving), our pursuit to understand it should correspond to its nature. On this basis we may describe basic questions that are at the core of our pursuits of biblical study, beginning with authorial intentions and moving through ecclesial history into our contemporary locations. In this light Bible study essentially attempts to pursue answers to these questions:

1. <u>Authorial Intention</u>: What was the meaning intended by the original author(s) for this particular passage? What is God's intention for including this scriptural passage within the whole of the biblical canon? Why was it so intended?
2. <u>Audience Reception</u>: What did the original audiences likely understand by this scriptural passage? How would the original audiences have understood this intention? How did they embody it, or might they have embodied it, and lived according to its directives and its implications? Why was this necessary for them to do so in the way directed by this scriptural passage?
3. <u>Historical Reception</u>: What meaning(s) has the church historically ascribed to this scriptural passage? How were these meanings embodied in ecclesial ministry and life historically? Why were they so embodied?
4. <u>Current Reception</u>: How is the church today to understand the authorial intention? How are we to appropriate it, that is, to be empowered by it so as to embody it and live it out? How are we today to reconcile past ecclesial interpretations with our own today?
5. <u>Implications</u>: What are the implications of our interpretation for understanding and ordering all of life today in our respective communities in the world?

VI. PRINCIPLES OF SCRIPTURAL STUDY

Based upon these methodological considerations of the ten attributes of Scripture, let me describe a set of fundamental presuppositions through the use of acronyms for ease of memorization. These presuppositions will inform our study of Scripture by helping us remain open to what is present in Scripture; they play prominently in each exegetical area and its tasks as described throughout this book.

First, there are two general interpretive principles that I learned from two of my exegesis professors. Professor Joseph Wang instilled in his students, among many other things, the principle of **CAP**—**C**onsider **A**ll **P**ossibilities. This dictum applies when considering and collecting relevant and pertinent exegetical evidence such as grammatical constructions, syntax, word meaning and usage, historical context, theological implications, and especially contextual considerations.[28] This latter type of evidence is decisive and is what Professor

> **CAP**—**C**onsider **A**ll **P**ossibilities.
> **CIE**—**C**ontext **I**s **E**verything.

---

[28] The consideration of all possibilities is what Bauer and Traina are advocating for when they write of "the willingness to gather evidence fully and openly for and against the premises stated and to accept them as conditional (when necessary), along with the acknowledgement that the inferences drawn are hypothetical and changeable." For this and more on the idea of "radical openness" as "the litmus test of the presence and practice of the inductive spirit," see Bauer and Traina, *Inductive Bible Study*, 23–25.

Bob Lyon called **CIE**—**C**ontext **I**s **E**verything. We know the truth of this firsthand when our own statements are related to others, but taken out of context. Political pundits on all sides too often rely on removing statements from their original context to arrive at new meanings in order to create or advance ideological extreme characterizations of their opponents. We know that context is critical for understanding the meaning of any statement.

In addition to CAP and CIE, we may consider a "family" of interpretive principles. The first two acronyms involve the foundational principles of **GRAMMA** (**GRAM**matical **M**ode of **A**nalysis) and **GRAMPS** (**GRAM**matical **P**rocedure of **S**tudy). These principles relate to the grammatical nature of Scripture and our need to interpret it accordingly by accessing accurately what was said in the original languages. The next two principles are **AUNT** (**AU**thority of the **NT**) and **UNCLE** (**U**nconditional **N**ature of the **C**anon for **L**ater **E**ras). These remind us that the focus of our interpretation centers around the revelation of Jesus Christ in the NT understood within the complete and closed Canon of Scripture inclusive of the Hebrew Scriptures as OT. To these principles, we need to add **MOM** (**M**ajor **O**n **M**ajors and **M**inor **O**n **M**inors) and **POP** (**P**riority **O**n **P**raxis). These two help interpreters pay attention to what is a central concern in Scripture—the faithful obedience of God's people. MOM alerts us that not all Scripture is equal in its application; POP reminds us that God in Christ through the Spirit enables our faithful obedience to grow and live in holy love. But, the family is not complete. There is also **SIS** (**S**cripture **I**nterprets **S**cripture) and **BRO** (**B**e **R**eaching **O**ut). The first affirms the need of interpretation to be self-referential in that passages of Scripture that are difficult to interpret should be interpreted by clear passages of Scripture. As much as possible, we let Scripture interpret Scripture. Also, BRO reminds us that Scripture is evangelistic and propels us to mission and outreach in the world. Notable also are the engendered principles **HIS** (**H**istory **I**nforms **S**cripture) and **HERS** (**H**istorical **E**nvironment of **R**oman **S**ociety). These two remind us of the social-religious-political location of God's ecclesial communities as they were inspired by God to write Scripture in history. Together this family of interpretive principles supports CIE and CAP.

THE FAMILY OF INTERPRETIVE PRINCIPLES

GRAMMA (**GRAM**matical **M**ode of **A**nalysis)
GRAMPS (**GRAM**matical **P**rocedure of **S**tudy).

AUNT (**AU**thority of the **NT**)
UNCLE (**U**nconditional **N**ature of the **C**anon for **L**ater **E**ras).

MOM (**M**ajor **O**n **M**ajors and **M**inor **O**n **M**inors)
POP (**P**riority **O**n **P**raxis).

SIS (**S**cripture **I**nterprets **S**cripture)
BRO (**B**e **R**eaching **O**ut).
HIS (**H**istory **I**nforms **S**cripture)
HERS (**H**istorical **E**nvironment of **R**oman **S**ociety).

VII. Core Interpretive Areas, Procedures, and Skills

In light of the above considerations and the nature of Scripture, it is possible to identify and organize the vast array of methods and procedures that biblical interpreters have historically used. Although each area of research is often well defined, what is not often indicated is their interrelation as a fluid movement. Here are what I deem to be the most helpful areas for research, study, reflection, and appropriation:

Steps **internal** to Scripture	1. Contextual Location
	2. Textual Comparisons
	3. Grammatical Study
	4. Semantic Analysis
Steps **outward** from and between scriptural passages	5. Lexical Research
	6. Literary Forms
	7. Historical Context
	8. Scriptural Correlations
Steps **toward** scriptural appropriation and embodiment	9. Interpretive Decisions
	10. Biblical Theology
	11. Evaluated Applications
	12. Presentation Brainstorm

These twelve areas will be treated as progressive Steps in the Interpretive Journey; they represent what I consider to be "best practices" for fruitful interpretation and appropriation. We begin "internal" and move "outward" to Scripture's broader environment. A decisive hinge point occurs with Step 9: Interpretive Decisions that bridges Scripture's initial, ancient embodiment and its present potential embodiment as we move to scriptural appropriation. Specifically, the ordering of the twelve exegetical Steps works to establish a context initially in Step 1: Contextual Location (remember CIE: Context Is Everything). Next we perform Step 2: Textual Comparisons in English and in Greek in order to identify if there are any significant textual variations among English translations and ancient Greek manuscripts—these variations would alert us to areas in need of careful attention. Step 3: Grammatical Study and Step 4: Semantic Analysis allow us to make careful observations and ask key questions that need resolution.

After looking carefully at Scripture internally, we will have been prepared to look outwardly to Scripture's "locatedness" within the ancient Mediterranean world. We will have identified important words for Step 5: Lexical Research. Continuing on, in Step 6: Literary Forms we investigate the scriptural passage within its broader literary environment since speech acts are conventional and utilize recognizable patterns of arrangement. In Step 7: Historical Context we consider the historical setting for the biblical writing based upon what can be known of the authors' and audiences' location and situation. We also evaluate how the biblical materials relate to their contemporaneous social and cultural *realia* (customs, events, artifacts, institutions, roles, etc.) since every ancient text is situated in a location and is "incarnated" in real life. This leads to Step

8: SCRIPTURAL CORRELATIONS where we observe any quotation, allusion, or thematic connection that the biblical passage has with other biblical passages and consider what meaning these have.

By this point in the interpretive journey, we will have done a lot of spadework and digging; we will have identified questions that remain unanswered and need interpretation. As we engage in STEP 9: INTERPRETIVE DECISIONS we first consider which questions are most necessary to answer in order to best understand and appropriate the biblical text. In light of evidence that we have gathered and in view of the history of interpretation as represented in commentaries, we will decide how best to answer key questions. As we interpret the scriptural passage, we have begun the critical process of appropriation. Next, after having come to more firm conclusions on the meaning of the passage by addressing its more pressing and answerable questions, we are ready for STEP 10: BIBLICAL THEOLOGY. Here we identify and synthesize the theological truth of the passage: What does the passage affirm about God, about Creation, about Humans, and the relationship between these entities? In the next STEP 11: EVALUATED APPLICATIONS, we evaluate the truths, commands, and practices of the passage for faithful application today: Are these transcultural or culture-bound? In what ways do the theological truths and practices relate to our society and human situation? How are we to apply and appropriate this passage in our communities? Finally, we consider how best to present our interpretive findings for teaching and preaching by performing STEP 12: PRESENTATION BRAINSTORM. Thoughtful and engaging communication that is consonant with the truth of Scripture will help people comprehend and envision better how to be faithful to God. Here one considers what illustrations, stories, examples, and analogies best compliment the biblical text. The goal of walking *In Step with God's Word* is faithful proclamation of the gospel of Christ and teaching about God's Kingdom within our respective locations. Thus, these last two interpretive STEPS take shape around the needs, concerns, and hopes of our respective communities.

Let me state here and now very clearly that for the typical interpreter it would be impractical, if not even impossible, to perform all twelve interpretive STEPS each time he or she studies the NT. When I teach through these twelve STEPS, I explain that *interpreters will need to be selective and adaptive about which tasks will be most needful in each circumstance*. This will vary depending on the passage and your time constraints. So, you should understand that as you learn and practice these twelve interpretive STEPS, they represent "best practices" in each area and ***the goal is for you to develop interpretive skills suitable for each STEP***.

In Step with God's Word attempts to promote honest, probing, and attentive observation of the text for faithful interpretation and holy, loving, and missional living. About "attention" Todd Oakley has said: "Of all the activities human beings undertake, perhaps none is more consequential for the performance of other activities than paying attention. When we attend, we perceive. When we attend and perceive, we remember. When we attend, perceive, and remember, we learn. When we learn, we can act deliberately and with forethought."[29] In particular, "[a]ttention is thus

---

[29] Todd Oakley, *From Attention to Meaning: Explorations in Semiotics, Linguistics, and Rhetoric*, European Semiotics 8 (Bern: Peter Lang, 2009), 25.

important for many activities, perception, voluntary recall, and the development of skill."[30] So, be prepared to be attentive and by this attentiveness to grow in your interpretive skills. One of the founders of Inductive Bible Study, Wilbert Webster White, depicted the centrality of careful observation of Scripture within the following chart.[31] Consider it carefully.

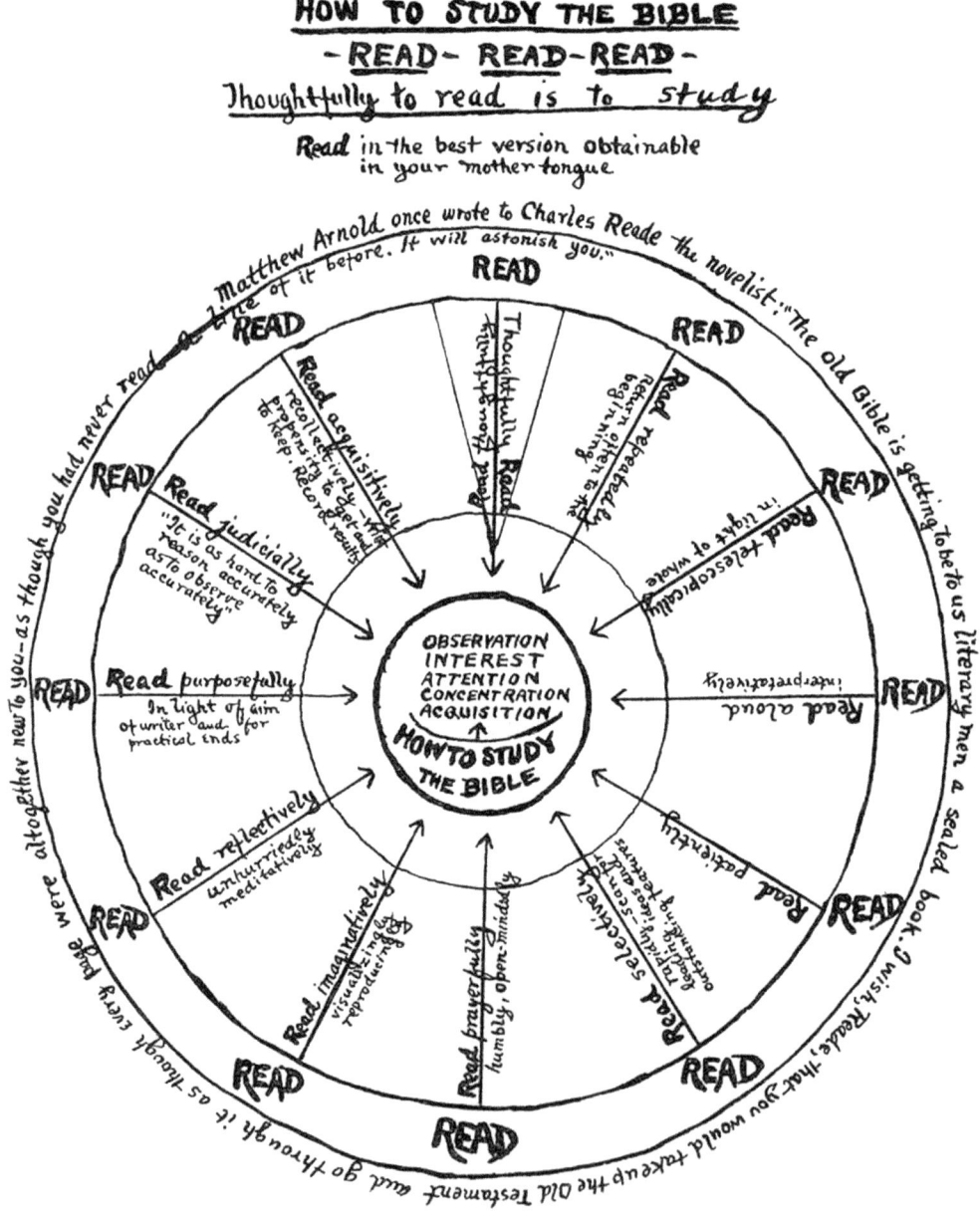

---

[30] Raja Parasuraman, *The Attentive Brain* (Cambridge: MIT Press, 1998), 3.

[31] This image has been modified for print and was the third draft (Oct 15, 1921) of White's depiction; the image is in the public domain and found at https://dlc.library.columbia.edu/catalog/cul:3tx95x6b2b accessed Aug 24, 2016, Columbia University Libraries, Union Theological Seminary, New York. For a history of the Inductive Bible Study movement and White's place, see David R. Bauer, "Inductive Biblical Study: History, Character, and Prospectus in a Global Perspective," *Asbury Journal* 68.1 (2013): 6–35.

Finally, let me conclude this CHAPTER ALPHA with stating these two core goals for your interpretive work. First, *seek to understand Scripture as it is and as it has come to us, and not as you want it to be.* This requires empathy, that is, yearning to understand and know something on its own terms and not our own terms. We are here acknowledging God's terms of self-disclosure and becoming known through the gospel in Scripture. The second concern is this: *Love God and humans conjointly and completely.* Love is the greatest of the faith, hope, and love triad (1 Cor 13:13). Love is what endures. Both of these aims should lead us to humility, to earnestness in the pursuit of truth, and to empathy in terms of love for those that are "others" and different. God has provided the model for us by seeking after and finding us when we were lost, by revealing himself sacrificially in human form, by talking truthfully to us using human idiom (languages and literary forms), and by providing forgiveness and reconciliation for us and one another. God shows us how to love, how to know this love, and what to do with that knowledge.

So we are now ready to take this interpretive journey together *In Step with God's Word*.

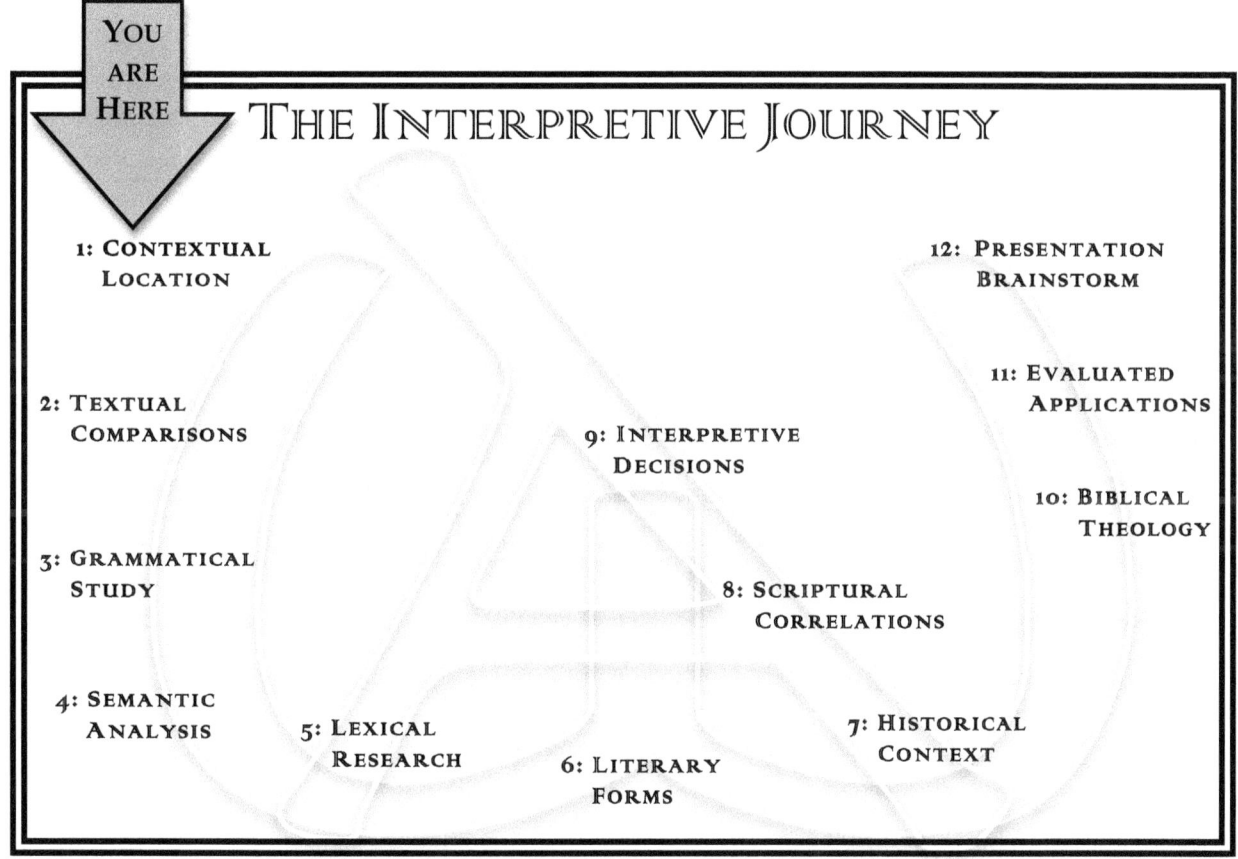

PART II:

WALKING INSIDE AND AROUND THE WORD

STEP 1

CONTEXTUAL LOCATION

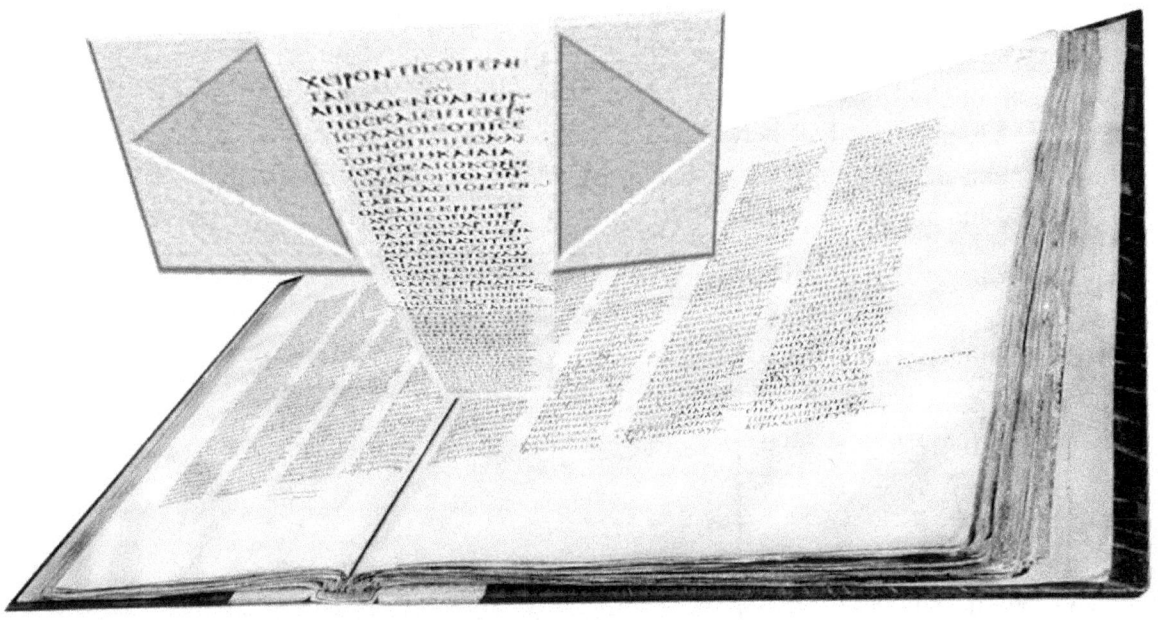

What are the three most important factors in buying real estate? Location. Location. Location.
—common adage

Introduction: Interpreting Scripture is like buying real estate. Location is everything. Thus, the starting place is the specific passage that you have chosen to investigate in its context. Traditionally, the passage is called the "pericope" (pl. pericopae, but pericopes is also used). Pericope (not to be confused with periscope that may result from your word processor's autocorrect function!) derives from the Greek noun περικοπή, "a cutting around/out." Pericopae were identified for the regular reading of Scripture in Jewish and early Christian services dating to the time of Jesus if not earlier. Each pericope was identified within the context of Scripture in a schedule of readings that formed what is called a lectionary. Unfortunately, it is very common for us as readers to "cut out" pericopae from their literary and scriptural contexts, orphaning them. Therefore, one of the most foundational tasks when interpreting a passage is to understand its context. Remember the acronym CIE, "Context Is Everything." This STEP 1: CONTEXTUAL LOCATION describes how to locate a pericope within its context, how to investigate important features of semantic relationships and contextual constraints, and how to perform an inductive book survey.

I. PRIMARY SURVEY

Orientation: The survey below provides an overview of the levels of context for a pericope and a discussion of the larger levels: book, corpora, and canon. The formation of the Christian Canon of Scripture is the most important overarching context. Thus, we will discuss the basic organization of Scripture and how laws of composition structure biblical materials. Our careful observation of these relationships allows us to ask incisive interpretive questions.

Bible as Structured, Sacred Literature: We most essentially encounter God's Word as literature; it comes to us literarily. Therefore, our study should involve observing the literary features of the biblical texts at multiple levels as carefully and as thoroughly as possible. These levels are described below and move from the smallest unit to the largest unit:

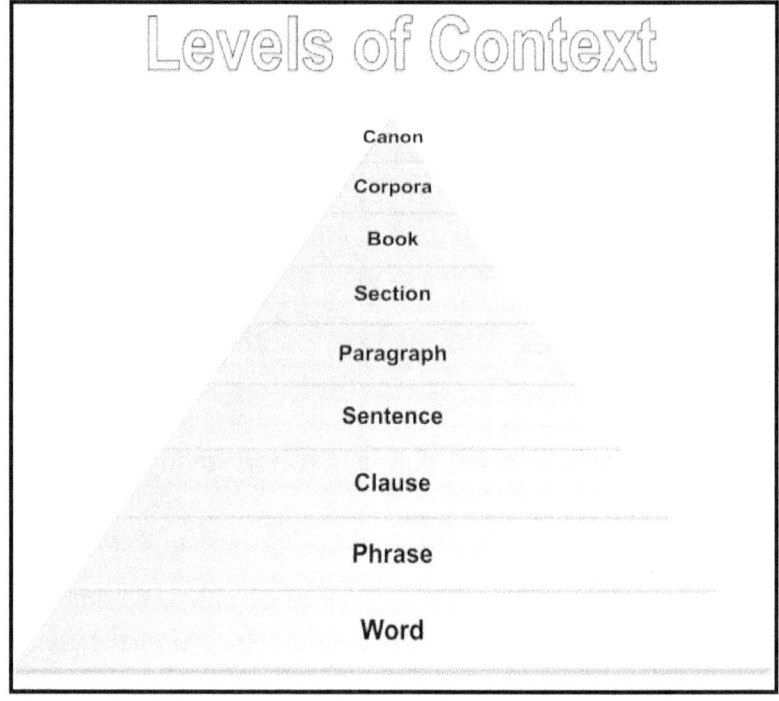

a. **Words** consist of smaller components; the study of word meaning is called lexicography. Yet, words have special meanings in actual use and occur within figures of speech, etc.
b. **Phrases, Clauses**, and **Sentences** entail sentence grammar, semantic relationships, and literary forms.
c. **Paragraphs, Units,** and **Sections** represent an even higher level of text organization; here you may study semantic relationships, literary form, and rhetorical patterns.
d. **Books** as a whole represent the discourse as a whole; you may here study semantic relationships, discourse grammar, rhetorical patterns, and the analysis of genre.
e. **Corpora** refers to the interrelation of books within a "corpus" on the basis of authorship, common issues, and/or thematic development. Important corpora in the NT include the Synoptic Gospels, Luke-Acts, Johannine Literature, Pauline letters, and Petrine letters.
f. **Canon** refers to the two Testaments, Old and New, in which you may study books within each Canon, discern theological patterns, and describe biblical theology.

If we might be more philosophical at this moment, we would add larger contextual levels above the levels of written "text":

g. **Church History** involves distinct ecclesial movements within world history.
h. **Culture** and **Society:** Culture refers to more specific, idiosyncratic expressions of human values, beliefs, and practices whereas society describes people(s) with shared customs, laws, and organization.
i. **Empire** refers to the overarching unifying governance of diverse populations situated above cultures and society and enacts the promotion of ideological, totalizing worldviews.
j. **World History** entails an even larger scale than empire by describing different locations, different time periods, and progressive human involvements involving cause-effect, etc.
k. **Created Order** or **Cosmos** is a broader view of human and creaturely existence inclusive of the created or natural world and "supra-natural/spiritual" realities.

<u>Canon, Testament, Corpora, Books</u>: It may be helpful to visualize how our Bible is organized. Below is a chart describing the contents of the Christian Bible, the Old Testament and New.

HEBREW BIBLE: *TaNaK (Torah, Nebi'im, Kethubim)* OR OLD TESTAMENT

		The **Law** (*Torah*)
Genesis **Exodus** **Leviticus** **Numbers** **Deuteronomy**	These five books are known as "the Law of Moses" or "the Pentateuch."	In the NT these books are treated as a collection; see, e.g., Matt 5:17; 7:12; 11:13; 22:40; Luke 16:16.
Joshua **Judges** **1 & 2 Samuel** **1 & 2 Kings**	"The Former Prophets" These six books are also called "the Deuteronomistic History."	The **Prophets** (*Nebi'im*) These books are also treated as a collection; see references above.
Isaiah **Jeremiah** **Ezekiel**	"The Major Prophets" Daniel also considered a major prophet by the church.	
Hosea, Joel, Amos, Obadiah, Jonah, Micah, Nahum, Habakkuk, Zephaniah, Haggai, Zechariah, and **Malachi**	"The Twelve Minor Prophets"	

Psalms	Called the "Psalter" by the church.	
Job Proverbs Song of Songs Ecclesiastes	Wisdom Literature	The **WRITINGS** (*Kethubim*) See Luke 24:44 "the Psalms"; and Matt 23:35 and 2 Chr 24:21.
Lamentations Esther Ruth Daniel	Historical Writings	

THE NEW TESTAMENT IN CANONICAL ORDER

Matthew Mark Luke	"The Synoptic Gospels"	The **FOUR GOSPELS** are ancient historical biography.
John		John belongs to "the Johannine Literature."
Acts	A biographical history of the early church; the second volume of Luke	
Romans* 1* & 2 Corinthians* Galatians*		The **PAULINE EPISTLES** are official, rhetorical letters using prescripts and postscripts of personal letters. Critical scholarship often divides the Pauline Epistles into the seven undisputed(*) and the six disputed letters.
Ephesians Philippians* Colossians	"The Prison Epistles" (including Philemon)	
1* & 2 Thessalonians		
1 & 2 Timothy Titus	"The Pastoral Epistles"	
Philemon*	With the Prison Epistles	
Hebrews	Considered to be by Paul in the early church	The **LATTER NT** (not necessarily the "later" NT) consists of other Epistles, Treatises, Sermons, and the Apocalypse.
James 1 & 2 Peter 1, 2, 3 John Jude	"The General or Catholic Epistles"	
Revelation	"The Apocalypse"	

Old Testament Corpora: The Old Testament (OT) is partitioned as Hebrew Bible into *Torah* (Law), *Nebi'im* (Prophets), and *Kethubim* (Writings), what is called *TaNaK*. The Prophets and Writings are further partitioned into corpora (smaller collections of books; former, major, and minor prophets; wisdom literature, etc.) to provide a context for interpretation. This ordering is different than our Protestant Bible's ordering, which is different than the Catholic ordering that also includes additional books called "deutero-canonical."[1] The Protestant Bible reorders these books.

THE PROTESTANT OLD TESTAMENT = 39 BOOKS[2]

Law = 5 Books	*History = 12 Books*	*Poetry = 5 Books*	*Prophecy = 17 Books*
Genesis	**Joshua**	**Job**	*Major Prophets= 5 books*
Exodus	**Judges**	**Psalms**	**Isaiah**
Leviticus	**Ruth**	**Proverbs**	**Jeremiah**
Numbers	**1 & 2 Samuel**	**Ecclesiastes**	**Lamentations**
Deuteronomy	**1 & 2 Kings**	**Song of Songs**	**Ezekiel**
	1 & 2 Chronicles		**Daniel**
	Ezra		*Minor Prophets= 12 books*
	Nehemiah		**Hosea, Joel, Amos, Obadiah, Jonah, Micah, Nahum, Habakkuk, Zephaniah, Haggai, Zechariah** and **Malachi**
	Esther		

New Testament Corpora: Likewise, the New Testament (NT) is comprised of smaller corpora as follows (with some overlap) that form larger contexts of meaning:
- Synoptic Gospels (Matthew, Mark, and Luke) with a typical working assumption that Matthew and Luke used Mark, which is considered the earliest form of the gospel.[3]
- Luke-Acts. Generally, it is now recognized that these books develop themes conjointly.

---

[1] The deutero-canonical books include historical tales (Tobit, Judith, 1 & 2 Maccabees), a prophetic book (Baruch with a letter of Jeremiah), wisdom literature (Wisdom and Ecclesiasticus), and additions to biblical books (Esther and Daniel). These books were included in the Septuagint (LXX) in the fourth-century AD, but this does not necessarily support the view that the church universal recognized them as Scripture. In fact, the church councils in the fifth-century excluded them. It was not until the Roman Catholic council of Trent in 1545–63 in response to the Protestant Reformation that these books were affirmed officially as deutero-canonical, in large part because they contain theology in support of particular Catholic doctrine (praying to the saints).

[2] The details of the chart slightly adapted are from John R. McRay, "Bible, Canon of the" in *Baker Encyclopedia of the Bible*, eds. W. A. Elwell and B. J. Beitzel (Grand Rapids: Baker, 1988), 300–306.

[3] This view remains the dominant working hypothesis; see, e.g., the excellent review of the evidence and the implications for interpretation in Robert H. Stein, *Studying the Synoptic Gospels: Origin and Interpretation*, 2nd ed. (Grand Rapids: Baker Academic, 2001); on the other hand, the church father Augustine related church tradition that Matthew wrote his gospel first in Hebrew or Aramaic and that the others were dependent on it; see John Wenham, *Redating Matthew, Mark, and Luke* (London: Hodder and Stoughton, 1991).

- Johannine writings include John's Gospel, 1, 2, and 3 John, and Revelation, although there is considerable dispute whether the same "John" is responsible for these books.
- Pauline Epistles consist of all thirteen letters that identify Paul as author.
- The undisputed Pauline Epistles are considered safely "authentic" and include Romans, 1 and 2 Corinthians, Galatians, Philippians, 1 Thessalonians, and Philemon. This view is still common, but is increasingly and rightly being questioned as more and more evidence comes forth to account for changes of style and content within the Pauline letters—Paul's use of secretaries, co-writers, varying circumstances, writing to different locales, etc.
- The disputed Pauline Epistles include Ephesians, Colossians, 2 Thessalonians, and the Pastorals. These have also been called the Deutero-Pauline Epistles. For some people, Hebrews belongs also in this category.
- The Corinthian Correspondence includes 1 and 2 Corinthians.
- The Prison Epistles include Ephesians, Colossians, Philippians, and Philemon.
- The Thessalonian Correspondence includes 1 and 2 Thessalonians.
- The Pastorals or Pastoral Epistles include 1 and 2 Timothy and Titus.
- The Catholic or General Epistles include James, 1 and 2 Peter, 1, 2, and 3 John, and Jude.
- The Petrine Epistles include 1 and 2 Peter.

Understanding that interpreters sometimes delineate their research along such corpora will help you contextualize their working assumptions as they themselves are attempting to properly contextualize evidence. So, you may pick up a book at Amazon.com on Paul and discover that only the "undisputed" or "authentic" Pauline letters are treated; this represents a bias, a position, or a concession to scholarly convention by that author. Also, the use of corpora may be beneficial when doing a word or theme study; the sheer quantity of Bible references may require a smaller pool for careful study, and these corpora provide such contexts. Likewise, when weighing evidence to interpret a passage, these corpora would help prioritize such evidence. For example, if I were interpreting a pericope in Matthew, and I found evidence in the Pastoral Epistles and contrary evidence in the Synoptic Gospels—I would need to give priority to the evidence in the Synoptic Gospels, all things being equal, since Matthew has some more intimate relation to Mark and Luke (regardless of whether I believe that Matthew or Mark was written first).

<u>Genre and Literary Forms</u>: As the survey above reveals, you can see that Scripture contains a variety of types of literature (called genres), and even within these interpreters have identified a variety of smaller conventional units called literary forms. Below is an essential list of genres:

- Apocalypse (e.g., Daniel 7–12, Book of Revelation)
- Wisdom (e.g., Proverbs, Job)
- Poetry (e.g., Psalms, parts of the Prophetic Corpus)
- Prophecy (e.g., Isaiah, Jeremiah, Malachi)
- Narrative
    - Historiography (e.g., 1 Samuel, Ezra, Nehemiah)

- Biography (e.g., Gospels, Acts)
- Short Story or Novella (e.g., Ruth, Jonah, Esther)
- Letter-Argumentative (e.g., Paul, Peter, Jude)
- Covenant formula with Laws (e.g., Exodus, Deuteronomy)
- Testament or Sermon (e.g., 1 John, Hebrews)

Part of the context of any particular passage is recognizing the book's genre and how that passage is appropriate or not to the conventions of the genre. Certain literary forms are also more fitting to certain genres than to others. Thus, because genre and literary form are so critical for interpretation, these are discussed in a distinct interpretive area, STEP 6: LITERARY FORMS. For now, just understand that CONTEXTUAL LOCATION involves at a rudimentary level the recognition of genre.

<u>Canon Formation</u>: A particular issue that is often raised is why some books were selected for inclusion into the canon of Scripture and others were not. The process, I would argue, was one not of selection, but of *recognition*.[4] Bruce Metzger argues that the church came "to recognize, accept, affirm, and confirm the self-authenticating quality of certain documents that imposed themselves as such upon the church."[5]

<u>OT Canon</u>: As far as Hebrew Scripture (Old Testament), there is debate when its books were closed as a canon. It is conventional to assign this closing to AD 90 at the meeting of Jewish leaders at the town of Jamnia just twenty years after the fall of the Jerusalem temple. However, because of the following evidence, I favor the view that the Jewish tripartite canon (TaNaK) was closed by the time of (or with) Jesus's teaching for the following reasons:

- In Luke 24:44 Jesus refers to all three sections of TaNak when saying: "These are My words which I spoke to you while I was still with you, that all things which are written about Me in the Law of Moses and the Prophets and the Psalms must be fulfilled." Psalms is the first book of the Writings section, and it only need to be assumed that "Writings" was not yet standardized as a title for this section. Additionally, Jesus in the next verse (24:25) can generalize Law, Prophets, and Psalms as "the Scriptures" (τὰς γραφάς).
- Jesus's teaching in Matt 12:6, 41, 42 affirmed that "someone/thing greater than the temple … Jonah … Solomon was here." In saying this, Jesus was referring to himself. Notable is the fact that each section of the Hebrew Bible is represented: temple = Law; Jonah = Prophets; Solomon = Writings (as purported author of Proverbs and Ecclesiastes).
- In Matt 23:34–35 Jesus forewarned his contemporaries before the tragic fall of Jerusalem: "Therefore, behold, I am sending you prophets and wise men and scribes; some of them you will kill and crucify, and some of them you will scourge in your synagogues, and per-

---

[4] For an accessible accounting of the NT canon formation, see Arthur G. Patzia, *The Making of the New Testament: Origin, Collection, Text & Canon* (Downers Grove, IL: InterVarsity, 1995) and more recently Lee Martin McDonald, *The Origin of the Bible: A Guide for the Perplexed* (London: T&T Clark International, 2011).

[5] Bruce M. Metzger, *The Canon of the New Testament: Its Origin, Development, and Significance* (Oxford, 1987), 287, quoted by Patzia, *Making of the New Testament*, 105.

secute from city to city, so that upon you may fall *the guilt of* all the righteous blood shed on earth, from the blood of righteous Abel to the blood of Zechariah, the son of Berechiah, whom you murdered between the temple and the altar" (NASB). The indictment is staggering when one realizes that Abel, the first human killed in the narrative of Scripture, represents the first book of the TaNaK (Genesis) whereas Zechariah represents the last person killed at that location (between the temple and the altar) in 2 Chr 24:20–21, the very last book of TaNaK. Basically, Jesus's indictment spans all of Hebrew Scripture, TaNaK.[6]

NT Canon Formation: A full-scale description cannot be given here, but I would argue that any consideration must recognize at least nine historical factors that contributed to the need and impetus to have such a canon. These historical factors are provided in the chart below:

HISTORICAL FACTORS IN NT CANON FORMATION

BY THE THIRD- AND SECOND- CENTURIES BC: 1. Secular libraries around the Greco-Roman world and literary critics were concerned with collections of "authentic" writings of classical authors; there were scholarly debates about what writings were "authentic" Homer, Plato, Aristotle, etc. Thus, a concern for authenticity and authoritative canons existed before and after the NT documents were written and themselves collected as a "canon." IN THE FIRST-CENTURY AD: 2. Multiple Gospels were written to faithfully preserve the teaching of Jesus and his apostles (Luke 1:1–3; cf. John 21). 3. Paul's letters were collected probably by Paul himself (cf. 1 Thess 5:27; 2 Cor 10:10; Col 4:16; 2 Pet 3:15–16).[7] 4. Believers understood that God spoke through Jesus (Heb 1:2); the Gospels were God's word; the Scripture quotation formula "has been written" (γέγραπται) is used for John's

---

[6] See discussion in Roger T. Beckwith, *The Old Testament Canon of the New Testament Church and Its Background in Early Judaism* (London: SPCK, 1985), who addresses also the surmountable difficulty of why Zechariah is identified as son of Berechiah, i.e., to refer to two Zechariahs, the martyr and the prophet.

[7] Stanley E. Porter, "When and How was the Pauline Canon Compiled? An Assessment of Theories," in *The Pauline Canon*, ed. S. E. Porter; Pauline Studies 1 (Leiden: Brill, 2004), 122–23. On the view that the earliest Pauline collection was created by Paul himself and consisted of Galatians, 1 and 2 Corinthians, and Romans (F. C. Baur's "authentic" Pauline letters), see David Trobisch, *Die Entstehung der Paulusbriefsammlung: Studien zu Anfängen Christlicher Publizistik*, NTOA 10 (Freiburg, Schweiz: Universitätsverlag, 1989) and idem, *Paul's Letter Collection: Tracing the Origins* (Minneapolis: Fortress, 1994). Trobisch is reviewed and discussed by Porter who disagrees with Trobisch's view, while supporting the conclusions of E. Randolph Richards, *The Secretary in the Letters of Paul* (WUNT 2/42; Tübingen: J.C.B. Mohr, 1991) that all thirteen letters were collected together early. Porter rightly surmises, "It is possible that Paul was involved in this process by virtue of his having produced copies of his letters" (125). Paul's use of a letter secretary supports this contention; see, esp. Richards, "The Codex and the Early Collection of Paul's Letters," *BBR* 8 (1998): 151–66.

> Gospel (John 20:31) and Luke's gospel and the subsequent proclamation of the apostles (Luke 24:46); thus, the use of γέγραπται signals the Gospels' scriptural status.
> 5. Hebrew Bible Canon is closed, at least by Jamnia in AD 90.
>
> IN THE FIRST- AND EARLY SECOND-CENTURY AD:
> 6. The church became increasingly Gentile (cf. AD 135), and thus there existed a need for an authentic canon for teaching new converts about a Jewish Jesus.
> 7. The gnostic Marcion in Rome (ca. AD 120s) created his own list of ten edited Pauline Letters adding to it Luke's Gospel (minus Luke's "Jewish" portions).
>
> IN THE MIDDLE TO LATE SECOND-CENTURY AD:
> 8. The growth and spread of heretical Gnostic teachings and spurious documents about Jesus increased dramatically thus increasing the need for a closed apostolic canon.
> 9. The Montanist Christian sect wrote down spoken prophecy that increasingly became canon for the adherents, but was recognized as heretical by significant early church fathers.

In short, the need for authentic writings was real and early, and served to help spread the gospel proclamation and solidify faith in Jesus of Nazareth. In view of such historical factors, many interpreters have described fundamental criteria that contributed to recognizing which books should be considered God's Word. These include the following:

- Apostolicity: A book's origin or source was from or related to the initial apostles.
- Spirituality: A book was edifying for faithful living and dying (even martyrdom).
- Historicity: A book faithfully portrayed the historical Jesus and initial gospel proclamation.
- Antiquity: A book was recognized for its age, and thus early attestation to apostolic truth.
- Catholicity/Universality: A book had broad geographic distribution and use.
- Doctrinal Veracity: A book was orthodox & consonant with the rule of faith (*regula fidei*).
- Unanimity: Each book was eventually affirmed by the ecclesial councils.

Not all these factors were as determinative for each individual book; but to the extent that each factor could speak in favor of a book, it contributed to recognizing that book's divine inspiration.

To conclude, canon, testament, corpora, and whole books provide the largest literary interpretive framework for any given pericope. When conducting research, such frameworks help delineate research (due to time constraints) and help prioritize evidence that impinges on the interpretation of a pericope.

Chapters, Versification, and Abbreviations: Recognizing the value of "chunking" texts into smaller units for readers of the Bible, scholars added chapter divisions and verse numbers (i.e., versification). Eusebius of Caesarea (fl. AD 265–340) developed "canons" of discrete units in the Synoptic Gospels that allowed comparison of parallel passages. Chapters were added ca. AD 1200 by Peter the Chanter and Stephen Langton; versification began in the late thirteenth-century and was codified by Robert Estienne (known as Stephanus, fl. 1503–59) in his Greek NT published in

1551. Generally, chapter and verse numbers provide a universal reference point so that interpreters can speak efficiently with one another about this or that chapter and verse. The convention is to separate chapter from verse with a colon. Thus, Matt 11:21 signifies Matthew chapter eleven verse twenty-one. If you are adding an additional chapter and verse or even a different NT book with chapter and verse, separate each with a semi-colon (;). Also, it is standard to present book references in canonical order and numerical sequence, except when one might prioritize Mark as the source for the other Synoptic Gospels. For example, "Jesus repeatedly refers to himself as 'the Son of Man' (e.g., Mark 9:9//Matt 17:9; Luke 6:22; John 1:51; 13:31; cf. Acts 7:56)." This example illustrates also the use of two other conventions. First, the two back slashes (//) indicate passages in the gospels in parallel with one another (i.e., parallel passages); the verses are identical or nearly so in content. Second, you will commonly find other abbreviations such as "cf.". So, when writing, follow these conventions for efficiency and clarity. Abbreviations of biblical books are given below followed by abbreviations of Common English versions and common abbreviations.[8]

STANDARD ABBREVIATIONS OF BIBLICAL BOOKS
ACCORDING TO THE SOCIETY OF BIBLICAL LITERATURE (SBL)

OT = Old Testament				NT = New Testament			OT Apocrypha	
Gen	Isa	Nah	Ruth	Matt	Phil	1-2-3	1-2-3-4	1-2-3-4
Exod	Jer	Hab	Song	Mark	Col	John	Kgdms	Macc
Lev	Ezek	Zeph	Eccl	Luke	1-2 Thess	Jude	Add Esth	Pr Azar
Num	Hos	Hag	Lam	John	1-2 Tim	Rev	Bar	Pr Man
Deut	Joel	Zech	Esth	Acts	Titus		Bel	Sir
Josh	Amos	Mal	Dan	Rom	Phlm		1–2 Esdr	Sus
Judg	Obad	Ps (Pss)	Ezra	1-2 Cor	Heb		4 Ezra	Tob
1–2 Sam	Jonah	Job	Neh	Gal	Jas		Jdt	Wis
1–2 Kgs	Mic	Prov	1-2 Chr	Eph	1-2 Pet		Ep Jer	

ABBREVIATIONS FOR COMMON ENGLISH TRANSLATIONS

ASV = Authorized Standard Version	NIV84 or NIV = New International Version 1984 or 2011
CEB = Common English Bible	NJB = New Jerusalem Bible
ESV = English Standard Version	NKJV = New King James Version
JB = Jerusalem Bible	NLT = New Living Translation
KJV = King James Version	NRSV = New Revised Standard Version
NASB = New American Standard Bible 1995	RSV = Revised Standard Version
NET = NET Bible	TNIV = Today's New International Version
NIV = New International Version 2011	TEV = Today's English Bible (Good News)

---

[8] See *The SBL Handbook of Style Second Edition: For Biblical Studies and Related Disciplines* (Atlanta: SBL Press, 2014).

COMMON ABBREVIATIONS
(see *SBL Handbook of Style* 8.1.3)

cf. = *confere* = "compare with"	**b.** = a date a person is born
e.g. = *exempli gratia* = "for example"	**fl.** = *floruit* = "flourished" or a person lived at this time
f. = the following verse (as in Matt 12:31f. = Matt 12:31–32)	**c.** = century
ff. = the following two verses (Matt 12:31ff. = Matt 12:31–33)	**ca.** = *circa* = approximately (in dating)
	cj. = a conjecture (i.e., an educated guess)
s.v. = *sub verbo* or *sub voca* = "under the word/voice" just referred to	**n.d.** = no date available
	n.p. = no page available

EXERCISE 1–A: Render these cumbersome statements into the appropriate simplified forms using the conventional abbreviations:

a. "I was reading yesterday James chapter five verse thirteen in my New International Version."

b. "A most eloquent translation of Psalm twenty-three verse two is in the King James Version."

c. "Paul's definition of God's will as sanctification in terms of sexual purity in First Thessalonians chapter four verses three and four is startling; I wonder how it reads in the original Greek New Testament?"

d. "In the New American Standard Bible 1995 edition the word 'compassion' is found in Paul's writings three times (Colossians chapter three verse twelve and Romans chapter nine verse fifteen and Philippians chapter two verse one)."

<u>The Impact of Topical Headings?</u>: Modern translations have added another reading aide: topical section headings. But, when all is said and done even as helpful as they may be at times, we must recognize that adding chapter divisions, versification, and topical headings impose "structure" onto the text that *are very interpretive*. At best, these are a helpful convention for quick reference or basic orientation to the topics addressed; at worst, however, *chapter divisions, versification, and topical headings may actually mislead readers to wrongly envision a setting, context, or division*. But hopefully now, you will not be mislead. Let me provide an example of each where I have found there to be some level of potential misunderstanding if not even interpretive problems. First, compare how major translations place topical headings on 1 Tim 2:1–15. The NIV states "Instructions on Worship"; the NRSV has "Instructions concerning Prayer"; the NASB labels 2:1–8 "A Call to Prayer" and 2:9–15 "Women Instructed." After my careful study of the passage, if I were to create a label, it would be "Prayer and Conduct for Proper Witness to the Roman Culture"—by which I mean the passage concerns having a prayerful and behavioral stance within the Roman empire that is winsome for outsiders including especially how women behaved, who, if perceived as "insubordinate" (i.e., too much independent of a husband), would have raised a large

red flag for the new religious movement.⁹ Second, the decision to start ch. 11 within 1 Corinthians at 11:1 was probably mistaken since most commentators and Bible translations treat 11:1 with ch.10.¹⁰ Finally, where a verse ends and begins varies in Eph 1:4–5. The phrase *"in love"* is literally stuck in between, and translations versify differently depending on interpretation. Thus, the KJV and the GNT critical edition of Nestle-Aland places "in love" at the end of v. 4: "He hath chosen us in him ... that we should be holy and blameless before him *in love…*" making "in love" modify "chosen" or more likely "holy and blameless" as a characteristic of believers. But many modern translations punctuate and versify the sentence differently and place "in love" in v. 5 (NIV and RSV). Thus the RSV reads: "He predestined us *in love...*" making God's predestination carried out "in love." The point is this: versification, chapters, and topical labeling are interpretive. Each involves an interpretive decision that may have theological significance.

EXERCISE 1–B: Compare how major English translations divide or use topical headings for Eph 5:21–22. Additionally, certain English Versions or Bibles may provide notes there. If you know some Greek, also consult the various editions of the Greek NT and then consider the syntactical relationship between these two verses. (**Hint**: look at the verbs.)

<u>Words, Grammar, Syntax, and Discourse</u>: Traditionally, the study of a pericope was synonymous with the study of individual sentences within that pericope. Study then has been partitioned into lexical or philological (study of words), grammatical (word functions within the sentence), and syntactical (clause relations within sentences). However, in our complete interpretative work we are concerned with more than just the structure of individual sentences (i.e., subject, verb, direct object, etc.). It is now understood that meaning is conceived, conveyed, received, and perceived at higher levels than just individual words within sentences or just phrases/clauses, even though words, phrases, and sentences are themselves fundamental to communication. Another level of significant meaning exists at a "discursive" level where we may observe higher patterns of organization across paragraphs, unites, and books as a whole. Furthermore, we are increasingly appreciating biblical materials as originally a spoken piece of communication that was orally performed.¹¹ Discourse analysis or "text-linguistics" are fields of study that research these aspects of text. Theoretically, these fields can be very complex; however, a simpler approach is possible.

<u>Semantic Relationships</u>: To help understand how a text means what it does or what we

---

⁹ For a description of this history in relation to the NT texts that treat husband-wife relationships, see the dated but still helpful work of David L. Balch, *Let Wives Be Submissive: The Domestic Code in 1 Peter*, SBLMS 26 (Chico, CA: Scholars Press, 1981).

¹⁰ Anthony C. Thiselton, *The First Epistle to the Corinthians: A Commentary on the Greek Text*, NIGC (Grand Rapids: Eerdmans, 2000), 779–95. So also the NIV; but the NASB includes 11:1 with ch. 11 and has the heading "Christian Order."

¹¹ In fact, a newer field of study for the NT is called "performance criticism" that looks particularly at performance features and dynamics embedded within the discourse in the selection of descriptive words, setting, dialogue, etc. For an excellent short example of performance critical study, see Kelly R. Iverson, "A Centurion's 'Confession': A Performance-Critical Analysis of Mark 15:39," *JBL* 130 (2011): 329–50.

might call the text's "meaning" (i.e., "semantics"), many interpreters have identified and described **semantic relationships**[12] or **laws of composition**.[13] These relationships vary in name and number from one interpreter to another, but here is a basic list: repetition, introduction, comparison, contrast, causation, substantiation, purpose, climax, generalization, particularization, interrogation, cruciality, and summarization.[14] Semantic relationships are found in all human communication—visual, oral-aural, literary, or otherwise sensory (if even such communication exists for gustatory, olfactory, or tactile senses!). These semantic relationships have been described at different points in human history from different fields of study, including rhetoric, art, music, compositional and literary studies, linguistics, and cognitive development. These semantic relationships are described below in TERTIARY RESEARCH and once again in STEP 4: SEMANTIC ANALYSIS.

Asking Questions: One goal when reading and studying Scripture is to seek understanding, and this always will require the asking of questions. Asking questions begins the process of understanding. The type of questioning, however, should not be initiated by our own agenda, as if we are already inclined to know the answer. Rather, the types of questioning should arise out of our careful, inductive observation of the details of the pericope—this type of questioning allows Scripture to set the agenda as much as possible, and this should drive our investigation, rather than letting our investigation be driven by our own concerns and questions. In fact, much poor or bad interpretation occurs because we come to the Scriptures with questions that Scripture is not addressing at that moment. While walking *In Step with God's Word*, you are always encouraged to ask questions about the meaning and significance of the text. Remember the questions that you raise—some will be resolved but others will be reoccurring and thus should be brought forward as you progress through the interpretive areas. In STEP 9: INTERPRETIVE DECISIONS, you will choose specific questions for answering in consultation with your collected evidences and in conversation with biblical specialists or commentators (those who write commentaries). These commentators may or may not address the question(s) that you choose to resolve. The determination of the best interpretation will be based upon the evidence that you have gathered from your interpretive work in STEP 1: CONTEXTUAL ANALYSIS, STEP 2: TEXTUAL COMPARISONS, STEP 3: GRAMMATICAL STUDY, STEP 4: SEMANTIC ANALYSIS, STEP 5: LEXICAL RESEARCH, STEP 6: LITERARY FORMS, STEP 7: HISTORICAL CONTEXT, and STEP 8: SCRIPTURAL CORRELATIONS.

Types of Questions: Crucial types of questions to ask have been described in Bauer and Traina and include the following: definitional (What? When? Where?); modal (how?); rational (why?); and implicational (So what? What are the implications?). It is always important to allow the careful observations and specifics of the pericope determine the questions being asked. Specifically, questions may be asked around the meaning or implications of semantic relationships.

---

[12] These are also called "structural relationships"; see Traina, *Methodical Bible* Study, passim. Traina and peers (such as Jenson) learned from Wilbert Webster White at the Theological Seminary at New York; for a history of this Bible Study movement, see David L. Thompson, *Bible Study that Works*, rev. ed. (Nappanee, IN: Evangel, 1995).

[13] This is what Kay Arthur in her many interpretive books has called in her adaptation of what was taught at Union Theological Seminary.

[14] Bauer and Traina, *Inductive Bible Study*.

Exercise 1–C: Read the Beatitudes in the Sermon on the Mount in Matt 5:3–12 given below (WEB translation) and follow the procedures that follow.

³ Blessed are the poor in spirit, for theirs is the Kingdom of Heaven.

⁴ Blessed are those who mourn, for they shall be comforted.

⁵ Blessed are the gentle, for they shall inherit the earth.

⁶ Blessed are those who hunger and thirst after righteousness, for they shall be filled.

⁷ Blessed are the merciful, for they shall obtain mercy.

⁸ Blessed are the pure in heart, for they shall see God.

⁹ Blessed are the peacemakers, for they shall be called children of God.

¹⁰ Blessed are those who have been persecuted for righteousness' sake, for theirs is the Kingdom of Heaven.

¹¹ Blessed are you when people reproach you, persecute you, and say all kinds of evil against you falsely, for my sake.

¹² Rejoice, and be exceedingly glad, for great is your reward in heaven. For that is how they persecuted the prophets who were before you.

1. First, identify where you observe these five semantic relationships. **Note**: These five semantic relationships are in increasing difficulty to recognize and describe.

    a. reoccurrence (repeated elements),
    b. substantiation (the logical support for a previous claim),
    c. climax (high point of intensity),
    d. contrast (differentiated elements), and
    e. comparison (describing elements as being similar).

2. Second, describe as best you are able the significance of these semantic relationships in context and how they influence and relate to one another.

3. In view of this, third, summarize the main message of 5:3–12 in three sentences.

4. Fourth, write down questions arising from your study of 5:3–12: what, where, when, how, why, and so what?

PRIMARY INTERPRETIVE PROCEDURES:

1. Read the whole NT book of your pericope. In what corpora does your NT book belong?
2. Identify the basic genre of the book given the basic categories supplied above that include apocalypse, wisdom, poetry, prophecy, narrative (history, biography, short story), letter-argumentative, covenant formula, and testament/sermon.[15] Consider how this basic identification may or may not bear upon understanding the context of the passage under investigation. Ask any questions here.
3. Identify and record the larger paragraph or section within which your pericope is located.
4. Consider whether or not or to what extent chapter divisions or section topical labels (found in most English Bibles) may have influenced your (pre-)understanding of the passage. Could these divisions or labels create a bias in your interpretation of the passage?
5. Record any significant observations and interpretive questions about the book as a whole, and the pericope's function within it.

II. SECONDARY STUDY

Orientation: The essential concern of CONTEXTUAL LOCATION is to consider the passage in its *complete* literary context *at the book-discourse level* as much as possible. Within any writing, all passages are linked together and contribute to the complete discursive performance of the author. So important is the ability to "track the argument" that one commentator, Thomas R. Schreiner, has stated while assessing other interpreters: "I am convinced that tracing the structure of the argument in the Pauline epistles is the most important step in the exegetical process. One of the weaknesses in many commentaries today is the failure to trace the argument in each paragraph, and the failure to explain how each paragraph relates to the preceding and following paragraphs."[16] As simple and basic as contextual location sounds, interpreters often disagree at this foundational level. Sometimes their understanding of the argument flow is transparent, but many times not; sometimes special attention is afforded to show and explain this structure, many times not. Sometimes commentators may be prevented from giving a straightforward discussion of this because the layout or length of the commentary does not allow it. So, we need to perform this work properly to orient ourselves to the passage and establish a sound foundation for further STEPS.

Beginning, Middle, and Closing Locations: Where a passage falls within a whole discourse is foundational for interpretation. As basic as this may sound, simply considering beginning-middle-closing locations is a helpful way to make observations of the text. Vernon K. Robbins describes this as "Beginning, Middle, and Closing Texture."[17] He uses the metaphor of "texture" be-

---

[15] Note: Genre is given specific treatment in STEP 6: LITERARY FORMS.

[16] Thomas R. Schreiner, *Interpreting the Pauline Epistles*, Guides to New Testament Exegesis (Baker: Grand Rapids, 1990), 97.

[17] See his books describing his interpretive analytics: *Exploring the Texture of Texts: A Guide to Socio-Rhetorical Interpretation* (Valley Forge, PA: Trinity Press International, 1996); *The Tapestry of Early Christian*

cause the richness inherent in any discourse can be helpfully studied from multiple perspectives. The beginning position often provides information that orients the audience and prepares them for what follows by introducing agents, actions, and ideas. Just how agents, actions, and ideas are introduced provides a framework and constrains the discussion that follows. The middle position functions to elaborate and develop the ideas previously introduced. Careful attention to how some agent, action, or idea is elaborated is critical for proper interpretation. Finally, the closing position functions to conclude a discussion—in this location closing material may summarize, generalize, serve as a transition, or point to further implications of what has been discussed (e.g., giving commands or exhortations). Such material leaves a lasting impression and/or transitions to the next section. Additionally, since the final closing material is privileged as the "last word," it may be used to express final positive feelings between authors and audiences; typically in NT documents this often entails sending greetings, conferring the grace of Christ and God's peace, and ascribing glory to God (e.g., Gal 6:18; 1 Cor 16:19–24; Rom 16:20–27; Eph 6:23–24; Phil 4:20–23).

<u>Material Before and After, Repetition, and Transitions</u>: With most passages, the rubric of beginning-middle-closing locations can be applied. The passage you are studying will often be the middle and sandwiched by material before and material after. Determining the boundaries of the pericope is important even if this is often open to debate. You need to consider what unifies a pericope. A pericope will be unified around an agent/actor or a theme; so you should pay attention to the subject of verbs and the presence of repeated words or similar ideas that identify a unifying theme. Thus, it is prudent to think about how the material before and after contributes to, but also delimits, the focus of meaning in any given pericope. Another matter to consider is the presence of **transitions**. Transitions will help link one pericope to another as well as mark where a new paragraph begins. Here are standard ways to detect major transitions:

1. change in theme
2. change in agent and/or grammatical person (first, second, or third; e.g., "we" to "they")
3. change in verb tense
4. change in tone or perspective
5. change in location or setting
6. the use of direct address (e.g., "Brethren, ...")
7. transitional conjunctions (e.g., "Therefore, ..." or "Now, ...")

These devices often occur in some combination together. So, the lesson here is not to rely primarily on chapters, versification (see, e.g., 1 Cor 11:1–2), or translation paragraph titles. Although helpful at times, these may also be misleading. Furthermore, these divisional breaks may not have arisen from the original manuscripts.

Discourse: Rhetoric, Society, and Ideology (London: Routledge, 1996). Within his understanding of "inner texture" he discusses beginning-middle-closing texture. A helpful description of "inner texture" with multiple examples of beginning-middle-closing texture is found at http://www.religion.emory.edu/faculty/robbins/SRI/Examples/textures/inner/index.cfm.

UBS⁴/⁵ Punctuation Apparatus: One helpful resource is the second apparatus at the bottom of the UBS Greek NT. There are three apparati. The first provides textual variants (see TEXTUAL COMPARISONS in STEP 2) and the third lists quotations, allusions, and significant parallels (see SCRIPTURAL CORRELATIONS in STEP 8). The second is the Punctuation Apparatus or what the UBS calls "discourse segmentation." Although one must become acquainted with the abbreviations used (see the UBS introduction), there is a wealth of information here. Five major critical editions of the Greek NT and eleven modern translations in English, French, German, and Spanish are compared in matters of punctuation (commas, periods, colons/dashes, parenthesis, questions, commands, exclamations, and poetic structure), clausal breaks, paragraph breaks, and section headings.

Contextual Constraints: Although word combinations in any language are virtually unlimited, the particular choice of words and their interrelation in phrases, sentences, paragraphs, and sections are limited. In fact, you might even say that recognizing the location of a pericope within a discourse places "constraints" on the possible viable interpretations of that passage. The Bible translator Ernst R. Wendland states, "the discourse itself operates both structurally and conceptually to limit the number of valid possible 'interpretations' of this (or any other) pericope."[18]

The idea of "constraint" has been a helpful one for me. We know that context is everything (CIE); what an author discusses in context delimits the referents and themes to that context. We will often hear statements from politicians that are taken out of context (and placed into a new one), and it changes the meaning completely; the statement is thus made to say things other than that to which they were initially delimited. *As faithful interpreters, we run the risk of "unrestraint" when making the text speak to our immediate situation.* Ironically, this occurs in large part because of our high view of Scripture (a personal devotion book, "a love letter" as Kierkegaard put it). But such a high view of Scripture, which *generalizes* it as a static whole, violates the very nature of Scripture as "incarnated" divinely-inspired (yes), but also humanly made, and particular. Scripture addressed situations "on the ground." Basically then, *this matter of constraint acknowledges that the original historical-social-cultural context affects and delimits our immediate appropriation and contemporaneous application of any pericope.* Stated another way, the issue is whether or not we should readily take what Scripture says as application-ready for immediate appropriation today. In other words, if studying a passage in James, we might ask, "Was James addressing a situation that may not sufficiently be like our own situations now, such that it would be problematic (or possibly even detrimental) for us to take what he said two-thousand years ago uncritically and to apply it unreflectively in our own lives today?"

> This matter of "constraint" acknowledges that the original historical-social-cultural context affects and delimits our immediate appropriation and contemporaneous application of any pericope.

---

[18] Ernst R. Wendland, "A Tale of Two Debtors: On the Interaction of Text, Cotext, and Context in a New Testament Dramatic Narrative (Luke 7:36–50)," in *Linguistics and New Testament Interpretation: Essays on Discourse Analysis*, ed. David Alan Black (Nashville: Broadman, 1992), 101–43.

<u>All Texts Have Contexts: Literary, Ideological, Cultural, and Social</u>: These contexts delimit or constrain the range of possible meanings through that text's being grounded in that initial setting. These areas are explored in STEP 7: HISTORICAL CONTEXT. Even if an author would offer more generalized ideas and envision larger implications, he or she would still do so while located and constrained *to some degree with factors/features of that initial setting.* (How could they not???) The human biblical authors were themselves space and time bound. Thus, the pericope's grounding in actual time and space persists even while biblical authors disclosed and revealed *generalized* and even *universal, transcultural* truths, themes, and networks of themes to address the particular needs of their original audiences. In STEP 11: EVALUATED APPLICATIONS we will discuss how to evaluate whether the truth of a pericope (properly interpreted by that point) is culture-bound (delimited) or transcultural (immediately application ready); and how that truth, even if culturally bound, may be generalized and thus brought forward for application and appropriation in our respective contexts.

However, at this stage in the interpretation process, it is not only possible to consider these contextual constraints, but mandatory to begin doing so. Our initial reflection on contextual constraints may need to guide and delimit our interpretation of the pericope's meaning, the significance we glean, the possibilities of various applications, and our appropriation of the meaning in our respective communities.

EXERCISE 1–D: First, compare seven English translations of 1 Cor 7:1. (Incidentally, this type of comparison is one type of TEXTUAL COMPARISONS covered in STEP 2.) Try to discern whether 7:1b is Paul's statement/question or the Corinthians' question/statement. Second, read all of 1 Cor 7. Then look at the underlying Greek of 7:1 and consider whether this may help answer this question (it may or may not). (Such Greek GRAMMATICAL STUDY is covered in STEP 3.) Third, consult two top tier commentaries and summarize their discussion and conclusions. What are the issues these identify? What evidences are supplied, if any? (INTERPRETIVE DECISIONS will be made in STEP 9.) Fourth, in view of your research what interpretation and translation do you think is best?

Now, let me try to give you an example of how a biblical context is delimited or constrained. Many have called 1 Cor 7, rightly or wrongly, the "marriage chapter." However, the fact that Paul was responding to a specific question or issue in 7:1 should constrain our interpretation to some degree. The difficulty is that we do not even know for certain what the question was, and whether 7:1 represents that question or Paul's response to it! Furthermore, we must ask, In his response was Paul treating *all* possible marriage scenarios? Probably not. For example, we notice that Paul did not allow divorce except in the case when the spouse was a non-believer and wanted to leave the marriage. However, we must ask, Did Paul have in mind an abusive, co-dependent situation, where one spouse physically hurts and threatens another with death? Probably not. And yet, 1 Cor 7 has been used to encourage wives to "hang in there," get beaten and bloodied up, and hope for the best. Given Paul's social-cultural context, we must ask, Could he have envisioned the concept of a "separation" in which the governing authorities would put a constraining order on the

STEP 1: SECONDARY STUDY

abusive spouse? I don't think so. In other words, in 1 Cor 7 Paul was speaking within a Greco-Roman-Jewish context and assuming fairly good relations between persons in marriage. So, the "marriage chapter" of 1 Cor 7 is constrained by at least these four factors:

- the initial question asked of him (probably seen in 7:1, but this is debated);
- his own social-cultural location, contemporaneous conceptions, and conventions of marriage, divorce, separation, etc.;
- the best wisdom on marriage according to Christ's own teaching preserved (in part) in the Gospels (see Paul's reference to these places at 1 Cor 7:10, 12, 25); and,
- and the Spirit's wisdom (7:40) to further extend godly principles/values onto "new" settings and situations (i.e., what one should do if married to a non-believer).

SECONDARY INTERPRETIVE PROCEDURES:

The following procedures incorporate 1.–4. from the PRIMARY INTERPRETIVE PROCEDURES above.

1. **Read the whole NT book of your pericope. In what corpora does your NT book belong?**
2. **Identify the basic genre of the book given the basic categories supplied above that include apocalypse, wisdom, poetry, prophecy, narrative (history, biography, short story), letter-argumentative, covenant formula, and testament/sermon.[19] Consider how this basic identification may or may not bear upon understanding the context of the passage under investigation. Ask any questions here.**
3. **Identify and record the larger paragraph or section within which your pericope is located.**
4. **Consider whether or not or to what extent chapter divisions or section topical labels (found in most English Bibles) may have influenced your (pre-)understanding of the passage. Could these divisions or labels create a bias in your interpretation of the passage?**
5. **What thematic elements are repeated or emphasized within the pericope? Give references.**
6. **Where is the pericope in the discourse's development (beginning, middle, conclusion)?**
7. **How does the preceding material prepare for and relate to this pericope? What transition occurs into the pericope?**
8. **How does this pericope prepare for and relate to subsequent material? What transition occurs from the pericope to the next one?**
9. **Based upon your findings thus far, what contextual "constraints" are placed upon the passage under consideration? Explain. How might these constraints affect the passage's interpretation and delimit application today?**
10. **Provide a summary of your most significant observations as well as any pivotal interpretive questions about the book as a whole and the pericope's function within it.**

---

[19] Note: Genre is given specific treatment in STEP 6: LITERARY FORMS.

III. TERTIARY RESEARCH

Orientation: One important exercise to better understand a pericope's context is to perform a Book Survey. At the heart of the methodology for book surveys as presented here is Inductive Bible Study (IBS) that seeks to observe the structure of books as wholes and recognize major structural relations organizing the material. Additional observations are also made that include historical-critical information about the author, audience, and situation, as well as the tone, atmosphere, and other significant observations. This level of interpretation will assume expertise about Major Semantic Relationships, and how to identify them at the book level.

Major Semantic Relationships (MSRs): All people, regardless of their language, rely on certain "universal" communication laws in order to understand each other. We organize our discourse consciously or unconsciously in regular ways. These laws of organization govern the selection and arrangement of words, phrases, clauses, paragraphs, sections, and units in relation to one another. In other words, *all levels of discourse are organized in observable ways*. Thus, "meaning" is conveyed subconsciously and consciously through the relationships of clauses to clauses, sentences to sentences, paragraphs to paragraphs, sections to sections, etc. The goal for the "observant" student of Scripture is to become aware of "the Laws of Composition" and how to identify them as they organize and are present in the largest units or among the smallest units of discourse. Here are brief definitions, descriptions, and examples of MSRs.[20]

MAJOR SEMANTIC RELATIONSHIPS[21]

Introduction—the giving of necessary background information that prepares the reader for the material that follows; e.g., Luke 1:1–4	**Recurrence**—the repetition of the same terms, phrases, clauses, or themes; repetition of word family; e.g., "holy" in Leviticus.
Particularization—the movement from general idea(s) to particular ideas. Usually one may detect a general statement that is then particularized; this is the converse of generalization.	**Pivot** or **Cruciality**—a movement of events or ideas to an unexpected crucial point on which subject matter turns in another direction; e.g., King David's sin with Bathsheba (2 Sam 11).
Generalization—the movement from particular ideas to a general statement or broad topic; this is the converse of particularization; e.g., Matt 28:18–20 (Make disciples, baptizing, teaching)	**Causation**—the move from cause to effect, from action to the result produced; this is the converse of substantiation; e.g., Rom 12:1; Key terms: *therefore*, *thus*, *consequently*, *then* (not temporal)
Summarization—An abridgment (summing up) either preceding or following a unit of material *by* reiterating specific elements or themes; e.g., Acts 1:8 summarizes major topics of Acts.	**Substantiation**—the move from effect to cause, from the result to the source; the basis or rationale of an argument; this relation is the converse of causation; e.g., Rom 1:16 Key Terms: *for*, *because*, *since*

---

[20] For a survey and history of the notion within the Inductive Biblical Studies movement, Fredrick J. Long, "Major Structural Relationships: A Survey of Origins, Development, Classifications, and Assessment," *The Journal of Inductive Biblical Studies* 1 (2014): 22–58 available at http://place.asburyseminary.edu/jibs/vol1/iss1/3.

[21] This lists are slightly adapted from David R. Bauer's lecture notes (1988–1990).

Instrumentality/Purpose—a reference to the means by which an end or goal is achieved; e.g., Matt 3:13. Key Terms: *in order that, so that*, and sometimes *that*	**Interrogation** or **Problem/Solution**—The movement from a problem to its solution or a question and its answer. This implicitly involves causation.
Comparison—the process of showing how two or more items/ideas/people are alike; e.g., Eph 5:1–2. Key Terms: *like, as, just as*	**Climax**—the movement from lower to higher and to highest intensity within a passage or book with focus on the highest or greatest point being realized; e.g., the Gospels narratives building to Jesus's crucifixion and resurrection.
Contrast—the process of showing how two or more items/ideas/people are different; e.g., 1 Cor 14:1–5. Key Terms: *but, however*	

SUPPORTING SEMANTIC RELATIONSHIPS THAT HELP CONVEY MSRs

Inclusion—beginning and ending a unit with the same words or ideas; this material "brackets" the section and may help to convey key topics of the passage or an entire book. See, e.g., Mark's Gospel and heavens and later the temple veil "torn apart" (1:10; 15:38).	**Chiasm**—discussing topics A...B...C and then continuing to discuss the same topics but by inverting their order C...B...A; so you have ABC-CBA. See, e.g., Mark 2:27 "The Sabbath was made for man, not man for the Sabbath."
Alternation or **Interchange**—going "back and forth" between material: ABABABAB; this is a good way to compare or contrast two ideas. See, e.g., 1 Cor 14:1–5 that supports contrast.	**Intercalation**—the insertion of seemingly unrelated material (B) in the middle of a larger narrative or argument (A): A-B-A. See, e.g., the account of John the Baptist's beheading surrounded by the sending and return of the twelve (Mark 6:7–32).

<u>Inductive Bible Study</u>: It is assumed here that students have gained proficiency at book level analysis through the employment of IBS methodology, as explained, e.g., by Robert A. Traina. There have been many other related practitioners or schools of IBS including Irving Jensen, Oletta Wald, David Thompson, Kay Arthur, T. Michael W. Halcomb, to name only a few (see bibliography below). To date, the most authoritative hermeneutical explanation and illustration of IBS has been written by David R. Bauer and Robert A. Traina, *Inductive Biblical Study* (2010).

It is my working assumption that any student of Scripture who has learned how to do an IBS book survey *should do so in some greater or lesser form when preparing to teach or preach through any given biblical book.* Such a survey will help inform and guide further research on particular pericopes. Additionally, it may be advisable to conduct a segment survey upon the broader section within which your pericope is found (even this presupposes having done a book survey). These surveys are tentative and should be considered "open" for revision as the evidence demands it. Indeed, Daniel P. Fuller argues, "a preliminary survey of a book should always be made at the out-set, though with fear and trembling."[22]

---

[22] *The Inductive Method of Bible Study*, 3rd ed. (Pasadena, CA: Fuller Theological Seminary, 1959), IV.10.

When to Perform a Segment Survey: If you are working with a sizable pericope (let's say, more than fifteen verses) or one that is difficult to understand or to relate to its broader literary context, then a segment survey may be especially helpful. Time constraints should also be considered. Here are some practical guidelines to help determine the boundaries of your segment survey:

1. Determine the larger section or segment (if any) within which our passage falls. You would benefit from having done a book survey. Do not rely on paragraph breaks or sectional headings that may be present in your Bible.
2. Generally, look for "cohesiveness" or not with what comes before or after your pericope. Consider the continuation of themes, perspectives, grammatical constructions, and rhetorical structures (chiasm, alternation, inclusion, or argument pattern).
3. At the same time, look for major structural breaks and transition points. These may or may not correspond with the English paragraph breaks. Do not rely on chapters, versification (see 1 Cor 10:33–11:2), or paragraph titles. Although helpful at times, they can also be misleading; these are not inspired. See the discussion of transitions above. For convenience, here again are some things that signal major transitions:

    a. change in theme
    b. change in person (first, second, or third; e.g., "we" to "they")
    c. change in verb tense
    d. change in tone or perspective
    e. change in location or setting
    f. the use of direct address (e.g., "Brethren, …")
    g. transitional conjunctions (e.g., "Therefore," "Now, …")

4. Once you have determined to what larger segment your pericope belongs, then perform a segment survey according to the steps described in TERTIARY RESEARCH.
5. **NOTE**: Detailed observation and more thorough investigation of the verses will occur in STEP 3: GRAMMATICAL STUDY and STEP 4: SEMANTIC ANALYSIS.

EXERCISE 1–E: Perform a Segment Survey on one of these segments:

Matt 1:1–17	Matt 5–7	1 Cor 12–14
Rom 9–11	Jas 4:1–5:10	Rev 1:8–3:22

EXERCISE 1–F: Perform a Book Survey on one of these books:

Mark	Ephesians	Philemon	2 Peter	Jude

TERTIARY INTERPRETIVE PROCEDURES: In addition to completing the SECONDARY INTERPRETIVE PROCEDURES, the following steps describe how to perform a Segment or Book Survey. Book Surveys take considerable time, but you will improve with practice.[23]

1. **Identify general literary form or genre (e.g., poetry, discursive and logical, letter, historical, parable, miracle, prophetic, legal, proverbial, apocalyptic).**
2. **Give a short, two or three word, accurate, but catchy title for each chapter of the biblical book or for each paragraph of the segment.**
3. **Locate and graphically depict the major divisions or sub-divisions of the book or segment.**
4. **Identify and briefly describe the Major Semantic Relationships (MSRs) operative across a majority of the book or the segment.** Remember that for a MSR to be "major," it must "govern" a majority of the book/segment, i.e., it must relate to or span a majority of the chapters in the biblical book; e.g., if there are four chapters, then two or more chapters must be governed.
5. **Ask interpretative questions for each MSR identified, but <u>don't</u> answer the questions now.**
6. **Summarize the Key Verses (be selective) for each MSR from the Survey.**
7. **Note Other Major Impressions, such as tone, atmosphere, figures of speech, or other structurally significant observations** *not already accounted for in the Survey thus far.*
8. **Additionally, for Book Surveys identify any information pertaining to authorship, audience, and provenance (i.e., the dating, location, and historical circumstances surrounding the writing) from specific details within the book itself and <u>not</u> using outside resources.**

IV. BIBLIOGRAPHY

Primary Survey

<u>Canon Formation</u>

Bruce, F. F. *The Canon of Scripture*. Downers Grove, IL: InterVarsity, 1988.

Patzia, Arthur G. *The Making of the New Testament: Origin, Collection, Text & Canon*. Downers Grove, IL: InterVarsity, 1995.

McDonald, Lee Martin *The Origin of the Bible: A Guide for the Perplexed*. London: T&T Clark International, 2011.

<u>Semantic/Structural Relationships, Careful Observation, and Interpretation</u>

Arthur, Kay et al. *The New How to Study Your Bible: Discover the Life-Changing Approach to God's Word*. Eugene, OR: Harvest House, 2010. [Teaches basic inductive approach to studying the Bible with attention to observation mark-up.]

Duvall, J. Scott, and J. Daniel Hays. *Grasping God's Word: A Hands-on Approach to Reading, Interpreting, and Applying the Bible*. 3rd ed. Grand Rapids: Zondervan, 2012.

Fee, Gordon D. and Douglas K. Stuart. *How to Read the Bible Book by Book: A Guided Tour*. Grand Rapids: Zondervan, 2002. [Reading guide for each book of the Bible.]

---

[23] See discussion/examples in Bauer and Traina, *Inductive Bible Study*; cf. Traina, *Methodical Bible Study*.

Halcomb, T. Michael W. *People of the Book: Inviting Communities into Biblical Interpretation*. Eugene, OR: Wipf & Stock, 2012. [Teaches an IBS approach for groups.]

Inductive Bible Study Website: http://inductivebiblestudy.seedbed.com/

Jensen, Irving Lester. *Independent Bible Study*. Rev. ed. Chicago: Moody, 1992. [Note that Jensen, a peer of Robert Traina, here describes his understanding of IBS.]

Thompson, David L. *Bible Study That Works*. Rev. ed. Nappanee, IN: Evangel, 1994. [[Provides a brief description of IBS history and its principles and basic workflow.]]

Virkler, Henry A. and Karelynne Ayayo, *Hermeneutics: Principles and Processes of Biblical Interpretation*. 2nd ed. Grand Rapids: Baker Academic, 2007. [Defines hermeneutics, reviews the history of biblical interpretation, and describes a process of biblical interpretation that moves to application.]

Wald, Oletta. *The New Joy of Discovery in Bible Study*. Rev. ed. Minneapolis: Augsburg Fortress, 2002. [A student of Robert Traina, she relies on his *Methodical Bible Study*.]

Secondary Study

Canon Formation

Beckwith, Roger T. *The Old Testament Canon of the New Testament Church and Its Background in Early Judaism*. London: SPCK, 1985.

McDonald, Lee Martin. *The Biblical Canon*. Peabody, MA: Hendrickson, 2007.

_____. *The Formation of the Biblical Canon*. 2 vols. London: Bloomsbury T&T Clark, 2017.

_____. *Forgotten Scriptures: The Selection and Rejection of Early Religious Writings*. Louisville: Westminster John Knox, 2009.

Metzger, Bruce M. *The Canon of the New Testament: Its Origin, Development, and Significance*. Oxford: Oxford University Press, 1987.

Inductive Biblical Study

Traina, Robert A. *Methodical Bible Study: A New Approach to Hermeneutics*. Wilmore, KY: Robert A. Traina, 1952 (repr., Grand Rapids: Zondervan, 2002). [Traina describes and exemplifies IBS; see also below the more hermeneutically explicit book by Traina and David Bauer (*Inductive Bible Study*).]

Tertiary Research

Inductive Biblical Study Methodology and Exegesis

Bauer, David R. and Robert A. Traina. *Inductive Bible Study: A Comprehensive Guide to the Practice of Hermeneutics*. Grand Rapids: Baker, 2010, esp. chs. 11–13 treating observation and book surveys.

Fee, Gordon D. *New Testament Exegesis: A Handbook for Students and Pastors*. 3d ed. Louisville: Westminster John Knox, 2002, pp. 9–12 (see bibliography, pp. 158–59).

The Journal of Inductive Biblical Study available for free download of articles at http://place.asburyseminary.edu/jibs/

STEP 2

TEXTUAL COMPARISONS

"And so important is it to perceive *differences* as well as resemblances, that in many languages the words denoting intellectual ability are mostly derived from words signifying *Distinction* and *Separation*. Such is the case in our own Language with the words '*Skill*,' '*Discernment*,' and '*Discretion*;' all of which originally meant *Separation*."[1]

—Richard Whately

Introduction: The NT was first written down in Greek and subsequently enjoyed a rich history of translation into Latin, Syriac, Ethiopic, etc. and eventually into English. In 1382 John Wycliffe made the first English translation based upon the Latin Vulgate. In 1526 William Tyndale published the first NT translated from the Greek text prepared by Erasmus (1516). Since then there have been over a hundred English translations produced. Today among the most commonly used English translations are the NIV, NET, KJV, NKJV, NLT, RSV, NRSV, NASB, and ESV, just to name a few. In STEP 2: TEXTUAL COMPARISONS students will investigate the NT to learn about its

---

[1] Richard Whately, *Introductory Lessons on Mind* (Boston: James Munroe, 1859), 109, emphasis original.

textual transmission by looking at English version notes, comparing English versions, and accessing data on textual variations as recorded in critical editions of the Greek NT.

I. PRIMARY SURVEY

<u>English Bibles and Their Notes</u>: To begin, *we must understand that every translation is interpretive*. That is, there is no such thing as a straightforward "perfect" translation from original languages into a target language like English. However, a person may learn a lot by comparing the English wording and the choices made when rendering words/ideas; we quickly learn what interpretive issues are present in our pericope. We might see words being translated in different ways—such words may be studied in more detail in STEP 5: LEXICAL RESEARCH. We might find different "logical" connections indicated that would give us pause and cause us to reflect more deeply about the passage. Furthermore, English translations often contain information in footnotes to increase our understanding. For example, the NET Bible is a newer version with very extensive notes. Other major English versions contain notes that are very valuable for the teacher and preacher. If a church uses a specific version as a pew Bible or if people prefer a particular version, a pastor should check these versions before preaching or teaching on a particular pericope.

<u>Textual Transmission and Different Verses</u>: Once we begin comparing Bible versions, we might become troubled to discover that certain verses are "missing" from our versions. The reason why verses are "omitted" has a simple explanation: It is due to the transmission history of our NT. Our NT was written, then copied and copied, translated into ancient languages, and then copied and copied some more. But, in fact, the NT is the most reliably attested set of documents from the ancient world; it has been carefully copied and preserved. In this transmission, however, changes in the text occurred—changes that were accidental or sometimes intentional. Certain biblical scholars dedicate their lives to studying and dating ancient copies of the NT in an attempt to recover the earliest version (called the autograph) of NT books. In fact, over a hundred and fifty years ago one of the most significant manuscript finds was made at a monastery at Mt. Sinai—codex "Sinaiticus" dating to the fourth-century preserves a very old version of the Greek NT. Moreover, we are still discovering old papyrus fragments of the NT!

<u>The King James Version</u>: The KJV was translated in 1611 and then subsequently revised many, many times. Since then, however, we have continued to find ancient manuscripts that preserve early versions of the NT. These older manuscripts are more accurate in preserving the original wording and reveal to us where the KJV needed revision in certain verses. The chart below shows which verses have been omitted from the KJV in modern translations *after* the publication of the Greek critical editions of B. F. Westcott and F. J. A. Hort (1881) and the *Novum Testamentum Graece* (1898, revised numerous times). I don't agree with all of these omissions. For example, Matt 9:34 is likely original, so are Luke 22:20, 24:12, and 24:40. So, what happened such that these verses were omitted in modern translations? You will notice that most of these omissions in recent English translations occur in the Gospels, and ***these verses have a parallel verse or verses in the same Gospel or in another Gospel***. So what most likely happened during textual transmis-

sion while copying these passages is that scribal copyists **added verses** that already existed in the Gospel accounts in order to "fill in" the story. So, while copying a parallel passage in one Gospel, a scribe added a verse or two already found elsewhere in another account. There are other instances where multiple verses are omitted, such as Mark 16:9–20 and John 7:53–8:11; most likely these longer passages were not original but were added to the Gospels after the initial composition. This explains why they are not found in the earliest manuscripts as noted in most modern translations.

"Extra" Verses: A Comparison of English Versions[2]

O = omitted in main text.
B = bracketed in the main text—The translation team and most biblical scholars today believe the verses were not part of the original text. However, these texts have been retained in brackets in the NASB and the HCSB.
F = omission noted in the footnote.
B+F = bracketed in the main text and omission noted in the footnote.

Passage \ Version	NIV	NASB	NKJV	RSV	NRSV	ESV	NCV	TLB	REB	HCSB	AMP	CEB	CJB	CEV	ERV	GW	EXB	GNT	Knox	LEB	MSG	Mounce	NET	NIrV	NLV	NLT	OJB
Matt 9:34 (12:24 //Mark 3:22 //Luke 11:15)									F																		
Matt 12:47 (Mark 3:32// Luke 8:20)			O	F	F				F	F		O	F			F	F									F	
Matt 17:21 (Mark 9:29)	F	B	F	O	O	F	O	F	F	B	F	O	O		O	F	O		O	O	O	O				F	
Matt 18:11 (Luke 19:10)	F	B	F	O	O	F	O	F	F	B	F	O	O		O	O	F	O		O	O	O	O			O	
Matt 21:44 (Isa 8:14, 15)			O	F		F			F	B	F		O	F	F	F	F	O								F	
Matt 23:14 (Mark 12:40// Luke 20:47)	F	B	F	O	O	F	O		F	B	F	O	O		O	O	F	O		O	O	O	O			O	
Mark 7:16 (Matt 13:9, 43; Mark 4:9, 23; Luke 8:8; 14:35; Rev 2:7, 11, 17, 29; 3:6, 13, 22; 13:9)	F	B	F	O	O	F	O	O	F	B	F	O	O		O	F	F	O		O	O	O	O			O	
Mark 9:44 (9:46; repeated in 9:48)	F	B	F	O	O	F	O	O	F	B	O	O	O		O	O	F	O		O	O	O	O			O	
Mark 9:46 (9:44; repeated in 9:48)	F	B	F	O	O	F	O	O	F	B	O	O	O		O	O	F	O		O	O	O	O			O	
Mark 11:26 (Matt 6:15//18:35)	F	B	F	O	O	F	O		F	B	F	O	O		O	O	F	O		O	O	O	O			O	B
Mark 15:28 (Luke 22:37)	F	B	F	O	O	F	O	F	F	B	F	O	O		O	O	F	O		O	O	O	O			O	B
Mark 16:9–20 (longer ending)		B	F	F	F	B	F	F		B	F	B	F	F			B	F		B	B		B		B		
Luke 17:36 (Matt 24:40)	F	B	F	O	O	F			F	B	F	O	O		O	O	F	O		O	O	O	O			O	
Luke 22:20 (Matt 26:29//Mark 14:24)								F	F								F					O				F	
Luke 22:43		B	F	O	F				B			F	F			F				B+F			B			F	
Luke 22:44		B	F	O	F				B				F	F	F		F			B+F			B			F	
Luke 23:17 (Matt 27:15//Mark 15:6)	F	B	F	O	O	F	O	O	F	B	F	O	O		F	O	O	F	O		O	O	O	O		O	B
Luke 24:12 (John 20:4–5)			O			F					F	O				F											
Luke 24:40			F	F	F		F									F											

---

[2] Slightly adapted from http://goo.gl/l9tV3C accessed 9-8-2012.

John 5:4	F	B	F	O	O	F	O	F	F	B		O	O			O	O	F	O		O	O	O	O		B	O	B
John 7:53–8:11		B	F	O	F	B	F	F		B	F	B					B			B+F		B					
Acts 8:37	F	B	F	O	F	F	O	F	F	B	F	O	O			O	O	F	O		O	O	O	O		B	O	B
Acts 15:34	F	B	F	O	O	F	O	O	F	O	F	O	O			O	O	F	O		O	O	O	O			O	B
Acts 24:7	F	B	F	O	O	F	O		F	B		O	O			O		O			O	O	O	O			O	B
Acts 28:29	F	B	F	O	O	F	O	O	F	B	F	O	O			O	O	F	O		O	O	O	O			O	B
Rom 16:24	F	B	F	O	O	F	O		F	B	F	O	O			O	O	F	O			O	O	O			O	B

<u>Translation Teams Must Make Decisions</u>: Additionally, English versions will vary in their decisions on which verses to include or not and whether to footnote these decisions. We must understand that each English version was created by a team of experts who had to make decisions about whether certain verses were most likely in the original manuscripts of our Greek NT. At the same time, version translation teams have worked with differing translation theories and representing various theological traditions—each of these factors affects decisions about which verses to include but also how to render these verses into English.

Let's look at the very popular NIV84. The twenty-two instances where the NIV84 is "missing" verses may be displayed as follows below with the explanatory notes included:

"MISSING" VERSES IN THE NIV WITH EXPLANATION IN FOOTNOTES[3]

Matt 5:44	**Some late manuscripts:** …bless those who curse you, do good to those who hate you…
Matt 17:21	**Some manuscripts:** But this kind does not go out except by prayer and fasting. …bless those who curse you, do good to those who hate you…
Matt 18:11	**Some manuscripts:** The Son of Man came to save what was lost.
Matt 23:14	**Some manuscripts:** Woe to you, teachers of the law and Pharisees, you hypocrites! You devour widows' houses and for a show make lengthy prayers. Therefore you will be punished more severely.
Mark 7:16	**Some manuscripts:** If anyone has ears to hear, let him hear.
Mark 9:44	**Some manuscripts:** Where their worm does not die and the fire is not quenched. (Isa 66:24)
Mark 9:46	**Some manuscripts:** Where their worm does not die and the fire is not quenched.
Mark 11:26	**Some manuscripts:** But if you do not forgive, neither will your father who is in heaven forgive your sins.
Mark 15:28	**Some manuscripts:** And the scripture was fulfilled which says, "He was counted with the lawless ones" (Isa 53:12)

---

[3] Slightly adapted from http://www.missingverses.com/ accessed 9–5–2012.

Mark 16:9–20	**Included with note:** [The earliest manuscripts and some other ancient witnesses do not have Mark 16:9–20]
Luke 17:36	**Some manuscripts:** Two men will be in the field; one will be taken and the other left.
Luke 22:43	**Included with note:** [Some early manuscripts do not have vv. 43–44]
Luke 22:44	**Included with note:** [Some early manuscripts do not have vv. 43–44]
Luke 23:17	**Some manuscripts:** Now he was obliged to release one man to them at the Feast.
John 5:4	**Some manuscripts:** And they waited for the moving of the waters. From time to time an angel of the Lord would come down and stir up the waters. The first one into the pool after each such disturbance would be cured of whatever disease he had.
John 7:53–8:11	**Included with note:** [The earliest manuscripts and many other ancient witnesses do not have John 7:53–8:11]
Acts 8:37	**Some manuscripts:** Phillip said, "If you believe with all your heart, you may." The eunuch answered, "I believe that Jesus Christ is the Son of God."
Acts 15:34	**Some manuscripts:** But Silas decided to remain there.
Acts 24:7	**Some manuscripts:** And wanted to judge him according to our law. But the commander, Lysias, came and with the use of much force snatched him from our hands and ordered his accusers to come before you.
Acts 28:29	**Some manuscripts:** After he said this, the Jews left, arguing vigorously among themselves.
Rom 16:24	**Some manuscripts:** May the grace of our Lord Jesus Christ be with all of you. Amen.
1 John 5:7	**Late manuscripts of the Vulgate:** Testify in heaven: the Father, the Word and the Holy Spirit, and these three are one. (***not found in any Greek manuscript before the sixteenth century***) And there are three that testify on earth: the…

A Basic Understanding of "Textual Criticism": Why is there such variation among modern translations? The answer is simply that our NT documents have been transmitted through 2,000 years across many languages and cultures. Originally, the NT documents were written in Greek, although there is some early church testimony that Matthew's Gospel may have been initially written in Aramaic or Hebrew. We have recovered thousands of fragments and manuscripts of the

Greek NT—the count is somewhere around 5,813.[4] Our oldest complete copy of the Greek NT was discovered in 1844 at St. Catherine's Monastery at Mt. Sinai by the Bible scholar Constantin von Tischendorf. More recently, NT fragments (purportedly dating to the second-century) have been discovered inside the cartonnage of mummy masks, but these are not yet published.

PALEOGRAPHY OF NEW TESTAMENT MANUSCRIPTS

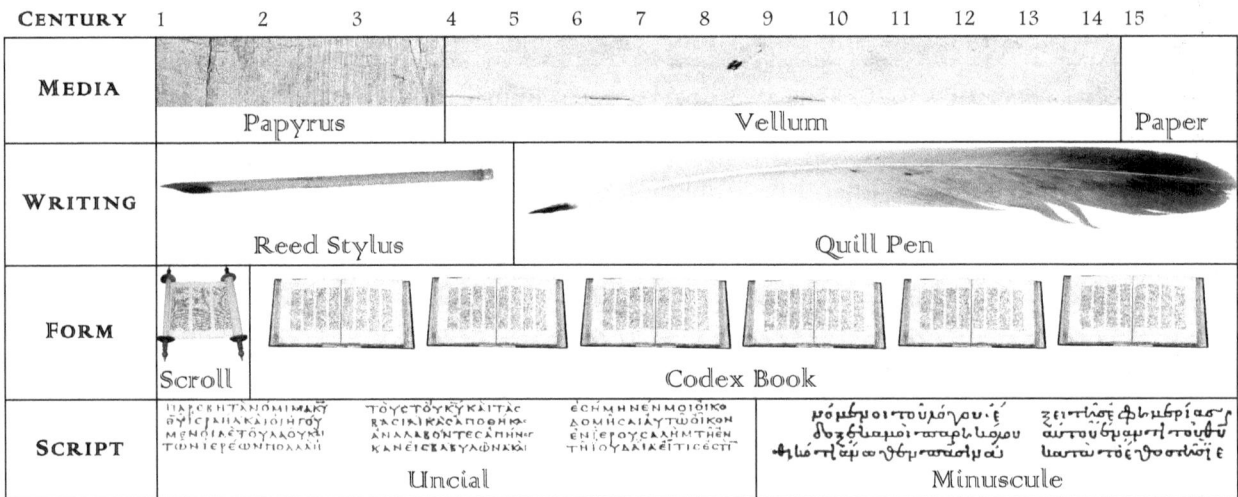

Experts have been carefully scrutinizing the Greek manuscripts, which then serve as the basis for modern English translations. All such manuscripts are dated and carefully compared to determine their character and relative accuracy. The discipline of study called textual criticism (also called "lower criticism") investigates the textual tradition and is concerned to discern what was most likely the "original text" based upon the available manuscripts.[5] Stated again, textual criticism is the field of scholarly work that attempts to understand how ancient manuscripts were transmitted through the creation of copies; copies were made by hand one at a time or sometimes with one person reading and many others copying (the first "photocopiers" or rather aural copiers). The goal of textual criticism is to discern which copies best testify to the original text, and by comparison of manuscripts to arrive at a text as close as possible to the original text. Unfortunately, we no longer have these originals or what are called "autographs." Nevertheless, *our NT is bar none the best attested text from the ancient world*, having over 5,500 fragments, portions, and whole Greek manuscripts that are "extant," i.e., in existence, on hand, or not lost(!), supporting it.

Developments across the Centuries: The excellent chart above shows developments by century (from left to right) in media upon which texts were copied (Papyrus to Vellum [= leather] to Paper), writing implements (reeds to quills), format (rolled up scrolls to codex or book form), and

---

[4] Stanley E. Porter, *How We got the New Testament: Text, Transmission, Translation* (Grand Rapids: Baker, 2013), 82–84.

[5] See the detailed review of this history within Kurt Aland and Barbara Aland, *The Text of the New Testament: An Introduction to the Critical Editions and to the Theory and Practice of Modern Textual* Criticism, trans. Erroll F. Rhodes, 2nd rev. ed. (Grand Rapids: Eerdmans, 1989).

writing style (Uncial=upper case letters with no spacing to Minuscule=lower case).[6] Very possibly the early Christians first began using the codex book form that dates to the mid-first-century AD.

<u>Types of Ancient NT Witnesses</u>: These fragments, portions, and whole manuscripts are classified into five categories: Papyri (written on the paper made from Egyptian Papyrus reeds), Uncials (using upper case letters), Minuscules (using lower case and cursive letters), Lectionaries (compiled church Scripture readings), and Ostraca (potsherd fragments). Additionally, we have manuscripts in various languages (e.g., 10,000+ Latin) and quotations from church fathers that are given approximations below and on the next page.[7] Numbers change as new discoveries are made.

EXTANT MANUSCRIPTS OF THE NT

NT GREEK	MANUSCRIPTS OF THE EARLY VERSIONS		
Uncials ≈ 325	Latin Vulgate ≈ 10,000+	Sahidic ≈ 150	Bohairic ≈ 100
Minuscules ≈ 2800	Ethiopic ≈ 2,000+	Arabic ≈ 75	Sogdian ≈ 3
Lectionaries ≈ 2200	Slavic ≈ 4,000	Old Latin ≈ 50	Old Syrian ≈ 2
Papyri ≈ 130 (+ new discoveries)	Armenian ≈ 2,600	Anglo Saxon ≈ 7	Persian ≈ 2
Recent Finds (Ostraca) ≈ 40	Syriac Peshitta ≈ 350+	Gothic ≈ 6	Frankish ≈ 1
TOTAL EXTANT ≈ 5,500	**TOTAL EXTANT EARLY VERSIONS ≈ 19,000**		

EARLY CHURCH FATHERS' QUOTATIONS OF THE NT

WRITER	GOSPELS	ACTS	PAULINE EPISTLES	GENERAL EPISTLES	REVELATION	TOTAL
Justin Martyr	268	10	43	6	3	**330**
Irenaeus	1,038	194	499	23	65	**1,819**
Clement	1,017	44	1,127	207	11	**2,406**
Origen	9,231	349	7,778	399	165	**17,922**
Tertullian	3,822	502	2,609	120	205	**7,258**
Hippolytus	734	42	387	27	188	**1,378**
Eusebius	3,258	211	1,592	88	27	**5,176**
TOTALS	19,368	1,352	14,035	870	664	36,289

---

[6] J. Harold Greenlee, *Introduction to New Testament Textual Criticism*, rev. ed. (Peabody, MA: Hendrickson, 1995), 23.

[7] These charts and statistics were gathered by a former colleague of mine, Rev. David Reed, and used by permission. I have updated them. ***Older*** data has been depicted graphically by Mark Barry at http://goo.gl/63QtoA.

Comparison of Classical Texts and the NT[8]

Ancient Author	Fragments or Copies	When Written	Earliest Copy	Time Span
Caesar (*History*)	≈33	100–44 BC	late 3rd century	≈400 yrs
Livy (*Annals*)	≈11	59 BC – AD 17	4th century	≈400 yrs
Plato (*Tetralogies*)	≈7	427–347 BC	12th century	≈1,450 yrs
Tacitus (*Annals*)	≈20	AD 100	12th century	≈1,000 yrs
Thucydides (*History*)	≈100	460–400 BC	3rd century BC	≈100 yrs
Herodotus (*Histories*)	≈50	480–425 BC	3rd century BC	≈100 yrs
Sophocles (≈120 known plays)	≈190	496–406 BC	3rd century BC	≈100 yrs
Lucretius	≈5	Died ca. 55 BC	2nd century AD	≈200 yrs
Euripides (≈65 known plays)	≈310	480–406 BC	3rd century BC	≈200 yrs
Demosthenes (speeches)	≈200	383–322 BC	3rd century BC	≈100 yrs
Aristotle	≈50	384–322 BC	AD 1100	≈1,400 yrs
Aristophanes	≈65	450–385 BC	1st century BC	≈400 yrs
Homer (Iliad and Odyssey)	≈1850	≈800 BC	3rd century BC	≈500 yrs
New Testament	≈24,000+	AD 40–90	2nd century	50–100 yrs

As helpful as these charts may be to bolster confidence in the textual basis of the NT, they are somewhat misleading. Why? The number of Greek manuscripts and fragments of the NT that date before AD 300 is less than one hundred.[9] Moreover, we continue to find more manuscript fragments of the NT and classical texts in, for example, mummy masks (the scrap paper was used to make them). The point, however, is to recognize how well-attested the NT documents are.

<u>Textual Variants or Readings</u>: If NT documents are so well attested, then what's the deal? Do you remember the telephone game that we all played in elementary school? A message was repeated around the circle until the last player recited it, and we all laughed at how "corrupted" the message had become. Well, "corruption" within biblical texts is quite serious; although scribes were generally careful when copying, some were less so and introduced "unintentional" errors while copying (errors of mis-seeing and mishearing, etc.); other scribes, however, added "intentional" changes (or errors) whether for simple clarification, for consistency with a parallel passage (as in the Synoptic Gospels [Matthew, Mark, and Luke]), for theological purposes (particularly later in the third- to fifth centuries with the ongoing theological debates), or for some unknown reason. These variations between copies of the same text are called "textual variants" or different

---

[8] Numbers may be found at the "Leuven Database of Ancient Books" (http://www.trismegistos.org/ldab) and these listed here are approximations based available information as much as I could verify.

[9] Philip Wesley Comfort and David P. Barrett treats about seventy in *The Text of the Earliest New Testament Greek Manuscripts* (Wheaton, IL: Tyndale House, 2001). In addition to these, more recently discovered early papyri, e.g., in the Green collection, will be published with Brill.

"readings." Textual variants are deviations of one copy from another copy. They have virtually all been catalogued. *Ninety-eight percent of these variants are not theologically significant*; that is, they would not overturn orthodox theology.[10] The types of errors have been logically cataloged (see below in TERTIARY RESEARCH). Thus, simply put, the goal of scholars trained in this field (called "textual critics") is to identify, organize, and evaluate textual variants in order to determine which variants are most likely original to the text and to understand the rise of those that are not.

EXERCISE 2–A: Below are NT verses that have textual variants for which our major English Bible versions will have notes. First, using three major English translations (e.g., the NIV, NASB, RSV, NRSV, and NET), identify what textual variants exist in these verses. Second, consider whether you can identify what may have motivated the creation of the variant readings: Was it for clarification, consistency, theological meaning, or some other (unknown) reason to you? Third, record any specific information that the versional notes provide to help evaluate or understand the variants. Which version provides the most help?

  a. 1 John 5:7–8
  b. Matt 13:13,15
  c. 1 Cor 2:1
  d. Acts 24:6–8

The Written or Electronic Word? The question was asked of me whether a pastor should prefer a written or electronic version of the Bible or Greek NT. As we discussed this, I asked how print or electronic versions might affect those to whom we minister. There is something "grounded" about seeing a physical book. It is more concrete and real. The younger generation is looking for authenticity—perhaps a book in paper might represent that to them. I am also amazed at how large the printed book trade continues to be. So, a book in a written physical form remains powerful. On the other hand, this "powerfulness" needs to be embodied in persons. So my concern is to wrongly focus on the facade than the real deal, which is Christ alive in us through the power of the Spirit. Christ in us is real and tangible; such realness results when God's people are prophesying (applying God's word to real life situations) and unbelievers become convicted and state, "God is truly among you!" (1 Cor 14:25). In this regard, I think of the very thought-provoking movie, *The Book of Eli* (that has some very violent scenes). The bad guy simply wanted the good Book for the power that he would have over people by merely possessing it. But the good guy had actually internalized it. How? If you want to know, read this from right to left or backwards (**Spoiler Alert until the end of the paragraph**): liarb ni ti gnidaer ti deziromem dna dnilb saw eh. When we movie watchers realized that, we marveled (or were supposed to, I think) at the miraculous way in which he overcame (okay—at times, butchered) his foes. In the end, however, the Bible was pre-

---

[10] For this reason, many have identified as sensationalist the work of Bart D. Ehrman, *Misquoting Jesus: The Story Behind Who Changed the Bible and Why* (New York: HarperOne, 2007). In fact, there is no conspiracy here by the church to hide this textual history.

served by being printed on a printing press and then shelved beside other "Holy Books" (Torah, Koran, Bhagavad Gita, etc.) and thus relegated to another *status quo* religion book. The movie was thought provoking about the written versus the internalized, powerful Word.

So the point is that we should always favor function over form, and substance over appearance. If people in the church pew attach more weight to a written physical book, then what does that mean? How deep is their understanding of the nature of God's ways? I heard once of a donor who wanted to give money for Bibles in Russia, but only if the Bibles were the KJV in English! Russian speaking people would be expected (apparently!) to learn Elizabethan English to read God's Word. What would be more impactful is the incarnated Word alive in believers; but people also need the Word in a language and form that they can understand. So, when offering pastoral care to an elderly person who has used the Bible in print form, it may be best for the pastor to hold in hand a print Bible to read to them during a home or hospital visit. But, in a youth group setting a cell phone or iPad will likely be fine. However, most importantly in either situation is that we live the Word, or rather that we allow the Word to live in us (Gal 2:20).

PRIMARY INTERPRETIVE PROCEDURES:

1. **Compare and record important differences from at least three major English versions (e.g., NIV11, NASB, NRSV, RSV and NET). Specifically, identify and record where the translations differ regarding key words that may need further study in STEP 5: LEXICAL RESEARCH. Ask Questions.**
2. **Search within Bible notes and record any significant information that pertains to translation and meaning. Ask Questions.**
3. **Search within Bible notes that may alert you to possible text critical variants in the Greek manuscript tradition. If present, list these by verse reference and consider whether they impact the meaning of the pericope.**
4. **Summarize your most important findings noting the most vital interpretive questions (if any) that you want to bring forward to STEP 9: INTERPRETIVE DECISIONS.**

II. SECONDARY STUDY

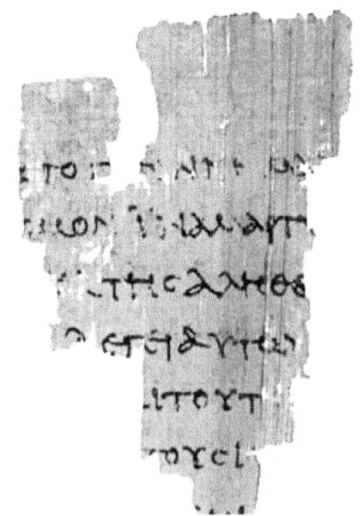

Orientation: TEXTUAL COMPARISONS at a secondary level involves looking at critical Greek editions of the NT in order to discover whether there are any significant textual differences (variants) between major manuscript witnesses within a pericope and then to consider whether these differences might assist our understanding or interpretation of the pericope. To the right is a picture of the famous Papyrus 52 fragment (verso–back side) of John's Gospel that is dated to the early second-century (public domain).

Why should a pastor consider whether any textual variants are present? Textual variants may reflect an early interpretive trajectory within the church.[11] The prodigious exegete Marcus Barth commenting on Ephesians has this to say: "the textual variants are a great aid in studying early interpretations. They help the modern expositor to realize where there are as yet insoluble problems. Each of them ... may vitally influence the interpretation of the whole epistle."[12] Robert F. Hull also helpfully explains:

> [T]textual variants have stories to tell about the problems the first Christians wrestled with: tensions between Jews and Gentiles; women in family life and church leadership; the divine/human nature of Jesus; the standardization of liturgical texts; social and sexual issues; and others.... The fact is that textual criticism affects the life of the church at its most basic level, for its results eventually filter down to the ordinary Bible-reading public in the translations in popular use.[13]

And, with only some orientation students can access both the more important variants and the important discussions of them.

Students should ideally read an introductory book on textual criticism (Greenlee's is an excellent overview), and then move to skim read the introduction to a critical edition of the Greek NT, either the United Bible Society 3rd, 4th or 5th edition (UBS$^{3/4/5}$) or the Nestle-Aland 26th, 27th, 28th edition (NA$^{26/27/28}$). There you will learn much about textual criticism. One of the foundational things to learn is that there are several types of witnesses to the Greek NT text. Over time, textual critics have settled on a symbol system for each set of types of witnesses (thankfully!). For example, papyri have a large cursive 𝔓 and are numbered 1–127 (see the helpful "List of NT Papyri" at Wikipedia), because this is how many we have found. But, Daniel Wallace has reported recently seven new papyri, six dated in the second-century and one portion of Mark's Gospel dated to the first-century apparently.[14] Obviously, such papyri would be some of the earliest witnesses to the NT to date, joining perhaps the earliest 𝔓^{52} (see previous page), the size of a half dollar.

<u>Major Types of Witnesses</u>: Supplementing what was presented above, here is a list of the major types of witnesses to the Greek NT:

1. **Papyri**: e.g., 𝔓^{66} is Bodmer Papyrus II containing John ca. AD 200; or 𝔓^{52} ca. AD 96–150.
2. **Codex/Codices**: e.g., Codex Sinaiticus (ℵ), Codex Vaticanus (B) ca. AD 300; given capital letters, some foreign letters, <u>and</u> numbers beginning with a zero (0XXX) ranging from 01 to

---

[11] See, e.g., Joël Delobel, "Textual Criticism and Exegesis: Siamese Twins?," in *New Testament Textual Criticism, Exegesis, and Early Church History: A Discussion of Methods*, ed. B. Aland and J. Delobel; CBET 7 (Kampen: Kok Pharos, 1994), 98–117 at 107–16.

[12] Markus Barth, *Ephesians 1–3*, vol. 1, 2 vols., AB 34 (Garden City, NY: Doubleday, 1974), 53.

[13] Robert F. Hull Jr., *The Story of the New Testament Text: Movers, Materials, Motives, Methods, and Models*, RBS 58 (Leiden: Brill, 2010), 3.

[14] See the announcement at http://www.dts.edu/read/wallace-new-testament-manscript-first-century/ accessed Feb 29, 2012 and more fully described at http://sheffieldbiblicalstudies.wordpress.com/2012/02/06/first-century-fragment-of-mark/ (with Hebrews 1 needing to be changed to Hebrews 11, and Romans 8–9 to 9–10).

0268; e.g., Codex Sinaiticus is known by this name, but also by the Hebrew letter א (*aleph*) and by the codex number 01.
3. **Minuscules (cursives)**: Codices are numbered as 1–2600 with no zero at the front.
4. **Ancient Versions**: e.g., Latin, Syriac, Coptic, Sahidic, etc. Each are abbreviated: thus vg = Vulgate; syr = Syriac, etc.
5. **Lectionaries**: Collections of scriptural texts for public reading are indicated by ℓ or l followed by numbers. It is difficult to differentiate the letter l (el) from the number 1 (one).
6. **Patristic Quotations**: e.g., Augustine, Clement of Alex., etc. who are given abbreviations.
7. **Other**: e.g., Ostraca, amulets, inscriptions, mosaics—often these are not included in the textual critical apparati of GNTs.[15]

Causes of Textual Variation: It is helpful to consider the varieties of mistakes or errors or changes that scribes made while reproducing texts. Scholars have categorized these in two ways: conscious or intentional changes and unconscious or unintentional changes.[16]

1. **Unconscious or Unintentional Changes**:
   a. *Faulty Word Division*: e.g., 1 Timothy 3:16: ὁμολογουμένως μέγα ("confessedly great") for ὁμολογοῦμεν ὡς μέγα ("we acknowledge how great").
   b. *Homoeoteleuton* ("similar ending")—skipping from one letter or word to the same letter or word further down the page; e.g., 1 John 2:23: here many manuscripts skip from the first occurrence of τὸν πατέρα ἔχει to the second.
   c. *Haplography* ("single writing")—writing a letter or word once when it should be written twice; e.g., in 1 Thess 2:7: ἐγενήθημεν ἤπιοι ("we became gentle") for ἐγενήθημεν νήπιοι ("we became infants").
   d. *Dittography* ("double writing")—writing a letter or word twice instead of once; e.g., in Mark 12:27: ὁ θεὸς θεὸς for θεὸς. Also, in Codex B at John 13:14 the word διδάσκαλος is repeated.
   e. *Metathesis* ("change of place") [*also called transposition]—changing the order of letters or words; e.g., in Mark 14:65: ἔλαβον ("received") for ἔβαλον ("struck").
   f. *Itacism*—confusing vowel sounds; e.g., in Rom 5:1: ἔχωμεν ("let us have") for ἔχομεν ("we have").
   g. *Homoioarchton* ("similar beginning")—like *homoeoteleuton* ("similar ending"), a scribe could anticipate the next letters or word (move the eye) and then come back to the same letters or word but skipping words or lines in between.

---

[15] For a brief discussion, see David C. Parker, *An Introduction to the New Testament Manuscripts and Their Texts* (Cambridge: Cambridge University Press, 2008), ch.3, "Other Types of Witnesses," pp.108–30.

[16] The majority is directly from David Alan Black, "Appendix 1: *Types of Errors in the New Testament Manuscripts*" *New Testament Textual Criticism: A Concise Guide* (Grand Rapids: Baker, 1994), 59–61. However, additions are marked with asterisk (*); see also Comfort, *Encountering the Manuscripts: An Introduction to New Testament Paleography & Textual Criticism* (Nashville: Broadman & Holman, 2005), 322–29.

*h. *Confusion of Letters*—Certain Greek letters or combinations looked similar and were sometimes confused. For the uncial script, these characters were commonly confused.[17]

COMMONLY CONFUSED UNCIAL LETTERS

ⲁ Δ λ	Α Δ Λ
Ε Θ Ο С	Ε Θ Ο Σ
ΙC Κ	ΙΣ Κ
Γ Τ	Γ Τ
ΙΙ Η Π Τ ΤΤ	ΙΙ Η Π Τ ΤΤ
Μ ΛΛ	Μ ΛΛ

2. **Conscious or Intentional Changes**:

   a. *Grammatical Improvements*; e.g., in Mark 6:29: ἦλθον for ἦλθαν.
   b. *Liturgical Changes*; e.g., in Matt 6:13 there is the addition/omission of the doxology in the Lord's Prayer.
   c. *Elimination of Apparent Discrepancies*; e.g., in Mark 1:2: ἐν τοῖς προφήταις ("in the prophets") is substituted for ἐν τῷ Ἡσαΐᾳ τῷ προφήτῃ ("in Isaiah the prophet") because the quotation in Mark 1:2–3 is from Malachi and Isaiah.
   d. *Harmonization of Parallel Passages*; e.g., Matt 19:17 in some ancient manuscripts has been added to in order to harmonize with Mark 10:18//Luke 18:19.
   e. *Conflation*—combining two or more variants into one reading; e.g., in Luke 24:53 αἰνοῦντες and εὐλογοῦντες may have been conflated to produce the reading αἰνοῦντες καὶ εὐλογοῦντες (although it is also possible that homoeoteleuton can account for the shorter readings).
   f. *Doctrinal Changes*; e.g., in 1 John 5:7–8, this "Heavenly Witnesses" passage has no good Greek manuscript support (certainly no early Greek manuscript support).

<u>Assessing Textual Variants</u>: Textual critics have developed two broad categories of criteria to help adjudicate between textual variants, to weigh evidence as to which reading is most likely original. The first concerns logical and contextual evidence within the text or discourse itself, what is called "internal criteria." The second type is called "external criteria" and concerns the character of physical manuscripts (age, location, distribution, etc.) discussed further below. Although external evidence has priority, I will treat internal evidence first.

<u>Internal Evidence</u>: After centuries of pondering logical likelihoods, textual critics have recognized the following criteria concerning internal aspects of the text. These provide evidence to be weighed when deciding which variant is most likely the original form of the text.[18]

1. The reading that best explains the rise of the other variant readings is to be preferred. See Col 2:2 (cf. 1:27) for an example of an explanatory reading.

---

[17] This chart is from Rich Elliott, "A Site Inspired by Encyclopedia of New Testament Textual Criticism," Online at http://www.skypoint.com/members/waltzmn/ShortDefs.html#EasConf accessed 1–7–2015.

[18] The examples given below after each principle are from Greenlee, *Introduction*, 112–14. For a more robust list of eleven internal criteria, see Stanley E. Porter, *Handbook to Exegesis of the New Testament*, NTTS 25 (Leiden: Brill, 1997), 62–63.

2. The harder reading is to be preferred. Why? Scribes tended to simplify difficulties in the text. Consider the harder reading in Mark 1:2.
3. The shorter reading is generally to be preferred. Why? Scribes tended to be additive rather than subtractive, although there is evidence that shortening the text also occurred.[19] See the shorter reading in an intentional change at 1 Cor 6:20; conversely see the longer reading in an unintentional change at 1 John 2:23.
4. The reading that is not harmonized or less parallel is to be preferred. See an example of this in Matt 19:16–18//Mark 10:17–19//Luke 18:18–20. Matthew's text is harmonized with Mark's and Luke's version of the account.
5. The reading more in line with the author's style and theology is to be preferred. Consider Mark 16:9 which reads πρώτη but Mark everywhere else uses μία to represent "the (number) one day of the week."

It is not uncommon that criteria are mixed and in opposition to one another. Also, a consideration of "style" involves subjective judgments. Finally, there are additional "external" criteria that can add further complexity to the puzzle of sorting out variant readings.

Christian Centers of Learning, Textual Activity, and Family Groupings: The current consensus is that certain locations were centers where Christians collected and copied their manuscripts; and thus, certain manuscripts can be shown to have certain relationships with others because of the theory of their "location" and the textual variant tradition that existed in that location. Remember that once a textual variant is introduced, the variant tends to have staying power, and those subsequent copies from that corrupted text carry the corruption with them. On this basis also, textual critics will group together manuscripts into families through the identification of "family resemblances" based upon textual characteristics of variations. On the next page, I have created A DEPICTION OF TEXT DISTRIBUTION THROUGH LOCALES for the transmission of Luke that has created the versions of the Greek NT that we have today. The arrowed lines represent textual copying.

The Caesarean text-type seems to be restricted to the Gospels and is identified with the church father, Origen (AD 185–254), who, after relocating to Caesarea (Maritima), noted some distinctive readings associated with this location. Some scholars don't even consider this a legitimate category; it is the least homogenous because it is a mixture of Alexandrian and Western readings. The Alexandrian text-type (sometimes called the "neutral text") is considered most reliable by many text-critics, because they are the earliest (being preserved in Egypt). The Western text type is early, but generally deemed unreliable because it consistently contains longer readings. The

---

[19] This principle has been recently questioned in the revised 1981 dissertation by James R. Royse, *Scribal Habits in Early Greek New Testament Papyri*, NTTSD 36 (Leiden: Brill, 2008), esp. 735. Royse proposes instead the following: "In general the longer reading is to be preferred, except where: a) the longer reading appears, on external grounds, to be late; or b) the longer reading may have arisen from harmonization to the immediate context, to parallels, or to general usage; or c) the longer reading may have arisen from an attempt at grammatical improvement." This conclusion is based upon his careful study of scribal tendencies among the earliest papyri to omit, rather than add, and to align/correct style in view of the immediate context.

Byzantine/Koine (also know as "Syrian") is considered less reliable since it is more expansive. More than eighty percent of our manuscripts are of the Byzantine text-type and thus also have a later dating beginning in the 8th century with most dated in the second millennium. This text-type became well-known in the later medieval era and was the base for Erasmus' Greek testament resulting in so many copies being made. In 1611 this text-type was the basis for the KJV. To consider the age, characteristics, text-type, and family relations falls within "external criteria."

DEPICTION OF TEXT DISTRIBUTION THROUGH LOCALES

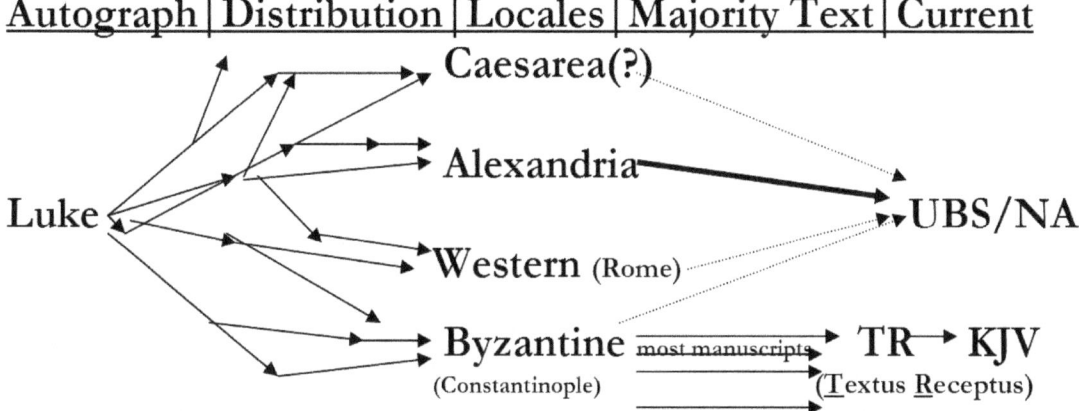

External Criteria for Evaluating Witnesses: Four basic principles for evaluating the quality of a textual variant are the age, quality, distribution, and number of witnesses. The first is rather obvious: The earlier a witness is in *age*, the closer it is to the original manuscript's dating and presumably has less chance of corruption (but this is still obviously possible). But this alone is insufficient especially when comparing manuscripts four hundred years removed from the original document; thus, the *quality* of a witness is important. What tendencies does a manuscript have? Does it have many variant readings due to sloppy copying? Does it tend to have expansive readings that harmonize (e.g., in a Gospel account) and so is less likely reliable in these instances? To what text-type and family does it belong? **Distribution** concerns how broadly distributed geographically a variant reading is. If one reading is found only in the western text-type, then it is less likely to be the original reading. If, on the other hand, a reading is found well-represented in several text-types (i.e., it is broadly distributed geographically) with older and better quality witnesses, then this would indicate that the reading is more likely original.[20] Finally, the *number of witnesses* is less important than the age and quality of them. Why? The Byzantine text type was popularized and multiplied making it the most common text type (about 80% of all extant manuscripts). If you simply added up witnesses in favor of a reading, this would always favor the Byzantine reading. So, you must consider the age, quality, and distribution and not just the number of witnesses.

---

[20] The mechanism historically would look like this—the proper reading "spread out" early among churches so that it could be found in many locales. This assumes also something quite important: individual "errors" (or perhaps tendencies) entered into the textual tradition by way of one location ***and thus would not have broader circulation***.

These principles may be illustrated with the telephone game analogy above, but by adding four columns of communication channels. Imagine that there were four columns of twenty students in rows of four each in the game, and one person who gave the initial message. Of course, at the end of each row there would likely be four different messages. The children closer to the starting person, irrespective of row, represent earlier witnesses in terms of age/dating. Among the eighty students, one might note that certain ones always liked to "foul up" the message—their quality of truly representing the message would be dubious; one could very possibly track the introduction of variant readings to these certain students. Once the message was corrupted, however, it would be passed along corrupted. If one tried to find out which reading was original in any given row, when all four students in the same row agreed even though in different columns, these four reflect the importance of broad (early) geographic distribution. Finally, adding up all the students within distinct groupings of variant readings would be analogous to considering the number of witnesses.

<u>Example of the Relevance of Textual Criticism in Eph 3:21</u>: John Muddiman commenting on Eph 3:21 observes, "The co-ordination of the Church and Christ and the precedence given to the former is striking and unparalleled in the New Testament. The variants, omitting the 'and' (D^c K L P) or reversing the order (D* F G), only serve to underline this fact."[21] Careful attention to this textual variant leads one to consider its implications, namely, that "Church" is placed forward before "Christ" in a statement about how God is being glorified *as if the church were more instrumental somehow now for that purpose*. Why was Ephesians worded in this manner? For many interpreters, such an emphasis on the Church reflects ecclesiological development and consequently a later dating with the implication being that Paul could not have written this letter. However, in the Mediterranean world cities and groups of people were deified, placed with other divinities, and depicted as such on statuary, etc. In particular, political entities in Asia Minor were personified, if not even "co-deified," in relation to the "gods" with whom they were related. So, for example, a city (the *demos*) is found as receiving the dedication on an altar used for sacrifices ("to the demos") typically used for the deity. Also, the Roman people were personified-deified as the goddess *Roma* and placed in close relationship to Caesar; her image was seen in temples, coinage, reliefs, and statuary, especially in Asia Minor, as the imperial cults spread vigorously in this area in the first half of the first-century. *The emperor Augustus refused any cult unless Roma was placed with his statue*. In conclusion, a text-critical "problem" (the word "church" is placed before Christ, and scribes attempted to change this) resulted in an interpretive question (Why would the church be placed first?) that led to my further research on personification of groups or political entities and the discovery of a very intriguing social-religious parallel: As Caesar was in relation to Roma, so Christ was in relation to the Church. It may have been that Paul, if the author (as I maintain), was attempting to provide an important identity indicator for the followers of Christ as Christ's personified and co-divine "body" since otherwise they would have no significant organization to which to belong having been expelled or disenfranchised from synagogues and pagan places of worship. So, paramount in Ephesians is the identity of believers as the church assembly of the exalted Christ.

---

[21] John Muddiman, *The Epistle to the Ephesians*, BNCT (London: Continuum, 2001), 175–76.

Which Critical Edition to Use? There are currently three editions of the Greek NT (GNT) that pastors should consider using. The first two are identical twins or "sister" texts in the truest sense of the word. These are the UBS[3/4/5] and the NA[26/27/28]. These two GNTs have the same text, but vary in punctuation (see immediately below). The recent update, the UBS[5] and NA[28], have only thirty-four differences in the Catholic Epistles.[22] The NA[28] follows the text of the second edition of the *Editio Critica Maior* (ECM) prepared by the University of Muenster (the Catholic Epistles are completed) and the University of Birmingham (currently working on John's Gospel).[23] For further discussion on the ECM and available resources, see TERTIARY RESEARCH below.

Comparison: For a helpful example illustrating the differences, consider 2 Cor 9:8–9. Below students can see how the UBS[4-5], NA[27-28], and SBL GNT punctuate, mark, and indicate text critical marks differently in 2 Cor 9:8–9, which includes a quotation from Ps 112:9 (LXX). I include my English translation below each that reflects the difference of punctuation.

1. The UBS[4-5] uses capitalization, **bold**, indentation, and parallel alignment to show a direct quotation. Also, καθὼς γέγραπται ends with a comma.

   8 δυνατεῖ δὲ ὁ θεὸς πᾶσαν χάριν περισσεῦσαι εἰς ὑμᾶς, ἵνα ἐν παντὶ πάντοτε πᾶσαν αὐτάρκειαν ἔχοντες περισσεύητε εἰς πᾶν ἔργον ἀγαθόν, **9** καθὼς γέγραπται,
   Ἐσκόρπισεν, ἔδωκεν τοῖς πένησιν,
   ἡ δικαιοσύνη αὐτοῦ μένει εἰς τὸν αἰῶνα.[e] [The [e] here is a punctuation note.]
   8 "Moreover, God is powerful to increase all grace to you, in order that, in all ways always all self-sufficiency having, you would increase in every good work, [9] just as it is written,
   "He scattered abroad, he gave to the poor;
   his righteousness remains forever."

2. The NA[27-28] does not use capitalization to introduce quotations, but *italics*, indentation, and parallel alignment. Also, καθὼς γέγραπται ends with a raised dot (·) like the SBL GNT.

   8 ⸀δυνατεῖ δὲ ὁ θεὸς πᾶσαν χάριν περισσεῦσαι εἰς ὑμᾶς, ἵνα ἐν παντὶ πάντοτε πᾶσαν αὐτάρκειαν ἔχοντες περισσεύητε εἰς πᾶν ἔργον ἀγαθόν, **9** καθὼς γέγραπται·
   ἐσκόρπισεν, ἔδωκεν τοῖς πένησιν,
   ἡ δικαιοσύνη αὐτοῦ μένει εἰς τὸν αἰῶνα⸆.
   8 "Moreover, God is powerful to increase all grace to you, in order that, in all ways always all self-sufficiency having, you would increase in every good work, [9] just as it is written:
   "He scattered abroad, he gave to the poor;
   his righteousness remains forever."

3. The SBL GNT uses neither italics, bold, indentation, or parallel alignment. Additionally, the editor Michael Holmes has placed 2 Cor 9:9 into parentheses (that end in 9:10) and con-

---

[22] For a brief description see http://www.nestle-aland.com/en/the-28–edition/revision-of-the-catholic-letters/.
[23] See the description of the EMC at http://www.uni-muenster.de/INTF/ECM.html.

cludes both 9:8 and 9:9 with a raised dot (·) rather than a comma and period, respectively. These editorial decisions involve interpretation. Holmes has presumably judged 9:9–10 to be an aside.

⁸ δυνατεῖ δὲ ὁ θεὸς πᾶσαν χάριν περισσεῦσαι εἰς ὑμᾶς, ἵνα ἐν παντὶ πάντοτε πᾶσαν αὐτάρκειαν ἔχοντες περισσεύητε εἰς πᾶν ἔργον ἀγαθόν·
⁹ (καθὼς γέγραπται· Ἐσκόρπισεν, ἔδωκεν τοῖς πένησιν, ἡ δικαιοσύνη αὐτοῦ μένει εἰς τὸν αἰῶνα·
⁸ "Moreover, God is powerful to increase all grace to you, in order that, in all ways always all self-sufficiency having, you would increase in every good work; ⁹ (just as it is written: "He scattered abroad, he gave to the poor; his righteousness remains forever;" ... ⁹:¹⁰....)

Also, each has its own system of representing textual variants (using different *sigla*) as well as the number of variants discussed. The NA$^{27/28}$ has far more textual variants listed in its apparatus, but generally has fewer (more strategic, representative) witnesses shown for each variant. The UBS$^{4/5}$ provides fewer textual variants (none above), but is much more selective to include the more disputed or important ones. Likewise, the UBS includes a rating of textual variants (A, B, C, D) in the 4th edition, with "A" being most certain of their results. These ratings have changed from the 3rd to the 4th editions generally in the favor of decisions being given more confidence; for instance, many D ratings are upgraded to C ratings. In this regard the UBS GNT is particularly helpful because it typically lists only the most important textual variants. The most contested variants are those scored {C} in the UBS$^{4/5}$ which were scored {D} in the UBS^{3} edition.

Historically, individuals worked to produce critical editions; but the UBS/NA text represented the work of five textual critics. Recently, Michael Holmes has created a new edition for the Society of Biblical Literature (SBLGNT) by comparing and making decisions on four sources—the editions of Westcott-Hort (WH), Tregelles (Treg), the Greek base for the NIV, and the Byzantine text of Robinson and Pierpont (RP). The result is a text that is free for download (http://www.sblgnt.com/). The impact of this is still to be seen; it essentially adds another layer of complexity and potential confusion for pastors and teachers. Another complicating factor is that newer editions will always be released as newer evidence is found. For example, the NA^{28} edition has incorporated more recently studied papyri fragments ($\mathfrak{P}^{117-127}$), although it will not include the most recent seven found ($\mathfrak{P}^{128-134}$), and the new fragments yet to be found. Apparently, Acts and the Catholic Epistles have notable textual differences in places due to the re-evaluation of textual evidence; in all over thirty changes have been made.

Example: Comparison of the Greek Testaments of 1 Cor 2:1–4: Below is a discussion of how textual variants are presented and discussed in the NA^{27}, UBS^{4}, SBLGNT, and the discussions in two commentaries (Gordon Fee and Ben Witherington). Immediately below in a chart are textual variants as found in the NA^{27} compared with the versional notes of the NASB.

NA²⁷ TEXTUAL VARIANTS IN 1 COR 2:1–5

	NA²⁷	NASB WITH TEXT CRITICAL NOTES
#1 #2 #3 #4	2:1 Κἀγὼ ἐλθὼν πρὸς ὑμᾶς, ἀδελφοί, ἦλθον οὐ καθ' ὑπεροχὴν λόγου ἢ σοφίας καταγγέλλων ὑμῖν τὸ ⸀μυστήριον τοῦ θεοῦ. 2 οὐ γὰρ ἔκρινά ⸂τι εἰδέναι⸃ ἐν ὑμῖν εἰ μὴ Ἰησοῦν Χριστὸν καὶ τοῦτον ἐσταυρωμένον. 3 κἀγὼ ἐν ἀσθενείᾳ καὶ ἐν φόβῳ καὶ ἐν τρόμῳ πολλῷ ἐγενόμην πρὸς ὑμᾶς, 4 καὶ ὁ λόγος μου καὶ τὸ κήρυγμά μου οὐκ ἐν ⸂πειθοῖ[ς] σοφίας [λόγοις]⸃ ἀλλ' ἐν ⸀ἀποδείξει πνεύματος καὶ δυνάμεως, 5 ἵνα ἡ πίστις ὑμῶν μὴ ᾖ ἐν σοφίᾳ ἀνθρώπων ἀλλ' ἐν δυνάμει θεοῦ.	1 And when I came to you, brethren, I did not come with superiority of speech or of wisdom, proclaiming to you the ¹testimony of God. 2 For I determined to know nothing among you except Jesus Christ, and Him crucified. 3 I was with you in weakness and in fear and in much trembling, 4 and my message and my preaching were not in persuasive words of wisdom, but in demonstration of the Spirit and of power, 5 so that your faith would not rest on the wisdom of men, but on the power of God. ¹ One early ms reads *mystery*
	FOUR VARIANTS	**VARIANTS TRANSLATED**
#1	⸀† μαρτυριον ℵ² B D F G Ψ 33. 1739. 1881 𝔐 b vg syʰ sa ┊ txt 𝔓⁴⁶ᵛⁱᵈ ℵ* A C pc ar r syᵖ bo; Hipp BasA Ambst	**Variant**: "The *testimony* of God" (KJV, RSV, NIV, ESV) ┊ **NA²⁷ Text**: "The *mystery* of God" (NRSV, NJB; NLT has "message")
#2	⸂ 2 1 ℵ A F G 048ᵛⁱᵈ. 6. 1175. 1241. 1505. 2464 al ┊ του ειδ.τι 1881 𝔐 ┊ ιδειν τι Ψ ┊ txt B C (D) P 33. 81. 365. 630. 1506. 1739 pc	**Variants**: "to know something" (change in word order) ┊ "(in order) to know" ┊ "to see something" ┊ **NA²⁷ Text**: "to know something"
#3	⸂πειθοις ανθρωπινης σοφ. λ. ℵ² A C Ψ (630) 𝔐 vgᶜˡ ┊ πειθοι ανθ. σοφ. λ. 1. 42. 440. (⸋2495) al ┊ πειθοις ανθ. σοφ. και λ. 131 ┊ πειθοις σοφ. 𝔓⁴⁶ F G pc ┊ πειθοι σοφιας *sine test.?* [i.e., *without testimony?*] ┊ txt (ℵ*) B D 33. 1175. 1506. 1739. 1881 pc vgˢᵗ (syᵖ)	**Variants**: "with persuasive words of human wisdom" ┊ "with persuasion of human wisdom with words" ┊ "with persuasive things of human wisdom and words" ┊ "with persuasive [things] of wisdom" ┊ "with persuasion of wisdom" ┊ **NA²⁷ Text**: "with persuasive words of wisdom"
4	⸀ αποκαλυψει D*·²	**Variant**: "in revelation of the Spirit and power" **NA²⁷ Text**: "in demonstration of the Spirit and power"

The UBS⁴/⁵ and NA²⁷/²⁸ texts are identical. However, the UBS⁴ lists only variants #1 (B rating) and #3 (C rating), but provides more detailed information about additional variants and the ancient authorities that support them (esp. church fathers). See the chart below. The UBS⁴ will also contain two other apparati—a Quotation and Allusion Apparatus (valuable for STEP 8: SCRIPTURAL CORRELATIONS) and a Punctuation Apparatus (valuable for STEP 1: CONTEXTUAL LOCATION). Read the introduction of the UBS⁴/⁵ for more information about these apparati.

UBS⁴ TEXTUAL VARIANTS AND APPARATI IN 1 COR 2:1–5

UBS⁴	UBS⁴ TEXTUAL APPARATUS
2 **1** Κἀγὼ ἐλθὼν πρὸς ὑμᾶς, ἀδελφοί, ἦλθον οὐ καθ' ὑπεροχὴν λόγου ἢ σοφίας καταγγέλλων ὑμῖν τὸ μυστήριον¹ τοῦ θεοῦ. **2** οὐ γὰρ ἔκρινά τι εἰδέναι ἐν ὑμῖν εἰ μὴ Ἰησοῦν Χριστὸν καὶ τοῦτον ἐσταυρωμένον. **3** κἀγὼ ἐν ἀσθενείᾳ καὶ ἐν φόβῳ καὶ ἐν τρόμῳ πολλῷ ἐγενόμην πρὸς ὑμᾶς, **4** καὶ ὁ λόγος μου καὶ τὸ κήρυγμά μου οὐκ ἐν πειθοῖ[ς] σοφίας [λόγοις]² ἀλλ' ἐν ἀποδείξει πνεύματος καὶ δυνάμεως, **5** ἵνα ἡ πίστις ὑμῶν μὴ ᾖ ἐν σοφίᾳ ἀνθρώπων ἀλλ' ἐν δυνάμει θεοῦ.ᵃ	**1** {B} μυστήριον 𝔓⁴⁶ ᵛⁱᵈ ℵ* A C 436 1912 itᵃʳ, ᵒ, ʳ syrᵖ copᵇᵒ slav Hippolytus Basil-Ancyra; Ambrosiaster Ambrose Paulinus-Nola Augustine // μαρτύριον ℵ² B D F G Ψ 0150 6 33 81 104 256 263 365 424 459 1175 1241 1319 1506 1573 1739 1852 1881 1962 2127 2200 2464 *Byz* [L P] *Lect* itᵇ, ᵈ, ᶠ, ᵍ vg syrʰ copˢᵃ arm ethᵖᵖ geo Basil Chrysostom Cyril; Jerome Pelagius // σωτήριον *l* 598¹/² *l* 593 *l* 599 ² **4** {C} πειθοῖς σοφίας λόγοις (ℵ* λόγος) B D 0150 33 1175 1506 1739 1852 1881 1912 itʳ vgʷʷ, ˢᵗ (arm) geo¹ Origenᵍʳ ⁴/⁷, ˡᵃᵗ ²/³ Eusebius Didymus¹/³ Chrysostom¹/² Severian; Ambrose¹/⁷ Jerome⁴/⁵ Pelagius Varimadum // πειθοῖς σοφίας 𝔓⁴⁶ F G Chrysostomᵐˢˢ (itᵇ, ᶠ, ᵍ πειθοῖ) // πειθοῖς ἀνθρωπίνης σοφίας λόγοις ℵ² A C Ψ 6 81 104 256 263 365 424 436 459 1241 1319 1573 (1962 σοφίας ἀνθρωπίνης) 2127 (2200 *omit* λόγοις) 2464 *Byz* [L P] *l* 592 itᵒ vgᶜˡ geo² slav Origenᵍʳ ¹/⁷, ˡᵃᵗ ¹/³ Ps-Athanasius Cyril-Jerusalem Apollinaris Didymus²/³ Chrysostom¹/² Cyril²/³; Ambrose²/⁷ // πειθοῖ ἀνθρωπίνης σοφίας λόγοις 205 209 (2495 σοφίας ἀνθρωπίνης) Cyril¹/³ // πειθοῖ σοφίας λόγων (itᵈ) syrᵖ Origenᵍʳ ¹/⁷, (¹/⁷) (Epiphanius); Ambrose¹/⁷, (³/⁷) Jerome¹/⁵
UBS⁴ Quotations and Allusions Apparatus **2.1** 1 Cor 1.17 **2** Ga 6.14 **3** Ac 18.9; 2 Cor 10.1 **4** 1 Th 1.5 **UBS⁴ Punctuation Apparatus** ᵃ **2.5** NO P: M // SP: WH // P: TR AD NA RSV Seg NJB REB	

The text of the SBLGNT differs; it treats variants #1–3, but for variant #1 reads μαρτύριον "testimony" contrary to the NA²⁷ μυστήριον "mystery"; for variant #2 it maintains the NA²⁷ reading; but for variant #3 it has the reading ἐν ⸂πειθοῖ σοφίας⸃ "with persuasion of wisdom," a conjectured reading with no manuscript support!

In his commentary Ben Witherington III does not discuss any textual variants. However, in his commentary Gordon Fee for variant #1 agrees with "testimony" (against UBS, NA, and Metzger's *Textual Commentary*) and for variant #3 decides on a reading that has no textual evidence:

"the persuasion of wisdom" (a conjecture). So, commentaries are written with different purposes and will differ in how much assistance they will provide when making text-critical decisions.

<u>Consulting Textual Commentaries and Other Commentaries</u>: Students of the NT should know that there are resources solely dedicated to comment on the more significant textual variants. These works are called textual commentaries. Their value is in providing expert analysis and often a decision about which variant reading is preferred in the most important instances. Such textual commentaries will complement discussions that you may find in commentaries. Below I provide a list of textual and other commentaries from most accessible to more technical and/or brief.

1. **Omanson**, Roger L., and Bruce M. **Metzger**. *A Textual Guide to the Greek New Testament: An Adaptation of Bruce M. Metzger's Textual Commentary for the Needs of Translators.* Stuttgart: Deutsche Bibelgesellschaft, 2006. This work is based upon Metzger's and is intended to simplify his discussion for Bible translators who have not had formal training in textual criticism. The value of Omanson's work is that it explains Metzger's analysis and contains discussions on "segmentation" (i.e., section breaks) of the Greek text (e.g., at 1 Tim 3:1, 15). However, Omanson's work does not render Metzger's obsolete, since Metzger's work lists many individual witnesses within his comments and also discusses more variants than are found in Omanson.

2. **Comfort**, Philip Wesley. *New Testament Text and Translation Commentary: Commentary on the Variant Readings of the Ancient New Testament Manuscripts and How They Relate to the Major English Translations.* Carol Stream, IL: Tyndale House, 2008. Comfort's work is very readable because he displays completely the main textual variants according to modern critical editions and then shows the most important supporting ancient witnesses.

3. **Metzger**, Bruce M., United Bible Societies. *A Textual Commentary on the Greek New Testament, Second Edition a Companion Volume to the United Bible Societies' Greek New Testament (4th Rev. Ed.).* New York: United Bible Societies, 1994. Since Metzger was one of the five textual critics on the committee for the GNT base of the UBS and NA$^{26/27}$ editions, it is helpful to have his summary analysis of the committee's decisions. Additionally, when he had (strong) disagreement with the committee's decision, Metzger places his assessment (and another on the committee that also agreed) in bracket's following his presentation of the evidence (see, e.g., Jude 5).

4. **Academic Commentaries**: Discussions of textual variants will be found in academic commentaries. The level of accessibility and quality of discussion will vary, however. For instance, the Baylor Handbook series will provide brief discussions of the more important variants. As time allows, you may find benefit to consult commentaries in addition to these dedicated textual commentaries. For example, the chart on the following page compares entries for a textual variant in 2 Cor 3:9 that each work above provides; included also are entries from the commentaries of Murray J. Harris[24] and Fredrick J. Long.[25]

---

[24] *The Second Epistle to the Corinthians,* NIGTC (Grand Rapids: Eerdmans, 2005), 281.

[25] *2 Corinthians: A Handbook on the Greek Text,* BHGNT (Waco, TX: Baylor UP, 2015), 67.

COMPARISON OF TEXTUAL VARIANT ENTRIES FOR 2 COR 3:9
IN TEXTUAL AND OTHER COMMENTARIES

\multicolumn{2}{l}{At issue is whether the noun "ministry" (διακονία) is in the dative or nominative case. The critical editions have that dative form that may be translated as location "in" (NET):}
	⁹ᵃ εἰ γὰρ τῇ διακονίᾳ τῆς κατακρίσεως δόξα, "For if there was glory in the ministry that produced condemnation,..." (NET).
Omanson & Metzger	3:9 τῇ διακονίᾳ {B} A majority of the Committee, impressed by the weight of the external evidence supporting τῇ διακονίᾳ, was inclined to regard the nominative as due to scribal assimilation to the preceding (and following) διακονία.
Comfort NU = the NA and UBS critical editions) TR = Textus Receptus Maj= Majority Text	The NU has the wording ει γαρ τη διακονια της κατακρισεως δοξα ("for if there was glory in the ministry of condemnation"). This has excellent testimony: 𝔓⁴⁶ ℵ A C D* F G 33 1739. TR WH, with the support of B D² Maj, read η διακονια via instead of τη διακονια, yielding the rendering: "for if the ministry of condemnation was glory." TR followed Maj, and WH followed B. The difference between the first reading and the second in the Greek is that the first is a dative, and the second a nominative. The variant is probably the result of scribal assimilation to the preceding and the following nominative η διακονια. The resultant reading is slightly bolder in that it equates the ministry of condemnation with glory, whereas the NU reading indicates that there was an element of glory in the ministry of condemnation.
Metzger	3:9 τῇ διακονίᾳ (in the ministry) {B} The external evidence strongly supports the reading in the text. The words τῇ διακονίᾳ were changed to the nominative case ἡ διακονία in a number of witnesses under the influence of the noun ἡ διακονία in v. 8 and again near the end of v. 9. The reading in the text, translated literally, is "For if [there was] glory in the ministry of condemnation." The variant reading, translated literally, is "For if the ministry of condemnation [was] glorious." As several commentators have remarked, the meaning is nearly the same, the variant perhaps giving a more positive view of Moses' ministry.
Harris	The external evidence supporting the dative τῇ διακονίᾳ (preferred by NA²⁶, ²⁷ and UBS³, ⁴) is early and varied (𝔓⁴⁶ ℵ A C D* F G Ψ 0243 33 104 326 630 1175 1739 *pc*[b] syr sa Ambrosiaster Pelagius) and stronger than the support for ἡ διακονία (B D² 1881 M a f vg bo), the reading preferred by NA²⁵ and UBS¹, ² (with a "C" rating) or διακονία (81 629* 1505 2464 *pc*). Moreover, it is arguable that the dative is the more difficult reading, since it breaks the sequence of nominatives (ἡ διακονία) in vv. 7–9, and the dative of possession or the locative dative (however the dative here be construed) is uncommon in the NT. If τῇ διακονίᾳ be taken as original, the nominative may be explained as an assimilation to the preceding and following διακονία (Metzger 509). Whether the dative or the nominative be preferred, the sense is basically the same: "if the ministry/dispensation that brought condemnation was glorious...."
Long	A sizable textual tradition has a nominative ἡ διακονία here (B D² M *pm*); however, the dative form is very well attested (𝔓⁴⁶ ℵ A C D* F G Ψ 33 *al*). The UBS⁴ upgraded its confidence rating from C to B.

STEP 2: SECONDARY STUDY 95

EXERCISE 2–B: Given the description of the textual variant in the chart on the previous page, consider these questions:

1. What is the interpretive payoff of understanding the textual variant, if any?
2. Would you mention and/or discuss the variant while preaching or while teaching a Sunday school class?
3. If not, is there another setting where this would have value to mention or discuss?

Decisions: As a pastor or teacher, you must decide whether we should preach from verses that were very likely not a part of the original documents or what translation to use. In the above example for 1 Cor 2:1, the variety of translations makes it likely that a good number of parishioners will have a Bible that reads "mystery" and others with "testimony." Should this be mentioned from the pulpit? How about in an adult Sunday school classroom?

Significant examples of textual variants involving large sections of texts (often included in our Bibles) include the following: Mark 16:9–20; John 7:53–8:11; Matt 23:14; 1 John 5:8. There are others. For myself, I will not preach from Mark 16:9–20, since I believe that it was not an original part of Mark's gospel; this portion is missing from the earliest manuscripts with no good reason why it would have been omitted. Moreover, these extra verses contain material that has been very divisive for the church (tongue speaking, snake handling). The story of the woman caught in adultery in John 7:53–8:11 is more difficult for me, since it seems as though this was a story about Jesus in circulation looking for a home; some manuscripts place it in Luke or at the end of John. My conviction is that it is a true account of Jesus's ministry, but was not an original part of John's gospel. So, I must decide whether to preach from this, and certainly if I do, I need to explain why. People in the pews will have their Bibles open and may read the footnote in the English Bible that says something like, "The earliest manuscripts do not have John 7:53–8:11" and perhaps will wonder what that means. What will you say about this from the pulpit? In a teaching setting, more probably something could and should be said.

So, the point is that pastors and teachers need to do some homework: As they are able, they should educate Christians about the careful transmission of the texts that are the basis of Bible translations. Christians do not claim that "no corruption" of the manuscripts has occurred, as Muslims may claim of the Koran; in fact, the Koran is only the Koran in its original Arabic and there have been many editions.[26] Not so with Christian Scripture; at its core the Bible is incarnational, being copied and translated into all languages as the Word of God (Go, Bible translators, go!), and thus accessible to all to hear the Gospel of Jesus who suffered, died, and is raised, the one Lord.

Variants are our Earliest Commentaries: Finally, students should understand that *textual variants may often function like our "earliest commentaries."* Why? Because they alert us to difficult passages where scribes simplified grammar, clarified theological points, attempted to harmonize parallel accounts, or supplied additional interpretive information. So, variants are valuable.

---

[26] In 2007 a text-critical edition of the Koran (Corpus Coranicum) was initiated. See http://www.dh2012.uni-hamburg.de/conference/programme/abstracts/corpus-coranicum-a-digital-landscape-for-the-study-of-the-quran/

SECONDARY INTERPRETIVE PROCEDURES:

The following procedures incorporate 1.–3. from the PRIMARY INTERPRETIVE PROCEDURES.

1. **Compare and record important differences from at least three major English versions (e.g., NIV11, NASB, NRSV, RSV, and NET). Specifically, identify and record where the translations differ regarding key words that may need further study in STEP 5: LEXICAL RESEARCH. Ask Questions.**
2. **Search within Bible notes and record any significant information that pertain to translation and meaning. Ask Questions.**
3. **Search within Bible notes that may alert you to possible text-critical variants in the Greek manuscript tradition. If present, list these by verse reference and consider whether they impact the meaning of the pericope.**

Note: Steps 4.–6. may be grouped together in your report for the sake of conciseness.

4. **Check for significant textual variants in the UBS$^{3/4/5}$ and record them.[27] If there are none listed in the UBS$^{4/5}$ and if time allows, then check the NA$^{27/28}$ and record them.**
5. **If variants are present, consult textual commentaries for any analysis of the variant(s).**
6. **Consult and summarize discussions of the textual variants (if any) from two or three more-academic commentaries.**
7. **Decide: Conclude your textual critical work by deciding whether you might agree with one major variant over another and whether any textual variants are significant enough to mention in a preaching setting or a teaching setting. Be clear and concise.**
8. **Summarize your most important findings noting the most vital interpretive questions (if any) that you want to bring forward to STEP 9: INTERPRETIVE DECISIONS.**

III. TERTIARY RESEARCH

<u>Orientation</u>: Advanced students should expect not simply to access the critical judgments of experts of textual criticism, but also to perform their own assessments of the manuscript tradition and transmission history as evidenced in all available witnesses (including the church fathers) for the purpose establishing the earliest text as possible. In some cases advanced students may uncover further evidence in favor of one reading as opposed to another or may even discover wrongly identified or assessed witnesses.[28] Furthermore, the digitization of ancient manuscripts with high quality images has reinvigorated interest in the field. Additionally, private donors have funded

---

[27] Remember that the most significant variants are generally those scored {C} in the UBS$^{4/5}$ which were scored {D} in the UBS^3 edition.

[28] Although such a claim may seem overreaching, in fact, have taught advanced students in textual criticism classes, this has been true on numerous occasions. Databases have been shown to be wrong; witnesses have been wrongly listed in support of a variant, etc.

searches for more ancient manuscripts: currently, there have been recently announced eight or so new papyri fragments that have yet to be published, dated, and integrated into scholarly research and discussion.

EXERCISE 2–C: Given this recto of Papyrus 52 at right, find the location in John's gospel and reconstruct the text around the fragment by estimating column width and character spacing.

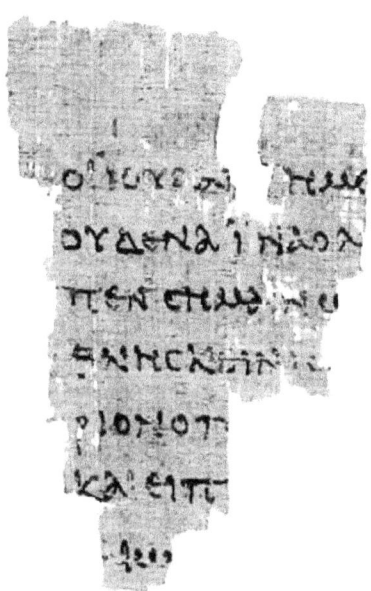

    The Goal(s) of Textual Criticism: Traditionally, the goal of textual criticism has been recovering the original text of the original manuscripts (called autographs) as authored by the initial authors. However, this goal has been adjudged as too optimistic and has increasingly been questioned on several grounds: unavailability of early texts from the first two centuries, uncertainty of the amount of variation in texts at this time, and questions about the "singular" publication of books like Acts, which may have been published in two forms—the short form as seen in the Alexandrian tradition and the longer edition as seen in the Western edition. Instead, textual critics like David C. Parker will advocate primarily for understanding the transmission of the "tradents" of the NT text and not necessarily the recovery of the original text, which in his view is too often a doubtful enterprise.

    Example of Rom 12:1–2: On the next page is Rom 12:1–2 from the Nestle-Aland (NA^{27}) critical edition; the textual variations are underlined. (Note that the $UBS^{3/4}$ text for Rom 12:1–8 contains no listing of variants!) Notice that the NA^{27} uses special *sigla* ($^s...^{\backprime}$, $^{\ulcorner}$, and $^{\top}$and many others) to demarcate where there are notable textual variants (also, the NA^{27} and UBS texts have been selective in which textual variants to include). The NA^{27} provides what the text-critical scholars have best decided was likely the original text. Let me discuss the variants in 12:1–2 verse by verse. Romans 12:1 involves only the transposition of two words ("pleasing" and "to God") without any change of meaning; the textual variant may stress "to God" since it is placed in a forward position. The listed witnesses supporting each variant indicate that there is strong evidence for each reading; in fact, the cross (†) for the textual variant alerts us that the earlier 25th edition chose it as the best reading, but was overturned in the newer editions. In 12:2a and 12:2b there are similar variants that involve the mood of the verb forms. The NA^{27} text reads imperative forms whereas the textual variants have infinitives, which could be understood as imperatival in use, but more likely are meant to create a list of infinitives beginning at 12:1 that would be translated like this: "I exhort you to present your bodies ... and not to be conformed ... but to be transformed.... (In a forthcoming book I provide a discussion of the logic of these sentiments in the SAMPLE STEP 3: GRAMMATICAL STUDY REPORT ON ROMANS 12:1–8.) The last variant in 12:2c involves the addition of "your." There are no listed variants for 12:2d.

Textual Variants of Rom 12:1–2 in the NA²⁷

NA²⁷	Greek Variant Texts (underlined)	Listed Witnesses
NA text	12:1 Παρακαλῶ οὖν ὑμᾶς, ἀδελφοί, διὰ τῶν οἰκτιρμῶν τοῦ θεοῦ παραστῆσαι τὰ σώματα ὑμῶν θυσίαν ζῶσαν ἁγίαν ⌐εὐάρεστον τῷ θεῷ⌐, τὴν λογικὴν λατρείαν ὑμῶν·	txt (𝔓⁴⁶) ℵ² B D F G Ψ 33. 1739. (1881) 𝔐; Tert
Textual Variant	12:1 Παρακαλῶ οὖν ὑμᾶς, ἀδελφοί, διὰ τῶν οἰκτιρμῶν τοῦ θεοῦ παραστῆσαι τὰ σώματα ὑμῶν θυσίαν ζῶσαν ἁγίαν ⌐τῷ θεῷ εὐάρεστον⌐, τὴν λογικὴν λατρείαν ὑμῶν·	† ℵ* A P 81. 1506 pc lat; Spec
NA text	12:2a καὶ μὴ ⌐συσχηματίζεσθε τῷ αἰῶνι τούτῳ,	txt 𝔓⁴⁶ ℵ B* L P 104. 365. 1241. 1739 pm; Cl
Textual Variant	12:2a καὶ μὴ ⌐συσχηματίζεσθαι τῷ αἰῶνι τούτῳ,	A B² D* F G Ψ 33. 81. 630. 1175. 1505. 1506 pm
NA text	12:2b ἀλλὰ ⌐μεταμορφοῦσθε	txt 𝔓⁴⁶ B* L P 104. 365. 1241. 1739 pm; Cl
Textual Variant	12:2b ἀλλὰ ⌐μεταμορφεῖσθαι	ℵ A B² D* D² F G Ψ 6. 81. 630. 1175. 1505. 1506. 1881 pm
NA text	12:2c τῇ ἀνακαινώσει τοῦ νοός ᵀ	txt 𝔓⁴⁶ A B D* F G 6. 630. 1739. 1881 pc; Cl Cyp
Textual Variant	12:2c τῇ ἀνακαινώσει τοῦ νοός ᵀ ὑμῶν	ℵ D¹ Ψ 33 𝔐 latt sy
NA text (no variants)	12:2d εἰς τὸ δοκιμάζειν ὑμᾶς τί τὸ θέλημα τοῦ θεοῦ, τὸ ἀγαθὸν καὶ εὐάρεστον καὶ τέλειον.	(none listed)

Important *Sigla* of GNT Critical Editions (not comprehensive)

NA	SBL GNT	UBS
° omitted word ⸀ ... ⸁ omitted words ⌐ replaced word ⸀ ... ⸂ replaced words ᵀ inserted word(s) ⸉ ... ⸊ transposed words † the reading of the NA²⁵ edition	⌐ or ⌐ or ⌐¹ a note pertains to a word ⸀ ...⸁ note pertains to replaced words [...] the enclosed text is doubtful	Footnote numbers indicate textual variants. Footnote letters indicate punctuation variation in the major translations.

STEP 2: TERTIARY RESEARCH

Manuscripts Identified by Text-Type Location: Working with an understanding that manuscripts were "located" in major centers of Christianity, scholars have classified manuscripts, church fathers, and ancient translations into geographic families: Alexandrian, Western (Rome), and Byzantine (Constantinople). Additionally, some will argue for a Caesarean family (e.g., J. Harold Greenlee). See also NA^{27} pages 58–63 in the introduction for a description and evaluation of the best manuscripts.

MANUSCRIPTS IDENTIFIED BY TEXT-TYPE LOCATION[29]

i. Alexandrian Witnesses

(1) Primary Alexandrian (or Proto-Alexandrian):
𝔓^{45} (in Acts) 𝔓^{46} 𝔓^{66} 𝔓^{75} B, Sahidic (in part), Clement of Alexandria, Origen (in part), and most of the papyrus fragments with Pauline text.

(2) Secondary Alexandrian (Later Alexandrian):
Gospels: (C) L T W (in Luke 1.1 to 8.12 and John) (X) Z Δ (in Mark) Ξ Ψ (in Mark; partially in Luke and John) 33 579 892 1241 Bohairic
Acts: 𝔓^{50} A (C) Ψ 33 (11.26–28.31) 81 104 326
Pauline Epistles: A (C) H I Ψ 33 81 104 326 1739
Catholic Epistles: 𝔓^{20} 𝔓^{23} P A (C) Ψ 33 81 104 326 1739
Revelation: A (C) 1006 1611 1854 2053 2344; less good, 𝔓^{47}, ℵ

ii. Western Witnesses

Gospels: 𝔓^{69} ℵ (in John 1.1–8.38) D W (in Mark 1.1–5.30) 0171, the Old Latin, (syr^s and syr^c in part), early Latin Fathers.
Acts: 𝔓^{29} 𝔓^{38} 𝔓^{48} D E 383 614 1739 syr^{hmg} syr$^{pal\ ms}$ cop^{G67} early Latin Fathers, Ephraem
Epistles: the Greek-Latin bilinguals D F G, Greek Fathers to the end of the third-century, Old Latin mss and early Latin Fathers, Syrian Fathers to about AD 450
Revelation: It will be observed that for the book of Revelation no specifically Western witnesses have been identified.

iii. Byzantine Witnesses

Gospels: A E F G H K P S V W (in Matthew and Luke 8.13–24.53) Π Ψ (partially in Luke and John) Ω and most minuscules
Acts: H L P 049 and most minuscules
Epistles: L 049 and most minuscules
Revelation: 046 051 052 and most minuscules

iv. Caesarean Witnesses (listed in the 1st edition of Metzger's *Textual Commentary*)

Pre-Caesarean: 𝔓^{45} W (in Mark 5:31—16:20) $f^1 f^{13}$ 28
Caesarean Proper: Θ 565 700 arm geo Origen (in part) Eusebius Cyril-Jerusalem

---

[29] The following list is from Metzger, *Textual Commentary*, xxix-xxx.

General Principles of Textual Criticism to Remember: (EC=External Criteria; IC=Internal)

1. The reading that has the best manuscript support (early, quality, distribution, family relationship) is to be preferred (EC); *weigh* manuscript support; do not *count* it.
2. The shorter reading is often to be preferred (IC) because the tendency is to *add* not *subtract*.
3. The more difficult reading (grammatically and theologically) is to be preferred (IC).
4. The reading that best explains the origins of the other readings is to be preferred (IC).

Helpful Charts and Information in Kurt & Barbara Aland's *The Text of the New Testament* (2nd ed.): I have found this information helpful:

1. Variant Free Verses in GNT according to the seven critical editions: 62.9% variant free (p. 29)
2. Summary of the Textual Transmission History (a la Aland) (pp. 67–71)
3. Distribution of Greek Manuscripts by Century (p. 81)
4. Descriptive List of Papyri (pp. 96–102)
5. Descriptive List of Uncials (pp. 107–28)
6. Description of Correctors (p. 108)
7. Descriptive List of Minuscules (pp. 129–38)
8. A Review of Text Manuscripts (Papyri, Uncials, Minuscules) by Category (I, II, III, IV, V) Date (century), Content, and Length (ten folios plus are in bold): (pp. 159–62)
9. Twelve Principles of Textual Criticism Summarized (pp. 280–81)
10. Charts 5–6 Textual Contents of Papyri and Uncials (within the "end matter")

The *Editio Critica Maior* (ECM) and the Coherence-Based Genealogical Method: For TERTIARY RESEARCH we need to understand the scope, methodological approach, and resources available with ECM initiative at the University of Münster:

> Each volume of the ECM includes "Text", "Supplementary Material", and "Studies". In addition, a digital platform is in the development process that will give online access to all data that is collected in the process of producing the ECM. The data will primarily consist of diplomatic transcripts of all manuscripts cited in the apparatus and the databases from which the edition is produced. Moreover, the transcripts will be successively linked to photos made available in the Virtual Manuscript Room. A further program within the digital platform will allow individual users to access the data and apply the Coherence-Based Genealogical Method on his/her own. The first ECM volume contains the Catholic Letters. By now, the parts "Text" and "Supplementary Material" are available.[30]

The Coherence-Based Genealogical Method is an emerging model generator of probable textual witness relationships (suggesting transmission history) based on tracking variants in ancient witnesses. By entering the texts of ancient manuscripts into a single database, the method will pro-

---

[30] http://www.uni-muenster.de/INTF/ECM.html accessed October 23, 2015.

duce a branching tree diagram depicting relations of witnesses based on the presence or absence of variants, not the dating of the manuscript. Importantly, "The Coherence-Based Genealogical Method makes no textual decisions. It merely reveals an image of the tradition which emerges from a text-critical philological study of all the variants."[31]

Computer Software Databases and CNTTS: Increasingly, Bible Software will provide access to textual critical resources such as, e.g., the database created by the Center for NT Textual Studies that is available in Accordance, BibleWorks, and Logos. This CNTTS database catalogues textual variants by (likely) type of error; but interpretive judgments have been made concerning how to categorize these textual variants. You will find a wealth of information, yet mistakes have been found in the database and there is a learning curve to using it. Still, this is a very helpful resource. Many other features may be found, but they should be used with caution, double-checking critical information with actual manuscripts or high quality (color) images of them.

TERTIARY INTERPRETIVE PROCEDURES:

Below are procedures for determining this fundamental exegetical question, "How is the text established?"[32] Judgments are required as you consider the following questions:

1. **Are there variants in the passage? List them.**
2. **What is the number of witnesses for the different variants?**
3. **What is the age of the witnesses for the different variants?**
4. **What is the geographic distribution for each variant?**
5. **What is the validity of the witnesses? Notice the type of text to which the witnesses belong.**
6. **What is the shorter reading (= *lectio brevior*)? This is not always the preferred reading.**
7. **Are unconscious causes of error possible reasons for variants (especially mechanical errors arising from the *scriptio continua*)?**
    a. exchange of letters for reasons of form or sound
    b. haplography (i.e., the omission of letters)
    c. doubling of letters
    d. homoeoteleuton (i.e., the same or similar ending), e.g., where two or more words in a row with same ending result in an omission of a word by accidental skipping to the next word
    e. dittography, e.g., the doubling of words or restarting at same place twice
    f. wrong dissolution of an abbreviation
    g. wrong understanding of an earlier correction
    h. wrong understanding of a marginal note
    i. wrong demarcation of sentence or clause

---

[31] *Ibid*.

[32] From Dieter Georgi, "Scheme of Questions for an Exegesis of NT Texts" from unpublished notes for graduate students (1970), slightly revised and edited by Julian Hills, September, 1988, and myself subsequently.

8. **Are <u>conscious alterations</u> the causes of certain variants?**
   a. alterations influenced by OT parallels
   b. alterations influenced by NT parallels esp. in the Synoptic Gospels and Disputed-Paulines
   c. corrections of language, e.g., grammar, style, or textual-critical corrections
   d. theological "corrections"
9. Which is the more <u>difficult reading</u> (= *lectio difficilior*)? (cf. also 6. and 8.; what is said under 6. sometimes contradicts the rule of the greater age of the *lectio difficilior*).
10. Which reading is to be taken as the best, <u>as the reason/source for all the others</u>? (Question 10. supports question 11.)
11. Which reading is demanded by language/style of the author and the literary context? (Note that 11. is in tension with questions 8. and 9.)
12. Which reading fits best with the social-communal location of the author and audience based upon what can be known of them?
13. What can the variants tell us about the difficulties of the text?
14. What can the variants tell us about the history of interpretation?

IV. BIBLIOGRAPHY

Primary Survey

<u>English Bibles that may provide some very limited knowledge of Greek or Ancient Witnesses</u>
    NET Bible
    NASB
    NIV, and many others.

<u>Textual Criticism</u>
    Stewart, Robert B., ed. *The Reliability of the New Testament: Bart Ehrman and Daniel Wallace in Dialogue*. Minneapolis: Fortress, 2011.
    Wegner, Paul D. *A Student's Guide to Textual Criticism of the Bible: Its History, Methods & Results*. Downers Grove, IL: InterVarsity, 2006.

Secondary Study

<u>Critical Editions of and Commentary on the GNT</u>
    The Greek New Testament. B. Aland, *et al.* eds. 4th ed. New York: United Bible Societies, 1994.
    The Greek New Testament. B. Aland, *et al.*, editors. 5th ed. German Bible Society, 2014.
    Holmes, Michael W. *The Greek New Testament: SBL Edition*. Society of Biblical Literature, 2010.
    Metzger, Bruce M. *A Textual Commentary on the Greek New Testament, Second Edition a Companion Volume to the United Bible Societies' Greek New Testament*. 4th Rev. ed. London: United Bible Societies, 2005.

Omanson, Roger L., and Bruce M. Metzger. *A Textual Guide to the Greek New Testament: An Adaptation of Bruce M. Metzger's Textual Commentary for the Needs of Translators*. Stuttgart: Deutsche Bibelgesellschaft, 2006.

History, Theory, and Practice of Textual Criticism

Black, David Alan. *New Testament Textual Criticism: A Concise Guide*. Grand Rapids: Baker, 1994.

Bauer, David R. *An Annotated Guide to Biblical Resources for Ministry*. Annotated Guides 16. Peabody, MA: Hendrickson, 2003, pp. 202–204 for a guide to NT textual criticism.

Comfort, Philip Wesley. *Encountering the Manuscripts: An Introduction to New Testament Paleography & Textual Criticism*. Nashville: Broadman & Holman, 2005.

Greenlee, J. Harold. *Introduction to New Testament Textual Criticism*. Rev. ed. Peabody, MA: Hendrickson, 1995.

Hull, Jr., Robert F. *The Story of the New Testament Text: Movers, Materials, Motives, Methods, and Models*. Resources for Biblical Study 58. Leiden: Brill, 2010.

Porter, Stanley E., and Andrew W. Pitts. *A Handbook for the Textual Criticism of the New Testament*. Eerdmans NT Greek Series. Grand Rapids: Eerdmans, 2015.

Wachtel, Klaus and Michael W. Holmes, eds., *The Textual History of the Greek New Testament: Changing Views in Contemporary Research*. Society of Biblical Literature Text-critical Studies 8. Atlanta: SBL Press, 2011.

Tertiary Research

Critical Editions and Commentary on the GNT

CNTTS NT Critical Apparatus available in Accordance Bible Software (see http://www.accordancebible.com/buzz/articles/cntts.php) and BibleWorks.

Comfort, Philip Wesley and David P. Barrett, *The Text of the Earliest New Testament Greek Manuscripts*. Rev. ed. Wheaton, IL: Tyndale House, 2001. [Available in Logos Bible Software and BibleWorks.]

Comfort, Philip Wesley. *New Testament Text and Translation Commentary: Commentary on the Variant Readings of the Ancient New Testament Manuscripts and How They Relate to the Major English Translations*. Carol Stream, IL: Tyndale House, 2008. [Available in Accordance Bible Software.]

Nestle, E. and K. Aland *et al.*, eds. *Novum Testamentum Graece*. 27th ed. Stuttgart: Deutsche Bibelgesellschaft, 1995. [The text is identical to the UBS^4, but with a textual apparatus indicating more variants, but often providing less witnesses in support in comparison.]

Aland, Barbara *et al.*, eds. *Novum Testamentum Graece*. 28th rev. ed. Stuttgart: Deutsche Bibelgesellschaft, 2012.

Pierpont, William G., and Maurice A. Robinson. *The New Testament in the Original Greek: According to the Byzantine/Majority Textform*. Roswell, GA: The Original Word Publishers, 1995.

Tischendorf, Constantin. ed. *Novum Testamentum Graece, ad antiquissimos testes denuo recensuit apparatum criticum omni studio perfectum apposuit commentationem isagogicam praetexuit Constantinus Tischendorf, editio octava critica maior.* 2 vols. 8th ed. Leipzig: Gieseke and Devrient, 1869–94. [Out of print, but available in BibleWorks and other Bible Software; has idiosyncratic system different from the UBS and NA editions, but still useful because of its detailed textual apparatus.]

Tregelles, Samuel Prideaux. *The Greek New Testament, Edited from Ancient Authorities, with their Various Readings in Full, and the Latin Version of Jerome.* London: Bagster; Stewart, 1857–1879.

Westcott, B. F. and F. J. A. Hort, *The New Testament in the Original Greek*, vol. 1: *Text*; vol. 2: *Introduction* [and] *Appendix*. Cambridge: Macmillan, 1881, 1886. [Westcott and Hort were eighteenth-century English scholars who pioneered modern developments of textual criticism; their text is heavily dependent on Codex Vaticanus (B). Available here http://archive.org/details/newtestamentinth027928mbp.]

History, Theory, and Practice of Textual Criticism

Aland, Kurt, and Barbara Aland. *The Text of the New Testament: An Introduction to the Critical Editions and to the Theory and Practice of Modern Textual Criticism.* Translated by Erroll F. Rhodes. 2nd Rev. Grand Rapids: Eerdmans, 1989.

Metzger, Bruce M. and Bart D. Ehrman. *The Text of the New Testament: Its Transmission, Corruption, and Restoration.* 4th ed. New York: Oxford University Press, 2005.

Parker, David C. *An Introduction to the New Testament Manuscripts and Their Texts.* Cambridge: Cambridge University Press, 2008.

There are a number of Helpful Websites for Textual Criticism

The *Liste* website, with updates cataloging the NT Manuscripts: www.unimuenster.de/NTTextforschung/ or in English at http://egora.uni-muenster.de/intf/index_en.shtml

International Greek New Testament Project: http://www.igntp.org/

Center for NT Textual Studies (CNTTS): Database: http://www.nobts.edu/cntts/ and described here: http://www.youtube.com/watch?v=id9a3c1uVJc

Online Encyclopedia of NT Textual Criticism conceived by Rich Elliott at http://www.skypoint.com/members/waltzmn/

A "Catalogue of New Testament Papyri & Codices 2nd–10th Centuries" by K. C. Hanson is located here http://www.kchanson.com/papyri.html

The "Leuven Database of Ancient Books" at http://www.trismegistos.org/ldab.

STEP 3
GRAMMATICAL STUDY

"The skill of writing is to create a context in which other people can think."
— Edwin Schlossberg

Introduction: NT authors were inspired and skilled writers. Language and grammar are finite and fixed, yet infinite in possibility. Studying grammar is foundational for understanding what is "meant." Grammatical study of the NT is best done in the original Greek language. Obviously, without knowing Greek such study cannot take place and will be limited to English grammar, which nevertheless pays great dividends. This STEP is sizeable because it is foundational to interpretation. The PRIMARY SURVEY gives an overview of English grammar in some detail. The purpose of such detail is to help facilitate attentive and accurate observation and analysis of the text. Often such observation will not only aide your understanding, but will also lead to important questions that need to be answered later. The PRIMARY SURVEY concludes with describing a method of "constituent marking" that facilitates efficient observation of any given pericope. In SECONDARY STUDY constituent marking is applied to the Greek text. Here Greek students will be shown how to investigate many aspects of Greek grammar. In TERTIARY RESEARCH I will introduce linguistic concepts of information structure, word order, the use of the article, and emphatic and pragmatic constructions. The interpretive principles GRAMMA (GRAMmatical Mode of Analysis) and GRAMPS (GRAMmatical Procedure of Study) are at the core of this work.

I. Primary Survey

<u>Grammar, Words, and Relevance</u>:[1] Communication is efficient while also aiming at optimal effect. Communicators consciously and unconsciously use word-meanings, grammar, and rhetorical "systems" to impact their audiences. Language use is creative (novel) and conventional (established). The communication guides audiences through explicit use of language ("explicatures") to arrive at proper implications (or "implicatures") for understanding. At the same time, speakers and audiences share a "context" or cognitive environment, and so not every word will need careful explanation. For an "outsider" listening in on the conversation—whether to text messages or phone conversations today or to written documents 2,000 years old—considerable "gaps" will exist, and we are left re-imagining the meaning and may even completely miss the meaning because we do not share the language conventions nor the full conversational context.

<u>**Exercise 3–A**</u>: Below are two unrelated text-messages.[2] Consider the questions that follow.

1. Evening v good if somewhat event laden. Will fill you in, don't you worry... Head ok but throat wrecked. See you at six then!

2. Thankyou for ditchin me i had been invited out but said no coz u were cumin and u said we would do something on the sat now i have nothing to do all weekend i am a billy no mates i really hate being single

   a. What efficiencies of communication are observed in each text message?
   b. What gaps of contextual knowledge exist? How could we fill the gaps to reconstruct events?
   c. What are the most important questions to ask and answer for a more complete understanding of what is being communicated?

<u>Routine and Non-Routine Words</u>: When reading and studying any piece of text, you must consider how an author intended a particular word or words to be understood. Are the words "routine" words or "non-routine" ones? Non-Routine words are more unusual, may be more difficult to understand, and may bear special significance for understanding the passage. In general, our attention is drawn to the new and the unusual. However, even routine words may be used in quite significant ways, if repeated, qualified, or used in special ways. For example, Luke Timothy Johnson has observed how the rather routine terms "Lord" and "teacher" are strategically used to convey important truths about Jesus's identity as affirmed by others in the Gospels of Mark and Matthew:

---

[1] This summary draws generally from the field of linguistics called pragmatics and specifically Relevance Theory. See, e.g., Dan Sperber and Deirdre Wilson, *Relevance: Communication and Cognition*, 2nd ed. (Oxford; Cambridge, MA: Blackwell, 2001) and Gene L. Green, "Relevance Theory and Biblical Interpretation," in *The Linguist as Pedagogue: Trends in the Teaching and Linguistic Analysis of the Greek New Testament*, ed. Stanley E. Porter and Matthew Brook O'Donnell, New Testament Monographs 11 (Sheffield: Sheffield Phoenix, 2009), 217–40.

[2] These two examples are from Caroline Tagg, *Discourse of Text Messaging: Analysis of SMS Communication* (New York: Continuum, 2012), 76–77.

> We have seen ... that in Mark's Gospel everybody calls Jesus Teacher, whether opponents (Mark 12:14, 19, 32), those who encounter him but fail to follow (10:17–31), those who encounter him and believe (9:17), or the disciples (4:38; 9:38; 10:35; 13:1). On the other hand, Mark never has disciples or opponents call Jesus Lord; only the afflicted give him that title. Matthew's discrimination is finer. Who calls Jesus Teacher? Always outsiders, whether opponents such as the scribes (8:19; 12:38), Pharisees (12:38; 22:16, 36), Jewish tax collectors (17:24), Herodians (22:16), Sadducees (22:24), or those who encounter Jesus but do not follow, like the rich young man (19:16). Jesus is never called Teacher by the disciples, the afflicted, or those coming to faith in him. The disciples (8:25; 14:28; 16:22; 17:4; 18:21) and those coming to faith in Jesus (8:2, 6, 8; 9:28; 15:22, 25, 27; 17:15; 20:30) always call him Lord (but see 26:18).
>
> ...The only apparent exception to this rule confirms it. The term "Lord" is never found on the lips of the betrayer, Judas. When Jesus predicts his betrayal at the last supper, the other disciples ask, "Is it I, Lord?" (26:22). Judas asks, "Is it I, Rabbi?" (26:25). And when he greets Jesus in the garden to arrest him, it is with these words, "Hail, Rabbi" (26:49). Matthew subtly but effectively portrays Judas as an outsider.[3]

This example illustrates how language may be used beyond a word's meaning; here we observe larger strategies to communicate something of who Jesus is and how one should best relate to him as Lord. So, the point is to understand that even routine words that are seemingly unimportant in and of themselves may be used across a discourse in quite important ways.

<u>Figurative Use of Language</u>: Words can be used to convey meaning beyond a simple one-for-one correspondence to what they often refer. For example, "I took a rabbit trail when researching this paper!" Obviously, "rabbit trail" is used beyond its primary significance (a winding long path made by rabbits). In this sentence "rabbit trail" refers to an unproductive long period of research or wasted time. Notice that even "wasted time" is a metaphor treating "time" as a commodity that can be "squandered." Indeed, the figurative use of language abounds in the field of writing. Thus, when interpreting discourse, we need to consider whether words or phrases are used in a more literal way where there is a one-for-one correspondence at this point of reference, or, whether the word or phrase is used in order to make broader conceptual associations that move beyond a one-for-one association. If the latter, we should consider whether a word or phrase is used within a figure of speech. Actually, figures of speech are like trees in the forest of discourse; they are quite common and diverse in kind. Regularly used figures include the following:

1. *metaphor*—comparing two seemingly unrelated entities or things (without *like* or *as*)
2. *simile*—comparing two entities or things using the words **like** or **as**
3. *irony*—saying one thing but meaning something else
4. *parody*—imitating a standard practice or behavior in jest, often mockingly or for effect.

---

[3] Luke Timothy Johnson and Todd C. Penner, *The Writings of the New Testament: An Interpretation*, rev. ed. (Minneapolis: Fortress, 1999), 195.

5. *hyperbole*—exaggeration in order to make a point
6. *personification*—attributing personal attributes and characteristics to non-personal entities
7. symbolism—indicating that some word has broader reference than the simple meaning of it

Many other types of special figures or tropes have been described.[4] This list is sufficient for now.

EXERCISE 3–B: Below is 1 Thess 5:4–11 (NASB).
[4] But you, brethren, are not in darkness, that the day would overtake you like a thief; [5] for you are all sons of light and sons of day. We are not of night nor of darkness; [6] so then let us not sleep as others do, but let us be alert and sober. [7] For those who sleep do their sleeping at night, and those who get drunk get drunk at night. [8] But since we are of *the* day, let us be sober, having put on the breastplate of faith and love, and as a helmet, the hope of salvation. [9] For God has not destined us for wrath, but for obtaining salvation through our Lord Jesus Christ,[10] who died for us, so that whether we are awake or asleep, we will live together with Him.[11] Therefore encourage one another and build up one another, just as you also are doing.

   a. Identify what you consider to be non-routine words.
   b. Identify any figurative use of language.

Parts of Speech:[5] The *parts of speech* are the basic building blocks of sentence grammar. Greek, like English, has many parts of speech. The English language is an Indo-European language. As such, English has been greatly influenced by many languages, including Greek. Thus, the two languages are very similar with regard to their parts of speech.

THE PARTS OF SPEECH

1. <u>noun</u>: a person, place, or thing; e.g., *house, woman,* or *Jesus* (a proper noun)
2. <u>pronoun</u>: stands in the place of a noun. The previous noun to which a pronoun refers is called the antecedent. If the referent occurs afterwards, it is called the postcedent. Many types of pronouns exist; here is an essential list:

   a. <u>personal</u>: *I, my, me, we; you, your; he, she, it, they, his, hers, their*
   b. <u>reflexive</u>: *myself, yourself, herself, themselves* (note: relates back to subject)
   c. <u>demonstrative</u>: *this, these; that, those* (note: a pointer)
   d. <u>interrogative</u>: *Who? What? Why? Where?*
   e. <u>indefinite</u>: *someone, anyone, a certain one*
   f. <u>relative</u>: *who, which, what* (note: begins a subordinate clause)

---

[4] See http://penelope.uchicago.edu/Thayer/E/Roman/Texts/Rhetorica_ad_Herennium/4B*.html for a summary of figures described in the first century Roman Rhetorician Quintilian. See also E. W. Bullinger, *Figures of Speech Used in the Bible* (London: Eyre & Spottiswoode, 1898) and the entry "Figure of Speech" in Wikipedia.

[5] The review of English grammar here relies heavily on my *Koine Greek Grammar: A Beginning-Intermediate Exegetical and Pragmatic Handbook*, Accessible Greek Resources and Online Studies (Wilmore, KY: GlossaHouse, 2015), ch.1.

3. adjective: modifies a noun; it tells the reader more information about that particular noun; e.g., *noisy cat, good woman, righteous man*. Under the category of adjectives, you may also consider what are called "determiners" that point or specify a noun or substantive: *the rooster, this clock* (the latter is an adjectival use of the demonstrative pronoun).
4. preposition: a word that begins a prepositional phrase. Common prepositions include the following: *out, of, from, through, for, along side, up (to), with, over, at, to*. These prepositions form prepositional phrases, which modify either a noun (hence, called *adjectival* use) or the action of the verb (called *adverbial* use). For example, The woman *in the house* walked *into the garage*. Consider also the prepositional phrases in Rom 5:2: *Through Christ* we have also obtained *by faith* our introduction *into this grace*. In both examples can you identify which prepositional phrases are adjectival and which are adverbial?
5. verb: The verb explains the action or state of being in a sentence. Critical concepts for verbs are tense (in English, this indicates time of action; present, past, progressive past, perfect, pluperfect, and future) and modality (whether the action is a simple statement, command, or potential action). Consider the verbs of Gal 3:11–12: [11] *Now that no one is justified by the Law before God is evident; for, "The righteous man shall live by faith."* [12] *However, the Law is not of faith; on the contrary, "He who practices them shall live by them."*
6. adverb: modifies most often the action of the verb, but may also modify adjectives or other adverbs. For example, Rom 5:7: *For one will hardly die for a righteous man; though perhaps for the good man someone would dare even to die*.
7. conjunction: connects sentences, clauses, or phrases in some logical relationship. For example, here are some common conjunctions: *and, but, however, therefore, for, because, if*. In Gal 3:11–12 above, the words and expressions *for*, *However*, and *on the contrary*, function as conjunctions.
8. interjection: an exclamation; e.g., *Wow!, Alas!, Behold!*

Basics of the English Sentence: The simplest English sentence must have both a subject and a verb; e.g., *Jesus wept*. Even the command *Go!* has an understood subject *(You) go!* The subject may be a noun or a pronoun or any word that acts like a noun. Sometimes in English, and especially in Greek, certain parts of speech may act like nouns (adjectives, prepositional phrases, verbals [infinitives and participles]) and, therefore, may function as the subject. In addition to a subject and verb, one may describe a direct object (DO) that receives the action of the verb (see below). Essentially, everything else in the sentence—prepositional phrase, adverbs, adjectives, appositives, subordinate clauses, etc.—are modifiers. Much special meaning and nuance is conveyed by these modifiers and the relationship that they have to what they modify (see below).

More on English Verbs: Verbs are complex; they convey action or state of being. Sentences are usually built around the verb. In English and Greek, the endings will help indicate number (singular or plural); also there will sometimes be changes in the verb stem to indicate tense or aspect: e.g., "says" and "said." Verbs in these languages have many features including the following:

Important Characteristics of Verbs

Tense (Time)	a. past—*I healed*
	b. present—*I heal*
	c. future—*I will heal*
Aspect (Type of Action)	a. simple—*I heal*
	b. progressive—*I am healing*
	c. perfective/resultative—*I have healed*
Voice	a. active—*I heal*
	b. passive—*I am (being) healed*
	c. reflexive middle—*I heal myself*
Mood	a. command—*Be healed!*
	b. fact—*I was healed.*
	c. possibility—*Could I be healed?*
	d. wish—*Oh, to be healed!*
Person and Number (singular//plural)	a. first—*I // we*
	b. second—*you // you*
	c. third—*he, she, it // they*

When studying a foreign language like Greek, it is often necessary to learn other grammatical "categories" like those in the table above. It can be dizzying. Additionally, these categories are recognizable by different verb endings on the verb stem. Within the English Language these endings are also present, but they are "native" to us unlike those in Greek, Latin, and Hebrew. However, the English verb system is often difficult for those learning it as a second language; the proper use of English verbs differentiates those who write poorly or write well.

Transitive and Intransitive Verbs: Some verbs transfer action from the subject to another noun. These are called transitive verbs. Verbs that do not transfer action from the subject to another noun are called intransitive verbs. From the example above, the verb *wept* is intransitive. Some examples of transitive and intransitive verbs are given below.

1. transitive: *to hit, to put, to send, to visit*. Here are some examples: *He hit the ball. She put the pencil on the table. He sent the apostles. Jesus visited them. He baked a cake.*
2. intransitive: *to walk, to sit, to laugh, to be*. Here are examples: *Peter walked (across the street). Julie sat (quietly). We laughed (together). He is good* (*good* is an adjective).

Notice how for transitive verbs the subjects *act* upon and/or produce the other nouns. The verbs above describe this transference of action. Intransitive verbs do not transfer the action to an object. Notice how some verbs may act either transitively or intransitively depending on the sentence. For example, *He walked* is intransitive and *He walked the dog* is transitive.

As stated above, transitive verbs involve the subject performing some activity with another noun. This other noun is called a **direct object** (DO). The direct object is often produced or acted upon by the subject. For example, *Peter healed the man*, and *He called the woman a disciple*. The direct objects are *the man* in the first sentence and *the woman* and *a disciple* in the second sentence. The *man* receives the action; he was healed. The *woman* was ascribed a status, *a disciple*. It should be noted that transitive verbs may have two direct objects, one external to the action (here *the woman*) and one internal or produced by the action (the name *disciple*). Another example of an internal direct object would be *She sang a song* where the *song* is produced by the action. In this case the direct object would also be a *cognate*, i.e., derived from the same word root (sang » song).

Occasionally the action done by the subject is done *to* or *for* someone or something. The noun *to whom* and *for whom* an action is done is called the **indirect object** (IO). For example, *The man bought a bone for the dog* and *She gave the speech to them*.

The Critical Concept of Modifiers: All the parts of speech—but especially adjectives, adverbs, prepositional phrases, pronouns, and verbals (participles and infinitives)—may function in the sentence to modify the subject, verb, and direct or indirect object by providing more specialized information about them. Therefore, modifiers are extremely important in interpretation because they give further description and clarification to any particular word in the sentence. Additionally, a word may have multiple modifiers. Consider all the underlined modifiers in Rom 5:11: *And not only this, but we also exult in God through our Lord Jesus Christ, through whom we have now received the reconciliation....*

Scope and Extent: Another helpful set of observations to make concerns the logical limiting or delimiting relationship of the modifier (adjectival or adverbial) to what they modify in terms of scope and extent. Types of scope would entail whether an item is inclusive (***all***), exclusive (***only***), or limited (***few, some, many***). Types of extent would entail whether something is complete (***whole, all***), partial (***part, some***), or nothing at all.

Apposition is one Kind of Modification: A noun placed after another noun giving it further description or explanation is said to be *in apposition* to the first noun. Normally the noun in apposition immediately follows the noun that it is describing. In English the noun in apposition is typically set apart by commas and may also be indicated by statements like ", that is," or ", namely,". Here is an example:

2 Cor 1:1 Παῦλος ἀπόστολος Χριστοῦ Ἰησοῦ,... καὶ Τιμόθεος ὁ ἀδελφὸς
Paul, *an apostle of Christ Jesus*,... and Timothy, *the brother*,

Both *an apostle* and the *brother* are in apposition to the nouns immediately before them. Each further explains just who Paul and Timothy are: an apostle and a brother.

Main Clauses (Sentences), Dependent Clauses, and Phrases: Once we understand the parts of speech, we now know the main components of a sentence. Each sentence is composed of a main clause, which may or may not have dependent clauses. A *clause* is any group of words having a verb in it, usually with a subject. The main sentence, which may be comprised of a subject, verb, modifiers, and objects, is called the *main clause*. The main clause is able to stand on its own and be grammatically correct; it can be spoken by itself and make sense. On the other hand, a *dependent clause* (also called a *subordinate clause*) cannot stand on its own and make sense; it must be understood with a main clause.

EXERCISE 3–C: In the two sentences below from Rom 5:6–7, try to identify the main sentence and dependent clause. The answer is provided in this footnote below.[6]

[6] For while we were still helpless, at the right time Christ died for the ungodly.
[7] For one will hardly die for a righteous man; though perhaps for the good man someone would dare even to die.

Thus, there are two types of clauses: main clauses and dependent clauses. Finally, a *phrase* is any group of words that belong together, but have no verb. From Rom 5:6–7 above, there are several phrases: *at the right time, for the ungodly, for a righteous man, for the good man*.

Conjunctions: Thus far we have learned terms that describe the basic English sentence: subject (S), verb (V), direct object (DO), indirect object (IO), and modifiers (M). But how do conjunctions function in the sentence? Basically, *conjunctions* link words, phrases, clauses, sentences, and paragraphs together and convey various semantic relationships.

1. **Sometimes conjunctions coordinate two more or less equivalent components**; e.g., *Peter and John went to the tomb*. Here two subjects are joined by *and*; thus we have what is called a *compound subject*. A *compound sentence* is when two or more main clauses are joined into one expression. For example, *They went to the tomb, but Mary left it*.
2. **A conjunction may be used to connect two or more unequal parts**. This can be most easily seen in the following example: *She came to the tomb in order to see him*. Here, the subordinate clause *in order to see him* is initiated with the conjunction *in order that* linking the idea of *see him* with the main clause. The conjunction *in order that* expresses the semantic relation of *purpose* and thus explains the intended goal or purpose for which they went to the tomb. A sentence that has a subordinate clause is called a *complex sentence*.
3. **Thus, conjunctions may be classified into two categories: coordinating and subordinating**. Coordinating conjunctions connect two or more equal components or sentences. Subordinating conjunctions connect a subordinate clause to the main sentence. A few examples of each are given below:

   coordinating: *and, but, however, either...or, for* (when not a preposition!)
   subordinating: *if, that, because, while, after, (al)though, in order that, so that*

---

[6] **ANSWER**: There are four clauses. The first and the fourth are dependent or subordinate clauses. The second and the third are the main sentences: **First Clause=** *For while we were still helpless,* **Second Clause=** *at the right time Christ died for the ungodly.* **Third Clause=** *For one will hardly die for a righteous man;* ["for" here is a conjunction]; **Fourth Clause=** *though perhaps for the good man someone would dare even to die.*

Types of Clausal Connections: It is possible to be even more precise in delineating types of clausal relationships. These relationships are usually recognized by conjunctions or adverbs. Below is a taxonomy of clausal relationships, which overlap somewhat with what will be described further below as semantic relationships:

TYPES OF CLAUSAL CONNECTIONS

1. **Temporal or chronological connectives**—give the text a sense of time, order, and/or chronology. Key words in this connective: *after* (Rev 11:11), *as* (Acts 16:16), *before* (John 8:58), *now* (Luke 16:25), *then* (1 Cor 15:6), *until* (Mark 14:25), *when* (John 11:3), *while* (Mark 14:43)
2. **Local or geographical connectives**—help provide a setting for a portion of a text. Key words: *where* (Heb 6:20); also *near, beside, along (side of)*
3. **Emphatic connectives**—used to express emphasis and importance. Key words: *indeed* (Rom 9:25), *only* (1 Cor 8:9)
4. **Logical connectives**—used to express important logical relationships
    a. **Reason**. Key words: *because* (Rom 1:25), *for* (Rom 1:11), and *since* (Rom 1:28)
    b. **Result**. Key words: *so* (Rom 9:16), *then* (Gal 2:21), *therefore* (1 Cor 10:12), *thus* (1 Cor 8:12)
    c. **Purpose**. Key words: *in order that* (Rom 4:16), *so that* (Rom 5:21)
    d. **Contrast**. Key words: *although* (Rom 1:21), *but* (Rom 2:8), *much more* (Rom 5:15), *nevertheless* (1 Cor 10:5), *otherwise* (1 Cor 14:16), *yet* (Rom 5:14)
    e. **Comparison**. Key words: *also* (2 Cor 1:11), *as* (Rom 9:25), *as-so* (Rom 5:18), *just as* (Rom 11:30–31), *likewise* (Rom 1:27), *so also* (Rom 4:6)
    f. **Series of facts or Lists**. Key words: *and* (Rom 2:17–19), *first of all* (1 Tim 2:1), *last of all* (1 Cor 15:8), *or* (2 Cor 6:15)
    g. **Condition**. Key words: *if* (Rom 2:19)
    h. **Concession**. Key Word: *although* (Rom 1:21–22)
    i. **Alternative**. Key Word: *either, or* (Matt 12:32)

Types of Phrasal Meanings: Phrases are smaller units of words that do not have a verb; often we think of prepositional phrases. Here are some of the major types of phrases. The observation and determination of how a phrase functions is often very helpful in interpretation:

TYPES OF PHRASAL MEANINGS

1. **Agency**—the person(s) performing the action. Key words: *through, by*
2. **Cause, Basis**—the basis on which an action is done. Key words: *because of, on account of*
3. **Means**—the thing by which the action is completed. Key words: *through, by, with*
4. **Direction**—movement to or from something or someplace. Key Words: *to, towards, away, from*

5. **Beneficiary**—the person(s) for whom some action is done. Key words: *for, on behalf of*
6. **Reference**—specifying or relating one item or action to a particular person or thing. Key words: *concerning, about*
7. **Origin** or Source. Key words: *from, of*
8. **Manner**—indicating how something is done. Key words: *by, with*
9. **Association**—indicating who relates with whom. Key word: *with*
10. **Substitution**—who is replacing whom, etc. Key word: *in place of, for*
11. **Apposition**—one noun is further defined by another noun (comma)

Contextual and Narrative Relationships: What has been presented above constitutes areas for careful observation of a text. Typically, these observations would be at the sentence or possibly paragraph level. However, broader observations may be made across sentences and paragraphs, especially in stories or narratives or in writing that may contain features like a story. Types of observations to make would include the following:

BASIC OBSERVATIONS FOR NARRATIVES OR STORIES

1. **Setting**: When and where
2. **Identifying the Purpose** of the Discourse: What Problem, Question, and Focus is given?
3. **Identifying Main Characters**—the **Protagonists** and their **Antagonists**: Who?
4. **Actions/Roles** of People and especially of God: What do they do? What roles do they have?
5. **Characterization** of People: What are they like? How are they characterized and why?
6. **Episodic Connections** (miracle events, parables, etc.): What leads to what? Why?
7. **Plot Development**: What moves the plot forward? What question, issue, or dilemma persists throughout the telling of the story?
8. **Dialogue** (conversation) vs. **Monologue** (one person speaking)
9. **Story Shifts**: Major Breaks and Pivot Points. What causes these changes? Why?
10. **Climactic development** and/or resolution to the problem, question, or issue

Other types of narrative observations are possible, but these are starting points upon which to build a more comprehensive understanding of the meaning and purpose of a passage.

Constituent Marking for Analyzing English Sentences: When analyzing sentences, it is helpful to know how each element or constituent functions and how it is related to the constituents around it. The method below is a fairly efficient one that can be applied to sentences in print or electronic form. If the text is printed out, then you may hand-write the marking. If the text is within a word processor, such as Microsoft Word, you may add the different types of underlining, parentheses, brackets, arrows, curved lines, and different types of boxes.[7]

---

[7] The "Constituent Marking" described here is slighty adapted from Long, *Koine Greek Grammar*, §4.7.

English Grammar and Constituent Marking

<u>Verbs</u> and <u>subjects</u>	Both subject and its verb are single underlined.
<u>Direct Objects</u> (double underline)	Direct object receives a double underline.
<u>Indirect Objects</u> (dotted underline)	Indirect object receives a dotted underline.
[Conjunctions] and [Interjections]	Place a box around conjunctions and interjections.
[Adverbs] (dashed box)	Place dashed boxes or draw a circle around adverbs; draw an arrow to what the adverb modifies.
(Prepositional Phrases)	Place prepositional phrases within parentheses, and then decide what each modifies and draw an arrow to it.
Verb ← Modifier Noun ← Modifier	Modifiers are either adverbial (modifying a verb) or adjectival (modifying a noun). Draw an arrow to what is being modified, especially if this is unclear.
[Subordinate Clauses] [¹… [²… [³…³] …²] …¹]	Place brackets around subordinate clauses and, if unclear, draw an arrow to what it modifies. If more than one subordinate clause exists, then number them. See example below for John 3:16.
Noun = Appositional Phrase	Place an equal sign (=) to indicate apposition (i.e., one noun abutted to another noun to further explain it).
antecedent ambiguous postcedent pronouns	Draw a dotted line to the antecedent of the pronoun, especially relative pronouns which also begin a clause.
unobvious antecedent ← [relative pronoun clauses]	Place relative pronoun clauses within brackets […], since it is a subordinate clause. Draw a dotted line to its antecedent; if it is unclear, add a question mark.
Adjectives and Direct Address	The marking of these depends on which noun they are modifying grammatically or logically.

Example Constituent Marking of John 3:16 with Observations: Below is a constituent marking of John 3:16. You may want to try doing this first and then compare it with my work.

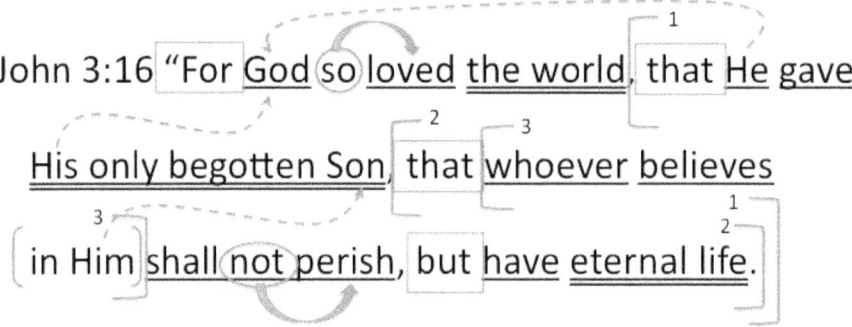

Having accomplished this constituent marking, you observe that John 3:16 contains one main clause and three dependent clauses. The main sentence is "God loved the world." This sentence is modified by an adverb "so" and has dependent clause #1 modifying it: "that He gave His only begotten Son." Then there is dependent clause #2 that also begins with "that: "that whoever believes in Him shall not perish, but have eternal life." Finally, within this second dependent clause there is a third clause "whoever believes in Him." The "whoever…" is a bit difficult to understand because it is equivalent to "he who…." It is helpful to separate the "he" and the "who." The "he" here is the subject of "shall not perish, but have eternal life"; the "who" is a relative pronoun that begins a subordinate clause "who believes in Him." This relative pronoun clause is a subordinate clause that delimits the "he" who shall not perish but shall have eternal life. Notice that the "but" indicates a contrasting pair of ultimate fates—perish vs. eternal life; furthermore, since "eternal" is a non-routine word, consider performing a word study on "eternal life" in STEP 5: LEXICAL RESEARCH. Also, what would this word/idea/concept have meant for believers in the first-century? Consider answering this question in STEP 9: INTERPRETIVE DECISIONS. Having eternal life is dependent on one's believing in "Him," who refers back to "His only begotten Son"—Jesus in context. The "Son" is modified by both "His" (=God the Father) and "only begotten," which is a verbal idea that describes a special or unique progeny. "Only begotten" is an odd and controversial idea and worth performing a word study on in STEP 5: LEXICAL RESEARCH.

The word "that" in English is also tricky (cf. Webster's Dictionary); it can indicate a demonstrative pronoun ("*That* is his dog"), adjective ("I hate *that* dog"), or adverb ("I would not go *that* far"); but none of these is its use here. Rather, it functions as a conjunction signaling four possible types of dependent clauses: indirect statements or content ("He said *that*…"); reason or cause ("He was pleased *that* his dog came home"); purpose ("He did this [in order] *that* it would happen…"); or result ("He did this [with the result] *that* it happened"). What is the meaning in each instance here? In English sense, the first "that" means cause ("God so loved the world, because he sent His Son"), result ("God so loved the world, with the result that He sent His Son"), or content ("God loved the World thus: that he gave His Son…"). Here most likely the descriptive content of God's love is indicated. The second "that" indicates purpose (the Greek confirms this). How does this knowledge affect your understanding of the passage?

PRIMARY INTERPRETIVE PROCEDURES:

1. Working with an enhanced understanding of English grammar, choose an English version and mark up verses using the <u>constituent marking method</u>.
2. Identify and describe the function of any <u>conjunctions</u>; remember that some conjunctions may signal the presence of a subordinate clause.
3. Locate the <u>main clause</u> in each sentence; is it a command, simple statement, or possibility?
4. Identify any <u>subordinate clauses</u>; what does each modify and how does it do so?
5. Identify any modifiers such as <u>prepositional phrases</u> and <u>adverbs</u>; what sentence element does each modifier modify and how does it modify the element?
6. Finally, <u>consolidate</u> your most important findings by summarizing key points, noting key words for further study, and identifying questions needing interpretation. (For word study, see STEP 5: LEXICAL RESEARCH; for the selection and answering of important questions, see STEP 9: INTERPRETIVE DECISIONS.)

II. SECONDARY STUDY

<u>Orientation</u>: The study of Greek grammar, syntax, and text-linguistic features lies at the heart of Greek exegesis. You may feel like this ancient student of Greek, but don't give up! It is time to open your eyes to see the hope in your labor![8] Presented below is a prioritized description of the most fruitful areas to explore the underlying Greek of the NT beginning with constituent marking that assists careful observation of the text.

<u>Constituent Marking</u>: The same English constituent marking may be used for the analysis of the Greek Text with some minor adjustments. Such marking helps to clarify the interrelation of the various sentence elements or constituents. The marking allows you to visualize the function of the words and will "prime the pump" for your subsequent careful study of the Greek text. Below is the legend for marking a Greek sentence; following that is an example with John 3:16. What one observes is that, although the marking of the English translation of John 3:16 above had three subordinate clauses, the underlying Greek text has only two subordinate clauses.

---

[8] Artwork was created by Sophy Hollington and is used with permission; the image appeared in James Romm's NY Times article, "Beginning Greek, Again and Again" (accessed 1–5–2015 at http://goo.gl/UuVL9p). Notice the ΕΛΠΙΣ ("hope") on the top of the stack of papers.

GREEK GRAMMAR AND CONSTITUENT MARKING

Verb|s and subjects	Both subject and its verb are single underlined; also "chop off" verb endings.
⬜Conjunctions⬜ and ⬜Interjections⬜	Place a box around conjunctions and interjections.
⸨Adverbs⸩	Place a dashed box or circle around adverbs.
Direct Objects	Direct objects receive a double underline, which are often in the accusative case, but some verbs use the dative or genitive case.
Indirect Objects	Indirect object receives a dashed underline.
Noun ⟵ Genitive Modifier	Draw an arrow to what is modified. You can also apply this rule to all modifiers that may be ambiguous (adverbs, prepositional phrases)
Noun = Appositional Phrase	Place an equal sign (=) to indicate apposition.
(Prepositional Phrases)	Place prepositional phrases within parentheses (…).
{Special uses of Cases} including {Vocatives}	Place curly braces around special case functions, including the vocative. Draw arrows to what is modified if these are present.
[Subordinate Clauses] [¹… [²… [³…³] …²] …¹]	Put brackets around subordinate clauses. Add superscript numbers for more than one clause and close off the clause with the same number.
antecedent ambiguous postcedent pronouns	Draw a dotted line to the antecedent or the postcedent of an ambiguous pronoun. If you are uncertain, use a question mark.
unobvious antecedent [relative pronoun clause]	Place relative pronoun clauses within brackets […], since it is a subordinate clause. Draw a dotted line to its antecedent; if it is unclear, add a question mark.
Adjectival Modifiers	Mark these in like manner as the noun to which they are linked grammatically or logically.

Example of Constituent Marking of John 3:16 with Observations: Compare this marking with the English constituent marking performed above.

STEP 3: SECONDARY STUDY

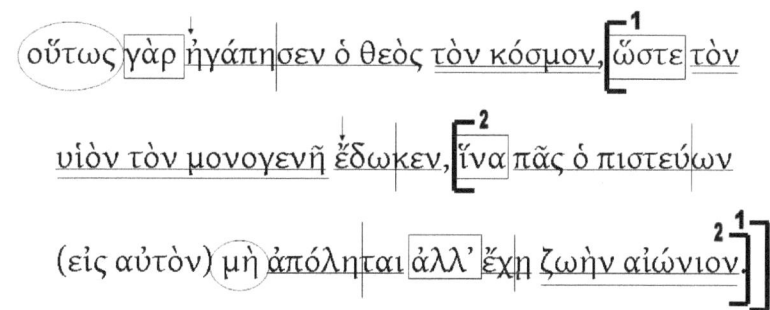

We observe one main clause that begins with the postpositive conjunction γάρ *for* that provides support for the previous claim in 3:15. Then we observe two subordinate clauses [¹ [² ... ²] ¹] beginning with subordinating conjunctions: ὥστε *that* and ἵνα *that*. In the English there was some ambiguity as to the meaning of the two "thats," but in Greek we can see that ὥστε lies behind the first one working with οὕτως *thus* to provide a "description" of God's love and that ἵνα *in order that* lies behind the second one and indicates "purpose." So, God's sending of Jesus illustrates God's love for the World, and the purpose of Jesus's coming was for the ones believing not to perish, but to continue having life everlasting. This last point is emphasized by the use of pair μή ... ἀλλά *not that ... but this* that stresses the final outcome of *life everlasting*. This simple sentence is given more clarity simply by observing and understanding the conjunctions; they are critical.

EXERCISE 3–D: Perform constituent marking on this Greek sentence with a translation below.

Matt 5:3 Μακάριοι οἱ πτωχοὶ τῷ πνεύματι, ὅτι αὐτῶν ἐστιν ἡ βασιλεία τῶν οὐρανῶν.

Blessed are the poor in spirit, because theirs is the Kingdom of the Heavens.

Particles and Conjunctions: After constituent marking, you should carefully consider all the particles and conjunctions in the passage. **Particles** are indeclinable words that signal discourse nuances and relations, which includes adverbs and conjunctions. **Conjunctions** are thus a subset of particles that connect discourse sections, sentences, clauses, phrases, or words. What is tricky in Greek is that certain words that we don't normally consider to be conjunctions will function like conjunctions; sometimes this is true of adverbs like τότε *then* and also of improper prepositions used alone like ἕως, ἄχρι, and μέχρι (each incidentally meaning *until*) or of proper prepositions in special constructions with infinitives (μετά meaning *after*, πρό meaning *before*, etc.).

Coordinating and Subordinating Conjunctions: Two sub-classifications of conjunctions are coordinating and subordinating. **Coordinating conjunctions** connect "equivalent" items within a sentence or relate sentences/paragraphs to one another. As such, conjunctions may help you discern a flow of thought. According to Daniel B. Wallace "The most common *coordinating* conjunctions are (in order): καί, δέ, γάρ, ἀλλά, οὖν, ἤ, τε, οὐδέ, οὔτε, and εἴτε."[9] **Subordinating con-**

---

[9] Daniel B. Wallace, *Greek Grammar Beyond the Basics: An Exegetical Syntax of the New Testament* (Grand Rapids: Zondervan, 1996), 669. The same page summarizes subordinate conjunctions.

junctions will relate a sub-clause to the main clause within a single sentence. According to Wallace, "The most common *subordinating* conjunctions that usually govern the *indicative* mood are (in order): ὅτι, εἰ, καθώς, ὡς, γάρ, and ὅτε. The most common *subordinating* conjunctions that usually govern the *subjunctive* mood are: ἵνα, ὅταν, ἐάν, ὅπως, ἕως, μή, and μήποτε." Traditionally, conjunctions have been described by semantic sense (see chart below).[10]

"SEMANTICS" OF COORDINATING & SUBORDINATING CONJUNCTIONS

	SEMANTICS:	temporal	causal	purpose	result	content	conditional	inferential	continuative	adversative	explanatory	emphatic
COORDINATING FUNCTIONS	ἀλλά									but		certainly
	ἄρα							therefore				
	γάρ		for								now	indeed
	δέ								and, now	but	now	indeed
	διό							wherefore				
	καί								and	but		even
	μέντοι									however		indeed
	οὖν							therefore	then, now	however	now	indeed
	πλήν									nevertheless		
	τέ								and			
	τοίνυν							therefore				
	ὥστε							therefore				
SUBORDINATING FUNCTIONS	ἄχρι	until										
	διότι		because									
	ἐάν						if					
	εἰ						if					
	ἐπεί		since									
	ἐπειδή	when	since									
	ἵνα			in order that	so that	that						
	ὅπως			in order that								
	ὅτε	when										
	ὅτι		because			that						
	πρίν	before										
	ὡς	when, as	since	in order that		that		so then				
	ὥστε				so that							

<u>Processing Constraints</u>: However, a purely semantic understanding of conjunctions is inadequate if not even misleading. First, conjunctions will not uncommonly work in combinations. Second, sometimes the assigned meanings are incompatible if not even contradictory. For example, how can καί inherently mean both "and" and "but"? Also, compare the various semantic meanings assigned to the conjunction οὖν in the chart above: *therefore, however, then, now, indeed*. How is "however" (adversative or contrastive) compatible with "therefore" (inferential)? It isn't. So, instead, these "meanings" are derived *from the possible translational sense from the broader discourse context and thus are not inherently marked by the conjunction οὖν itself.*

---

[10] The chart is reconstructed from Harvey E. Dana and Julius R. Mantey, *A Manual Grammar of the Greek New Testament* (New York: Macmillan, 1927), 257.

Instead of a "semantic" approach, Stephen H. Levinsohn has begun describing Greek conjunctions and the lack of a conjunction (asyndeton, marked Ø) in pragmatic terms as providing **processing constraints** that help *readers/hearers properly process the information conveyed in the interlinked clauses, sentences, paragraphs, and even sections*: "A different constraint is associated with each conjunction."[11] Thus, Levinsohn finds unacceptable meanings or "senses" attributed to conjunctions that "cannot be reconciled with this constraint." For example, it is problematic to assign to καί and οὖν an adversative sense ("but") and to δέ a supportive sense ("for"). Steven E. Runge, too, has adopted Levinsohn's framework and provides a helpful discussion of asyndeton and the more frequent coordinating conjunctions.[12] I find this approach particularly helpful.

Processing Constraints of Coordinating Discourse Markers: While calling for more research in the area, Cynthia Long Westfall has rightly said, "Conjunctions are often neglected in discussions of structure, but they provide some of the best formal indications of how the author intended the discourse to be processed."[13] More work is necessary to describe the use of particles as discourse markers of intra-, inter-, and extra-sentential relations. Since then, Levinsohn has presented research on coordinating inferential conjunctions in Paul and coordinating conjunctions in Rom 6.[14] Most recently Christopher J. Fresch has investigated a handful of conjunctions alone or in combination in the LXX (including one subordinating conjunction set εἰ μή or ἐὰν μή) as "discourse markers" (DMs). He summarizes the rationale of such research as follows: "[R]ather than attributing the semantics of surrounding contexts to the DMs, I posited core discourse-pragmatic functions that could be consistently observed across the data sets. These descriptions focus, then, on how each DM instructs the reader to build their mental representation of the discourse and process the text."[15] Drawing upon these studies and my own research, the chart on the next page provides a summary of the basic processing constraints of coordinating conjunctions. However, you must understand that while there is some consensus with many of these conjunctions and their descriptions, there is no uniformity of nomenclature and much room for refinement exists. For a more complete picture of the processing constraints of each conjunction, see the resources cited above and the explanations beginning below the chart.

---

[11] *Discourse Features of New Testament Greek: A Coursebook on the Information Structure of New Testament Greek*, 2nd ed. (Dallas: Summer Institute of Linguistics, 2000), 69–131.

[12] See *Discourse Grammar of the Greek New Testament: A Practical Introduction for Teaching and Exegesis* (Peabody, MA: Hendrickson, 2010), 57 (Table 3).

[13] Cynthia Long Westfall, "A Method for the Analysis of Prominence in Hellenistic Greek," in *The Linguist as Pedagogue: Trends in the Teaching and Linguistic Analysis of the Greek New Testament*, ed. Stanley E. Porter and Matthew Brook O'Donnell, New Testament Monographs 11 (Sheffield: Sheffield Phoenix, 2009), 75–94, esp. 84–86 (quotation from p. 84).

[14] "'Therefore' or 'Wherefore': What's the Difference?," in *Reflections on Lexicography: Explorations in Ancient Syriac, Hebrew, and Greek Sources*, ed. Richard A. Taylor and Craig E. Morrison, Perspectives on Linguistics and Ancient Languages 4 (Piscataway, NJ: Gorgias, 2014), 325–43; idem, "Holistic Approach to Romans 6" (presented at the The International Conference of the Society of Biblical Literature, London, England, July 2011).

[15] Christopher J. Fresch, "Discourse Markers in the Septuagint and Early Koine Greek with Special Reference to The Twelve" (St. Edmund's College University of Cambridge, 2015), 222. See summary in pp. 227–28.

Processing Constraints of Coordinating Connectors

	Constraints:	corrective	strengthen	inferential	distinctive or development	continuative or additive	alternative	forward pointing	adversative	consequence	sameness	result or conclusion	specific thematic	concurrence	subsequence	intensive or emphatic	Suggested English Translations
Coordinating Connectors	ἀλλά	+															But
	ἄρα			+						+							Therefore, Wherefore
	γάρ		+			+											For
	δέ				+												And, Now, Moreover, Furthermore
	διὰ τοῦτο			+								+					For this reason
	διό			+		+		+									So then
	διόπερ			+		+										+	So then indeed
	ἤ						+										Or
	καί					+											And; also
	μέν					+		+									indeed
	μέντοι							+	+							+	However, Nevertheless
	οὖν			+	+												Therefore, Then (resumption)
	πλήν								+							?	Nevertheless
	τέ					+					+						both/and (with similar items)
	τοίνυν													+		+	Hence (now)
	τοιγαροῦν			+	+											+	For this very reason, then
	τότε (used in narrative)				+										+		Then, Afterward, Subsequently
	ὥστε			+						+		+					To conclude, In sum

Let me provide further explanation for these discourse connectors and markers:

- **ἀλλά** will commonly follow a negative adverb like οὐ or μή to signify a correction: "not that … but this." The purpose of the correction is not necessary to negate the existence of the former but to emphasize the latter.
- **ἄρα** "constrains what follows to be interpreted as a consequence of what has already been stated in the context" … it "typically introduces a direct logical consequence of, usually, a single proposition" (Levinsohn, "Therefore," 331 and 336).
- **γάρ** indicates support or strengthening of the previous statement. The support may entail explanation and not simply providing a logical cause or an inferential basis.
- **δέ** is a new development marker that functions at various discourse levels: new scene, new segment, off-topic material, or small steps in arguments (Fresch, "Discourse Markers," 227). One particular and not infrequent use of δέ is to connect two parallel statements entailing two contrasted paralleled elements: e.g., "I will boast for the sake of such a person, but [δέ] I will not boast for my own sake" (2 Cor 12:5).

- διὰ τοῦτο, although technically a prepositional phrase, when occurring at the start of a sentence, this functions to advance the argument inferentially by reference to a specific thematic topic signified by the τοῦτο.
- διό "typically introduces an expository or hortatory THESIS that is inferred from what has already been stated.... It contrasts with οὖν in that it does not move the argument on to a new point" (Levinsohn, "Therefore," 329, emphasis original).
- διόπερ intensifies διό with περ adding "intensive and extensive force" (BDAG s.v.).
- ἤ denotes an alternative, either explicitly stated or implied from the context.
- καί is a continuative connector that "connects two items of equal status, constraining them to be closely related to one another" (Runge, *Discourse Grammar*, 24). Not infrequently, καί works more adverbially meaning "also" or "even" to mark a "thematic addition" to the topic of the discourse (Runge, *Discourse Grammar*, ch. 16).
- μέν "1) alerts readers to forthcoming necessary, corresponding, and semantically-related material that needs to be processed together with the host utterance in which μέν occurs and 2) instructs readers to build their mental representation of the discourse by regarding the resultant grouping as a coherent discourse unit that provides relevant information about a preceding or presupposed topic" (Fresch, "Discourse Markers," 228). This use of μέν is readily observed in the μέν ... δέ construction, although μέν also has this function when alone.
- μέντοι is often understood simply as an adversative *however, although*; however, it may entail a similar constraint as μέν although made more intensive by the suffix –τοι, "a marker of emphasis on the reliability of a statement" (BDAG, s.v.).
- οὖν "constrains what follows to be interpreted as a distinct point that advances an argument in an inferential way." After a supportive statement involving γάρ, an οὖν will "introduce a distinct point that advances an earlier theme" (Levinsohn, "Therefore," 327). This is called resumption. For an example of this latter scenario, see the οὖν at Matt 5:19.
- πλήν functions like ἀλλά to mark a contrastive statement and may be more intensive.
- τέ, when pairing items or used in lists, marks +sameness of kind grammatically (Long, *Koine Greek Grammar*, 275). When alone, τέ "adds distinct propositions that are characterized by *sameness*, in the sense that they refer to different aspects of the same event, the same occasion, or the same pragmatic unit" (Levinsohn, *Discourse Features*, 106–7; emphasis original).
- τοίνυν "signals a switch of attention to or back to the current situation" (Levinsohn, "Therefore," 339).
- τοιγαροῦν combines constraints marked by τοί (emphasis), γάρ (strengthening), and οὖν (distinct, inferential point); for example, it is used twice in the NT to draw a forceful exhortative conclusion (1 Thess 4:8; Heb 12:1).
- τότε **(in narrative)** Whereas δέ is the default new development marker, τότε "makes explicit that the development that follows is *temporal* in nature" (Runge, *Discourse Grammar*, 38 italics original).
- ὥστε "When ὥστε introduces an independent clause or sentence ... the logical relation with the context is less direct and, quite often, the input for the result introduced by ὥστε is more than one proposition." (Levinsohn, "Therefore," 335).

Processing Constraints of Subordinating Connectors: Let me say that much more research is necessary regarding subordinating conjunctions. However, with this caveat in mind I offer the following chart as a summary of my best thinking on their basic processing constraints.[16]

PROCESSING CONSTRAINTS OF SUBORDINATING CONNECTORS

	CONSTRAINTS:	time until which	time during which	time before which	strengthen	expectation of intention or content	consequence	expectation of content or cause	situational contingency (conditional)	exception	comparison	certainty	intensive or emphatic	Suggested English Translations
SUBORDINATING CONNECTORS	ἄχρι μέχρι	+												until, as far as
	διότι				+									since, because
	ἐάν								+					if
	εἰ								+					if
	εἰ μή ἐὰν μή									+				except, unless
	ἐπεί				+									since, because
	ἐπειδή				+							+		since (in fact)
	ἐπειδήπερ				+							+	+	since (in fact) indeed
	ἵνα					+								(in order) that
	καθώς				+						+			just as
	ὅπως					+								in order that, how
	ὅτε		+											when
	ὅτι				+			+						that, because
	πρίν			+										before
	ὡς		+								+			as, like, while
	ὥστε						+							so that

Asyndeton (Ø) or Lack of Coordinating Conjunctions: Asyndeton is typically significant varying with the particular NT author. The lack of *demarcating* a connection between sentences or units of discourse obligates audiences to supply a connection and thus requires greater cognitive processing and internalization of conceptions that may produce greater communicative effect.

- Isolated instances of asyndeton may signal section breaks especially if there is a sudden shift of topic and the presence of other discourse indicators that usually help signal such (e.g., vocatives of direct address, "Brothers").
- If there does not appear to be a major section break, then asyndeton may reflect a relationship between propositions that is beyond or different from what may be conveyed via the available connectors. Such relationships may entail providing an **evaluation**, moving from

---

[16] See discussions of select subordinate conjunctions in my *Koine Greek Grammar*, chs. 4, 8, 14–16, 22–23, 26.

STEP 3: SECONDARY STUDY   125

general to specific, or **summarization**.[17] One kind of evaluation in Paul occurs within diatribe amidst questions and their answers; asyndeton may reflect a different speaker in such contexts and/or answers provided to questions posed (e.g., Rom 3:2, 4, 9b, 27, 29; 6:1–2, 15–16; 1 Cor 6:12a, 13a, 18b [perhaps]).

- o Additionally, the motivation for asyndeton may be **emotional**, signaling intense feeling and focus on a particular topic.
- o Finally, asyndeton may occur in **lists with a sequence of verbal actions** that produces "a vivid and impassioned effect" (BDF §460).

EXERCISE 3–E: Given this English translation of 1 Cor 14:22–25 that identifies all conjunctions, so-used adverbs, and asyndeton inside brackets, consider the constraint/function of each.

²² To conclude this unit [ὥστε], tongues are a sign not [οὐ] with respect to the ones believing but [ἀλλά] with respect to unbelievers; additionally [δέ] prophecy is a sign, not [οὐ] to unbelievers but [ἀλλά] to those who believe.

a. ὥστε =   c. δέ =
b. οὐ ... ἀλλά =   d. οὐ ... ἀλλά =

²³ Therefore [οὖν], if [ἐάν] the whole church assembles together and [καί] all speak in tongues, and [καί] ungifted men or [ἤ] unbelievers enter, will they not say that [ὅτι] you are in a pagan religious frenzy?

a. οὖν =   d. καί =
b. ἐάν =   e. ἤ =
c. καί =   f. ὅτι =

²⁴ Moreover, [δέ] if [ἐάν] all are prophesying, and [καί] an unbeliever or [ἤ] an ungifted man enters, he is convicted by all, [∅] he is called to account by all, ²⁵ [∅] the secrets of his heart are disclosed, and [καί] so he will fall on his face and worship God, declaring that [ὅτι] God is certainly among you.

a. δέ =   e. ∅ ... ∅ [lack of conjunction] =
b. ἐάν =   f. καί =
c. καί =   g. ὅτι =
d. ἤ =

Punctuation and Paragraphing: The importance of studying coordinating conjunctions or asyndeton has application for understanding unit breaks and boundaries or what might be called "paragraphing" and "segmentation" of the discourse. The interpretation of passages may depend on properly identifying the unit boundary and theme.[18] One helpful place to consider punctuation

---

[17] Levinsohn, *Discourse Features*, 119–20. This discussion is adapted from my *Koine Greek Grammar*, 281.

[18] For example, for 1 Tim 2:11–15, the asyndeton at 2:11, and its significance in the argument progression of 1 Tim 2 generally, see my article, "A Wife in Relation to a Husband: Greek Discourse Pragmatic and Cultural Evidence for Interpreting 1 Tim 2:11–15," *The Journal of Inductive Biblical Studies* 2.2 (2015): 6–44.

and paragraphing is the "punctuation apparatus" of the UBS GNT. This apparatus shows you how various scholarly editions of the Greek NT and major modern Bible translations (KJV, RSV, NIV, NASB, etc.) have decided to punctuate and partition the text. One must understand how to decipher this apparatus. For example, right after 1 Cor 14:21 a footnote in the UBS[4] indicates "**21** P: NIV TOB" which indicates that the NIV (1983 2nd ed.) and the *Traduction Oecuménique de la Bible* French translation have a paragraph break here. Then, after 14:25 the UBS[4] indicates: "**25** NO P: AD // SP: WH // P: TR NA M RSV Seg Lu REB NRSV." The double lines // indicate the next piece of punctuation datum. So, the "NO P:" indicates that the AD (Greek Bible Apostoliki Diakonia, 1988) has no paragraph break here; the "SP:" indicates that the WH (Westcott-Hort) Greek edition has a sub-paragraph break here; and finally the "P:" shows Greek editions and versions that have a paragraph break here rather than a major section break as the UBS[4] has.

Other Modifiers and Adjuncts: **Prepositional phrases** and other modifiers add depth and color to sentences. Since these are not strictly needed, their semantic and pragmatic contribution is typically significant for the message of the text. You should consider what these are modifying and what is their semantic contribution to the sentence. As needed, consult Greek lexicons and intermediate or advanced grammars. Likewise, pay attention to any **adverbs**, and consider what they are modifying and what is their semantic contribution to the sentence; consult Greek lexicons and intermediate/advanced grammars as needed. The chart below provides semantic categories that describe PHRASAL MODIFYING RELATIONS appropriate to prepositional phrases and adverbs.[19] Be sure to think through the dynamics of each to draw appropriate implications.

PHRASAL MODIFYING RELATIONS

Location ("in, out, at")	Reference ("concerning")	Origin or Source ("from")
Temporal ("at, before")	Instrumental ("by, through")	Manner (describing "how")
Direction ("towards, away")	Agency ("through, by")	Association ("with")
Purpose ("for, to")	Cause ("because, on acc. of")	Substitution ("in place of")
Beneficiary ("on behalf of, for")		

Pronouns: Pronouns tell a story and have exegetical significance. Below is a list of major and minor pronouns in the GNT organized by type and relative frequency: Consider the semantic value of **special pronouns** (reciprocal, reflexive, possessive, correlative, demonstratives, etc.). Also consider what emphasis is added by **emphatic pronoun forms** (accented forms). Identify whether there are any special uses of the personal pronoun (αὐτός, αὐτή, αὐτό). For example, be sure to note the **redundant nominative forms** of the personal pronoun, which are not required, since the finite verb has a "default subject." What emphasis is indicated? Note the occasional uses of intensive meaning ("-self") or identical meaning ("same"). Relative pronouns may be necessary to **restrict** or clarify the reference or may be **non-restrictive** to explain an event or noun attribute.

---

[19] From David Alan Black, *Linguistics for Students of New Testament Greek: A Survey of Basic Concepts and Applications*, 2nd ed. (Grand Rapids: Baker, 1995), 111–12.

GREEK PRONOUNS (WITH OCCURRENCES IN THE GNT)

Personal (8468)	Demonstrative (1652 +10)	Relative (1406+144)	Correlative (57+14+110+1)	Interrogative (579+33+27)	Indefinite (510)	Reflexive (399)	Possessive (116)	Reciprocal (100)
ἐγώ ἡμεῖς *I; we* σύ ὑμεῖς *you* αὐτός *he, she, it; they*	οὗτος *this* ἐκεῖνος *that* + ὅδε *that* →	ὅς *who* + ὅστις *whoever*	τοιοῦτος *of such a kind* + οἷος → *such a one* + ὅσος → *how many* + τοιόσδε *such as this*	τίς *who? what? why?* + ποῖος *what sort of?* + πόσος *how much of?*	τις *someone*	ἐμαυτοῦ σεαυτοῦ ἑαυτοῦ *-self*	ἐμός *my* ἡμέτερος *our* σός *your* ὑμέτερος *your*	ἀλλήλων *one another*
• look for nominative forms w/ verbs • look for emphatic forms (e.g., μου–ἐμοῦ) • special uses (*same, self*)	• intensified article • pointer of what? • forward or backward referent	• begins elaborative clause • where end? • ὅστις may describe *nature* and provide *support*[20]	• very significant in context • οἷος and τοιοῦτος stresses quality • ὅσος stresses quantity	• τί can mean *why?* or *what?* • ποῖος stresses quality • πόσος stresses quantity	• open referent • scope is inclusive	• no nom. forms • reflects back on subject • plural are the same	• most emphatic form for possession • fairly rare	• speaks to mutuality • reminds us of our corporate body life

Greek Verbs: Paying careful attention to central features of the Greek verb will often pay good exegetical dividends. Although there has been considerable debate about the nature of the Greek verb, it is possible to summarize the discussion and the exegetical benefits rather succinctly in terms of these five areas:

1. voice of verbal action (active, middle, passive);
2. verbal aspect (imperfective, perfective, resultative-stative, and future);
3. choice of tense to represent past time within historical narrative;
4. the choice between the Present Tense (imperfective aspect) or the Aorist Tense (perfective aspect) in the non-Indicative Moods; and
5. the semantics and special uses of the non-Indicative moods.[21]

Voice of Verbal Action: Greek verbs may express action as completed by the subject (active), as completed by the subject in some relation to the subject (middle voice), or as completed for or to the subject (passive). The active and passive voices are the most comprehensible for English speakers. The active verbal voice, although the most common Greek voice, still is significant

---

[20] Maximilian Zerwick, *Biblical Greek: Illustrated by Examples*, trans. by Joseph Smith; 4th ed.; Scripta Pontificii Instituti Biblici 114 (Rome: Editrice Pontificio Istitutio Biblico, 1963), 68 (§163): "ὅστις either shares the indeterminate status of its antecedent or, if the antecedent is itself determinate, regards it not as individual but as of such a nature. In this latter case ὅστις may easily have a causal sense ('in as much as') or consecutive one ('such as'). The distinction is therefore one which affects the sense, and does so in much the same way as the presence or absence of the article...."

[21] The following material is slightly modified from various discussions in my *Koine Greek Grammar*.

because it specifies the "agent" performing the action; just who is acting may be quite important for the message. However, if an author chooses to render a statement using the passive voice rather than the active voice (especially when the active was a possible choice), we should wonder why. The passive voice allows for the option of leaving the "agent" unspecified and implied (sometimes this is God in what is called the "divine passive" use). The significance of the middle lies in the responsibility and action of self-interest or benefit (for good or bad) that the subject has in performing the action; we should ask why the middle voice was used.

EXERCISE 3–F: Given these examples where verbal voice is specified inside the brackets, consider the implications or nuances of why the verbal voices were chosen to describe the action. You may need to consider the statements in context.

2 Tim 4:15 You guard yourself [M] against him, for he vigorously opposed [A] our teaching.

1 Cor 6:7 Why not rather let yourselves be wronged [M]? (Yes!) Why not rather let yourselves be defrauded [M]? (Yes!)

2 Cor 1:4 God encourages [A] us in all our affliction in order that we would be able to encourage [A] the ones in affliction through the encouragement with which we ourselves are encouraged [P] by God.

Matt 5:7 Blessed are the merciful, for they shall be shown mercy [P].

<u>Verbal Aspect</u>: "Verbal aspect is, in general, the portrayal of the action (or state) as to its *progress*, *results*, or *simple occurrence*."[22] A scholarly consensus is beginning to emerge around these categories and definitions. Grammarians have described **verbal aspect** in relation to Greek verbs as follows:

Aspect	Greek Tenses
a. **Imperfective**: action as viewed internally as in progress or incomplete	**Present, Imperfect**
b. **Perfective**: action as viewed as a whole externally or as complete (but not necessarily completed)	**Aorist**
c. **Resultative-stative**: action reflects "a given (often complex) state of affairs"[23]	**Perfect, Pluperfect**
d. **Future**: action reflects expectation/intention of occurrence in the future	**Future**

<u>*Aktionsart* or "Categories" of Verb Tense Usage—A CAUTION</u>: Aspect Theory as summarized above represents an emerging consensus. Additionally, however, Wallace and many others will describe verbal *Aktionsart*, that is, multiple "Specific Uses" for each verb Tense:

It is important to distinguish aspect from Aktionsart. In general, we can say that ***aspect is***

---

[22] Wallace, *Greek Grammar*, 499, emphasis original.
[23] Porter, *Idioms of Greek New Testament*, 2nd ed. (Sheffield: Sheffield Academic Press, 1994), 21–22.

Step 3: Secondary Study

*the unaffected meaning while **Aktionsart** is aspect in combination with lexical, grammatical, or contextual features*. Thus, the present tense views the action from within, without respect to beginning or end (aspect), while some uses of the present tense can be iterative, historical, futuristic, etc. (all of these belong to Aktionsart and are meanings of the verb affected by other features of the language).[24]

Wallace's categories by Aspect (with Future placed with the Aorist tense) may be summarized in the chart below. As can be seen, two *Aktionsart* categories <u>Ingressive</u> and <u>Gnomic</u> repeat across all aspect boundaries. Also, the *italicized* categories occur across two or more tenses.

Common Verbal Aspect and *Aktionsart* "Categories"

PROGRESSIVE ASPECT (INTERNAL VIEW)		SIMPLE OCCURRENCE ASPECT (EXTERNAL)		RESULTATIVE ASPECT (PERFECTIVE)	
PRESENT	*IMPERFECT*	*FUTURE*	*AORIST*	*PERFECT*	*PLUPERFECT*
-Instantaneous	-Instantaneous	-Predictive	-Constative	-Intensive	-Intensive
-Progressive	-Progressive	-Imperatival	-Consummative	-Extensive	-Extensive
-Extending-From-Past	-<u>Ingressive</u>	-Deliberative	-<u>Ingressive</u>	*-Aoristic*	*-Simple Past Pluperfect*
-<u>Gnomic</u>		-<u>Gnomic</u>	-<u>Gnomic</u>	-<u>Gnomic</u>	
-Iterative	-Iterative	-Miscellaneous Subjunctive Equivalents	-Epistolary	*-Perfect with Present Force*	
-Customary	-Customary		*-Proleptic*	*-Proleptic*	
-Historical			-Immediate Past	-in Allegory	
-Perfective	-*"Pluperfective"*				
-Conative	-Conative				
-In Progress, but not Complete	-In Progress, but not Complete		[Proleptic means "futuristic"]		
-Not Begun, but About/Desired to be Attempted	-Not Begun, but About/Desired to be Attempted				
-Futuristic					
-Completely Futuristic					
-Mostly Futuristic					
-Retained in Indirect Discourse	-Retained in Indirect Discourse				

This atomization of categories is problematic: Grammarians may be ascribing "too much" to the verbal forms. In other words, we are mistaken to think that Greek authors intended these "Specific Meanings of the Present Tense" (Wallace essentially identifies ten of them!) to be marked grammatically in the Present Tense verb form. Indeed, Wallace above rightly posits the influence of "contextual features" that must be taken into account to discern these special uses. *However, to the extent that one must appeal to explicit external contextual indicators (i.e., other words in the context) to support the identification of this or that specific use of the Present Tense, the more unlikely it is that the specific uses are actually indicated by the grammatical form of the Present Tense.*

---

[24] Wallace, *Greek Grammar*, 499. The chart below is compiled from p. 768.

Additionally, beyond semantic meaning and contextual indicators *pragmatic constraints* govern an author's choice to use one verb tense instead of another. These may include, e.g., rhyming, style, tone, sentence arrangement, and prominence effect. These pragmatic constraints have not been consistently taken into account in terms of what is essentially marked by each verb tense. So, let's consider what discursive significance may be conveyed by choosing one tense instead of another.

<u>Tense Use in Historical Narrative</u>: In the Indicative Mood the Aorist is the default past time tense; it typically carries forward the mainline of the narrative. When encountering other past time tenses such as the historic present, imperfect, perfect, or pluperfect, you should then pay careful attention and ask why they are used. The following chart and discussion summarizes what is signified or marked by the choice of tense in narrative discourse.[25]

VERBAL ASPECT AND PRAGMATIC FUNCTIONS OF TENSES IN NARRATIVES

	Augment	Aspectual Semantic Significance			Pragmatic Effect		
	Remoteness (There-ness)	Perfective	Imperfective	Resultative-Stative	Main line	Fore-ground	Front-ground
Aorist	+	+			+		
Historic Present			+			+ + subsequent focus	
Imperfect	+		+			+ + vividness + open	
Perfect				+			+
Pluperfect	+			+			+

<u>Aorist Tense</u>: The Aorist Indicative is suitable to mark the mainline of the narrative—the Aorist Indicative moves the narrative forward. All other tenses are unmarked for mainline although they may carry it forward; but they are marked for some kind of prominence in the narrative.

<u>Historic Present (HP) is Forward Pointing</u>: The HP has the pragmatic effect to highlight the unfolding, subsequent events, actions, or speech. The *imperfective aspect of "incompleteness"* opens up the narrative to look forward to subsequent speech or action. In this respect the Historic Present is to be differentiated from the Imperfect Tense that instead preserves an imperfective verbal aspect in relation to the verbal action itself. Also, the location of the HP may be at the start of a new unit, but also need not be.

<u>Imperfect Tense</u>: The Imperfect Tense represents the verbal action as *imperfective*, that is, as internal and ongoing without view of beginning and ending. As such, the presence of the Imperfect Tense alerts audiences to envision such *ongoing past action* in relation to the verbal action itself. This distinguishes the Imperfect Tense from the HP that rather points forward to something subsequent in the narrative. In terms of pragmatic effect, since Imperfect Tense verbs are marked +*internal and ongoing*, it may add vividness to highlight significant events in the narrative and/or

---

[25] Slightly modified from Long, *Koine Greek Grammar*, 245–47. Porter discusses background, foreground, and frontground in *Idioms of the Greek New Testament*, 2nd ed. (Sheffield: Sheffield Academic Press, 1994), 23.

it may serve to introduce a new scene by keeping the verbal action "open" and ongoing.

Perfect and Pluperfect Tenses: Since the Perfect Tense has *resultative-stative aspect*, its use emphasizes a resultant effect or state of actions. To put this resultant effect or state into remote, distant, past time, an augment may be added in the formation of the Pluperfect Tense. Because of their rarity and the complex resultative aspect, the Perfect and Pluperfect Tenses are the most prominent of the tenses. By their use, authors indicate important actions/states.

Summary of Tenses: The **augment** marks +remoteness and typically past time in the Aorist Tense, Imperfect Tense, and Pluperfect Tense (although absent occasionally) in the Indicative Mood. In narratives the perfective aspect (i.e., *complete[d] action*) of the **Aorist Tense** indicates mainline material or the storyline that is *not marked for prominence* (Porter calls this *background*). The **Imperfect Tense** in narrative shows imperfective aspect (i.e., *action in progress* or *incomplete*) and makes vivid and *foregrounded* the verbal event itself; it may "open up" an ensuing scene. The **Pluperfect Tense** represents stative aspectual actions that are *frontgrounded*, but have remoteness, i.e., have already occurred in the past and have (*already*) had stative results that have since concluded. Also having stative aspect, the **Perfect Tense** represents actions that are *frontgrounded* but are not-marked for remoteness. In other words, the resultant stative effects are typically still persisting and/or these results are prominently presented. Finally, the **Historic Present** with imperfective aspect (i.e., *action in progress* or *incomplete*) highlights the narrative's immediately unfolding subsequent speech or actions. Thus, each tense makes a distinctive contribution to narrative discourse that corresponds both to the semantics of the tense form (e.g., "remoteness" signaled by augmentation) and to the pragmatics of verbal aspect in contextual use.

Verb Tenses in Non-Narrative Materials: The description above pertains primarily to narrative materials, but in many respects we may extend the principles to non-narrative discourse (such as Paul's letters) with the main exception being that the aorist tense is backgrounded and the mainline material is the present tense; also there is no historic present usage. In Paul we observe switches between past, present, and future time frames depending on the argumentative needs in each context. For example, in Rom 5:8–10 Paul linked Christ's past death to our future salvation. This is communicated via verb tenses.

EXERCISE 3–F: Given Rom 5:1–2, what is the pragmatic function of the verb tense: background, foreground, and frontground? You will have to convert the Greek tense form to its verbal aspect.[26]

¹ Therefore, having been justified [Aorist Tense] by faith, we have [Present Tense] peace with God through our Lord Jesus Christ, ² through whom also we have obtained [Perfect Tense] our introduction by faith into this grace in which we stand [Perfect Tense]; and we exult [Present Tense] in hope of the glory of God.

---

[26] The example is from Porter, *Idioms*, 23. "Being justified by faith" (aorist) is the background for the foregrounded "we have peace with God" (present) and the frontgrounded "we have had access by faith into grace by which we have stood" (both verbs are perfect). Then, Paul foregrounds "exulting" in hope of glory.

Non-Indicative Moods: Finally, we consider the verbal aspect and special functions of the non-Indicative Moods, in which we may include participles (verbal adjectives) and infinitives (verbal nouns). These moods have the following frequencies: participles (6,659), infinitives (2,291), subjunctive (1,860), imperatives (1,618), and optative (68). For comparison sake, the frequency of the indicative mood is 15,613. The chart below visualizes these Moods and Tenses and provides frequencies based upon searching Logos Bible Software's tagging of the NA[28].

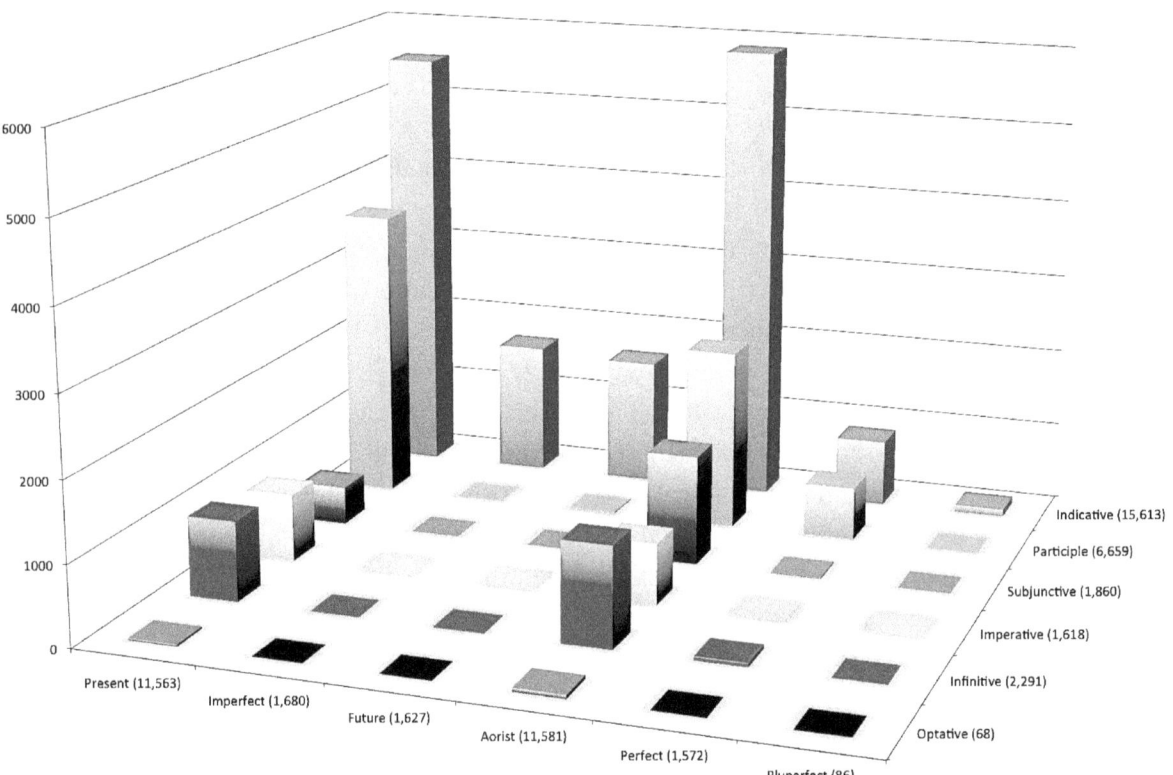

FREQUENCY OF GREEK VERB TENSES AND MOODS

Verbal Aspect of Non-Indicatives: As you can see in the chart above, apart from the Indicative Mood (the back row), we mainly find Present and Aorist Tenses (the front columns 1 and 4 from left to right), with a few Perfect tense forms occurring as participles. Within the non-Indicative Moods, the Present Tense carries special significance because it indicates progressive, on-going, or regular-intermittent action; also the Perfect Tense (much less common) is significant because it indicates a resultant state. These two tenses are marked in distinction from the Aorist Tense that is used when the author views the action/event simply as a whole or as complete.

Special Constructions of the Non-Indicative Moods: Although technically participles and infinitives are not "moods," they are often treated as such. Key uses and constructions may be summarized in an outline format starting with the most frequent mood (excluding the Indicative): participles, then infinitives, subjunctives, imperatives, and optatives.

STEP 3: SECONDARY STUDY   133

PARTICIPLE FUNCTIONS (frequency 6,659). Participles are verbal adjectives. Because of their high frequency, examples are provided below.

1. **Adjectival Functions**: The participle will mostly have the article with it in this use.

   a. <u>Substantive Use</u>: Participles may be turned into a substantive (a noun) when accompanied by an article and standing alone. You should consider why a person has been represented by this *verbal* adjective as opposed to simply a noun or substantive adjective.

   John 12:45 καὶ <u>ὁ θεωρῶν</u> ἐμὲ θεωρεῖ <u>τὸν πέμψαντά</u> με.
   And <u>the one beholding</u> me beholds <u>the One that sent</u> me.

   b. <u>Attributive Use</u>: The Participle may modify a substantive like an adjective. You should consider why a person/entity has been modified by this *verbal* adjective as opposed to simply an adjective.

   Luke 3:7 Ἔλεγεν οὖν <u>τοῖς ἐκπορευομένοις ὄχλοις</u> βαπτισθῆναι ὑπ᾽ αὐτοῦ· γεννήματα ἐχιδνῶν, τίς ὑπέδειξεν ὑμῖν φυγεῖν ἀπὸ <u>τῆς μελλούσης ὀργῆς</u>;
   Therefore, he was saying <u>to the outcoming crowds</u> to be baptized by him, "Brood of vipers! Who showed you to flee from <u>the coming wrath</u>!"

2. **Circumstantial (i.e., adverbial) Participles**: This use of the participle is very common and there is much to think about exegetically. *When so used, the participle will never have an article with it*. Thus, a participle that does not have an article should be considered initially as circumstantial, although there are some exceptions. This use of the participle is commonly described as "adverbial," but grammarians and interpreters too often confuse *what is modified* (the verb) with *adverbial options of modification* (such as cause, condition, concession, time, etc.). ***In fact, the adverbial, or better, the circumstantial participle is unmarked for adverbial meanings.*** Any sense of adverbial meanings comes from the context; for a listing of these senses, see below. So, it is better to conceive of participles as filling out the "circumstances" surrounding the actions of the main verb. Moreover, the location of the participle delimits the function of the participle: Does it occur before (pre-nuclear) or after (post-nuclear) the main verb?

   a. <u>Pre-nuclear (before)</u>: In pre-nuclear locations circumstantial participles may:
      i. mark a **transitional segue** showing *continuity* with the previous narrative; and/or
      ii. provide an **important framework** for the main verb that is otherwise unnecessary; and/or
      iii. provide **procedurally** or **logically necessary action** prior to the main verb.

Matt 2:11 καὶ ἐλθόντες εἰς τὴν οἰκίαν εἶδον τὸ παιδίον μετὰ Μαρίας τῆς μητρὸς αὐτοῦ, καὶ πεσόντες προσεκύνησαν αὐτῷ καὶ ἀνοίξαντες τοὺς θησαυροὺς αὐτῶν προσήνεγκαν αὐτῷ δῶρα, χρυσὸν καὶ λίβανον καὶ σμύρναν.

And [after] coming into the house [SEGUE], they saw the child with Mary, his mother, and falling down [PROCEDURAL] they made obeisance to him, and opening their treasure chests [PROCEDURAL], they offered gifts to him, gold and frankincense, and myrrh.

  b. <u>Post-nuclear (after)</u>: Two main uses of post-nuclear circumstantial participles are:
     i. by **redundant** statements **to point forward and emphasize subsequent speech**; or
     ii. to **explicate** or **specify particulars** of the main verbal action.

Matt 10:5 Τούτους τοὺς δώδεκα ἀπέστειλεν ὁ Ἰησοῦς παραγγείλας αὐτοῖς λέγων· εἰς ὁδὸν ἐθνῶν μὴ ἀπέλθητε καὶ εἰς πόλιν Σαμαριτῶν μὴ εἰσέλθητε·
Jesus sent out these twelve, instructing [EXPLICATE/QUALIFY] them, saying [REDUNDANT]: "Do not depart into the way of the Gentiles and do not go into the city of the Samaritans."

  c. <u>Adverbial Contextual Senses</u>: It may be that you may discern a contextual adverbial sense. These are the categories commonly identified with *English translations*.

     i. **Temporal**; the Aorist Tense participle will be used for "time prior" (*after*) whereas the Present Tense participle will be used for "time contemporaneous" (*while, when*)
     ii. **Substantiation (sometimes called Causal)** (*because*)
     iii. **Purpose (Instrumental)** (*in order that*)
     iv. **Concession** (*although, even though*)
     v. **Conditional** (to form an *if* clause),
     vi. **Result** (*so that*, or *resulting in*)
     vii. **Means** (*by means of*)
     viii. **Manner** (indicates *how* in terms of manner)

4. **Genitive Absolute Circumstantial Participle**: There are some three-hundred instances when a circumstantial participle is placed into the genitive case and has a genitive "subject" present or implied that is different than the subject of the main verb. Typically, these constructions will be pre-nuclear in location and thus have pre-nuclear functions.

Matt 5:1b καὶ καθίσαντος αὐτοῦ προσῆλθαν αὐτῷ οἱ μαθηταὶ αὐτοῦ.
And after he sat down, his disciples came to him.

5. **Periphrastic Participles**: One special use is the *periphrastic participle* (with a form of εἰμί or equivalent) that is essentially a roundabout way of creating a verbal statement via a participle functioning like a predicate adjective. *This construction would seem to stress the verbal action as an attribute of the subject more than a simple verb would do.* In other words,

the author deliberately creates such a construction presumably for the effect of verbalizing an attribute onto an agent or subject.

Matt 19:22 ἦν γὰρ ἔχων κτήματα πολλά
For he was having [had] many possessions

Matt 10:22 καὶ ἔσεσθε μισούμενοι ὑπὸ πάντων διὰ τὸ ὄνομά μου.
And you will be hated by many because of my name.

6. **Complementary Participles**: A final use of the participle that is not terribly common in the GNT is called the complementary participle. Here the participle participates integrally with the main or nuclear verb to form a whole verbal idea. The complementary participle may be classified as a type of supplementary participle. What distinguishes this use from the periphrastic participle (also a sub-class of supplementary participles) is that certain nuclear verbs semantically may need to use the participle to complete their meaning, whereas the nuclear verb in the periphrastic construction (εἰμί or γίνομαι) does not need the participle; instead, the periphrastic construction is simply one option for conveying verbal action.

Eph 1:18a οὐ παύομαι εὐχαριστῶν ὑπὲρ ὑμῶν…
I do not cease giving thanks for you…

<u>INFINITIVE FUNCTIONS</u> (frequency 2,291). Infinitives are verbal nouns.

1. **Complementary**: Completing the meaning of Verbs ("I am able…to do"); also some nouns or adjectives will take an infinitive ("authority…to do").
2. **Substantival Infinitives** are infinitives that act as nouns.
3. **Infinitives of Indirect Discourse or Content/Noun Clauses**. In places where you might expect a ὅτι *that*, you will occasionally find a infinitive with accusative subject translated "that" expressing the content of what is said, thought, felt, etc. or further defining an idea.
4. **Adverbial Infinitives** form adverbial subordinate clauses.
   a. *Conjunction Construction*: With ὥστε the infinitive is used to express result (or sometimes Purpose).
   b. *Preposition Constructions*:   **Luke 2:27b** ἐν τῷ εἰσαγαγεῖν τοὺς γονεῖς τὸ παιδίον…
   when the parents led inside the child…
      i. <u>Purpose</u>: εἰς (fairly common) and πρός (rare) are both used to mean *in order that*.
      ii. <u>Substantiation</u>: The prepositions διά (less common) and ἕνεκεν (very rare; see 2 Cor 7:12) mean *because*.
      iii. <u>Temporal</u>: A temporal meaning is conveyed by the following prepositions.
         α. ἐν *while, when* (most common)   γ. πρό *before* (rare)
         β. μετά *after* (less common)   δ. ἕως *until* (very rare)
      iv. <u>Substitution</u>: The preposition ἀντί (very rare) means *in stead of* (Jas 4:15).
      v. <u>Source or Basis</u>: The preposition ἐκ (very rare) means *from, on the basis* (2 Cor 8:11).

c. *Articular and Anarthrous Infinitives*: The infinitive alone (anarthrous or articular) is found in contexts where the adverbial senses of purpose and result (much less commonly) are present. Inherently, however, the infinitive is unmarked for purpose or result. Articular infinitives in a context of **purpose** occur 33 times and with a sense of **result** only 2–5 times. If present, the article is genitive neuter singular (τοῦ). The anarthrous infinitive is found in contexts of specific or general **purpose** 253 times and of **result** 12 times.[27]

SUBJUNCTIVE FUNCTIONS (frequency 1,860). The Subjunctive Mood is used for possibility, volition, and deliberation. Unfortunately, there is no single way to translate all Subjunctive Mood verbs into English—it truly depends on the construction in which one finds them. Often students will be taught or will opt for "may" or "might"; you should avoid this! So, we need to think through the semantics involved in each construction before we can translate the idea into English or any other language.

1. **Dependent Subjunctives** are found in subordinate clauses beginning with subordinating conjunctions, adverbs, or pronouns.
    a. <u>Purpose</u> meaning "*in order that*" with ἵνα or ὅπως or negatively with μή alone "*lest*" (i.e., "*in order that not*").
    b. <u>Result</u> meaning "*so that*" with ἵνα. This is somewhat rare, and usually a meaning of purpose or content should be considered first (if not even to be preferred).
    c. <u>Content</u> "*that*" with ἵνα providing the content of something said, thought, wanted, prayed, etc. Usually the ὅτι ("*that*") conveys this, but if there is some potentiality or purpose involved, then ἵνα seems to be used.
    d. <u>Conditional</u> with ἐάν ("*if*"), ὅταν ("*whenever*"), or ὃς ἄν or ὅστις ἄν ("*who(so)ever*"). Here ἐάν and these related forms are used to present a supposition (the "*if*-clause") that is a subordinate clause to the main clause (the "*then*-clause").
    e. <u>Temporal</u> with constructions such as μέχρις οὗ ("*until*") (rare) that can convey the notions of destination, goal, and purpose.

2. **Independent Subjunctives** are used to form their own main clause. Four such uses exist:
    a. *Hortatory Subjunctive*: This use occurs exclusively with a 1st person plural Subjunctive verb. The Hortatory Subjunctive is a polite injunction or command: *"<u>Let</u> us do this...."*
    b. *Prohibition with μή*: The Aorist Subjunctive with the negative particle μή is used for a negative command: *"Don't do that...!"*
    c. *Deliberative Question*: A sentence asking an open-ended question: *"What <u>should</u> I do?"*
    d. *Emphatic Negation*: To make a very emphatic denial, authors would use both negative particles οὐ μή (in this order) with the Subjunctive Mood (or on occasion the Future Tense): *"Such and such <u>will never ever happen</u>...."* This is an emphatic denial.

---

[27] Clyde W. Votaw, "The Use of the Infinitive in Biblical Greek" (Ph.D. diss., The University of Chicago, 1896), 10–13, 4–849. The number of specific or general purpose infinitives combines Votaw's "Distinct and Specific" with "Modified and General" categories.

IMPERATIVE FUNCTIONS (frequency 1,618).

1. **General Use**: The imperative mood in Greek can be used for prayers, petitions, requests, and commands. Generally speaking, the present tense indicates repetition or recurring actions expected, whereas the Aorist tense views the commanded action simply as a whole or complete. The choice to issue a command with the Present Tense as opposed to the Aorist Tense is often exegetically significant.

2. **Mitigation and Potency of Exhortations**: Not all commands and exhortations are the same. Some are mitigated; others are potent. Levinsohn applies two terms, **potency** and **mitigation**, to discuss exhortations: "One way to distinguish different forms of exhortation is on the basis of their relative potency. Wendland (2000:58) defines the potency of an exhortation as 'its relative directness, urgency, or degree of mitigation'. 'Mitigate' means 'make less severe' (*OED*)."[28] Altogether, the factors affecting the potency of exhortations include the mood of the exhortation, the person (first 'Let us...", second "You...!", or third "Let him..."), clause type (direct vs. indirect), and the presence of any qualifiers that may intensify or alternatively may mitigate the exhortation. In combination such factors may be in tension; e.g., in Eph 4:17 Paul "says that" believers should not walk like the nations (an indirect command); yet he adds hugely intensifying elements "I *testify* with the *Lord*."

FACTORS AFFECTING THE RELATIVE POTENCY OF EXHORTATIONS[29]

EXHORTATION MOOD	PERSON	POTENCY	CLAUSE TYPE	QUALIFIERS
Imperative	2nd	MOST	Independent (direct)	Intensifying
Subjunctive		↑		
Indicative	1st	↕		
Infinitive	3rd	LESS	Dependent (indirect)	Mitigating

OPTATIVE FUNCTIONS (frequency 68). The Optative Mood expresses *wish*, *potential future occurrence*, and even *deliberation* (which overlaps considerably with the Subjunctive Mood.) In fact, in the NT era the Optative Mood is being replaced by the Subjunctive Mood and the Future Indicative. In the GNT it occurs 68 times and fifteen of these mainly occur in Paul's letters as the conventional negative exclamatory expression Μὴ γένοιτο, *May it not be!* This statement is an extremely strong denial and helps underscore important points Paul makes.

---

[28] Stephen H. Levinsohn, *Self-Instruction Materials on Narrative Discourse Analysis* (Dallas: SIL International, 2012), 73–81. He cites Ernst R. Wendland, "'Stand fast in the true grace of God!' A Study of 1 Peter," *Journal of Translation and Textlinguistics* 13 (2000): 25–102 and the *Oxford English Dictionary* (OED) s.v.

[29] See the discussion in my *Koine Greek Grammar*, §25.3. The chart is found on p. 504.

Use Charts to Display Data Clearly: Consider using a chart to help display information. Below is a portion of Rom 12:6 illustrating the utility of charts:

Verse & Verb	Parsing	Tense or Mood	Significance for Exegesis
v.6 ἔχοντες	PAP MPN	Present participle	Functioning as main verb with an implied form of εἰμί from v. 5: "[we are] having…." This is an implied periphrastic construction. The participle alone is a bit shocking; it intimately connects the notion of our being mutually co-members of the body (v.5) with "having gifts acc. to grace…" (v.6). In other words, what we have is for mutually serving one another.
τὴν δοθεῖσαν	APP FSA	Aorist Passive Participle functioning attributively	modifies "grace" and is a divine passive— Grace is given **by GOD** to believers for believers.

SECONDARY INTERPRETIVE PROCEDURES:

Since these involve accessing the Greek text, they do <u>not</u> involve the primary procedures.

1. Copy and paste in the Greek text from the UBS or NA.
2. Perform the <u>constituent marking method</u> on the passage or the most important verses.
3. Note all the <u>conjunctions/particles</u> in the passage and consider how they function.
4. Note the <u>verbal person</u> (1st, 2nd, or 3rd) of the verbs; From what perspective is the discourse being narrative or argued?
5. Consider each <u>pronoun</u>. What types are used? Why? What "story" is being told in the "persons" specified?
6. Note all the <u>prepositional phrases</u> in the passage; then consider what they are modifying and what is their semantic contribution to the sentence.
7. Note all the <u>adverbs</u> in the passage; then consider what they are modifying and what is their semantic contribution to the sentence.
8. Notice any special significance of <u>verb tenses</u>, especially Imperfect, Perfect, and Pluperfect Tenses (in all moods); then consider the distinction between Present Tense and Aorist Tense in the non-Indicative Moods.
9. Consider all the <u>non-Indicative Mood verbs</u> (participles, infinitives, subjunctives, and imperatives) and any special constructions with important semantics associated with them.
10. Summarize your main findings perhaps even in a way that non-Greek users can understand. Keep record of any significant questions for STEP 9: INTERPRETIVE DECISIONS.

III. TERTIARY RESEARCH

Overview: At this level of research students are expected to work with secondary perspectives and procedures with even greater ability and discernment. At a minimum researchers should be able to engage scholarly commentaries on issues of interpretation, discerning what are the most important critical discussions and being able to summarize them in concise, helpful ways. Furthermore, you may track connectives and understand their contribution to the discourse's information structure. Additional areas of investigation include word order, the presence or absence of the article, and marked constituents that indicate nuance or emphasis. Finally, this level of research may entail deploying a discourse model to perform text linguistic analysis.

Connectives: Building upon the presentation above that describes conjunctions as connectives or discourse markers, you may carefully track the course of argumentation to discern unit boundaries, the nature of propositions, and the progression of argumentation. Both coordinating and subordinating conjunctions should be investigated as to their processing constraints. In a number of specialized studies Levinsohn has tracked the information structure as suggested by connectives.[30] Following his analysis of 1 Tim 1:3–2:10 may illustrate how to track the information structure and its benefits. Levinsohn also works constituent-by-constituent offering comments on matters of word order, contextual meaning, and translation notes. He describes the structure of 1:3–11 ("Timothy should command people to stop teaching the Scriptures incorrectly") and 1:12–17 ("Paul's gratitude to Christ Jesus") as follows:

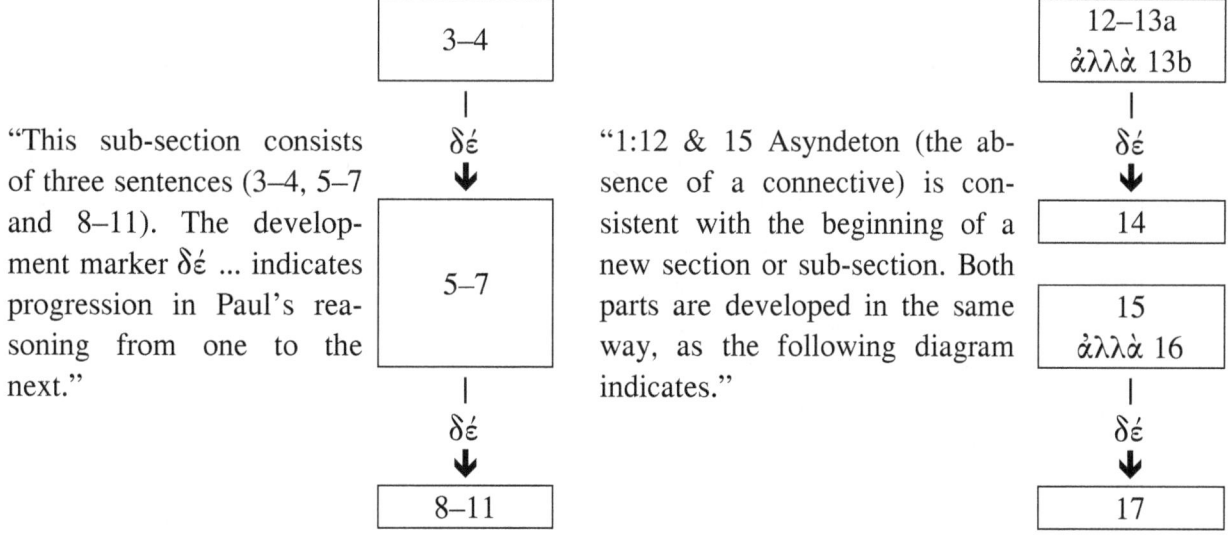

"This sub-section consists of three sentences (3–4, 5–7 and 8–11). The development marker δέ ... indicates progression in Paul's reasoning from one to the next."

"1:12 & 15 Asyndeton (the absence of a connective) is consistent with the beginning of a new section or sub-section. Both parts are developed in the same way, as the following diagram indicates."

---

[30] In addition to several studies cited above, see the following that may be available online: Stephen H. Levinsohn, "The Relevance of Greek Discourse Studies to Exegesis," *Journal of Translation* 2.2 (2006): 11–21; *Some Notes on the Information Structure and Discourse Features of 1 Corinthians 1–4* (Dallas: SIL International, 2009); *Some Notes on the Information Structure and Discourse Features of 1 Thessalonians* (Dallas: SIL International, 2009); *Some Notes on the Information Structure and Discourse Features of 1 Timothy* (Dallas: SIL International, 2009); *Some Notes on the Information Structure and Discourse Features of Luke 22 and 6:20–49* (Dallas: SIL International, 2009).

So, δέ indicates new developments (1:5, 8, 14, 17) and asyndeton indicates new subunits (1:3, 12, 15). Furthermore, in 1:12–17 each use of ἀλλά in 1:13b and 1:16 does not occur in a standard οὐκ ... ἀλλά construction, but ἀλλά "corrects" descriptions of Paul's former blaspheming, persecuting, and sinful behaviour and occurs with the verb ἠλεήθην *I was shown mercy*. These repeated statements point to an important affirmation: Human sinfulness is met by God's mercy. Thus, ἀλλά is used twice here to make this central point in the discourse. In such analysis it is important to notice that Levinsohn does not treat coordinating conjunctions that are found within subordinate clauses (e.g., relative pronoun clauses) such as the δέ in 1:9 and the καί in 1:10—such "buried" coordinating conjunctions are not on equal terms as far as tracking the information structure.

Continuing on, Levinsohn depicts 1:18–2:10 together since he sees the οὖν at 2:1 as resumptive of the mainline argument seen at 1:18–19a:

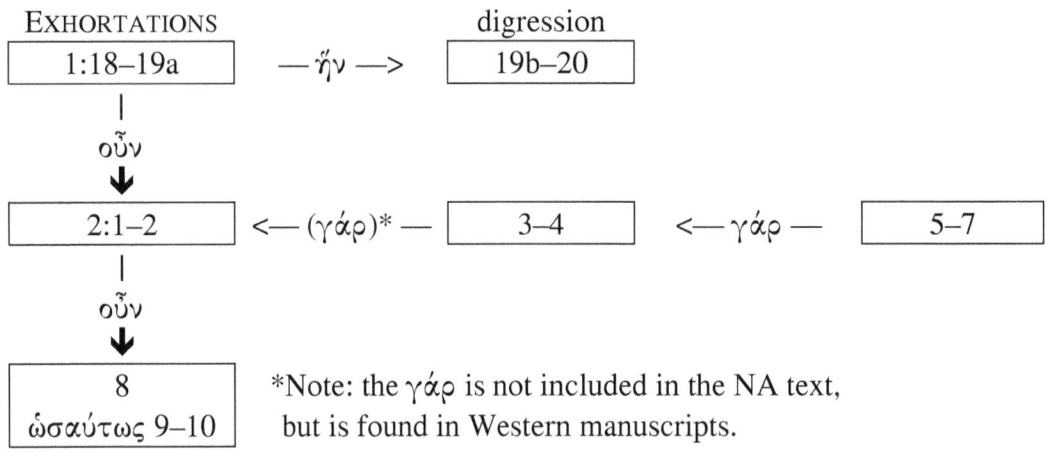

The relative pronoun ἥν in 1:19b begins a digression on "good conscience" and those wrecking it. The οὖν marks an inferential development that resumes 1:18. This observation that 2:1 resumes the mainline argument of 1:18 is significant because at 1:18 Paul entrusts "this instruction" (ταύτην τὴν παραγγελίαν) to Timothy. The phrase is preposed and the demonstrative is fronted before the noun; thus, the phrase has prominence. But what is "this instruction"? It refers to the whole letter; thus the phrase is a general statement. "Instruction" is the focus of 1 Timothy: Paul began the letter recalling his earlier instruction to Timothy by using the verb form παραγγέλλω *I instruct, command* (1:3–4) and then Paul defines this in 1:5: "Moreover [δέ], the goal of the instruction [τὸ τέλος τῆς παραγγελίας] is love from a clean heart and a good conscience and unhypocritical faith." So, 1 Timothy is "this instruction" and 1:18 resumes focus on this instruction and 2:1 continues with Paul's exhortation. Strengthening statements are made with γάρ in 2:3–4 and 2:5–7 (although the first γάρ is attested only in the Western manuscripts, hence Levinsohn places it in parentheses). At 2:8 Levinsohn explains the information structure: "Οὖν again marks the resumption of the main theme-line, following the strengthening material of 3–7." The ὡσαύτως in 2:9 connects the exhortations of women to those of the men and requires the audience to bring forward the implied verb βούλομαι *I want*. To try your hand at this, see EXERCISES 3–G below.

Step 3: Tertiary Research

Word Order: Notice any prominence related to **word order**.[31] Emphasis is generally indicated by a forward placement relative to other sentence components, or placement at the very end of the sentence for "final emphasis," which is especially true of verbs. The type of emphasis may be described at various levels: the sentence, the clause, or the phrase.

Word Order Variations and Prominence

Sentence Level: Generally, the default sentence order is Verb-Subject-Object (VSO).	
Preposed Position	Unless when a clause functions as a segue or a point of departure, when some sentence constituent occurs before the verb, emphasis attends that constituent whether it be a subject, object, or modifier (subordinate clause, prepositional phrase, adverbs, etc.).
Final Position	"Final emphasis" is achieved by the strategic placement of a sentence constituent at the clause's very end for effect. This is the last word and may function as a transition for the subsequent discourse.
Left (Dis)Location of Topics (LDT) or Frames (LDF)	A not uncommon occurrence in Greek is the extreme fronting to the left of some sentence constituent (word, phrase, or clause) to the sentence initial slot, but then in the main clause a "trace element" will refer back to the left (dis)located constituent. My research of the GNT indicates that LDTs mark both +immediate alternative discontinuity and +larger discourse continuity, whereas LDFs simply introduce important complex adverbial frameworks marked +discontinuity.
Clause Level: The relative positioning of clauses may indicate stress.	
Elaborative Clause	Any relative pronoun clause or participle clause that is strictly not necessary and is non-restrictive (i.e., disambiguating the referent) disrupts the sentence flow and gains prominence.
Conditional Clause	Typically, the protasis or supposition ("if" part of a conditional sentence) occurs before the main clause; but emphasis attends the protasis when it occurs after the main clause. This final position is always where exceptive clauses with εἰ μή are found and as such they stress "the exception."
Phrase Level: In general, modifiers placed before what they modify draw more attention to their modification; this gives more prominence to the modifier.	
Discontinuous Modifiers	The disruptive separation of a modifier from its substantive draws attention to one or the other or to both constituents.
Other Modifiers, including Adjectival, Demonstrative, & Genitive Modifiers	When placed in front of their substantive, this draws more attention to their modification. This may also apply to πᾶς, πᾶσα, πᾶν. In general, more research is necessary in this area.

---

[31] This discussion summarizes various treatments of word order in *Koine Greek Grammar*.

<u>Discourse Pragmatic Use of the Article or its Absence</u>: The discussion below will treat Proper Names of Participants, Proper Names of Places, and General Nouns before providing some Examples and concluding with a comment about textual variants involving the article. Given the nature of the subject, this discussion pertains especially to narrative material.

<u>Proper Names of Participants</u>: A complicating factor to a more traditional understanding of the Greek article has been to recognize that the presence or absence of articles functions pragmatically to signal discourse activation, status, and emphasis of participants. *Activation* concerns whether a participant (person) has been brought on stage in a scene (i.e., within a limited range of verses) or the entire discourse. *Status* concerns whether participants remain on the stage in the scene or move off when another takes the stage. *Emphasis* concerns prominence afforded to participants that are already activated. The basic discourse principles explained below summarize the discussion of Jenny Read-Heimerdinger and Levinsohn.[32]

1. **Initial Introduction/Activation of Participant is through Anarthrous Identification**. A participant or unique entity is typically introduced or "activated" onto a scene within a narrative without the article (anarthrous). Importantly, direct speech represents a new scene, so participants will generally need to be activated within them (i.e., be anarthrous) from the perspective of the audience of the speech.
2. **Continued Activation through Arthrous (Articular) Identification**. In that scene, as long as that participant or unique entity remains activated, he/she will normally be articular.
3. **Global VIP Status is Assumed through Continuous Arthrous Identification**. Some participants may be granted "global VIP" (Very Important Participant) status in the narrative—i.e., they are assumed known or important throughout, like God—and need no activation in the discourse or reactivation; so, such participants will normally be found with the article (i.e., arthrous).
4. **Local VIP Status is Maintained through Arthrous Identification**. Even if a participant disappears for a time from the narrative, once returning, the participant enters articular. Your observation of this phenomenon helps identify a participant with Local VIP status. For example, in Acts 13–28 Paul goes on and off stage throughout, yet is frequently arthrous on his return. This is because (apparently) he is being viewed as a Local VIP for this portion of Acts, although he is not a global VIP in the same sense as God is.[33]
5. **Unless the participant is a Global or Local VIP, his/her Removal from a Scene Requires Re-Activation later via Anarthrous Identification**. (= principle #1) A participant can be deactivated by removal from the scene and/or by being "upstaged" by another partic-

---

[32] Read-Heimerdinger gave a presentation entitled "The Discourse Use of Articles with Personal Names in Acts" at the Discourse Studies Workshop sponsored Logos Bible Software and co-organized by her and Steven Runge before the annual meeting of the Society of Biblical Literature Nov 22, 2013 in Baltimore. Her presentation was a summary of her more detailed study in her book, *The Bezan Text of Acts: A Contribution of Discourse Analysis to Textual Criticism*, JSNTSS 236 (London: Sheffield Academic, 2002), 116–44. Levinsohn, *Discourse Features*, ch.9.

[33] This example was provided by Read-Heimerdinger while reading through and critiquing this material.

ipant being activated. Then, re-activation of a previously activated participant without global or local VIP status is through anarthrous identification.

6. **Emphasis is given to an activated participant through Anarthrous Identification**. Participants that have been activated through anarthrous referent may continue to be highlighted or emphasized as a "local VIP" through anarthrous reference (see Levinsohn 156–58). The type of emphasis must be determined from context: it may include contrast with another participant or highlighting some important action or speech of the participant.

7. **Exceptions to these principles include the following**:
   a. "Set phrases" may be anarthrous, such as "in the name of Jesus (Christ)" (ἐν τῷ ὀνόματι Ἰησοῦ Χριστοῦ), where we might otherwise expect to find Jesus articular in Acts since he is the global VIP.
   b. Indeclinable names may be (unexpectedly) articular since the article may be provided to indicate the noun's case (Wallace 240). So, in Matt 1:18 the first occurrence of Joseph is articular (τῷ Ἰωσήφ); in Acts 7:8 at the first mention of Isaac, we find τὸν Ἰσαάκ (examples from Levinsohn 151). In this latter case the accusative article indicates that Isaac is not the subject, but the direct object of the verb. Alternatively, you may account for these articles on the basis of the knowledge of the audience in Matthew (Joseph is a known person or knowable from the genealogical context) and the Jewish audience who was listening to Stephen's speech in Acts 7.[34]

Cities and Regions: Jenny Read-Heimerdinger maintains, "names of cities ... are usually (but not always) anarthrous at first mention whereas names of regions/provinces/countries are arthrous."[35] For example, the region of Samaria is always articular (John 4:4, 5, 7; Acts 1:8; 8:1, 5, 9, 14; 9:31; 15:3), except one instance in Luke 17:11 (διὰ μέσον Σαμαρείας καὶ Γαλιλαίας).

General Nouns: The introduction of a place, space, or situation will also assume the items/persons commonly understood as present therein; therefore, when explicitly mentioned, such items/persons will be articular, even though it is their first mention. For example, an entity like *a home* may imply the existence of other entities, like *the atrium* in the home or *the master* of the home, etc. So, once a *home* is introduced in the discourse, then afterwards the first reference will be made to *the* atrium (articular) or *the* master (articular) since these are assumed as known in the previous reference to the home.

Examples: In general, Levinsohn's work reveals some interesting observations in the Gospels and Acts (151–55):

- In Matthew and Mark once Jesus has been activated by anarthrous reference in Mark 1:9 and Matt 1:16 (shown above), he then shows a global VIP status and is never again reactivated, *EXCEPT* after his resurrection (Matt 28:9 is anarthrous, but thereafter arthrous in 28:10, 16, 18).

---

[34] Read-Heimerdinger has proposed this alternative explanation in a private conversation.
[35] In an email correspondence.

- In Luke 1–3 Jesus is always anarthrous, but after activation at the start of his ministry in 4:1 (anarthrous), Jesus achieves global VIP status (arthrous in 4:4, 8, 12, 14 etc.) until his resurrection, after which he is reactivated by being anarthrous (24:15).
- In Matt 14 Herod the tetrarch is activated by anarthrous reference in 14:1, and thereafter remains on stage with articular reference (14:3, 6a, 6b).
- In Mark 15 Pilate is activated by anarthrous reference in 15:1, and thereafter remains on stage with articular reference (15:2, 4, 5, 9, 12, 14, 15, etc.).
- In Luke 9 Peter is reactivated with anarthrous reference (9:28) and thereafter remains on stage with articular reference (9:32, 33; and 12:41 and 18:28).

Other examples may be found. In Acts 9:2 Saul asks for *letters* (anarthrous) from the high priest *for Damascus* (εἰς Δαμασκὸν, anarthrous) to be carried along *to the synagogues* (πρὸς τὰς συναγωγάς, arthrous); then in 9:3, Paul traveled and approached near to *the Damascus* (τῇ Δαμασκῷ). The explanation according to the principles above is as follows: *letters* are anarthrous because they are not specific letters previously mentioned; they are simply letters. Since *Damascus* is a city, its first reference is anarthrous (more common), but the second is arthrous (probably anaphoric). *The synagogues* are arthrous because they have a distinct referential identity being known to exist in the setting of the city of Damascus that has already been introduced.

In 1 Tim 2:15 Paul's articular reference to "the childbearing" (τῆς τεκνογονίας) has presented interpreters with problems. With the article Paul was indicating specificity of an entity that is known or knowable in the discourse context; but what? Although some have suggested *this childbearing* refers to Christ's incarnational birth through Mary, it is simpler to understand that Paul has been discussing a husband in relation to a wife in 2:11–15, and so *the childbearing* referred to would naturally occur from the marriage relationship.[36]

<u>Textual Critical Matters Regarding the Article</u>: Read-Heimerdinger has rightly urged me to let students know the following:

> Some mention is needed of the large amount of variant readings regarding the presence of the article in the Gospels and Acts—esp. with proper names. The editors of the NA edition … made their choice of [best] readings without the knowledge of the 'principles' you present here, but instead adopted the reading that was most in line with the author's 'style'—which your principles show is not relevant or applicable in the case of the article.[37]

Also, when discussing the use or absence of the article (see ch. 9), Levinsohn shows awareness of variant readings that are sometimes, and sometimes not, shown in the critical editions of the GNT.

<u>Marked Constituents for Prominence and Discourse Pragmatics</u>: Time does not allow any full treatment here, although several of these items are discussed above. These areas of "emphasis"

---

[36] For the full interpretation of this passage, see my, "A Wife in Relation to a Husband" cited above.

[37] Read-Heimerdinger offered this while reading through and critiquing this material (slightly edited for clarity).

and "pragmatics" may overlap with one another; the lists come from the Subject Index of my *Koine Greek Grammar* (with page and section numbers) and deserve careful investigation.

EMPHATIC AND PRAGMATIC CONSTRUCTIONS INDICATING PROMINENCE

Emphasis (types of), defined (66), as listed in John 13:31–35 (314)	**Pragmatic(s)**, xvi, xvii, xviii, xix, 23, 161, 317, 369
Additive, with καί meaning *also* (82–83)	Ἀποκρίνομαι, §18.5 TAKING CONTROL OR "ANSWERING BACK" IN CONVERSATION: Ἀποκρίνομαι
Ἄν, if added to expressions in NOTES ON VOCABULARY 26 (518)	*Apposition*, with possible elaborative emphasis (100)
Appositional Target, with Ὅτι (160)	*Article*, §21.4 DISCOURSE PRAGMATIC USE OF THE ARTICLE OR ITS ABSENCE
Attributive, with adjectival modifiers (137–38, 143), 394	*Asyndeton*, 280–81
Cognate Accusative, due to repetition of lexeme (466)	Αὐτός, 385
Comparative and Superlative, §25.6 COMPARATIVE AND SUPERLATIVE EMPHASIS	*Conditional Sentence Structure*, 519–20
Correlative, 279, 338, 349, 427, 519, 530; §15.6 CORRELATIVE EMPHASIS: LISTS AND COORDINATED CONNECTIVES	*Conditions (Temporal-Functional)*, 521–22
	Conjunctions, §1.4 CONJUNCTIONS: LEXICAL MEANINGS, CONSTRAINTS, & PRAGMATIC EFFECTS; 51, 275, 285
Demonstrative, 334, adjectival use in fronted position (228)	*Demonstrative Pronouns*, 224–30
Elaborative, with apposition (100); with relative pronouns (173–74); with participle in second attributive position (324–25)	*Ellipsis*, §9.4 ELLIPSIS: SUPPLYING AN IMPLIED WORD
Genitival, 78, 98 (in Matt 15:28), 129, 130, 235, 288	*Exception Clauses*, 534–38
	Exhortations, §25.3 THE POTENCY OF EXHORTATIONS: PRAGMATIC CONSIDERATIONS
Intensive and Identical with Αὐτός, §20.3 INTENSIVE AND IDENTICAL USES OF Αὐτός	*Genitive Absolute*, 388–91
Interrogative, §14.3 INTERROGATIVE EMPHASIS	*Historic Present*, 124, §6.6 HISTORIC PRESENT (HP) AND DISCOURSE PRAGMATICS
Morphological, with compounded prepositions (113–14), on Οὐχί and Μήτι (257–58), with Κάθως (292), with –περ (520n1)	*Imperfect Tense*, 153
	Left (dis)location, 406–408
Negative, 435, 455; §22.6 NEGATIVE EMPHASIS	*Metacomments*, with Οἶδα (195–96); §10.8 METACOMMENTS AND PRAGMATICS
Qualitative, 224; §26.4 QUALITATIVE EMPHASIS	*Narrative Past Time*, §13.5 DISCOURSE PRAGMATIC OPTIONS TO REPRESENT PAST TIME IN THE INDICATIVE MOODS
Quantitative, 224, 541; §12.4 QUANTITATIVE EMPHASIS	
Participant, with article (416–17)	*Nominative (Pendent, Suspended)*, 402
Periphrastic, with participle (374–76)	*Participles (adjectival)*, 323–26
Position Final, 77–78, 285, 368, in exception clauses (533)	*Participles (circumstantial)*, 328–32
Position Fronted (preposed), 66, 77, 258, 313–14, 325, 368, 394, 538, with respect to protasis (541)	*Participles (genitive absolute)*, 388–91
	Participles (periphrastic), 374–76
Possessive, 364–68.	*Participles (redundant)*, 333–34, 349
Pronominal, by emphatic form (167)	*Prepositions as Verbal Object*, 145
Redundant Participle, 333	*Recitative* Ὅτι, 158–59
Subject (grammatical), with redundant pronouns (168–69), 520n1	*Relative Pronouns*, 172–74
	Verbal Aspect, 50–51
Thematic Address, vocatives with ὦ (98)	*Vocatives*, 95–98

As an example of a pragmatic feature, Levinsohn maintains that ἀποκρίνομαι *I answer* is used to show taking back control of a conversation or controlling it by making an important statement.[38] For example, in Acts 8:18–24 Peter urges Simon Magus to repent because he wants to purchase the ability to bestow the Holy Spirit: "May you perish with your silver!" However, Simon "answers back" (ἀποκριθείς) entreating Peter **instead** to pray that nothing would befall him as Peter indicated. So, is Simon repenting here or taking control and still thinking like a magician by appealing to Peter who spoke the judgment upon him to now pray for him? I think it is the latter.

EXERCISE 3–G: Given Eph 5:1–6 below with all boxed conjunctions, all main or subordinate verbs underlined, and each main clause numbered/left-justified, perform the following analyses:

    a. Depict and describe the information structure in the space at the right.
    b. Identify any word order variations and discuss areas of prominence.
    c. Account for the discourse pragmatic use of the article.
    d. Identify and discuss any emphatic or pragmatic constructions indicating prominence.

5:1 Γίνεσθε [οὖν] μιμηταὶ τοῦ θεοῦ [ὡς] τέκνα ἀγαπητὰ

2 [καὶ] περιπατεῖτε ἐν ἀγάπῃ, [καθὼς] [καὶ] ὁ Χριστὸς

   ἠγάπησεν ἡμᾶς [καὶ] παρέδωκεν ἑαυτὸν ὑπὲρ ἡμῶν

   προσφορὰν [καὶ] θυσίαν τῷ θεῷ εἰς ὀσμὴν εὐωδίας.

3 Πορνεία [δὲ] [καὶ] ἀκαθαρσία πᾶσα [ἢ] πλεονεξία

   [μηδὲ] ὀνομαζέσθω ἐν ὑμῖν, [καθὼς] πρέπει ἁγίοις,

4a [καὶ] αἰσχρότης [καὶ] μωρολογία [ἢ] εὐτραπελία, ἃ οὐκ ἀνῆκεν,

4b [ἀλλὰ] μᾶλλον εὐχαριστία.

5 τοῦτο [γὰρ] ἴστε γινώσκοντες, [ὅτι] πᾶς πόρνος

   [ἢ] ἀκάθαρτος [ἢ] πλεονέκτης, ὅ ἐστιν εἰδωλολάτρης,

   οὐκ ἔχει κληρονομίαν ἐν τῇ βασιλείᾳ τοῦ Χριστοῦ καὶ θεοῦ.

6a Μη[δεὶς] ὑμᾶς ἀπατάτω κενοῖς λόγοις·

6b διὰ ταῦτα [γὰρ] ἔρχεται ἡ ὀργὴ τοῦ θεοῦ ἐπὶ τοὺς υἱοὺς τῆς ἀπειθείας.

---

[38] *Discourse Features*, 231–35.

TERTIARY INTERPRETIVE PROCEDURES:

1. Identify <u>connectives</u> and <u>asyndeton</u> and depict and describe the information structure.
2. Identify any <u>word order variation</u> and consider any associated prominence.
3. Consider the <u>article's use</u> for activation status or emphasis.
4. Consider the presence of <u>marked and emphatic constituents</u> and any <u>discourse pragmatic features</u> that bring constituents into great prominence. How do these instances work together to achieve optimal communicative impact?
5. Consult the more <u>academic commentaries</u> for valuable discussions of Greek grammar and syntax. They will also likely raise and discuss important questions for interpretation. Such commentaries include WBC, AB, Hermeneia, ICC, and NIGTC.
6. Summarize the main interpretive issues and questions arising from these commentaries.

IV. BIBLIOGRAPHY

Primary Survey

<u>Language Observations and Figures of Speech</u>

Bullinger, Ethelbert William. *Figures of Speech Used in the Bible*. London: Eyre & Spottiswoode, 1898.

Traina, Robert A. *Methodical Bible Study*. Wilmore, KY: Robert A. Traina, 1952. 31–49.

<u>Beginning Greek Grammars</u>

Black, David Alan. *Learn to Read New Testament Greek*. 3rd ed. Nashville: Broadman & Holman, 2009.

Croy, N. Clayton. *A Primer of Biblical Greek*. Grand Rapids: Eerdmans, 1999.

Long, Fredrick J. *Koine Greek Grammar: A Beginning-Intermediate Exegetical and Pragmatic Handbook*. Wilmore, KY: GlossaHouse, 2015 and its accompanying workbook. [See the description and examples of Constituent Marking §§4.7; 9.5; 18.4 and CHECK POINT 5.3–6, and the many exercises throughout the exercises with answer keys.]

Secondary Study

<u>Intermediate Greek Grammar Resources</u>

Black, David Alan. *It's Still Greek to Me: An Easy-to-Understand Guide to Intermediate Greek*. Grand Rapids: Baker, 1998.

_____. *Linguistics for Students of New Testament Greek: A Survey of Basic Concepts and Applications*. 2nd ed. Grand Rapids: Baker, 1995.

_____. *Using New Testament Greek in Ministry: A Practical Guide for Students and Pastors*. Grand Rapids: Baker, 1993.

Fee, Gordon D. *New Testament Exegesis: A Handbook for Students and Pastors*. 3rd ed. Louisville: Westminster John Knox, 2002, Section II.2–3, pp. 59–78.

Long, Fredrick J. *Koine Greek Grammar: A Beginning-Intermediate Exegetical and Pragmatic Handbook*. Wilmore, KY: GlossaHouse, 2015.

_____. *2 Corinthians: A Handbook on the Greek Text*. Baylor Handbook on the Greek New Testament. Waco, TX: Baylor University Press, 2015. [See especially the introduction that provides a comprehensive view of marked emphasis and prominence.]

Moule, C. F. D. *An Idiom Book of New Testament Greek*. 2nd ed. Cambridge: Cambridge University Press, 1959.

Porter, Stanley E. *Idioms of the Greek New Testament*. 2nd ed. Sheffield: Sheffield Academic Press, 1994.

Runge, Steven E. *Discourse Grammar of the Greek New Testament: A Practical Introduction for Teaching and Exegesis*. Peabody, MA: Hendrickson, 2010.

_____. *The Lexham Discourse Greek New Testament*. Bellingham, WA: Logos Bible Software, 2008.

Wallace, Daniel B. *The Basics of New Testament Syntax: An Intermediate Greek Grammar, The Abridgment of Greek Grammar Beyond the Basics*. Grand Rapids: Zondervan, 2000.

Young, Richard A. *Intermediate New Testament Greek: A Linguistic and Exegetical Approach*. Nashville: Broadman & Holman, 1994.

Zerwick, Maximilian. *Biblical Greek*. Rome: Scripta Pontificii Instituti Biblici, 1963.

Tertiary Research

Advanced Greek Grammars

Blass, F. and A. Debrunner. *A Greek Grammar of the New Testament and Other Early Christian Literature*. Trans. Robert Funk. Chicago: University of Chicago Press, 1961. [=BDF]

Moulton, J. H., W. F. Howard, and Nigel Turner. *A Grammar of New Testament Greek*. 4 vols. Edinburgh: Clark, 1908–76.

Campbell, Constantine R., and D. A. Carson. *Advances in the Study of Greek: New Insights for Reading the New Testament*. Grand Rapids: Zondervan, 2015.

Robertson, A. T. *A Grammar of the Greek New Testament in the Light of Historical Research*. Nashville: Broadman, 1934.

Wallace, Daniel B. *Greek Grammar Beyond the Basics: An Exegetical Syntax of the New Testament*. Grand Rapids: Zondervan, 1996.

Verbal Aspect

Campbell, Constantine R. *Basics of Verbal Aspect in Biblical Greek*. Grand Rapids: Zondervan, 2008.

_____. *Verbal Aspect, the Indicative Mood, and Narrative: Soundings in the Greek of the New Testament*. Studies in Biblical Greek 13. New York: Peter Lang, 2007.

_____. *Verbal Aspect and Non-Indicative Verbs: Further Soundings in the Greek of the New Testament*. Studies in Biblical Greek 15. New York: Peter Lang, 2008.

Fanning, Buist M. *Verbal Aspect in New Testament Greek*. Oxford Theological Monographs. New York: Oxford University Press, 1991.

Porter, Stanley E. *Verbal Aspect in the Greek New Testament: With Reference to Tense and Mood*. New York: Peter Lang, 1993.

Linguistics, Prominence, Information Structure, Discourse Pragmatics

Porter, Stanley E. *Linguistic Analysis of the Greek New Testament: Studies in Tools, Methods, and Practice*. Grand Rapids: Baker, 2015.

Levinsohn, Stephen H. "Adverbial Participial Clauses in Koiné Greek: Grounding and Information Structure" presented at the International Conference on Discourse and Grammar (DG2008) Illocutionary force, information Structure and Subordination between Discourse and Grammar, Universeit Ghent, Belgium, May 2008.

_____. "A Fresh Look at Adjective-Noun Ordering in Articular Noun Phrases" presented at the International Conference of the Society of Biblical Literature, London, England, July 2011.

_____. *Discourse Features of New Testament Greek: A Coursebook on the Information Structure of New Testament Greek*. 2nd ed. Dallas: Summer Institute of Linguistics, 2000.

_____. "Holistic Approach to Romans 6" presented at the International Conference of the Society of Biblical Literature, London, England, July 2011.

_____. *Self-Instruction Materials on Narrative Discourse Analysis*. Dallas: SIL International, 2012.

_____. *Self-Instruction Materials on Non-Narrative Discourse Analysis*. Dallas: SIL International, 2011.

_____. *Some Notes on the Information Structure and Discourse Features of 1 Corinthians 1–4*. Dallas: SIL International, 2009.

_____. *Some Notes on the Information Structure and Discourse Features of 1 Thessalonians*. Dallas: SIL International, 2009.

_____. *Some Notes on the Information Structure and Discourse Features of 1 Timothy*. Dallas: SIL International, 2009.

_____. "'Therefore' or 'Wherefore': What's the Difference?" Pages 325–43 in *Reflections on Lexicography: Explorations in Ancient Syriac, Hebrew, and Greek Sources*. Edited by Richard A. Taylor and Craig E. Morrison. Perspectives on Linguistics and Ancient Languages 4. Piscataway, NJ: Gorgias, 2014.

_____. "The Relevance of Greek Discourse Studies to Exegesis." *Journal of Translation* 2.2 (2006): 11–21.

Louw, Johannes P. *Semantics of New Testament Greek*. Philadelphia: Fortress, 1982.

Smith, Robert E. "Recognizing Prominence Features in the Greek New Testament." *Selected Technical Articles Related to Translation* 14 (1985): 16–25.

STEP 4

SEMANTIC ANALYSIS

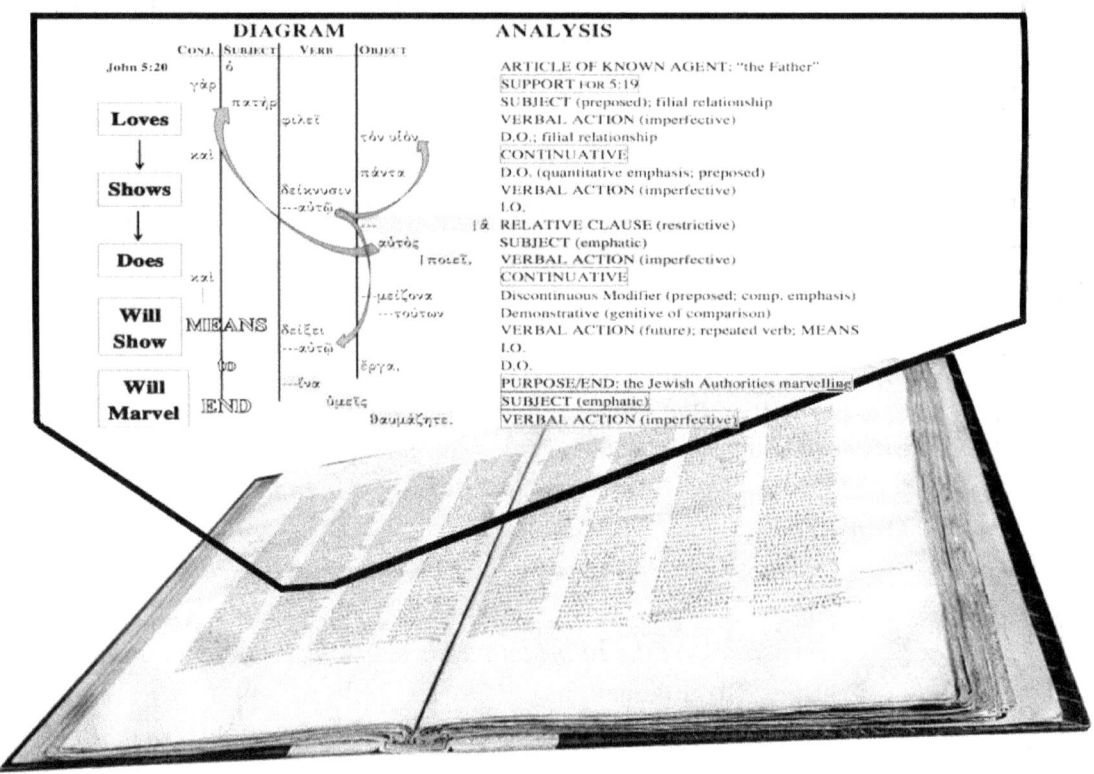

"I know all those words, but that sentence makes no sense to me."
—Matt Groening

"The limits of my language means the limits of my world."
—Ludwig Wittgenstein

Introduction: Moving beyond grammatical study, semantic analysis looks more intently at words in relation to semantic relationships between clauses, sentences, and paragraphs. The word *semantic* concerns the notion of *meaning*; hence, STEP 4: SEMANTIC ANALYSIS has a goal to clarify the meaning of sentence components in relation to each other within the context of the surrounding sentences. One effective procedure for this is to perform semantic diagraming that facilitates close examination of the verses; this is followed by semantic analysis where you consider the meaningful interrelations of words, phrases, and clauses. **Semantic diagramming** involves aligning and layering each constituent of a sentence in order to show the relations of these constituents with respect to one another. **Semantic analysis** considers the grammatical meanings, semantic relationships, and organizational patterns between these constituents. Semantic diagramming and analysis may be performed in English or in Greek; the goal of such diagramming and analysis is to answer these essential questions:

1. *What* are the main constituents in each clause (if present), i.e., the initial conjunction, subject, verb, compliments, and modifiers?
2. *What* relates to what or *what* modifies what?
3. *How* does the modifier qualify what it modifies?
4. *Why* does the modifier qualify what it does *in the way* it does?
5. *What* larger structural patterns exist in between clauses that reflect additional levels of relationships and meanings?

By closely examining sentence patterns and paragraph structure, our attention will more likely be attuned to the most prominent and important semantic features of the discourse as a whole. This in turn will likely assist us in discovering the most essential, foundational "preaching points" of the pericope. After all, the discourse was composed to set forth important points and to speak truth into real life situations. The interpretive principles GRAMMA (GRAMmatical Mode of Analysis) and GRAMPS (GRAMmatical Procedure of Study) are at the core of this work. Also, the principle CAP "Consider All Possibilities" applies.

I. PRIMARY SURVEY

<u>Semantic and Other Relationships</u>: Written discourse (and all discourse) is organized using "relations" within and between phrases, sentences, paragraphs, and sections. Interpreters have described these possible relationships under the various designations like "Laws of Composition," "Structural Relationships," or "Semantic Relationships." Although these relationships were provided in STEP 1: CONTEXTUAL LOCATION, they are important enough to include here once again.[1] The assumption is that all people—regardless of their language—utilize "universal" communication laws to arrange utterance and convey meaning. In other words, "meaning" is communicated explicitly and implicitly in this way. Although these laws do not account for all of the meaning in communication, they convey much. The goal for the "observant" student of Scripture is to become aware of semantic relationships and how to identify them between the largest units of Scripture all the way down to the smallest units of clauses, phrases, and words in relation to each other in sentences. Below is a brief definition and description of semantic relationships.

---

[1] For a historical survey, see Long, "Major Structural Relationships," 22–58.

MAJOR SEMANTIC RELATIONSHIPS[2]

Introduction—the giving of necessary background information that prepares the reader for the material that follows; e.g., Luke 1:1–4	**Recurrence**—the repetition of the same terms, phrases, clauses, or themes; repetition of word family; e.g., "holy" in Leviticus.
Particularization—the movement from general idea(s) to particular ideas. Usually you may detect a general statement that is then particularized; this is the converse of generalization.	**Pivot** or **Cruciality**—a movement of events or ideas to an unexpected crucial point on which subject matter turns in another direction; e.g., King David's sin with Bathsheba (2 Sam 11).
Generalization—the movement from particular ideas to a general statement or broad topic; this is the converse of particularization; e.g., Matt 28:18–20 (Make disciples, baptizing, teaching)	**Causation**—the move from cause to effect, from action to the result produced; this is the converse of substantiation; e.g., Rom 12:1; <u>Key terms</u>: *therefore*, *thus*, *consequently*, *then* (not temporal)
Summarization—An abridgment (summing up) either preceding or following a unit of material *by* reiterating specific elements or themes; e.g., Acts 1:8 summarizes major topics of Acts.	**Substantiation**—the move from effect to cause, from the result to the source; the basis or rationale of an argument; this relation is the converse of causation; e.g., Rom 1:16 <u>Key Terms</u>: *for*, *because*, *since*
Purpose/Instrumentality—a reference to the means by which some end or goal is achieved; e.g., Matt 3:13. <u>Key Terms</u>: *in order that*, *so that*, *that* (possibly; be careful!)	**Interrogation** or **Problem/Solution**—The movement from a problem to its solution or a question and its answer. This implicitly involves causation.
Comparison—the process of showing how two or more items/ideas/people are alike; e.g., Eph 5:1–2. <u>Key Terms</u>: *like*, *as*, *just as*.	**Climax**—the movement from lower to higher and to highest intensity within a passage or book with focus on the highest or greatest point being realized; e.g., the Gospel narratives build climactically to the crucifixion and resurrection of Jesus.
Contrast—the process of showing how two or more items/ideas/people are different; e.g., 1 Cor 14:1–5. <u>Key Terms</u>: *but*, *however*	

SUPPORTING SEMANTIC RELATIONSHIPS TO HELP CONVEY MSRs

Inclusion—beginning and ending a unit with the same words or ideas; this material "brackets" the section and may help to convey key topics of the passage or an entire book. See, e.g., Mark's Gospel and heavens and later the temple veil "torn apart" (1:10; 15:38).	**Chiasm**—discussing topics A...B...C and then continuing to discuss the same topics but by inverting their order C...B...A; so you have ABC-CBA. See, e.g., Mark 2:27 "The <u>Sabbath</u> was made for <u>man</u>, not <u>man</u> for the <u>Sabbath</u>."
Alternation or **Interchange**—going "back and forth" between material: ABABABAB; this is a good way to compare or contrast two ideas. See, e.g., 1 Cor 14:1–5 that supports contrast.	**Intercalation**—the insertion of seemingly unrelated material (B) in the midst of a larger narrative or argument (A): A-B-A. See, e.g., the account of John the Baptist's beheading in the midst of the sending out and return of the twelve (Mark 6:7–32).

---

[2] This lists are slightly adapted from David R. Bauer's lecture notes (1988–90).

These semantic relationships have been identified and discussed in multiple interpretive contexts. First, in the ancient rhetorical treatises of Aristotle, Cicero and several others, these semantic relationships are discussed under what is called argumentative topics or rhetorical *topoi* ("places") for a person to go to in order to help construct an argument for a speech.[3] Second, modern linguistics within the field of discourse analysis and text-linguistics in 1958 took a large step in moving beyond "sentence grammar" to consider discourse grammar.[4] Linguists identified that certain languages grammatically marked meaning at the paragraph level; this development was linked to the dissemination and publication of Inductive Bible Study (IBS) principles.[5] Third, in modern "Conceptual Integration Theory" (a field within cognitive science) linguists recognize the existence of "vital relations" that are meaning making organizing principles in our mental landscape.[6] These incidentally overlap significantly with the semantic relationships of IBS.[7] For example, children are able to make meaning by correlating objects and entities to one another by these "vital relations;" a child can look at a semi-circle with a triangle above it and "identify" it as a boat (semi-circle) with a sail (the triangle). This implicitly involves comparison. Hence, what Asbury Theological Seminary has been teaching in IBS courses appears to be a universal human grammar of meaning making that may be observed at all levels and in all kinds of human communication.

EXERCISE 4–A: Matt 5:13–16: It may be helpful for you to try to identify MSRs in a familiar passage. Below is the text from the NIV84. The following MSRs are present: comparison, contrast, causation, problem/solution, and purpose. Before looking at the next page, see if you can identify these MSRs operative in the passage below.

13 You are the salt of the earth. But if the salt loses its saltiness, how can it be made salty again? It is no longer good for anything, except to be thrown out and trampled by men.
14 You are the light of the world. A city on a hill cannot be hidden.
15 Neither do people light a lamp and put it under a bowl. Instead they put it on its stand, and it gives light to everyone in the house.
16 In the same way, let your light shine before men, that they may see your good deeds and praise your Father in heaven.

---

[3] The correlation of various topical theories in ancient rhetorical theory is described comprehensively in Fredrick J. Long, *Ancient Rhetoric and Paul's Apology: The Compositional Unity of 2 Corinthians*, SNTSMS 131 (Cambridge: Cambridge University Press, 2004), 62–70.

[4] James Loriot and Barbara Hollenbach, "Shipibo Paragraph Structure," *Foundations of Language* 6 (1970): 43–66. They wrote the paper in 1958 (according to fn.2): "It is the thesis of this paper, however, that linguistics goes beyond the domain of individual sentences, and that explicit statements can be made about relations across sentence boundaries. These statements, rather than appealing to style or context, make use of formal criteria" (43).

[5] As related to me by my colleague Joseph R. Dongell.

[6] Gilles Fauconnier and Mark Turner, *The Way We Think: Conceptual Blending and the Mind's Hidden Complexities* (New York: Basic Books, 2002).

[7] Fredrick J. Long, "Vital Relations and Major Structural Relationships: A Heuristic Approach to Observe and Explore Biblical and Other Discourse." Presented Sunday November 22 at a session of Cognitive Linguistics in Biblical Interpretation at the Annual SBL, Atlanta, 2015.

Discussion of Matt 5:13–16: This pericope has three discrete sections: The first two are in parallel with two metaphors (salt and light) and the third section brings the discussion to an exhortative conclusion. Let me describe each section by depicting the MSRs, discussing them briefly, asking questions, and then concluding with the fruit of other findings doing LEXICAL RESEARCH.

A. First Section (5:13): Metaphor of Salt with *Comparison, Contrast, & Caused Question*

1. First Metaphor: "You are the salt of the earth." This entails *comparison* between "you" and "salt." Since these two entities are not obviously comparable, we anticipate an explanation of some kind, which in fact follows.
2. This is elaborated by way of *contrast* articulated as a *question* indicating an underlying problem (how to be restored) that involves a move from cause to effect (*causation*):

"But if the salt loses its saltiness, how can it be made salty again?"

"It is no longer good for anything, except to be thrown out and trampled by men."

B. Second Section (5:14–15): Metaphor of Light with *Comparison, Contrast, & Causation*

1. Second Metaphor: "You are the light of the world." Again, this entails *comparison*.
2. This is elaborated by way of another implicit *comparison* (you are a city) within a statement of denial followed by another dual *comparison* (lamp is to city as hidden is to being under a bowl) and a *contrast* ("instead") that describes a positive *causation* (lamp on stand → gives light to everyone in the house.).

Denial: "A city on a hill cannot be hidden." (implicit *comparison*)
Comparison: 15 "Neither do people light a lamp and put it under a bowl."
Contrast: "Instead they put it on its stand, and it gives light to everyone in the house."

C. Third Section (5:16): Final Exhortation with *Comparison, Purpose, & Solution*.

16 In the same way, let your light shine before men,

(in order) that they may see your good deeds and praise your Father in heaven.

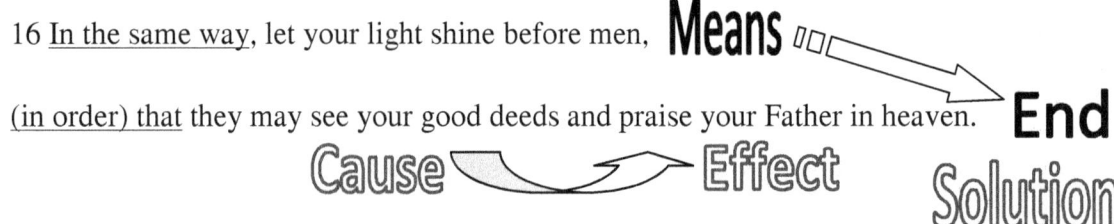

D. Some Interpretive Questions: What is signified by all these comparisons and movements from cause to effect? What does light shining in the world mean? How are the problems of losing saltiness or not casting light resolved in the final exhortation and purpose statement?

E. Further Observations and Findings for Lexical Research (Step 5):

1. The expressions "salt of the earth," "light of the world," "gives light to everyone," and "shine before men" all suggest that a real and necessary benefit is being offered to other people. Arguably, God arranged the world such that grace was to be bestowed to people through other people. No wonder there is now so much misery; due to sin we fail to bless and bestow grace to others. Rather, we hurt each other and fail to shine our light.
2. The two metaphors are elaborated so that they address two potential threats to fulfilling our God-given calling: Salt can become tainted and trampled on (Does this refer to sin and public shame in us?) and light may be hidden (Are we afraid to stand out/be seen?).
3. Jesus likens his followers "to a city" (5:14; cf. Gal 4:26; Heb 12:22; Rev 21:9–10) and carries over the notion of "light" into the final exhortation (5:16). This seems significant, especially since God's people in the OT were to walk in God's light (Isa 2:5), but due to their failure (Isa 5:20), it was prophesied that the awaited Messiah was to bring light (9:2–6), even light to the nations (42:6; 49:6). This vocation of being "light" in the world comes to believers through the Messiah Jesus (1 Thess 5:5; 2 Cor 4:6; 6:14; Rom 13:12; Eph 5:8; 1 John 2:8–10; cf. Isa 59:20–60:3), who is the true light of the world (Matt 4:16=Isa 9:2; Luke 2:32; Acts 26:23; John 1:4–9; 8:12; 9:5; 12:35–36).

<u>Detailed Semantic Diagramming and Analysis</u>: A formal process of arranging sentence elements in relation to one another may facilitate observation. In what follows I present a robust approach to identifying the main sentence, any subordinate clauses and modifying expressions, their interrelationship, any meaning gained, and interpretive questions needing to be answered. This can be done in English or in Greek. What is described below was inspired by George H. Guthrie's text-linguistic method performed on Hebrews (1994).[8] I had seen Guthrie's approach and adapted it to analyze a portion of the classical Attic Greek Historian Thucydides' *The Peloponnesian War* in a masters thesis.[9] Recently, I have described semantic diagramming and analysis with procedures and examples elsewhere.[10] For similar diagramming approaches, see the following works:

- Fee, Gordon D. *New Testament Exegesis: A Handbook for Students and Pastors*. 3rd ed. (Louisville: Westminster John Knox, 2002) [1st ed. 1983]), 41–58 ("Structural Analysis").
- Guthrie, George H. and J. Scott Duvall, *Biblical Greek Exegesis* (Grand Rapids: Zondervan, 1998).
- Kaiser, Walter C. Jr. *Towards an Exegetical Theology: Biblical Exegesis for Preaching and Teaching* (Grand Rapids: Baker, 1981), 165–81.
- Louw, J. P. *Semantics of New Testament Greek*. Semeia Studies (Philadelphia: Fortress, 1982), ch. 10.

---

[8] George H. Guthrie, *The Structure of Hebrews: A Text-Linguistic Analysis*, NovTSup 73 (Leiden: Brill, 1994).

[9] Fredrick J. Long, "A Discourse Analysis of the Tyrannicides Digression: Thuc. VI:53–61" (Thesis for MA in Classics, University of Kentucky, 1995).

[10] Long, *Koine Greek Grammar*, § 16.4.

Caveat on Imitating and Innovating: Let me provide a caveat here. *The goal is not to perform semantic diagramming identically to any particular person per se, but for you to understand how and why such diagramming and analysis is important, and to learn how to adapt this for yourself.* In particular, you need to learn the following:

1. What are the main sentence elements?
2. What is modifying each element (if anything)?
3. How does each modifier qualify what it modifies?
4. Why each modifier qualifies what it does and how it does so in the context of the discourse?
5. And, what are the implications for understanding the passage, applying it, and presenting this understanding to others?

It may very well be that students will make substantial innovations in their semantic diagramming work. Go for it! An important consideration, however, is clarity and repeatability—in other words, could someone else be taught how to do what you did and end up with very similar results? If your work is unclear and not repeatable, then there is a problem—you have created your own universe. So, what follows below is a description of how to perform semantic diagraming and analysis in English before describing it in Greek in SECONDARY STUDY AND TERTIARY RESEARCH.

Sentences, Slot Zones, Aligning, and Layering Greek Sentence Elements: One of the first conceptual landmarks of semantic diagramming is identifying distinct sentences. Look first for the main sentences. Next is the concept of **zones as slots** within which to place and align the appropriate sentence elements. The basic zones from left to right are: verse reference numbers, initial coordinating conjunction, subject, main verb, and verbal complements (including predicate nominatives). These elements may or may not be present; they may be implied in the sentence. If they are not expressed, the elements may be represented as null (ø). For example, the subject is often implied in the verbal ending; or, the verb may itself be implied from the context. These slots are arranged as vertical zones and preserve word order by layering elements horizontally (with a hard return in a word processor). So, students will be expected to align and layer the sentence elements into perceivable *zones* and *relative positions* while preserving sentence word order.

Basic Sentence Components and Zones Slots: You begin with aligning into zones or slots the basic sentence parts that include initial coordinating conjunction, subject, main verb, and object compliments, if present.

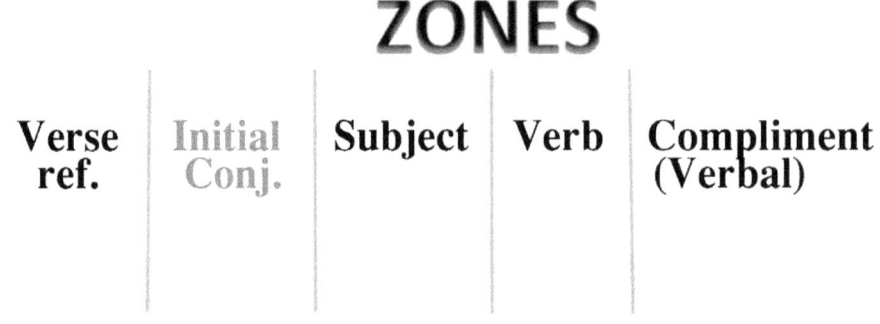

Step 4: Primary Survey

Two further points can be made here. First, it may be advantageous to layer sentence elements in order to provide room to note observations, questions, and other interpretive comments to the right within brackets [...] for each element.

ZONES Layered with Comments

Verse ref.	Initial Conj.	Subject	Verb	Compliment
John 3:16	For *[substantiation of 3:17]*			
		God *[divine subject]*		
			loved *[simple past; affective sense?]*	
				the world

Second, the content of speech, thought, or feeling in either direct or indirect statements is placed in the verbal complement zone. Consider the equivalence of the two sentences below placed in zones as follows (no verse reference is needed).

And	Jesus	said	"something" (= direct object)

And	Jesus	said,	"We [NOTE: Relative Zones]
			   are going
			     ---to Jerusalem"

The second sentence entails direct discourse ("We are going to Jerusalem") that is placed within the verbal complement zone; in this regard it functions to fill the complement (i.e., the "something" that is said) from the first sentence. Notice, too, that "---to Jerusalem" (indicating destination) is a modifier (see immediately below) and so is layered under the verb "are going" and indented three spaces (---). This direct discourse shows relative zones for each clause. In these examples you first have the main clause ("And Jesus said *something*") and then the subordinate clause of direct discourse ("We are going to Jerusalem"). See further examples below.

<u>Modifiers</u>. Then you continue by layering/placing any modifiers (such as indirect object, adverbs, adjectives, prepositional phrases, and subordinate clauses) into relative positions under or above the sentence elements they modify. The modifiers are indented three spaces from the start of the element, which may be indicated by three dashes (---) and helps to set them apart. Students may improvise here, adding lines, arrows, or other markings to help set off and demarcate modifiers. Decisions must be made about what modifies what—e.g., Does a preposition modify the verb or some noun? If you are ever uncertain, leave a question mark in the semantic diagram and make a note. Below is a hypothetical diagram.

ZONES

Verse ref.	Initial Conj.	Subject	---modifier² Verb	---modifier¹ Compliment

Notice that the diagram became more complex. In this depiction there are two modifiers, one adjectival and the other adverbial. The first one from top down is placed on top of the verbal compliment. Why? Because it occurred first in the sentence. After the verse reference, the hypothetical sentence would have read like this: (discontinuous) modifier¹, initial conjunction, subject, modifier², verb, and object compliment. You can always see the sentence word order from top to bottom and left to right. The second modifier is adverbial since it is aligned on top of the verb. Notice that it extends into the next zone. This intrusion is incidental, and depends on how wide you make the zones. For some students this extension into another zone is intolerable; so they will widen their zones in order to try to keep modifiers within the boundaries of their zone. This is fine (good luck!). There is flexibility here. The point, however, *is to understand 1) what are the main sentence elements (initial conjunction, subject, verb, object complement), 2) what are the modifiers, and 3) what each modifier modifies.* The image below depicts the zones with modifiers that receive *brief comments of analysis* in brackets [...].

ZONES Layered with Modifiers

Verse ref.	Initial Conj.	Subject	Verb	Compliment
John 3:16	For	God	--- so [*manner*] loved	the world
			--- so that... [*result*]	

<u>Types of Modifiers</u>: It may be helpful to reflect on what types of modifiers English regularly deploys. These can be broadly categorized as adjectival (modifying nouns), adverbial (modifying verbs or adverbs), and sentential (modifying sentences or larger units of discourse).

TYPES OF MODIFIERS

Adjectival (Nouns)	Adverbial (Verbs and Adverbs)	Sentential (Sentences and Discourse)

o article ("a" or "the")
 o adjective (red, all, good, happy)
 o any type of pronoun (his, our), esp. relative pronoun (who, which…)
 o possessive noun (the ball <u>of John's</u>)
 o prepositional phrase (<u>at home</u>)
 o appositional phrase (e.g., "John, =<u>the mailman</u>, was at home.")
	o adverbs (well, happily)
	 o indirect object
	 o prepositional phrase
	 o subordinate clauses, including these types:
	   ▪ conjunctive
	   ▪ adverbial participle
	   ▪ infinitive constructions
		o conjunctions
		 o interjections
		 o direct address (e.g., "<u>John</u>, come here!")
		
		 [NOTE: It may be difficult to know where to place direct address or interjections.]

<u>Subordinate Clauses and "Relative" Zone Slots</u>: Because of the complexity added by the presence of subordinate clauses, they receive special treatment here. Indeed, the same zone slots apply in the formation of subordinate clauses—but *the slot zones begin at the point of modification where the subordinate clause begins*. For subordinate clauses beginning with conjunctions, the zone slots start with the conjunction; thus these clauses and their zones are relative to the location of the subordinating conjunction. For relative pronouns that modify a noun, the relative pronoun will be aligned under this noun three spaces over, and then from this location the subordinate clause will build "around" the relative pronoun with its own "relative" zones. This can get tricky. Be sure to see the **SUGGESTED ANSWER** for the semantically diagramming of John 3:17 below.

Relative ZONES for Subordinate Clauses

Verse ref.	Initial Conj.	Subject	Verb	Compliment		
John 3:16	For	God	--- so [*manner*] loved	the world		
Relative ZONES begin with Subordinate Clauses ⟶			--- so that CONJ.	he SUBJ.	gave VERB	His Son… OBJECT

We can see above that John 3:16 ends with a subordinate clause that continues (…) and this subordinate clause modifies the main verb "loved", yet starts its zones (conj., subj., verb, object) right where the clause begins; thus, the subordinate clause has "relative zones," i.e., zones that start right where the subordinate clause begins. I like to highlight (in shades of grey) subordinate clauses to offset them from the main clause. Students may choose whatever method they prefer as long as it is clear (e.g., placing subordinate clauses inside a large box, or putting it in bold text).

EXERCISE 4–B: In the space given below, make a layered semantic diagram of John 3:16 and 3:17 using this English translation. Look for subordinate clauses. Check your work against the **SUGGESTED ANSWER** provided further below.

3:16 For God loved the world in this way, that He gave His unique Son, in order that the one who believes in Him would not perish, but would have eternal life.

Ref.	Conj.	Subj.	Verb	Complement Zone
3:16				

STEP 4: PRIMARY SURVEY

3:17 For God did not send the Son into the world in order to judge the world, but in order that the world would be saved through Him.

Ref.	Conj.	Subj.	Verb	Complement Zone
3:17				

<u>Using Paper or Computer to Make Observations</u>: Semantic diagramming should be accompanied with semantic analysis. If you have done the diagramming in a word processor, I recommend printing it out and then writing out your analysis on it. Alternatively, you can embed interpretive questions and observations using a word processor, but this can be time-consuming to draw arrows, add color, etc. However, many of my students have created stunning and effective computer-prepared analyses. Types of observations to record during this analysis include:

1. particular modifying expressions and the meaning they have;
2. significant words or themes for further word study;
3. significant points of grammar, syntax, and usage to be studied and pondered;
4. larger structural observations spanning several verses;
5. other observations that may contribute to your understanding of the passage;
6. interpretive questions that should be answered to better understand the passage; and then
7. conclude by summarizing the most significant observations and questions.

EXERCISE 4–C: Within your semantic diagramming work above on John 3:16–17, perform semantic analysis by adding comments for each sentence element, making observations, and asking questions. Compare your work with the **SUGGESTED ANSWER** provided immediately below.

SUGGESTED ANSWER: Subordinate clauses are shown in grey highlighting. In 3:16 there are three layers of grey shading that reflect three layers of subordinate clauses. Remember that within subordinate clauses, the zones are relative starting right where the clause begins. Absent but implied sentence elements are indicated by null ø and placed within brackets [...]. At the right, observations and brief analysis are italicized within brackets. John 3:17 has more extensive comments.

Ref.	Conj.	Subj.	Verb	Complement Zone
3:16	For			
		God	loved	
				the world,
			---in this way	
Subordinate Clause I			--- that	[*conjunction of result; relative zones begin*]
			He	
				gave
				--- His
				--- unique
				Son,
Subordinate Clause II				--- in order that [*conjunction of purpose*]
				the one [*qualified by believing*]
Subordinate Clause III				--- who believes in Him
Subordinate Clause II (Continued)				would
				--- not [*DENIAL*]
				perish,
				---but ø [= in order that] [*CONTRAST*]
				ø [= the one] would have ---eternal
				[*AFFIRMATION*] life.

Ref.	Conj.	Subj.	Verb	Complement Zone
3:17	For			
		God	did --- not send	[*DENIAL: What God's purpose is not*]
				the Son [*referent identity of Jesus*]
				--- into the world [*location of mission*]
				--- in order to [*conjunction of purpose; relative zones begin*]
				ø [= he] judge
				the world,
	but	ø [= God]	ø [= sent]	ø [= the Son] [AFFIRMATION: *What God's purpose is*]
				--- in order that [*conjunction of purpose; relative zones begin*]
				the world [*recipient of salvation*]
				would be saved [*passive voice*]
				--- through Him. [*agency of Jesus*]

STEP 4: PRIMARY SURVEY   163

Practice and Adapt the Diagramming: It is important to practice and personalize this diagramming within limit; keep it simple and useful to you and those you may teach. Below in EXERCISE 4–D I offer a semantic diagram of Rom 5:10–11 (NASB) with lines connecting subordinate clauses to their main clauses. The main verbs are double underlined.

EXERCISE 4–D: Perform semantic analysis of this semantic diagram of Rom 5:10–11. Subordinate clauses have been given darker shading. Further below you will be able to compare your work with my work.

Rom 5:10 For if while we were enemies we were reconciled to God through the death of His Son, much more, having been reconciled, we shall be saved by His life.

```
10 For
            ┌ if      ┌ while we were enemies
              we were reconciled
                  ---to God
                  ---through the death
                          ---of His Son,
         ---much more,
            ┌ having been reconciled,
     we shall be saved
         ---by His life.
```

Rom 5:11 And not only this, but we also exult in God through our Lord Jesus Christ, through whom we have now received the reconciliation.

```
11 And not only this,
     but
         we
             ---also
             exult
             ---in God
             ---through our Lord
                     =--Jesus
                         =--Christ,
                 ---through whom
             we
                 ---now
                 have received
                         the reconciliation.
```

Some Additional Suggestions and Final Reminders: First, avoid tabbing over since this will cause problems should you ever want to resize your fonts and print your work. Use only hard returns and spaces to align words. Second, remember that the order of sequencing from left to right is this, if the element is present: **verse # | conjunction | subject | verb | object complement**. Third, sometimes because of modifiers these elements will need to be layered on different lines, but try to imagine where they would fall respectively to the other basic elements and align them accordingly. So, a direct object is placed in alignment one space after the verb even if on a different line. Then, modifiers are spaced three spaces to the right of what they modify. Fourth, it is difficult to decide whether to place adverbial modifiers with the main verb or the helping verb. For example, in "they were throwing wildly," "were" is the helping verb and "throwing" the main verb; so, you have to choose where to place "wildly," but try to be consistent. Fifth, modify the method to help you understand the logic and flow of the passage. Adapt it; consider using color-coding, etc. but don't waste too much time learning how to manipulate the text electronically. Paper and pen is fast. Finally, be sure to differentiate the scriptural text from your observations. Below, the scriptural text uses normal type whereas I have placed my analysis in **bold** type.

SEMANTIC ANALYSIS OF ROM 5:10–11

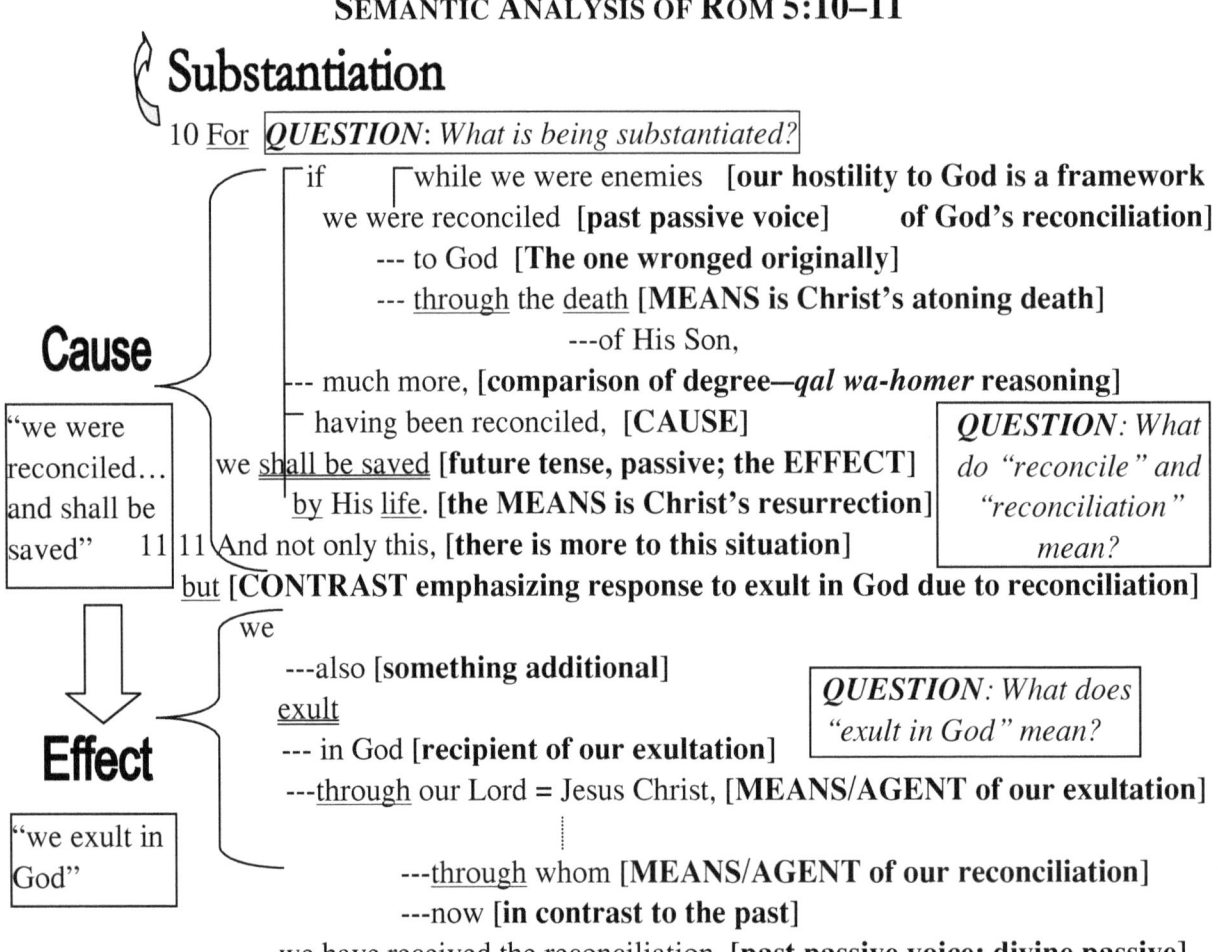

STEP 4: PRIMARY SURVEY   165

Key Observations and *Questions* of Rom 5:10–11:

1. Key word: *Reconcile*. Question: *What does reconcile mean?*
2. Christ is the AGENT and His Death is the MEANS of our reconciliation; his life is the MEANS of our future salvation; thus, he is the MEANS/AGENT of our exultation in God.
3. This reconciliation has already happened, yet some aspect of our salvation is still in the future and this salvation is assured through Christ's resurrection.
4. We are passive recipients of all this as indicated by the passive voice verbs.
5. We start out as enemies to God, but end up exulting in God through Christ.
6. Question: *What does "exult" mean?*

Other Databases are Available to Consult and Compare: With the increased awareness of semantics, publishers are producing commentaries and databases that encode and even display semantic relationships or something quote comparable. However, be aware that when consulting these, you are viewing someone's (or some group's) interpretation of the data and their choice to represent the data: It may be wrong, flawed, or incidentally mistaken.

Logos Bible Software's "Propositional Outline" Flow: To give but one example of the kinds of logical outlines available in books or software, as explained by Logos, "Propositional Flow offers a visual filter that reformats Bible text into an outline that shows how ideas fit together, how the text flows, and how each line relates to the next. Each line is defined with an easy-to-understand label along with definitions for each label. Text is indented to show the flow of thought and illustrate which groups of text fit together." Below is the "propositional outline" of Rom 5:10–11 (NASB). Notice that the semantic relations are given on the left. Hovering over the relation inside the software will reveal a definition, but these are often easy to understand. Verse numbers and lower case letters help to track the suggested connections.

10	a	Reason (9c)	For if
	b	Background-Status (c)	while we were enemies
	c	Continuation (a)	we were reconciled to God through the death of His Son,
	d	Comparison	much more,
	e	Background-Experience (f)	having been reconciled,
	f	Continuation (d)	we shall be saved by His life.
11	a	Qualification	And not only
		Supplied	*this*, [["*this*" has been supplied in the translation]]
	b	Suggestion	but we also exult in God through our Lord Jesus Christ,
	c	Instrument	through whom we have now received the reconciliation.

Compare this outline flow with my example on the previous page on the same verses. Notice that much is missed: the larger move from CAUSE to EFFECT (5:10a-e to 5:10f and 5:11), the smaller semantics of MEANS to END, AGENT, and CONTRAST (that is rather called "Suggestion"), and a few other smaller observations as well as asking important questions. So, learn not to rely on such resources *first*. Instead, develop skills to make your own incisive observations and questions.

Primary Interpretive Procedures: (Semantic Analysis in English)

1. **If possible, put the Scripture text into a word processor for easy manipulation. (But, this is not necessary.)** I prefer to use the NASB since it tries to follow the original sentence structure of the underlying Hebrew and Greek. (This does not make the NASB a better translation; rather, this type of translation is preferred for this kind of work.)
2. **Next, continue by isolating individual sentences. This will not often match verse numbers.**
3. **After this, identify the main sentence and any subordinate clauses (sometimes called dependent clauses).** This will require both that you understand how to locate verbs within the sentence and also that you are able to distinguish between the main verb and a verb used in a subordinate clause. If needed, find someone to help you identify these.
4. **Proceed next to isolate any initial coordinating conjunctions or similar type expressions** (e.g., direct address "Brethren, ...").
5. **Then, align the main sentence (Subject | Verb | Object Complement) into their appropriate zone slots. Don't worry about modifying expressions yet** (e.g., subordinate clauses, prepositional phrases); these will be dealt with next.
6. **Place the modifiers over or under what they modify and indented 3 spaces. Consider using dashes to demarcate this spacing (---). If you are uncertain what some element is modifying, note this and ask a question. You have now performed a semantic diagram.**
7. **Next, move to semantic analysis. In this phase make comments on each sentence element by describing its sentence function and contribution, by making semantic observations, by identifying structural and logical relations, and by asking interpretive questions.**
8. **It may be helpful for you to draw connecting lines, arrows, etc. as well as add other observations around the text to help explain and describe it.**
9. **Look for repeated words/ideas and observe larger patterns of arrangement.**
10. **Finally, provide a summary of your most significant findings as well as any important questions that may need resolved as you continue your interpretive work.**

II. Secondary Study & III. Tertiary Research

<u>Greek Semantic Diagramming and Analysis</u>: Working this closely with the Greek text brings Secondary Study and Tertiary Research together. In what follows you will receive additional helps for diagramming in Greek that are very similar to what has been provided for English. Be patient with yourself since this will take some time to master. Also, you may need to adapt this to enable yourself to make good and clear observations. Study the many examples carefully.

<u>How to Align and Layer a Greek Sentence</u>: A basic premise of semantic diagramming is to preserve the original Greek sentence order as much as possible. (Traditional sentence diagramming does not do this.) Postpositive conjunctions like δέ and γάρ will be layered to remain placed in the

first zone in the diagramming. Another important premise is to align and layer the sentence into perceivable zones and relative positions while preserving sentence word order. Essentially, you align the basic sentence parts (initial coordinating conjunction, subject, main verb, object compliment) into relatively fixed zones and then layer the modifiers (indirect objects, adverbs, adjectives, prepositional phrases, and subordinate clauses) into relative positions under or above the words they modify indented three spaces over using dashes (---) if this helps.

Types of Modifiers in Greek: It may be helpful to reflect on what types of modifiers Greek regularly deploys. These can be broadly categorized as adjectival (nouns and substantives), adverbial (verbs and adverbs), and sentential (sentences and discourse).

TYPES OF GREEK MODIFIERS

ADJECTIVAL Modifiers of Nouns and Substantives	ADVERBIAL Modifiers of Verbs and Adverbs	SENTENTIAL Modifiers of Sentences and Discourse

o article
o attributive adjective and equivalent
o any type of pronoun, but especially these types:
  ▪ genitival
  ▪ possessive
  ▪ demonstrative
  ▪ relative (begins clause)
o genitive noun
o prepositional phrase
o appositional phrase
o vocatives
	o adverbs
	o indirect object
	o prepositional phrase
	o adverbial uses of the noun cases—genitive, accusative, dative (e.g., dative of means)
	o subordinate clauses, including these types:
	  ▪ conjunctive
	  ▪ adverbial participle (including genitive absolute)
	  ▪ infinitive constructions
		o conjunctions
		o interjections
		o vocatives

On the next page is a graphic called TYPES OF MODIFIERS AND ZONES that will illustrate the zones and what possible modifiers may be found there.

Articles: Technically, the article is a modifier and could be diagrammed as such layered and indented. I tend to keep the article with its substantive for simplicity sake rather than layering the diagram and making it taller; to separate and layer it adds more complexity. But you may want to align articles as modifiers under what they qualify, and this is technically more accurate.

Substantives: It should be reminded here that many types of modifiers may function as nouns as substantives (often so marked by the article); as such, these substantives may function like subjects and object compliments. For example, an adjective may function as a substantive (ὁ δίκαιος "the righteous one"), and then function as the subject of the clause.

Sentence Level Modifiers: Such modifiers are sometimes difficult to diagram. Some **interjections** like ἰδοῦ "behold" may function to introduce the whole sentence; as such, they may be well placed in the initial conjunction zone. Also, **vocatives** give prominence to what follows in the clause. In such cases I recommend treating the vocative like an initial conjunction. However, sometimes vocatives will have an explicit referential relationship to a sentence element (like the subject or an implied subject) while also supplying critical information about the (perception of the) identity of the persons so specified. In such cases, the vocative may probably be better diagrammed as an appositional modifier. For example, consider below the proximity of the vocative to its logical referent in 2 Cor 6:11. In such a case I recommend treating the vocative as modifying the substantive appositionally (=) and diagrammed like this:

Types of Modifiers and ZONES

	Sentential	Adjectival	Adverbial	Adjectival
Verse ref.	Initial Conj.	**Subject**	**Verb**	Object Compliment
	◆Interjections (e.g., ἰδοῦ) ◆Vocatives (?)	◆Articles ◆Adjectives ◆Some Pronouns ◆Genitives ◆Prep. Phrases ◆Apposition ◆Vocatives (?)	◆Adverb ◆Indirect Object ◆Prep. Phrase ◆Adv. Case Uses ◆Subordinate Clauses with Conjunctions, Participles, & Infinitives	◆Articles ◆Adjectives ◆Some Pronouns ◆Genitives ◆Prep. Phrases ◆Apposition ◆Vocatives (?)

2 Cor 6:11 Τὸ στόμα ἡμῶν ἀνέῳγεν πρὸς ὑμᾶς, <u>Κορίνθιοι</u>, ἡ καρδία ἡμῶν πεπλάτυνται·
Our mouth has been opened to you, <u>Corinthians</u>; our heart has been expanded.

2 Cor 6:11 Τὸ στόμα
  ---ἡμῶν |
          | ἀνέῳγεν
          | ---πρὸς ὑμᾶς,
          | =--<u>Κορίνθιοι</u>,
  ἡ καρδία
  ---ἡμῶν |
          | πεπλάτυνται·

<u>Romans 3:21–23 Diagrammed</u>: Now I'll demonstrate these principles on Rom 3:21–23. Each sentence will be semantically diagrammed with relative zones, alignment marks, comments, and notes. **Warning**: This may look more difficult than it actually is, so hang in there! Here is the Greek and English text of these verses.

Romans 3:21 Νυνὶ δὲ χωρὶς νόμου δικαιοσύνη θεοῦ πεφανέρωται μαρτυρουμένη ὑπὸ τοῦ νόμου καὶ τῶν προφητῶν, [22] δικαιοσύνη δὲ θεοῦ διὰ πίστεως Ἰησοῦ Χριστοῦ εἰς πάντας τοὺς πιστεύοντας. οὐ γάρ ἐστιν διαστολή, [23] πάντες γὰρ ἥμαρτον καὶ ὑστεροῦνται τῆς δόξης τοῦ θεοῦ,

STEP 4: SECONDARY STUDY & TERTIARY RESEARCH

Romans 3:21 But now apart from the Law *the* righteousness of God has been manifested, being witnessed by the Law and the Prophets, [22] even *the* righteousness of God through faith in Jesus Christ for all those who believe; for there is no distinction; [23] for all have sinned and fall short of the glory of God, (NASB)

Reference	Conj. Zone	Subj. Zone	Verb Zone	Complement Zone
Rom 3:21			--- Νυνὶ	
	δὲ		--- χωρὶς νόμου	
		δικαιοσύνη --- θεοῦ	πεφανέρωται	
			--- μαρτυρουμένη	*[**NOTE**: a circumstantial participle]*
			--- ὑπὸ τοῦ νόμου καὶ τῶν προφητῶν,	
22	δὲ	δικαιοσύνη --- θεοῦ	ø [=*has been manifested*] --- διὰ πίστεως --- Ἰησοῦ =-- Χριστοῦ --- εἰς --- πάντας τοὺς πιστεύοντας.	
	γάρ	ø [=*there*]	--- οὐ ἐστιν	διαστολή,
23	γάρ	πάντες	ἥμαρτον καὶ ὑστεροῦνται	τῆς δόξης --- τοῦ θεοῦ

Notes:
- When the coordinating conjunction καί is not clause initial but connects two sentence elements, the καί is indented and placed between what it coordinates, as, for example, with the καί within the prepositional phrase in 3:21 (ὑπὸ τοῦ νόμου καὶ τῶν προφητῶν) and connecting the verbs 3:23 (ἥμαρτον καὶ ὑστεροῦνται).
- In 3:22a the verb is elliptical (null ø), and may be indicated within brackets in English ([= *has been manifested*]). Similarly, in 3:22b the subject [=*there*] is implied in the verbal ending.
- In 3:22, the adjective πάντας modifies τοὺς πιστεύοντας *those that believe*.
- In 3:23, the verb ὑστεροῦνται takes the genitive for its object complement.

EXERCISE 4–E: Make a semantic diagram (SD) and perform semantic analysis (SA) on Eph 2:17–18 and then Eph 2:19–22 first in English and then in Greek. Be mindful of subordinate clauses and what they modify. Compare your work with my work in the video links below; but understand that I have continued to develop SD and SA so that these earlier video examples may vary in method.

SD English of Eph 2:17–18 http://screencast.com/t/807eNGAtPh4
SD Greek of Eph 2:17–18 http://screencast.com/t/K9caI94KcmM1
SD Greek and English Part 1 of Eph 2:19–22 http://screencast.com/t/pzcAnfb7U
SD Greek and English Part 2 of Eph 2:19–22 http://screencast.com/t/0F6HReZgOBIA
SD Greek and English Part 3 of Eph 2:19–22 http://screencast.com/t/sNiwtqyONuF0

<u>Further Examples from Gal 2:19 and 2:20</u>: Below I offer semantic diagrams and analyses of Gal 2:19 and 2:20. Consider practicing these on your own first before looking at what I provide.

2:19 ἐγὼ γὰρ διὰ νόμου νόμῳ ἀπέθανον, ἵνα θεῷ ζήσω. Χριστῷ συνεσταύρωμαι·
2:19 *For I died through the law to the law, in order that I would live for God. I have been crucified with Christ.*

Ref.	Conj.	Subj.	Verb	Complement
2:19		ἐγὼ		[emphatic pronoun use stressing Paul as agent and example]
	γὰρ			[support for claim in 2:18b that Paul's repentance proves him a sinner]
			---διὰ νόμου	[intermediate agency; How? Paul admits the law is right about universal sin? see Rom 3:1–19]
			---νόμῳ	[dative of reference; νόμου νόμῳ abutted; aural impact]
			ἀπέθανον,	[Aorist tense; perfective aspect complete(d) action]
			---ἵνα	[purpose subordinate clause —"dying to the law" is the MEANS for Paul's END, "living to God"]
			---θεῷ	[dative of reference or advantage?]
		∅	ζήσω.	[Aorist subjunctive mood verb]
	∅			[Asyndeton! Why? Emotional highpoint?]
			Χριστῷ	[Object of compound verb with συν-]
		∅	συνεσταύρωμαι·	[Perfect tense; resultative! Paul co-identifies with Christ in crucifixion; how???]

Summary Conclusion and Key Questions:

a. Emphatic use of ἐγώ draws attention to Paul as agent and as an example to imitate.
b. The abutting of forms of νόμος would suggest a focal point, and "law" as an intermediate means to bring about Paul's death (past complete[d] action).
c. Living for God is the Purpose of Paul's death via the law. How is this accomplished?
d. Asyndeton and perfect tense emphasizes Paul's co-crucifixion with Christ.

STEP 4: SECONDARY STUDY & TERTIARY RESEARCH 171

2:20 ζῶ δὲ οὐκέτι ἐγώ, ζῇ δὲ ἐν ἐμοὶ Χριστός· ὃ δὲ νῦν ζῶ ἐν σαρκί, ἐν πίστει ζῶ τῇ τοῦ υἱοῦ τοῦ θεοῦ τοῦ ἀγαπήσαντός με καὶ παραδόντος ἑαυτὸν ὑπὲρ ἐμοῦ. [ζῶ (1st sg.) and ζῇ (3rd sg.) from ζάω]

2:20 *Moreover, I myself no longer live; but Christ lives in me. Additionally, that which now I live in the flesh, I live in faithfulness to the Son of God, the one loving me and giving himself on behalf of me.*

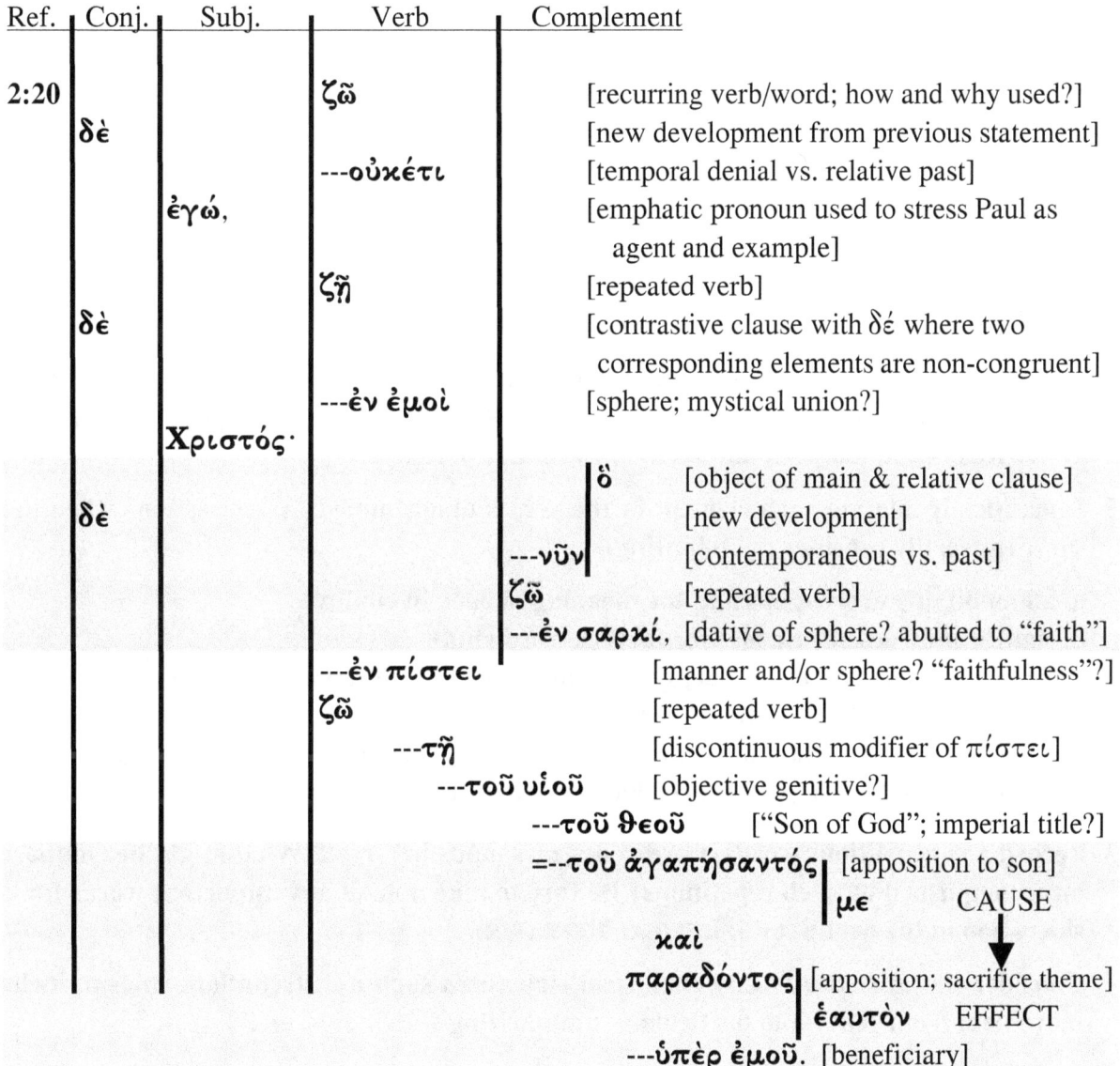

Summary Conclusion and Key Questions:

1. Repetition of the verb ζάω "I live"—why? Why is this important in context?
2. How are the prepositional phrases "in flesh" and "in faith(fullness)" related? Are they being contrasted? Why are they abutted?

3. Implicit contrast between Paul's past and the current "now."
4. The identity of Jesus Christ as "the Son of God" is stressed by the discontinuous modification that then allows it to be stated after the verb as the object of Paul's "faith(fulness)." Also, the Son of God is given explicit elaboration through the appositional description of what Christ has done ("he loved and has given himself" for Paul), which has sacrificial overtones (cf. Eph 5:1–2). Is there any implicit contrast to the imperial title of the current Caesar as "son of the deified one" (Latin: *divi filius*)? Consider researching this in STEP 7: HISTORICAL CONTEXT.
5. Repetition of Paul as referent through the emphatic pronoun (ἐγώ) with the verb ζῶ, the prepositional phrase ἐν ἐμοί, the verb form ζῶ again, and finally Paul signified through the pronouns as the beneficiary (ὑπὲρ ἐμοῦ) of Christ's sacrificial love (με). Why is there such a focus on Paul? In what way would these repetitious references help identify Paul as an example for the Galatian believers?

SECONDARY AND TERTIARY INTERPRETIVE PROCEDURES:

1. For SECONDARY STUDY choose two or three key verses and diagram them semantically. If it would be helpful, also complete the PRIMARY INTERPRETIVE PROCEDURES. For TERTIARY RESEARCH diagram and analyze the entire pericope.

2. Semantically analyze each element in the verses diagrammed. Ask questions when necessary. Especially consider the following:

   a. all modifying expressions and the meaning of each in context
   b. significant words or themes for further word study
   c. significant points of grammar, syntax, and usage to be further studied and pondered
   d. larger structural observations spanning several verses or the entire pericope
   e. other observations that may contribute to your understanding of the passage
   f. questions needing to be answered later to understand the passage.

3. Record any repetitious words, word roots, or sounds in Greek. What might be emphasized or accomplished by such repetitions? Be sure to take note of any important words for consideration in the next STEP 5: LEXICAL RESEARCH.

4. Consider the existence of any rhetorical structures such as alternation, chiasm, inclusio, movement from general to particular, summarizing statements, etc.

5. Summarize key findings and the most important questions that you may need to address in STEP 9: INTERPRETIVE DECISION.

IV. BIBLIOGRAPHY: See books cited above (p. 155) by Kaiser, Louw, Fee, and Guthrie.

Part III:

Exploring Around and Outside the Word

The Interpretive Journey

1: Contextual Location

2: Textual Comparisons

3: Grammatical Study

4: Semantic Analysis

5: Lexical Research

6: Literary Forms

7: Historical Context

8: Scriptural Correlations

9: Interpretive Decisions

10: Biblical Theology

11: Evaluated Applications

12: Presentation Brainstorm

You Are Here (↑ at step 5: Lexical Research)

STEP 5

LEXICAL RESEARCH

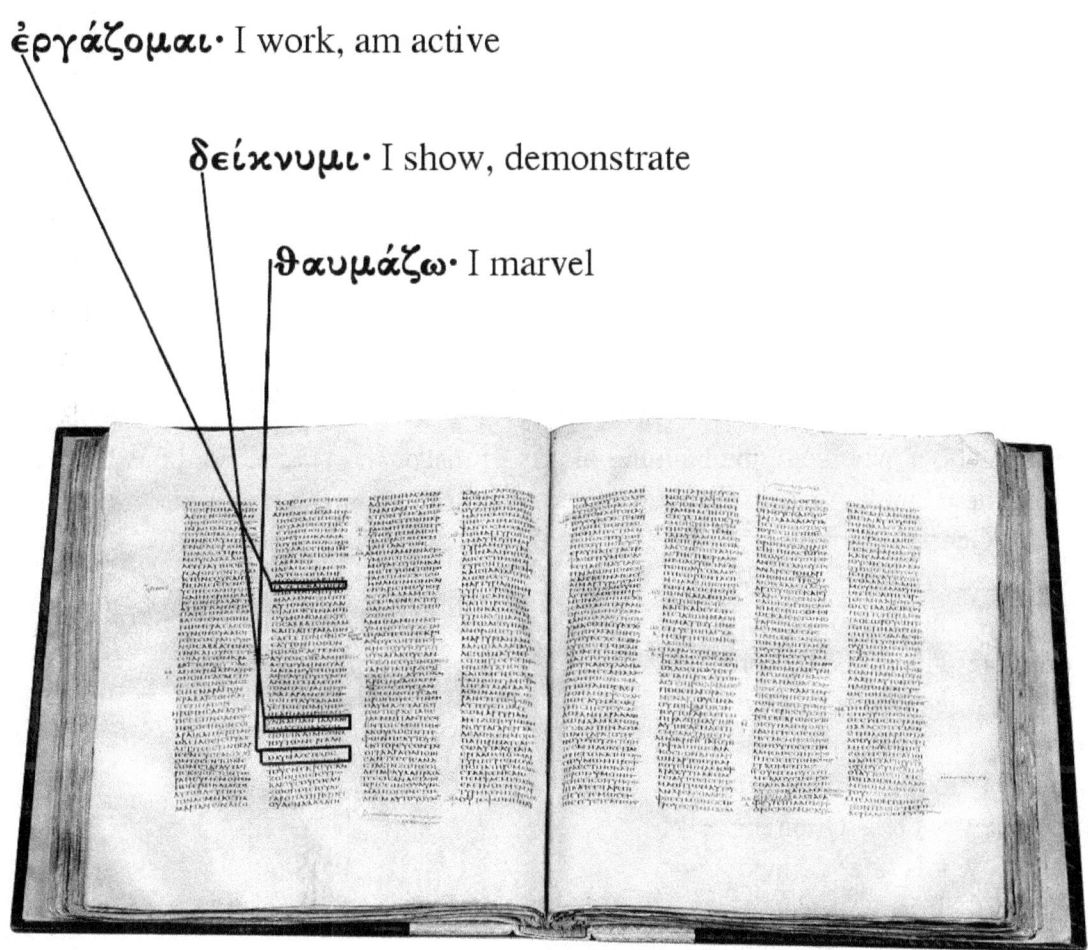

ἐργάζομαι· I work, am active

δείκνυμι· I show, demonstrate

θαυμάζω· I marvel

"But the Hebrew word, the word *timshel*—'Thou mayest'—that gives a choice. It might be the most important word in the world. That says the way is open. That throws it right back on a man. For if 'Thou mayest'—it is also true that 'Thou mayest not.'"

—John Steinbeck, *East of Eden,* from the mouth of Lee, the Chinese servant of Adam Trask

Introduction: God's Word is conveyed through individual words. While every word contributes to the message of God's Word, certain words are more pivotal for exploration than others. *Simply put, studying key words allows you to access to the main ideas of the Bible.* We should particularly study words that are critical for a proper interpretation of any given passage, but also words that have important implications for our proper theological, social, and moral formation. John Steinbeck's classic novel *East of Eden* hinges on and concludes with the meaning of the Hebrew verb *timshel* in Gen 4:7 painstakingly researched by the servant Lee who dedicated years to learn Hebrew to resolve how English versions translated the word differently. He also discussed it with fellow Chinese sages and Jewish Rabbis for years. Biblical authors used words strategically. Importantly, "a word's context must always be the means for determining its meaning."[1] As an interpretive step, LEXICAL RESEARCH attempts to locate and study these critical words in context. In SECONDARY STUDY AND TERTIARY RESEARCH you access the original Greek; this is a great benefit of learning biblical Greek—to be able to identify and research key words. Principles that particularly apply are CIE "Context is Everything," AUNT "Authority of the NT," UNCLE "Unconditional Nature of the Canon for Later Eras," and MOM "Major on Major (word)s."

I. PRIMARY SURVEY

Orientation: Words are the building blocks of discourse. God's Word has been communicated using these building blocks; some words are vital for gaining a proper interpretation and perspective on God's purposes and God's intended life for us. However, we have "blind spots" that delimit our pre-understanding for good or too often for bad. One reason to learn biblical languages is to be able to perform word studies on key words. Often in dictionaries, words are defined using simple "glosses" typically providing the most common meanings first. However, words are used in complex ways with nuances of meanings. Yet, with a little bit of knowledge and some due caution, one can perform good word studies based upon the original languages.

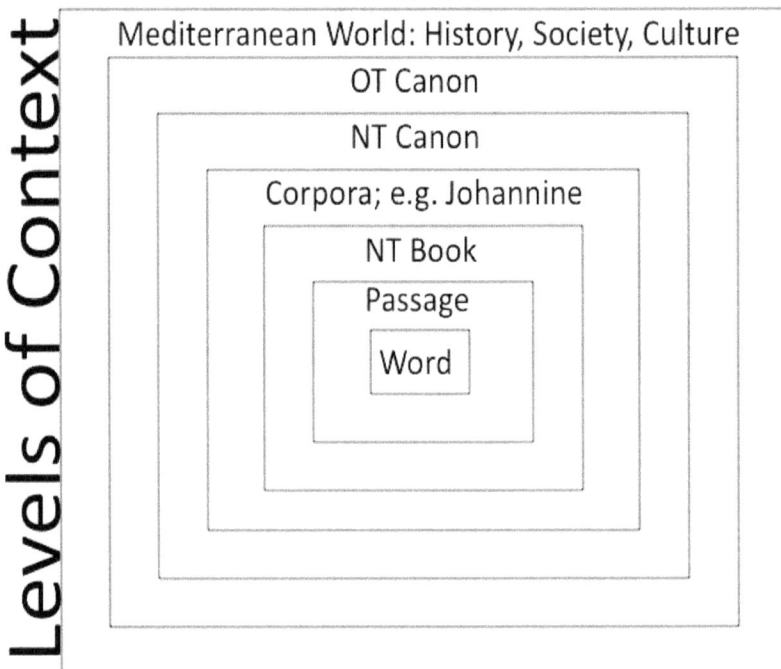

---

[1] Fuller, *Inductive Method*, V-12.

Context is Everything (CIE): *Word studies should be done in context, i.e., the meaning of a word in a passage should be determined by its use in the immediate context.* After all, authors choose words that are fitting for the context; had another context been in view, another word would have been more appropriately chosen. The levels of context may be conceptualized starting with the word in its clause (with or without modifiers) that occurs within a paragraph; then there are successively higher levels of structure within a book. Also, books belong to corpora within the NT canon within the biblical canon that was created within the ancient Mediterranean world and this environment falls within broader world history and the created order.

Words Cohere within a Network of Concepts: In addition to literary contexts, recent research into the rhetoric of communication and the conception of ideas indicates that words are used in relation to other words to form "networks" of meaning.[2] Such networks allow for communicative meaning, efficiency, and efficacy. When one word is used, other words and ideas are assumed or even more likely to be used. Words and ideas travel together. For example, consider this sentence: *Farms are really smelly.* In your mind you may begin to envision why this is true. You may think of cattle, pigs, horses, and manure. These smelly animals immediately populate in your mind's eye, *if you have knowledge of standard North American farming.* But, what if you don't have this knowledge because you think of "fish" farming with tilapia? Well, this may be smelly, too. So, we may miss a significant aspect of the text because we envision it differently.

Let me provide you with a scriptural example. Ever since I became a follower of Jesus, Eph 2:10 has been one of my favorite verses. Let me give you a fairly typical translation: "For we are God's workmanship, created in Christ Jesus for good works that God prepared in advance that we would walk in them." The verse is fairly understandable—it describes believers created in God's plan in Christ to live and walk in good works. This fits nicely into a Christian worldview in which each believer needs to be a good person in the world as a result of God's saving work in Christ. However, upon further research I discovered that the verb "created" (κτίζω) and its related noun forms (κτίστης *a founder, restorer*) were very commonly used to describe the founding of a people, colony, city, cult, religious group, etc. (LSJ 1002). It is a ubiquitous social-political word group. Then I learned that some of the Roman philosophers and political thinkers understood that the "gods" had formed the Roman people as a "work" (*opus*) through political rulers who exemplified justice, wisdom, and performed good deeds (*bene facta*); this ruler was to be followed as an example. In fact, this Roman view of politics and its origins had drawn more broadly from a stock formula of the founding of nations that is even found in the OT (e.g., Deut 4:1–10). So, Eph 2:10 reflected a network of ideas—common political themes—that *we today don't readily recognize.* (See the bibliography and my extensive de-

> When studying words, we need to attempt to re-conceptualize which networks of ideas existed around them that are connected to human activity and space.

---

[2] For a description of such a view, see Vernon K. Robbins, *The Invention of Christian Discourse: From Wisdom to Apocalyptic*, Rhetoric of Religious Antiquity 1 (Blandford Forum, UK: Deo, 2009).

scription below under TERTIARY RESEARCH.) Once again, we need to consider the context of Ephesians where Paul had just described the audience's past of being influenced by an evil political ruler within a social context (2:2–3) and then Jesus's forming a new humanity that unites Jew and non-Jew into one body politic that is metaphorically like a temple of God (2:11–20) and grows together into Jesus the head, the Christ, and the Son of God (4:11–16). Ephesians is quite political.

<u>Networks Re-envisioned and Blending</u>: So, what this idea of "networks of ideas" means is that when we study words, we need to try to re-conceptualize which networks of ideas existed around them. Such networks are not static, but often linked to real, lived-in human experience within time, space, cultures, and society. Moreover, we readily use words of human physical activity to describe non-physical events. Imagine one adult saying to another: "Stop pushing me around!" Words are very dynamic; networks of relations develop, persist, and become a part of our social-cultural heritage often without our explicit awareness. Moreover, within discourse these networks will often "blend" with other existing networks to aide in comprehension of communication—taking what is known and familiar and merging this with new ideas. Particularly with authors and socio-political movements that are charting a new course, these "conventional" networks of ideas will be modified within their discourse, if not even subverted and turned on their head.

<u>EXERCISE 5–A</u>: Below is 1 Thess 5:8–11 (NASB). Read and answer the questions below.

⁸ But since we are of *the* day, let us be sober, having put on the breastplate of faith and love, and as a helmet, the hope of salvation.
⁹ For God has not destined us for wrath, but for obtaining salvation through our Lord Jesus Christ,
¹⁰ who died for us, so that whether we are awake or asleep, we will live together with Him.
¹¹ Therefore encourage one another and build up one another, just as you also are doing.

a. What networks of ideas from human (physical) activity and space have been blended together?
b. What is the purpose of the blending?

Even while recognizing "networks," you should not expect an exact one-for-one parallel as if the whole network were needing to be provided and explained in detail for the audience. Communication is as complete as it needs to be; it is efficient. We like efficiency. So we should pay particular attention to the modifications and "extra material" that are present: These extra pieces of information may very well be close to the heart of the "messaging" and "nuancing" of the author.

<u>Study Important Words and Phrases</u>: Obviously, you should study words and phrases that are critical for a proper interpretation of any given passage. By this point in the Interpretive Journey, you will likely have identified such words. Additionally, you should study words that have important implications for our proper theological, social, and moral formation. We should be willing to move outside our comfort zones and "interest zone." In other words, when doing word studies, be careful not to select the same types of words to study. For example, you may be very interested in eschatology (the study of the end times); however, you may be doing yourself and those under your preaching and teaching a disservice *always* to gravitate to such notions and words.

EXERCISE 5–B: Consider how these phrases are defined in their respective contexts:

a. "eternal life" in John 17:3   b. "God's will" in 1 Thess 4:3–4   c. "fine [white] linen" in Rev 19:8

<u>Word Studies should be done in Context</u>: As the diagram of the Levels of Context depicts above, words are co-related to successive levels of context from the sentence within a passage, to the whole book, to the corpora, etc. Which context is most determinative for the meaning of a word? Essentially, the meaning of a word should be determined in reference to its immediate context. Sometimes words are even defined in their context. How large is this immediate context? It depends in each instance. Although the formation of a word and its history of use in other documents (prior and subsequent) may provide important "constraints" upon meaning (see Tertiary Research), *a word's immediate literary context is most foundational. Also of extreme importance is the social-cultural environment that, however, is more difficult to access and must be reconstructed* (see Step 7: Historical Context). Two types word studies may be conducted.

<u>Passage Word Study</u>: Once having chosen a passage, you may study a key word's meaning primarily from that passage and the book's context. The **benefit** of this approach is that you work primarily within that one literary context; thus, the focus of the study is more manageable (one literary context primarily). On the other hand, a **weakness** may be that your investigation of the other occurrences of the word outside that passage and its book may be influenced by the "interpretive view" of that singular passage. Thus, the results of your study will pertain primarily to the meaning of the word in that one passage and you may fail to recognize the larger network of ideas.

<u>Thematic Word Study</u>: You may choose to study a morally or theologically significant word across the NT and in other corpora (such as the LXX and extra-biblical literature and documents—see further below). The **benefit** is that, after a careful investigation of the word's many contexts, you will have a significant understanding of the varied use(s) of that word. This requires a lot of work. A **weakness** is that such study may be overwhelming and you *may not adequately study* each specific context where the word is found due to the amount of labor involved. Thus, your word study may become in some ways "superficial" and consequently not very accurate or truly reflective of the breadth of the word's usage.

<u>Classification When Studying Occurrences of Words</u>: Words are symbols that refer to entities readily comprehensible by the intended audiences. Eugene A. Nida says "By observing the correspondences between lexical units [i.e., words] employed and the referents they designate, we recognize certain sets of correspondences, and on the basis of these correspondences we acquire the meaning or meanings of such lexical units."[3] Thus, one of the critical processes in word study is study of individual occurrences, but also what else attends these words. At the core of semantic analysis is "classification" that consists of "(1) lumping together those units which have certain features in common; (2) separating out those units which are distinct from one another, and (3) de-

---

[3] *Componential Analysis of Meaning*, ed. Thomas A. Sebeok; Approaches to Semiotics 57 (The Hague; Paris; New York: Mounton, 1975), 64.

termining the basis for such groupings."[4] This ability to discern likeness and distinction is critical for studying how authors use words in context.

EXERCISE 5–C: Given Matt 6:25–34 below (NASB), circle the words that you think are important to study. Why did you choose them? Are you attracted to repeated words, difficult ideas, social-cultural concepts, theological notions, and/or morally formative words?

25 For this reason I say to you, do not be worried about your life, *as to* what you will eat or what you will drink; nor for your body, *as to* what you will put on. Is not life more than food, and the body more than clothing?

26 Look at the birds of the air, that they do not sow, nor reap nor gather into barns, and *yet* your heavenly Father feeds them. Are you not worth much more than they?

27 And who of you by being worried can add a *single* hour to his life?

28 And why are you worried about clothing? Observe how the lilies of the field grow; they do not toil nor do they spin,

29 yet I say to you that not even Solomon in all his glory clothed himself like one of these.

30 But if God so clothes the grass of the field, which is *alive* today and tomorrow is thrown into the furnace, *will He* not much more *clothe* you? You of little faith!

31 Do not worry then, saying, 'What will we eat?' or 'What will we drink?' or 'What will we wear for clothing?'

32 For the Gentiles eagerly seek all these things; for your heavenly Father knows that you need all these things.

33 But seek first His kingdom and His righteousness, and all these things will be added to you.

34 So do not worry about tomorrow; for tomorrow will care for itself. Each day has enough trouble of its own.

<u>Basic Tools for Word Studies I: Concordances</u>: The most essential tool for doing a word study is not a dictionary or lexicon (surprisingly!), but a concordance. A concordance provides all the occurrences of a word in the NT by giving scriptural references and sometimes even the portion of a verse in which the word is found. There are English-based concordances and Greek-based concordances; there are also concordances with English text based on Greek words.[5] The classic and now quite dated combination of English concordance based upon the Greek text is *Strong's Exhaustive Concordance* that employed a numbering system for each Hebrew and Greek word that you could use to study a Greek word. The resource is still being updated in print.[6] Alternatively, the publishing company Zondervan published its own concordance and numbering system edited by John R. Kohlenberger and Edward W. Goodrick based upon the NIV text and its underlying

---

[4] Nida, *Componential Analysis*, 66. Classification is the final step of the process with the first three being naming, paraphrasing, and defining (64–66).

[5] See, e.g., George V. Wigram, *The Englishman's Greek Concordance of New Testament: Coded with Strong's Concordance Numbers*; reprinted (Peabody, MA: Hendrickson, 1996).

[6] See James Strong, *The New Strong's Expanded Exhaustive Concordance of the Bible*; expanded ed. (Thomas Nelson, 2010).

Hebrew and Greek text.[7] Hence, the numbering system is called the G/K system from their last names. What this means, however, is that there are competing numbering systems, editions, versions, etc. and this can be quite confusing.

Now with the advent of electronic media, print editions of concordances have a more limited application. Likewise, on the Internet you may find search engines that contain English concordances based upon an underlying Greek word.[8] These may be limited to the KJV and the NASB (1971). Additionally, the searches may be faulty. Let me explain. For example, one website boasts searches in 100 languages and versions among which is included the Greek NTs by Stephanus, Scrivener, Westcott-Hort, and the SBLGNT. However, you must type in the exact Greek word "form" with breathing and accent marks. You are thus searching for one particular form of a Greek word rather than all the occurrences of the word itself. For example (using an English example), if you wanted to search for all occurrences of the verb "to sing," you would have to search for "sing," "sings," "sang," "sung," etc. Thus, to search properly, you must know alternative forms of a Greek word—but such knowledge requires that you have learned Greek sufficiently; even for beginning students, to produce all the proper forms and accents can be tricky.

Another website has a multiple version concordance search, and also provides Strong's and Englishman's searches for Greek and Hebrew.[9] It contains an interlinear version with active links directly to the Englishman's concordance providing one with results showing all the occurrences of that particular word form (not all the forms of the word), but then shows a link to a complete listing based on Strong's numbering that then shows all forms of the word.

<u>Software "Concording" Options</u>: Here computer software offers more robust searching options on the most recent English versions and the most recent critical Greek editions (UBS$^{3/4/5}$, NA$^{27/28}$, and SBLGNT). In addition to the broadly available KJV and NASB version, the NIV, RSV, NRSV, ESV among others are "tagged" to the underlying modern-critical Greek NT editions. There are a number of software options for accessing and searching the Greek NT. The top three in alphabetical order are Accordance, BibleWorks, and Logos. The searching interface varies considerably between the three; each has its respective searching strengths and access to results data, apart from considering the complete software package. However, whichever platform you choose, it is incumbent to learn how best to use your software. These companies often have video tutorials available online as well as user blogs and live help options. These companies are eager to teach you how to use their software. Also, fellow students and professors can be excellent resources to learn how to use Bible software.

<u>Dangers with English Concordances and Other Concordances</u>: One serious problem arises when we ask this question: What is the underlying Greek text upon which the concordance is based? Is the Greek text the more recently established critical text that has considered *every* Greek

---

[7] Edward W. Goodrick and John R. Kohlenberger III, *The Strongest NIV Exhaustive Concordance* (Grand Rapids: Zondervan, 2004). It has been variously revised.

[8] For example, see Strong's Concordance online at http://www.biblestudytools.com/concordances.

[9] See http://biblehub.com/concordance.

manuscript found, every quotation in the Church Fathers, all the early versions, and all the available evidence? Or, is the concordance based on the KJV-based Greek text, i.e., the Majority or Byzantine text? If necessary, read once again STEP 2: TEXTUAL COMPARISONS. The problem with these freely available online concordances is that *they probably do not allow you direct access to the most recently established critical editions of the Greek NT* since these texts are copyrighted.[10] So, you must understand that when using these online concordances, you are likely searching inferior Greek editions. How detrimental will this be? Well, probably 99.8% of the time it isn't a problem. However, occasionally you may find "discrepancies" of word occurrences. For instance, if doing a word study on the word translated "mystery" (μυστήριον) using online concordances, you would probably not find 1 Cor 2:1, because the Byzantine Greek textual tradition that is the basis for the KJV and some other translations has the word "testimony" (μαρτύριον) instead.

Basic Tools for Word Studies II: Lexicons: After concordances, the most important tool for lexical research are dictionaries or lexicons. These will provide a basic range of meanings that a word has, which is called a word's **semantic range**. One problem in use, however, is that students will be tempted to use the lexicon as *if it were a smorgasbord from which to select a word meaning for the passage they are interpreting*. They may feel quite justified to do this, and the meaning they select and supply will support the interpretation they envision or want for the passage. However, is such a "selected" meaning arrived at with careful scrutiny and weighing of evidence and interpretive options? If not, such selection is rather circular. This may very well violate both the principles of CIE: CONTEXT IS EVERYTHING and CAP: CONSIDER ALL POSSIBILITIES.

However, we must understand that lexicons by nature are limited in their ability to represent fully the nuances, meanings, and contextual significance of words as deployed by the wide variety of authors in that language. However, scholarly lexicons will provide lengthier entries in the attempt to capture some of these nuances. Even so, Daniel P. Fuller articulates the limitations of lexicons very well,

> It is obvious, then, that a dictionary or lexicon can provide only partial assistance in coming to terms with words. Their only service is to show the various possible meanings that a word may have. Even then they do not always show the process meaning a word has in a particular context, for authors (and Biblical authors are no exception!) often impart a unique emphasis to a word so that it can become the means whereby they can communicate the new concept which they have in their minds.[11]

The particular merits of various lexicons are briefly discussed below in IV. BIBLIOGRAPHY. Typically, lexicons are identified by their authors' last names that are often abbreviated. For example, the abbreviation L&N is the lexicon by Johannes Louw and Eugene Nida.

---

[10] This is addressed by Porter in ch. 1 of his book, "Who Owns the Greek New Testament? Issues That Promote and Hinder Further Study," *Linguistic Analysis of the Greek New Testament: Studies in Tools, Methods, and Practice* (Grand Rapids: Baker Academic, 2015).

[11] Fuller, *Inductive Method*, V-11–12.

EXERCISE 5–D: Compare below the lexical entries of the noun χάρις commonly glossed *grace*. The *italics* and **bold** formatting of the entries are preserved. How uniform are the meanings between the lexicons? What would happen if you only consulted one lexicon and not any others?

A. Strong's Concordance: (Located at the back of the concordance proper; very dated)
graciousness (as *gratifying*), of manner or act (abstract or concrete; literal, figurative, or spiritual; especially the divine influence upon the heart, and its reflection in the life; including *gratitude*):—acceptable, benefit, favour, gift, grace (-ious), joy liberality [sic], pleasure, thank (-s, -worthy).

B. James Swanson:[12] (a modern lexicon that succinctly summarizes other lexicons)
  1. **kindness**, grace
  2. **gift**
  3. **thanks**
  4. **good will**, favor towards someone

C. BDAG: (the standard NT lexicon focusing on the NT and Apostolic Fathers)
  1. **a winning quality or attractiveness that invites a favorable reaction,** *graciousness, attractiveness, charm, winsomeness*
  2. **a beneficent disposition toward someone,** *favor, grace, gracious care/help, goodwill*
  3. **practical application of goodwill,** *(a sign of) favor, gracious deed/gift, benefaction*
  4. **exceptional effect produced by generosity,** *favor*. Of effects produced by divine beneficence which go beyond those associated with a specific Christian's status.
  5. **response to generosity or beneficence,** *thanks, gratitude* (a fundamental component in the Greco-Roman reciprocity system…)

D. LSJ: (standard classical Greek lexicon covering literature before, during, and after the GNT)
  I. in objective sense, *outward grace* or *favour, beauty*, properly of persons or their portraits
  II. in subjective sense, *grace* or *favour felt*, whether on the part of the doer or the receiver
   1. on the part of the doer, *grace, kindness, goodwill for* or *towards* one
   2. more frequently on the part of the receiver, *sense of favour* received, *thankfulness, gratitude*
   3. *favour, influence*, opposed to force
   4. *love-charm, philtre*
  III. in concrete sense,
   1. *a favour* done or returned, *boon*
   2. especially in erotic sense, of *favours granted*
  IV. *gratification, delight in* or *from* a thing
  V. For the phrase δαιμόνων χάρις (literally "grace of the gods/goddesses") *homage due* to them, their *worship, majesty*; 2. *thank-offering*
  VI. Various other uses (e.g., as a preposition).

---

[12] *Dictionary of Biblical Languages with Semantic Domains: Greek (New Testament)* (Oak Harbor: Logos Research Systems, 1997).

Limiting the Study Range by Corpus: If there are too many occurrences to study—more than thirty, but this will vary depending on your ability and time available—then consider limiting your study. You may limit by corpus (e.g., Gospels-Acts, Paul, or Latter NT), attributed author (Johannine, Pauline, Petrine, or Luke-Acts), or to a specific book (e.g., Mark). In other words, if necessary, limit your research to the particular biblical book upon which you are focusing or to the corpus of the particular biblical author (e.g., the Johannine Corpus includes the Gospel of John, 1–3 John and Revelation).

Word Study Fallacies: With the increased ease of access to the Greek NT, anyone can begin to study words. From the start, however, we must understand and avoid common problematic assumptions and questionable practices when doing word studies. Before I provide a step-by-step approach for word studies, it will be instructive to think about common types of problematic assumptions and mistakes when doing word studies. For a thorough discussion on this topic, see D. A. Carson, *Exegetical Fallacies*, 2nd ed. (Grand Rapids: Baker, 1996), 27–64. The names of the fallacies below do not necessarily come from Carson.

1. **Part-Whole Fallacy**: *It is problematic to assume that by studying one particular word, a whole concept has been studied*. In reality, a single theme may be represented by several different words or phrases, and the totality of a certain truth/theme is usually not represented in one word. To study a theme may also involve studying **cognates** (words built from the same Greek root), **synonyms** (other words having similar or overlapping meanings and uses), and even **antonyms** (words with the opposite meaning). Lexicons will often be helpful in identifying cognates and related forms. A particularly helpful resource for identifying synonyms and antonyms is Louw and Nida's Greek-English lexicon (L&N) (see bibliography below). To illustrate this point, consider the chart generated by Logos Bible Software 4 on the word "body" from the NASB—the one English word in the NT can be a translation of eight different Greek words, even though the largest pie portion is from only one word σῶμα "body."

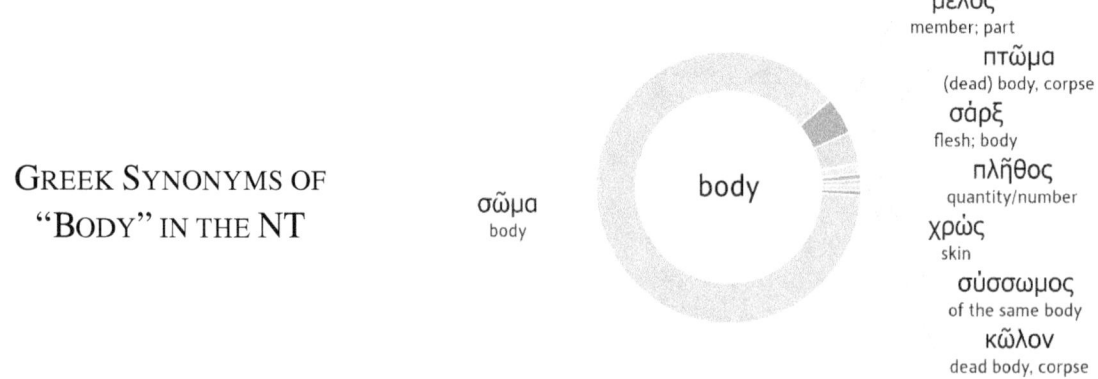

2. **One Meaning Fallacy**: *It is erroneous to assume that a word has only one meaning in all its occurrences*. In other words, some will argue that a Greek word, whenever it is used, must carry the same meaning and translation. However, this view involves a naïve understanding of how communication takes place. We use the same words often in different ways and meanings, even

within the same sentence or document. Even under divine inspiration, Greek words may have various meanings when used within the same book. For example, within 1 Corinthians the word *spirit* (πνεῦμα) by itself (i.e., with no other modifiers) may mean God's Spirit (2:10; 12:4, 8, 11, 13), a person's spirit (5:5), or the prophets' spirits (14:32). So, you need to consider alternative meanings when looking at each occurrence of a word.

3. **Lexicon Fallacy**: *It is not always true that a lexicon provides the definitive list of word meanings or uses*. Lexicons may not provide enough definitions or sufficiently nuanced definitions; or, their definitions may be too interpretive. Indeed, calling for a new lexicon for the NT a century earlier, the gifted philologist G. Adolf Deissmann said,

> The scientific attitude towards lexicography begins the minute we learn that the meaning of a given word cannot always be got straight from the dictionary, that every word presents a problem in itself, and that we have no right to speak scientifically about a word until we know its history, *i.e.* its origin, its meaning, and how meanings have been multiplied by division or modification.[13]

The degree of the lexicon fallacy will depend on the quality and thoroughness of the lexicon consulted. Actually, lexicons normally attempt to provide merely a listing of *the basic range of meanings*. Some lexicons provide only glosses (basic definitions). So, we must understand the limitations of our lexicons. Special word "nuances" are not often listed in lexicons; however, one may find that a more technical lexicon "creates" a special meaning to explain/interpret a unique use in a difficult passage; e.g., BDAG for σῶμα in Col 2:17 (the only reference given) offers "substantive reality" (def.4); better is def. 5. So, we must be very cautious, when arriving at a "new" word meaning, to establish such a nuance by actual usage elsewhere.

4. **Etymological Fallacy**: *A word's meaning in the NT is determined by the etymology of its component parts and its previous meaning*. In other words, it is questionable whether a word's root or the history of use of a Greek word provides the definitive insight into the NT Greek word's meaning. For example, a Greek word's use in Homer (eighth-century BC) **may** or **may not** have any bearing on a word's meaning in the NT. The problem is that Greek words were used over centuries and in various contexts. Remember that the *Koine* NT Greek is but one type of Greek—it represents a single slice of Greek usage across time. NT authors likely were not intimately familiar with a word's root and were certainly not aware of how a word was used historically. Therefore, although a word's root or history of use may be valuable evidence for what a word in the NT may mean, neither its root or its history automatically determines a word's meaning; rather, the word's meaning is most fundamentally determined by its use in context.

5. **Anachronistic Fallacy**: *It is problematic to think that a word's meaning can be transported back from our current English use of a cognate form to determine or illuminate a Greek word's*

---

[13] G. Adolf Deissmann, *Light from the Ancient East the New Testament Illustrated by Recently Discovered Texts of the Graeco-Roman World*, trans. L. R. M. Strachan, 2nd ed. (London: Hodder & Stoughton, 1910), 412.

meaning. For example, the English word *dynamite* denotes something very *powerful* and *explosive*. It would be wrong to conclude necessarily that the Greek word δύναμις carries an *explosive* meaning.

6. **Overload Fallacy**: *It is a common mistake to think that all the possible meanings of a particular word given in a lexicon are found in each and every occurrence of that word.* This reflects, again, a very poor understanding of how communication normally occurs. Every word spoken does not mean three, four, or five things *simultaneously*. Normally, an author communicates a singular meaning with a word. Conversely, the NT authors understood that their audiences were diverse, and that words may communicate richly to different vantage points. Ultimately, then, in order to understand the meaning of a word, we must consider two things: (1) whether a word's meaning would reasonably be in the original author's repertoire of understanding; and (2) whether the original receptor audience(s) would have been able to understand this meaning from the literary context and their shared cognitive historical environment with the author(s).

Conclusion: Follow due diligence and be careful when performing word studies. Allow the evidence to guide your conclusions; keep thinking about the original context and how the first audiences would have "heard" and understood the words. *A biblical word now should not mean what it never meant then.*

PRIMARY INTERPRETIVE PROCEDURES: (Some facility with Greek is needed.)

1. **Starting with a specific passage or as part of a theme you want to study, choose an important word to study.** Consider investigating words that have theological, spiritual-moral formative, and practical social dimensions.
2. **Locate the underlying Greek word and Strong's Number or K/H number in order to identify the Greek word being studied.**
3. **Record the range of possible meanings from three Greek Lexicons.** In addition to the range supplied by Strong's or the K/H resource, look at Thayer's (which is older), but especially newer lexicons that are keyed to Strong's or K/H numbers, like Swanson and Zodhiates.
4. **Using a Concordance, find all occurrences of the word in the NT (not just one form of the word) and record these occurrences by making a chart by author and/or corpora (e.g., Gospels, Luke-Acts, Johannine Corpus, Pauline Corpus, Latter NT).**
5. **Decide on the scope of your research: Does time allow for you to study all the NT occurrences? If not, then delimit your study by corpora or by individual NT book.**
6. **Study carefully each occurrence of the word(s) in context: This can be performed in two stages. First, study and take notes. Second, if possible, organize your findings under headings of meanings and usage.** To study, look at each word in context to "inform" or "broaden" your understanding of the use of this word. As you study these occurrences, record what you are learning about the word. Here are some particular considerations to bear in mind:

STEP 5: PRIMARY SURVEY 187

   a. "Seek for any definition, explanation, or description the author may give to the word in question."[14]
   b. Notice the surrounding structure of each passage where the word is found. For example, is the word involved in a parallel structure that helps define the word? Is it being contrasted or compared with other words? Is the word a part of a command or the conclusion of an argument so that it helps to summarize the previous discussion? Or, is the word part of a preparatory statement that may provide a general idea that is elaborated upon in what follows?
   c. Notice how the word functions and relates to other words grammatically.
   d. Notice how the word is being modified. Is it being defined or nuanced in some way?
   e. Ask questions like these: Are there synonyms or antonyms used in the context? Should these synonyms and/or antonyms also be studied?
   f. Consider how a word's meaning may be developed through a NT book. For example, if you are performing a Passage Word Study, consider how the *previous occurrences* of a word contribute to the word's meaning later in the NT book. Then also consider how the word's meaning is developed progressively in the individual occurrences throughout the book.
   h. Generally, be analytical and discerning of patterns of usage across the NT canon.
7. **Record and summarize your general findings:** Provide a summary of your most significant findings as well as any pivotal interpretive questions that resulted from your work. Consider using a chart to represent your findings. Include observations and insights from the following questions and considerations:
   a. Which meanings are most common? And in which NT author are they found? Consider why. Systematize or categorize the use(s) of this word.
   b. Also notice any patterns you might have observed. Are there other ideas or words that are commonly found with your particular word? What are the implications?
   c. Which passages are most helpful or important for understanding the word or its importance?
   d. On a larger scale how does your word study change your understanding of God, the nature of people, the world, or affect your living and relationship to God, people, and the world?
8. **Determine the best meaning/interpretation of the word in the context of your pericope:** If studying a particular passage, consider how your findings inform the particular usage and meaning of the word in that passage.
9. **Significance of findings and considerations for application:** Having just canvassed the word's use in the GNT, you are in a good position to consider points of contact between the biblical world and your world. What new understandings of God, Jesus, the Holy Spirit, creation, and the first Christians emerge? How are you challenged to live differently?

---

[14] This is the first step of how to study a word in Daniel Fuller, *Inductive Method*, V-12. His subsequent steps, which correspond with some of mine, are in order: 2. Note the word's syntactical relationships; 3. Note the words used in parallel or antithesis to the word in question; 4. See how the word is used in the immediate context; 5. Note the way a word is used in parallel passages; 6. Note the way the word is used in other passages in the Bible; and 7. Investigate the roots of a word that may be found in parent or cognate languages (V-12 – V-14).

II. SECONDARY STUDY

Orientation: Within secondary study, students are able to work directly with the Greek text. It is expected that students will be able to identify a Greek word's lexical form, to locate all instances of a Greek word (not simply a particular form of a word), and to access standard scholarly resources for careful lexical research. Additionally, at this level of study students should be able to identify cognate forms of Greek words that are built off of the same root or stems and decide whether to research these words. Moreover, synonyms and antonyms may fruitfully be studied.

Consider Studying Closely Related Cognates, Synonyms, or even Antonyms: When studying a word, it may be beneficial to look at related words according to derived form (cognates) or according to sense (synonyms and antonyms). Cognates may be formed by *compounding* two or more *different* roots; however, these roots may not be readily apparent. For example, κληρονόμος "heir, beneficiary" is from κλῆρος "lot (for casting votes); allotment" and νέμομαι "have/hold as one's own possession" is not from νομός "law."

Cognates: Meaning across a discourse can be constructed through the use of semantically related words that are derived from the same Greek root. Such words are called cognates. **Cognates** are words that are built from the same Greek root: e.g., δικαιοσύνη is a cognate noun related to the verb δικαιόω. The search for cognates might on occasion uncover a broader association of meanings in a passage. Consider, for example, the οἰκ- Greek root in Eph 2:19–22, in which the stem is found six times in six different words with a variety of meanings. The root conveys generally the idea of "house(hold)" and these six words help communicate powerfully the Gentiles' changed social status of once being "aliens" (πάροικοι) but who are now in Christ "household members" (οἰκεῖοι) who are being built (ἐποικοδομηθέντες and συνοικοδομεῖσθε) into a structure (οἰκοδομή) which is a temple (κατοικητήριον) of God. *However, importantly not all cognates will carry a similar range of meaning, so you must be careful in selecting which cognate words are worthy of further investigation.*

Synonyms and Antonyms: Words that have overlapping meanings are called **synonyms**. To adequately study a broader network of ideas, you may need to a look at synonyms. Additionally, **antonyms** are words that have an opposite meaning. Some of these may be cognates that are built with the same root but with an ἄλφα *privative* prefix that effectively "negates" the Greek root. For example, ἀ-δίκως means *unjustly*.

Finding Cognates, Compounds, and some Antonyms: You should be able to find most cognates by looking in the lexicon/dictionary entries next to the word you are studying that are in alphabetical order. Scan up and down. Some lexicons will provide the "word root" from which the particular word is formed (LSJ, Intermediate LSJ, Zodhiates, Strong's, Thayer's, and sometimes BDAG). Also understand that some cognates won't be so easy to find using alphabetical order because they have one or more prefixes added to them (a prefix is something added to the front). There are many prefixes, but these are common: 1) α- (called *alpha* privative which often negates the concept), 2) ευ- (which means "good"), and, 3) prepositions, which may radically alter the meaning and thus render it less valuable as a cognate to study.

Software Databases: Databases may be searched to take into account such prefixes. For example, the BibleWorks BGM database is linked to lexical forms and can be searched to find cognates using this template: .*stem , where the period (.) starts the word search, the asterisk (*) is a wildcard, and then "stem" is the basic stem before any endings. *Verbs* often can take prepositional affixes (and thus are called compound verbs); the same searching technique will probably yield good results: .*basicverbstem. For example, consider the verb περιπατέω "I walk/live" and how to study its usage. If you know some Greek, you recognize that the περι- prefix is an affixed preposition; so you could then conduct a search by typing .*πατεω in the search string. When limiting the search to the NT, you will find all occurrences of the verbs πατέω, ἐμπεριπατέω, καταπατέω, and περιπατέω. These are all cognates. So, the next consideration would be to determine whether these cognates are similar enough in meaning for you to investigate each of them as you perform your word study; just click on the given references in the hits list in BibleWorks to quickly scan the usage of these cognates to determine this.

Another convenient resource is *The Lexham Analytical Lexicon to the Greek New Testament* in Logos Bible Software. It lists cognates under each word's lexical entry. These and other resources inside software become especially powerful since one can hover over or click on words to quickly access information on lexical meaning and sometimes the occurrences of a word.

Finding Synonyms: You may also want to discover synonyms built from a different Greek-root that may contribute to understanding the "moral theme" or "theological concept" behind your chosen word. Spiros Zodhiates' *The Complete Word Study Dictionary* often provides cognates, synonyms, and antonyms. Additionally, Louw and Nida, *Greek-English Lexicon based on Semantic Domains* (L&N), is particularly helpful here because words are arranged by "semantic domain" (i.e., related fields of meaning). Words are grouped together into broader definitions in lists, regardless of cognate status or not, but also sometimes including cognates so that you can find cognates looking that way, too. For example, under the domain of "**A Behavior, Conduct (41.1–41.24)**" there are twenty-four entries of words. Among these you will find the following:

41.3 διάγω; ἀγωγή, ῆς *f*; ἀναστρέφομαι; ἀναστροφή, ῆς *f*: to conduct oneself, with apparent focus upon overt daily behavior—'to live, to conduct oneself, to behave, behavior, conduct.'

41.11 περιπατέω[b]; πορεύομαι[d]: to live or behave in a customary manner, with possible focus upon continuity of action—'to live, to behave, to go about doing.'

41.12 στοιχέω: to live in conformity with some presumed standard or set of customs—'to live, to behave in accordance with.'

Let me point out a few things. First, one can see in 41.3 four different words that L&N have classified together; if you were doing a word study on one, you may want to consider studying the others. Second, in 41.11 the two Greek words have superscripts that indicate that these words are found in other semantic domains. See L&N Volume 2 for a listing of each word and what domains it is in. Third, in 41.12 only one word is found; but there is a cognate noun, στοιχεῖα, that is found in three different domains (a. natural substances [2.1]; b. supernatural powers [12.43]; c.

basic principles [58.19]), one of which relates to what this verb in 41.12 signifies; so, you would find it by considering cognates.

EXERCISE 5–E: Find and assess the cognates and synonyms for the word περιπατέω *I walk, live*.

<u>Caution about studying Cognates, Synonyms, and Antonyms</u>: In a good number of cases cognates and compounds will not overlap significantly enough with the range of meanings of your main word to warrant further study. In other words, such words *might have a quite different semantic meaning/field*, and if this is the case, they have limited relevance for your study. For example, υἱοθεσία "adoption" is derived from υἱός "son" and τίθημι "to set, place." This latter verb has quite a different basic meaning and is very common; thus, it would likely not be helpful in a study on υἱοθεσία. The bottom line is this—*Be careful: Cognates, synonyms, and antonyms may or may not help your study, but they will certainly increase your workload.*

<u>Expanding Study to the LXX and Hebrew Text</u>: If time permits and you believe there is benefit to do so, you may also track down the use of the word in the LXX, and then study it in the word study. *In fact, if your NT word is found within an OT quotation, then you should probably study the LXX because it translates the Hebrew.* So, your work will now have a broader focus of research—what Hebrew word from the OT quotation does the Greek word translate? And what meaning does that Hebrew word have? But your work may also have a narrower scope of research. Consider the question: When the NT authors use this particular Greek word elsewhere, do they possibly have the OT quotation in mind? In general, then, when researching a Greek word back into the LXX, a student should consider how the NT authors may or may not be influenced by the LXX and Hebrew word meanings. This will require some facility in Hebrew word study. Still valuable, also, is Edwin Hatch and Henry A. Redpath, *A Concordance to the Septuagint and the Other Greek Versions of the Old Testament (including the Apocryphal Books)*, 2nd ed. (Grand Rapids: Baker, 1998), which provides a listing of Hebrew words that lie behind the LXX Greek words identified in each word occurrence by verse. It is a very handy resource. This resource is surpassed by Bible software, such as Logos' "Bible Word Study" reports, e.g., here for περιπατέω.

LXX Usage Graphic for Περιπατέω

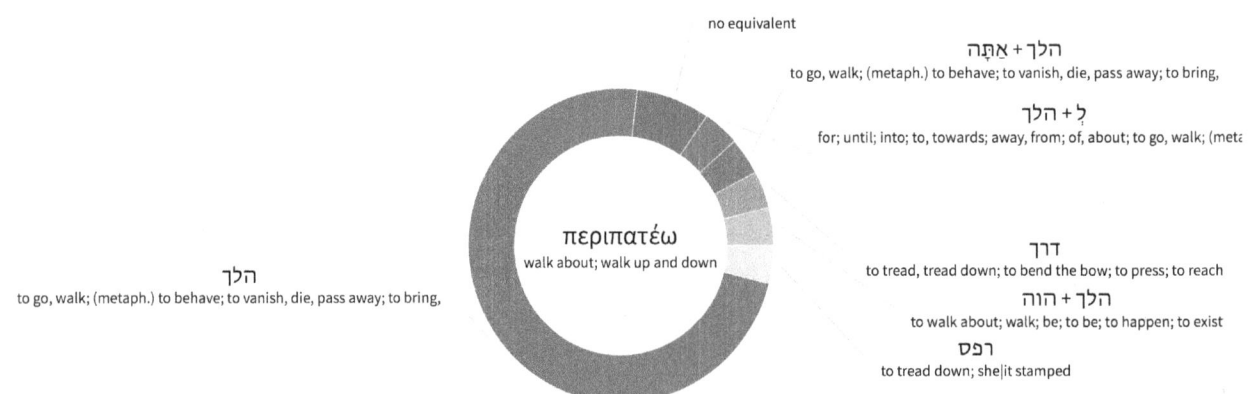

Secondary Interpretive Procedures:[15]

1. **List key words or phrases bringing forward previous observations: Choose one or two most important ones to study.** Consider investigating words that have moral formative or practical dimensions, not only theological purport. Also, for the sake of proclamation in the church, avoid purely "academic" words motivated by scholarly questions. (I have been guilty of this!) Be sure to distinguish between "routine" and "non-routine" words; non-routine words will generally (although not always) be more fruitful for closer investigation.
2. **Identify important cognates and compounded forms; check for synonyms and antonyms.**
   a. First, check whether any cognates and compounded forms exist. If time allows (i.e., if there are not any or many cognates or compounds), then consider identifying synonyms and antonyms.
   b. Second, assess their lexical meanings for congruency with the main word being studied, and then find how many occurrences these others words have in the Greek NT.
   c. Decide whether to perform further study on any cognates, compounded forms, synonyms, and antonyms. Are these close enough in meaning to warrant further study?
3. **Record semantic range of possible meanings.** Within two or more Greek Lexicons (see the list below), look up all the possible meanings for the words (your base word, and any cognates or synonyms that you choose to study). Record these. I highly recommend BDAG (the standard NT lexicon currently) and LSJ (the standard Classical lexicon). These two lexicons overlap in coverage, but come out of two different respective traditions of scholarly focus based upon the subject matter.
4. **Evaluate and decide which words from 1.–3. warrant further study in contextual use.**
5. **Using a concordance, find all occurrences of the words you have chosen to study in the NT and record these occurrences distinguishing each word by making a chart by author and/or corpora (e.g., Gospels, Luke-Acts, Johannine Corpus, Pauline Corpus, Latter NT).** Preliminarily, consider any patterns of location across the NT. For example, is this a Pauline concept? Or, is it found mainly in Luke-Acts? What might this imply?
6. **Determine the scope of your word study.** How much time do you have time to work? Consider working with occurrences less than one hundred times. If needed, delimit your contextual study by author, corpora, or testament (NT with or without portions of the LXX).
7. **Study carefully each word occurrence contextually.** Look at each word in context to "inform" or "broaden" your understanding of the use of this word. As you study these occurrences, record what you are learning about the word. Here are some particular considerations:
   a. "Seek for any definition, explanation, or description the author may give to the word in question."[16]
   b. Notice how the word functions and relates to other words grammatically.

---

[15] If you would like additional help with lexical research, see Fee, *NT Exegesis*, section II.4, pp. 79–95.

[16] This is the first step of Fuller's description of how to study a word (*Inductive Method*, V-12).

c. Notice how the word is being modified. Is it being defined or nuanced in some way?

d. Notice the surrounding structure of each passage where the word is found. For example, is the word involved in a parallel structure that helps to define the word? Is it being contrasted or compared with other words? Is the word a part of a command or the conclusion of an argument, so that it summarizes the previous discussion? Or, is the word part of a preparatory statement that provides a general idea that is elaborated upon in what follows?

e. Are there synonyms or antonyms used in the context? Should these synonyms and/or antonyms also be studied? See discussion of synonyms and antonyms above.

f. Consider how a word's meaning may be developed throughout a particular NT book.

g. Also consider how the *previous occurrences* of a word contribute to the word's meaning in a later portion of the NT book.

h. Finally, consider how the word's meaning may be *progressively developed* in the individual occurrences throughout the book.

i. Generally, **be analytical and discerning of patterns of usage across the NT canon**. For example, one of my students noted that the term "temple" ναός through the NT canon is at first a referent to the physical temple structure in Jerusalem (in the Synoptic Gospels), then applied to Jesus's own person (John 2:21), next "God needs no temple to dwell in" (Acts 17:24), then God's People are God's temple (Paul's Letters), and Revelation ends with "And I saw no temple in the city, for its temple is the Lord God the Almighty and the Lamb" (21:22 ESV).

8. **Record and summarize your general findings.** Provide a summary of your most significant findings as well as any pivotal interpretive questions that resulted from your work. Consider using a chart to represent your findings. Include observations and insights from the following questions and considerations:

    a. Which meanings are most common? And in which NT author are they found? Consider why. Systematize or categorize the uses of this word.

    b. Also notice any patterns you might have observed. Are there other ideas or words that are commonly found with your particular word? What are the implications?

    c. What passages are the most helpful for understanding the word and its importance?

    d. On a larger scale how does your word study change your understanding of God, the nature of people, the world, or affect your living and relationship to God, people, and the world?

9. **Determine the best meaning/interpretation of the word in the context of your pericope.** If studying a particular passage, consider how your findings inform the particular usage and meaning of the word in that passage.

10. **Significance of Findings and Considerations of Places of Application**: Having just canvassed the word's use in the GNT, you are in a good position to consider points of contact between the biblical world and your world. What new understandings of God, Jesus, the Holy Spirit, creation, or the early Christian movement in its life and mission in the world emerge? How are you challenged to live differently?

III. TERTIARY RESEARCH

Orientation: The scope and necessary work of Greek word study/philology greatly increases when we move outside of the NT and the LXX. This vast world includes instances of the Greek language preserved on literature, papyri, coins, inscriptions, tablets, potshards, mosaics, etc. In TERTIARY RESEARCH you may learn how to access, search, and analyse the Greek language historically and by locations across the Mediterranean world. In what follows, I provide a brief overview of some philological perspectives on word meanings in use. This is immediately followed by brief descriptions of the main corpora of the ancient Greek language and some resources for conducting research. Within this discussion I will intersperse examples of my own philological research.

Lexicography Revisited: Increasingly, scholars recognize the need for better lexicography, i.e., creating word entries in lexicons. John A. L. Lee, after surveying the history of NT lexicography has shown significant deficiencies: the dependence on prior lexicons, the influence of translation traditions, and methodological inadequacies.[17] In my research I have found several words inadequately "glossed" or defined in BDAG. Not sufficiently accounted for is the broader "classical" Mediterranean word usage. See below my example with κτίζω "I create." The history of Christian lexicography has "constrained" the glosses theologically, sometimes for the good, of course, and sometimes for the not-so-good. Also, interpreters have given preferential treatment for word meanings derived from the LXX as a translation of the Hebrew OT rather than understanding the broader connections to the Hellenistic world. For example, further below I will argue that our present "church" understandings of σωτήρ "savior" in Ephesians reflects an "individualistic" (me, myself, and I) understanding of the title of Christ and interpreters primarily appeal to the LXX background for the notion almost entirely at the expense of considering the extensive surrounding context of the Greco-Roman world.

Lexical Pragmatics and Conventional Schemas: Within the field of Biblical Studies, Gene L. Green has recently urged interpreters to understand "lexical pragmatics" that explores "the way word meaning is modified in use, and the notion of *ad hoc* concept formation." Studying actual usage and ad hoc concept formation, argues Green, "provide useful and, indeed, essential perspectives for the interpretation of any communication, including the interpretation of biblical literature."[18] Additionally, words in a discourse depend on *a shared cognitive environment* where conventional schemas or networks of ideas undergo meaning development contextually in ad hoc concept formation by way of "narrowing," "broadening," "category extension," "reference assignment," "disambiguation," and "enrichment."[19]

From the perspective of Relevance Theory, words have three "entries" in mental represen-

---

[17] John A. L. Lee, *A History of New Testament Lexicography*, StBibGreek (New York: Peter Lang, 2003).

[18] Gene L. Green, "Lexical Pragmatics and Biblical Interpretation," *JETS* 50.4 (2007): 799–812 at 800.

[19] Green, "Lexical Pragmatics," 805–8; and *idem*, "Lexical Pragmatics and the Lexicon," *BBR* 22 (2012): 315–33. The CAT example is from Green.

tation: logical, encyclopedic, and lexical.[20] The logical entry (the most basic and simple) "only points to the irreducible properties of the concept, nothing more."[21] For example, the furry household pet that purrs when petted would have the logical entry of CAT. For the next entry, Green explains, "The *encyclopedic entry* of a concept, according to Sperber and Wilson, 'contains information about its extension and/or denotation: the objects, events and/or properties which instantiate it.'"[22] This entry is large, open-ended, and very culturally dependent. In fact, the statement above ("the household pet that purrs when petted") is part of a larger encyclopedic lexical entry—it is culturally dependent. Finally, the lexical entry Green explains (quoting Sperber and Wilson) is "information about the natural-language counterpart of the concept: the word or phrase of natural language which expresses it."[23] In our example, "cat" is the lexical entry. Sometimes the lexical entry will entail a whole phrase as in "the kingdom of God" or "the Son of Man."

Example of "Head-Body" in Ephesians 1:22 (cf. Col 2:17):[24] I have argued that Paul deliberately and extensively used political terms, ideas, and concepts to advance an understanding of God acting in the world through the Lord Jesus as political head of the church assembly that counters and even trumps the Roman imperial rule.[25] The description of Christ "as Head [κεφαλή] over all things for the church assembly" (1:22) deploys a well-known political metaphoric schema, already found in some form in the notion of "head/tail" (Deut 28:13, 44)[26] and "head" as "ruler" (ἄρχων) in the LXX (see esp. Psalm 18 [LXX]).[27] The head-body analogy was more formally developed in Hellenistic, Stoic political thought seen in the first- and second- centuries AD (see, e.g., Tacitus, *Ann.* 1.12.12; Plutarch, *Galba* 4.3; Curtius Rufus, *Historiae Alexandri Magni Macedonensis* 10.9.1; Philo, *De Praem. Et Poen.* 114, 125).[28] The metaphoric schema is promi-

---

[20] Green summarizes here the work of Dan Sperber and Deirdre Wilson, *Relevance*, 86.

[21] Green, "Lexical Pragmatics," 801.

[22] Ibid.

[23] Green, "Lexical Pragmatics," 803.

[24] This material comes from my Ephesians commentary research for the new series Rhetoric of Religious Antiquity edited by Vernon K. Robbins and Daune F. Watson published with Deo and SBL Press.

[25] For descriptions of this political background, see Nijay K. Gupta and Fredrick J. Long, "The Politics of Ephesians and the Empire: Accommodation or Resistance?," *JGRChJ* 7 (2010): 112–36; and especially, Fredrick J. Long, "Ephesians: Paul's Political Theology in Greco-Roman Political Context," in *Christian Origins and Classical Culture: Social and Literary Contexts for the New Testament*, ed. S. E. Porter and A. W. Pitts, The New Testament in its Hellenistic Context (Leiden: Brill, 2012), 255–309.

[26] Markus Barth overstates the case when he says, "The proclamation of Christ's resurrection in Eph 1:20–23 is made in political terms, couched in the political language of OT royal psalms; the term "head" has a distinctly political meaning which is not Greek but Hebrew…" (*Ephesians*, AB 34 [Garden City, NJ: Doubleday, 1974], I.169).

[27] Schlier, "κεφαλή," *TDNT* 3:674–76.

[28] References are from Andrew T. Lincoln who supports this background (*Ephesians*, WBC 42 [Dallas: Word, 1990], 69; cf. the discussion and conclusions of Charles H. Talbert, *Ephesians and Colossians*, Paideia (Grand Rapids: Baker, 2007), 86–88. Likewise, dismissing the Gnostic-redeemer position of Heinrich Schlier ("κεφαλή," *TDNT* 3:676–79) and drawing upon references such as are discussed in Edward Schweizer ("σῶμα, σωματικός, σύσσωμος," *TDNT* 7:1038–39), James D. G. Dunn surveys options and concludes regarding the origins of the language of headship in relation to Christ, "Most likely the emphasis on Christ as head emerged, initially at least, from

nently utilized in Seneca *De Clementia* (I.3.5; I.5.1; II.2.1) dated ca. AD 55, written for the newly ascended emperor Nero. As Nero's court philosopher, Seneca described the Roman people as the "body" of the emperor and so the emperor was their soul and head.[29] This usage is contemporaneous for Paul. For example, Seneca (I.3.5) made a request of Nero: "For if ... you are the soul of the state and the state your body [*corpus*], you see, I think, how requisite is mercy: for you are merciful to yourself when you are seemingly merciful to another. And so even reprobate citizens should have mercy as being the weak members [*membris*] of the body."[30] Political headship is explicitly related to power: "For while Caesar needs power, the state also needs a head [*caput*]" (Sen. *Clem.* I.4.3). This is so because, as Allan P. Ball argues, "considered as the head of the empire, the imperial figure was a concrete illustration of the principle of a world-wide Providence."[31] The background of this schema indicates that "head-body" thinking in Ephesians finds nearer provenance, and thus relevance, to the imperial political rhetoric of the mid-first-century rather than to (proto-) gnostic thought of the late first- and early second-century that has been postulated by commentators of Ephesians. Indeed, elsewhere in Paul the political metaphor of body parts of the Church members (1 Cor 12) are placed in relation to Christ as the "head" (11:1–16).[32]

Example of "created upon good works" in Eph 2:10: God "created" (κτίζω) us in Christ Jesus not "for good works" indicating purpose (so all modern translations), but rather "upon good works" (ἐπὶ ἔργοις ἀγαθοῖς), where ἐπί with the dative much more naturally carries this sense of "upon" as the basis.[33] Thus, 2:10 describes believers as "having been created in Christ Jesus up-

---

the first factor [stoic thought], since the Stoic concept of both state and cosmos as a body could include also thought of the ruler of the state or the divine principle of rationality in the cosmos (Zeus or the logos) as the head of the body" ("'The Body of Christ' in Paul" in *Worship, Theology, and Ministry in the Early Church*, ed. M. J. Wilkins and T. Paige; JSNSSS 87 [Sheffield: Sheffield Academic Press, 1992], 160). See also the very carefully argued dismissal of the Gnostic background to the head-body imagery in J. Paul Sampley, *'And the Two Shall become One Flesh': A Study of Traditions in Ephesians 5:21–33*, SNTSMS 16 (Cambridge: Cambridge University Press, 1971), 61–66.

[29] See also the discussion of Michelle V. Lee, *Paul the Stoics, and the Body of Christ*, SNTSMS 137 (Cambridge: Cambridge University Press, 2006), 37–38.

[30] The quotation is from Sampley, *Two Shall Become One Flesh*, 65; the other translations of Seneca *De Clementia* are from John W. Basore, *Seneca Moral Essays*, 3 vols. (LCL).

[31] Allan P. Ball, "Caesar Cult," 307.

[32] See Margaret M. Mitchell, *Paul and the Rhetoric of Reconciliation: An Exegetical Investigation of the Language and Composition of 1 Corinthians*, HUT 28 (Tübingen: J.C.B. Mohr, 1991), 68–83, 157–64 and Dale Martin, *The Corinthian Body* (New Haven: Yale University Press, 1995), 38–68 and 87–103. See also the discussion of Anthony C. Thiselton who rightly concludes: "However Paul may have wished to utilize the language for theological purposes, it would be *heard by the addressees* as language traditionally used to argue for *unity on the basis of a hierarchical political structure*" (*First Epistle*, 990–94, at 992 emphasis original). Ancient support for the political use of the metaphor include Plato, *Rep.* 5.470C-D and 2.370A-B; cf. 1.352E-54 and Dio Chrysostom, *Or.* 1.32; 3.104–7; 17.19; 34.23; 50.3.

[33] This corresponds with "ἐπί" BDAG defn. 6 "marker of basis for a state of being, action, or result, *on*" or possibly 1.b.β. "a marker of location" if Eph 2:10 evokes a construction scene, something built upon good works. BDAG, however, in a less frequent usage (defn.16) lists ἐπί with the dative to indicate purpose in Gal 5:13, 1 Thess 4:7, 2 Tim 2:14, and Eph 2:10; but each of these instances can themselves be disputed; Gal 5:13 builds upon 5:1 and could as easily indicate "basis upon"; 1 Thess 4:7 clearly parallels ἐπί with ἐν, where ἐν does not carry a telic sense;

on the basis of good deeds." The verb κτίζω in LSJ (1002) has as its first two meanings to "*people a country, build houses and cities in* it," and next "of a city, *found, build*." The verb and cognate forms (such as κτίστης "founder") had broad social recognition as a schema, as attested numerously in the inscriptions to describe beneficial deeds to found and (re-)establish colonies, cities, and the like. Summarizing this usage is Werner Foerster: "In NT days the word group is used particularly for the founding of cities, houses, games, and sects, and for the discovery and settlement of countries.... Founding is a task for the ruler, esp. the Hellenistic ruler with his autonomous glory and his approximation to divinity."[34] The Roman emperor easily steps into this role. An inscription in Asia Minor, *Tralles* 32 (26–25 BC) reads: [Αὐτο]-κράτορι Καίσαρι [θεοῦ] υἱῶι θεῶι Σεβασ[τῶ κ]τίστη καὶ τῆι Τύχη αὐτοῦ ἡ γερουσία. "To ruling Caesar of God, Son of God, Augustus Founder, and to his Fortune, the Senate." So also *TAM* V,2 1098 (Thyatira in Lydia Asia Minor, ca. 2 BC) praises Caesar Augustus as "Savior, Benefactor, Restorer [κτίστης], and Father of the Fatherland." So Nero is called "Benefactor and Founder" (*CIG* 3991 in Lycaonia in Asia Minor; n.d.). There are thousands of examples where the verb and agent forms from the κτισ- root are found on inscriptions in Asia Minor from varying dates and locales describing the restoring/founding of fatherlands, cities, cults, associations, walls, etc.

Associated with founding and restoring cities and peoples are the good deeds of rulers who administer justice, bring peace, establish institutions of law, and build religious places of worship (shrines and temples). Thus, Romulus the founder of Rome, bringing peace out of war and providing "equal laws" (*aequata...iura*), places "the Roman State upon a strong foundation" (*fundamine mango res Romana*; Ovid *Metamorph.* 14.805–9). Julius Caesar performed "civic deeds" (*domi gestae*) "in war and peace;" but his "greater work" (*maius opus*) was providing his son, the emperor Augustus, "ruler of matters for the human race" (*praeses rerum humano generi*; Ovid *Metamorph.* 15.745–59). Augustus performs "services" (*merita*; 15.838) and "good deeds" (*bene facta*; 15.850, cf. 15.758–59); Augustus left us his *Res Gestae* "Deeds of Accomplishment" in thirty-five paragraphs as a memorial upon his death (AD 14) in several locales (Rome, Ancyra the capital city of Anatolia, Apollonia and Antioch in Pisidia). Virgil's unidentified and hoped for "messiah" in *Eclogues* 4.46–54 was addressed as the "dear offspring of the gods, mighty descendent of Jupiter," who by "the fixed will of Destiny" will usher in the golden age through his praiseworthy "deeds" (*facta*). Earlier than each of these texts, however, was Cicero's summary of who

---

and the ἐπί with the dative in 2 Tim 2:14 more likely supports (meaning "because of") the previous ἐπί clause "do not wrangle with words which is no use *because of* the ruin of those hearing." However, G. H. R. Horsley indicates that there are uses of ἐπί ἀγαθοῖς in letters in the context of prefectural visits, which have a seemingly telic force (*New Documents Illustrating Early Christianity: A Review of the Greek Inscriptions and Papyri Published in 1976*, vol. 1 [North Ryde, Australia: Macquarie University, 1981], 46). But these involve a sufficiently different context than in Eph 2:10 with "founding" (κτίζω) working with ἐπί ("upon"). Also, in the LXX the only three instances of ἐπί with ἔργον in the dative supports this interpretation: Ps 103:31 (LXX) "the Lord will rejoice in his good things" (on the basis of; because of); Isa 17:8 "they will in no way trust in their altars, nor in the works of their hands" (on the basis of); Sir 39:14 "bless the Lord for all his works" (i.e., on the basis of/because of).

[34] Foerster "κτίζω κτλ," *TDNT* 3:1025–6.

qualifies for entry into the heavenly abodes: those who perform "beneficial services for the fatherland" (*bene meritis de patria*; VI.24.26) and "the best tasks ... for the safety of the fatherland" (*opitmae curae de salute patriae*; *Rep.* VI.26.29). It is partly on the basis of the Gospels' recording the "good deeds" of Jesus that they are identified as ancient biographies (*Bioi*) that highlighted the deeds of important (often political) figures—such works served the civic purpose of promoting imitative courage, wisdom, and piety for the greater good.[35]

This evidence suggests that Eph 2:10 develops a schema of founding an institution with a network of ideas as it describes God's founding activity of Christ's church body, His *magnum opus* "best work." Commonly, the founding of people groups and cities involved the notable exemplary conduct of a political head, the King and lawgiver, who through "good deeds" established the community. In Ephesians Christ accomplished good deeds of forgiveness and loving sacrifice (see 2:13–17; 4:32–5:2; 5:23–27). Yet, a transformation has occurred, an enrichment, since Christ abolishes the law (2:13–14), yet becomes the "standard measure" of maturity for the body (4:13, 20–24). God's people, Christ's church body, are expected to walk in such deeds as Christ has modeled for them.

Further Philological Reflections on Word Meanings: I submit these thoughts, questions, and ideas tentatively for further reflection on how words gain meaning and how we might discover such meaning in biblical usage. These reflections may be inadequate and are certainly incomplete, yet I offer them as fruitful areas to consider for research. The discussion proceeds progressively and historically from word derivation to the history of interpretation and then to contemporaneous research tools. In this regard, the last three items below (H., I., and J.) describe a first, second, and third step workflow for philological research. We must remember that word meaning is constrained and properly determined primarily by a consideration of contextual usage (E.)

A. ***Etymology***: Concerns the building blocks of the Greek word (root, stem, affixes).
  1. Not infrequently a word's etymology may be debatable; see, e.g., ἀνακεφαλαιόω which may be understood as derived from κεφάλαιον ("main point") or κεφαλή ("head").[36]
  2. Also, there is too often the fallacy of thinking that the word's meaning is equal to the sum of its parts. Words are used so commonly and reflexively that such parts are often forgotten.
  3. And yet, ancient philosophers and "commentators" were at times cognizant of word roots and attempted to explain the meaning of words, sometimes quite allegorically, based upon supposed etymological derivations. This is seen especially in the extant scholia, i.e., commentaries on ancient texts such as Homer, Hesiod, Pindar, Aristophanes, and a few others.

B. ***Prior Historical Usage***: Concerns how words were used historically prior to biblical usage.
  1. First, we don't have every instance of a word's use recorded. What we have mainly are literary sources often reflective of the educated elite and the social upper classes, as seen in literature, literary papyri, inscriptions, coinage, etc. How might these differ from oral usages of

---

[35] Warren Carter discusses the concept of "great deeds" as a feature of *bioi* in relation to John's Gospel (*John and Empire: Initial Explorations* [New York: T&T Clark, 2008], 137–39).

[36] For discussion, see Hoehner, *Ephesians: An Exegetical Commentary* (Grand Rapids: Baker, 2002), 220–21.

the common person, of which we have much less material, i.e., the documentary papyri?
   2. Yet, even these socially elite uses may have trickled down to more common usage and could be evident in NT usage.
   3. Consider whether particular NT authors had access to earlier traditions of word usage. For example, even though Homeric writings date to the eighth-century, these works continued to be used in Greco-Roman education in the NT era. See also Contemporaneous Usage below.
C. *Contemporaneous Usage*: Concerns usage inside and outside the NT documents.
   1. Consider locations. Are sources found in the same location?
   2. Are there thematic relationships between the NT authors? What might this signify? An emerging Christian intellectual/literary scribal culture?
   3. Consider whether the Greek word might relate to or be translated from another contemporaneous language such as Aramaic, Hebrew, or Latin.
   4. Consider whether it is likely that the NT author would draw on this or that ancient source or on contemporaneous sources that might have used these ancient sources.
   5. Consider Intertextuality. See Richard B. Hays's seven criteria of intertextuality in *Echoes of Scripture in the Letters of Paul* that are discussed in STEP 8: SCRIPTURAL CORRELATIONS.
D. *Authorial Usage*: Concerns a word's use elsewhere by an author or in a closely related corpus.
   1. Is the word or related words used elsewhere by the author or in their corpus of writings?
   2. Is the word defined there anywhere? How are these uses across the corpus related in sense?
   3. If there are (quite significant) differences of meaning, might these differences result from the respective contexts of each word's occurrence?
E. *Contextual Usage*: Concerns the word's usage in the immediate context and in the entire book.
   1. Consider progressive use of the word throughout the discourse.
   2. Notice how the word functions and relates to other words grammatically.
   3. Notice how the word is being modified. Is it being defined or nuanced in some way?
   4. Notice the surrounding structure of each passage where the word is found. For example, is the word involved in a parallel structure that helps to define the word? Is it being contrasted or compared with other words? Is the word a part of a command or the conclusion of an argument so that it summarizes the previous discussion? Or, is the word part of a preparatory statement that provides a general idea that is elaborated upon in what follows?
   5. Consider whether there are synonyms or antonyms used in the context. Should these synonyms and/or antonyms also be studied? See discussion of synonyms and antonyms above.
   6. Consider how a word's meaning may have developed throughout a particular NT book.
   7. Also consider how the *previous occurrences* of a word contribute to the word's meaning in a later portion of the NT book.
   8. Finally, consider how the word's meaning may be *progressively developed* in the individual occurrences throughout the book.
F. *Subsequent Usage*: Concerns how a word was used in subsequent occurrences in history.
   1. Where and in what distribution is the word found in subsequent usage? Is this a unique Chris-

tian word found mainly or exclusively in the Church Fathers and commentators of Scripture, or does the word continue to have broader usage in the Greco-Roman world?
2. What relationship does the word's subsequent usage have to its prior usage?
3. Is there an aspect of meaning that is preserved by later writers or interpreters? For example, St. John Chrysostom compares the seal of the Holy Spirit with the seal soldiers received as a tattoo (possibly, SPQR= *Senatus Populusque Romanus*); "καθάπερ γὰρ στρατιώταις σφραγίς, οὕτω καὶ τοῖς πιστοῖς τὸ πνεῦμα ἐπιτίθεται [trans. "For just as a seal for soldiers, thus also the Spirit is set {as a sign} for believers" *Homily* on 2 Cor 3:7]. Might this indicate something of Paul's use of "sealed" in Eph 1:13, since he speaks of the collective body of believers as an army (cf. Eph 6:10–20)?

G. *Interpretation of Others*: Concerns how interpreters of Scripture have understood the word.
  1. How has the word been understood across church history?
  2. How has the word been more recently understood in modern/contemporaneous scholarship?

H. *Lexicons*: Concerns how Greek lexicographers have defined and described Greek words. Here we have in mind the major Greek Lexicons: BDAG, LSJ, L&N, and Thayer's (although dated).
  1. These are a "First Stop" when considering a word's possible range of meaning.
  2. Lexicons will often try to take into account the above considerations by looking at a word's broader usage.
  3. However, lexicons are fallible. It is often wrongly thought that interpreters need only appeal to a meaning cited in the lexicon to decide an interpretive matter. However, not all word occurrences are (equally) considered.
  4. Avoid the common "overload fallacy" in which it is thought that every instance of a word carries with it all the lexical meanings of that word.
  5. Remember to consider the localized rhetorical contexts of the NT book under investigation.
  6. Also remember that words are often used in context within networks of ideas.

I. *Theological and Exegetical Dictionaries and Specialized Studies*: Concerns more expansive treatments of (select) NT words often in multiple volumes. See the list immediately below.
  1. Such works are a "Second Stop" but well worth it.
  2. You will notice in BDAG, for example, that articles from these reference works will be cited in support of this or that lexical entry or specialized usage. It has been nearly two decades since BDAG (2000) has been edited and printed; so, there are many important articles and essays written that advance our understanding of word meanings.
  3. Theological Lexicons are usually multi-volume works often with multiple contributors. These are typically concerned with all the areas discussed above in their surveys of word usage in secular, biblical, and patristic eras. The last three listed below investigate especially the Greek inscriptions and other archeological finds.

     a. Gerhard Kittel, ed., ten volume *Theological Dictionary of the NT* (*TDNT*)
     b. Colin Brown, ed., three volume *New International Dictionary of NT Theology* (*NIDNTT*)
     c. H. Balz and G. Schneider, eds., three volume *Exegetical Dictionary of the NT* (*EDNT*)

d. Ceslas Spicq, three volume *Theological Lexicon of the NT* (*TLNT*)
e. James H. Moulton and George Milligan, *Vocabulary of the Greek NT* (MM)
f. G. Adolf Deissmann, *Bible Studies* and *Light from the Ancient East*.

J. **Electronic and Internet Databases for Searching Use of Terms in History**: These are a "Third Stop" for primary database researching, but time consuming and yet quite necessary and often quite fruitful. Indeed, much research is still needed across and between these databases to gain a rich understanding of the social-cultural-political-religious nature of NT vocabulary.

Perseus: One website that is attempting to link several types of ancient texts and artifacts together is the Perseus Project located at www.perseus.tufts.edu. As stated, the opening statement of the Mission of Perseus is as follows: "Our larger mission is to make the full record of humanity —linguistic sources, physical artifacts, historical spaces—as intellectually accessible as possible to every human being, regardless of linguistic or cultural background."

Greek Literature: The *Thesaurus Linguae Graecae* (TLG): The TLG is a repository database of all extant Greek literature from Homer (ca. eighth-century BC) through to the fall of Byzantium in AD 1453. It contains over 12,000 entries and offers limited free access and paid subscription access to the full database (individuals or institutions).[37] I cannot stress enough the immense importance of this database that continues to improve features and search capabilities. Many a dissertation's research has depended on the TLG.[38] The TLG formerly was made available on CDs; the last ones were TLG-Disk D and TLG-Disk E that you could then access through a software interface. A particularly helpful interface is called Diogenes that when connected to the internet provides parsing of words through the Perseus website engine and also the complete LSJ lexicon.[39] Combining parsing and lexical help within one interface is incredibly helpful. Also, Diogenes can house several other databases for searching and researching: The Coptic NT, a limited and out-dated inscriptional database that is surpassed by the online PHI Searchable Inscriptions database (see description below), and the Latin Literature equivalent to the TLG.

Latin Literature: The PHI Searchable Latin Database: If your research extends into Roman writers and the Latin language, you have access to the Latin equivalent to the TLG funded by the Packard Humanities Institute. It is located here: http://latin.packhum.org. You must first agree to the terms of use. At one point the Latin database was available as a CD (the PHI CD 5 database; updatable to 5.3). This database integrates also with Diogenes.

Greek and Latin Inscriptions (Epigraphy): Preserving honorific decrees and other civic records (e.g., rules of the association), inscriptions or epigraphy is an important area of research for NT and Classical studies. Frederick W. Danker—editor of BDAG—earlier, after his careful and detailed lexico-grammatical study of "official and semi-official" inscriptions concerning benefac-

---

[37] http://stephanus.tlg.uci.edu.

[38] For myself, the TLG database was instrumental to research the ancient Greek rhetorical tradition, specifically, forensic rhetoric in my published dissertation *Ancient Rhetoric and Paul's Apology*.

[39] http://www.dur.ac.uk/p.j.heslin/Software/Diogenes. Diogenes was created by P. J. Heslin,

tion, argues, "To do hermeneutical justice, then, to public documents like those found in the Pauline corpus—including even Philemon—it is necessary to interpret them first of all in the light of linguistic data that would have been available to the larger public and which would have provided the necessary semantic field for understanding the argument of a versatile communicator like Paul...."[40] Of particular note, Danker concluded, "No document in the New Testament bears such close resemblance in its periodic style to the rhetoric of inscriptions associated with Asia Minor as does the letter to the Ephesians."[41] There are a number of online searching sites; what is provided below is not comprehensive.

1. *PHI Searchable Inscriptional Database*: The PHI Searchable Inscriptional Database is an incredible resource funded by the Packard Humanities Institute that continues to gather the available discovered inscriptions into a searchable database by location. It is available at http://epigraphy.packhum.org. You must first agree to the terms of use. An out-dated version of this database is found on PHI CD 7 that can be used in conjunction with Diogenes with all the attending benefits of parsing and lexical help.
2. *Trismegistos*: http://www.trismegistos.org/index.html. This website provides an interdisciplinary portal of papyrological and epigraphical resources from Egypt, but now expanding to the ancient world more generally. Trismegistos gives external links to related databases.
3. U.S. Epigraphy Project: Lists collections of Greek and Latin inscriptions in the USA and provides links to databases here http://usepigraphy.brown.edu/projects/usep/links, some of which are described below.
4. The *Epigraphic Database Heidelberg*: This database "contains the texts of **Latin and bilingual** (i.e. Latin-Greek) **inscriptions of the Roman Empire**. The epigraphic monuments are collected and kept up to date on the basis of modern research. With the help of search functions specific queries can be carried out—e.g. a search for words in inscriptions and/or particular descriptive data. The search results are often displayed together with photos and drawings."[42] The search provides access to three databases: epigraphic texts, photographs, and bibliography.
5. *Epigraphik-Datenbank Clauss-Slaby*: Provides access to "almost all Latin Inscriptions." For access and instructions, go to http://www.manfredclauss.de/gb/index.html.

Papyri: Ancient Egyptian papyri are still being found and sometimes even re-found in libraries, old and new, containing portions or complete copies of ancient texts, letters, and documents. Papyri may be classified as documentary (letters of various kinds, business transactions, family communications, or imperial correspondence) and literary or non-documentary (i.e., consisting of ancient literary works). The value of papyri for understanding the NT is well illustrated

---

[40] Danker, *Benefactor: Epigraphic Study of a Graeco-Roman and New Testament Semantic Field* (St. Louis: Clayton, 1982), 28.
[41] *Benefactor*, 451.
[42] From http://edh-www.adw.uni-heidelberg.de/home?lang=en accessed 2–25–2017.

in the writings of the great philologist G. Adolf Deissmann.[43] The most famous collection of papyri was found at Oxyrhynchus, Egypt and has been published by B. P. Grenfell and A. S. Hunt (available at the Internet archive).[44] One site, www.papyri.info, has gathered links to the major searchable websites and provides searching of them all:

1. Advanced Papyrological Information System (APIS)
2. Duke Databank of Documentary Papyri (DDbDP)
3. TRISMEGISTOS
4. Heidelberger Gesamtverzeichnis der griechischen Papyrusurkunden Ägyptens (HGV)
5. Bibliographie Papyrologique (BP)

Numismatic Research—Coin Issues: Greek and Roman coins were broadly disseminated and functioned to express local civic pride, provincial fidelities, and imperial ideology.[45] Coins contain (abbreviated) words in the legends as well as imagery and personifications of virtues and political ideals as deities. As such, coins become a resource for the meaning of important words and ideologies. Numismatic scholars Harold Mattingly and Edward A. Sydenham argue:

> In the development of reverse types the coinage of the Roman Empire far surpassed anything that numismatic art had produced previously.... An aspect of the imperial coinage which is peculiarly Roman and accounts largely for the varied character and historical importance of the reverse types is that, besides being the medium of exchange, the coins were used to disseminate knowledge of current events and propaganda of various kinds—they were, in short, the newspapers of the day.[46]

Likewise, Michael McCormick maintains, "The facet of imperial propaganda which remains most accessible to us today is embodied in the Roman coinage. It was the coinage which relayed to the farthest reaches of the empire the kind of themes embodied in the monuments of the capital and provincial centers."[47] Indeed, Jesus himself is reported as making appeal to the image and legend on a coin (see Mark 12:13–17//Matt 22:15–22//Luke 20:20–26). A number of NT interpreters have

---

[43] G. Adolf Deissmann, *Bible Studies: Contributions, Chiefly from Papyri and Inscriptions, to the History of the Language, the Literature, and the Religion of Hellenistic Judaism and Primitive Christianity*, trans. A. Grieve, 2nd ed. (Edinburgh: T&T Clark, 1903); *New Light on the New Testament, from Records of the Graeco-Roman Period*, trans. L. R. M. Strachan (Edinburgh: T&T Clark, 1907); *The Philology of the Greek Bible: Its Present and Future*, trans. L. R. M. Strachan (London: Hodder and Stoughton, 1908); and *Light from the Ancient East*.

[44] *The Oxyrhynchus Papyri* vols. I-XV (London: Egypt Exploration Fund, 1898–1926).

[45] See, e.g., Andreas Alfoldi, "The Main Aspects of Political Propaganda on the Coinage of the Roman Republic," in *Essays in Roman Coinage Presented to Harold Mattingly* (Oxford: Oxford University Press, 1956), 63–95; Michael Grant, "Roman Coins as Propaganda," *Archeology* 5 (1952): 79–85.

[46] Harold Mattingly and Edward Allen Sydenham, *The Roman Imperial Coinage: Vol. I Augustus to Vitellius*, vol. 1, 12 vols. (London: Spink & Son, 1923), 22.

[47] McCormick, *Eternal Victory: Triumphal Rulership in Late Antiquity, Byzantium, and the Early Medieval West*, Past and Present Publications (Cambridge: Maison de Sciences de l'Homme and Cambridge University Press, 1986), 26.

explored the relationship of coinage to the NT.[48] There are a number of online search sites and/or sites dedicated to specific topics; what is provided below is not comprehensive:

1. American Numismatic Database at http://numismatics.org.
2. Caesar's Coins: http://www.humanities.mq.edu.au/acans/caesar/Home.htm
3. Coins of Roman Egypt: http://www.coinsofromanegypt.org/html/collection.htm
4. Buildings on Roman Coins: http://www.romancoins.info/VIC-Buildings.html

<u>Abbreviations Galore</u>: The world of Classical Greek and Latin literature entails numerous abbreviations of ancient documents, inscriptions, etc. as well as of modern journals and reference works. The PHI searchable databases will provide descriptions of these. But, when reading articles, essays, and monographs, you may need assistance. Consider consulting the frontal material of LSJ, the *Oxford Latin Dictionary* (*OLD*), and the *Oxford Classical Dictionary* (*OCD*). Additionally, you may find helpful the journal abbreviations in *L'Année Philologique* online.[49]

<u>The LXX *or* Classical Word Usage?</u> The LXX is obviously an extremely relevant resource for understanding the NT. Most of the quotations of the OT in the NT appear to draw from the LXX, indicating good familiarity with the LXX by the NT authors. However, we must ask, is the LXX always the most relevant background for the initial original audiences of the NT documents? *Good communication uses language and ideas that are familiar to the audience.* For the apostle Paul, the young converts to Christianity certainly included a good number of Jews, but the majority were from among the Gentiles as his affirmations indicate (Rom 1:5,13; 11:13; 15:8–19 *et passim*). Although (some of) these converts may have been exposed to or even taught from the LXX, knowledge of the LXX should not necessarily be assumed as primary. So, we should carefully consider whether the NT author intended to refer to the LXX and/or used the common vocabulary of a region within the Greco-Roman world. Again, we must evaluate whether words participate within a network of ideas and what other words are being used in tandem.

EXERCISE 5–F: Conduct research on one of the following words.

1. πανήγυρις in Heb 12:23. Consider its usage in the broader context of Heb 12. Conduct research in the PHI and other databases. Be sure to read Spicq's entry in *TLNT*.
2. εὐεργέται in Luke 22:25. Conduct research in the PHI and other databases. If time allows, consult Frederick W. Danker, *Benefactor: Epigraphic Study of a Graeco-Roman and New Testament Semantic Field* (St. Louis: Clayton, 1982).

---

[48] E.g., Richard E. Oster, "Numismatic Windows into the Social World of Early Christianity: A Methodological Inquiry," *JBL* 101 (1982): 195–223; Larry J. Kreitzer, "A Numismatic Clue to Acts 19.23–41 the Ephesian Cistophori of Claudius and Agrippina," *JSNT* 9 (1987): 59–70; idem, *Striking New Images: Roman Imperial Coinage and the New Testament World*, JSNT 134 (Sheffield: Sheffield Academic, 1996); Lawrence E. McKinney, "Coins and the New Testament: From Ancient Palestine to the Modern Pulpit," *Review & Expositor* 106.3 (2009): 467–89; Harry O. Maier, *Picturing Paul in Empire: Imperial Image, Text and Persuasion in Colossians, Ephesians and the Pastoral Epistles* (New York: T&T Clark, 2013), *passim*.

[49] http://www.annee-philologique.com/files/sigles_fr.pdf.

Example of σωτήρ "savior" in Eph 5:22–24: Paul very strategically places Christ in the center of a crafted chiasm—a literary form that arranges phrases and statements in inverted order: ABCD-E-DCBA. The number of elements may vary; see the discussion of Chiasms in STEP 6: LITERARY FORMS. The prominence features in the text draw our attention primarily to Christ and the *Ekklesia* and secondarily to the husband's role to care for his wife as his own body. Thus, I would maintain that the primary agent is Christ in relation to the Church, and secondarily the husband in the relation to his wife. Yet interpreters would have us focus on human-scale marriage, while under-appreciating and not exploring more completely two of the most prominent expressions in the pericope: First, in 5:23 the referent of Christ "himself (being) savior of the body" and, second, in 5:27 the church as "glorious" (ἔνδοξος). I will have an extended discussion of ἔνδοξος in STEP 7: HISTORICAL CONTEXT. Here, however, I would like to focus on σωτήρ "savior."

Let's review how some important commentators have understood σωτήρ "savior." Harold W. Hoehner will ask and then answer, "What, then, did this unique phrase mean for the believers in Ephesus? In fact, it is an ancillary comment to reinforce Christ as the head...."[50] He further explains that the phrase means "Christ's redemption of individual sinners resulting in reconciliation to God and also to each other within the body of believers." True enough, but is there more to this phrase than individualistic salvation? Is this how the term was used and commonly understood? Hoehner further explains that Christ as Savior has some applicability to the husband's relationship to his wife, to protect her physically and spiritually, but he cannot save her "from eternal doom as Christ does the church but rather acts as her protector in a temporal sense." About the title "Savior" Peter T. O'Brien has very little to say, except to clarify that the Savior role is Christ's alone and not the husband's and "His saving activity, especially his sacrificial death (2:14–18; cf. 5:2), was for the deliverance of men and women in dire spiritual peril (2:1–10)."[51] Frank Thielman correctly identifies the phrase αὐτὸς σωτήρ is "emphatic" and also says of this phrase:

> Paul seems to have caught himself drifting away from the practical to the theoretical in the final clause of 5:23 'He himself is the Savior of the body.' With ἀλλά (*alla*, but) he pulls his train of thought quickly back on track just as he will at the end of the passage in 5:33: 'In any case, you too—every single one of you—must love his own wife.' Both phrases are evidence that Ephesians started life as an oral discourse that, although not unorganized, was also not planned in meticulous detail.[52]

However, no broader social-political significance is affirmed of σωτήρ; Thielman correctly, but *only*, relates the title to earlier statements of Christ's supreme position for the church in Ephesians (1:22–23; 4:15–16) and to God-in-Christ's saving activity (2:5, 10).[53]

---

[50] Hoehner, *Ephesians*, 743.

[51] O'Brien, *The Letter to the Ephesians*, Pillar New Testament Commentary (Grand Rapids: Eerdmans, 1999), 414–15. Despite the retraction of this commentary, the view expressed here is commonly held.

[52] Thielman, *Ephesians*, BECNT (Grand Rapids: Baker Academic, 2010), 378–79.

[53] This latter reference is buried in a footnote in Thielman, *Ephesians*, 379 fn. 17.

CHIASTIC STRUCTURE OF EPH 5:22–24

5:22 αἱ γυναῖκες [*submitting*] τοῖς ἰδίοις ἀνδράσιν   Wives *submitting* to their own husbands
     ↑ ὡς τῷ κυρίῳ,   [COMPARISON]   as to the Lord

23 ὅτι ἀνήρ ἐστιν κεφαλὴ	**A**	Husband is head
τῆς γυναικὸς	**B**	of Wife
ὡς καὶ ὁ Χριστὸς κεφαλὴ	**C**	as Christ is head
τῆς ἐκκλησίας,	**D**	of Ekklesia
CENTER αὐτὸς σωτὴρ	**E**	He is Savior
τοῦ σώματος·	**E**	of the Body
24 ἀλλὰ ὡς ἡ ἐκκλησία ὑποτάσσεται	**D**	As Ekklesia submits
τῷ Χριστῷ,	**C**	to Christ
οὕτως καὶ αἱ γυναῖκες	**B**	thus also Wives
τοῖς ἀνδράσιν ἐν παντί.	**A**	to Husbands

Rudolf Schnackenburg understands σωτήρ as a metaphor prompted by and introduced into the metaphor of Christ as head of the church while discussing marriage; however, the meaning and significance of "savior" is eclipsed by Schnackenburg's interest on the church as a Body, the origins of which remains uncertain. Although he considers Gnostic notions of Head-Body, he concludes this is "doubtful."[54]

Ernest Best briefly reviews the possible background for σωτήρ even admitting, "It was widely used in the contemporary world being applied to the Roman emperor, the Ptolemies, Asclepius, and the Heavenly Man."[55] But, he quotes affirmingly A. D. Nock's assessment, "… its frequent employment in the Septuagint as a predicate of God or of the Messiah seems to supply the most natural antecedent for its Christian usage."[56]

However, let's consider the merits of Nock's view. The word σωτήρ occurs only forty-one times in the LXX being used to translate מוֹשִׁיעַ "deliverer, savior" six times (Judg 3:9, 15; 12:3; 1 Kgdms 10:19; 2 Esd 19:27; Isa 45:21). Otherwise, σωτήρ translates יֵשַׁע "help" eleven times and יְשׁוּעָה "help, acts of salvation" four times.[57] The remaining LXX occurrences of σωτήρ are outside

---

[54] Schnackenburg, *Ephesians: A Commentary*, trans. H. Heron (Edinburgh: T&T Clark, 1991), 247–48.

[55] Best, *Ephesians*, ICC (New York: T&T Clark International, 1998), 536.

[56] A. D. Nock, "Early Gentile Christianity and Its Hellenistic Background," in *Essays on the Trinity and the Incarnation*, ed. A. E. J. Rawlinson (London: Longmans, Green, 1928), 52–156 at 92.

[57] Respectively, Ps 23:5; 24:5; 26:1, 9; 64:6; 78:9; 94:1; Micah 7:7; Hab 3:18; Isa 17:10; 62:11; and then Deut 32:15; Ps 61:3, 7; Isa 12:2.

the Hebrew OT within the OT Apocrypha and Pseudepigrapha.[58] Although God is indeed identified as the (eternal) Savior, rarely is σωτήρ messianic, i.e., referring to God's Messiah (possibly only Isa 62:11). So, Nock's claim is problematic on this basis alone. In the NT the words for salvation may be summarized in the chart below.

Σωτήρ AND CLOSE COGNATES IN THE NT

	GOSPELS/ACTS	PAULINE	LATTER NT
σωτήρ "savior" (24x)	Luke 1:47; 2:11; Acts 5:31; 13:23; John 4:42	Eph 5:23; Phil 3:20; 1 Tim 1:1; 2:3; 4:10; 2 Tim 1:10; Titus 1:3, 4; 2:10, 13; 3:4, 6	2 Pet 1:1, 11; 2:20; 3:2, 18; 1 John 4:14; Jude 25
σωτηρία "salvation" (45x)	Mark 16:8; Luke 1:69, 71, 77; 19:9; Acts 4:12; 7:25; 13:26, 47; 16:17; 27:34; John 4:22	Rom 1:16; 10:1, 10; 11:11; 13:11; 2 Cor 1:6; 6:2; 7:10; Eph 1:13; Phil 1:19, 28; 2:12; 1 Thess 5:8, 9; 2 Thess 2:13; 2 Tim 2:10; 3:15	Heb 1:14; 2:3, 10; 5:9; 6:9; 9:28; 11:7; 1 Pet 1:5, 9, 10; 2:2; 2 Pet 3:15; Jude 3; Rev 7:10; 12:10; 19:1
σωτήριος "saving" (5x)	Luke 2:20; 3:6; Acts 28:28	Eph 6:17; Titus 2:11	
σῴζω "I save" (106x)	Matt 1:21; 8:25; 9:21, 22; 10:22; 14:30; 16:25; 19:25; 24:13, 22; 27:40, 42, 49; Mark 3:4; 5:23, 28, 34; 6:56; 8:35; 10:26, 52; 13:13, 20; 15:30, 31; 16:16; Luke 6:9; 7:50; 8:12, 36, 48, 50; 9:24; 13:23; 17:19; 18:26, 42; 19:10; 23:35, 37, 39; John 3:17; 5:34; 10:9; 11:12; 12:27, 47; Acts 2:21, 40, 47; 4:9, 12; 11:14; 14:9; 15:1, 11; 16:30, 31; 27:20, 31	Rom 5:9, 10; 8:24; 9:27; 10:9, 13; 11:14, 26; 1 Cor 1:18, 21; 3:15; 5:5; 7:16; 9:22; 10:33; 15:2; 2 Cor 2:15; Eph 2:5, 8; 1 Thess 2:16; 2 Thess 2:10; 1 Tim 1:15; 2:4, 15; 4:16; 2 Tim 1:9; 4:18; Titus 3:5	Heb 5:7; 7:25; Jas 1:21; 2:14; 4:12; 5:15, 20; 1 Pet 3:21; 4:18; Jude 5, 23

Delimiting our focus to the uses of σωτήρ in the Pauline Epistles, we see that the title occurs first in Eph 5:23 and Phil 3:20 and then only in the Pastorals. Altogether, these letters are dated towards the end of Paul's ministry, and all these letters but Philippians are disputed. *Why would σωτήρ only*

---

[58] Jdt 9:11; Wis 16:7; Sir 51:1; Bar 4:22; 1 Macc 4:30; 3 Macc 6:29, 32; 7:16; Odes Sol. 2:15; 4:18; 9:47; Pss. Sol. 3:6; 8:33; 16:4; 17:3.

occur in the later Pauline Epistles? Surveying these Pauline instances, the title is used equally in reference to God (1 Tim 1:1; 2:3; 4:10; Titus 1:3; 2:10; 3:4) and Christ (Eph 5:23; Phil 3:20; 2 Tim 1:10; Titus 1:4: 2:13; 3:6), with Titus 2:13 referring to God or to Christ. In these uses the activity of Savior is in reference to the past time describing salvific benefits rendered (2 Tim 1:10; Titus 3:4, 6), to the present reality of the Savior's oversight, position, and command (Eph 5:23; 1 Tim 1:1; 2:3; Titus 1:3, 4; 2:10), and to the future hope of kindness, grace, and glory offered to believers at the appearing of the Savior (Phil 3:20; 1 Tim 4:10; Titus 2:13).

Furthermore, we can consider the distribution of word usage across various corpora and media from the eighth-century BC through the first-century AD by searching some of the databases described above (see the chart below). By no means is this chart's numerical results sufficient to determine word meanings; however, my point here is to establish currency, relevancy, and ubiquity of notions of "salvation" and "savior" *since Paul's Gentile audiences would more readily supply meanings of σωτήρ and its closest cognates from the broader social-cultural environment.* The results show that σωτήρ and its close cognates occur 748 times in the NT and LXX. Searching the other databases, we find some 16,000 occurrences of these words, which is inclusive of the 748 since these were also found in the TLG database search. Also, among these 16,000 occurrences are included a handful of instances within the Jewish Pseudepigraphal works (such as Greek editions of 1 Enoch 10:2; 14:2), which may (or may not) show the influence of the LXX. However, not included in these occurrences are the innumerable depictions of Savior and Salvation as Greco-Roman ideas specified textually or represented in coins, statuary, temples, and reliefs.

Σωτήρ AND CLOSE COGNATES BEFORE THE SECOND-CENTURY AD

	BIBLICAL		ANCIENT MEDIA			
GREEK WORD SEARCHED	NT	LXX	TLG LITERATURE	PHI INSCRIPTIONS	COINS	PAPYRI
"σωτηρ" σωτήρ "savior" σωτηρία "salvation" σωτήριος "saving"	24 45 5	41 155 35	1904 3618 688	over 5,000 of the stem "σωτηρ"[59]	The title Σωτηρ occurs on **many** coins in different centuries/locales	over 400 results, including some personal names
σώζω "I save"	106	336	approx. 3465	over 500	Not specified, but visualized in triumphal marches, protection, etc.	over 200 results
APPROXIMATE TOTALS=	748		16,000 (approximately) not including countless coins and other representations of "saviors" on statuary, reliefs, and other artifacts			

---

[59] Also, we could add a couple dozen or so instances of the Latin *Soter*.

Returning to Nock, his own position was more nuanced if we read it in context. On the same page he states his views once more (emphasis mine):

> We conclude therefore that the application of the title Soter to Jesus is not in origin connected with non-Jewish religious use of the word. **At the same time, converts from the Gentile world must have felt in the term something opposed to other appropriations of it.** For them Jesus was Soter as the deliverer from disease and demoniac possession, the deliverer from subjection to inferior divine powers, the deliverer from sin, and the giver of happy immortality; for them He was Soter as, and more than as, Asclepius, Emperors, and mystery-gods; to them He gave peace, but not merely an earthly peace; to them He gave also what philosophers looked on as soteria.

Certainly, Nock rightly placed σωτήρ within this broader context, which, in fact, very well may have been Paul's point in using the title in the first place. In other words, the horizon of God as Savior (from the OT and LXX) certainly informed what it meant for Jesus to be the Savior of God's people, who saves them from the oppressing power of sin. Yet, simultaneously this affirmation merged with and necessarily supplanted the prevailing alternative social-cultural-political notions of human rulers acclaimed as savior and providing benefits for the people. This fits within the context of Ephesians where the verb σῴζω earlier occurs in 2:5, 10. In 2:1–10 and 2:11–22 Paul made it clear that salvation is social-political by providing mercy, making peace, and unifying humanity. Moreover, the gentile believers have been saved from living "according to the [human] Ruler related to the Authority of the Air [=Zeus-Jupiter], the spirit…." (2:2).[60]

In this social-cultural context one Roman imperial title was "savior" (σωτήρ), of which Deissmann can summarize: The title "Saviour of the world … was bestowed with sundry variations in the Greek expression to Julius Caesar, Augustus, Claudius, Vespasian, Titus, Trajan, Hadrian, and other Emperors in inscriptions of the Hellenistic East."[61] The title "Zeus Savior" is lavished upon Nero in AD 67 for liberating Greece.[62] One inscription published by the Asian League in 9 BC across Asia Minor at Priene, Apameia, Eumeneia, Dorlyaion, and the rather small town of Maioneia praised Caesar Augustus for many things, not least of which was his being "savior." At Halicarnassus in Asia Minor in 2 BC another inscription praised Augustus as "Savior of the common human race [σωτῆρα τοῦ κοινοῦ τῶν ἀνθρώπων γένους]" because he embodied the "sur-

---

[60] See Fredrick J. Long, "Roman Imperial Rule under the Authority of Jupiter-Zeus: Political-Religious Contexts and the Interpretation of 'the Ruler of the Authority of the Air' in Ephesians 2:2," in *The Language of the New Testament: Context, History and Development*, ed. S. E. Porter and A. W. Pitts, Linguistic Biblical Studies 6; Early Christianity in its Hellenistic Environment 3 (Leiden; Boston: Brill, 2013), 113–54.

[61] Deissmann, *Light*, 369; "σωτήρ" LSJ def. 3; Cf. Paul Wendland, "ΣΩΤΗΡ," *ZNTW* 5 (1904): 335–53 and Dominique Cuss, *Imperial Cult and Honorary Terms in the New Testament*, Paradosis: Contributions to the History of Early Christian Literature and Theology 23 (Fribourg: University Press, 1974), 63–67. For comments on the possibility of compiling instances of σωτήρ as found in the inscriptions, see Deissmann, *Bible Studies*, 83.

[62] *GG* VII 2713; SIG³ 814; translated in Sherk, *Roman Empire*, 110–12 (no. 71).

passing benefits for humankind" and provides "for living a blessed life."[63] Praise of political rulers for protection and provision was common for the Ptolemy kings of the third- and second- centuries BC; Ceslas Spicq rightly summarizes, "the prince is conceived as representing the divinity and procuring the welfare of his subjects, who look to him for everything—security and happiness."[64]

But why would Paul co-relate Christ as Savior and the Church body to the marriage relationship in the context of the household codes? Well, if my argument is correct, that σωτήρ is used to supplant alternative claims to "savior," then the elevated status of the *Ekklesia* in Ephesians, especially here as likened to the bride of Christ, would supplant a concurrent common social-cultural entity. But what? Well, an alternative political couple was well represented in Asia Minor and its environs: Caesar in relation to *Roma*, the personification of the Roman state.[65] The Caesar-savior (σωτήρ) had an actively and strategically depicted ceremonial relationship with Rome as deified *Roma*. The importance of this relationship, *Roma* with Caesar, was seen across the empire, because as Duncan Fishwick explains, "in the provinces the regulation was that temples were acceptable only if Dea Roma shared in the cult" with the emperor (Suetonius *Aug.* 52).[66]

Ronald Mellor explains the history and religious significance of Roma:

> The goddess Roma had always played a political role…. Roma existed solely as a divine embodiment of the Romans themselves and thus would not be honored by them…. She [Roma], like *patria*, symbolized Rome past as well as Rome present. This use of Roma enabled the destinies of the imperial house to be linked with those of the state—the title *pater patriae* is one expression of this and the association of Roma and Augustus is another. The goddess was represented as a traditional divinity. Sometimes a warrior, sometimes a mother-figure, she had always to draw on the attributes of other gods since she herself had no history, no myth.[67]

In relation to Ephesus, Mellor summarizes, "Ephesus shows the clearest historical development of the cults of Roma: first, Roma alone; then Roma and [the Roman Proconsul Publius Servilius] Isauricus; then the provincial temple of Roma and Julius Caesar (29 BC); and finally, by 5 BC, a municipal cult of Roma and Augustus. The cult of Roma was important at Ephesus and a temple of the goddess is likely."[68] The two entities were joint religious figures, and their statues shared temples in Asia Minor as occurred in 29 BC with Roma/Julius at Ephesus and Nicaea and Augus-

---

[63] BMI 894.

[64] "σωτήρ" *TLNT* 3:353.

[65] On the development of the cult of Roma, see Ronald Mellor, *ΘΕΑ ῬΩΜΑ: The Worship of the Goddess Roma in the Greek World*, Hypomnemata: Untersuchungen zur Antike und zu ihrer Nachleben Heft 42 (Göttingen: Vandenhoeck & Ruprecht, 1975). He explains the scope of the cult, "Suetonius [*Augustus* 52] tells us that this marriage [between Roma and Augustus] was required in provincial cults by imperial command, but a similar pattern filtered down to the municipal cults as well" (195).

[66] Fishwick, "Dio and Maecenas: The Emperor and the Ruler Cult," *Phoenix* 44 (1990): 267–75 at 270

[67] Mellor, *Θεα ΡΩΜΗ*, 199–200.

[68] Mellor, *Θεα ΡΩΜΗ*, 138.

tus/Roma in Pergamum (see Tacitus, *Ann*. 4.37.4) and Nicomedia.[69] In Ancyra of Galatia a cult to Caesar and Roma existed during the reign of Tiberius,[70] and an altar for the pair was found even in the small village of Choriani near Hierocaesareia.[71] Herod also built a very notable temple at Caesarea Maritima with statues of Caesar Augustus (in imitation of Jupiter Olympius) and Roma (like Juno at Argos) that could been seen from the sea as one came into the harbor (Jos. *Wars* 1.414; *Ant*. 15.339).[72] It was at this very location that the apostle Paul was held after delivering the collection offering of the Gentile churches to Jerusalem. It was at Caesarea Maritime that Paul appealed to Caesar and was subsequently transported to Rome for trial (Acts 23:23; 25:8–12, 21; 26:32; 27:24; 28:19). In conclusion, I would argue that Paul's use of σωτήρ "savior" paired with the *Ekklesia* as the bride in Eph 5:23–24 was intended to supplant Roman offers of "salvation."

ARTIFACTS OF THE EMPEROR AND ROMA CULT[73]

This Cistophorus coin of Pergamum minted 41–54 AD under Claudius shows him on the obverse. On the reverse, he is shown in the temple of Augustus and Roma being crowned, possibly by Roma or Fortuna.

Dating to AD 37–41, this 1 1/16 inch sardonyx cameo (now placed within a seventeenth-century setting) shows Caligula with cornucopia (symbolizing abundance) enthroned next to Roma.

---

[69] Nock, "Σύνναος Θεός," *HSCP* 41 (1930): 1–62 at 43.

[70] *OGIS* 533, translated by Robert K. Sherk, *The Roman Empire: Augustus to Hadrian* (Cambridge: Cambridge University Press, 1988), 73–75 (no. 38).

[71] Thomas R. S. Broughton, "Roman Landholding in Asia Minor," *TAPA* 65 (1934): 207–39 at 216.

[72] Fishwick, "Dio and Maecenas," 270; Kenneth G. Holum, "Caesarea's Temple Hill: The Archaeology of Sacred Space in an Ancient Mediterranean City," *Near Eastern Archaeology* 67 (2004): 184–99. Helpful is the description as summarized by Mahlon H. Smith ("Caesarea Maritima" webpage of *Into His Own: Perspective on the World of Jesus*, OCLC catalog no. 62046512; accessed Oct. 16, 2008 at http://virtualreligion.net/iho/caesarea.html) "Caesarea was designed as a model Roman city, complete with aqueducts, sewers, a forum, mosaic walkways covered with marble colonnades, a racetrack [hippodrome], an amphitheater (larger than the Coliseum in Rome) & a large temple dedicated to Augustus & Roma. It was Herod's tribute to his Roman patrons. After Herod's son Archelaus was deposed, it became the Roman capital of Judea & Samaria. A stone with a dedication by Pontius Pilate found in the theatre provides physical evidence that it was the primary base of the Roman prefects." Smith provides these references in Josephus, *Ant*. 15.293, 339; 16.13; 19:343–365; *War* 1.80; 2.16–17, 282–296, 457–459.

[73] Cistophorus (RIC 1 Claudius 120) courtesy of www.cngcoins.com. The picture of the Caligula Cameo is in the public domain; the artifact is located in the Kunsthistorisches Museum in Vienna (IXa 59).

TERTIARY INTERPRETIVE PROCEDURES:

1. **Compare the word's meanings within major lexicons. This is a "first stop" when considering a word's possible range of meaning.**
2. **Preliminarily, on the basis of the following criteria consider the possible presence of a network of related ideas and/or the extent of any conventional schema.**
   a. the repetition of related concepts that may reflect or generate a recognizable schema;
   b. the relative density of related concepts within a delimited discourse space;
   c. the strategic and progressive use of related concepts in important discourse locations;
   d. the amplification of related concepts by marked and emphatic constructions;
   e. the situational relevance of the related concepts within the shared cognitive environment; and
   f. the satisfying insight gained with respect to these related concepts in terms of communicative efficiency and maximal impact on the audience(s).

NOTE: In procedure 12. below you will return to re-consider the possible presence of schema or network of ideas after having conducted more extensive lexical research.

3. **Consult theological and exegetical dictionaries and specialized studies for possible (extended) discussions of a word and its use and meaning. Such works are a "second stop."**
4. **Next, in view of the possible schema research the word's usage in *history* and *location* across available corpora and media in the electronic searchable databases: literary works, inscriptional remains, papyri, coins, and other artifacts. These databases are a "third stop" for lexical research and require expertise, skill, and time.**
5. **Consider the word's etymology, i.e., the building blocks of the Greek word (root, stem, and any affixes).**
   a. Beware: Not infrequently a word's etymology may be debatable.
   b. Also, there is too often the fallacy of thinking that the word's meaning is equal to the sum of its parts. Words are used so commonly and reflexively that such parts may be forgotten.
   c. And yet, ancient philosophers and "commentators" were at times cognizant of word roots and attempted to explain the meaning of words, sometimes quite allegorically, based upon supposed etymological derivations.
6. **Consider the word's prior historical usage.**
   a. First, understand that we don't have every instance of a word's use recorded; what we have mainly are literary sources that are often reflective of the educated elite and the social upper classes as seen in literature, literary papyri, inscriptions, coinage, etc. How might these differ from oral usages of the common person, from which we have much less material? For an example of such material, see the documentary papyri.
   b. Yet, even these uses among the socially elite may have reflected the broader culture and usage among the broader populace. Likewise, such social-elite meanings may have trickled down to more common usage and then could be evident in the NT.

c. The LXX and other Jewish Intertestamental literature will have special relevance for the NT. However, your research into these sources should not be at the expense of the broader Greco-Roman sources since NT authors were writing to diverse audiences.

d. Consider whether particular NT authors had access to earlier traditions of word usage. For example, although the Homeric writings date to the eighth-century, these works continued to be used within Greco-Roman education during the NT era. See also Contemporaneous Usage below.

7. **Investigate the word's contemporaneous usage inside and outside the NT documents.**
   a. Consider locations. Are sources found in the same location?
   b. Are there thematic relationships between the NT authors? What might this signify? An emerging Christian intellectual/literary scribal culture?
   c. Consider whether the Greek word may relate to or be translated from another contemporaneous language such as Aramaic, Hebrew, or Latin.
   d. Consider whether it is likely that the NT author would draw on this or that ancient source or on contemporaneous sources that might have used these ancient sources.
   e. Consider Intertextuality. See Richard B. Hays's seven criteria of intertextuality in *Echoes of Scripture in the Letters of Paul* that are discussed in STEP 8: SCRIPTURAL CORRELATIONS.

8. **Consider the word's use by an author and within a closely related corpus.**
   a. Is the word or related words used elsewhere by the author or in a corpus of their writings?
   b. Is the word defined there anywhere? How are these uses across the corpus related in sense?
   c. If there are (quite significant) differences of meaning, do these differences result from the respective contexts of each word's occurrence?

9. **Carefully observe the word's (immediate) contextual usage**.
   a. Notice how the word functions and relates to other words grammatically.
   b. Notice how the word is being modified. Is it being defined or nuanced in some way?
   c. Notice the surrounding structure of each passage where the word is found. For example, is the word involved in a parallel structure that helps to define the word? Is it being contrasted or compared with other words? Is the word a part of a command or the conclusion of an argument so that it summarizes the previous discussion? Or, is the word part of a preparatory statement that provides a general idea that is elaborated upon in what follows?
   d. Are synonyms or antonyms used in the context? Should these synonyms and/or antonyms also be studied? See discussion of synonyms and antonyms above.
   e. Consider how the *previous occurrences* of a word contribute to the word's meaning in a later portion of the NT book.
   f. Finally, consider how the word's meaning may be *progressively developed* in the individual occurrences throughout the book.

10. Research the word's subsequent usage.

a. Where and in what distribution is the word found in subsequent usage? Is this a unique Christian word found mainly or exclusively in the Church Fathers and commentators of Scripture or does the word continue to have broader usage in the Greco-Roman world?

b. Is there an aspect of meaning that is preserved by later writers or interpreters?

c. What relationship does the word's subsequent usage have to its prior usage?

11. Consider the word's history of interpretation as may be reflected in ancient and modern commentaries.

a. How has the word been understood across church history?

b. How has the word been more recently understood in modern/contemporaneous scholarship?

12. Determine the lexical pragmatics and ad hoc concept formation in the passage(s) under investigation.

a. Has any schema or network of ideas been utilized? Revisit procedure 2. above. How is the schema present in the pericope under investigation?

b. Consider how the word concept has developed in terms of "narrowing," "broadening," "category extension," "reference assignment," "disambiguation," and "enrichment."[74]

c. Finally, what implications does this have for understanding the ideological messaging of the pericope?

IV. BIBLIOGRAPHY

Primary and Secondary Resources

Concordances

In Bible Software: E.g., Accordance, BibleWorks, Logos

Online: Strong's concordance online at http://www.biblestudytools.com/concordances/. See also Biblios.com at http://concordances.org.

Print:

Goodrick, Edward W. and John R. Kohlenberger III, *The Strongest NIV Exhaustive Concordance*. Grand Rapids: Zondervan, 2004.

Kohlenberger III, John R. *The Greek-English Concordance of the New Testament*. Grand Rapids: Zondervan, 1993.

Moulton, W. F., A. S. Geden, H. K. Moulton, and I. Howard Marshall. *A Concordance to the Greek Testament*. 6th ed. Edinburgh: Clark, 2002.

Strong, James. *The New Strong's Expanded Exhaustive Concordance of the Bible*. Expanded ed. Nashville, TN: Thomas Nelson, 2010.

Wigram, George V. *The Englishman's Greek Concordance of New Testament: Coded with Strong's Concordance Numbers*. Reprinted. Peabody, MA: Hendrickson, 1996.

---

[74] See the articles by G. Green, "Lexical Pragmatics and Biblical Interpretation" and "Lexical Pragmatics and the Lexicon."

Recommended Greek Lexicons (See also esp. Bauer, *Biblical Resources*, 195–200.)

 Bauer, Walter and F. W. Danker, W. F. Arndt, and F. W. Gingrich (BDAG). *Greek-English Lexicon of the New Testament and Other Early Christian Literature.* 3rd ed. Revised. Chicago: The University of Chicago Press, 2000. [This is the standard scholarly Greek NT Lexicon.]

 Liddell, H. G., R. Scott and H. S. Jones (LSJ). *A Greek-English Lexicon.* 9th ed. revised. Oxford: Clarendon, 1996. [The previous edition, which is the same but missing a supplement, can be accessed on the web at various locations such as at www.perseus.tufts.edu.

 Liddell, H. G. *A Lexicon: Abridged from Liddell and Scott's Greek-English Lexicon.* Oxford: Clarendon, 1963. An abridgment that still contains word derivation information in parentheses.]

 Louw, Johannes and Eugene Nida (L&N). *Greek-English Lexicon of the New Testament Based on Semantic Domains.* 2nd ed. New York: United Bible Societies, 1988. [A very valuable lexicon which allows one to find synonyms and antonyms; has its own numbering system based upon semantic domains.]

 Swanson, James. *Dictionary of Biblical Languages With Semantic Domains: Greek (New Testament).* Electronic ed. Oak Harbor, WA: Logos Research Systems, 1997. [Very accessible lexicon using Strong's numbering and referencing other lexicons and theological dictionaries.]

 Thayer, Joseph Henry. *Thayer's Greek-English Lexicon of the New Testament.* Electronic ed. International Bible Translators (IBT), 1998–2000. [Prior to BDAG, Thayer's was the standard Greek NT lexicon. It is dated, but still contains some insightful information, e.g., for some words the underlying roots are given in the formation of the word.]

 Zodhiates, Spiros. *The Complete Word Study Dictionary: New Testament.* Chattanooga, TN: AMG, 1992. [Not recognized as an academic lexicon, nevertheless Zodhiates is still helpful to provide a perspective on the possible meanings of a word as well as listing synonyms and antonyms and often the roots used in the formation of the word.]

Tertiary Resources

See the books and online resources provided in the discussion above.

STEP 6

LITERARY FORMS

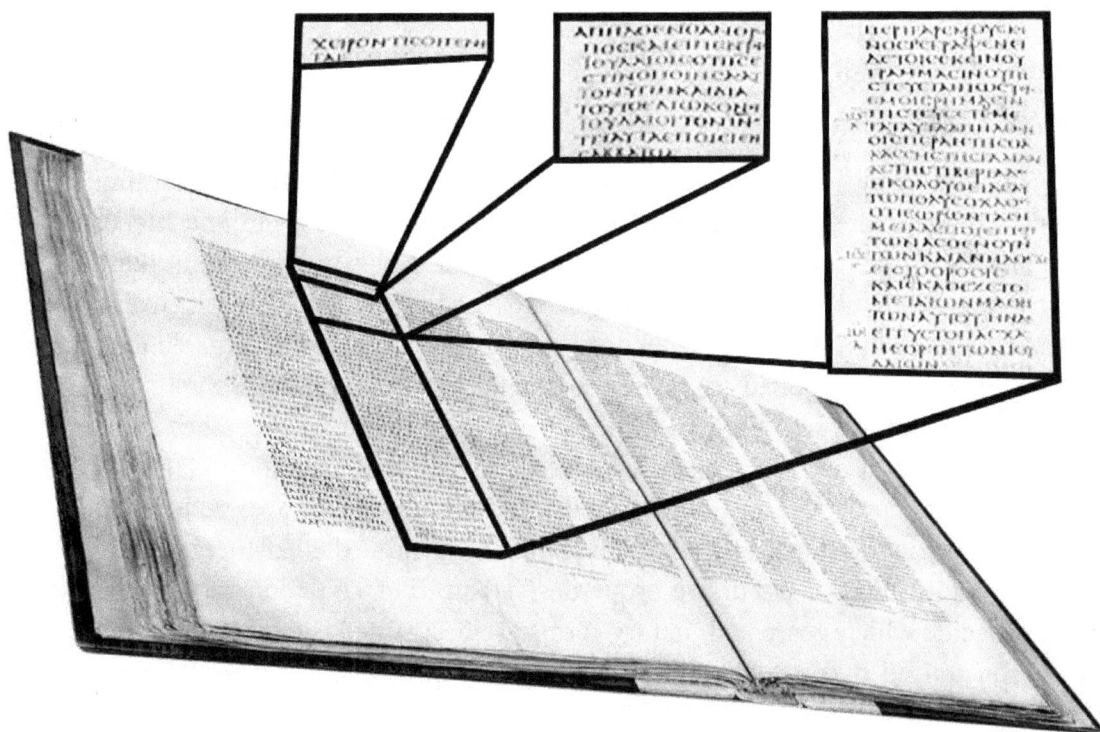

"[G]enres are agents of ideological closure—they limit the meaning-potential of a given text...."[1]
—John Hartley

"Different genres specify different 'contracts' to be negotiated between the text and the reader ... which set up expectations on each side for the form of the communication (e.g. narrative, debate), its functions (uses and gratification), its epistemology ..., and the communicative frame (e.g. the participants, the power of the viewer, the openness of the text, and the role of the reader)."[2]
—Sophia Livingstone

---

[1] "Genre" in Tim O'Sullivan et al. *Key Concepts in Communication and Cultural Studies*, 2nd ed., Studies in Culture and Communication (London: Routledge 1994), 128.

[2] "The Rise and Fall of Audience Research: An Old Story with a New Ending" pages 247–54 in Mark R. Levy and Michael Gurevitch eds. *Defining Media Studies: Reflections on the Future of the Field* (New York: Oxford University Press, 1994), 252–53.

Introduction: A commonly underappreciated yet fruitful avenue for biblical interpretation is studying genre and literary form. Understanding a book's genre and any literary form(s) present in a passage helps readers have proper assumptions and guides their interpretive approaches. Eugene A. Nida has said, "The type of text (or discourse genre) always contributes significantly to the meaning of a discourse, for it provides important clues as to interpretation."[3] Our study should correspond as much as possible to what we are studying in order to interpret it rightly. For example, one should not read an editorial piece in a newspaper as if it were history; nor when someone says to us, "Knock, knock," should we expect to receive a piece of advice. *The context of communication, genre, and literary form guide our expectations and reception of what we read and hear.*

I. PRIMARY SURVEY

Orientation: Conventions of Genre and Literary Form: Ancient writers set limits on the interpretation of their writing by utilizing established conventions of genre and literary forms that were recognizable to their audiences whether through reading or more often in the public "hearing" of what was written. To organize writings into "books" was one such convention.[4] Recognizable conventions of writing are called *genres* and *literary forms*. When applied to a whole book, we speak of **genre**; when applied to a discrete smaller portion of a book, we speak of **literary form**. Tzvetan Todorov argues, "[G]enres, indeed, are nothing but such choices among discursive possibilities, choices that a given society has made conventional"; he adds, "[i]n a given society, certain discursive properties are institutionalized, and individual texts are produced and perceived in relation to the norm constituted by that codification. A genre, whether literary or not, is nothing other than the codification of discursive properties."[5] Thus, before the creation of their discourse, authors must decide which genre and literary forms are best suited to convey their message. Thus, authors are constrained by societal-cultural conventions; otherwise, how would people recognize what they are communicating?

EXERCISE 6–A: Reflect on the general phenomenon of genres within your life-setting.

1. What genres are most common in your social-cultural setting?
2. How are such genres recognized in terms of settings, features, and context?
3. Are you able to provide a definition and accurate generalized description of each genre?
4. How would understanding such information about a specific genre help with interpretation?

---

[3] Eugene A. Nida, *Style and Discourse: With Special Reference to the Text of the Greek New Testament* (Roggebaai, Cape Town: Bible Society, 1983), 53.

[4] Luke's writing of his Gospel and Acts into two "books" within a single "work" followed literary conventions of the day. Furthermore, to include frontal material (a prologue) to orient readers as to methods and content was also customary; in fact, the Jewish historian, Josephus includes prologues to his two books in his work "Against Apion" which are strikingly similar to Luke's.

[5] *Genres in Discourse*, trans. C. Porter (Cambridge: Cambridge University Press, 1990), 9 and 18–19, cited in Tom Thatcher, *Riddles of Jesus in John: A Study in Tradition and Folklore* (Atlanta: SBL Press, 2000), 99.

Genre Identification and Major Biblical Genres: John Barton argues that at the heart of biblical interpretation is the identification of genre.[6] Knowing the genre of the book will provide an essential framework and basic guidelines for interpreting any passage within the book through understanding how the text coheres together and what can be known of the author's intentions.[7] For instance, if you are looking at poetry, then you might identify coherent features that are particular to poetry—such as metaphoric language and parallelism—and what interpretive significance these have in conveying the author's intentions. If you were looking at a historical work, you would want to identify features of historical writing operative during the time period in which that historical work was written. Universal features of historical writing would include reference to time, characters (protagonists and antagonists), events, causes and effects, and general elaborative description. However, each culture varies in what constitutes "proper" historical writing because specific conventions differ from time to time and place to place. (This variability is also true of all genres.) Western historians and readers may favor strict chronology and read the Gospels with that expectation; however, this was not necessarily the case in ancient Mediterranean cultures. Below are major categories of biblical genres along with representative examples for each.

MAJOR BIBLICAL GENRES

- Apocalypse (e.g., Daniel 7–12, Book of Revelation)
- Wisdom (e.g., Proverbs, Job)
- Poetry (e.g., Psalms, parts of the Prophetic Corpus)
- Prophecy (e.g., Isaiah, Jeremiah, Malachi)
- Narrative
  - Historiography (e.g., 1 Samuel, Nehemiah)
  - Biography (e.g., Gospels, Acts)
  - Short Story or Novella (e.g., Ruth, Esther)
- Letter-Argumentative (e.g., Paul, Peter, Jude)
- Covenant formula with Laws (e.g., Exodus, Deuteronomy)
- Testament or Sermon (e.g., 1 John, Hebrews)

> Certain genres will "attract" certain literary forms; thus the recognition of literary forms will often help identify the genre of a book.

EXERCISE 6–B: Given the list of biblical genres above, answer the following questions:

1. Which biblical genres are most foreign to you? Why do you think that might be?
2. Are there any genres that should be added to this list of biblical genres?
3. What might it mean that the Bible contains so many different types of genres? What might we learn about God and our relationship with God from this diversity of expression?

---

[6] John Barton, *The Nature of Biblical Criticism* (Louisville: Westminster John Knox, 2007), 5. It is stated as the first of his ten theses: "Biblical Criticism is essentially a literary operation, concerned with the recognition of genre in texts and with what follows from this about their possible meaning. It is thus also focused on semantics, but the semantics of whole texts as well as of individual words or sentences."

[7] Barton, *Nature of Biblical Criticism*, 24.

Literary Forms: At a reduced scale, literary form refers to shorter communication units with distinctly recognizable features. Substantial evidence exists that writers composed entire works via discernible smaller units or episodes. *Certain genres will "attract" certain literary forms; thus the recognition of literary forms will often help identify the genre of a book.* Smaller units may be used so frequently or have such importance that they acquire a particular and somewhat standardized "form"; they become conventional as literary forms. For instance, an utterance "knock, knock" belongs to what category of communication? Does this form exhibit a particular structure? While a "spoken joke" is a general category of genre, a "knock, knock joke" represents a particular form within that category; usually such jokes occur within particular contexts. In your estimation, when and where typically are knock, knock jokes spoken? By whom and for whom are they told? By recognizing the literary forms, people can begin to evaluate what is expected of them and also anticipate and comprehend other communicative cues as an interpretive framework within which to understand the meaning of what is communicated as a whole. Children often tell knock, knock jokes; yet, such jokes are not limited to them and create a friendly atmosphere.

Miscommunication and Wrong Identification: Communicators and conversation partners anticipate and know what to expect because of the use of conventional forms of speech. If, however, a person misreads the type or style of conversation, at some level this will result in a failure of communication leading to misunderstanding. By analogy, interpreters may misunderstand and assume the wrong literary form for a passage thus misinterpreting it. For example, D. A. Carson, speaking to fallacies of interpretation, comments: "One of the most common errors preachers make in the area of literary genre occurs in their handling of Proverbs. A proverb is neither a promise nor case law. If it is treated that way, it may prove immensely discouraging to some believers when things do not seem to work out as the 'promise' seeks to suggest."[8] For the remainder of this initial discussion within PRIMARY SURVEY, I will describe two common and important literary forms that are worth careful study: lists and parables.

Lists—A Guide to Study a Literary Form: One basic and important literary form is the "list." Even today, our lives consist of many lists whether written out, typed in, or impressed upon our minds. When my wife and I owned our Milwaukee house (a 1927 duplex), we created a list with thirty-five items to repair or replace. (I remember the list and numbers vividly!) It was a mix of general and prioritized items after a brainstorming session of what needed to be done, but additional items were subsequently added. In our minds, we came to prioritize the list, and began successively to cross items off one by one. Today, I sometimes use "Tasks" in my Gmail account to remember and prioritize what I should be doing. Finishing this chapter is top on my list today.

Lists Defined and Described: Most basically, a list may be defined as follows: *three or more items presented together to provide greater understanding about what is deemed important.* By this definition, two items do not constitute a list, although this should not lessen their interpretive importance as "a doublet." Lists implicitly involve the semantic relationship of reoccurrence of three or more items, the importance of which is typically guaranteed by the space and promi-

---

[8] D. A. Carson, *Exegetical Fallacies* (Grand Rapids: Baker, 2003), 138.

nence awarded them in a discourse. *The proper interpretation of biblical lists will always contribute to the proper interpretation of the entire passage and for understanding the overarching concerns of the biblical authors.* The Scriptures contain many lists, whether of persons or agencies (genealogical, biographical, etc.), places (geographical), events (chronological, grouped, etc.), processes (steps, stages, etc.), attributes (qualities, etc.), or concepts (moral, theological, etc.).

The use of lists is as old as human communication. Geoffrey W. Bakewell, before giving a survey of the "Written Lists of Military Personnel in Classical Athens," offers these comments on the history of the use of lists in antiquity:

> The appearance of written lists frequently accompanies a culture's attainment of a certain basic level of literacy. This is partly because such lists provide a substantial payoff. They require relatively little grammatical or literary sophistication to create; they are, depending on the inscriptional medium, easily corrected and maintained; and they are accessible to a broad range of readers, including those with minimal literacy skills. Yet at the same time such lists comprise a valuable tool for classifying, quantifying, and ordering the world. It is thus not surprising that they also formed a significant part of the writing generated by classical Athens.[9]

Lists are found much earlier than at Athens. The Jewish Scriptures contain many lists. Indeed, Bakewell cites Jack Goody, *The Domestication of the Savage Mind*, who has a chapter dedicated to "What's in a list?"[10] While discussing different broad categories of lists (personnel, administrative, events, etc.), Goody demonstrates that the development of "writing" encouraged more sophisticated forms and use of lists. Well, not surprisingly, biblical materials are *full* of lists! Although biblical writers used lists for a variety of purposes and each purpose must be determined in context, the use of lists can be related to what cognitive scientists and linguists describe as "information structure." Lists function to organize and prioritize items that often also provide easier recollection. Within biblical materials, lists function to make reference to what has been already discussed (backward referencing), to what will be discussed (forward referencing), or possibly to both (transitional or medial). When I see a biblical list, I stop and consider what it tells me about the nature of life and being a follower of Christ. Before reading further, perform the next exercise.

EXERCISE 6–C: How would you describe this list in Eph 4:31? Is there a particular order?

"Let all bitterness and rage and anger and brawling and slander be removed from yourselves along with all malice."

---

[9] Geoffrey W. Bakewell, "Written Lists of Military Personnel in Classical Athens" pages 89–101 in *Politics of Orality*, ed. Craig R. Cooper; Orality and Literacy in Ancient Greece 6; Mnemosyne: Bibliotheca classica Batava Supplementum 280 (Boston: Brill, 2007), 89.

[10] Jack Goody, *The Domestication of the Savage Mind*, Themes in the Social Sciences (Cambridge: Cambridge University Press, 1977), ch. 5.

When I read the list in Eph 4:31, I can now see an exemplary, conceptualized vice list describing an inner to outer progression. It starts and builds inwardly with "bitterness," then moves to "rage" (θυμός), and "anger" (ὀργή), with the latter being more outwardly expressed. Then the list moves even more outwardly by first describing "brawling" (κραυγή lit. "shouting")—presumably against the individual with whom one is angry—and then by infecting third parties with "slander." Bitterness is triangulated to others! Finally, the list climaxes with "all malice" presumably directed against the one hated, although perhaps more broadly directed to others, perhaps even to God.[11]

On occasion, the observation of a list has led me to make larger contextually significant observations. For example, in the list of five items in Eph 2:12, Paul described concisely what the Gentiles once were lacking: 1) separated from Christ, 2) excluded the commonwealth of Israel, 3) strangers to the covenants of promise, 4) having no hope, and 5) without God in the world. Upon closer inspection, I discovered that at the end of the pericope in 2:18–22 each listed item was obtained through the sacrificial work of Jesus Christ. Furthermore, I discerned that 2:11–22 is carefully structured as a chiasm. See my depiction of this in TERTIARY RESEARCH further below.

<u>Purpose Behind the Lists</u>: It is my conviction that NT lists are always purposeful and thus worthy of careful interpretation. The significance of lists would apply more broadly to other writings. For example, my colleague, Tony Headley, who in light of this concept of "purposeful lists" in the Apostle Paul's writings, has published on such lists in John Wesley that strategically describe an *ordo salutis* or "order of salvation."[12] Headley has noted that Wesley was thoroughly aware of the inner-to-outer movements of God's salvific work in us and this is represented in lists found in his writings. When interpreting lists, you should investigate the following areas:

FEATURES OF BIBLICAL LISTS

1. **Material Content**
   a. *persons* or *agencies* (genealogical, biographical, etc.)
   b. *places* (geographical, etc.)
   c. *events* (chronological, grouped, etc.)
   d. *processes* (steps, stages, etc.)
   e. *attributes* (qualities, etc.)
   f. *concepts* (moral, theological, etc.)

2. **Scope**
   a. *exhaustive (inclusive)*—all possible items are included in the list.
   b. *massive (majority)*—many but not all.
   c. *open (indefinite)*—unrestricted and open; any or some.

---

[11] See further my chapel homily "The Bitterness of Anger and God's Way Out" from June 7, 2011 at Asbury Theological Seminary.

[12] Anthony J. Headley, *Getting It Right: Christian Perfection and Wesley's Purposeful List*, Asbury Theological Seminary Series in World Christian Revitalization Movements in Pietist/Wesleyan Studies 14 (Lexington, KY: Emeth, 2013).

d. *limited (exclusive)*—selected items are included in the list.
   i. *representative*—items are a sampling of general representation.
   ii. *exemplary*—the most critical or important items are included.
   iii. *Are there other types of limitation?*
3. **Referencing**
   a. *backward*—primarily related to what precedes.
   b. *forward*—primarily related to what follows.
   c. *dual*—both backward and forward referencing.
      i. *transitional*—bridging what comes before to the new coming afterwards.
      ii. *medial*—occupying middle position in the development of argument.
4. **Formal Structure**. Often more than one characteristic applies simultaneously:
   a. *collective*—the group of items coheres together evenly.
   b. *grouped*—items within a list are paired or grouped together among other groupings.
   c. *progressive*—items build upon one another in a development.
   d. *prioritized*—one or more item is preeminent to the others (initial, center, final).
   e. *inner-outer movement*—related to above, the list describes intra-personal realities and moves to inter-personal realities or vice versa.
   f. *alternating*—items are presented back and forth between two poles or vantage points.
   g. *chiastic*—items are arranged around a central notion in ABC-CBA fashion.
   h. *bracketed*—the list begins and ends with the same/similar item.
5. **Semantic (Structural) Relations**. Implicitly, lists involve reoccurrence, but may also involve one or more of the following semantic relations:[13]
   a. *climactic*—items culminate with a high point (determined from literary context).
   b. *particularizing*—items provide details of a general notion.
   c. *generalizing*—items move from specific to more general concepts.
   d. *contrastive*—items are contrasted with one another.
   e. *comparative*—items are compared to one another.
   f. *causative*—items lead consequently to something.
   g. *purposive means*—items are intended as a means to something.
   h. *manner*—items describe the "manner" of something (like behavior or action).
   i. *resultative*—items come from or result from something.

Learning these categories and features above will allow you to analyze and describe list quite efficiently. For practice, perform EXERCISE 6–D on the next page. For a sample analysis of a list, consider also my discussion of the Beatitudes from Matt 5:3–12.

---

[13] Cf. Robert A. Traina, who related some structural relationships to the interpretation of what he called "series of facts." He indicated, "Comparison, contrast, enumeration, or progression from the general to the specific may be involved in this type of relation" (*Methodical Bible Study*), 42 n26.

EXERCISE 6–D: Observe and describe this following list that is punctuated following the underlying Greek text according to material content, scope, referencing, and semantic relationships.

> ²² But the fruit of the Spirit is love joy peace, patience kindness goodness, faithfulness ²³ gentleness self-control. Against such things there is no law.

For example, on "The Fruit of the Spirit" in Gal 5:21–22 one could summarize: The <u>material content</u> consists of nine moral concepts (virtues); the <u>scope</u> is limited and representative (5:22 describes these virtues as "such things," using a correlative pronoun of quality); the <u>referencing</u> is dual, occupying a medial position in the development of Paul's contrast between walking in the flesh versus in the Spirit; the <u>formal structure</u> is grouped (three triads; many commentators agree on this), but also prioritized ("love" is placed first); the <u>semantic relationships</u> are particularizing (5:22a "fruit" and 5:23b "such things"), resultative (from the Spirit; 5:16–18, 22, 25), and contrastive to "the deeds of the flesh" (particularized in 5:19–21).

<u>Example—The Beatitudes List</u>: Now, let me briefly describe one of my favorites NT lists, perhaps the most important of lists—the Beatitudes in the Sermon on the Mount (Matt 5:3–12). The verses are provided here so that you can practice (again) or follow my analysis more easily.

> ³ Blessed are the poor in spirit, for theirs is the Kingdom of Heaven.
> ⁴ Blessed are those who mourn, for they shall be comforted.
> ⁵ Blessed are the gentle, for they shall inherit the earth.
> ⁶ Blessed are those who hunger and thirst after righteousness, for they shall be filled.
> ⁷ Blessed are the merciful, for they shall obtain mercy.
> ⁸ Blessed are the pure in heart, for they shall see God.
> ⁹ Blessed are the peacemakers, for they shall be called children of God.
> ¹⁰ Blessed are those who have been persecuted for righteousness' sake, for theirs is the Kingdom of Heaven.
> ¹¹ Blessed are you when people reproach you, persecute you, and say all kinds of evil against you falsely, for my sake.
> ¹² Rejoice, and be exceedingly glad, for great is your reward in heaven. For that is how they persecuted the prophets who were before you.

In terms of <u>material content</u>, this list contains nine moral dispositions or attributes each begun with "blessed" (μακάριοι) and supported with favorable consequences ("because they will…" or "because theirs is…"). In terms of <u>scope</u>, the list is exclusive/limited, but exemplary; the list is not inclusive (containing every single moral disposition or attribute), but exemplary describing distinct, pivotal stages of development. In terms of <u>referencing</u>, the list is forward looking; it prepares for the rest of the Sermon on the Mount, possibly speaking in general terms of the moral virtues and conduct to be embodied by one who would follow Jesus.

In terms of <u>formal structure</u>, first, the list shows an inner-to-outer movement that is progressive (see further below) and bracketed (5:3, 10). The first items of the list at 5:3–10—"poor in spirit," "mourning," "gentle," "hungering and thirsting for righteousness," "merciful," "pure in heart," "peacemaking," and "persecuted for righteousness"—move from inward to outward relations (self to others) as well as depict a progression initially concerning internal spiritual poverty ("poor in spirit" and "mourning") but then concerning relating to the poverty of others (being "gentle," then "merciful," being "pure in heart," then "peacemaking," then "being persecuted"). Indeed, I have described these beatitudes as providing an *ordo salutis*, not in terms of earning salvation, but in terms of receiving it and working for the comprehensive salvation of others. The list achieves an initial culmination with "peacemaking" (5:9), i.e., trying to reconcile two or more parties at odds. This will involve identifying problems, points of responsibility, and even sin. Peacemaking works for mutual acknowledgement of the problem and for confession of sin for the purpose of reconciliation. The difficulty with peacemaking is that too often not everyone will take responsibility for his or her part in the conflict. If and when this happens, persecution against the peacemaker will often result, which is what the eighth beatitude in 5:10 depicts: "Blessed are those who are persecuted for the sake of righteousness."

A second feature of the formal structure is that the list builds to the last "blessed" item in 5:11—"Blessed are you when people insult ... persecute ... falsely say ... because of me." This final beatitude is differentiated 1) by something being done against the disciples, 2) by switching to second person plural "You," 3) by repeating the content of the previous beatitude ("persecuted"), 4) by containing its own list ("insult ... persecuted ... say falsely against"), 5) by explicit reference to Jesus ("me"), 6) by altering the repeated pattern in 5:3–10 of "Blessed are the.... because they/theirs..." (μακάριοι οἱ ... ὅτι αὐτοὶ/αὐτῶν), 7) by placement after the bracketing achieved by the statement "because theirs is the Kingdom of Heaven" in 5:3 and 5:10, and 8) by being given further elaboration in 5:12 ("Rejoice and be glad...!"). When we recognize that 5:11–12 is climactic, we have begun already to make observations about the semantic relationships of the list.

In terms of semantic (structural) relationships, the list concerns a reoccurrence of moral dispositions or attributes that are substantiated with a description of their favorable consequences ("because they will..." and "because theirs is..."). Moreover, the first seven items (5:3–9) progressively provide causation for the last two descriptions, which are climactic moral attributes ("being persecuted") in 5:10–12. Additionally, the first eight attributes are more general and stated in third person ("they"), leading to the more particular second person ("you") in 5:11–12. The attention and climactic "punch line" for the beatitudes is in the final, ninth beatitude that brings Jesus's teaching "close to the hearers" by using "You"—"blessed are YOU, when you are persecuted for righteousness...." Then, Jesus compares those who would embody the beatitudes (the YOU) with the prophets who were also persecuted. Jesus envisions and calls his followers to fully participate in the *ordo salutis,* which once embodied will involve peace-making (calling people to reconciliation) that all too often will result in persecution. Although much more can be said about the beatitudes, we have covered much ground here in our analysis.

A Catalog of NT Lists: Every NT book has one or more lists; intriguingly, the least populated are the Johannine writings (excluding the Book of Revelation) which have a propensity for doublets and oppositional pairings. Also, it is interesting to observe that Paul's earliest letters have significantly fewer lists (Galatians, 1 and 2 Thessalonians), while his major and latter letters have the most (1/2 Corinthians, Romans, Ephesians, and the Pastorals). Below are verses containing lists from each NT book; I have searched more thoroughly in some books than in others, especially the NT letters. Generally, the Gospels are underrepresented. Most of these lists are excellent for careful study; some occur at critical points in the argument and function to consolidate the main points of a pericope. In order to fully recognize and appreciate some of the lists (depending on the English translation), it may be necessary to consult the Greek (e.g., Mark 5:25–27, 33).

A Catalog of NT Lists

Matt 4:17–22; chs. 5–7; ch. 13; 15:19; chs. 23–25; 28:18–20
Mark 3:13–19; 5:25–34; 7:21–22; 8:30–34; 9:31; 10:33–34
Luke 3:1–2, 7–18; 6:20–26; 21:10–28; 23:1–4; 24:44–49
John 16:5–11; 18:20; 19:20; 20:27; 21:15–17
Acts 1:8; 2:1–12, 17–21, 42–47; 6:1–6; 17:34; 28:26–27
Romans 1:29–31; 3:9–20; 5:3–5; 7:12; 8:28–30, 31–39; 9:3–5; 11:1; 12:1–2, 3–8, 9–21; 13:9, 13; 15:8–13; ch. 16
1 Corinthians 1:12–13, 20, 22–24, 26–29, 30; 2:3; 3:6, 11–16, 21–23; 4:7–13; 5:9–13; 6:9–11; chs. 12–14 on the various gifts of the Spirit, the description of love, etc.; 15:1–11, 35–44
2 Corinthians 4:7–12; 6:1–13; 11:4, 25–33; 12:19–21; 13:11 and 14
Galatians 1:13–14, 1:15–2:14; 3:28; 4:10; 5:19–23, 26
Ephesians 4:1–3, 4–5, 17–19, 20–24, and 25–32 (or including also 5:1–2); 5:3–9, 15–22
Philippians 2:1–2; 3:1–16; 4:8–9
Colossians 1:9–12, 13–20; 2:20–23; 3:5–17, 3:18–4:1;
1 Thessalonians 1:3; 4:16–17; 5:14, 15–22, 23
2 Thessalonians 2:1–2; 3:6–12
1 Timothy 1:8–11, 13, 17; 2:1, 7, 9–10, 15; 3:1–15, 16; 4:12–13; 5:9–10, 13–14; 6:3–5, 11
2 Timothy 2:1–7, 11–13, 22; 3:1–9, 10–11, 16; 4:1–5, 7
Titus 1:5–16; 2:1–10, 12, 15; 3:1–3
Philemon 1–2, 22–23
Hebrews 1:2–4, 5–14; 2:3–4, 6–8; 6:1–2, 4–6; 7:26; 8:10–11; 9:2; 10:19–25, 29; ch. 11; 12:18-24; ch. 13.
James 1:11, 19; 2:1–4, 14–16; 3:7–8, 15–18; 4:7–10; 5:12
1 Peter 1:2; 2:1–3, 9, 17; 3:3, 8–12, 22; 4:1–4, 15; 5:1–3, 10
2 Peter 1:2–11; ch. 2; 3:3–4, 10
1 John 1:1; 2:11, 12–14, 16; 5:7–8; 2 John 3; 3 John 10
Jude 2, 5–16, 19, 20–21, 22–23, 25
Revelation 1:4–6, 8, 9, 11, 12–16, 19; chs. 2–3; 4:5–7, 9, 11; 5:11–13; 9:21; 21:8; 22:15

NOTA BENE: I have identified most lists here but not always in specificity particularly for the Gospels and those places where whole chapters are given. However, for the Pauline Epistles my identification is fairly thorough. In a few places lists will span across whole chapters, e.g., when Paul is recounting his narrative of movements and interactions in Gal 1:15–2:14.

A Procedure for Studying Lists: Based upon my experience interpreting NT lists and thinking about how best to describe them according to the taxonomy presented above, I would recommend the following procedure for anyone who might consider interpreting a NT list:

1. Locate the list within its **literary context** and ask, Is this list backward referencing, forward referencing, or both?
2. Identify the **material content** of the items of the list: Does it contain persons, places, events, processes, concepts, or a mix of these? If the latter, consider initially why it is mixed.
3. Determine the **scope** of the list—exhaustive or limited; if limited, consider how is it limited. Does the literary context help in this determination?
4. Study the **formal structure** of the list itself; consider the types of formal structures described above. Look especially for how the literary context may describe the structure or priorities of the list itself by statements before and after the list.
5. Consider what major **semantic relationships** are operative within the list itself and surrounding the list; consider how the list may be introduced or referred back to within the literary context.
6. Based upon material content, scope, formal structure, and semantic relationships, conduct further research on **key terms and ideas** of the list as they may occur within the biblical book, corpus, testament, canon, and/or in relation to the first-century social-cultural milieu.
7. Determine the **rhetorical purpose and meaning** of the list as plausibly intended by the author for the original audience(s). Be sure to major on the majors, and minor on the minors.
8. Finally, **evaluate** the major findings from your study and how the list may encourage us to live differently today and consider how you might **apply** and **appropriate** the list.

Jesus's Teaching Methods: Although we commonly associate "parables" with Jesus's teaching, in fact he used a variety of approaches to teaching depending on the setting and audience. Parables, although his most common type of teaching, are still only one type of teaching; see further below. In this respect, the Greek word for "parable" (παραβολή) reflects a broader range of meanings not unlike the underlying Hebrew word *Mashal*: comparisons, proverbs, illustrations, analogies, and fictitious narratives to convey a religious or moral lesson (as found in LSJ). The following chart categorizes Jesus's main types of teaching.

TEACHING FORMS OF JESUS

1. **Parable** (fictitious story to convey a lesson or lessons); e.g., Parable of Mustard Seed (Mark 4:30–33); the Good Samaritan (Luke 10:30–37)
2. **Allegorical Story** (many elements have meaning); e.g., Parable of Sower and many locations (Matt 13:3–9)
3. **Aphorism** (personal proverb); e.g., Heart's treasure (Matt 6:21); one who has will have taken away (Luke 8:18)
4. **Use of OT Scripture** (quoting or strongly alluding to the OT); e.g., Jesus begins his ministry (Luke 4:16–21)

> 5. **Hyperbole** (overstatement); e.g., plank in eye (Matt 7:3–5)
> 6. **Illustrations** (using object lessens); e.g., "Who is the greatest?" and presents a child (Mark 9:35–37)
> 7. **Paradoxical or Enigmatic Sayings** (seemingly nonsensical); e.g., "the first must be last" (Mark 9:35)
> 8. **Encountering Life Situations**; e.g., settling an inheritance dispute (Luke 12:13–15)
> 9. **Metaphoric Statements**; e.g., "I am the bread of life…" (John 6:35)
> 10. **Syllogistic Reasoning** ("If…, [then]…"); e.g., "If God were your father, (then) you would love me" (John 8:42)
> 11. **Rhetorical Questions**; e.g., How can saltiness be restored? (Mark 9:50); What is the source of John's Baptism? (Luke 20:3–4)

EXERCISE 6–E: Identify the following types of teaching (yes, even in the apostle Paul):

Matt 4:10; 5:29; 16:25; 17:20; 21:28–31; 22:19–21

Mark 2:27; 4:26–29; 12:1–10

Luke 6:32; 7:31–32; 9:23; 11:19; 20:41–44

John 6:26–27, 35; 7:16–19, 37–38; 9:3–5; 10:34–36; 11:9–10, 25–26

2 Cor 2:14–15; 3:7–8, 9; 6:1–2, 14–18; 11:2–3; 12:10b

<u>Parables as a Literary Form</u>: Jesus used a Jewish technique of relating short stories known as parables. However, interpreters have struggled how best to interpret them. In the early church, allegorical interpretation was one common approach. In a rather well-know example, the church father Augustine thoroughly deployed an allegorical method to interpret the Good Samaritan parable in Luke 10:30–37; see his creative interpretation on the following page. His attempt is not unlike our own attempts to bring Scripture into our own world; we too often allegorize Scripture. However, what is the cost of doing this? When interpreting Scripture allegorically, are we reading passages as intended by the original authors? Arguably not. In 1899 Adolf Jülicher argued vigorously against allegorizing parables maintaining that make one and only one point.[14] This pendulum swing is understandable in light of the abuses of allegorizing parables. However, this "singular meaning approach" does not correspond to how Jesus himself and the Gospel writers treated his parables since they allegorically explained certain elements of some parables (such as main agents and actions). For example, in Matt 13:18–23, 36–43, 49–50 Jesus explained the meaning of his parables in this fashion. Thus, more recently NT interpreters have reevaluated how best to interpret parables mediating between the extremes of allegorizing or the one-point approach.

---

[14] Adolf Jülicher, *Die Glieschnisreden Jesu*, 2 vols. (Freiburg: Mohr, 1899).

AUGUSTINE'S ALLEGORICAL INTERPRETATION OF GOOD SAMARITAN PARABLE[15]

The man going down to Jericho = Adam	Priest = Priesthood of the Old Testament (Law)
Jerusalem, from which he was going = City of Heavenly Peace	Levite = Ministry of the Old Testament (Prophets)
	Good Samaritan = Christ
Jericho = The moon which signifies our mortality (this is a play on the Hebrew terms for Jericho and moon which both look and sound alike)	Binding of wounds = Restraint of sin
	Oil = Comfort of good hope
	Wine = Exhortation to spirited work
Robbers = Devil and his angels	Animal = Body of Christ
Stripping him = Taking away his immortality	Inn = Church
Beating him = Persuading him to sin	Two denarii = Two commandments to love
Leaving him half dead = Because of sin, he was dead spiritually, but half alive, because of the knowledge of God	Innkeeper = Apostle Paul
	Return of the Good Samaritan = Resurrection of Christ

Craig L. Blomberg has provided helpful guidelines for parable interpretation. The principles are fairly simple. You must recognize that parables develop important points around the main persons or entities in the parable. Blomberg offers this classification: triadic (three), dyadic (two), or monadic (one) along with the presence or not of hierarchical structure (monarchic or non-monarchic).

BLOMBERG'S DESCRIPTION OF COMMON PARABLES STRUCTURES[16]

MONADIC =	one main character	**EXAMPLE:**	Treasure Hunter (Matt 13:44–46)	
DYADIC = *type 1* *monarchic*	superior | subordinate	**EXAMPLE:**	Farmer | (Mark 4:26–29) Seed Growing Secretly	
type 2	good example — bad example	**EXAMPLE:**	Tax Collector — Pharisee (Luke 18:9–14)	
TRIADIC = *type 1* *monarchic*	master ╱╲ good subordinate bad subordinate	**EXAMPLE:**	Father (Luke 15:11–32) ╱╲ Prodigal Son Older Brother	
type 2	master subordinate sub-subordinate	**EXAMPLE:**	King (Matt 18:21–35) Servant forgiven large debt Other Servant not forgiven small debt	
type 3	good example – unifier – bad example	**EXAMPLE:**	Samaritan — Man — Priest (Luke 10:30–37) in ditch Levite	

---

[15] From Robert Stein, *The Method and Message of Jesus' Teaching*, rev. ed. (Louisville: Westminster John Knox, 1994), 46.

[16] This table slightly adapts and combines the two charts of information in Craig L. Blomberg, *Jesus and the Gospels: An Introduction and Survey* (Nashville: Broadman & Holman, 1997), 259 and 261.

EXERCISE 6–F: Given this parable from Luke 16:19–31 (NASB), perform the following steps:

1. Determine the main characters and/or events.
2. Is this parable triadic, dyadic, or monadic?
3. Determine the point being made surrounding each person or entity. Is the parable introduced or explained in such a way to clarify the point(s)?
4. How do these points relate to the surrounding context?
5. What interpretive questions do you have about the meaning or social-cultural background?

[19] "Now there was a rich man, and he habitually dressed in purple and fine linen, joyously living in splendor every day. [20] "And a poor man named Lazarus was laid at his gate, covered with sores, [21] and longing to be fed with the *crumbs* which were falling from the rich man's table; besides, even the dogs were coming and licking his sores. [22] "Now the poor man died and was carried away by the angels to Abraham's bosom; and the rich man also died and was buried. [23] "In Hades he lifted up his eyes, being in torment, and saw Abraham far away and Lazarus in his bosom. [24] "And he cried out and said, 'Father Abraham, have mercy on me, and send Lazarus so that he may dip the tip of his finger in water and cool off my tongue, for I am in agony in this flame.' [25] "But Abraham said, 'Child, remember that during your life you received your good things, and likewise Lazarus bad things; but now he is being comforted here, and you are in agony. [26] 'And besides all this, between us and you there is a great chasm fixed, so that those who wish to come over from here to you will not be able, and *that* none may cross over from there to us.' [27] "And he said, 'Then I beg you, father, that you send him to my father's house— [28] for I have five brothers—in order that he may warn them, so that they will not also come to this place of torment.' [29] "But Abraham said, 'They have Moses and the Prophets; let them hear them.' [30] "But he said, 'No, father Abraham, but if someone goes to them from the dead, they will repent!' [31]"But he said to him, 'If they do not listen to Moses and the Prophets, they will not be persuaded even if someone rises from the dead.'"

<u>A Procedure for Studying Parables</u>: I offer here a five-step process for studying parables.

1. Consider the **literary structure** of the parable identifying the **main agents** and **turns of events**, while also paying careful attention to the **semantic/structure relationships**.
2. If needed, conduct research on the **socio-cultural background** (see STEP 7: HISTORICAL CONTEXT) to make sense of these agents, actions, etc. For some parables this may not be necessary while for others this will be the only way to properly determine its (original) meaning.
3. Consider the **point that each major agent or turn of event represents** that sometimes is made clear by an explicit explanation; otherwise, this will need to be determined from the context.
4. Then, consider the **parable's contribution to the thematic development** in the context: How does the parable support, develop, or advance the main themes?
5. If time allows, **compare the version of the parable found in your passage with what may be found in another Gospel; note the differences**. These differences may help further relate the parable to its surrounding context. However, be careful not to harmonize the various versions of the parable; that is not the point and may obscure the meaning of the parable in context. All in all, be sure to understand that differences between parallel parables may or may not be due to the fact that the gospel writers edited them differently; differences may instead reflect that Jesus taught a parable repeatedly (probably) and taught them differently in differing settings.

Researching Literary Forms: If you can (safely) identify within a passage a particular "form," then you are well along the way to understanding the structure and meaning of the passage. Remember too that literary forms will help inform the genre of the whole book since genres attract and invite particular literary forms. Lists and parables are common and productive types of literary forms to study. There are others certainly to identify; presented below in SECONDARY STUDY is an extensive chart of types of literary forms found in the Bible. The next step would be to research the literary form identified to see what scholars have said about it in general or in relation to your passage. Also, it is possible that your passage contains a significant variation from the form, which is usually for some emphasis, and so you ought to pay attention to that difference and ask why it is there. Or, a literary unit may combine elements of two or more forms to create a hybrid; again this combination has interpretive significance. So, you should probe how the forms interrelate in order to stress points (see the example of Eph 2:11–22 in TERTIARY RESEARCH below).

Avoiding a "Cookie-Cutter" Approach to Literary Forms: Finally, we need to avoid presupposing a structure and overlaying a form onto the passage. This is like pressing a cookie-cutter onto rolled-out dough. You must always be cautious and willing to adjust your understanding to correspond to the evidence—i.e., what *actually* is observed—and not to what you want to find. Remember that literary forms prepare our expectations for how to read and interpret the passage in context. If we wrongly assign a form and structure, we will often find ourselves reading the passage against its grain (to use a wood metaphor) and also against its proper role in the immediate context. However, when properly observed and recognized, literary forms will guide our interpretation and help to clarify what was originally intended in the initial composition of the discourse.

PRIMARY INTERPRETIVE PROCEDURES:

1. **Based upon previous identification of the genre of your book under STEP 1: CONTEXTUAL LOCATION (if completed), re-evaluate that initial identification and bring forward any questions you might have had.**
2. **Consult recent commentaries (specialized verse-by-verse treatments of biblical books) or resources (like books, articles, or essays) that might attempt to determine the literary form of the passage and genre of the NT book.** Read and take notes about that genre and/or literary from two or three sources; Bible commentaries or dictionaries may be helpful. Additionally, there are many fine NT Introductions and specific books summarizing NT genres (see chapter Bibliography).
3. **In light of new information learned about the particular features of the genre and literary form, re-read the book as a whole (or significant surrounding portions) noting features of the genre that relate particularly to your pericope.** How does your pericope relate to the book as a whole in terms of genre? How does the pericope support genre determination?
4. **If a parable or list is present in the pericope, follow the procedures on pp. 225 and 228.**
5. **Record any significant observations and interpretive questions raised by considering the genre of the book as a whole and your pericope's function within it.**

II. SECONDARY STUDY

Orientation: The identification of literary genres and literary forms is one of the most beneficial aspects of critical scholarship. Much ink has been spilled on the subject to describe their proper characteristics and functions socially and culturally. For the average Christian or pastor, it is easy to get lost in the scholarly discussions and to wonder about the relevance. Although some debates have been more-or-less settled with discussion continuing about sub-categories of genres (e.g., the Gospels as ancient biography), other debates continue (e.g., diatribe; and the nature of Paul's letters). In SECONDARY STUDY, we will review the major issues of NT genres and literary forms while directing interpreters to the most fruitful areas of study.

The Gospels as Historical Biography: An example of a somewhat established matter concerns the Gospels as "ancient biographies" (βίοι)—something scholars had considered before, but Richard Burridge has settled.[17] A sizable majority of Gospel scholars agree with this assessment, even though debate continues about what sub-genre of biography and whether the NT gospels are historical or romantic (i.e., fictional) biography. However, Craig S. Keener continues to show convincingly how the Gospels are best understood as historical.[18]

> Although ancient biographies varied in their historiographic practice, in the early Empire biographies about figures who lived in the generation or two before the biographer included substantial historical information about the figure. This observation may be particularly relevant for biographies about sages. Schools often preserved considerable information about their founders' teachings; ancient memory practices exceeded what is typical today, and disciples often preserved and passed on considerable information. Researchers should neither treat the Gospels more skeptically nor demand from them greater precision than we would from comparable works of their era.[19]

Diatribe (Conversational Exchanges) in Paul: Even after Rudolf Bultmann's identification and description of the popular philosophical teaching technique of diatribe in Paul's writings a century ago,[20] modern interpreters are still debating the finer details of how and when diatribe was used, in what social setting, and what implications this has for identifying the auditor or interlocutor with whom Paul is dialoguing (hypothetically) throughout Rom 1–11.[21] Thus, the interpretation

---

[17] Richard A. Burridge, *What Are the Gospels? A Comparison with Graeco-Roman Biography*, 2nd ed. (Grand Rapids: Eerdmans, 2004).

[18] Craig S. Keener, *The Historical Jesus of the Gospels* (Grand Rapids: Eerdmans, 2009). See also his, "Otho: A Targeted Comparison of Suetonius's Biography and Tacitus's History, with Implications for the Gospels' Historical Reliability," *BBR* 21.3 (2011): 331–55.

[19] Craig S. Keener, "Assumptions in Historical-Jesus Research: Using Ancient Biographies and Disciples' Traditioning as a Control," *Journal for the Study of the Historical Jesus* 9.1 (2011): 26–58, from the abstract.

[20] Rudolf Karl Bultmann, *Der Stil der paulinischen Predigt und die kynisch-stoische Diatribe*, FRLANT 13 (Göttingen: Vandenhoeck & Ruprecht, 1910).

[21] See, e.g., Stanley Kent Stowers, *The Diatribe and Paul's Letter to the Romans*, SBLDS (Chico, CA: Scholars Press, 1981); idem., *A Rereading of Romans: Justice, Jews, and Gentiles* (New Haven: Yale University Press,

of (parts of) Romans hinges upon these debated points. The same is true of 1 Corinthians: What represents Paul's voice? And, what represents the interlocutor's voice which may reflect a viewpoint contrary to Paul's? On this difficulty, consider the exercise below.

EXERCISE 6–G: First Corinthians 6:12–20 begins a new unit. Given below is my own translation with the expected answers to rhetorical questions given in brackets [...]. Consider these questions:

1. Can you identify Paul's voice and the interlocutor's voice? How easily?

2. If so, how would you distinguish features of each voice?

3. Are these voices in conversation or strong opposition to one another?

> ¹² All things are lawful for me, but not all things are profitable. All things are lawful for me, but I will not be mastered by anything.
> ¹³ Food is for the stomach and the stomach is for food, but God will do away with both of them. Moreover, the body is not for immorality, but for the Lord, and the Lord is for the body.
> ¹⁴ Furthermore, God has not only raised the Lord, but will also raise us up through His power.
> ¹⁵ Don't you know that your bodies are members of Christ? [Surely yes!] Shall I then take away the members of Christ and make them members of a prostitute? May it never be!
> ¹⁶ Or don't you know that the one who joins himself to a prostitute is one body? [Surely yes!] For He says, "THE TWO SHALL BECOME ONE FLESH."
> ¹⁷ But the one who joins himself to the Lord is one spirit *with Him*.
> ¹⁸ Flee immorality. Every sin that a person commits is outside the body, but the immoral person sins against his or her own body.
> ¹⁹ Or don't you know that your body is a temple of the Holy Spirit who is in you, whom you have from God, and that you are not your own? [Surely yes!]
> ²⁰ For you have been bought with a price. Therefore, glorify God in your body.

Indeed, recognizing the presence of diatribe places a necessary constraint upon our interpretation.

<u>How to Study Paul? Ancient Rhetoric vs. Epistolary Criticism</u>: Obviously, Pauline and other NT epistles show the opening, transitional, and concluding features of ancient "personal" letters. See further below for clear evidence of this. However, the ancient letter tradition was diverse and includes official letters and didactic/literary letters in addition to personal letters. Most typically, Paul's epistles have been compared to the personal or documentary letter tradition. However, Paul's letters show great variance from the existing personal letter tradition and what is recommended by the literary critic "Demetrius" (authorship is uncertain) when discussing "plain" style in *On Style* (first-century BC) which may be summarized in what follows:[22]

1997); Runar M. Thorsteinsson, *Paul's Interlocutor in Romans 2: Function and Identity in the Context of Ancient Epistolography* (Stockholm: Almqvist & Wiksell International, 2003), and Changwon Song, *Reading Romans as Diatribe*, SBL 59 (New York: Peter Lang, 2004).

[22] See Carol Poster, "A Conversation Halved: Epistolary Theory in Greco-Roman Antiquity," in *Letter-*

LENGTH: Paul's epistles have an average of 2,500 words in contrast to the 955 word average of Seneca's letter length and 295 of Cicero's in his published letters.[23] Demetrius says, "The length of a letter, no less than its range of style, should be restricted" (*On Style* 228).
STYLE: Paul is more lively and conversational and not graceful and plain (*On Style* 224–26).
ADDRESSEES: Paul addresses communities within regions (e.g., "Achaia" in 2 Cor 1:1), not typically individuals as is the case in the personal documentary letters.
CONTENT: Paul addresses communal concerns and rigorously and argumentatively engages philosophical, theological, and ethical ideas in contrast to subjects in personal letters.

Certainly, Paul's epistles may be investigated as letters as a genre with particular literary forms within the letter as a whole (see below GRECO-ROMAN PERSONAL DOCUMENTARY LETTER FORMS). *However, what accounts for the significant characteristics and features of Paul's epistles that are not accounted for by documentary-epistolary theory?*

Ancient Rhetoric in Paul: In dispute is whether and to what extent Paul's epistles reflect the influence of ancient rhetorical practices either intentionally (i.e., Paul utilized such rhetoric) or unintentionally (i.e., "rhetoric was in the air").[24] Interpreters want explicit proof of the use of formal rhetoric in Paul. Yet, according to the very tenets of the rhetorical theorists, especially those in the first-centuries BC and AD surrounding the NT, *one flaunted their use of rhetoric at risk of being identified as a sophist trying to persuade for bad reasons.*[25] Thus, it is not surprising that Paul's epistles do not so overtly reflect rhetorical forms, even though under careful scrutiny one may detect rhetorical structure, forms, strategies, and "idioms" (expressions) that are from the tradition.[26] This "hiddenness" of Paul's rhetoric is what we should expect. And yet Paul openly and unabashedly admitted that he "persuades" in 2 Cor 5:11 using πείθω, a technical verb (the goddess of persuasion is Πειθώ), although earlier disavowing such with regard to his preaching of the Gospel in 1 Cor 2:1–4. So, we are in a bit of a conundrum since he disavowed it and then admitted it. The solution is a rather simple one: *Paul was not beholden to rhetoric (to display it openly) especially in his person while preaching; and yet Paul could organize discourse and argue rhetorically in his epistles.* This polarity lies behind the "evaluation" from his critic in 2 Cor 10:10 where we find this assessment of Paul and his letters: "On the one hand, his letters are weighty and strong, but on the other hand, his personal presence is unimpressive and his speech contemptible." In the end, Paul's epistles are more than simply letters—they contain a variety of literary forms that show influence from the rhetorical tradition. Therefore, Paul's letters may be deemed "rhetorical epistles" and

---

Writing Manuals and Instruction from Antiquity to the Present: Historical and Bibliographic Studies, ed. C. Poster and L. C. Mitchell, Studies in Rhetoric/Communication (Columbia: University of South Carolina Press, 2007), 23–24.

[23] These numbers are from the very helpful article by Paul J. Achtemeier, "Omne Verbum Sonat: The New Testament and the Oral Environment of Late Western Antiquity," *JBL* 109 (1990): 3–27.

[24] See recently my critique: "Review of Ryan S. Schellenberg, *Rethinking Paul's Rhetorical Education: Comparative Rhetoric and 2 Corinthians 10–13*," *RBL* [http://www.bookreviews.org] (2014).

[25] See a detailed accounting of the rhetorical tradition in my *Ancient Rhetoric and Paul's Apology*, 32–33.

[26] In addition to my work cited above, see, e.g., Margaret M. Mitchell, *Paul and the Rhetoric of Reconciliation*. See also the many writings of Ben Witherington III that illustrate dependence on ancient rhetoric.

should be studied as such. For further discussion, see TERTIARY RESEARCH.

Epistolary Features: Just as modern letters are recognizable by particular features, so ancient letters had characteristic features. Below summarizes the personal/documentary letter form.[27]

GRECO-ROMAN PERSONAL/*DOCUMENTARY* LETTER FORMS[28]

I. INTRODUCTORY SALUTATION:
  A. Sender
  B. to Addressee
  C. Greetings (χαίρειν "greetings")
  D. A Wish for Good Health, often with a prayer to a certain deity on behalf of the Addressee

II. BODY OF LETTER:
  A. Usually introduced with characteristic formulae
  B. Comments are often brief.

III. CLOSING:
  A. Final Greetings (includes people other than addressee)
  B. Good wishes, especially for people other than addressee
  C. Concluding greeting or prayer
  D. Sometimes a date

IV. ADDRESS ON THE REVERSE SIDE OF THE LETTER (letter was usually folded)

Some of these features are quite old. For example, the fourth-century BC Greek historian Xenophon in his work "The Education of Cyrus" (*Cyropaedia* 4.5.27–33) contains a letter written that opens with Κῦρος Κυαξάρῃ χαίρειν "Cyrus to Cyaxares, Greetings!" and then concludes with travel plans to come visit him before the standard goodbye: ἔρρωσο "Farewell" (lit., "Be strong!").

EXERCISE 6–H: Consider modern types of letters:

a. How many types (and sub-types) of modern letters can you identify?

b. What are the shared characteristics of each type of letter?

c. What are unique or distinctive features? Do these particular features especially inform the purpose of the specific letter type?

Epistolary and Rhetorical Forms: Scholars have very carefully compared Paul's Epistles to ancient epistolary and rhetorical conventions. In my estimation, it is possible to correlate these epistolary formal features (left column) with rhetorical dispositional structures (right column). You must remember that in actual performance you will find variations and innovations.

---

[27] See the excellent survey of the ancient letter tradition by Hans-Josef Klauck, *Ancient Letters and the New Testament: A Guide to Context and Exegesis*, trans. Daniel P. Bailey (Waco, TX: Baylor University Press, 2006).

[28] Slightly adapted from Michael R. Cosby, *Apostle on the Edge: An Inductive Approach to Paul* (Louisville: Westminster John Knox, 2009), 91.

PAULINE EPISTOLARY AND RHETORICAL FORMS

EPISTOLARY FORMAT	RHETORICAL DISPOSITION

I. Introduction: Typically includes five elements:
  A. the sender,
  B. to the recipient,
  C. initial greeting "Grace and peace" (χάρις καὶ εἰρήνη)
  D. a thanksgiving, and/or
  E. a prayer, which may build to an eschatological climax
Note: The letter's main themes may be seen in D. and E.
	I. *Prooemium/Exordium/Proem*
	
	Purposes: to establish the good will of the audience and to orient them to the basic issue(s) to be addressed

II. Transition to the letter body: *May be* marked by a disclosure statement such as "I want you to know...." This statement may signal the presence of a *narration*.	**II. *Narration*** (optional) in past time Purpose: to give the basic facts of the situation relevant for gaining optimal persuasion **III. *Proposition/Prothesis***: one thesis **Partition**: multiple theses heads Purpose: to state the thesis or summarize the main argument point(s) that will be addressed in the *probatio*

III. Letter Body:
  A. The body of the letter may have two sections: doctrinal and hortatory/parenetic or ethical. But there are some exceptions.
  B. In addition to disclosure statement, other formulas are:
    1. Appeal Formula with "I exhort" (παρακαλέω)
    2. Confidence Formula (e.g., "I am confident that...")
    3. "Now concerning..." Formula with περὶ δέ...
    4. "Finally" Formula with λοιπόν or τὰ δὲ λοιπά
	IV. *Probatio/Proofs* (main argument):
	Purpose: to elaborate the theses as presented in the *prothesis* or *partition* prototypically in the same order as given in the *partition*
	
	V. *Refutation* (optional)
	Purposes: to refute objections to the *probatio*/main argument and to address and debunk one's opponents
	
	VI. Self-Adulation (optional)
	Purpose: to speak favorably of oneself

IV. Closing: Typically includes several of these elements:
  A. final greeting (e.g., "I also send greetings...")
  B. exchange of greetings (e.g., "others send greetings")
  C. request for prayer
  D. travelogue (e.g., "I hope to pass through Macedonia")
  E. signature (e.g., "See what large letters I use")
  F. benediction (e.g., "Grace and peace be to you all...")
  G. doxology (e.g., "Now to God be the glory...")
	VII. *Peroration/Epilogue*
	
	Purposes: to make a final emotional appeal and/or to summarize the most important points of the discourse

STEP 6: SECONDARY STUDY 235

EXERCISE 6–I: Given Paul's letter to Philemon with the paragraphs and spacing breaks as given in the RSV, identify epistolary and rhetorical literary forms in the space available to the right.

¹ Paul, a prisoner for Christ Jesus, and Timothy our brother,

To Philemon our beloved fellow worker ² and Apphia our sister and Archippus our fellow soldier, and the church in your house:

³ Grace to you and peace from God our Father and the Lord Jesus Christ.

⁴ I thank my God always when I remember you in my prayers, ⁵ because I hear of your love and of the faith which you have toward the Lord Jesus and all the saints, ⁶ and I pray that the sharing of your faith may promote the knowledge of all the good that is ours in Christ. ⁷ For I have derived much joy and comfort from your love, my brother, because the hearts of the saints have been refreshed through you.

⁸ Accordingly, though I am bold enough in Christ to command you to do what is required, ⁹ yet for love's sake I prefer to appeal to you—I, Paul, an ambassador and now a prisoner also for Christ Jesus— ¹⁰ I appeal to you for my child, Onesimus, whose father I have become in my imprisonment. ¹¹ (Formerly he was useless to you, but now he is indeed useful to you and to me.) ¹² I am sending him back to you, sending my very heart. ¹³ I would have been glad to keep him with me, in order that he might serve me on your behalf during my imprisonment for the gospel; ¹⁴ but I preferred to do nothing without your consent in order that your goodness might not be by compulsion but of your own free will.

¹⁵ Perhaps this is why he was parted from you for a while, that you might have him back for ever, ¹⁶ no longer as a slave but more than a slave, as a beloved brother, especially to me but how much more to you, both in the flesh and in the Lord. ¹⁷ So if you consider me your partner, receive him as you would receive me. ¹⁸ If he has wronged you at all, or owes you anything, charge that to my account. ¹⁹ I, Paul, write this with my own hand, I will repay it—to say nothing of your owing me even your own self. ²⁰ Yes, brother, I want some benefit from you in the Lord. Refresh my heart in Christ.

²¹ Confident of your obedience, I write to you, knowing that you will do even more than I say. ²² At the same time, prepare a guest room for me, for I am hoping through your prayers to be granted to you.

²³ Epaphras, my fellow prisoner in Christ Jesus, sends greetings to you, ²⁴ and so do Mark, Aristarchus, Demas, and Luke, my fellow workers.

²⁵ The grace of the Lord Jesus Christ be with your spirit.

Literary Form and Modes of Persuasion: From the very start of ancient rhetorical education, every attempt was made to harness the form of the discourse to be maximally persuasive in the respective situation. We must remember that the goal of discourse is to move the audience to adopt a certain view of reality that has corresponding beliefs, attitude, affections, and actions. *But the user was never a slave of the form, but the form was subject to the use.* A failure to understand this dictum has lead interpreters to "over interpret" the forms by being slavishly tied to them and not understanding the variety of arrangements of forms and mixtures of forms required by the situation. For example, Aristotle (rightly!) maintained that narrative material should be placed wherever needed in the discourse. Analogously, Quintilian thought that partitions (brief summaries of the subsequent material) should not be restricted in placement after the narrative material, but should used and placed wherever needed in the discourse. So, it is not surprising that within the rhetorical tradition considerable thought was given to *how persuasion is best achieved*. As a starting point, it is helpful to recreate a diagram by Jakob Wisse (slightly modified) that describes the relation of *ethos* (ethical character), *logos* (logical reasonableness), and *pathos* (emotional impact) to the speech event.[29] To the diagram "means" are added by which each mode may be achieved.

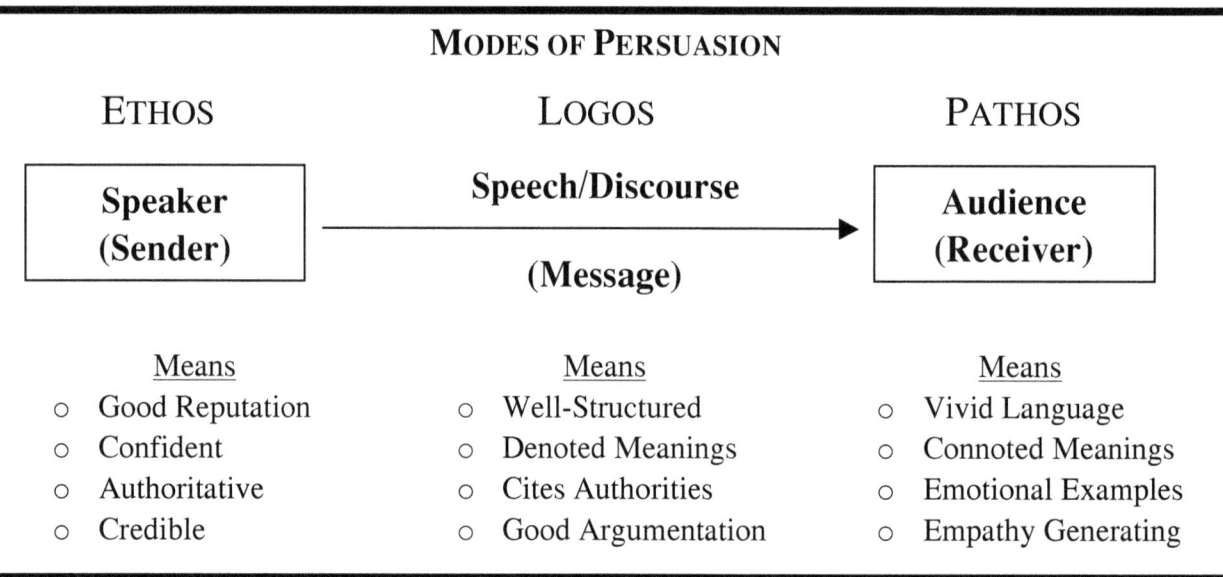

Orality and Oral Patterning: Despite the fact that we today most often encounter the NT as a written document, the first audiences would have experienced it audibly. The documents would have been read, if not even "performed" with proper enunciation, intonation, body positioning and gestures. So important was the final performance of rhetorical speeches that the rhetorician Quintilian in his monumental summary of the rhetorical tradition in the multivolume *Institutio Oratoria* ("Oratorical Instruction" ca. AD 90) devotes separate sections to memorization and to gestures.

---

[29] Jakob Wisse, *Ethos and Pathos: From Aristotle to Cicero* (Amsterdam: Hakkert, 1989), 6.

Chiasm: The arrangement of material such that elements are repeated in inverted order is called a chiasm or chiasmus and has the pattern AB … BA.[30] Just how many elements are present varies according to an author's elaboration of the chiastic schema.[31] Thus, chiasms may have multiple corresponding elements and become rather complex, such as ABCDEFGH…HGFEDCBA. A much simpler and more common oral-literary form that carried aural impact would be lists and parallelism. However, chiasms require more effort to create and to receive. They are purposive.

The earliest explanation of chiasmus is the first-century BC manual of rhetoric, *Rhetorica ad Herennium* 4.39 which describes the basic, contrastive literary figure called *commutatio* ("[ex]change") as in "One should eat to live, not live to eat."[32] See also Quintilian *Inst.* 9.3.85 who used the Greek name ἀντιμεταβολή ("transposition"). Contrast was key. Instances of this compact contrastive form can be found in the NT, e.g., the concluding *punch line* of Jesus in Mark 2:27 "The Sabbath was for humanity and not humanity for Sabbath" (τὸ σάββατον διὰ τὸν ἄνθρωπον ἐγένετο καὶ οὐχ ὁ ἄνθρωπος διὰ τὸ σάββατον).[33]

Criteria for Observing Chiasmus: Many scholars have (claimed to have) observed chiastic structures in biblical literature, real or imagined.[34] Although certainly chiasmus may only exist in the eye of the beholder, I would argue that *interpreters should not form chiasms but chiasms should inform interpreters*. Not surprisingly, there is need to provide "controls" for observing chiasms. Craig L. Blomberg has provided nine **"Criteria for Detecting Extended Chiasmus."**[35] John D. Harvey in the midst of his discussion of chiastic oral patterns likewise develops criteria. More recently, Craig A. Smith in his Ph.D. dissertation "Criteria for Biblical Chiasms: Objective Means for Distinguishing Chiasm of Design from Accidental and False Chiasm" (University of Bristol, 2009) has shed further light on the subject by differentiating designed chiasms crafted intentionally by the author(s), accidentally generated chiasms, and falsely attributed chiasms by interpreters. In his research, Smith develops five objective criteria by which to validate the authenticity of a chiasm.[36]

> Interpreters should not form chiasms, but chiasms should inform interpreters.

---

[30] Material here is adapted from my essay, "The Oral, the Textual, and the Visual (or, The Good, the Bad, and the Ugly) in Jesus's and Paul's Chiastic Performance of Scripture in 2 Corinthians, Ephesians, and Mark" in an edited volume of the International Orality Network, *forthcoming*.

[31] Harvey, *Listening to the Text. Oral Patterning in Paul's Letters*, Evangelical Theological Society Studies 1 (Grand Rapids: Baker, 1998), esp. ch. 5. Harvey has investigated "oral patterns" in the Pauline Epistles delineating essentially various sub-types of chiasm (AB … etc. … BA) and inclusion (A … etc. … A). Harvey's list of possible patterns includes chiasmus, inversion, alternation, inclusion, ring composition, word chain, refrain, and concentric symmetry.

[32] Bullinger, *Figures of Speech*, 99.

[33] For other examples, see Bullinger, *Figures of Speech*, 299–303.

[34] See the overview by Harvey, *Listening to the Text*, 98–104.

[35] Craig L. Blomberg, "The Structure of 2 Corinthians 1–7," *CTR* 4 (1989): 3–20.

[36] In the following summary, I am particularly indebted in thought and wording of portions to the review of Smith's dissertation by Roger G. DePriest found online at: http://ntresources.com/blog/wp-content/uploads/2010/08/RGD-ReviewSmithDissChiasm.pdf.

SMITH'S OBJECTIVE CRITERIA TO EVALUATE CHIASMS

1. **Coherence with other structures in the passage.** Chiasms may be nested within structures and consecutive and complement the macro-structure of a passage, but they should not be in competition with them.
2. **Significant correspondences between respective elements.** These correspondences from most to least objectivity include verbal (same word/root), syntactical, form, scene/setting, concept, and phonetic.
3. **Significant symmetry between each half of the Chiasm.** In this criteria, Smith introduces mathematical formulae to evaluate the chiasm. Four places to consider include
    a. arrangement of units,
    b. macro-balance between panels,
    c. micro-balance between units, and
    d. symmetrical distribution of verbal elements.
4. **Discernable function consonant with the author's purposes.** Four purposes would include mnemonic/organizational, aesthetic, rhetorical, and semantic, with this later being the most important and including semantic emphasis, rhetorical development, and completion or illumination of thought.
5. **Discernable authorial affinity**, i.e., does the author elsewhere show chiastic arrangement?

<u>The Ideology of Chiasm</u>: The use of chiasmus and extended chiasmus aids the elaboration of themes, the correlation of ideas, and the memorization of ideas. Moreover, the use of contrastive chiasmus is often jarring ideologically. Ivo Strecker in a fascinating essay on "Chiasmus and Metaphor" discusses the power of chiasmus to alter ways of thinking by juxtaposing ideas, often to contrast them, as if in a mirror; thus by this mirroring of ideas, "chiasmus provides a means to deal with 'life's paradoxes and problems'."[37] Strecker also argues that chiasmic thinking and expression is historically conditioned, being especially motivated by difficult or pressing circumstances to represent paradoxical thinking:

> we see it [chiasmus] as a figure of surprise and emphasis, and already the fact that it is 'mind opening' ... indicates that it may have some dramatic effect in our brain.... We can generalize, and say that each historical period allows—even demands—its own chiasmus.... This '*kairos* of chiasmus' can be observed on a grand historical scale.... But, of course, it also applies to social interaction on a minute scale, in fact to all 'rhetorical situations' (Bitzer 1968) in which the assertion of will and the exercise of social power play a role.[38]

Here Strecker considers two examples: Albert Einstein's dictum "People were not created for the state, but the state for the people" that confronted modern totalitarianism; and the Green Move-

---

[37] "Chiasmus and Metaphor," in *Chiasmus and Culture*, ed. B. Wiseman and A. Paul; Studies in Rhetoric and Culture 6 (New York: Berghahn, 2014), 69–88 at 83. Greg L. Bloomquist alerted me to this fascinating essay.

[38] Strecker, "Chiasmus and Metaphor," 85–86.

ment's: "Do I have all I need? Do I need all I have?" that confronts consumerism. In a very similar way we observe NT persons and authors producing discourse that contains chiasmus in the midst of conflict, contrast, paradox, social power, revolutionary movement, and the assertion of will.

<u>A Catalogue of Biblical Literary Forms</u>: Below are Dieter Georgi's notes on NT literary forms passed along through his student, Julian Hills (an instrumental professor in my life), to me and other students. It has been slightly modified and expanded.

TYPES OF LITERARY FORMS IN THE NT

1. Prophetic saying (salvation or woe)	11. Rhetorical Disposition:	25. Audition
2. Apocalyptic saying	a. *Proemium*	26. Vision:
3. Proverb (wisdom)	b. *Narratio*	a. Dream
4. Legal saying:	c. *Prothesis* or *Partitio*	b. Vision proper
a. Casuistic legal maxim	d. *Probatio*	27. Vocation story
b. Apodictic legal maxim	e. *Refutatio*	28. Autobiographical statement:
5. Parable (in general):	f. Self-Adulation ("for oneself")	a. *Res gestae* (accomplishments)
a. Illustrative speech	g. *Peroratio*	b. Catalogue of *peristaseis* (circumstances faced)
b. Hyperbole	12. Structural Presentation:	
c. Paradox	a. Chiasm (ABC-D-CBA)	c. Fool's speech
d. Metaphor	b. Inclusio (A [....] A)	29. Epistolary Conventions
e. Comparison proper	c. Alternation (ABABABAB)	a. Appeal Formula ("I exhort")
f. Simile	d. Repetition (A.A.A.A.)	b. Confidence Formula
g. Parable in particular	13. Apophthegm/chreia:	c. "Now concerning…" Formula
h. Exemplary story	a. Biographical	d. Conclusion Formula ("Finally")
i. Figurative speech	b. Discussions	30. Greetings
j. Allegory	14. Miracle story:	31. Doxology
6. Words of	a. Paradigmatic miracle story	32. Prayer:
a. Self-presentation	b. Novelistic miracle story	a. Intercession
b. Self-recommendation	15. Kerygmatic formula (X died/raised)	b. Confession of sins
7. Legend:	16. Confession	c. *Berakah* (blessing)
a. Biographical	17. Acclamation (amen, Abba, etc.)	d. *Hodayah* (thanksgiving)
b. Cultic	18. Hymn	e. Benediction
8. Martyr story	19. Parenesis (exhortation)	f. Curse
9. Epiphany	20. Catalogue of virtues	33. Genealogy
10. Rhetorical argumentation:	21. Catalogue of vices	34. Use of the OT:
a. Epicheireme/*ratiocinatio*	22. Rules of church discipline	a. OT quotation with formula
b. Amplification of a theme	23. Standards for officials	b. Midrashic Interpretation
c. *Ekphrasis*/*Enargeia* (vivid descript.)	24. *Haustafeln* (household codes)	35. Portends and Prodigies

Some of these forms were explicitly recognized, analyzed, and taught by ancient authors. For example, the rhetorical handbooks and progymnasmata exercises discuss rhetorical argumentation, apophthegm/chreia, narratives, formulating laws, and proverbs.[39] Basic familiarization with these literary forms will usually yield fruit when considering how your pericope would have been recognizable to ancient Mediterranean audiences. The purpose of a writer using a literary form is as a vehicle to convey critical, if not central, points. Some forms are rather obvious structurally (lists, alternation, etc.); other forms are identified by their theme (greetings, genealogy, etc.). Mira-

---

[39] See, e.g., George A. Kennedy, *Progymnasmata: Greek Textbooks of Prose Composition and Rhetoric*, Writings from the Greco-Roman World 10 (Atlanta: Society of Biblical Literature, 2003).

cle stories often have a basic form of four elements: setting, problem/need, healing, and response. However, variation also exists and such variation may suggest special significance and nuance.

<u>How to Identify and Understand Literary Forms</u>: In addition to consulting the chart on the previous page of Types of Literary Forms in the NT, first, you must recognize that discourses are often "chunked" or constructed in discernable paragraph units. For example, in Paul's writings you can discern each of these units as a "cameo" (a short literary unit designed to communicate effectively) using Kenneth E. Bailey's term.[40] Second, these chunks are thematically focused and so we should expect unifying elements of person (as in verbal person and agency), time frame, location, representational viewpoint, and repetitions that can help demarcate the unit. Breaks occur when the theme changes. Third, authors used connectors/conjunctions (or their absence) to mark unit boundaries. Recall the Processing Constraints of Coordinating Connectors in Step 3: Grammatical Study (page 122). Fourth, biblical commentators will often try to identify literary forms—but beware that sometimes their approach becomes too narrow or rigid, like a cookie-cutter applied to a larger spread of dough. So, if you consult commentaries, do so critically and let the passage itself best guide you. Finally, fifth, conduct research on the meaning and significance of the literary form. For information about a particular literary form, see the bibliography at the end of this chapter (especially Aune and Bailey/Vander Broek) and consult the major and more recent Bible dictionaries. You may need to search Bible dictionaries broadly to find entries or extended discussions of the literary form. Some terms will have distinct headings such as "Paraenesis" and "Midrash." But, you will need to develop the certain skill of research and recognition and then more research and so continue to grow in this area. Below are basic considerations for understanding and recognizing literary forms.

GUIDANCE FOR IDENTIFYING THE PRESENCE OF LITERARY FORMS

1. Authors use literary forms that are recognizable and appropriate for their audiences.
2. Literary forms are utilized to help convey central or critical points that the author intends.
3. Literary forms are recognized by structure and/or by the content of important themes.
4. More than one literary form may be employed simultaneously within a pericope.
5. Variations in literary form may indicate an important aspect of the intended meaning.
6. Beware that parody—the playful, but subversive, imitation of a literary form—may be present. For example, Paul's foolish boast in 2 Cor 11:16–12:10 parodies a defendant's self-praise at the end of a defense speech.[41] So, recognizing the formal structure is not that same as understanding why it is used and its significance in context. Exigency and context is everything.

---

[40] Kenneth E. Bailey, *Paul Through Mediterranean Eyes: Cultural Studies in 1 Corinthians* (Downers Grove, IL: IVP Academic, 2011). Bailey demonstrates how carefully Paul structured his discourses. Working on 2 Corinthians with my students, we have found numerous instances of chiasms based lexically, both of inner-sentential nature (2 Cor 9:6, 7, and esp. 9:8; 12:7, 9) but also extending over a chapter (7:2–16, the center in 7:8). Charles H. Talbert also sees 5:23–24 as chiastic (three layers), with 5:23c being central but also parenthetical (*Ephesians and Colossians*, Paideia: Commentaries on the New Testament [Grand Rapids: Baker, 2007], 140).

[41] See my revised doctoral dissertation *Ancient Rhetoric and Paul's Apology*, 186–90.

STEP 6: SECONDARY STUDY 241

Tag and Bag? The goal of identifying literary forms is not to "tag and bag" the text by labeling it a certain way—that is, to render it dead and ready for consumption! Nor is the goal to apply rigidly a cookie-cutter approach to the text imposing a literary form at the expense of careful observation. Such are standard critiques against those who identify and rely too uncritically on literary forms. Nor is the goal to restrict a passage by focusing on only this dimension of the pericope or perhaps to see one and only one literary form. In actual communication, the merging of forms is common. So, we must allow the possibility that a particular passage under investigation may contain several literary forms merged together. See the example discussion of Eph 2:11–22 in TERTIARY RESEARCH below. In every case you should ask, "Why is this form used and possibly so used in conjunction with others?" All in all, literary form and genre studies provide perspectives that are critical for the interpretation of texts. *What is most important is how literary forms will bring our interpretive attention to the central, foundational ideas in the passage.* If they do not facilitate this, we would rightly question whether the identification of the form is legitimate.

EXERCISE 6–F: In the following passages, consider what literary form(s) may be present. Consider what research may be needed to help identify the forms and to describe them more completely.

Matt 13:24–30; 2 Cor 1:8–16; 9:6–8; Rom 12:9–21; 1 Pet 2:6–10; 1 John 2:18; Rev 1:4–6; 9:1–12

SECONDARY INTERPRETIVE PROCEDURES:

The following procedures incorporate 1.–3. from the PRIMARY INTERPRETIVE PROCEDURES above.

1. **Based upon previous identification of the genre of your book under STEP 1: CONTEXTUAL LOCATION (if completed), re-evaluate that initial identification and bring forward any questions you might have had. Basic options include apocalypse, wisdom, poetry, prophecy, narrative (history, biography, short story), letter-argumentative, covenant formula, and testament/sermon.**
2. **Consult recent commentaries (specialized verse-by-verse treatments of biblical books) or resources (like books, articles, or essays) that might attempt to determine the genre of the NT book. Read and take notes about that genre from two or three sources; Bible commentaries or dictionaries may be helpful. Additionally, there are many fine NT Introductions and specific books summarizing NT genres (see chapter Bibliography).**
3. **In light of new information learned about the particular features of the genre, re-read the book as a whole (or significant surrounding portions) noting features of the genre that relate particularly to your pericope.**
    a. **How does your pericope relate to the book as a whole in terms of genre?**
    b. **How does the pericope support genre determination?**
4. **What literary forms may be present in the passage? How are they distinctly identified?**

5. What variations in literary form(s) may be present? What possible significance do these differences have for interpreting the pericope?
6. How does the identification of literary form(s) affect your interpretation of the passage?
7. What is the relationship between book genre and literary form of the pericope? How does each mutually inform each other? How does the particular literary form contribute to the purposes of the discourse as a whole?
8. Provide a summary of your most significant findings as well as any pivotal interpretive questions raised about the genre of the book as a whole and your pericope's literary form, and its function within the book as a whole.

III. TERTIARY RESEARCH

<u>Orientation</u>: Are ancient texts reducible simply to discernible genres and literary forms? After all, rarely does a "pure" literary form exist. Instead, one finds much innovation and adaptation for each circumstance or exigency (the rhetorical situation and need). In actual use, genres and literary forms are quite diverse. Also, one observes the merger of genres and literary forms. Then too, often the identification of literary forms and genres is disputed between interpreters.

In view of the interpretive gridlock that may attend studying literary forms and historical reconstructions associated with them, Vernon K. Robbins has set forth a new model of socio-rhetorical interpretation (SRI) that urges interpreters to move beyond the identification of genre and literary form to investigate rhetorical themes/topoi in networks of themes called rhetorolects. These rhetorolects are fundamental topics that cohere around conventional places of human experience and interaction. These modes of discourse as rhetorolects are diverse, but principally in biblical materials have been described as wisdom (the home and cosmos), priestly (temple), prophetic (kingdom), precreation (empire; cosmos), apocalyptic (empire), and miracle (the human body). Potentially, there are other major rhetorolects and sub-rhetorolects such as imperial (empire) and creedal (ecclesial space).[42] Pivotal for SRI is the recognition of networks of themes in relation to physical, lived in, and contested spaces informed by critical spatiality theory.[43] On the following page is provided Robbins' BLENDED SPACES & LOCATIONS IN EARLY CHRISTIAN RHETOROLECTS. The first SRI commentaries are appearing in the *Rhetoric of Religious Antiquities* series.[44]

---

[42] Robbins is a prolific writer and his view of SRI and rhetorolects are found in numerous writings; see esp. *Invention of Christian Discourse* and the essays in Vernon K. Robbins, Robert H. Von Thaden, Jr., and Bart B. Bruehler, eds., *Foundations for Sociorhetorical Exploration: A Rhetoric of Religious Antiquity Reader*, Rhetoric of Religious Antiquities (Atlanta: SBL Press, 2016).

[43] These three spaces (although variously described among theorists) correspond roughly with 1st, 2nd, and 3rd space. See, e.g., the works of Edward W. Soja, Henri Lefebvre, and Homi K. Bhabha.

[44] Roy Jeal, *Exploring Philemon: Freedom, Brotherhood, and Partnership in the New Society*, Rhetoric of Religious Antiquities (Atlanta: SBL Press, 2015) and B. J. Oropeza, *Exploring Second Corinthians: Death and Life, Hardship and Rivalry*, Rhetoric of Religious Antiquities (Atlanta: SBL Press, 2016).

STEP 6: TERTIARY RESEARCH

BLENDED SPACES & LOCATIONS IN EARLY CHRISTIAN RHETOROLECTS[45]

Rhetorolects (Cultural Frames)	1st Space — Social, Cultural, & Physical Realia	2nd Space — Visualization, Conceptualization, & Imagination of God's World	3rd Space (Space of Blending) — Ongoing Bodily Effects and Enactments: Blending in Religious Life	Generic Space — Spaces of Mental Conceptions
Wisdom	household, vegetation, living beings	God as Father-Creator (Progenitor), Wisdom (light) as Mediator, People as God's children, Jesus as God's Son	human body as producer of goodness & righteousness	Cause-effect, change, time, identity, intentionality, representation, part-whole. **Formal argumentative topics**: opposites, grammatical forms of the same word, correlatives, more and less, time, turning back upon the opponent, definition, varied meanings, division, induction, previous judgment, parts, consequence, contrast, openly and secretly, analogy, same result, before and after, purpose as cause, for and against, implausible probabilities, contradictions, cause of false impression, cause and effect, better, doing contrary to what has been done, mi takes, meaning of a name. from Aristotle, *Rhetoric* II.23.1–29 (1397a-1400b); G. A. Kennedy, *Aristotle, On Rhetoric: A Theory of Civic Discourse* (New York: Oxford University Press, 1991) 190–204.
Prophetic	political kingdom, prophet's body	God as King, God on kingly throne in heavenly court, Selected humans as prophets, Selected people as God's kingdom, Jesus as Prophet-Messiah selected and sent by God	human body as distributor and receiver of justice (food, bodily needs, honor)	
Apocalyptic	political empire, imperial temple, imperial army	God as Almighty (*Pantokrator*), Jesus as King of King and Lord of Lords, multiple heavenly assistants to God	human body as receiver of resurrection & eternal life in a "new" realm of well-being	
Precreation	political empire & emperor's household	God as Eternal Emperor-Father, Jesus as God's Eternal Son	human body as receiver of eternal life through friendship (belief & loyalty) with God's eternal son	
Miracle	human body & unexpected phenomena & transformations in the natural world	God as Transforming Power, Selected humans as agents of God's transforming power, People as healed and transformed by God, Jesus as Healer & Miracle-Worker	human body as healed and amazingly transformed	
Priestly	altar, temple & temple city	God as Holy and Pure, God on priestly throne in heavenly temple, Selected humans as priests, People as God's holy & pure priestly community (assembly, city, kingdom), Jesus as Priest-Messiah	human body as giver of sacrificial offerings and receiver of beneficial exchange of holiness and purity between God and humans.	

[45] This is a reconfiguration of Figure 2 in Robbins, *Invention*, 109.

Envisioned Locations for Rhetorical Situations: What Robbins has drawn our attention to is the intersection of rhetoric with space which intriguingly originated in ancient Greek rhetoric. Thus, Aristotle systematized rhetoric according to conventional human spaces: the courtroom (forensic or judicial), the political assembly (deliberative or political), and the formal ceremony (epideictic or demonstrative). In each location topics may be identified that are best and most likely to gain persuasion in the audience: for the courtroom, what is just or unjust; for the assembly, what is beneficial or expedient; for the ceremony, what is honorable or shameful. Drawing upon other ancient authors and envisioning additional settings, let me augment Aristotle's locations as possible "Arenas" of Rhetoric to explore as well as propose "Areas" for investigating ancient Greco-Roman rhetoric. I present these to help people envision ancient spaces and rhetoric suitable for them.

"ARENAS" OF ANCIENT RHETORICAL INVENTION

1. "Master Teacher"; Sophists, like Gorgias, and the contrast between Isocrates and Plato
   - Display ("fictitious") pieces (e.g., Gorgias' *Helen*, Antisthenes' *Ajax*, etc.)
   - Disciples and Dialogues of Plato (e.g., *Pheadrus, Gorgias*; the *Apology*)
2. Courtroom (Forensic; Judicial); many extant speeches and ancient handbooks.
   - Accusation
   - Defense/Apology
3. Political Assembly (Deliberative; Political); many extant speeches and ancient handbooks.
   - Persuasive of benefit or expediency
   - Dissuasive of benefit or expediency
4. Ceremonial Speech (Demonstrative; Epideictic) in various settings: before a battle, funeral orations, festival speeches, etc.
   - Praise
   - Blame/Vituperative
5. Didactic-Educational Settings. See the summary of FIRST-CENTURY MEDITERRANEAN EDUCATIONAL SYSTEMS found in PRIMARY SURVEY in STEP 8: SCRIPTURAL CORRELATIONS.
   - Anticipating the Greek educational system (*Rhetorica Ad Alexandrum*)
   - Centers of learning such as existed at Athens, Alexandria, Rome, Rhodes, Tarsus, etc.
   - Atticism and Asiatic Rhetoric
   - *Progymnasmata* Exercises: Theon (1st BC), Hermogenes (2nd AD), Aphthonius (4th)...
6. Entertainment Settings; Public spectacle.
   - *Declamatio* (100 BC→ Cicero→Quintilian→Augustine)
   - *Suasoriae* (fictitious deliberative speech) and *Controversiae* (fictitious legal speech) (Seneca the Elder mid-late first-century BC); See Murphy, *Synoptic History*, 231–32.
7. Voluntary Associations; cultic-religious (synagogue and ekklesia), civic, philosophical, etc.
   - *Homilies* and Letters of correspondence
   - Hymns of praise and choral dances (hymnodes; the Dancing Cowherders of Pergamum)
   - Commemorative and honorific praise, e.g., on inscriptions
   - Orders of conduct

"Areas" for Investigating NT Rhetoric[46]

1. **Determination of Rhetorical Species.** Caution: often disputed and the usefulness is limited.
   - forensic
   - deliberative
   - epideictic
   - mixed
2. **Invention and Stasis Theory**
   - the essential issue or question
   - the basis of argumentation (*pathos*, *ethos*, *logos*)
   - *topoi* (places) of arguments
3. **Argumentative nature of Paul's Letters**
   - epicheiremes
   - enthymemes
   - use of artificial and inartificial proofs
4. **Dispositional Analysis of Pauline Letters**
   - *proemium*
   - *narratio*
   - divisio (statement of issue that may be distilled to a question)
   - *partitio* or thesis statement
   - *probatio*
   - *refutatio*
   - self-adulation ("concerning oneself")
   - *peroratio*
5. **Rhetorical Stylistics** (use of conventional figures of speech)
   - schemes
   - tropes
6. **Progymnasmata Exercises** (see esp. Theon's descriptions)
   - chreia and elaboration in the Gospels and Acts
   - *prosopopoieia* (speech in person) in the Gospels and Acts
7. **Memory** and **Rhetorical Performance**
   - e.g., Gal 3:1: "Christ was portrayed visibly as having been crucified."

Greek Rhetorical Education: Warrant for investigating the influence of Greco-Roman rhetoric in the NT is the ubiquitous and energetic environment of rhetorical training and display for centuries before, during, and after the writing of the NT. Ancient rhetorical training began in the fifth-century BC and gained momentum throughout the fourth-century BC and throughout the entire NT era. The earliest form of education involved exemplary speeches (e.g., Gorgias in the late

---

[46] A very helpful survey of the ancient Greco-Roman rhetorical tradition is by James J. Murphy et al., *A Synoptic History of Classical Rhetoric*, 4th ed. (New York: Routledge, 2013).

fifth-century BC) and technical handbooks by a variety of teachers. In the fourth-century these works and "sophists" (a derogatory label) were critiqued in the dialogues of Plato and then the writings of Aristotle, who nevertheless himself provided a superior systemization of rhetoric. From the fourth-century through the first-century AD, rhetorical theory continued to proliferate in the form of published speeches and handbooks even as it continued to develop theoretically (e.g., "stasis theory" of Hermogenes of Temnos in the second-century BC). Also, elementary exercises called *Progymnasmata* developed, of which we have five extant versions beginning in the first-century BC (by Theon) and through to the fifth-century AD.[47]

Also, great centers of learning were spread across the Roman Empire and included Athens, Alexandria, Rome, Ephesus, and Tarsus, the hometown of the Apostle Paul who self-identified as its citizen (Acts 21:39; 22:3). When Paul was endangered from deadly opposition in Jerusalem having just become a Christ follower, he was sent to Tarsus (Acts 9:30). In fact, Tarsus was "a university town" that rivaled Athens with its philosophers, poets, and linguists. In his book *Geography*, Strabo, who lived between 63 BC–AD 24, said the following:

> The people at Tarsus have devoted themselves so eagerly, not only to philosophy, but also to the whole round of education in general, that they have surpassed Athens, Alexandria, or any other place that can be named where there have been schools and lectures of philosophers. But it is so different from other cities that there the men who are fond of learning, are all natives, and foreigners are not inclined to sojourn there; neither do these natives stay there, but they complete their education abroad; and when they have completed it they are pleased to live abroad, and but few go back home…. Further, the city of Tarsus has all kinds of schools of rhetoric…. (14.5.13, LCL)

Strabo's report is followed by two lengthy paragraphs naming important philosophers.

Thus, ancient rhetoric began much earlier than what is reflected in the epistolary handbooks. Rhetorical education was much more ubiquitous, even among Jews, and especially Jews like Paul from Tarsus who traveled among Gentiles in the urban centers of the Greco-Roman world. In my assessment, then, both ancient rhetorical and epistolary conventions should inform our study of NT epistles provided that such study is carefully conducted and evidentially based.

<u>Types of Ancient Letters and Personal Letter Types</u>: It should come as no surprise that ancient letters were of different kinds, which Hans-Josef Klauck broadly categorizes as follows:[48]

1. **Non-literary or documentary**, which are "occasional" and not written for broader public or for posterity; these are preserved on the original papyrus, and contain many letters between family members and business associates. Ancient epistolary theorists like Ps(eudo) Demetrius (1st-2nd century AD) and Ps(eudo) Libanius (4th century AD) catalogued personal

---

[47] See the recent translation by George A. Kennedy, *Progymnasmata*.
[48] Hans-Josef Klauck, *Ancient Letters and the New Testament*, 68–69. M. Luther Stirewalt provides more specificity: official, personal, technical, essay, school exercise, and entertainment (*Studies in Ancient Greek Epistolography*, RBS 27 [Atlanta: Scholars Press, 1993]).

letter into 21 and 41 types, respectively, with some overlap. Ps.Demetrius includes friendly*, commendatory*, blaming*, reproachful*, consoling*, censorious*, admonishing, threatening*, vituperative, praising*, advisory, supplicatory, inquiring*, responding, allegorical, accounting, accusing, apologetic, congratulatory*, ironic* and thankful* (those with asterisks are also found in Ps.Libanius). The most prominently discussed letter type for Ps.Demetrius is the friendly type to foster friendship; for Ps.Libanius it is the parenetic type that exhorts to pursue (encouragement) or to avoid something (dissuasive).[49]

2. **Official and diplomatic letters** (royal or imperial), with a slight distinction between the official letter addressing everyday particular circumstances and the diplomatic letter carrying much more political significance as is testified by their inclusion on monuments or reproduced in literary works of history, etc.

3. **Literary letters**, which have been copied and handed down to us; rhetorical exercises, forgeries for propaganda, poetic pieces, letters within novels, and philosophical treatises.

The problem with NT analysis is that Paul's Epistles have primarily been studied against the background of non-literary documentary letters that came prominently to light around AD 1900 in the papyrus findings at Oxyrhynchus Egypt. The enthusiasm of G. Adolf Deissmann directed subsequent interpreters to view Paul's writings as "non-literary" (except perhaps Romans) comparable to such letters.[50] Particularly important for Deissmann was the private nature of personal letters versus the public nature of "epistles"; yet this assessment does not square with the fact that Paul's letters addressed congregations across geographic regions (e.g., Gal 1:2; 2 Cor 1:1) and also were circulated (Col 4:16; cf. 1 Thess 5:27; 2 Thess 2:2). Likewise, John L. White, one of the first NT scholars to study ancient letters intensively in relation to the NT, commenting on the literary letter tradition maintains, "The use of rhetorical techniques, especially in the theological body of Paul's letters, indicates that a knowledge of these traditions is quite relevant to the study of early Christian letters."[51] Helpful also for resolving the matter is M. Luther Stirewalt who has studied ancient letters according to their setting (normative, extended, and fictitious). By normative, Stirewalt means specific actual correspondence between parties. Extended settings involve the letter envisioning an "extended" broader audience. Fictitious settings entail the impersonation of the author addressing a conceived situation. Stirewalt concludes that Paul's epistles are reflective of *official normative letters*; I would agree as long as we recognize that certain of his epistles envision extended audiences at times, and at least one, Philemon, is closer to a personal letter, although one that is quite rhetorically conceived (as evidenced in EXERCISE 6–I above).[52]

Example of Eph 2:11–22: What literary form(s) may be observed in this pericope? Well, in my estimation, perhaps as many as five! These reflections come after researching Ephesians inten-

---

[49] The discussion of letter types is summarizing Carol Poster, "A Conversation Halved," 27–30.

[50] G. Adolf Deissmann, *Light from the Ancient East*, e.g., 64, 147; see esp. 219–34, where Deissmann's views are clearly stated before reviewing the letters of the Pauline corpus.

[51] John L. White, *Light from Ancient Letters*, Foundations and Facets (Philadelphia: Fortress, 1986), 3.

[52] M. Luther Stirewalt, *Paul, the Letter Writer* (Grand Rapids: Eerdmans, 2003).

sively for over a decade now. First, let me begin with a formal rhetorical argumentative form. In an ancient rhetorical handbook written in the first-century BC, there is an argument form consisting of five steps (given below) called the deductive argument (*Rhet. Her.* 2.19.28). The summarization of the argumentation of Eph 2:11–22 conforms nicely to the deductive argument:

> *Thesis:* 2:11–13 You Gentiles, once alienated, were now brought near by the blood of the Messiah.
> *Reason:* 2:14a For [γάρ] Christ himself is our Peace,
> *Proof of the Reason:* 2:14b–16 who made both Jews and Gentiles into one body by destroying hostility and annulling the law of commandments, in order to create a unified humanity.
> *Elaboration:* 2:17–18 And [καί] Christ preached peace to those far away and peace to those near because both have access to the Father through Christ and in one Spirit.
> *Conclusion:* 2:19–22 Therefore [Ἄρα οὖν] You Gentiles are not foreigners, but co-citizens, household members of God, a holy temple and dwelling place of God in Christ in the Spirit.

What this suggests is that Paul was carefully presenting material for the Gentile audience to apprehend. It focuses our attention on the conclusion which is stressed with two conjunctions (Ἄρα οὖν), each translatable as "therefore." Paul purposefully advances an argument here.

Second, in 2:17 we see Paul strongly alluding to Isa 57:19—"And he came and preached peace to you who were far off and peace to those who were near." We further observe that the Isaian notions of "near" and "far" have shaped the previous verses (2:11–16); thus we understand that Paul is interpreting Isaiah in a "midrashic" fashion. This observation of literary form helps us understand particularly Paul's originating thought processes: He has deliberately evoked Hebrew Scripture and interpreted it in light of Christ's work and the particular themes in 2:11–22 in the context of Ephesians. The observation of midrashic interpretation should cause us to ask why Paul used this particular OT text and where else this particular OT text (Isa 57:19) was used in Paul's day. These questions lead us to consider intertextual and doctrinal correlations which is the distinct exegetical task of STEP 8: SCRIPTURAL CORRELATIONS.

Third, in addition to being midrashic, the material in 2:11–22 is "kerygmatic." Paul has interpreted Isa 57:19 in light of Christ's coming, preaching, and suffering death. Paul is proclaiming the accomplishments of Jesus's sacrificial work. Typically, we think of *kerygma* as "Jesus died, Jesus rose from the dead, and Jesus ascended to the right hand of God." But, if Paul elaborates upon Christ's sacrificial benefits offered in his death, then this passage is kerygmatic. Why does it take the particular form that it does here? Why is resurrection missing? Or, has Paul already addressed Christ's resurrection in 1:19–21?

Fourth, the content of 2:11–16 and 2:17–22 is replete with "political-civic" themes associated with unity, citizenship status, leadership structure, temple building, sacrifice, etc. Does this constitute a literary form? Maybe; the language is distinctive and builds on other political themes across Ephesians that support my contention that Ephesians reflects pervasively the presence of an imperial-political rhetorolect. One wonders to what extent Paul was deliberately incorporating these themes to help form the Christian identity of Gentile believers, so that they may properly function as Christ's political body on earth carrying on God in Christ's mission in the world (see esp. 4:1–16). So, thus far we see that 2:11–22 is a combination of midrashic scriptural interpretation merged with kerygmatic proclamation within a political rhetorolect supporting the view that God in Christ has achieved a peace and (re)formed "one new humanity" in Christ as a temple space.

Fifth, the passage is arranged chiastically in an ABCDEF-G-FEDCBA pattern. This observation arose from my semantic diagramming and analysis work of STEP 4.[53] Technically, this chiasm could be described more fully in that STEP—but one may argue that chiasms are a distinct, ancient literary form since they are found across all types of ancient Mediterranean literature.

CHIASM OF EPHESIANS 2:11–22

A 11 Διὸ μνημονεύετε ὅτι ποτὲ ὑμεῖς τὰ ἔθνη ἐν σαρκί, οἱ λεγόμενοι ἀκροβυστία ὑπὸ τῆς λεγομένης περιτομῆς ἐν σαρκὶ χειροποιήτου,	A 11 "Therefore, remember that once you, the gentiles in flesh, who are called uncircumcision by the so-called handmade circumcision in flesh," [Gentiles are cultically and socially separated by human conditions "in flesh" and agency by speech.]
B 12 ὅτι ἦτε τῷ καιρῷ ἐκείνῳ ① χωρὶς Χριστοῦ, ② ἀπηλλοτριωμένοι τῆς πολιτείας τοῦ Ἰσραὴλ καὶ ③ ξένοι τῶν διαθηκῶν τῆς ἐπαγγελίας, ④ ἐλπίδα μὴ ἔχοντες καὶ ⑤ ἄθεοι ἐν τῷ κόσμῳ.	B 12 "that you were at that time ① without Messiah, ② alienated from the citizenship of Israel and ③ foreigners of the covenants of the promise, ④ having no hope and ⑤ being godless in the world." [The Gentile audience had an alienated status in that they were lacking various attributes.]
C 13 νυνὶ δὲ ἐν Χριστῷ Ἰησοῦ ὑμεῖς οἵ ποτε ὄντες μακρὰν ἐγενήθητε ἐγγὺς ἐν τῷ αἵματι τοῦ Χριστοῦ.	C 13 "But now, in Messiah Jesus you who once were far away have come near by the blood of the Messiah."
D 14a Αὐτὸς γάρ ἐστιν ἡ εἰρήνη ἡμῶν,	D 14a "For He is our peace," [stated positively; "peace" is opposite to "enmity" in D'—16b]
E 14b ὁ ποιήσας τὰ ἀμφότερα ἓν	E 14b "who made both groups one"
F 14c καὶ τὸ μεσότοιχον τοῦ φραγμοῦ λύσας, τὴν ἔχθραν ἐν τῇ σαρκὶ αὐτοῦ,	F 14c "even by destroying the dividing wall of hostility, that is, the enmity by means of his flesh" ["Destroying" and "enmity" are opposite to "creating" and "peace" in F'—15b]
G 15a τὸν νόμον τῶν ἐντολῶν ἐν δόγμασιν καταργήσας,	G 15a "by having annulled the law of commandments in decrees" [forward position—center of chiasm]
F' 15b ἵνα τοὺς δύο κτίσῃ ἐν αὐτῷ εἰς ἕνα καινὸν ἄνθρωπον ποιῶν εἰρήνην	F' 15b "in order that he would create in himself one new humanity making continuous peace" ["creating" and "peace" are opposite to "destroying" and "enmity" in F—14c]

---

[53] This chiasm is discussed and included in the Appendix of Long, "Ephesians," 308–9.

E' 16a καὶ ἀποκαταλλάξῃ τοὺς <u>ἀμφοτέρους</u> ἐν <u>ἑνὶ σώματι τῷ θεῷ</u>	E' 16a *"and would reconcile to God <u>both groups</u> in <u>one body</u>"*
D' 16b διὰ τοῦ σταυροῦ ἀποκτείνας τὴν <u>ἔχθραν</u> ἐν <u>αὐτῷ</u>.	D' 16b *"by killing through the cross the <u>enmity in himself</u>"* [stated negatively; "enmity" is opposite to "peace" in D—14a]
C' 17 καὶ ἐλθὼν εὐηγγελίσατο εἰρήνην ὑμῖν <u>τοῖς μακρὰν</u> καὶ εἰρήνην <u>τοῖς ἐγγύς</u>·	C' 17 *"And when he came, he proclaimed peace <u>to you far away</u> and peace to those <u>near</u>,"*
B' 18–20 ⑤ & ④ ὅτι <u>δι' αὐτοῦ</u> ἔχομεν τὴν προσαγωγὴν οἱ ἀμφότεροι ἐν ἑνὶ πνεύματι πρὸς τὸν πατέρα. ¹⁹ ③ Ἄρα οὖν οὐκέτι ἐστὲ <u>ξένοι</u> καὶ πάροικοι ἀλλὰ ② ἐστὲ <u>συμπολῖται</u> τῶν ἁγίων καὶ <u>οἰκεῖοι</u> τοῦ θεοῦ, ²⁰ ἐποικοδομηθέντες ἐπὶ τῷ θεμελίῳ τῶν ἀποστόλων καὶ προφητῶν, ① ὄντος ἀκρογωνιαίου αὐτοῦ <u>Χριστοῦ Ἰησοῦ</u>,	B' 18–20 *"④ & ⑤ because through him we both have access in one Spirit to the Father. ¹⁹ ③ Therefore then, no longer are you <u>foreigners</u> and aliens, ② but you are <u>co-citizens</u> of the saints and ⑤ <u>household members</u> of God, ²⁰ being built upon the foundation of the apostles and prophets, ① with <u>Messiah Jesus himself</u> being the capstone,"*
A' 21–22 ⑤ ἐν ᾧ πᾶσα οἰκοδομὴ συναρμολογουμένη αὔξει εἰς <u>ναὸν ἅγιον</u> ἐν κυρίῳ, ²²ἐν ᾧ καὶ <u>ὑμεῖς</u> συνοικοδομεῖσθε εἰς <u>κατοικητήριον</u> τοῦ θεοῦ <u>ἐν πνεύματι</u>.	A' 21–22 *"⑤ in whom the whole structure being bound together grows into <u>a holy temple</u> in the Lord, ²² in which even <u>you</u> are being built into <u>the dwelling place</u> of God <u>in the Spirit</u>."* [Gentiles are cultically converted and bound by divine action in the Messiah Jesus by the Spirit.]

The importance of observing this chiasm is that it helps to focus our attention on the literary center—Christ's role of annulling of the law in the commandments with human decrees in 1:15a—as the means by which the Gentiles are brought into the political body and familial fellowship of the saints. Furthermore, the chiasm emphasizes this pivot point in order to underscore the radical social-religious-political transformation of the Gentiles needed for them to enter fully and equally into God's family. These Gentiles are reconceived as a "holy temple-space" and obtain co-citizenship status along with the saints. Thus, the chiasm reflects Paul's deep understanding of the socially sacred transformative power of Christ's sacrificial work to unify all people—Jew and Gentile—into one body politic in the proclamation of the gospel.

EXERCISE 6–G: Given Eph 2:11–12 above, consider these questions:

1. What significant spaces are envisioned? What view of God is presented?
2. What rhetorolects are present and blended together? Why are they blended in this way?
3. If Greco-Roman and Jewish rhetoric are present, what may be said about the education level of the author and audience(s)?
4. Given the ideological significance of chiasms, what might this suggest about the function of this passage?

TERTIARY INTERPRETIVE PROCEDURES:

Supplementing the SECONDARY INTERPRETIVE PROCEDURES above, consider the following:

1. <u>Socio-Rhetorical Investigation</u>: Extending your analysis beyond literary forms, investigate the passage from the perspective of Socio-Rhetorical Interpretation.
   a. Identify the primary agents, spaces, and their conceptual configuration(s).
   b. What view of God is present?
   c. Is there a discernible "constellation of topoi" supporting the presence of "rhetorolects" as envisioned by Vernon Robbins? Such rhetorolects include, but are not limited to:
      i. Wisdom
      ii. Prophetic
      iii. Apocalyptic
      iv. Precreation
      v. Miracle
      vi. Priestly
   d. Are there discernible emergent sub-rhetorolects that may be fruitful to explore?
      i. Imperial or Political
      ii. Creedal
      iii. Others?
   e. What storyline of God and His People is assumed and/or developed here?
   f. How does the text relate to its surrounding culture as well as ideologically address it?

2. <u>Ancient Rhetorical Influences</u>: In view of the "ARENAS" OF ANCIENT RHETORICAL INVENTION (p. 244) and the "AREAS" AND FOR INVESTIGATING NT RHETORIC (p.245), probe the passage for rhetorical influences.
   a. What formal "rhetorical" influences may be detectable based upon the ancient rhetorical tradition as described in the extant speeches, rhetorical handbooks, and/or the progymnasmata exercises?
   b. Is direct or indirect dependence on such traditions or practices likely? Be careful to show how such influence is warranted.
   c. If influences are present, what may this tell us of the social location of the NT author and the audience(s)?

3. <u>Ancient Jewish Rhetoric</u>: **Consider the influence of ancient Jewish rhetoric; this area needs further research.** Consider also, e.g., the description of Jewish exegetical techniques discussed in STEP 8: SCRIPTURAL CORRELATIONS.

4. <u>Orality and Culture</u>: After reading pp.225-33 on ancient literacy and libraries, how does your passage contribute to understanding ancient orality, literacy, and education levels?

IV. BIBLIOGRAPHY

Primary Survey

Duvall, J. Scott and J. Daniel Hays. *Grasping God's Word: A Hands-on Approach to Reading, Interpreting, and Applying the Bible*. 3rd ed. Grand Rapids: Zondervan, 2012.

Fee, Gordon D. and Douglas Stuart. *How to Read the Bible for All Its Worth*. 3rd ed. Grand Rapids: Zondervan, 2003. [Discusses hermeneutics and method as well as biblical genres in the OT and NT.]

Ralph, Margaret Nutting. *And God Said What?: An Introduction to Biblical Literary Forms*. Rev. ed. Mahwah, NJ: Paulist, 2003.

Ryken, Leland. *Words of Life: A Literary Introduction to the New Testament*. Grand Rapids: Baker, 1987. [Describes the literary nature of the NT and discusses perspectives and strategies for reading the NT in terms of respective genres of individual books.]

Stein, Robert H. *Playing by the Rules: A Basic Guide to Interpreting the Bible*. Grand Rapids: Baker, 1994. [Discusses hermeneutics of Bible study and develops the metaphor of "game" and "rules" in relation to describing different biblical genres and literary forms in OT and NT.]

_____. *An Introduction to the Parables of Jesus*. Philadelphia: Westminster, 1981.

Secondary Study

Aune, David Edward. *The New Testament in Its Literary Environment*. Library of Early Christianity 8. Philadelphia: Westminster, 1987.

_____. *Greco-Roman Literature and the New Testament: Selected Forms and Genres*. Sources for Biblical Study 21. Atlanta: Scholars, 1988.

Bailey, James L. "Genre Analysis." Pages 140–65 in Joel B. Green, ed., *Hearing the New Testament: Strategies for Interpretation*. 2nd ed. Grand Rapids: Eerdmans, 2010.

Bailey, James L., and Lyle D. Vander Broek. *Literary Forms in the New Testament: A Handbook*. Louisville: Westminster John Knox Press, 1992. [This book also recommends additional resources specific to each literary form.]

Blomberg, Craig L. "The Diversity of Literary Genres in the New Testament," Pages 507–32 in *New Testament Criticism and Interpretation*. ed. D. A. Black and D. S. Dockery. Nashville: Broadman & Holman, 2001.

Virkler, Henry A. and Karelynne Ayayo, *Hermeneutics: Principles and Processes of Biblical Interpretation*. 2nd ed. Grand Rapids: Baker Academic, 2007. [See esp. the discussions in ch.6 "Special Literary Forms: Similes, Metaphors, Proverbs, Parables, and Allegories" and ch.7 "Special Literary Forms: Prophecy, Apocalyptic Literature, and Types."]

Tertiary Research

Consult the scholarly resources discussed above, especially the work of Vernon K. Robbins.

STEP 7

HISTORICAL CONTEXT

"It is self–evident that any word, concept, or document must be interpreted in its own historical setting."[1]

—George Eldon Ladd

Introduction: An exciting dimension of scriptural study is learning about ancient history, society, and culture. Some people enjoy this more than others. However, knowing the historical and the social-cultural influences within a passage has a tremendous bearing, not only on arriving at sound interpretation (see STEP 9: INTERPRETIVE DECISIONS), but also on how we appropriate Scripture in our lives (see STEP 11: EVALUATED APPLICATIONS). Scriptural passages constantly in-

---

[1] George Eldon Ladd, *The New Testament and Criticism* (Grand Rapids: Eerdmans, 1967), 171.

tersect with the ancient Mediterranean cultures—metaphors, analogies, social roles, customs (such as athletic, military, financial terms, etc.), various procedures, foods, occupations, genres, literary forms, etc. Basically, a full spectrum of social-cultural values, roles, and practices has influenced and is reflected in the biblical materials that remains unfamiliar to us; new insights are being gleaned everyday as new information from archaeological discoveries or ancient sources are correlated with biblical materials. It is a slow and difficult process for this information to disseminate and eventually impact Bible translations, if it ever does. Our failure to understand the historical context may cause us to lock the Bible in a cultural freeze-frame so that we canonize ancient cultural practices without truly understanding God's contextualized message to His people. *In scriptural interpretation, what we don't see may blind us.* Our starting presuppositions may mislead us. The principles that inform this exegetical area are **HIS** "History Informs Scripture" and **HERS** "Historical Environment of Roman Society."

> In scriptural interpretation, what we don't see may blind us.

I. Primary Survey

Basic Chronology and Dates: A thorough historical context to the NT cannot be given here; but you should be aware of important dates even if they are disputed. Here, I want to present some important dates first from the OT era that provide an important framework deserving of its own book, then from what is called the Intertestamental period, then from the NT itself, and then some post-NT dates. We will conclude finally with a more detailed NT chronology.

Important OT Dates (with *Biblical Sources*)

Creation (*Genesis*; see also *Psalm 104; 136; Isaiah 40:12–31*)
The Fall-Noah-Babel (*Genesis*)
2000–1800 BC–Call of Abraham (*Genesis; Job?*)
1250 BC (or **1450 BC**)–Moses and Exodus Event (*Exodus, Leviticus, Numbers,* and *Deuteronomy*)
1200–1060 BC (or **1400–1050 BC**)–Conquest and Occupation of the Land (*Joshua* and *Judges*)
1050 BC–Kingship Begins: Saul, David, Solomon (*Ruth; 1* and *2 Samuel; 1 Kings 1–11; Psalms, Proverbs, Ecclesiastes, Song of Solomon*)
967 BC–First Temple Construction begins (*1 Kings 1–11*)
933 BC–Divided Kingdom (*1 Kings 12–25; 2 Kings; 2 Chronicles 10–36; Obadiah* and *Joel*)
720 BC–Northern Kingdom into Exile by Assyria (*2 Kings 17; Amos, Hosea, Micah, Jonah, Isaiah*)
587–586 BC–Southern Kingdom into Exile by Babylon and First Temple Destroyed: (*2 Kings 24–25; 2 Chronicles 36; Nahum, Zephaniah, Habakkuk, Jeremiah, Lamentations, Ezekiel,* and *Daniel*)
530s BC–Fall of Babylon by the Persian King Cyrus (*Isa 45:1*) and Cyrus' Decree (*Esther, Haggai,* and *Zechariah*)
516 BC–Second Temple Completed (*Ezra*)
458 BC–Return from Babylon (*Nehemiah*)
~430 BC–Close of the OT Prophets (*Malachi*)

STEP 7: PRIMARY SURVEY 255

When reading through the Hebrew Scripture, it is interesting to recognize that other non-biblical books are mentioned as sources: *The Generations of Adam* (Gen 5:1); *The Book of the Wars of the Lord* (Num 21:14); *The Book of Jashar* (2 Sam 1:18); *The Book of the Acts of Solomon* (1 Kgs 11:41); *The Book of the Chronicles of the Kings of Israel* (1 Kgs 14:19; 2 Kgs 1:18; 2 Chr 20:34); *The Book of the Chronicles of the Kings of Judah* (1 Kgs 14:29; 2 Kgs 8:23); *The Annals of Jehu* (2 Chr 20:34); *The Vision of Isaiah* (2 Chr 32:32); *The Book of the Kings of Judah and Israel* (2 Chr 16:11; 25:26; 27:7). Indeed, the Bible writers relied on other ancient historical accounts.

IMPORTANT INTERTESTAMENTAL DATES

332 BC–Alexander the Great conquers Jerusalem and the process of Hellenization begins

323 BC–Alexander dies and his empire was split between rival generals (the Diadochi) and is eventually divided among three dynasties in the Greek East: the Attalids (Pergamum), the Seleucids (Babylonia), and the Ptolemies (Egypt).

192–188 BC–Romans defeated the Seleucid empire and gained control of Greece.

167 BC–The Desecration of Temple occurred by Antiochus IV Epiphanes ("god manifest").

167–64 BC–The Maccabean Revolt occurred.

164 BC–Hanukkah (Festival of Lights) is initiated at the rededication of the Temple.

164–63 BC–Hasmonean Dynasty; Qumran community separates; Sadducees and Pharisees form.

63 BC–Roman General Pompey conquers Jerusalem and annexes Syria into the Roman Empire.

These events are described in some books of the OT Apocrypha (the word apocryphal means "hidden; spurious"). There are fourteen book collections: *1–4 Maccabees, 1–2 Esdras, Wisdom of Solomon, Baruch, Additions to Esther, Ecclesiasticus (or Wisdom of Sirach), The Letter of Jeremiah, Tobit, Judith, The Prayer of Azariah, The Prayer of Manasseh, Psalm 151*, and two short legends about Daniel (*Susanna* and *Bel and the Dragon*).

IMPORTANT NT DATES (WITH *BIBLICAL SOURCES*)

6–4 BC–Birth of John and Jesus (*Four Gospels*)

AD 29–33–Ministry of Jesus culminating in his death and resurrection (*Four Gospels*)

AD 33–Pentecost (*Acts 1–2*)

AD 33–67–Conversion and Ministry of Paul <u>and</u> others (*Acts 9–28; Pauline Epistles* and *Latter NT*)

AD 67–70–Jewish War and Fall of the Second Temple (*Mark 13; Matthew 24; Luke 21; Revelation?*)

IMPORTANT POST-NEW TESTAMENT DATES (WITH *SOURCES*)

AD 90–Bishop Clement of Rome wrote to the Corinthians (*1-2 Clement*).

AD 90s–The *Didache* (*The Teaching of the Twelve Apostles*) was written.

AD 94–Josephus published *Jewish Antiquities*.

AD 108–Martyrdom of Bishop Ignatius of Antioch under the emperor Trajan (see *Letters of Ignatius*)

AD 111–Governor Pliny wrote to Emperor Trajan about the Christians in Bithynia.

AD 132–35–Revolt of Bar Kochba, Simon ben Kosiba, and the Roman ban of Jews living in Judea (Justin Martyr's *Dialogue with Trypho*)

A More Detailed NT Chronology

with possible dates of NT Books

6–4 BC	Birth of Jesus; Herod's death (**4 BC**)	
AD 28/29	John the Baptist prepares the way.	**29** John the Baptist beheaded (Mark 6:14–29)
AD 30	Jesus begins ministry at about 30 years of age.	**30–33** Jesus's ministry, death, and resurrection
AD 31–33		
AD 33/34	Stephen stoned (Acts 7)	**33–48** Peter is leader of the church in Jerusalem along with James and John.
AD 34	Saul persecutes the church and meets the risen Christ (Acts 9); Paul travels to Arabia, Damascus, Cilicia, and Syria (Gal 1:15–21)	
AD 37	Paul first visits Jerusalem (Gal 1:18–19)	
AD 44		**44** James, the brother of John (Zebedee), is martyred (Acts 12:1–2).
AD 45–46	**James**, the brother of the Lord, writes a letter	
AD 47	Paul's famine relief trip (Acts 11:25–30)	**47–48** Paul's first missionary Journey to Galatia and Asia Minor (Acts 13:2–14:28)
AD 48	Paul writes **Galatians**	
AD 49	○ Jerusalem Council (Acts 15) ○ Jews ejected from Rome by Emperor Claudius	**49–52** Paul's second missionary journey and first visit to Macedonia and Achaia (Acts 15:40–18:23)
AD 50–51	**1 & 2 Thessalonians**	
AD 52		**51** Paul on trial before Gallio (Acts 18:12–17)
AD 53		**53–57** Paul's third missionary journey and second visit to Macedonia and Achaia (Acts 18:23–21:16)
AD 54	**1 Corinthians**	
AD 55	**2 Corinthians**	
AD 56	**Romans**	
AD 58	**Ephesians, Colossians, Philemon**	**58–60** Paul arrested and moved to Caesarea Maritima (Acts 21:17–26:32)
AD 59		
AD 60	**Philippians**	**60–62** Paul moved to Rome to appeal to Caesar (Acts 27–28)
AD 61	**Jude?**	
AD 62	**1 Peter** **Luke–Acts?**	**62–64** Paul's fourth missionary journey to Spain
AD 63	**2 Peter; 1 Timothy**	
AD 64	**Mark's Gospel?**	

AD 65–67	**Titus**
	                1–2–3 John?
	                Revelation?
	2 Timothy
	                Hebrews?
	                Matthew's Gospel?
		64–68 Persecution of the church under the emperor Nero; Peter (**64/65**) and Paul (**67**) die in Rome under the Emperor Nero

AD 67–70	The Jewish Revolt against Rome	
AD 70	The fall of Jerusalem and second temple destroyed **Mark's Gospel?**	

AD 80s	**Hebrews?**
	                Luke–Acts?
	                Matthew's Gospel?
	                Revelation?	

AD 90s	**John's Gospel?** **1–2–3 John?**	

Disputed Dates: BC refers to "before Christ" and AD refers to the Latin *anno Domini* meaning, "In the year of the Lord ____"; thus AD precedes the date given. More recently, scholars commonly have adopted another convention that removes "Christ" from the dating abbreviations: BCE (before the common era) and CE (common era) instead of BC and AD, respectively. In some scholarly publications it is mandatory to use BCE and CE.

Although some of the dates in the charts above are fairly certain, others have more than one possible option with good scholarship on each side of the debate. For example, was the Exodus event earlier (~1450 BC) or later (~1250 BC)? Also, the exact date of Jesus's birth is hard to determine because King Herod the Great died in 4 BC, and yet Luke indicates (presumably) that the census taken before Jesus's birth occurred while "Quirinius was governor of Syria" (Luke 2:2) who became governor in AD 6 and had the census then; likewise, nowhere else is there reported an earlier financial census by ancient historians. Scholars may quickly see Luke in error, but the reputable NT scholar I. Howard Marshall has stated, "[H. Schürmann] warns against too easy acceptance of the conclusion that Luke has gone astray here; only the discovery of new historical evidence can lead to a solution of the problem."[2] Luke has been shown to be quite an excellent historian, despite the skeptical views that persist even still today.[3] Colin J. Humphreys has argued that a "census of allegiance" to Augustus was required of each Roman Province one year before Herod's death (Josephus, *AJ* XVII.2.4);[4] moreover, the new moving star from the east that "remained over" Bethlehem to guide the Magi from the East is consistent with ancient Greco-Roman descriptions of comets and their visibility (being seen for months) and paths (from east to south and then west)—such a comet is recorded as occurring in Chinese astronomical history in 5 BC.[5]

Bible Atlases: Atlases are important resources to understand geography over time. They will show territorial boundaries of different time periods, summarize routes travelled, and identify the (likely) location of cities. Atlases may treat the whole Bible, the OT, or the NT.

Historical Data: Cold Hard Fact or What's the Story? Historical writers of the Bible were not always concerned to provide (exact) dates for events; indeed, to do so was not always their primary purpose. However, this is not to say they were unconcerned with historical events and their factuality—yet, to provide a verifiable and chronological accounting of events was not necessarily their primary purpose in writing. Luke, however, shows good historical acumen by dating events in relation to identifying those holding various political positions of the day.

---

[2] I. Howard Marshall, *Luke: Historian and Theologian* (Grand Rapids: Zondervan, 1971), 69 n5.

[3] See, e.g., the statements on the trustworthiness of Luke by the once skeptical scholar William M. Ramsay, *St. Paul the Traveler and the Roman Citizen* (Grand Rapids: Baker, 1982), 4–10. Today the historicity of the Book of Acts is discounted on genre considerations, i.e., that Acts is novella writing akin to ancient romance literature. This view is not convincing nor has garnered much scholarly support, although it has a few loud proponents.

[4] Colin J. Humphreys, "The Star of Bethlehem—a Comet in 5 BC–and the Date of Christ's Birth," *TynB* 43.1 (1992): 31–56.

[5] See the article of the same name but with more astronomical data by Colin J. Humphreys, "The Star of Bethlehem—a Comet in 5 BC—and the Date of Christ's Birth," *Quarterly Journal of the Royal Astronomical Society* 32 (1991): 389–407.

EXERCISE 7-B: Read and observe the various ways that Luke dates an event and then consider the following questions.

Luke 3:1–2 Now in the fifteenth year of the reign of Tiberius Caesar, when Pontius Pilate was governor of Judea, and Herod was tetrarch of Galilee, and his brother Philip was tetrarch of the region of Ituraea and Trachonitis, and Lysanias was tetrarch of Abilene, ² in the high priesthood of Annas and Caiaphas, the word of God came to John, the son of Zacharias, in the wilderness.

1. What is the event being dated?

2. Which political-religious leaders are listed here? Is there any significance to the listing?

3. Consider the significance of Luke dating this event in the way he has.

With the advent of the practice of modern history (1700s), scholars were quite optimistic about recovering pure facts within history. Such a view is called historical positivism. At the same time, true history was concerned to reconstruct only verifiable events within the stream of *human* historical causality; divine interventions (by definition) were automatically deemed "unhistorical" since God does not interfere with human affairs nowadays (this was the view of Deism). With such a view of history, scholars when investigating biblical books articulated more and more skepticism that questioned the historical reliability of Scripture and especially even the primary events of the biblical narrative like the Exodus out of Egypt or the very existence of Jesus (let alone his resurrection). Such views persist today within the field of biblical studies and our high school and university students may be subjected to such views subtly or quite overtly by Bible or Religion professors who make it their goal to challenge their "naïve" view of Scripture.

However, conservative scholars have challenged such a pessimistic view of history while also defending the credibility of Scripture. For instance, Craig S. Keener has written persuasively (and quite extensively) in a 1172 page book that the NT accounts are credible in their reporting of miracles; such should not be discounted outright while pursuing serious historical investigation on philosophical and historiographical grounds since sound eyewitness accounts of miracles exist today as well as in antiquity.[6] Moreover, more recent historians and philosophers have challenged the view (and goal) of historical research to recover "pure" isolated facts since even these "facts" are not always interpreted the same way by people and thus do not mean the same thing depending on one's viewpoint. "There is no pure historical data, only subjective data seen from each one's vantage point." Taken to an extreme, this view results in epistemological "relativism" as reflected in this common belief: What is true for you is not true for me; we have our respective truths.

---

[6] Providing a rebuttal of historical skepticism with respect to miracles as well as providing evidence that miracles persist today, see the massive two volume work of Craig S. Keener, *Miracles: The Credibility of the New Testament Accounts*, 2 vols. (Grand Rapids: Baker Academic, 2011).

Fortunately, we can escape the extremes of skepticism and relativism by adopting a critical realist view of history that accounts for the importance of humans as story-creating beings located within narratives of meaning. N. T. Wright, drawing upon Ben F. Meyer's application of "critical realism" to NT interpretation,[7] has described the possibility of serious historical investigation within the context of story and worldview.[8] *Critical realism involves an observer's ability to study an object self-reflectively (critically) in an attempt to be true to what is truly observed.*

CRITICAL-REALISM AND HISTORICAL INQUIRY[9]

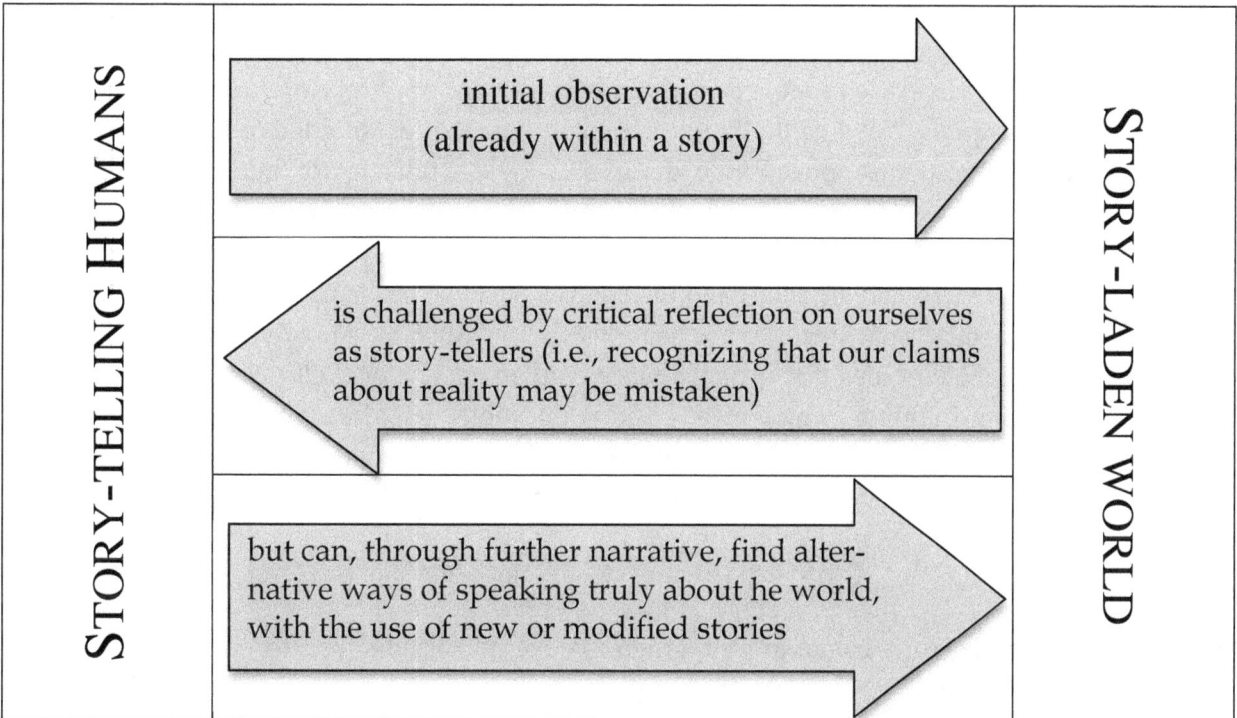

In addition to critical realism, Wright adds the notion of stories and worldviews: People find themselves within larger stories and narratives that promote a certain view of the world in which ultimate questions are given answer and are expressed "in cultural symbols" and "include a praxis, a way-of-being-in-the-world."[10] These stories are "normative: that is, they claim to make sense of the whole of reality."[11] While events happen, they are recalled and conveyed within this narrative

---

[7] Ben F. Meyer, *Critical Realism and the New Testament*, Princeton Theological Monograph Series 17 (Alison Park, PA: Pickwick, 1989).

[8] N. T. Wright, *The New Testament and the People of God*, Christian Origins and the Question of God 1 (Minneapolis: Fortress, 1992), esp. chs. 2–4. The rest of the book and the series attempts to apply these methodological perspectives to understand Jesus and the emerging Christian movement.

[9] The content of this diagram is from Wright, *People of God*, 44; however, I have entitled the exchange.

[10] Wright, *People of God*, 123–24. Worldviews entail stories, questions/answers, symbols, & praxis/conduct.

[11] Wright, *People of God*, 41.

framework whether or not one is aware of the story. However, by accepting a critical realist view of historical inquiry, one can reconstruct foundational features of the story in the worldview with careful and reflective observation and inquiry. Wright describes a reflective "back and forth" between the observing human and the world (see above the diagram CRITICAL-REALISM AND HISTORICAL INQUIRY). Thus, humans are story-telling creatures and will assimilate people, events, and historical "facts" within their understanding of the world in order to make sense of the world. However, this innate human capacity to connect facts, events, and agents together within a story *can actually become a detriment to reading Scripture since we may inappropriately overlay our stories onto the story of Scripture.*[12] We naturally fuse together these stories for good or for bad.

> Critical realism involves an observer's ability to study an object self-reflectively (critically) in an attempt to be true to what is truly observed.

Controlling Presuppositions: While discussing logical fallacies of interpretation, Carson describes a fallacy of "world-view confusion": "The fallacy in this case lies in thinking that one's own experience and interpretation of reality are the proper framework for interpreting the biblical text, whereas in fact there may be such deep differences once we probe beyond the superficial level that we find quite different categories are being used...."[13] Such may involve **anachronism**, i.e., the imposition of a modern idea that is out of place onto an ancient one. Closely related to this are "fallacies of question-framing," which means asking questions that already presuppose answers at the outset. Thus, one must be self-reflective and discerning of presuppositions that may cause one to look at biblical materials myopically seeing only what one wants to see.

<u>EXERCISE 7–B</u>: Consider Mark 10:25 below and answer the following questions.

Jesus said, "It is easier for a camel to go through the eye of a needle than for a rich man to enter into the kingdom of God."

1. What have you heard or learned about what "the eye of the needle" is? Is this literally a needle used for sewing? If so, what implication would this have for application today?

2. It is commonly related in preaching today that "the eye of the needle" was the popular name of a gate into Jerusalem that could only be entered by removing one's possessions from a camel's back and having the camel kneel (humbly) and crawl through the gate. Research this further.

3. What worldview or societal narratives would motivate adopting one interpretation or another?

4. How important is historical research for interpreting and appropriating this scriptural passage?

---

[12] As compelling as much of Wright's interpretive work is, he has been liable to criticisms (and I agree at times) with overlaying his reconstructed narrative story unto biblical materials, e.g., the parable of the Prodigal Son.

[13] Carson, *Exegetical Fallacies*, 104.

Example—A Wife in 1 Tim 2:11: Paul admonishes, "Let a woman learn quietly in all submission" (1 Tim 2:11). We often come to this passage with huge gaps in our understanding. Such gaps are encouraged by the section headings in our Bibles that would place Paul's admonitions within a framework of "church worship"; yet Paul is concerned with missionary outreach and social decorum.[14] Women were not highly educated in society (with exceptions), and yet Paul commanded that a woman learn with two qualifiers: "quietly" and "in all submission." What do these mean? Why did Paul add these? Here we must observe that Paul was likely addressing "an individual wife" since he moves from plural "women" generally in 2:9–10 to a singular woman (or wife) in 2:11. That an individual wife is in view is also indicated by "in all submission" since culturally it was paramount that a wife be in submission to her own husband and *not to all men*; the NT repeatedly affirms this (Col 3:18; 1 Pet 3:1–7; see also 1 Cor 14:34–35), even as such submission is drastically re-understood in light of Christ as "mutual submission" (Eph 5:21–33). Furthermore, historically and culturally we need to understand that wives were carefully watched in public; their dress, their behaviors, and their purchases were scrutinized and there was even a city magistrate in many Greek cities called a *gunaikonomos* ("controller of women") to ensure that they were conducting themselves befittingly.[15] In this regard, culturally women were expected to be "quiet" in public since silence was considered a woman's virtue; the playwright Sophocles is quoted by Aristotle on this point: "Silence is a woman's glory, but this is not equally the glory of man" (*Pol.* 1.XIII). Other ancient authorities nearer to the NT times also attest to this, e.g., Plutarch who advises, "A wife ought to speak only to her husband or through her husband…" (*Advice to Bride and Groom*, 32).[16] So, Paul in 1 Tim 2:11 reflects cultural mores of his time—women should be quiet and wives should submit to their own husbands—while also moving beyond these mores by commanding a wife to learn. Why would Paul straddle this fence? First, women are created in God's image and are equally as gifted and valuable as men; everyone benefits if they learn. Second, Paul respected and accommodated the Mediterranean culture for the sake of sharing the good news of the Lord Jesus to others, especially unbelieving husbands who would be carefully observing their wives' behavior within this new religious movement—this is the missionary context of the preceding verses in 1 Tim 2:1–7: God wants all people to be saved (2:4).

Historical Context: As discussed in STEP 1: CONTEXTUAL LOCATION, the complete literary context places a "contextual constraint" on the interpretation of the passage. Likewise, the historical context places a "historical constraint" because the specific situations of the author(s) and the audience(s) have constrained the focus and direction of the discourse. The authors of our NT documents were writing within a historical location and addressing historical circumstances facing the

---

[14] The following is a summary of the salient historical context that is presented in my article, "A Wife in Relation to a Husband" available at http://place.asburyseminary.edu/jibs/vol2/iss2/3/.

[15] For a description, see "Appendix: *Gynaikonomoi*, 'Controllers of Women'" in Daniel Ogden, *Greek Bastardy in the Classical and Hellenistic Periods* (Oxford: Clarendon, 1996), 364–76.

[16] Plutarch's treatise is much more dynamic than this and is well worth reading in its entirety to understand the complexity of customs and expectations of wives in relation to their husbands. The full text can be found at this website: http://penelope.uchicago.edu/Thayer/E/Roman/Texts/Plutarch/Moralia/Coniugalia_praecepta*.html.

audiences. What was happening at that time both prompted and inspired the writing of the NT document in the first place in the way that it was written. The historical specificity becomes a part of the way the text was written out, and so we should not ignore this fundamental reality.

<u>Authors, Audiences, and Provenance</u>: It is helpful to consider details pertaining to the life and circumstances of the author(s), if knowable: their history, past travels, and future travel plans, as well as any relationships they had with others that are mentioned. Additionally, you should consider the audiences' locations and the possible significant events (recent or pressing) that may have a bearing on *why* that particular NT document contains the particular themes that it does. This information of author, audience, and provenance/setting may have already been gathered (in whole or in part) in the book survey for STEP 1: CONTEXTUAL LOCATION described in TERTIARY INTERPRETIVE PROCEDURES. You may need to re-read the NT book to glean important relevant details.

<u>NT Introductions</u>: Helpful resources for students of Scripture are NT Introductions that specialize in providing such information. Experts who have devoted their lives to studying the texts and contexts and weighing the available evidence write such books. The quality, perspective, and detail of NT Introductions varies considerably. You must be discerning.

<u>Circularity</u>: Additionally, we don't have complete records, or even sufficient records, to provide definitively decisive historical reconstructions, and yet this may not prevent scholars from proposing "confident" reconstructions that may be completely wrong or may perhaps only approximate the situations facing the ancient authors and audiences. Image how complex life is now in communities; it was the same then. So, we must be aware that circularity may exist between historical evidence, reimagined reconstruction, and interpretation of the historical evidence. We must constantly ask ourselves, Is the evidence driving the interpretation or is the (pre-)interpretation driving the selection and use of evidence? Such hermeneutical circularity at some level is unavoidable; it happens among both liberal and conservative interpreters. So, you must read more than one source of information, read trusted sources, and discern between sources and evidences supplied.

EXERCISE 7–C: A very helpful book treating important NT historical contexts has been written by Warren Carter, *Seven Events That Shaped the New Testament World* (Grand Rapids: Baker Academic, 2013). The seven events are the following:

1. The Death of Alexander the Great (323 BCE)
2. The Process of Translating Hebrew Scriptures into Greek (ca. 250 BCE)
3. The Rededication of the Jerusalem Temple (164 BCE)
4. The Roman Occupation of Judea (63 BCE)
5. The Crucifixion of Jesus (ca. 30 CE)
6. The Writing of the New Testament Texts (ca. 50–ca. 130 CE)
7. The Process of "Closing" the New Testament Canon (397 CE)

a. How would you critique Carter's selections?

b. What important events are arguably missing?

Interesting Tidbits of History or Game Changing Perspectives: Although learning history around and in the biblical texts is interesting, some historical information opens up new perspectives, if not even vast horizons, on what NT authors are saying. Two of the most important events, yet controversial events, are Jesus's resurrection and the fall of Jerusalem. Jesus's resurrection confirmed his message and showed God's victory over death; a new era of God's deliverance had begun. Correspondingly, the fall of Jerusalem entailed the destruction of the temple. In the NT, it does not surprise me that Jesus is recorded as weeping twice: at the death of a close friend in view of the reality of resurrection (John 11:35) and the death of a city representing God's people who had rejected Jesus's message of peace and consequently faced judgment (Luke 19:41). Aligning with the prophets of God's people, Jesus's greatest mission was to call Israel to repentance lest God judge the nation (19:41–44), something which John the Baptist also foresaw and warned about (3:7–9). John foresaw "the coming *wrath*"—a word only elsewhere used in Luke's Gospel when Jesus predicted the "great distress upon the land and *wrath* against this people" (21:23) and the besieging and fall of Jerusalem (21:20–24). John indicated that "the axe is already at the root of the tree" (3:9). I once worked for a tree removal service and have hacked out a good number of trees and shrubs the old-fashioned way by using a grub hoe, a mattock. But why not simply cut the tree down? Why cut out the roots? Well, by cutting out the roots, *the tree is removed*. As uncomfortable as John's message was, it forms a critical historical framework for understanding the NT and the message of God in Jesus. Jesus also foresaw this event and wept for the city (19:41).

Stories as Frameworks of Meanings: God in Scripture is self-revealing. As God interacts with humanity and the world, we learn of God's purposes in the story of unfolding history. God discloses information about the nature of the world, the problems of the world, solutions to these problems, and where we are headed. There are several important frameworks that can inform our reading of Scripture. More will be said about these in STEP 10: BIBLICAL THEOLOGY. However, several are worth mentioning here because of their ability to help us grasp important dimensions of the big picture of Scripture.

- **Old Testament**: In Sandra Richter's *The Epic of Eden* (Downers Grove, IL: IVP Academic, 2008) you will find a very accessible and cogent description of God's plan of redemption as revealed to Adam, Noah, Abraham, Moses and David in the form of covenants.
- **Missional Outreach**: Brian D. Russell sets forth a reading of Scripture from the perspective of God's mission in the world in his book *(re)Aligning with God: Reading Scripture for Church and World* (Eugene, Or: Cascade, 2015). What we find in Scripture is a God who is seeking to save the lost.
- **Spiritual Realm**: Michael S. Heiser in his *The Unseen Realm: Recovering the Supernatural Worldview of the Bible* (Bellingham, WA: Lexham, 2015) traces the opposition to God's ways by the rebellious spiritual forces, fallen creatures of God, with which humans are involved in a struggle. Heiser shows the pervasiveness of this perspective that is sometimes obscured or even removed by our modern translations.
- **Political Ideology**: In my readings of Scripture, I have repeatedly and increasingly ob-

served the profound political aspects of the human world, the worst manifestations of evil, and God's involvement to save while confronting and subverting common, imperial, harmful political ideas and thoughts. A classical statement of the broader issue is found in Klaus Wengst, *Pax Romana and the Peace of Jesus Christ* (Philadelphia: Fortress, 1987). Also, see the numerous books authored and edited by Richard A. Horsley, which however often reflect a more "liberal" understanding of Christianity, yet still remain helpful.

EXERCISE 7–D: What do these words, ideas, and titles have in common in the first-century Mediterranean World? The answer is given in this footnote written backwards.[17]

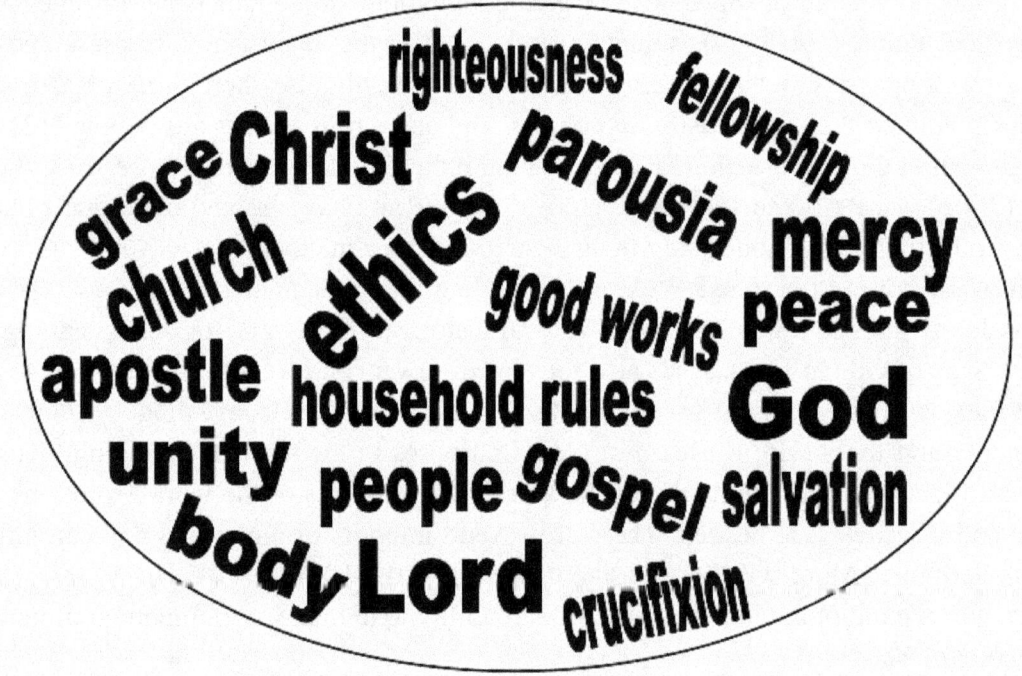

What words would you use that would characterize your contemporary understanding of the faith?

The Field of Archeology: More and more work is being conducted to uncover and recover artifacts from the ancient world. This is the field of archeology made popular for many of us by the movie *The Raiders of the Lost Ark*. However, much archeological work remains to be done. During my visit to Turkey (June 2016), I saw amazing things at biblical places like Pergamum, Ephesus, Miletus, Sardis, Thyatira, Laodicea, Hierapolis, and Perga. At Ephesus, whole areas of houses have yet to be excavated. The ancient city of Colossae remains completely unexcavated. Additionally, we are still interpreting the data uncovered and correlating it with biblical materials. For example, at the Istanbul Archeological Museum is one of the few remains from the destruction of the Jewish temple in AD 70—surrounding the Jewish temple was a balustrade barring entrance except at specific locations which had this inscription stone (approx. 22 x 33 inches) with a warning.

---

[17] .thguoht lacitilop tneicnA. Commonly students say this is "the core of Christian faith" or "Paul's teaching."

Warning Inscription on Foreigners entering the Jewish Temple Area[18]

The Greek text written with lower case letters, accents, and breathing marks is translated below.

μηθένα ἀλλογενῆ εἰσπο-	*No foreigner shall enter*
ρεύεσθαι ἐντὸς τοῦ πε-	*inside the balustrade*
ρὶ τὸ ἱερὸν τρυφάκτου	*around the temple*
καὶ περιβόλου· ὃς δ' ἂν λη-	*and enclosure; and whoever*
φθῇ, ἑαυτῷ αἴτιος ἔσ-	*is caught will have the blame*
ται διὰ τὸ ἐξακολου-	*in himself because of*
θεῖν θάνατον.	*the death resulting.*

This viewpoint of this inscription informs several NT passages including those on the next page.

---

[18] I took this photo June 2016 at the Istanbul Archeological Museum (Inv. 2196 T) modified to grayscale.

EXERCISE 7–E: What significance does this inscription have for understanding each of these NT passages? You will gain greater insight by looking at the broader literary context of each passage.

Mark 11:16–18 And Jesus would not allow anyone to carry merchandise through the temple. [17] And he was teaching and saying to them, "Is it not written, 'MY HOUSE SHALL BE CALLED A HOUSE OF PRAYER FOR ALL THE GENTILES'? But you have made it a ROBBERS' DEN." [18] The chief priests and the scribes heard and were seeking how to destroy Him; for they were afraid of Him, for the whole crowd was astonished at His teaching.

Acts 21:27–29 The Jews from Asia, upon seeing Paul in the temple, were stirring up the entire crowd and laid hands on him, [28] shouting, "Men of Israel, help! This is the person who preaches to all everywhere against our people and the Law and this place; and besides he has even brought Greeks into the temple and has defiled this holy place!" [29] For they had previously seen Trophimus the Ephesian in the city with him, and they supposed that Paul had brought him into the temple.

Eph 2:11–14, 21b–22 Therefore remember that formerly you, Gentiles in the flesh, who are called "Uncircumcision" by the so-called "Circumcision" performed in the flesh by human hands—[12] that you were once separate from Christ, excluded from the citizenship of Israel, and strangers to the covenants of promise, having no hope and without God in the world. [13] But now in Christ Jesus you who were formerly far off have been brought near by the blood of Christ. [14] For He Himself is our peace, who made both people one and broke down the barrier of the dividing wall, ... [21b] [you are] growing into a holy temple in the Lord, [22] in whom you also are being built together into a dwelling of God in the Spirit.

Resurgence of Background Studies: With access to ancient artifacts becoming more and more available electronically along with the recognition of the value of such as providing an essential context for Biblical Studies, a number of excellent resources give access to such information for students of Scripture. Keener's *IVP New Testament Background Commentary* (now in its 2nd edition, 2014) is an invaluable aid to concisely relate the most germane background information (in his view) for interpreting the NT. Additionally, Keener often provides brief incisive interpretive comments along with important OT references to help fill out the meaning for broader application today. Unfortunately, Keener does not often provide the references to the specific Greco-Roman sources from which he has derived information on social-cultural backgrounds. A resource with more information at times by providing more primary sources and numerous images is Clinton E. Arnold, ed., *Zondervan Illustrated Bible Backgrounds Commentary*, 4 vols. (Grand Rapids: Zondervan, 2002). See also Ben Witherington's many socio-rhetorical commentaries that contain accessible, readable, good summaries of background information and especially bibliographies to find primary treatments of background information.

Primary Interpretive Procedures:

1. Read the introductory material in a good NT introduction for the particular NT book to learn general and particular details of the historical background pertaining to the author(s), audiences, and circumstances: who, where, and when, and what?
2. Consult a Bible backgrounds commentary for your passage and summarize the most important pieces of information.
3. If time allows, consult two good quality commentaries for general and specific historical information.
4. From your reading and research above, summarize what is the most important historical background information regarding the following, if such is knowable:
    a. the locations of the author and of the audiences;
    b. the recent circumstances and future situations facing the author(s);
    c. The situation(s) facing the audience(s).
5. Specifically, from your research above, consider how the historical context has affected the writing of the particular pericope and the audiences' likely or plausible reception of what was being communicated to them.
6. Consolidate (not necessarily summarize) your findings and identify any unresolved questions that may need addressing during STEP 9: INTERPRETIVE DECISIONS.

II. SECONDARY STUDY

Orientation: Pastors have limited time and often resort to internet accessible commentaries. A problem with this is that such commentaries are often outdated and may contain erroneous background information. However, since the history surrounding the text informs its interpretation and helps its proper appropriation, our ability to access accurate and helpful information is imperative. People in the pew enjoy learning about the biblical cultures especially when it helps bring Scripture to life. Such background information helps to convey the relevancy of Scripture.

Identifying and Researching Historical-Social-Cultural Contexts: It may be helpful to understand that ideas conveyed in Scripture may be described as having broader *social* currency (i.e., understood across diverse people within a society) or a more limited *cultural* meaning (i.e., within a culture within a broader society). So, as you read the passage and study the commentaries, consider this question: What words, phrases, or ideas in this passage seem to have particular social or cultural significance in order to illuminate the passage? Then research the word, phrase, or idea in a suitable Bible dictionary, Bible encyclopedia, theological wordbook (e.g., *Theological Dictionary of the New Testament*, ed. by G. Kittel), commentary, or other resource. Explore the reference section of the library under commentaries. The better commentary series will likely touch upon pivotal socio-cultural and historical matters and point you to other important books and/or articles. If you have time, locate and read these secondary resources. Browse the main section of the library that has books and other resources for your particular NT book. Often, library personnel will gladly assist you in your research.

Example of the Suffering Servant in Isaiah: To give one example of such a context that must be recovered by us today, John H. Walton investigates the puzzling description of "the Suffering Servant" person in Isa 52:13–53:12 who is deformed, beaten down, and takes upon himself the iniquity of people, and yet God will exalt him. Indeed, interpreters have struggled to understand the background or network of ideas. For many Christians, Isaiah's vision reveals the sacrificial suffering of Jesus Christ to atone for the sins of each one of us, and rightly so. However, there is much more to be understood here. Walton argues, "the imagery, background, and obscurities of the fourth song [of the Suffering Servant] can be adequately resolved when the passage is read in light of the substitute king ritual motifs known from Mesopotamia as early as the Isin period (early second millennium) and as late as Alexander the Great [ca. 323 BC]."[19] In fact, Isaiah mimics these well-known traditions of ritual substitution only to subvert them. Isaiah opposes the standard depictions of royal power and privilege. Walton concludes, "Turning away from royal prerogative, covenant laurels and Davidic pedigree, Isaiah forges a new image drawing on ancient Near Eastern materials that emphasize God's prominence in the kingship equation. The Servant would then not be a messianic figure in the sense of representing continuity with the Davidic line as much as he would be messianic in the sense of representing what an ideal anointed monarch would look like." Isaiah's vision of the coming Jewish Messiah is both like and unlike King David, something which Jesus himself knew (Matt 22:41–46). What this vision signified is that God's Messiah would provide a different understanding of power and leadership and would thus transform how God's people are to view themselves and their mission in the world.

Book Reviews and Monographs: One way to stay in tune with current scholarship and important books is through reading book reviews. The *Review of Biblical Literature* (RBL) produced by the Society of Biblical Literature (SBL) is one resource providing reviews of published books. Also, many scholarly journals will conclude each issue with book reviews. Often book reviews will provide succinct summaries of the books describing the most salient ideas. If important enough, you can then decide to read the book. Thus, reviews of books are like reading the Cliff Notes to these books, which are also, however, never fully a substitute for the whole book.

Journal Articles and Essays: I would encourage pastors regularly to read articles or essays (in books) treating biblical passages. By reading merely 10–20 pages, you may glean seminal insights from scholars who have invested months, even years(!), reflecting on the meaning and significance of biblical texts. So, an investment of one hour of reading may discover insights made possible from a lifetime of study. One online resource where you can download and read excellent research is the Bulletin of Biblical Research (BBR) by the Institute of Biblical Research (IBR).[20] Many other excellent journals exist such as *New Testament Studies* and *Novum Testamentum*.

---

[19] Walton, "The Imagery of the Substitute King Ritual in Isaiah's Fourth Servant Song," *JBL* 122 (2003): 734–43. The quotations are from the first and last page respectively.

[20] https://www.ibr-bbr.org/bulletin-biblical-research.

STEP 7: SECONDARY STUDY

EXERCISE 7–F: The Epistle of James comes to a striking climax in 5:1–6.

Jas 5:1–6 (ESV) [1] Come now, you rich, weep and howl for the miseries that are coming upon you. [2] Your riches have rotted and your garments are moth-eaten. [3] Your gold and silver have corroded, and their corrosion will be evidence against you and will eat your flesh like fire. You have laid up treasure in the last days. [4] Behold, the wages of the laborers who mowed your fields, which you kept back by fraud, are crying out against you, and the cries of the harvesters have reached the ears of the Lord of hosts. [5] You have lived on the earth in luxury and in self-indulgence. You have fattened your hearts in a day of slaughter. [6] You have condemned and murdered the righteous person. He does not resist you.

1. Does this betray a social-economic crisis? If so, when? Or, is this just railing against the rich?

2. Consult two or more essays or articles on the Letter of James. For radically differing opinions of the historical setting, see R. W. Wall, "James, Letter of" pages 545–61 in *Dictionary of the Later New Testament and its Background*, 1st ed. (Downer's Grove, IL: IVP, 1997) and Dale C. Allison, Jr. "Blessing God and Cursing People: James 3:9–10," *Journal of Biblical Literature* 130 (2011): 397–405.

3. If you are preaching or teaching through this passage, how would you reconcile and summarize the different historical reconstructions of these proposed settings behind 5:1–6?

<u>Sociological Areas of Inquiry</u>: Truly, more and more we are able to understand social and cultural dimensions of the biblical world, although our interpretations will still vary. The benefit of such research is that it often helps us better relate to biblical authors and their audiences; it helps us better understand how Scripture is fully embodied, fully human. Here, social sciences have a direct bearing on interpreting the biblical text: "The branch(es) of science that deal with the institutions and functioning of human society and with the interpersonal relationships of individuals as members of society; anthropology, economics, political science, and sociology are chief branches."[21]

It may be helpful to summarize some areas of this research both to introduce and orient one to these dimensions of the texts. A pioneer, Howard Clark Kee, posited seven areas of investigation: boundaries (in vs. out groups, etc.), authority/power/leadership, status/role, rituals (e.g., initiation, celebration, transition), social implications of literary production (use of genre, themes, etc.), group functions/dynamics/identity, and the group's symbolic universe and social construction of reality.[22] Richard L. Rohrbaugh (ed.) organizes sociological study with essays from various contributors according to Part I: Core Values of Honor and Shame, Understanding New Testament Persons, Kinship, and Clean/Unclean, and Purity (Pure/Polluted, and Holy/Profane), Part 2: Social Institutions of the Preindustrial City, the Ancient Economy, and Patronage and Clientage, and Part

---

[21] John H. Elliott, *What Is Social-Scientific Criticism?* (Minneapolis: Fortress, 1993), 134. Elliot provides a very detailed description of possible areas of research in his Appendices 2–4.

[22] *Knowing the Truth: A Sociological Approach to New Testament Interpretation* (Minneapolis: Fortress, 1989), 65–69. Each topic is several questions to answer.

3: Social Dynamic of Meals, Food, and Table Fellowship, Millennialism, and Ancient Reading.[23] More recently, David A. deSilva has described from ancient perspectives (interacting with Greco-Roman and Jewish authors) honor-shame, patron-client, pollution-purity, and fictive kinship and persuasively shows how such ideas pervade and illuminate NT texts.[24] For a rich description of the ancient Greco-Roman World, many notable books are available.[25] Also, a "Social-Science Commentary" series is being written by Bruce J. Malina, Richard L. Rohrbaugh, and John J. Pilch, each of whom has written numerous books, articles, and essays from this perspective.[26]

EXERCISE 7–G: In 1 Cor 11:2–16 Paul discourages men from being veiled and women from being unveiled. Below is my translation of 11:4–6, 10b, and 15b in which I translate "woman" as "wife."

11:4–6 Every man who prays or prophesies with his head covered dishonors his head. ⁵ And every wife who prays or prophesies with her head uncovered dishonors her head—it is just as though her head were shaved. ⁶ If a wife does not cover her head, she should have her hair cut off; and if it is a disgrace for a wife to have her hair cut or shaved off, she should cover her head.

11:10b The wife ought to have authority over her head because of the messengers/angels.

11:15b Long hair is given to her as a covering.

Consider how knowledge of the following social values, roles, and practices may impact your understanding of the verses given above.[27]

1. One's dress and appearance reflected one's social and religious status.
2. Pagan priests veiled their heads in official functions; the emperor is often depicted veiled as the *Pontifex Maximus*, the "Highest Priest"; men aspired to gain status by being like him.
3. Women's hair was an object of lust in antiquity.
4. Women with their hair down in public were considered unmarried or sexually promiscuous.
5. To shave a woman's hair was one punishment for committing adultery.
6. The Roman marriage ceremony consisted of "veiling" the bride's head.
7. Head coverings were expected of married women in public settings.
8. Women in the first-century were increasingly displaying their hair in creatively beautiful ways although still partially covering their hair with various head coverings (see next page).
9. Informants and officials ("controllers of women") could identify breaches of social decorum.

---

[23] Richard L. Rohrbaugh, ed., *The Social Sciences and New Testament Interpretation* (Peabody, MA: Hendrickson, 1996).

[24] David Arthur deSilva, *Honor, Patronage, Kinship & Purity: Unlocking New Testament Culture* (Downers Grove, IL: InterVarsity, 2000).

[25] My preference is for Albert A. Bell, *Exploring the New Testament World: An Illustrated Guide to the World of Jesus and the First Christians* (Nashville: Thomas Nelson, 1998); but see also Moyer V. Hubbard, *Christianity in the Greco-Roman World: A Narrative Introduction* (Peabody, MA: Hendrickson, 2010).

[26] E.g., this volume is in its second edition by Bruce J. Malina and Richard L. Rohrbaugh, *Social-Science Commentary on the Synoptic Gospels*, 2nd ed. (Minneapolis: Fortress, 2003).

[27] These listed items reflect the research and ideas of the excellent work of Bruce W. Winter, *Roman Wives, Roman Widows: The Appearance of New Women and the Pauline Communities* (Grand Rapids: Eerdmans, 2003).

<u>Varieties of Head-Coverings</u>: Below are diverse head-coverings from the Greco-Roman period.[28] As you can see, head coverings are quite varied among Greek and Roman women. Some allowed for more hair to be displayed in a decorative way. Sometimes the hair itself is wrapped up to cover the head and functioning somewhat like a veil. In Paul's instructions on head coverings, he affirms the wife's responsibility for how she wears her hair, which, he argues, is given to her as a covering (i.e., a veil). It seems conceivable that the earliest believers, who were from various cultures and sub-cultures, had slightly different expectations of what was public space and private space and what constituted proper veiling. In private women could wear their hair down; but at a church meeting inside a house, was this location considered private or public space?

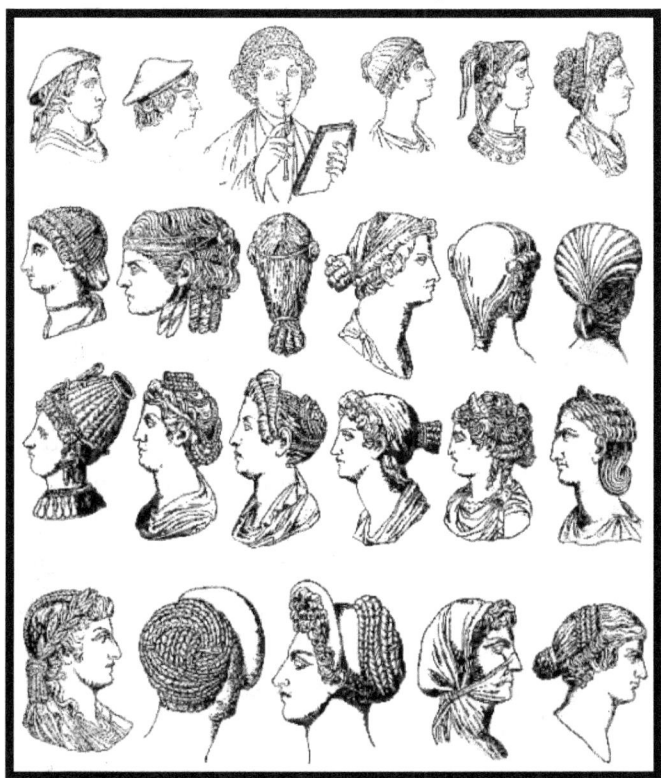

EXERCISE 7–H: To the right is the grave stele of the deceased Zotichos, who stands between his reclining parents.[29] It reads,

"I have departed from life, Zotichos, son of Milon, having lived for twenty-five years and eleven months." We, his parents, Milon and Eia, have erected this gravestone in his memory. Farewell, traveller!

The upraised hands at the top beseech the gods to avenge his untimely death.

1. Which figure depicted is his mother?

2. How is honor and shame represented here?

---

[28] The image, which includes reconstructions from statuary from the Imperial family, is slightly modified from M. A. Racinet, *Le Costume historique,* 6 vols. (Paris: Librairie de Firmin-Didot et cie, 1888), vol. 2, n.p.

[29] Picture taken and slightly modified by the author from the Istanbul Archeological Museum (Inv. 5466 T).

SECONDARY INTERPRETIVE PROCEDURES:

The following procedures incorporate some elements of the PRIMARY INTERPRETIVE PROCEDURES.

1. **Return to and reassess any prior work you may have done that treated the historical background and circumstances of the book. For instance, such information may have been identified during a Book Survey in STEP 1: CONTEXTUAL LOCATION. Also, you may have discovered historical information in STEP 5: LEXICAL RESEARCH and in STEP 6: LITERARY FORMS.**
2. **Consult two or more top quality commentaries and one introductory survey for the NT book to learn general and particular details of the historical context pertaining to the author(s), audiences, and circumstances: who, where, and when, and what?**
3. **Consult a Bible backgrounds commentary for your passage and summarize the most important pieces of historical-social-cultural information for understanding the passage.**
4. **Next, conduct research on the possible connections your passage may have to social, cultural, and historical materials (*realia*) of its time. Research these topics in the library and other available media (e.g., Bible software). Find and read journal articles, entries in Bible dictionaries, essays in books, and specific books or monographs treating the topic(s).**
5. **Specifically based upon your research above, consider how the historical context has affected the writing of the particular pericope and the audiences' reception of what was being communicated to them.**
6. **Consolidate (not necessarily summarize) your findings and identify any unresolved questions that may need to be addressed during STEP 9: INTERPRETIVE DECISIONS.**

III. TERTIARY RESEARCH

Orientation: At the highest levels of research, students of Scripture access primary materials in the original languages such as Hebrew, Aramaic, and Semitic languages generally, as well as Classical and Koine Greek, and Latin (if needed). Also, they are able to read secondary studies in German, French, and perhaps other modern languages, such as Italian and Spanish. Historical research may be extended more deeply in two ways: first, by accessing archaeological data in various media such as inscriptions, papyri, statuary, coins, mosaics, architecture, temple construction and locations, house structures and artifacts, city plans, and other realia; and, second, by engaging in research on the social history of the era and/or social-scientific study or exegesis of the biblical materials. The integration of anthropological or social-scientific perspectives with texts has helped interpreters provide a "thick description" of them.[30] Clifford Gertz has described the rich thickness

---

[30] The phrase is from Gilbert Ryle and was given rich description by Clifford Geertz, "Thick Description: Toward an Interpretive Theory of Culture," in *The Interpretation of Cultures: Selected Essays* (New York: Basic Books, 1973), 3–30.

of cultural analysis this way: "[M]ost of what we need to comprehend a particular event, ritual, custom, idea, or whatever is insinuated as background information before the thing itself is directly examined.... There is nothing particularly wrong with this, and it is in any case inevitable. But it does lead to a view of anthropological research as rather more of an observational and rather less of an interpretive activity than it really is."[31] It is difficult for us to access and assess modern as well as ancient data. Speaking to the latter, David E. Aune has helpfully summarized two types of social investigation with regard to ancient texts: sociological research and social-historical study:

> Given the empirical character of sociological research..., early Christianity cannot be the object of primary analytical research. It can only be the object of sociological research in the sense that theoretical models, formulated on the basis of modern empirical studies, may be applied secondarily to relevant data of early Christian history and literature. The secondary application of sociological theory is primarily of heuristic value in that it enables the scholar to see correlations, functions and explanations which would not otherwise be apparent.... The *social-historical* approach to ancient literature and history, on the other hand, can either use a particular text as a window through which to view the social realities of which it was part, or the social dimensions of the text can be explored with a view to providing a more adequate understanding of the text itself.[32]

<u>Sociological Criticism and Social-Historical Study</u>: H. Robert Mulholland, Jr. has described five levels of sociological investigation of the NT while providing brief examples.[33]

1. Preliminarily and descriptively, you can *reconstruct the social setting* as a descriptive exercise by accessing ancient archaeological realia in the areas of economics, politics, religion, education, social status, etc.; e.g., the role and authority of the scribes of Jesus's day.
2. More analytically, you can discern *"sociological dynamics" of "any human social matrix"* where old structures meet, interact, and conflict with new structures resulting in "emergent structures"; consider, e.g., the economic disruption at Ephesus in relation to Paul's gospel (Acts 19:23–27).
3. Both descriptively and analytically, you can *utilize sociological models to investigate social relations and the "multifaceted sociological matrix"* of individual and group interaction within the NT world. The Philippian Christians were an outcast group, having as their founder Paul who was beaten and escorted out of the city, and meeting in the house of a foreign woman.
4. *This process of investigation continues throughout the NT*, so that "[m]eaning of the words and symbols of the text are sought within the sociological matrix of the New Testament

---

[31] Geertz, "Thick Description," 9.
[32] "The Social Matrix of the Apocalypse of John," *BR* 26 (1981): 16–32 at 16, emphasis original.
[33] "Sociological Criticism," ch.8 in David Alan Black and David S. Dockery, eds., *Interpreting the New Testament: Essays on Methods and Issues* (Nashville: Broadman & Holman, 2001), 175–76.

world and not in a set of 'external, unchanging meanings' inherent in the terms and symbols themselves." For example, "Paul's use of 'mystery' terminology throughout his writings can only be understood within the pervasive presence of mystery religions in the Roman world." (I heartily agree, although this is not a commonly held view.)

5. Finally, the sociological critic and interpreter of the NT is *concerned to bridge the horizons of the NT with their own world of sociological meaning and significance*. This allows the message of the NT to have a bearing and influence on living in our respective "life matrix"; e.g., Paul calls believers not to be subjected to "the elemental principles of the world" (Col 2:20) corresponding to the "prevailing cultural perspectives, values, and structures" today.

Mulholland's "levels" of investigation are programmatic: He begins inductively through description, then utilizes models, and finally moves to modern appropriation.

Social-Scientific Exegesis: In addition to socio-historical research, it is possible to engage in historical investigation of biblical texts from a social-scientific perspective. While social history describes the history of social relations based upon explicit data, "*the social scientific approach takes two facts into account: (1) cultural meanings are more often held tacitly than explicitly; (2) the larger patterns of cultural meaning, equally tacit, provide a more ample basis for interpretation than the individual symbols, symbolic actions and texts.*"[34] John H. Elliot helpfully explains, "Social-scientific criticism … studies the text as both a reflection of and a response to the social and cultural settings in which the text was produced. Its aim is the determination of the meaning(s) explicit **and implicit** in the text, meanings made possible and shaped by the social and cultural systems inhabited by both authors and intended audiences" (**bold** added).[35]

Social Theory—Paradigms, Perspectives, and Models: Elliot helpfully distinguishes paradigm from perspective from model within sociological theories. Given a particular theory and perspective, "Models are … conceptual vehicles for articulating, applying, testing, and possibly reconstructing theories used in the analysis and interpretation of specific social data."[36] Stated together,

> "Models" are tools for transforming theories into research operations. "Perspectives" are more encompassing ways or "styles" of theorizing. And "paradigms" refer to the traditions, presuppositions, and methods of a discipline as a whole. For a parallel in the field of exegesis, the prevailing contemporary *paradigm* is the so-called historical-critical method. Within this paradigm there are, for instance, different *perspectives* concerning Gospel source theory, and *styles of theorizing* about Gospel relationships. According to these varying perspectives or theoretical styles, different *models* are used for construing and interpreting

---

[34] Leland J. White, "Grid and Group in Matthew's Community: The Righteousness/Honor Code in the Sermon on the Mount," ed. John H. Elliott, *Semeia* 35 (1986): 64, italics original.

[35] Elliott, *What Is Social Scientific Criticism?*, 8.

[36] John H. Elliott, "Social-Scientific Criticism of the New Testament: More on Methods and Models," ed. John H. Elliott, *Semeia* 35 (1986): 5.

synoptic properties and relationships (e.g. Synoptic textual parallels; two or four source models). Such a distinction between paradigm, perspective, theory and model will be of use not only for discussing and using models but also, on a larger scale, for facilitating cross-disciplinary communication and collaboration.[37]

Cautions and Caveats: John Barton has shown both the benefits and the dangers of sociological analysis, with the latter often corresponding to the benefits that have already been described: 1) anachronism (faultily applying an inappropriate model to an ancient setting); 2) loss of distinctiveness of the passage by the overlaid dominating model; 3) claiming too much by the model; 4) reductionism by focusing on one ancient dynamic in the passage at the expense of others; and, 5) using models drawn from the Enlightenment's anti-supernatural or atheistic assumptions.[38] So, like any method or model adopted for interpretation, you must evaluate its inherent assumptions, cautiously qualify your claims, and always let the model correspond to the evidence and not "force" the ancient evidence to fit into the model. With these cautions being said, my experience has been that students have conducted excellent research and brought great illumination to biblical materials through careful, evidential deployment of sociological exegesis.

Example: Patrons and Clients in 2 Cor 8–9: Elliot's essay describing "Patronage and Clientage" provides a rich description of the exchange of goods, services, and honor between a patron and his clients; such analysis is warranted for the NT because of the extensive NT vocabulary reflecting exchange of favor, thanks, and good works.[39] Bruce W. Winter has argued that believers in the NT are urged to be private benefactors.[40] The NT uses a robust vocabulary that Caleb Wang (a former student) described 2 Cor 8–9 from the perspective of patron-client relationships, showing that Paul depicted God as Patron, Jesus as Broker, and local Christian communities as co-clients, who in turn may become patrons to one another, but not for their own praise (as was customary practice), but for God's praise. Paul was at pains to help the Corinthians gain a proper perspective on their role in the exchange of goods while affirming God as the giver and they as the secondary agents, but acting in such a way that leads to much thanksgiving and praise to God (9:12–15).

Social-Cultural-Ideological Topoi: Robbins has described ancient themes in terms of social, cultural, and ideological topoi. Such may be discerned within biblical texts.[41] A **topos** is a rhetorically [inf]used idea, a conventional place from which to conceive information for communicative import, that is, for rhetorical persuasion. "Social" pertains to that which enjoys the broadest circulation of currency in a society. Diverse members of that society broadly recognize it. For ex-

---

[37] Elliott, "Social-Scientific Criticism," 7–8.

[38] Barton, "Historical Criticism and Social Scientific Perspectives in New Testament Study" pages 34–64 in *Hearing the New Testament: Strategies for Interpretation*, ed. J. B. Green, 2nd ed. (Grand Rapids: Eerdmans, 2010), 47–49.

[39] Ch. 7 in Rohrbaugh, ed., *Social Sciences*; the vocabulary is provided on p. 152.

[40] Winter, *Seek the Welfare of the City: Christians as Benefactors and Citizens*, First-century Christians in the Graeco-Roman World (Grand Rapids: Eerdmans, 1994).

[41] See the overview of SRI by Robbins, "Socio-Rhetorical Interpretation," in *The Blackwell Companion to the New Testament*, Blackwell Companions to Religion; ed. D.E. Aune (Chichester, U.K.: Wiley-Blackwell, 2010), ch. 13.

ample, the ancient letter form was recognizable across the Roman Empire; it was a convention that people widely knew and recognized. Commonly known, too, was Roman armor. The institution of a family unit consisting of husband and wife, any children, and household slaves was also ubiquitous. "Cultural" refers to that which is known (really) only to a sub-group within a society, a cultural group. Here, we are thinking of a variety of cultural groups from the NT era: Roman, Greek, and Jew. Of course, even within these broadly recognized groups, we should also identify subgroups that may or may not arise in part from geographic regions—Italian Romans, colonized Romans, free-born Romans, Egyptian Greeks, Asian Greeks (Asia Minor), Achaean Greeks, Diaspora-Hellenistic Jews, and Judean Jews. Certain ideas, customs, words, practices, jokes may only be fully recognizable within one of these cultural groups. "Ideological" refers to ideas that are only fully understandable within a smaller group of the broader cultural group within a society. What might be recognizable for a Christian Jew would not be fully known to a non-Christian Jew.

Example—Eph 2:10: Looking at this verse from the perspective of social, cultural, and ideological topoi led me to reconsider the meaning conveyed as follows:

SOCIAL, CULTURAL, AND IDEOLOGICAL TOPOI IN EPH 2:10					
αὐτοῦ γάρ ἐσμεν ποίημα,	κτισθέντες	ἐν Χριστῷ Ἰησοῦ	ἐπὶ ἔργοις ἀγαθοῖς	οἷς προητοίμασεν ὁ θεός,	ἵνα ἐν αὐτοῖς περιπατήσωμεν
For we are his handiwork	founded ("created")	in Christ Jesus	upon good works	that God prepared beforehand	that we would walk in them.
Social	**Social**	**Ideological**	**Social**	**Cultural**	**Cultural**

The first sentence (*For we are God's workmanship*) contains a social topos that God/gods are makers of humanity (see Diog.Lear. 1.35.8; cf. Acts 17:28; Braun, *TDNT*, 6.458–59). Such need not be held by all in the society for this notion to be a social topos recognized by most. Additionally, the notion of *founded upon good works* is likely a social topos in which the best human institutions were created/founded on such good works of their founding leader(s) (Corp.Herm. 12.5; 13.14; Braun, *TDNT*, 6.473). The ideas of *God's preparation of good deeds* and *God's intention that we humans walk in them*, as I currently assess these topoi, are both cultural arising particularly out of Jewish Scripture and subsequent thought (cf. W. Grundmann, *TDNT*, 2.704–706; although see Epictetus, *Ench*. 52). *In Christ Jesus* is the most specific topos, ideological in nature, reflecting the viewpoint of Paul informed by the coming of Jesus as the Messiah, the political founder of the renewed people of God. We might quibble a bit over my designations of what constitutes social as opposed to cultural, but taken as a whole Eph 2:10 displays a distinctive ideological blend of all three types of social, cultural, and ideological topoi by which Paul effectively describes God's establishment of a people group founded upon good works, the church assembly, as God's handiwork with its political head being *Jesus the Messiah* for the purpose of further encouraging walking in good works. The broader social and cultural topoi are now incorporated and blended into the text's particular ideological and sacred texture, i.e., what it affirms about God in Christ and God's people following Christ and living in the world.[42]

Archaeological Sources of Material Culture: In this chapter I have illustrated just a handful of media for research to which many others may be added including inscriptions, coins, ancient texts (including the NT), stele reliefs, architecture, city planning, mosaics, wall paintings, eating implements, and statuary. For example, at Corinth a statue of "the god Augustus" stood in the center of the forum; I have argued that this image relates to Paul's reference to "the god of this age" that blinds unbelievers from seeing the glory of Christ as Lord and the image of God.[43]

IMAGE OF A DENARIUS COIN MINTED UNDER TIBERIUS[44]

The coin above was minted at Lugdunum (Lyons, France) during AD 14–37 under Tiberius.[45] It shows the laureate head of the reigning emperor on the obverse side with the legend TI CAESAR

---

[42] Commenting on how the ideological texture of texts functions, Gregory L. Bloomquist makes a similar point before his analysis of the ideological topoi in Rom 1: "it is my contention that ideological texture deals with what authors do with preexisting topoi: alter, confirm, nuance, reshape, etc..... a writer or speaker uses existing socially or culturally intelligible *topoi* and their argumentation ideologically to reshape the *topoi* and/or existing arguments." ("Paul's Inclusive Language: The Ideological Texture of Romans 1" pages 165–93 in *Fabrics of Discourse: Essays in Honor of Vernon K. Robbins*, eds. David B. Gowler et al. (Harrisburg, PA: Trinity Press International, 2003), 175.

[43] Fredrick J. Long, "'The God of This Age' (2 Cor 4:4) and Paul's Empire-Resisting Gospel," in *The First Urban Churches: Volume 2: Roman Corinth*, ed. James R. Harrison and Laurence L. Welborn (Atlanta: SBL Press, 2015), 219–69.

[44] Coin image found at http://www.wildwinds.com/coins/ric/tiberius/RIC_0030.82.jpg accessed Aug 13, 2016 and used by permission.

[45] The general description is from http://numismatics.org/collection/1941.131.691. The reference numbers is BMC.48 or RIC.30.

DIVI AVG F AVGVSTVS ("Tiberius Caesar, august son of the god Augustus") and on the reverse side shows a divine female figure with the legend being PONTIF MAXIM meaning "Highest Priest." The coin was blasphemous from a Jewish perspective and should not have been handled since it hailed the deceased emperor Augustus as a god and Tiberius as this god's son.

EXERCISE 7–I: When Jesus was debating with the religious authorities, he was asked whether it was right to pay taxes to Caesar. Given Jesus's response, consider the questions that follow.

Luke 20:23–35 But He detected their trickery and said to them, [24] "Show Me a denarius. Whose likeness and inscription does it have?" They said, "Caesar's." [25] And He said to them, "Then render to Caesar the things that are Caesar's, and to God the things that are God's."

1. What pieces of historical information does this exchange depend upon a person knowing?

2. How significant is it that Jesus is accused of being a Galilean and encouraging tax revolts (see Luke 23:2)?

3. On the previous page is the denarius coin type that was very possibly referred to: What made this blasphemous for Jews to touch or possess?

Numismatics: The field of studying coins is called numismatics. This is a massive field with great complexity due to the various denominations of coins, diverse materials used, various locations of the mints, time periods of operation, types of mints (municipal, provincial, etc.), the rich imagery and sometimes abbreviated words inscribed, and the possibility of ancient and modern forgery. The particular importance lies in the fact that coins were designed to reflect and promote prevailing ideologies. See the select bibliography on numismatics below.

Example of ἔνδοξος "glorious" in Eph 5:22–27:[46] As we conclude this chapter, I would want to reiterate the need for careful observation of biblical materials. Your ability to understand the subtleties of the Greek language will guide you into fascinating areas of needed research. At this stage, observations from various investigative STEPS may combine powerfully to guide our investigations: STEP 3: GRAMMATICAL STUDY and STEP 4: SEMANTIC ANALYSIS prepare for STEP 5: LEXICAL RESEARCH, which along with STEP 6: LITERARY FORMS, points for the need of knowledge of STEP 7: HISTORICAL CONTEXT. On the next page I provide a STRUCTURAL DEPICTION OF EPH 5:22–27 in which chiastic pairings feature and emphasize Christ and the Church assembly. This caused me to ask questions that led to lexical research that suggested to me that further social-historical research was needed. A SUMMARY OF KEY OBSERVATIONS AND QUESTIONS FOR EPH 5:22–33 is given on the following page along with an extended discussion.

---

[46] I originally presented this research at a Rhetoric of Religious Antiquities seminar hosted by Brigitte Kahl at Union Seminary, NY, June 21, 2013 with Vernon Robbins presiding.

STEP 7: TERTIARY RESEARCH   279

STRUCTURAL DEPICTION OF EPH 5:22—27

```
5:22 αἱ γυναῖκες [submitting] τοῖς ἰδίοις ἀνδράσιν     Wives submitting to their own husbands
          ↑ ὡς τῷ κυρίῳ,       [COMPARISON]              as to the Lord
 23    ὅτι ἀνήρ ἐστιν κεφαλὴ              [A]  because a Husband is head
           τῆς γυναικὸς                   [B]  of the Wife
               ὡς καὶ ὁ Χριστὸς κεφαλὴ    [C]  as also Christ is head
                   τῆς ἐκκλησίας,         [D]  of the Ekklesia,
                       αὐτὸς σωτὴρ        [E]  He is Savior
   CENTER             τοῦ σώματος·        [E]  of the Body
 24            ἀλλὰ ὡς ἡ ἐκκλησία ὑποτάσσεται   [D]  But as the Ekklesia submits
                   τῷ Χριστῷ,             [C]  to Christ
               οὕτως καὶ αἱ γυναῖκες      [B]  thus also the Wives
           τοῖς ἀνδράσιν ἐν παντί.        [A]  to the Husbands in every respect.

 25 Οἱ ἄνδρες, ἀγαπᾶτε τὰς γυναῖκας,    [COMPARISON] Husbands love the wives
              καθὼς καὶ ὁ Χριστὸς          [A]  just as also Christ
                      ἠγάπησεν             [B]  loves
                           τὴν ἐκκλησίαν   [C]  the Ekklesia
                           καὶ
   CENTER                  ἑαυτὸν          [C]  Himself (Christ)
                      παρέδωκεν            [B]  He offers
                 ὑπὲρ αὐτῆς,               [A]  for her (the Ekklesia)

 26  ἵνα αὐτὴν ἁγιάσῃ          [A]  in order to sanctify her (the Ekklesia)
          καθαρίσας
              ↑ τῷ λουτρῷ      [B]  cleansed (with three items)
              ↑ τοῦ ὕδατος
              ↑ ἐν ῥήματι,
 27           ἵνα παραστήσῃ         in order that … would present
                  αὐτὸς              [C]  he (Christ) himself
                  ἑαυτῷ              [D]  for himself
   CENTER        ἔνδοξον             [D]  glorious
                  τὴν ἐκκλησίαν,     [C]  the Ekklesia
              μὴ ἔχουσαν
                  ↑ σπίλον           [B]  not having blemish (list of three items)
                  ↑ ἢ ῥυτίδα
                  ↑ ἤ τι τῶν τοιούτων,
          ἀλλ᾽ ἵνα ᾖ ἁγία καὶ ἄμωμος.
              [A]  but in order that she would be holy and blameless.
```

SUMMARY OF KEY OBSERVATIONS AND QUESTIONS FOR EPH 5:22–33

REFERENTS & VERB (explicit and pronominal, i.e., not implied in the verb forms)	REPEATED					SUBJECT OF EXPLICIT VERBS	ABUTTED ITEMS	CENTER OF CHIASM
	5:22-24	5:25-27	5:28-30	5:31-33	total			
Christ/Lord/Savior/He/Head	6x	4x	2x	1x	13x	6x	5x	3x
Church/Body (glorious, holy, blameless)	3x	6x	2x	1x	12x	4x		
Wife-Wives	3x	1x	2x	4x	10x	2x	4x	
Husband(s)/head/he	4x	1x	5x	9x	19x	7x		
Prominent VERB "to love"		2x	3x	1x	6x			

1. Which elements have the most extensive and prominent nomenclature? **Christ** and **Church**.
2. Which elements are repeated the most? **Husbands**.
3. Which element is most described adjectivally? **Church**.
4. Which elements are in prominent semantic structures? **Christ-Church** (comparison, purpose).
5. What elements are abutted? **Christ and Church**, but also **husbands and wives**.
6. Which are chiastically central? **Christ and Church**.
7. Which action/verb occurs most frequently? **Love** (highlighted in STRUCTURAL DEPICTION).
8. What referents and relationships call for our attention? **Christ/the Church** and **husbands**.

<u>Observations on Eph 5:22–27</u>: We observe the referents of Christ and the Church repeatedly abutted—but why? Well, we need to look at what is affirmed of each: Christ "himself is the Savior of the (church) body" (5:23) who "loves the church and gives himself for her" (5:25) "in order that he himself would present the church to himself as glorious" (5:27). This last culminating idea is a purpose statement and translated in various ways: in order to present the church "in splendour" (RSV, ESV), "radiant" (NIV), "glorious" (KJV, NET), "in all her glory" (NASB). This word ἔνδοξος is a rare in the NT (only Luke 7:25; 13:17; 1 Cor 4:10; Eph 5:27). What did the word convey socially? Why would Paul describe Christ's goal to present the Church "glorious"?

To begin, BDAG (s.v.) suggests two connotations for the word ἔνδοξος: 1. "being held in high esteem, *honored, distinguished, eminent*"; 2. "possessing an inherent quality that is not ordinary, *glorious, splendid*" (italics original). The first definition is social, concerning not merely outward appearance, but honor; the second concerns an internal quality. However, this divide between internal and external may misguide us by assuming a Platonic dualism; it may be that both dimensions are present since the means of presenting visibly the church as ἔνδοξος (5:27) is sanctifying cleansing, a metaphor addressing internal purity (5:26). It would thus seem that ἔνδοξος is the final act of visible honor predicated upon an internal sanctifying cleansing. The word "glorious" adequately expresses both ideas.

Search Results from the PHI Searchable Inscriptional Database

Observing the intricate chiastic structure and understanding the socio-political nature of Ephesians, I postulated that ἔνδοξος was a socially significant word in the world of Asia Minor. So, when searching the Packard Humanities Institute's (PHI) "Searchable Greek Inscriptions," I found hundreds of matches concentrated mostly in Asia Minor, of which I translated only a couple below and on the next page: TWO SAMPLE INSCRIPTIONS OF THE ROMAN IMPERIAL PERIOD WITH ἔνδοξος (see next page), a word denoting innate honor; both translated inscriptions pertain to the emperor—is this coincidental? *This would suggest that more research is necessary.*

778 matches.			1-250 251-500
	24	0.0019%	Attica (IG I-III)
	18	0.0072%	Peloponnesos (IG IV-[VI])
	28	0.0044%	Central Greece (IG VII-IX)
	16	0.0090%	Northern Greece (IG X)
	25	0.0123%	Thrace and the Lower Danube (IG X)
	4	0.0048%	North Shore of the Black Sea
	74	0.0065%	Aegean Islands, incl. Crete (IG XI-[XIII])
	493	0.0403%	Asia Minor
	4	0.0136%	Cyprus ([IG XV])
	57	0.0939%	Greater Syria and the East
	26	0.0116%	Egypt, Nubia and Cyrenaïca
	9	0.0065%	Sicily, Italy, and the West (IG XIV)

IG II² 851   Attica

| ενδοξ | --all regions-- | Browse |

Two Sample Inscriptions of the Roman Imperial Period with ἔνδοξος[47]

***I.KAUNOS* 140,** Honorific inscription for Iatrokles, son of Zenon. Rectangular block of gray limestone; molding at top and bottom on the front face. *Caria — Rom. Imp. period*

1 [ὁ δῆμος ὁ Κα]υνίων ἐπαινεῖ καὶ στεφανοῖ καὶ [ἡ] [γε]ρουσία χρυσῷ στεφάνῳ, τειμᾷ δὲ καὶ εἰκόνι χαλκῇ ['Ια]τροκλέα Ζήνωνος τοῦ Ἰατροκλέους Καρπασυανδέα, [ἄ]νδρα εὐγενῆ καὶ φιλόπατριν, προγόνων ἐπιφα- 5 νῶν καὶ <u>ἐνδόξων</u>, ἀρχιερατεύσαντα τῶν Σε-βαστῶν καὶ ἀγωνοθετήσαντα καὶ ταμιεύσαν-τα καὶ στρατηγήσαντα, πρεσβεύσαντα πρὸς τοὺς Σεβαστοὺς δωρεὰν ἀρετῆς ἕνεκεν καὶ εὐ-νοίας ἧς διὰ παντὸς ἐπεδείξατο. τὴν δὲ 10 [ἀ]νάστασιν τοῦ ἀνδριάντος ἐποιήσατο Λητοδώρα Πάππου, κατὰ θυγατροθε-σίαν δὲ Ἀριστοδήμου, Καυνία, ἡ γυνὴ αὐτοῦ.	1 The Caunian demos praises and crowns and the council of elders with a golden crown, and honors also with a bronze image Iatrokles Zanonos, the son of Iatrokles Karpasyandea, a man of good lineage and love of country, from a manifest 5 and <u>honored</u> ancestry, **holding the high priesthood of the *Sebastoi*** and directing athletic games and acting treasurer and acting strategos, ruling over the gifts for the Sebastoi because of virtue and good mind, which he showed through all. 10 .....

---

[47] The Greek text and descriptions, both slightly reformatted, are from PHI http://epigraphy.packhum.org/.

> **IG II² 1110 From Attica ca. AD 180–192**
>
> | | |
> |---|---|
> | frg. a.1 [Α]ὐτοκράτωρ Καῖ[σαρ — —]... | frg. a.1 "Emperor Caesar — —]... |
> | frg. b.1 — — — — — α καὶ | frg. b.1 — — — — — and |
> | [μυστηρίω]ν κεκοινωνηκὼς | having shared in the mysteries |
> | [ὥ]στε ἐξ ἐκείνου δίκαιος | so that from that I would be righteous/just |
> | ἂν εἴην ὁμολογῶν καὶ τὸ | confessing also |
> | 5 Εὐμολπίδης εἶναι. ἀναλαμ- | 5 to be Eumolpidian. Moreover, I assume |
> | βάνω δὲ καὶ τὴν τοῦ ἄρχοντο[ς] | also the friendly name of "ruler," |
> | προσηγορίαν, καθ' ἃ ἠξιώσατε, | according to which you deemed worthy, |
> | ὡς τά τε ἀπόρρητα τῆς κατὰ τὰ | as indeed the forbidden things |
> | μυστήρια τελετῆς <u>ἐνδοξό-</u> | of the initiation according to the mysteries, |
> | 10 <u>τερόν</u> τε καὶ σεμνότερον, | 10 a name both <u>rather honored</u> and revered, |
> | εἴ γέ τινα προσθήκην ἐπιδέ- | if indeed I receive some assistance, |
> | χοιτο, τοῖν θεοῖν ἀποδοθεί- | it would be given back to the gods |
> | η καὶ διὰ τὸν ἄρχοντα τοῦ τῶν | also on account of the ruler |
> | Εὐμολπιδῶν γένους, ὃν προ- | of the race of the Eumolpidae, |
> | 15 εχειρίσασθε, αὐτός τε μὴ δο- | 15 whom you chose—and he himself was not |
> | κοίην, ἐνγραφεὶς καὶ πρότε- | expecting—was engraved also formerly |
> | ρον εἰς τοὺς Εὐμολπίδας, | for the Eumolpidae, |
> | παραιτεῖσθαι νῦν τὸ ἔργον | to request now the work |
> | τῆς τειμῆς, ἣν πρὸ τῆς ἀρχῆς | of honor, which before this rule |
> | 20 [τα]ύτης ἐκαρπωσάμην. | 20 I bore fruit. |
> | 21 ἔρρωσθε. | 21 Be strengthened! |

<u>History of Interpretation of Eph 5:22–33</u>: Prominent features of the text are first Christ and the *Ekklesia* and next the husband's role to love his wife as his own body. Thus, I would maintain that the primary agent is Christ in relation to the Church, and secondarily the husband in the relation to his wife. Yet interpreters would have us focus on human-scale marriage *while underappreciating and not exploring more completely two of the most prominent expressions in the pericope*: First, in 5:23 the referent of Christ "himself (being) savior of the body" and, second, in 5:27 the church as "glorious" (ἔνδοξος). Remember, too, that we as interpreters should investigate not only what is textually explicit, but also what is implicit from the shared cultural environment.

The final statement of 5:23, αὐτὸς σωτὴρ τοῦ σώματος "He himself being the Savior of the body" has puzzled interpreters; it is the only occurrence of "savior" in Ephesians and seems out of place. J. Paul Sampley laments that the statement breaks up an otherwise nice chiastic structure in 5:23–24 and concludes that the phrase functions parenthetically to distinguish the husband/wife relationship from the Christ/church relationship.[48] However, Sampley is assuming that the chiastic

---

[48] J. Paul Sampley, *"And the Two Shall Become One Flesh": A Study of Traditions in Ephesians 5:21–33*, SNTSMS 16 (Cambridge: Cambridge University Press, 1971), 124–26.

center is ***not*** a paired element—in Ephesians there may be a singular central item or paired items,[49] but here there are paired items—Christ and the Body. Rather, the center is pivotal to Paul's ideological point in context providing a substantiation for the claim the Christ is the Head of the *Ekklesia* precisely because he is the Savior of the Body.[50] Yet, Sampley's research into the Christ-Church relationship has uncovered a core ideological comparison seen by him, however, only from a Jewish perspective: "It remains that the author's predominant concern ... is an explication of the relationship of the hieros gamos of YHWH and Israel."[51] The church is the holy marriage partner of Christ. Yet, what was the closest analogy to such a pairing in Asia Minor? ***Caesar and Roma.***

Rudolf Schnackenburg understands this first phrase "Savior of the Body" as a metaphor prompted by and introduced into the metaphor of Christ as head of the church while discussing marriage; however, the meaning and significance of "savior" is eclipsed by Schnackenburg's interest in the church as a body, the origins of which remains uncertain, although he considers Gnostic notions of Head-Body but concludes this is "doubtful."[52] Ernest Best briefly reviews the possible background for σωτήρ even admitting, "It was widely used in the contemporary world being applied to the Roman emperor, the Ptolemies, Asclepius, and the Heavenly Man."[53] But, he quotes affirmingly A. D. Nock's assessment, "… its frequent employment in the Septuagint as a predicate of God or of the Messiah seems to supply the most natural antecedent for its Christian usage."[54] However, we must consider the density of the usages in inscriptional notions of σωτηρ- (4,995) compared with the LXX frequency for σωτήρ (37x) and σωτηρία (151x). Also, we could add a couple dozen or so instances of the Latin *Soter*. Please refer to my extended discussion of σωτήρ and cognates earlier in III. TERTIARY RESEARCH under STEP 5: LEXICAL RESEARCH (pp. 204-10).

Returning to "Savior of the Body," Harold Hoehner will ask and answer explicitly, "What, then, did this unique phrase mean for the believers in Ephesus? In fact, it is an ancillary comment to reinforce Christ as the head...."[55] He explains that the phrase means "Christ's redemption of individual sinners resulting in reconciliation to God and also to each other within the body of believers." True enough, but is there more? Hoehner explains that Christ as Savior has some applicability to the husband's relationship to his wife, to protect her physically and spiritually, but he cannot save her "from eternal doom as Christ does the church but rather acts as her protector in a temporal

---

[49] For a chiastic presentation of 2:11–22, see CHIASM OF EPHESIANS 2:11-22 in STEP 6: LITERARY FORMS; additionally, the chiastic center of 4:4–6 is 'One Lord.' The chiastic center of 4:7–16 is in 4:13 'the perfect man' within the complex of political titles "the Son of God, the perfect Man, ...the Messiah" into which the body politic of the Church is to grow, employing ideal ruler ideology; so also, Talbert, *Ephesians and Colossians*, 115–17.

[50] Cf. the chiasm of only five elements (vv. 23a, 23b, 23c, 24a, and 24b) in Talbert, *Ephesians and Colossians*, 140. Andrew T. Lincoln states that he does not agree with the assertion that this serves as a chiastic focal point but rather that is "simply to provide an additional description of Christ's relationship to the Church" (*Ephesians*, WBC 42 [Dallas: Word, 1990], 370–71).

[51] Sampley, *Two Shall Become One Flesh*, 133 (cf. 37–42).

[52] Schnackenburg, *Ephesians*, 247–48.

[53] Best, *Ephesians*, 536.

[54] Arthur Darby Nock, "Early Gentile Christianity," 92.

[55] Hoehner, *Ephesians*, 743.

sense." About the title "savior" Thielman affirms that the phrase is "emphatic," and yet he also says of this phrase,

> Paul seems to have caught himself drifting away from the practical to the theoretical in the final clause of 5:23 'He himself is the Savior of the body.' With ἀλλά (*alla*, but) he pulls his train of thought quickly back on track just as he will at the end of the passage in 5:33: "In any case, you too—every single one of you—must love his own wife.' Both phrases are evidence that Ephesians started life as an oral discourse that, although not unorganized, was also not planned in meticulous detail.[56]

No further significance to σωτήρ is offered; it is rightly, but only, seen in relation to Christ's supreme position for the church (1:22–23; 4:15–16) and God-in-Christ's saving activity (2:5, 10).[57]

Concerning the adjective "glorious" (ἔνδοξος), Sampley understands the term mainly by way of the beauty associated with the terms "without blemish" and "without wrinkle." He expends considerable effort explaining these metaphors.[58] Following Sampley's lead, Best indicates that ἔνδοξος is "a word whose precise meaning needs to be derived from its context.... In v.27 it probably means 'beautiful.' Brides are supposed to be beautiful, at least in the eyes of their groom.... he, Christ, is the beautician who has prepared the bride, as God beautified Israel in Ezek 16:10–14."[59] So similarly Charles H. Talbert.[60] Best admits that "the beauty of the bride ... is of course not physical but moral and spiritual." Yet, Best maintains, "The remainder of the verse spells out ἔνδοξος...." referring readers to Sampley's study and then detailing the kind of skin the church is to have—without blemish or wrinkle.[61] Hoehner briefly recaps a few meanings from classical texts before providing a taxonomy of the biblical usage (LXX and NT), reporting that the adjective is used to translate fifteen Hebrew words; in the end his translation is "all-glorious."[62] Peter O'Brien translates ἔνδοξος as "in splendor" and sees in the description a reflection of God's clothing Israel "in magnificent apparel and jewelry" as a bride in Ezek 16:10–14.[63] Schnackenburg understands ἔνδοξος as "splendid" but muses over the merging of images of "the bridal bath" and "holy marriage," considering Gnosticism and Mystery Cults before reviewing somewhat favorably, but as incomplete, Sampley's work with Ezek 16:8–14. He concludes, "Even with this background we must assume a transformation of the metaphor because of the reality of Christ and Church. Possibly the author has fused different ideas."[64] Frank Thielman spends considerable time expounding the possible imagery of a bridal bath from the water reference in 5:26, and defines ἔνδοξος as

---

[56] Thielman, *Ephesians*, at 378 and 379, respectively.
[57] And this latter reference only in fn. 17 on p. 379.
[58] Sampley, *Two Shall Become One Flesh*, 67–74.
[59] Best, *Ephesians*, 546.
[60] Talbert, *Ephesians and Colossians*, 142.
[61] Best, *Ephesians*, 546.
[62] Hoehner, *Ephesians*, 758–59.
[63] O'Brien, *Ephesians*, 424–25.
[64] Schnackenburg, *Ephesians*, 250–51; quotation at 251.

"brilliant" (BDAG 332) and elaborates this as signifying "dazzling beauty" possibly involving "especially beautiful garments."[65] He explains, "The whole image is reminiscent of the elaborate toilet for both bride and groom that accompanied ancient weddings in Greek and Roman cultures."[66] However, a problem emerges when this bathing scenario does not match the description:

> The difference here is the unusual picture of the groom bathing the bride (Eph. 5:26) and presenting her in all her splendor to himself (v.27). The metaphor has taken this turn because the picture of a typical wedding has merged with the imagery of Ezek. 16:8–14. There God images Israel as his young bride, whom he has bathed, cleansed, anointed, and clothed with finery and jewels. Here in Ephesians, Christ takes the place of God in that imagery, and the church fills the place of Israel. Again, however, Paul breaks the boundary of a traditional image. In Ezek. 16 the imagery of the bride is part of a prophecy against Israel for its unfaithfulness to God: once made beautiful by God, Israel became a prostitute through its promiscuous alliances with their nations and their gods. Paul's image runs in the opposite direction: those who compromise the church were once stained, but through the death of Christ and the preaching of the gospel, Christ has cleansed them and set them apart for himself, just as a young and dazzlingly beautiful bride, in all her finery, is presented to the groom.

Thielman interprets the imagery in moral terms, "holy and blameless" (cf. Eph 1:4), and the church is "to live in a way that is consistent with this status."[67]

In the end, both the expression "he himself is Savior of the Body" and "glorious" are more prominent in the discourse than interpreters have acknowledged. Moreover, very little attention has been given to the social import of both terms and their relevance for the audience. To review, the concepts are prominent for various reasons at multiple levels for the following reasons:

1. Within the discourse, they entail further description of the most prominent agents in relation to one another in the pericope; they have discursive prominence in terms of referentiality.
2. They occur centrally within their respective chiasms; they reflect a patterned emphasis.
3. They each involve emphatic grammatical features, summarized for 5:23 and 5:27 below:

5:23 a. "he is Savior of the Body" is appositional to "Head of the Church" thus having emphasis.
    b. Sampley rightly comments, "The intensive pronoun αὐτός that opens the statement in v. 23c may function not only as emphasizing but also as contrasting. It may differentiate the last subject mentioned (Christ) from the earlier subject (the husband)."[68]
    c. Thielman thus correctly states, "Paul restates it [Christ's position of authority] in terms that are both emphatic and explicit: 'He himself ... is Savior of the body...'."[69]

---

[65] Thielman, *Ephesians*, 385–86.
[66] Thielman, *Ephesians*, 386.
[67] Thielman, *Ephesians*, 387.
[68] *Two Shall Become One*, 125.
[69] *Ephesians*, 378.

5:27 a. The center of the chiasm entails an emphatic pronoun with a reflexive pronoun, as Sampley explains: "The emphatic personal pronoun αὐτός in v. 27a makes it especially clear that Christ is the one who is the subject of the verb παρίστημι. The emphasis upon Christ's action is expressed further by the occurrence of ἑαυτῷ as the indirect object of the verb παραστήσῃ."⁷⁰
    b. Of the forwarded placement of ἔνδοξος, Hoehner states, "It is placed before the article and the noun τὴν ἐκκλσίαν, making it emphatic in its description of what kind of church Christ was to present to himself."⁷¹
    c. It is a socially prominent notion in Asia Minor as attested to its numerous occurrences in inscriptions (see above the SEARCH RESULTS FROM THE PHI SEARCHABLE INSCRIPTIONAL DATABASE).

For too many interpreters the title "savior" has primarily an individualistic, salvific dimension (a la Protestant reformation theology). Also, the depicted marriage and analogy to Christ is dominated by interpretive research and imagination that undervalues the overt political connotations in favor of a romantic fascination with the husband-wife relationship (a la romanticism and individualism), especially concerning the appearance of the bride/church as "without blemish or wrinkle" in 5:27.

But would Paul relegate the only occurrence of σωτήρ in Ephesians to such a romantic function? In its placement the phrase builds on the repetitively important Head-Body political metaphor from 1:22–23, 2:16, and 4:4, 12, 16 and is the chiastic center of 5:23–24. A more satisfactory explanation is that Paul wanted to make a further political point of comparing Christ-Savior/Church to Caesar-Savior/Roma. The Emperor as savior (σωτήρ) had a gamos relationship with Rome that was actively and strategically depicted as deified Roma throughout Asia Minor.⁷² Across Ephesians the Church assembly is exalted and personified as Christ's consort/bride.⁷³ Several social-religious phenomena account for why Paul paired Christ and the Church as an ideological counterpart to Caesar-Roma here within household relationships. First, there was imperial "interest" in the household as evidenced in Augustan legislation pertaining to the household. Second, the Imperial cult in Asia Minor featured the Emperor and Roma, and its priesthoods used married

---

⁷⁰ *Two Shall Become One*, 134.

⁷¹ *Ephesians*, 758. Hoehner adds that commentators treat the expression as a tertiary predicate to be translated "in order that he might present or render the church to himself, glorious" which "further emphasizes the qualitative character of the glory in which Christ is going to present the church" (759).

⁷² See the historical development of this relationship in Ronald Mellor, *ΘΕΑ ῾ΡΩΜΑ: The Worship of the Goddess Roma in the Greek World*, Hypomnemata: Untersuchungen zur Antike und zu ihrer Nachleben Heft 42 (Göttingen: Vandenhoeck & Ruprecht, 1975). On the official nature of the pairing, Mellor explains: "Suetonius [*Augustus* 52] tells us that this marriage [between Roma and Augustus] was required in provincial cults by imperial command, but a similar pattern filtered down to the municipal cults as well" (195).

⁷³ For a treatment of the common ancient practice of personification of groups and "the church assembly" in Ephesians, see my forthcoming essay, "*Ekklesia* in Ephesians as God-like in the Heavens, in Temple, in Cosmos, and in Armour: Ideology and Iconography in Ephesus and Its Environs," in *The First Urban Churches: Volume 3: Ephesus*, ed. James R. Harrison and Laurence L. Welborn (Atlanta: SBL Press, 2017).

couples. Third, Roma was otherwise depicted in armor, strong and fierce—a power to be contended with that is also countered in the Church donning God's armor, advancing the peace of the Gospel of Christ and supporting Paul, an ambassador in chains, through active prayer (6:10–20).

TERTIARY INTERPRETIVE PROCEDURES:

1. After performing careful structural observations and noting marked constructions giving emphasis and prominence to sentence elements, ask questions about the meaning and significance of these elements historically and social-scientifically .
2. What social roles, institutions, customs, cultural meanings, etc. may be implied in the text? Probe and ask questions about these.
3. Consider how best to answer these questions. Consult secondary research on the passage to see how others interpreters have approached it and what method(s) they used.
4. Consider what historical area(s) or sociological model(s) are available that would help you develop a framework to interpret the available data to help answer these questions.
   a. What warrants exist for your research into the area or use of the sociological model?
   b. Find other examples of those researching the historical area and/or those using the sociological model and learn from their research attempts.
   c. Understand and learn from the history of such historical research.
   d. Account for the development of the sociological model and consider its appropriateness for use given the particular data under investigation.
   e. Consider how best to refine the historical research and/or sociological model in light of criticisms and/or newer perspectives, if available.
5. Conduct thorough research in the historical area and/or using the sociological model.
   a. Consider literary, papyrological, inscriptional, and numismatic evidence.
   b. Consider available archaeological data reflecting material culture such as mosaics, architecture, temple construction and locations, house structures and artifacts, city plans, and other realia.
6. Finally, return to your initial questions and state how your research has (or has not) answered them. Consider also what questions still remain unresolved.
7. Consider how and why the NT author has reflected this context.
   a. What ideology or ideologies is/are being espoused and also resisted in the broader society or immediate local culture(s)?
   b. What are important implicit dimensions of the NT text as situated within its original social-historical context (as much as can be known)?
8. Finally, after having conducted your research, revisit the issue of researching within the historical area and/or using the sociological model (3. above) since refinement of the research approach and/or model may be one significant outcome of your work from which others may benefit.

IV. BIBLIOGRAPHY

Primary Survey

Bible Atlases

Lawrence, Paul. *The IVP Atlas of Bible History*. Downers Grove, IL: InterVarsity, 2006.

Rasmussen, Carl. *Zondervan Essential Atlas of the Bible*. Grand Rapids: Zondervan, 2013.

NT Introductions

Achtemeier, Paul J., et al., *Introducing the New Testament: Its Literature and Theology*. Grand Rapids: Eerdmans, 2001.

Brown, Raymond E. *An Introduction to the New Testament*. Anchor Bible Reference Library. New York: Doubleday, 1997.

Carson, D. A., et al. *An Introduction to the New Testament*. 2nd ed. Grand Rapids: Zondervan, 2005.

deSilva, David A. *An Introduction to the New Testament: Contexts, Methods & Ministry Formation*. Downers Grove, IL: IVP, 2004.

Guthrie, Donald. *New Testament Introduction*. Rev. ed. Downers Grove, IL: IVP, 1990.

Martin, Ralph P. *New Testament Foundations: A Guide for Christian Students*. 2 vols. Rev. ed. Grand Rapids: Eerdmans, 1986.

Johnson, Luke Timothy. *The Writings of the New Testament: An Interpretation*. Rev. ed. Minneapolis: Fortress, 2002.

_____. *The New Testament: A Very Short Introduction*. Very Short Introductions. New York: Oxford University Press, 2010.

Powell, Mark Allan. *Introducing the New Testament: A Historical, Literary, and Theological Survey*. Grand Rapids: Baker Academic, 2010.

_____. *Fortress Introduction to the Gospels*. Minneapolis: Fortress, 1997.

Dictionaries and Encyclopedias

Achtemeier, Paul J. *HarperCollins Bible Dictionary*, San Francisco: HarperSanFrancisco, 1996. [An updated edition of 1985 *Harper's Bible Dictionary*]

Bromiley, G. W., ed. *The International Standard Bible Encyclopedia*. Grand Rapids: Eerdmans, 1979–82.

Brown, Colin, ed. *The New International Dictionary of New Testament Theology*. 3 vols. Grand Rapids: Zondervan, 1975—.

Buttrick, G. A. *The Interpreter's Dictionary of the Bible*, New York: Abingdon, 1962 with 1976 supplement.

Evans, C. A. and S. E. Porter, eds. *Dictionary of New Testament Background: A Compendium of Contemporary Biblical Scholarship*. Downers Grove, IL: InterVaristy, 2000.

Freedman, D. Noel, ed., *Eerdmans Dictionary of the Bible*. Grand Rapids: Eerdmans, 2000.

Green, Joel B., et al. eds. *Dictionary of Jesus and the Gospels*. Downers Grove, IL: IVP, 1992.

Hawthorne, G., et al. eds. *Dictionary of Paul and His Letters*. Downers Grove, IL: IVP, 1993.

Martin, R. P. and P. H. Davids, eds. *Dictionary of the Later New Testament and its Developments*. Downers Grove, IL: InterVarsity, 1997.

Sakenfeld, K. D. *New Interpreter's Dictionary of the Bible*. 5 Vols. Nashville: Abingdon, 2006–2009.

Wood, D. R. W., ed. *New Bible Dictionary* 3rd ed. Downers Grove, IL: InterVarsity, 1996.

Overviews of NT History, Society, and Culture

Banks, Robert J. *Paul's Idea of Community: The Early House Churches in Their Historical Setting*. Grand Rapids: Eerdmans, 1980.

Bell, Albert A. *Exploring the New Testament World*. Nashville: Thomas Nelson, 1998.

Byatt, Anthony. *New Testament Metaphors: Illustrations in Word and Phrase*. Edinburgh: Pentland, 1995.

deSilva, David Arthur. *Honor, Patronage, Kinship & Purity: Unlocking New Testament Culture*. Downers Grove, IL: IVP, 2000.

Hubbard, Moyer V. *Christianity in the Greco-Roman World: A Narrative Introduction*. Peabody, MA: Hendrickson, 2010.

Jeffers, James S. *The Greco-Roman World of the New Testament Era: Exploring the Background of Early Christianity*. Downers Grove, IL: InterVarsity, 1999.

Witherington III, Ben. *New Testament History: A Narrative Account*. Grand Rapids: Baker Academic, 2001.

Background Commentaries

Arnold, Clinton E., ed. *Zondervan Illustrated Bible Backgrounds Commentary*. 4 vols. Grand Rapids: Zondervan, 2002.

Keener, Craig S. *The IVP Bible Background Commentary: New Testament*. 1st ed. Downers Grove, IL: IVP, 1993.

_____. *The IVP Bible Background Commentary: New Testament*. 2nd ed. Downers Grove, IL: InterVarsity, 2014.

Background Primary Texts

Barrett, C. K. *New Testament Background: Texts and Documents*. Rev. ed. San Francisco: Harper and Row, 1989.

Evans, Craig A. *Ancient Texts for New Testament Studies: A Guide to the Background Literature*. Peabody, MA: Hendrickson, 2005.

Ferguson, Everett. *Backgrounds of Early Christianity*. 3rd ed. Grand Rapids: Eerdmans, 2003.

Secondary Study and Tertiary Research

Databases for Searching Essays and Articles: ATLA, JSTOR, and EBSCO databases.

Dictionaries
- Freedman, D. Noel., et al. ed. *The Anchor Bible Dictionary*. 6 Vols. New York: Doubleday, 1992.
- Kittel, G. and G. Friedrich, eds. *Theological Dictionary of the New Testament*. Translated by G. Bromiley. Grand Rapids: Eerdmans, 1964–.

Commentaries
- Boring, M. Eugene, et al. *Hellenistic Commentary to the New Testament*. Nashville: Abingdon, 1995.
- Keener, Craig S. Various commentaries available for Matthew, 2 Corinthians, Romans, etc.
- Lightfoot, John. *A Commentary on the New Testament from the Talmud and Hebraica, Matthew—1 Corinthians*. Peabody, MA: Hendrickson, 1989.
- Malina, Bruce J., and John J. Pilch. *Social-Science Commentary on the Book of Acts*. Minneapolis: Fortress, 2008.
- Malina, Bruce J., and John J. Pilch. *Social-Science Commentary on the Book of Revelation*. Minneapolis: Fortress, 2000.
- Malina, Bruce J., and John J. Pilch. *Social-Science Commentary on the Letters of Paul*. Minneapolis: Fortress, 2006.
- Malina, Bruce J., and Richard L. Rohrbaugh. *Social-Science Commentary on the Gospel of John*. Minneapolis: Fortress, 1998.
- Malina, Bruce J., and Richard L. Rohrbaugh.. *Social-Science Commentary on the Synoptic Gospels*. 2nd ed. Minneapolis: Fortress, 2003.
- Witherington, Ben III. His various Social-Rhetorical Commentaries by Eerdmans on Mark, 1–2 Corinthians, Galatians, etc.

Social-Historical-Religious Backgrounds:
- Klauck, Hans-Josef. *The Religious Context of Early Christianity: A Guide to Graeco-Roman Religions*. Studies of the New Testament and its World. Edinburgh: T&T Clark, 2000.
- Koester, Helmut. *Paul & His World: Interpreting the New Testament in Its Context*. Minneapolis: Fortress, 2007.
- Meeks, Wayne A. *The First Urban Christians: The Social World of the Apostle Paul*. 2nd ed. New Haven: Yale University Press, 2003.
- _____. *The Moral World of the First Christians*. Library of Early Christianity 6. Philadelphia: Westminster, 1986.
- Sampley, J. Paul. *Paul in the Greco-Roman World: A Handbook*. Harrisburg, PA: Trinity Press International, 2003.
- Stambaugh, J. E. and D. L. Balch, *The Testament in its Social Environment*. Library of Early Christianity 2. Philadelphia: Westminster, 1986.

NT Introductions, History, and Methods

- Aune, David E., ed. *The Blackwell Companion to the New Testament*. Blackwell Companions to Religion. Oxford: Wiley-Blackwell, 2010.
- Koester, Helmut. *Introduction to the New Testament*. 2 Vols. New York: De Gruyter, 1982. [Note: Volume 1 entitled "History, Culture, and Religion of the Hellenistic Age" is an excellent survey.]
- Kümmel, Werner Georg. *Introduction to the New Testament*. Rev. ed. trans. Howard Clark Kee. Reprint of 1975 edition: Nashville: Abingdon, 1996.
- Schürer, Emil, *History of the Jewish People in the Age of Jesus Christ (175 B.C.–135 A.D.)*. Translated by T. A. Burkhill et al. Revised and edited by Geza Vermes and Fergus Millar. Edinburgh: T&T Clark, 1973–1986 (3 vols. in 4).
- Stegemann, Ekkehard and Wolfgang Stegemann. *The Jesus Movement: A Social History of Its First Century*. Minneapolis: Fortress Press, 1999.
- Theissen, Gerd. *The New Testament: A Literary History*. Minneapolis: Fortress, 2011.

Numismatics

- Aarts, Joris. "Coins Money and Exchange in the Roman World: A Cultural-Economic Perspective." *Archaeological Dialogues* 12 (2005): 1–28. [See the responses to Aarts in the same issue.]
- Crawford, Michael. "Money and Exchange in the Roman World." *JRS* 60 (1970): 40–48.
- Grant, Michael. *From Imperium to Auctoritas: A Historical Study of Aes Coinage in the Roman Empire, 49 B.C.–A.D. 14*. London: Cambridge University Press, 1969.
- _____. *Roman Anniversary Issues: An Exploratory Study of the Numismatic and Medallic Commemoration of Anniversary Years 49 B.C.–375*. Cambridge: Cambridge University Press, 1950.
- *Kreitzer, L. Joseph. *Striking New Images: Roman Imperial Coinage and the New Testament World*. Sheffield, England: Sheffield Academic Press, 1996.
- Manders, Erika. *Coining Images of Power: Patterns in the Representation of Roman Emperors on Imperial Coinage, A.d. 193–284*. Leiden: Brill, 2012.
- Mattingly, Harold. *Roman Coins from the Earliest Times to the Fall of the Western Empire*. 2nd ed. Chicago: Quadrangle, 1960.
- Mattingly, Harold, and Edward Allen Sydenham. *The Roman Imperial Coinage: Vol. I Augustus to Vitellius*. Vol. 1. 12 vols. London: Spink & Son, 1923.
- *Oster, Richard E. "Numismatic Windows into the Social World of Early Christianity: A Methodological Inquiry." *JBL* 101 (1982): 195–223.
- *Schaps, David M. *Handbook for Classical Research*. London: Routledge, 2011, ch. 16 on Numismatics.
- *Van Meter, David. *The Handbook of Roman Imperial Coins: A Complete Guide to the History, Types and Values of Roman Imperial Coins*. Nashua, NH: Laurion Numismatics, 1991.

*Wenkel, David H. *Coins as Cultural Texts in the World of the New Testament*. London: Bloomsbury T&T Clark, 2016.

Sociological and Social Historical Studies

Blasi, Anthony J., et al. eds. *Handbook of Early Christianity: Social-Science Approaches*. Walnut Creek, CA: Altamira, 2002.

Elliott, John H. *What Is Social-Scientific Criticism?* Minneapolis: Fortress, 1993.

Esler, Philip F., ed. *The First Christians in Their Social Worlds: Social-Scientific Approaches to New Testament Interpretation*. London: Routledge, 1994.

Horrell, David G., ed. *Social-Scientific Approaches to New Testament Interpretation*. Edinburgh: T&T Clark, 1999.

Neufeld, Dietmar, and Richard E. DeMaris, eds. *Understanding the Social World of the New Testament*. London; New York: Routledge, 2010.

Neyrey, Jerome H. and Eric C. Stewart, eds. *The Social World of the New Testament: Insights and Models*. Peabody, MA: Hendrickson, 2008.

Pilch, John J., ed. *Social-Scientific Models for Interpreting the Bible*. Leiden: Brill, 2001.

Rohrbaugh, Richard L., ed. *The Social Sciences and New Testament Interpretation*. Peabody, MA: Hendrickson, 1996.

Statuary, Imagery, and Architecture

Friedland, Elise A., et al. eds. *The Oxford Handbook of Roman Sculpture*. New York: Oxford University Press, 2015.

Maier, Harry O. *Picturing Paul in Empire: Imperial Image, Text and Persuasion in Colossians, Ephesians and the Pastoral Epistles*. New York/London: T&T Clark/Bloomsbury, 2013.

Reinach, Salomon. *Répertoire de La Statuaire Grecque et Romaine*. 4 in 5 parts vols. Paris: E. Leroux, 1897.

_____. *Répertoire de Reliefs Grecs et Romains*. 3 vols. Paris: E. Leroux, 1909.

Ward-Perkins, J. B. *Roman Imperial Architecture*. Reprint edition. New Haven; London: Yale University Press, 1992.

Zanker, Paul. *Roman Art*. Los Angeles: J. Paul Getty Museum, 2012.

_____. *The Power of Images in the Age of Augustus*. Translated by Alan Shapiro. Jerome Lectures 16. Ann Arbor: University of Michigan Press, 1988.

STEP 8

SCRIPTURAL CORRELATIONS

"Nothing comes from nothing …; no story comes from nowhere; new stories are born from old—it is the new combinations that make them new."[1]
—Salman Rushdie

"[T]here is no creation without tradition; the 'new' is an inflection on a preceding form; novelty is always a variation on the past."[2]
—Carlos Fuentes

---

[1] *Haroun and the Sea of Stories* (London: Penguin, 1991), 86.
[2] *Myself with Others: Selected Essays* (New York: Farrar, Straus and Giroux, 1990), 19.

Introduction: An ancient interpretive principle was "Let Scripture interpret Scripture" which may be simplified in the acronym SIS: "Scripture interprets Scripture." Every passage of Scripture is connected canonically to every other passage. Sometimes the connection is explicit: "As it is written in Isaiah the prophet,..." (Mark 1:2–3 quoting from Mal 3:1 and Isa 40:3). At other times it is implicit as when the Apostle Paul in Gal 1:15–16 describes God setting him "apart from his mother's womb ... to preach to the nations," which matches Jeremiah's description of his own calling (Jer 1:5); thus Paul seemingly compared God's purposes for him with Jeremiah. The goal of STEP 8: SCRIPTURAL CORRELATIONS is to identify and study any parallel accounts, quotations, allusions, or thematically related passages in order to see what fuller illumination of the passages may be discovered, whether the biblical authors intended the connection(s) or not. Within the field of Biblical Studies such research is called "intertextuality."

I. PRIMARY SURVEY

Scripture Using Scripture: As funny as it may sound, Scripture refers back to itself; sometimes biblical authors rewrote the story. This is most obviously true of Deuteronomy ("Second Law") that retells the Exodus and God's giving of the Law for the next generation. Deuteronomy thus stands in a special relationship with the Book of Exodus. The Psalms at times reflects on and summarizes God's history with Israel. First Chronicles re-chronicles the story of God with humanity, beginning with genealogies going back to Adam and then tracing the Davidic and priestly genealogies to the point of the narrative of King Saul's death and David assuming the kingship and reigning that culminated in the preparations for building the temple before passing the task to Solomon. Second Chronicles continues the narrative with Solomon on the throne finishing the temple, and then describes the divided kingdoms—the fall of the Northern Kingdom of Israel to the Assyrians (720 BC) and then the fall of the Southern Kingdom of Judah to the Babylonians (586 BC). Finally, 2 Chronicles ends with a brief mention of King Cyrus of Persia who defeated the Babylonians and would allow the Jews to rebuild the Jewish temple. What themes do 1 and 2 Chronicles help readers attend to? Their rewriting was purposeful; we would do well to focus on these important themes that shaped their narrative development.

Gospel Relationships and Parallel Accounts: Within the NT, certain books have a close relationship to one another. Most obviously these include the Four Gospels, Romans/Galatians, Ephesians/Colossians (very possibly written by Paul at the same time and location), and 2 Peter/Jude (drawing on similar traditions or one on the other). The Gospels relate the life of Jesus from their own sources and perspectives. Three of them—Matthew, Mark, and Luke—follow a similar timeline and are called the "Synoptic" Gospels ("syn" means "with" and "optic" means "view," i.e., "the same view"). The Synoptic Gospels present Jesus as going to Jerusalem once, whereas John's Gospel shows Jesus in Jerusalem four times (2:13–25; 5:1; 7:2–14; 11:55–12:19). What we learn by comparing the Synoptics and John is that the Synoptics focus on Jesus's one momentous journey to Jerusalem in which he would confront the religious authorities at the temple knowing that he would die there. In contrast, in John's Gospel most of Jesus's teaching ministry takes place at Jerusalem; otherwise, he is only outside Judea in Galilee (2:1–12, 4:1–2, 4:43–54, and ch.6) and in Samaria (4:4–42).

EXERCISE 8–A: In Luke's Gospel, Jesus's travel to Jerusalem is very pronounced and organizes the narrative; e.g., 9:51 marks a turning point in the Gospel. Given these references in Luke that track Jesus heading to Jerusalem, consider the following questions:

Luke 9:31, 51, 53; 13:22–25, 33–35; 17:11; 18:31; 19:11, 28, 41–45.

1. What does Jesus himself say about his travel to Jerusalem? How does Jesus prepare to go there?
2. What does Jesus teach in view of going to Jerusalem?
3. What effect does Luke's constant reference to Jesus's travel have? How is 19:41–45 climactic?

<u>Synoptic Gospels and the Four Source Theory</u>: We might wonder why the Synoptics show Jesus traveling once to Jerusalem. I believe it is because of the presentation of Mark's Gospel that frames Jesus's life and ministry by quoting Mal **3:1a** and Isa 40:3 in Mark 1:2–3. The prophet Malachi updates Isaiah's prophecy and depicts the Lord suddenly coming to the Temple for judgment in Mal **3:1b**—what is not quoted explicitly in Mark.[3] In fact, it would appear that Matthew and Luke each used Mark as their backbone, since 97% of Mark is found in them. Mark comprises 46% of Matthew and 42% of Luke; between them both, however, 97% of Mark is found. Luke and Matthew additionally have teaching material in common that is not found in Mark called the "double tradition" that adds up to 22–24% in each gospel. This material tracks progressively throughout Matthew and Luke somewhat in tandem. This has given rise to a theory that this teaching material was its own source that we now call "Q" (possibly

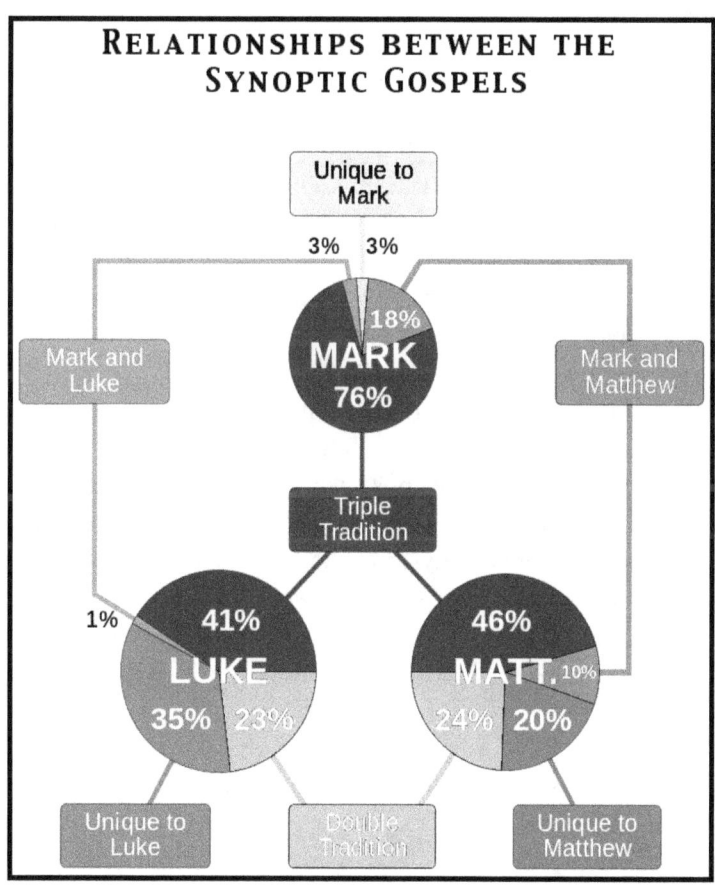

---

[3] For a discussion of this and the Isaianic themes, see Mark A. Awabdy and Fredrick J. Long, "Mark's Inclusion of 'For All Nations' in 11:17d and the International Vision of Isaiah," *The Journal of Inductive Biblical Studies* 1/2 (2014): 224–55 available for download at http://place.asburyseminary.edu/jibs/vol1/iss2/.

from the German Quelle "source"). Finally, about 35% of Luke is unique material (called "L" material) and 20% of Matthew is unique ("M" material). These percentages and relationships are displayed in the graphic above.[4] Currently, a majority of scholars hold to a four-source theory, that is, Matthew and Luke used 1) Mark's Gospel, 2) Q (as reflected especially in the double tradition), and their own source material, respectively, 3) M, and 4) L. Within Gospel studies, **Source Criticism** attempts to recover the "sources" of the gospels; **Redaction Criticism** studies how the Gospel writers arranged and edited source materials so as to recover their underlying theology and ideology. Key tools for such study are Gospel parallels.

<u>Gospel Parallels</u>: Reference books called "Gospel Parallels" will display the English or Greek text in parallel columns to help discover the similarities and differences between parallel passages. Such differences *may (or may not) reflect* a Gospel writer's intentional editing (called "redaction") that then may help us understand the writers' insight about Christ and their understanding of God and the world, i.e., their theology and ideology.

EXERCISE 8–B: Find major differences between the parallel passages given below (RSV) by underlining and/or by developing a color-coding system. Consider what important themes found in each Gospel may account for these differences.

MATT 3:13–17	MARK 1:9–11	LUKE 3:21–22
13 Then Jesus came from Galilee to the Jordan to John, to be baptized by him. 14 John would have prevented him, saying, "I need to be baptized by you, and do you come to me?" 15 But Jesus answered him, "Let it be so now; for thus it is fitting for us to fulfill all righteousness." Then he consented.	9 In those days Jesus came from Nazareth of Galilee and was baptized by John in the Jordan.	21 Now when all the people were baptized,
16 And when Jesus was baptized, he went up immediately from the water, and behold, the heavens were opened and he saw the Spirit of God descending like a dove, and alighting on him;	10 And when he came up out of the water, immediately he saw the heavens opened and the Spirit descending upon him like a dove;	and when Jesus also had been baptized and was praying, the heaven was opened, 22 and the Holy Spirit descended upon him in bodily form, as a dove,
17 and lo, a voice from heaven, saying, "This is my beloved Son, with whom I am well pleased."	11 and a voice came from heaven, "Thou art my beloved Son; with thee I am well pleased."	and a voice came from heaven, "Thou art my beloved Son; with thee I am well pleased."

---

[4] The image Relationship_between_synoptic_gospels.png created by Alecmconroyderivative work: Popadius - This file was derived from Relationship between synoptic gospels.png: CC BY-SA 3.0, and has been recolored and placed in greyscale for this work; https://commons.wikimedia.org/w/index.php?curid=27903558. The percentages are based upon the work of A. M. Honoré, "A Statistical Study of the Synoptic Problem," *NovT* 10.2–3 (1968): 95–147.

In the exercise above, one important difference is in the final sentence of each Gospel: Matthew places the heavenly statement in third person ("This is my beloved Son") whereas Mark and Luke place it in second person ("You are my beloved Son"), which is what probably was originally spoken. But, why did Matthew change this? Well, it appears that Matthew reports the *significance* of the heavenly affirmation *for our benefit; in his redaction Matthew depicts a further insight that God was displaying who Jesus is (the Beloved Son) for all to recognize.* Matthew was not trying to change the truth of what happened, but apply it so that we readers can understand the significance. This principle is an important one. As we will see, NT authors will sometimes explain the meaning of the OT Scriptures they are quoting within the quoted material itself. They will "tweak" the text to embed their interpretation of its significance. But, I am getting ahead of myself a bit. In EXERCISE 8–B above you should have noticed that in Luke's account Jesus received the "Holy Spirit" when baptized and while he "was praying"; both themes are important to Luke.[5]

Harmonizing the Gospel Accounts? It is reflexive for devout followers of Christ to want to harmonize the Gospel accounts into one account to form one great narrative weaving the sources together. The church father Tatian (ca. AD 120–180) created a work called the *Diatessaron* (meaning "Through the Four [Gospels]") that did precisely this; however, it did not survive except in fragments. But we should consider whether harmonizations are as helpful as they may seem. What would be the problem with harmonizing the accounts? Well, the original inspiration of the Gospels as Scripture occurred as distinct documents—to harmonize them removes their individual witness to God's presence and work in Christ. By patching together the Gospels into one narrative, we create our own vision of the Gospel while very likely obscuring the distinctive inspiration and theology of each Gospel. Certainly, we can learn something of the historical context of events—one Gospel may help explain background information. However, we must be careful to respect the integrity of each Gospel in relation to the others. So, *the best use of Gospel Parallels is not to harmonize the accounts, but to study the distinctive witness of each account to make God and Jesus known to the audience.*

> The best use of Gospel Parallels is not to harmonize the accounts, but to study the distinctive witness of each account to make God and Jesus known to the audience.

---

[5] Consider where the "Holy Spirit" occurs in the Gospels and Acts and you will see that Luke-Acts contains the largest majority of occurrences (in **bold**): Matt 1:18, 20; 3:11; 12:32; 28:19; Mark 1:8; 3:29; 12:36; 13:11; **Luke 1:15, 35, 41, 67; 2:25–26; 3:16, 22; 4:1; 10:21; 11:13; 12:10, 12;** John 1:33; 14:26; 20:22; **Acts 1:2, 5, 8, 16; 2:4, 33, 38; 4:8, 25, 31; 5:3, 32; 6:5; 7:51, 55; 8:15, 17, 19; 9:17, 31; 10:38, 44–45, 47; 11:15–16, 24; 13:2, 4, 9, 52; 15:8, 28; 16:6; 19:2, 6; 20:23, 28; 21:11; 28:25**. Also, Luke is particularly interested in "praying" as represented by the Greek verb προσεύχομαι, and especially Jesus praying, compared to the other Synoptic Gospels and Acts: Matt 5:44; 6:5–7, 9; 14:23; 19:13; 24:20; 26:36, 39, 41–42, 44; Mark 1:35; 6:46; 11:24–25; 12:40; 13:18; 14:32, 35, 38–39; **Luke 1:10; 3:21; 5:16; 6:12, 28; 9:18, 28–29; 11:1–2; 18:1, 10–11; 20:47; 22:40–41, 44, 46; Acts 1:24; 6:6; 8:15; 9:11, 40; 10:9, 30; 11:5; 12:12; 13:3; 14:23; 16:25; 20:36; 21:5; 22:17; 28:8**. Interestingly, John's Gospel does not use the verb προσεύχομαι or other words within the semantic domain of "praying" (L&N 33.178), but instead uses the verb ἐρωτάω "I request" to refer to praying (14:16; 16:26; 17:9, 15, 20).

EXERCISE 8–C: Perform a Gospel comparison of Matt 8:16–17, 12:1–8, and 16:13–21 with the parallel passages (if they exist) in Mark, Luke, and John.

1. Photocopy a Gospel Parallel or use computer resources to generate parallels (cite sources).

2. Note significant differences between the Gospels verse-by-verse in the three accounts.

3. Consider any particular nuances conveyed by one Gospel account as opposed to the others.

4. Does this raise any questions for the nature and study of the Gospels?

The Book of Acts and Paul's Epistles: It is often helpful to compare the descriptions of circumstances in the Book of Acts with other NT books, especially Paul's epistles. Details in Acts will help contextualize the community and sometimes the circumstances, although this may be debated. Positively, Paul's visit to Thessalonica recorded in Acts 17:1–9 is shortened since Paul is kicked out of town. Just how long Paul stayed there is uncertain, but Acts describes how Paul first went into the synagogue on three Sabbaths and reasoned with them from the Scriptures, before some of the Jews there organized a mob to cause an uproar leading to the city officials forcing Paul to leave. Acts mentions that "some Jews were persuaded" and "a large number of God-fearing Greeks and quite a few prominent women" (Acts 17:4). Paul's brief stay and being "run out of town" under persecution helps to explain why Paul wrote anxiously to the Thessalonians (1 Thess 3) and seems to boast of his upright character while distancing himself from the appearance of a traveling sophist and charlatan (2:3–12). But what is somewhat puzzling for interpreters is that Paul seems to be writing to people who were just formerly pagans "turning to God from idols to serve a living and true God" (1:9), when the first believers seem to have been Jews and God-fearers, people who already had turned away from idolatry. Paul's letter to the Galatians is also debated; how does it relate to Acts? Is the meeting described in Gal 2 the Jerusalem counsel meeting of Acts 15? Or, is Gal 2 describing Paul's relief fund trip of Acts 11:29–30? (I think the latter.) Still, it is often very helpful to read Paul's letters in view of his travels and interactions with the communities described in Acts. I think it is likely that Luke knew of Paul's letters, even though he nowhere mentions them. Luke mentions other letters (9:22; 15:23–30; 22:5; 23:25–35; 28:21), but why not Paul's? I would maintain that Paul's letters would have been perceived as politically subversive; if writing while Paul was imprisoned as a political prisoner (AD 66–67), Luke would not have wanted to draw attention to them.

Thematic Links and "Intertextuality": NT passages are thematically linked to passages in the OT and NT. English Bibles may provide footnotes to these places and identify what they deem the most important thematic parallels. However, we must understand that what one person identifies as a theme found elsewhere another may not agree or may correlate it to another passage. Scholars and theologians are particularly interested in such links because they are concerned to show the development and relationship of ideas. Yet, how helpful are these thematic links for our interpretation? Did the author intend the particular thematic link? And, even if we might conclude, "Yes, Paul had this theme in mind from this OT book," do we conclude that he intended the audience to have the theme in mind to properly interpret what he says? This area of research that identifies to what extent and why one text may refer to another text is called **intertextuality**; "inter" means "between" and intertextuality means "the reality of correspondence between texts."[6]

Prophecy, Fulfillment, and the Big Picture of God's Deliverance: Typically, we approach the relationship of the Old and New Testaments in terms of prophecy and its fulfillment: God spoke through the prophets (OT) who predicted the coming of the Messiah (NT). So, when Matt 1:22–23 says, "It is written, ..." and then quotes from Isa 7:14, we typically understand that this is taking place: A prophecy was given and its fulfillment reported. This connection involves a one-to-one correspondence: prophecy = fulfillment, especially where Jesus is involved.

However, when we look at the context of Isa 7, it is difficult to see a one-to-one correspondence. The prophet Isaiah was speaking into a contemporary situation involving the King Ahaz of Judah and his fear of being defeated by the northern Kingdoms of Israel and Syria; but the Lord gave him this sign in 7:14—"a virgin will be with child and bear a son, and she will call His name Immanuel." Moreover, Isaiah explains that before the child reaches the age of moral accountability, the two kings will be defeated, *but so will Judah* (to Ahaz's horror) by the same hand of the Assyrians (7:15–25). So, then, how can 7:14 be a prophecy for Judah's time and for Jesus's? The commentators Carl Friedrich Keil and Franz Delitzsch helpfully make this proposal:

> When Isaiah speaks of Immanuel as eating thickened milk and honey, like all who survived the Assyrian troubles in the Holy Land, he evidently looks upon and thinks of the childhood of Immanuel as connected with the time of the Assyrian calamities.... He [Jesus as Son of God] who became flesh in the fulness of time, did really lead an ideal life in the Old Testament history. He was in the midst of it in a pre-existent presence, moving on towards the covenant goal. The fact that the house and nation of David did not perish in the Assyrian calamities, was actually to be attributed, as Isa. 8 presupposes, to His real though not His bodily presence. In this way the apparent discrepancy between the prophecy and the history of the fulfilment may be solved.... The prophecy... is directly Messianic; it is a divine prophecy within human limits.[7]

Keil and Delitzsch explain that Isa 8–9 continues to reveal more about the central idea of Immanuel ("God among us"). In 8:8 and 8:10, Immanuel is mentioned once again; in 8:18 the prophet also states that he and his children are "signs." The prophecy then builds to a positive conclusion in Isa 9 with a climactic focus on the coming descendant of David, who is more than a descendant—in fact, he is called "wonderful Counselor, Mighty God, Everlasting Fa-

---

[6] Intertextuality was first introduced in Biblical Studies in full form in two work in 1989, Richard B. Hays, *Echoes of Scripture in the Letters of Paul* (New Haven: Yale University Press, 1989) and Sipke Draisma, ed., *Intertextuality in Biblical Writings: Essays in Honouof Bas Van Iersel* (Kampen, Neth.: Kok, 1989). The term *intertextualité* was first used by Julia Kristeva in $\Sigma\eta\mu\epsilon\iota\omega\tau\iota\varkappa\grave{\eta}$: *Recherches pour une sémanalyse*, Tel Quel (Paris: Éditions du Seuil, 1969), 113, 255; important essays were translated in her *Desire in Language: A Semiotic Approach to Literature and Art*, trans. Thomas Gora et al. (New York: Columbia University Press, 1980), 64–65.

[7] Carl Friedrich Keil and Franz Delitzsch, *Commentary on the Old Testament*, 10 vols. (Peabody, MA: Hendrickson, 1996), 7.147.

ther, and Prince of Peace." In context, these verses are as follow (Isa 9:6–7, ESV):

> ⁶ For to us a child is born,
>   to us a son is given;
> and the government shall be upon his shoulder,
>   and his name shall be called
> Wonderful Counselor, Mighty God,
>   Everlasting Father, Prince of Peace.
> ⁷ Of the increase of his government and of peace
>   there will be no end,
> on the throne of David and over his kingdom,
>   to establish it and to uphold it
> with justice and with righteousness
>   from this time forth and forevermore.
> The zeal of the LORD of hosts will do this.

So, Isaiah's vision of Immanuel in 7:14 anticipates ultimately a coming Davidic Messiah.

<u>Prophecy or Predictions?</u> Commonly people begin with a "literalistic" view of biblical prophecy that seeks to make every detail fit into the fulfillment; in so doing they may miss the gold nugget only to keep the much less important particulate matter. Such an approach resembles people interpreting the prophecies of Nostradamus (ca. AD 1555), the medical doctor who wrote down his prophecies in four-line quatrains grouped by hundreds called centuries. As summarized by Steve Bright, "These enigmatic quatrains contain old French terms, Latin terms, mythical Greek figures, historical allusions, unique words, anagrams, puns, odd spellings, odd syntax, partial words, inverted word order, and so on."[8]

A "PROPHECY" OF NOSTRADAMUS[9]

Prediction:
"The young lion will overcome the older one,
On the field of combat in a single battle;
He will pierce his eyes through a golden cage,
Two wounds made one, then he dies a cruel death."

What happened: In the summer of 1559 King Henry II of France (*older one*) lined up to joust the Comte de Montgomery (*young lion*), six years his junior, on the fields of France (*field of combat*). Both had lions on their shields. In their final pass Montgomery's lance tilted up, and

---

[8] "Nostradamus: A Challenge to Biblical Prophecy?" *Christian Research Journal* 25.2 (2002) n.p. found at http://www.equip.org/article/nostradamus/ accessed 8–26–2016.

[9] The prediction and what happened are quoted from "14 Famous Predictions by Nostradamus" accessed 8–26–2016 at http://www.businessinsider.com/predictions-of-nostradamus-2011-12#death-of-henry-ii-1. The rebuttal is from Steve Bright in the article cited in the previous footnote.

> burst through the king's visor splintering to pieces. Two shards, one through the eye (*pierce his eyes through a golden cage*), and one through the temple, lodged in the king's head (*Two wounds made one*). Henry suffered for 10 days (*then he dies a cruel death*) before dying in his bed.
>
> **Rebuttal by Steve Bright:** "Critics argue that the items in this quatrain are either not specific or just do not fit the event closely enough to support the accuracy ascribed to it. First, contrary to what the enthusiasts declare, the French never used the 'lion' as an emblem, so this figure of speech fits neither Henry nor the count in that respect. Second, 'young lion' versus 'old one' at best overstates the age difference between the two, Henry being at the most six years older; nor was Henry 'old,' being only 41. Third, 'The field of battle in single combat' could refer to any number of battles in history, and it is unlikely to be a reference to a friendly jousting competition at a marriage festival where, as James Randi points out, it was a serious *faux pas* even to draw blood.[10] Fourth, the shattered lance did not 'burst' Henry's eyes but entered his brain above only one eye. Fifth, 'a cage of gold' could only vaguely refer to a helmet of gold. In any case, neither competitor wore a gold helmet since gold is a metal too soft to be used for protective armor; nor is there any evidence Henry's helmet was gilt in gold. Sixth, the phrase 'two *fleets* one' presents a problem. The French word *classe* is translated 'fleet' everywhere else in the *Centuries*. Since 'fleet' does not fit anything in this event, the enthusiasts, without justification, find a similar sounding Greek word, *klasis*, which means "a fracture," and change the line from 'two *fleets* one' to 'two *wounds* made one,' meaning one wound for Henry and another for France who lost her king. Finally, the only line that is remotely descriptive of this event is that Henry 'died a cruel death' after days of suffering."

As seen above, those interpreting Nostradamus use a variety of techniques—transposing letters in words, interpreting words in different languages, using words with phonetic equivalence, adding up the values of dates and numbers, associating weakly connected ideas, etc. Additionally, Nostradamus' prophecies are random events—there is no connection between them in terms of providing a coherent narrative or moral purpose; they are not salvific or redemptive. Moreover, they give glory to Nostradamus not to God. In contrast, biblical prophecy calls people to covenantal faithfulness to God while describing the flaws and consequences of a lack of complete trust in Yahweh. For King Ahaz who had placed his trust in the King of Assyria rather than Yahweh, the prophecy of Isa 7–9 communicated both how the King of Assyria would turn on Judah while at the same time how God would not abandon his people, but send a Davidic Messiah to fulfill Immanuel. In context, Isaiah confronts the temptation to seek out information from illicit sources. He asks pointedly, "And when they say to you, 'Inquire of the mediums and the necromancers who chirp and mutter,' should not a people inquire of their God? Should they inquire of the dead on behalf of the living?" (Isa 8:19 ESV). We must remember that the Law of Moses condemned the use of such mediums and sources (Lev 20:6), as did Isaiah (19:3; 29:4; 44:25; 47:9, 12–13).

---

[10] James Randi, *The Mask of Nostradamus: The Prophecies of the World's Most Famous Seer* (Amherst, NY: Prometheus, 1993), 175.

The Gospel of Matthew and OT Prophecy and Fulfillment: At this point it would be helpful to investigate and discuss in some detail SCRIPTURE QUOTATION AND CITATION IN MATTHEW (below). We will learn much in this survey of Matthew's practice. No other NT book is more explicit and implicit in showing how Jesus fulfills scriptural prophecy, of which Jesus himself was aware (5:17; 26:24, 54–56). The fulfillment motif is explicitly found by using the verbs "fulfill" (πληρόω) and "written" (γράφω) to introduce an OT source, by making general reference to fulfilling the OT (5:17; 26:24, 54–56), and by implicitly connecting Jesus's ministry to Scripture.

SCRIPTURE QUOTATION AND CITATION IN MATTHEW

The asterisk (*) indicates an explicit fulfillment motif; + indicates an implicit fulfillment motif

Topic	Matthew	Old Testament Reference(s)
Virgin	1:22–23*	Isa 7:14; 8:10 (cf. Isa 9:6–7)
Bethlehem	2:5–6+	Micah 5:2
Out of Egypt	2:15*	Hos 11:1a (cf. Exod 4:22–23)
Weeping	2:17–18*	Jer 31:15
Nazarene	2:23*	????? (cf. Isa 11:1; Judg 13:5–7)
Voice in Wilderness	3:3+ 17:15+	Isa 40:3
The Father's Affirmation and Call	3:17	Isa 42:1; Ps 2:7; cf. Gen 22:2
Reply #1	4:4 +	Deut 8:3b
Temptation #2	4:6	Ps 91:11–12
Reply #2	4:7+	Deut 6:16
Reply #3	4:10+	Deut 6:13
Zebulun and Naphtali	4:15–16*	Isa 9:1–2
Not Commit Murder	5:21+	Exod 20:13//Deut 5:17
Not Commit Adultery	5:27+	Exod 20:14//Deut 5:18
Not Divorce	5:31+	Deut 24:1, 3; (cf. Jer 3:1)
Not Make False Vows	5:33+	Lev 19:12a; Num 30:2; Deut 23:21, 23
Eye for Eye	5:38+	Exod 21:24//Lev 24:20//Deut 19:21
Love Neighbor	5:43+	Lev 19:18b
Depart evildoer	7:23	Ps 6:8a
Took our Infirmities	8:17*	Isa 53:4a
Compassion not Sacrifice	9:13+	Hos 6:6
Cause Family Conflict	10:35–36+	Micah 7:6
Blind and Poor Helped	11:5	Isa 35:5–6a; 61:1
Messenger to Prepare Way	11:10+	Mal 3:1a
Rest for Souls	11:29	Jer 6:16b
Compassion not Sacrifice	12:7+	Hos 6:6
My Servant	12:17–21*	Isa 42:1–4; and Isa 11:10b (LXX); cf. Rom 15:12
Jonah 3 days	12:40+	Jonah 1:17
Dull Hearts	13:14–15*	Isa 6:9–10
Birds of Nest	13:32	Ezek 17:23; 31:6; Ps 104:12; Dan 4:12
Speak in Parables	13:35*	Ps 78:2

Righteous as Sun	13:43	Dan 12:3a
Honor Father and Mother	15:4	Exod 20:12a//Deut 5:16a and Exod 21:17//Lev 20:9
Lip Service; heart astray	15:7–9+	Isa 29:13
Repay according to deeds	16:27	Ps 62:12~Prov 24:12~Ps 28:4
The coming of Elijah	17:10–11+	Mal 4:5–6
Two or Three Witnesses	18:16+	Deut 19:15b
Male and Female One Flesh	19:4–5	Gen 1:27 (5:2) and 2:24
Certificate of Divorce	19:7	Deut 24:1
10 Commandments	19:18–19	Exod 20:13–16//Deut 5:17–20 and Lev 19:18
King on Donkey and Foal	21:4–5*	Zech 9:9; cf. Isa 62:11
Blessed is He	21:9+	Ps 118:26
House of Prayer & Den of Robbers	21:13+	Isa 56:7a and Jer 7:11a
Praise from Babes	21:16+	Ps 8:2 (cf. Ps 8:3 LXX)
Vineyard Parable	21:33+	Isa 5:1–2
Rejected Stone is the Capstone	21:42+	Ps 118:22–23
Sadducees' Question	22:24	Deut 25:5
Jesus's Answer, part 2	22:31–32+	Exod 3:6, 15, 16
Greatest Commandments	22:37, 39+	Deut 6:5 and Lev 19:18b
Jesus's Stumper Question	22:43–44+	Ps 110:1
Blessed is He	23:39+	Ps 118:26a
Abomination of Desolation	24:15+	Dan 9:27; 11:31; 12:11
Sun Darkened, Moon no light, Stars falling from heaven	24:29, 30+	Joel 2:10; 3:15; Isa 13:10; 24:23; Ezek 32:7; Amos 5:20; 8:9; Zeph 1:15
Son of Man coming on the Clouds and the tribes of the land mourning	24:30+	Dan 7:13 and Zech 12:10
Great Trumpet Gathers	24:31+	Exod 19:16; Deut 30:4; Isa 27:13; Zech 9:14
How the Son of Man departs	26:24	"as it is written."
Strike down the Shepherd	26:31+	Zech 13:7b
Jesus betrayed and taken	26:54–56*	"The Scriptures and the Prophets" fulfilled
Son of Man sitting & in the Clouds	26:64+	Ps 110:1a and Dan 7:13b
Potter's Field Purchased	27:9–10*	Zech 11:12–13; cf. Jer 32:6–9
Trusts in God	27:43+	Ps 22:8
Why have you forsaken me?	27:46+	Ps 22:1

<u>Important Aspects of the NT's use of the OT</u>: A close scrutiny of the chart serves to illustrate many important characteristics of the NT authors' use of the OT that will be discussed in the following pages. First, one's list of quotations and citations is insufficient to account for the use of the OT and the NT's dependency on it. Why? The OT has pervasively influenced the NT. For example, Matthew begins with the genealogy that summarizes God's history starting with Abraham through David, the Babylonian exile, and then building to the climax of Jesus (I am skipping many important details that are included in between). In the chart above, I had to make decisions about what constituted a scriptural quotation or reference; the point to consider is that ambiguity exists.

Second, Jesus is affirmed as the fulfilment of the awaited Messiah. This reflects the NT's affirmation of Jesus as the Messiah—what has been called a Christological hermeneutic. Thus, the first two stated fulfilled prophecies in Matt 1:22–23 and 2:5–6 concern Isaiah's "Immanuel" child from the line of David and Micah's vision of a ruler coming from Judah to shepherd his people. Both fulfilled prophecies effectively provide a framework for understanding the fulfilment motif in Matthew to be a Messianic one.

Third, the NT's use of any OT text must be studied within its broader book context and God's story of salvation. Thus, in Matt 2:15, when Jesus was a child, he was called out of Egypt just as God had called Israel out when He called Israel "My Son" (Hosea 11:1 restating Exod 4:22–23). There is a correspondence; such is called **typology** where a pattern repeats that gives significance to each of the corresponding events, *especially the latter event*. So, in Matt 2:15 Jesus's story corresponds to Israel's story, continuing it, even fulfilling it. Likewise, the followers of Christ are described in ways that identify them with Israel (esp. 1 Pet 2). Paul argued that "our fathers" of Israel flirted with idolatry and were punished as "types" to learn from (1 Cor 10:1, 6, 11).

EXERCISE 8–D: Look at the temptation of Jesus in Matt 4:1–11.

1. When tempted, from which scriptural passages did Jesus quote? What chapter range do they occupy and from what OT book?

2. Read these OT chapters in context. With whom is Jesus implicitly comparing himself? How might Jesus see his life in relation to God's people?

Fourth, it may be difficult to determine what exact reference is in mind; for example, Jesus quotes from the Ten Commandments that are found in more than one location. Also, Jesus in Matt 16:27 says that the Son of Man "will then repay every person according to his deeds" that reflects a sentiment found in several locations (Ps 62:12; Prov 24:12; Ps 28:4; cf. Sir 35:19). Likewise, Jesus clearly uses prophetic language in his description of events before the fall of the temple (Matt 24:29–30) that reflects various prophetic texts describing the fall of a city or nation (Joel 2:10; 3:15; Isa 13:10; 24:23; Ezek 32:7; Amos 5:20; 8:9; Zeph 1:15).

Fifth, NT authors would sometimes conjoin two or more Scriptures together in their quotation; sometimes the combination is seamless and one would never know. This practice was a common way for Jews to interpret Scripture—correlating passages together and actually citing them in tandem (see the discussion below on THE SEVEN RULES OF HILLEL within SECONDARY STUDY). Thus, it is quite appropriate in Matt 15:4 for Jesus to combine Exod 20:12a//Deut 5:16a with also Exod 21:17//Lev 20:9, since the latter describes punishments for those cursing their parents when they rather should have given them honor as commanded in the former passages.

Sixth, when quoting Scripture, authors might skip portions of verses or intervening verses. For example, in Matt 5:31 as Jesus condemns the common practice of divorcing one's wife, he quoted the OT passage and skipped a verse from Deut 24:1 to 24:3. Why? When quoting Scripture, the NT authors *focused on the points that they needed to make*. This practice is found among other Jewish interpretive communities; e.g., the Jews of the Qumran community (ca. 150–50 BC).

Seventh, the early Christians quoted from the wording of the Greek Septuagint (LXX) translation of the Hebrew text more commonly than from the Hebrew text and its wording. This is not too surprising since they wrote the NT in Greek. However, this observation attests to the broad influence of the LXX translation that at times shows variation from the Hebrew text. For example, in Matt 12:17–21 the final verse "and the nations will hope in his name" is only found in the Greek Septuagint (LXX) translation of Isa 11:10; it is not in the Hebrew. The Apostle Paul quotes from Isa 11:10 and not surprisingly reflects the wording of the LXX tradition. Also, at times it is difficult for us to know which textual tradition the NT used; sometimes it can be shown that the NT authors were influenced by the Aramaic translation (called Targums). This should not be too concerning, however, since adjustments to wording when quoting sources was allowable in Jewish interpretational practice (see below on THE SEVEN RULES OF HILLEL within SECONDARY STUDY).

Eighth, in their handling of the OT and reference to it, NT writers participated in contemporaneous social-cultural practices that involved play on words and word associations among other things. This is seen in the rather puzzling fulfilment statement in Matt 2:23, "and he came and lived in a city called Nazareth, to fulfill what was spoken through the prophets: "He shall be called a Nazarene." Yet, this statement is not a verse from any portion of known Scripture. Probably, the best solution is that Matthew utilized a play on words because "Nazarene" sounds like the Hebrew noun *nezer* meaning "branch" which recalls prophecies that the Messiah would descend from the branch of David (Isa 11:1; cf. Isa 4:2; Jer 23:5; 33:15; Zech 3:8; 6:12).[11]

Ninth, it is sometimes difficult to determine what is a quotation and merely what is called an allusion. An allusion is something less than a quotation. For example, consider the following statement of Jesus compared to Micah (NASB):

Matt 10:21–22	Micah 7:6–7
21 Brother will betray brother to death, and a father *his* child; and children will rise up against parents and cause them to be put to death.	6 For son treats father contemptuously, Daughter rises up against her mother, Daughter-in-law against her mother-in-law; A man's enemies are the men of his own household.
22 You will be hated by all because of My name, but it is the one who has endured to the end who will be saved.	7 But as for me, I will watch expectantly for the LORD; I will wait for the God of my salvation. My God will hear me.

Are we to think that Jesus had Micah in mind? Most certainly because each set of verses concludes with **enduring/waiting** for **salvation**. Moreover, three verses later in Matt 10:35–36 (see below) Jesus quotes from Micah 7:6 in first person thus making it a statement of purpose ("I came to…"):

34 Do not think that I came to bring peace on the earth; I did not come to bring peace, but a sword.
35 For I came to SET A MAN AGAINST HIS FATHER, AND A DAUGHTER AGAINST HER MOTHER, AND A DAUGHTER-IN-LAW AGAINST HER MOTHER-IN-LAW;
36 and A MAN'S ENEMIES WILL BE THE MEMBERS OF HIS HOUSEHOLD.

---

[11] Alternatively, scholars consider that Nazarene may refer to the Nazarite vow in Judg 13:5–7.

37 He who loves father or mother more than Me is not worthy of Me; and he who loves son or daughter more than Me is not worthy of Me.

38 And he who does not take his cross and follow after Me is not worthy of Me.

39 He who has found his life will lose it, and he who has lost his life for My sake will find it.

Tenth, NT authors interwove their interpretation of the passage with their quotation of it; that is, they combined Scripture with their own wording in order to make its meaning and relevance clear for the audience. In the case of his use of Micah 7:6 above, Jesus adds a first person perspective in the quotation; why? Well, he is not wanting to be identified with the speaker of Micah 7, who self admittedly is a sinner (7:9), but rather identifies himself as the One who brings an analogous inter-familial strife to the people of Israel in a similar context of awaiting for God's salvation. Jesus is a divine agent and he himself represents God to them as their only hope of having their sins pardoned that demonstrates God's unchanging love (7:18).

Eleventh, ancient authors did not have to cite their sources. As in Matt 10:35 above, Jesus seamlessly quotes from Scripture; one would not know it was Scripture unless one knew it was Scripture ahead of time. How might such be possible? Well, Jesus's age was a very oral one, and devout Jewish people heard Scripture read from birth. See also below the FIRST-CENTURY MEDITERRANEAN EDUCATIONAL SYSTEMS (p. 313) within SECONDARY STUDY.

Finally, NT authors might seemingly "wrongly" identify the sources of quotations; but by doing so, they are actually giving credit for the origin of the idea. Thus, Matt 27:9 indicates that the quotation is from Jeremiah, but actually it is from Zechariah. However, Jeremiah is the source of the original prophecy (Jer 32:6–10; cf. 19:1–4, 10–11). Similarly, Mark 1:2–3 indicates that the quotation is from Isaiah, but quotes first from Malachi and then Isaiah. Again, Isaiah is the earlier prophet and Malachi brings forward and updates Isaiah's prophecy. Another intriguing example illustrating the same phenomenon occurs at 1 Cor 14:21 when the Apostle Paul quotes from Isa 28:11–12 but introduces it as "In the Law it is written…." Isaiah described here the coming of the Assyrians that was initially foretold repeatedly in the Law of Moses (Lev 26:33; Deut 4:27–31; 28:36, 49, 52; chs. 29–30). So, in fact the Law was the source for Isaiah and Paul understood this.

MAJOR TYPES OF THE NT'S USE OF THE OT

1. **Direct Quotation of OT** that may or may not be accompanied by a *formal introduction* (e.g., "it is written…") and/or a *citation of the source* (e.g., "As David through the Holy Spirit in the Psalm said,…"). The nature and extent of introductions and citations (if present) are important.
2. **Allusions** have less direct wording in common and have no introduction or citation. The exact meaning and significance of allusions are often debated.
3. **Typology** involves implicit or explicit comparison of events and/or persons in order to show continuity in history and/or ideas; often such typological usage adds prominence to the latter event(s), person(s), or idea(s) in view of the former.
4. **Summaries** of or **References** to OT events or important OT people are not uncommon; e.g., Stephen's speech in Acts 7 effectively rehearses Israel's history of rebellion against God.

Bible Versions and Notes: Depending on the Bible, you may find footnotes in the text that would alert you to parallel passages, the identification and source of a quotation or strong allusion, and thematically related passages. Such notes may be located at the side, middle, or bottom of the scriptural text. Bibles will also have different ways to alert you to quoted sources and other wording that is likely a strong allusion in their estimation. *I cannot stress enough the importance of finding a translation that provides such information, although no single Bible does it perfectly.* Compare the following English versions and the information they provide.

COMPARISON OF FOOTNOTES OF SELECT MODERN ENGLISH TRANSLATIONS

VERSION	HEADING AND TEXT (LUKE 13:18–19)	INTERTEXTUAL NOTES	TYPE
NASB	*Parables of Mustard Seed and Leaven* **Luke 13:18** So ªHe was saying, "ᵇWhat is the kingdom of God like, and to what shall I compare it? 19 "It is like a mustard seed, which a man took and threw into his own garden; and it grew and became a tree, and ªTHE BIRDS OF THE AIR NESTED IN ITS BRANCHES."	ª *Luke 13:18, 19: Matt 13:31, 32; Mark 4:30–32* ᵇ *Matt 13:24; Luke 13:20* ª *Ezek 17:23*	parallel passages thematic strong allusion
NIV11	**The Parables of the Mustard Seed and the Yeast** 13:18,19pp—Mk 4:30–32 13:18–21pp—Mt 13:31–33 ¹⁸ Then Jesus asked, "What is the kingdom of Godʰ like?ⁱ What shall I compare it to? ¹⁹ It is like a mustard seed, which a man took and planted in his garden. It grew and became a tree,ʲ and the birds perched in its branches."ᵏ	 ʰ See Mt 3:2 ⁱ See Mt 13:24 ʲ Lk 17:6 ᵏ See Mt 13:32	parallel passages thematic thematic thematic thematic
ESV	**The Mustard Seed and the Leaven** ¹⁸ ʰHe said therefore, "What is the kingdom of God like? And to what shall I compare it? ¹⁹ It is like ⁱa grain of mustard seed that a man took and sowed in his garden, and it grew and became a tree, and the birds of the air made nests in its branches."	ʰ For ver. 18, 19, see Matt. 13:31, 32; Mark 4:30–32 ⁱ ch. 17:6; Matt. 17:20	thematic thematic

NRSV	*The Parable of the Mustard Seed* *(Mt 13:31–32; Mk 4:30–32)* [18] He said therefore, "What is the kingdom of God like? And to what should I compare it? [19] It is like a mustard seed that someone took and sowed in the garden; it grew and became a tree, and the birds of the air made nests in its branches."	[Apart from the parallel passages, there are no notes in this edition.]	parallel passages

Discussion of Bible Notes and Cross-Referencing Notes: As you can see, there are different conventions of how to represent data and what kinds of data. Also, the amount of data will vary by the particular edition of the English version. So, you should find a study Bible edition that will provide more thematic parallels and the like. An important feature of the NASB text is the use of SMALL CAPS to represent quotations and strong allusions. See the end of Luke 13:19 above. I particularly like this feature since it visually flags such material for careful study. Remember, however, that it is difficult to determine whether an author is alluding to a particular passage or simply connecting to a broader biblical theme. It depends on how similar and unique the wording is. The NASB decided that Luke 13:19b alludes strongly to Ezek 17:23. However, there is something more going on here. If you check the parallel passage in Matt 13:31–32, you will find that the NASB shows more scriptural references there: Ezek 17:23; Ps 104:12; Ezek 31:6; Dan 4:12. *So, be sure to check parallel passages.* Further study reveals that Jesus envisions God's kingdom as fulfilling Ezekiel's vision and as analogous, yet superior, to the vision of the Babylonian kingdom given to King Nebuchadnezzar; God's kingdom starts small but becomes an international empire.

Topical Bibles, Concordances, and Commentaries for identifying Bible Themes: Books exist that provide collections of themes such as *Nave's Topical Bible*[12] and *New Nave's Topical Bible*.[13] There is also the *Treasury of Scriptural Knowledge*.[14] These are massive books that collect tens of thousands of references together around scriptural topics. They may be hard to navigate because they contain so much information; also, not all the correlated passages are equally valuable. So, you must be discerning of the value of the correlations. Also, you may consider using English concordances to help find repeated words. Review the discussion of concordances (pp. 180-82) in STEP 5: LEXICAL RESEARCH. Finally, it is very helpful to consult Bible commentaries to identify parallel passages, quotations, allusions, or thematically related passages. Typically, commentators are very interested in such information in order to explain its significance.

---

[12] Orville J. Nave, *Nave's Topical Bible: A Comprehensive Digest of Over 20,000 Topics and Subtopics with More Than 10,000 Associated Scripture References* (McLean, VA: Hendrickson, 2002).

[13] James Swanson and Orville Nave, *New Nave's Topical Bible* (Oak Harbor, WA: Logos Research Systems, 1994).

[14] R. A. Torrey, *The Treasury of Scripture Knowledge*, 2nd ed. (McLean, VA: Hendrickson, 2002). See also Jerome H. Smith, *The New Treasury of Scripture Knowledge: The Most Complete Listing of Cross References Available Anywhere—Every Verse, Every Theme, Every Important Word* (Nashville: Thomas Nelson, 1992).

STEP 8: SECONDARY STUDY 309

EXERCISE 8–E: The writer to the Hebrews in 12:29 says, "For our God is a consuming fire."

1. Check the notes in two or three different Bibles to learn as much as you can about 12:29.

2. Is Heb 12:29 a quotation, allusion, or a thematically linked passage to the OT?

3. What story of God's relationship with humanity is being (re)told in Hebrews?

4. What significance does Heb 12:29 have in its surrounding context of chs. 12–13?

PRIMARY INTERPRETIVE PROCEDURES:

1. **Identify any parallel accounts. For parallels in the Gospels, use a Gospel Parallel or create your own and answer this question: What seems to be distinctive and possibly emphasized in your pericope?**
2. **Locate all quotations and strong allusions within your passage; be sure to check cross-references that are located in parallel passages (if there are any).**
3. **Next, study the original context(s) of the OT passage(s) quoted or alluded to and consider what important themes connect the OT and NT passages, especially God's saving plan and purposes to address human problems.**
4. **Then, identify thematically related passages. Use Bible notes or special resources such as Nave's Topic Bible. Be selective, create a chart that lists these related passages, check them in context, and discuss their relative worth for understanding the passage, if any.**
5. **Finally, provide a summary of what insights are gained from studying the parallel passages, quotations, allusions, and/or thematically related passages as well as any other significant questions arising for possible attention in STEP 9: INTERPRETIVE DECISIONS.**

II. SECONDARY STUDY

<u>Orientation</u>: The pastor's preparation for teaching and preaching requires a good knowledge of the OT's influence on the NT. This STEP 8: SCRIPTURAL CORRELATIONS will draw upon and enhance your capacity to recognize and interpret the significance of the NT's use of the OT. Specifically, you will consider how the OT quotation or allusion itself may be worded to suggest its proper interpretation and application in the NT context. This SECONDARY STUDY builds upon the PRIMARY SURVEY and then moves forward to understand how NT authors intended quotations and allusions to be interpreted and applied in their respective contexts.

<u>Classification of Types of the NT's Use of the OT</u>: To begin, let's review the types of the NT's use of the OT and also add some additional categories and examples. These categories of usage are presented below in order of the most explicit to least explicit reference to the OT passage.

1. **Direct Quotation (with or without formal introduction and with or without citation)**: Just where a quotation is found in the argument and whether it is introduced and credited to an au-

thor are always important for our interpretation. For example, in Heb 10:15–18 (NASB) consider how the author introduces the quotation of Jer 31:33–34:

> [15] And the Holy Spirit also testifies to us; for after saying,
> [16] "This is the covenant that I will make with them
> After those days, says the Lord:
> I will put My laws upon their heart,
> And on their mind I will write them,"
> *He then says,*
> [17] "And their sins and their lawless deeds
> I will remember no more."
> [18] Now where there is forgiveness of these things, there is no longer *any* offering for sin.

Identifying the speaker as "the Holy Spirit" adds gravity to what is said. Also, earlier in 8:8–12 the author of Hebrews had quoted the whole of Jer 31:31–34 and so the return in Heb 10 to further discuss the meaning is quite significant contextually. He stresses the forgiveness of the New Covenant and how this makes obsolete the sacrificial system of the Old Covenant.

2. **Interpreted OT Source**: Sometimes NT writers will explicitly interpret the OT passage quoted. This may entail explaining the meaning of phrases. There are various sub-classifications that will be discussed further below. For example, in Heb 12:26–29 (NRSV) see how the author of Hebrews quotes the text and proceeds to interpret the phrase "Yet once more" and apply its meaning for the audience.

> [12:26] At that time his voice shook the earth; but now he [God] has promised, "Yet once more I will shake not only the earth but also the heaven." [27] This phrase, "Yet once more," indicates the removal of what is shaken—that is, created things—so that what cannot be shaken may remain. [28] Therefore, since we are receiving a kingdom that cannot be shaken, let us give thanks, by which we offer to God an acceptable worship with reverence and awe; [29] for indeed our God is a consuming fire.

Despite this, interpreters debate what the meaning of "shaken once more" is.[15]

3. **Selective Summary of the OT**: NT authors sometimes show quite an extensive dependence on the OT by providing substantial summaries of OT materials. Perhaps the clearest examples are Stephen's speech in Acts 7 and the "Hall of Faith" in Heb 11. Each summary is selective and bears directly to the situation facing the audience.

4. **Simple Reference to OT Figures or Events**: Simple reference to an OT figure or event often recalls a complex of ideas. For example, in Matt 6:29 Jesus refers to "Solomon in all his glory" in contrast to the birds and flowers when discussing the need for one to trust in God's provision.

---

[15] For example, does this refer to Jesus's second coming or possibly to the very imminent Jewish War and the fall of the Jerusalem temple in AD 70? One's view of the dating of Hebrews will affect one's interpretation.

In 1 Cor 10:1–6 Paul discusses Moses and the Israelites to dissuade believers from idolatry.[16]

5. **Strong Allusion with Sound Verbal Parallels with no formal Introduction or Citation**: For example, Jesus begins to tell the story of the owner of the vineyard (Mark 12:1–12) by using the very wording of Isa 5:1–2 that begins the Vineyard Parable (Isa 5:1–7), but then Jesus develops the story in a new way.

6. **Echo (faint allusion) to Scripture**: In a seminal study Richard B. Hays notes that Paul's language is richly indebted to the OT Scriptures.[17] He argues that Paul appropriated scriptural phrases and motifs in ways that are contextually significant respective to each biblical context. When an echo is investigated, it usually "opens up" larger theological correspondences of themes between the two passages. This is true of explicit quotation, allusions, and fainter echoes. For example, in Eph 1:4 and 1:14 Paul describes the formation of the church body of Jews and Gentiles in terms of God's desire to have a "holy people for Himself" as "His special possession" and "His inheritance"—such wording echoes God's calling of Israel found in central covenantal passages like Exod 19:5–6, Deut 7:6, 14:2, etc.

7. **Important Thematic Connections**: Many NT texts have significant links to important themes and yet modern readers may not readily perceive these. The distinction between these thematic connections and an echo above has to do with the pervasiveness or uniqueness of the theme in the OT: Whereas an echo reverberates with other themes from the NT text originating from a single OT passage, thematic connections typically resonate with more than one OT passage. Consider this thematic connection: Jesus describes himself as the Good Shepherd (John 10:1–21) and the OT prophets described God as being like a shepherd (Isa 40:11; Ezek 34:11–16) and anticipated God appointing King David as a shepherd over his people (Ezek 34:23).

<u>Identifying Quotes or Strong Allusions</u>: English Bibles may identify Scriptural quotations using quotation marks (most Bibles), placing quotations and strong allusions in small caps (NASB), or using bold text (NET). Additionally, you can find lists of OT quotations and (strong) allusions in Greek Bibles (NA and UBS texts) as well as in books and other specialized resources. Within Greek Bibles, the printed text may help identify the presence of an OT quotation or allusion—the UBS uses **bold** and the NA texts uses *italics*. The NA Greek text also provides a listing of quotations, allusions, and thematically related texts in the side margin. The UBS provides references to quotations, (strong) allusions, and literary parallels at the bottom of the page in its Cross Reference apparatus. Additionally, the UBS has a very helpful appendix that shows OT quotations and (strong) allusions both from OT book into the NT and by NT book to the OT book. Electronically, the newest version of the NA[28] uses an asterisk (*) where it supplies OT references that one can hover over to see and click to go to (very handy!).

---

[16] In 10:7 Paul formally quotes Exod 32:6, but not until he makes a more general reference. Why? Probably because other lessons may be learned in addition to the one specifically given from Exod 32:6. Hence, Paul ends 1 Cor 10:6 with a general statement: "These things happened as examples and were written for our instruction."

[17] Hays, *Echoes of Scripture in the Letters of Paul* (New Haven: Yale University Press, 1989).

EXERCISE 8–F: Given below is Gal 3:6–14 (NET) verse-by-verse.

1. Identify which OT texts are used and classify the type of OT use in each case: direct quotation (with introduction or not and with citation or not), interpreted, selective summary, simple reference, strong allusion, echo, or thematic connection.

2. Do you think that Paul expected his audience(s) to know the contexts of these OT verses?

3:6 Just as Abraham *believed God, and it was credited to him as righteousness*,

3:7 so then, understand that those who believe are the sons of Abraham.

3:8 And the scripture, foreseeing that God would justify the Gentiles by faith, proclaimed the gospel to Abraham ahead of time, saying, "*All the nations will be blessed in you.*"

3:9 So then those who believe are blessed along with Abraham the believer.

3:10 For all who rely on doing the works of the law are under a curse, because it is written, "*Cursed is everyone who does not keep on doing everything written in the book of the law.*"

3:11 Now it is clear no one is justified before God by the law, because *the righteous one will live by faith*.

3:12 But the law is not based on faith, but *the one who does* the works of the law *will live by them*.

3:13 Christ redeemed us from the curse of the law by becoming a curse for us (because it is written, "*Cursed is everyone who hangs on a tree*")

3:14 in order that in Christ Jesus the blessing of Abraham would come to the Gentiles, so that we could receive the promise of the Spirit by faith.

Combined Quotations: E. Earle Ellis reports that Paul quotes the OT ninety-three times and alludes or parallels the OT and LXX texts one-hundred and eight times.[18] He summarizes, "Although the quotations are drawn from sixteen OT books, three-fourths of them are from the Pentateuch (thirty-three), Isaiah (twenty-five), and the Psalms (nineteen). The citations appear both singly and in combination."[19] Ellis helpfully delineates three ways this combining is done: "merged quotations (e.g. Rom. 3.10–18), chain quotation or *haraz* (e.g. Rom. 9:25–9), and looser midrashic commentary (cf. Rom. 9–11; Gal. 3)."[20] In EXERCISE 8–F we can see Paul's interpretive weaving together of OT texts (called midrash). Reading Scripture in view of Scripture is quite significant because Paul and other NT writers—indeed Jesus himself—herein reflect contemporaneous Jewish exegetical practices. But, the question remains, Would audiences have understood and appreciated the NT's sophisticated use of the OT? I think "yes" because Jewish communities enjoyed a high literacy rate. On ancient Mediterranean literacy, see my final discussion in TERTIARY RESEARCH.

---

[18] *Paul's Use of the Old Testament*, Twin Brooks Series (Grand Rapids: Baker, 1957), Appendix IA and IB. The LXX use is significant, too, in that some of the books included there are non-canonical such as Wisdom possibly alluded to in Rom 1:20–32; 9:21, etc. and Sirach possibly alluded at 1 Cor 6:12–13, etc.

[19] *Paul's Use*, 11.

[20] *Paul's Use*, 11 n5.

First-Century Mediterranean Educational Systems[21]

Element	Greek and Roman (Variations existed between Greek and Roman education and also from location to location.)	Jewish
Languages:	Greek and Latin	Hebrew
Core Curriculum:	Homer; Virgil (i.e., classical literature)	Torah
Location:	o Public, although Roman education was traditionally at home taught by the father, mother, and/or tutor o Girls were taught reading, writing and poetry.	o At home, but then for secondary level moved into schools in the second-century BC; by the first-century AD schools exited for both levels. o No girls received education generally.
Primary:	o 6 to 11 years of age with a slave "pedagogue" o gymnasium/athletics, reading, writing, music o dictation and writing	o 6 to 10 years of age o memorized written law *(bet seper)* o no dictation; students read aloud small torah samples *(megillah)*
Secondary Grammar:	o 12–15 years of age o reading, grammar, literature, exposition of poetry and mythology o some girls received this education, too.	o 10 to 13 years of age o studied oral torah in *midrash* (sustained commentary; *bet talmud*) and *mishnah* (topical arrangement; *bet midrash*) o chanted oral torah to memorize it
Secondary Rhetoric:	o 15–17 years of age (concluded with receiving the toga of manhood); o *Progymnasmata*= "the sayings of famous people *(chreia)*, maxims *(sententia)*, fables, mythological and historical narrative, development of commonplaces, encomium and denunciation, comparison, speech in character (impersonation), vivid description, thesis and discussion of the advantages or disadvantages of a law. These exercises were illustrated by famous prose works. Students would work each exercise using paraphrase, negation, pro and con, example and comparison." See Aelius Theon of Alexandria (1st or 5th century), Ps. Hermogenes of Tarsus (2nd), Libanius of Antioch (4th), Aphthonius of Antioch (4th), Nicolaus of Myra (5th) (see also Ronald F. Hock, "Chreia" in *ABD* I.912).	o Greek was not taught in Jewish education; it was acquired elsewhere in Israel or outside Jewish education. o Rhetorical training was sought in Alexandria or elsewhere. A school existed in Jerusalem from the third-century BC. o advanced study in Torah using Q/A method or students possibly pursued astronomy and mathematics o Informal education occurred in the synagogues with public readings, etc. o Generally, "These Jewish schools were probably both a counter to and imitation of the Greco-Roman education system" (Dennis L. Stamps, "Children in Late Antiquity," *DNTB[1]*, 200).
Tertiary:	One year of apprenticeship followed perhaps by further study of philosophy, history, medicine, law, or more rhetoric.	At the age of thirteen, the boy was to learn a trade from his father or be sent to someone else who could do so.

---

[21] Summarized from Duane F. Watson, "Education: Jewish and Greco-Roman," *DNTB[1]*, 308–13.

Ancient Education Valued: Jewish and Greco-Roman approaches to education are summarized on the previous page in FIRST-CENTURY MEDITERRANEAN EDUCATIONAL SYSTEMS. Jewish communities enjoyed a 30% literacy rate in terms of the ability to read and write. This contrasts with 10% typically suggested for the Greco-Roman populace;[22] *but this percentage seems too low to me* especially in the urban centers where the first Christian communities were established. At such locations an increasing book market and library system flourished. Read my discussion of orality and ancient libraries in TERTIARY RESEARCH below. Also, we must consider the impact of recited and performed "texts" in various settings, especially the synagogue where Scripture was read regularly. Something analogous occurred within Greco-Roman society where Homer's *Iliad* and *Odyssey* were standard works in education and texts were memorized for theater performance.

General Jewish "Modes" of Interpreting Scripture: Jewish modes of interpretation were in development in the centuries before and after Christ. Below are the main modes in the first-century that are not mutually exclusive; e.g., midrashic interpretation may be for the purpose of *halakah*.

1. **Mashal** (Hebrew meaning "comparison, parable, proverb"): "A story or saying that illustrates a truth using comparison, hyperbole, or simile. Can be a model, analogy, or example."[23] Jesus commonly spoke parables, some of which illustrate/explain his scriptural teaching. Isaiah 5:1–7 is an allegorical parable that Jesus retells as the vineyard tenants parable (Mark 12:1–12).
2. **Allegorical Interpretation**: Differing from crafting an allegory, this mode interprets story elements as having a significant difference from their meaning in the story. Paul employs such explicitly in Gal 4:21–31, although he may be turning his opponents' allegory back onto them.
3. **Typological-Analogical Interpretation**: The OT contains "types" that correspond to NT realities; e.g., in Luke 6:1–6 Jesus compares himself and his disciples to David and his band of men; in 1 Cor 10 Paul refers to Israel's struggle and punishment for engaging in idolatry.
4. **Halakah** (Hebrew "walking"): New applications or "broadening" of religious laws for conduct in everyday life; e.g., Jesus takes OT commands and reformulates them in Matt 5:17–48.
5. **Haggadah** (Hebrew meaning "telling"): The interpretation of OT narrative for edification; e.g., in Luke 11:29–32 Jesus made reference to Jonah and the people of Nineveh and to Solomon and Sheba, the Queen of the South (1 Kgs 10:1–3 and 2 Chr 9:1–12) to admonish the crowds.
6. **Pesher** (Hebrew meaning "interpretation"): Refers to the application-fulfillment of a prophetic passage to a contemporary community understood within an eschatological context; this approach is found in the Qumran community which wrote verse-by-verse commentaries on Nahum, Habakkuk, and the Psalms to explain the significance for the audiences; e.g., in Luke 4:18–21 Jesus reads Isa 61 and explains, "Today this Scripture is fulfilled in your hearing."
7. **Midrash** (Hebrew meaning "explanation"): This approach to Scripture is an extended, unfolding interpretation of a biblical passage or passages; see, e.g., Heb 3:7–19 where the author quotes Ps 95:7–11 and explains its meaning and significance for the audience.

---

[22] As discussed in William V. Harris, *Ancient Literacy* (Cambridge: Harvard University Press, 1989).

[23] David Seal, "Parable," ed. John D. Barry et al., *The Lexham Bible Dictionary* (Bellingham, WA: Lexham Press, 2016), n.p.

Step 8: Secondary Study

Exercise 8–G: In 2 Cor 6:2 Paul quotes Isa 49:8 somewhat unexpectedly (below from NASB):

6:1 And working together *with Him*, we also urge you not to receive the grace of God in vain— ²for He says, 'AT THE ACCEPTABLE TIME I LISTENED TO YOU, AND ON THE DAY OF SALVATION I HELPED YOU.' Behold, now is 'THE ACCEPTABLE TIME,' behold, now is 'THE DAY OF SALVATION.'"

Which of the general Jewish interpretive modes are reflected here?

<u>Embedded Interpretations and Applications</u>: Another very common practice of NT writers (and other ancient writers) is that they didn't quote their ancient sources as accurately as we might expect. However, this practice may be the result of deficient memories, different *Vorlagen* (original sources), or the acceptability of quoting material with an embedded interpretation. Evidence exists that the NT authors did work from memory, but also that they worked with different sources or variant translations, as it were. E. Earle Ellis has rightly stated, "Even where a variant text is apparently in view, Paul's textual aberrations in many cases have a hermeneutical purpose and often are closely tied to the immediate application of the citation."[24] *The possibility that NT authors are interpreting as they are quoting Scripture is essential for us to entertain in our interpretation.* So, when we observe differences between a possible *Vorlage* and the NT writer's quotation, we should consider what interpretive significance this may have. Why is this word changed? Why is this portion of the verse skipped over? Consult the better commentaries that will usually identify these differences and their interpretive significance.

> The possibility that NT authors are interpreting as they are quoting Scripture is essential for us to entertain in our interpretation.

<u>Early Christian Commentators</u>: Particularly adept at correlating and interpreting NT passages in light of the whole of Scripture, the church fathers are our earliest Christian commentators. They provide significant insights and may reflect a trajectory of interpretation not otherwise known; their writings may open up further avenues of understanding and research. The Ancient Christian Commentary on Scripture series published by InterVarsity Press with Thomas Oden as the general editor is a welcome resource to find such relevant ancient commentary. Otherwise, you may consult the Scripture indices of published translations of the church fathers.

Exercise 8–H: Consider why Paul in 1 Cor 9:9 quotes Deut 25:4 about the muzzling of oxen. How is this or isn't this a legitimate use of OT Scripture?

<u>Interpretive Rules of Jewish Scholars</u>: At the time of Jesus, midrashic interpretive strategies were developed and codified as "The Seven Rules of Hillel." These rules were first written down by the Jewish teacher Hillel (fl. ca. 20 BC—ca. AD 15), but probably existed in some form before then. They are quite important for NT study. In the second-century AD Rabbi Ishmael described thirteen and eventually the Rabbi Eliezer ben Yose the Galilean described thirty-two.[25]

---

[24] *Paul's Use*, 1.
[25] Craig A. Evans, "Midrash," *DJG*¹, 544–46.

THE SEVEN RULES OF HILLEL[26]

1. ***Qal wa-Homer*** (lighter and heavier) "What applies in less important cases will apply in more important ones."
   —E.g., Jesus argues that healing a person on the Sabbath is more valuable than circumcision of a child or saving a sheep on Sabbath (John 7:23; Matt 12:12).
   —See also Matt 6:26, 30//Luke 12:24, 28; Matt 7:11//Luke 11:13; Matt 10:25; John 10:24–36; 15:18–20. For Paul see Rom 5:8–9, 10, 15, 17; 11:12, 24; 1 Cor 9:11–12; 12:22; 2 Cor 3:7–9, 11; Phil 1:16; 2:12.
   —However, this is also a Greek form of argumentation. This raises the question to what extent has Jewish exegesis been influenced by Greek thought (Hellenization)?
2. ***Gezerah shawah*** (equivalence of expressions) "An analogy is made between two texts on the basis of a similar phrase, word or root."
   —For example, by comparing 1 Sam 1:11 to Judg 13:5 using the phrase "no razor shall touch his head" we may conclude that Samuel, like Samson, was a Nazarite.
   —Peter in Acts 2:25, 34 uses Ps 16:8–11 and 110:1 to support the resurrection of Jesus since both passages mention "at my right hand."
3. ***Binyan ab mikathub 'ehad*** (building of the father from one text) "One explicit passage serves as a foundation or starting point so as to constitute a rule (father) for all similar passages or cases."
   —E.g., Heb 9:11–22 applies "blood" from Exod 24:8=Heb 9:20 to Jer 31:31–34
4. ***Binyan ab mishene kethubim*** (building of the father from two or more texts) "Two texts or provisions in a text serve as a foundation for a general conclusion."
   —E.g., Paul in Rom 3:9–20 using a catena (i.e., string) of OT texts to establish a point.
5. ***Kela upherat*** (the general and the particular) "A general statement is first made and is followed by a single remark which particularizes the general principle."
   —E.g., Gen 1:27 makes a general statement which Gen 2:7, 21–23 particularizes.
6. ***Kayoze bo bemaqom 'aher*** (analogy made from another passage) "Two passages may seem to conflict until a third resolves the conflict." Consider the following examples.
   —Leviticus 1:1 "out of the tent of meeting" and Exod 25:22 "from above the ark of the covenant between the cherubim" seem to disagree until we see Num 7:89 where Moses entered the tent of meeting to hear God speaking from between the cherubim.
   —First Chronicles 27:1 explained the numerical disparity between 2 Sam 24:9 and 1 Chr 21:5.
   —Exodus 19:20 "YHWH came down upon Mount Sinai" seems to disagree with Deut 4:36 "Out of Heaven He let you hear His voice." But, Exod 20:22 reconciles the two by explaining that God brought the heavens down to the mountain and spoke.
7. ***Dabar halamed me 'inyano*** (explanation obtained from context) "The total context, not just the isolated statement, must be considered for an accurate exegesis." This is the principle CIE.

---

[26] The summary and examples are by James Trimm (slightly edited), originally accessed 1–31–2005 from http://www.nazarene.net/Hermeneutics/Hillel.html. The material is found in different web locations attributed to him. These rules of Hillel can be found discussed in many sources; e.g., Craig A. Evans, "Midrash," *DJG[1]* 544–45.

EXERCISE 8–I: Given these passages from Hebrews, consider the following questions.

1. In Heb 1:5–14 the author of Hebrews cites these OT texts: What Jewish exegetical rule is being used? What is the point being argued?
    Ps 2:7 = Heb 1:5
    2 Sam 7:14 = Heb 1:5
    Deut 32:43/Ps 97:7/(Neh 9:6) = Heb 1:6
    Ps 104:4 = Heb 1:7
    Ps 45:6–7 = Heb 1:8–9
    Ps 102:25–27 = Heb 1:10–12
    Ps 110:1 = Heb 1:13

2. What type of interpretive rule or argument is found in these passages?
    Heb 2:2–3
    Heb 9:13–14
    Heb 10:28–29
    Heb 12:9
    Heb 12:25

<u>Christology of Divine Identity</u>: Recently, Richard Bauckham has set forth an understanding of how the earliest Christians continued to understand Christ as God within the monotheistic affirmation of Judaism. What we find is that OT quotations that refer to God as Lord are applied to Jesus as Lord, thus affirming Jesus's identity as God (e.g., Rom 10:13 = Joel 2:32).[27]

EXERCISE 8–J: Consider the use of the OT in Eph 4:7–11 (NASB) and answer the questions.

⁷ But to each one of us grace was given according to the measure of Christ's gift.
⁸ Therefore it says,
    "WHEN HE ASCENDED ON HIGH,
    HE LED CAPTIVE A HOST OF CAPTIVES,
    AND HE GAVE GIFTS TO MEN."
⁹ (Now this *expression,* "He ascended," what does it mean except that He also had descended into the lower parts of the earth?
¹⁰ He who descended is Himself also He who ascended far above all the heavens, so that He might fill all things.)
¹¹ And He gave some *as* apostles, and some *as* prophets, and some *as* evangelists, and some *as* pastors and teachers,…

---

[27] Richard Bauckham, *God Crucified: Monotheism and Christology in the New Testament* (Grand Rapids: Eerdmans, 1999); he has developed this further in an unpublished paper "Paul's Christology of Divine Identity."

1. What OT passage is this from?
2. What changes and omissions are observed?
3. What may be the underlying *Vorlage* (Hebrew, Greek, or other)?
4. What interpretation may be embedded in the quotation? Why?
5. What mode(s) of Jewish interpretation are present?
6. What is being affirmed about Christ's identity?

SECONDARY STUDY PROCEDURES:

The following procedures incorporate some elements of the PRIMARY INTERPRETIVE PROCEDURES.

1. **Identify any parallel accounts.** For parallels in the Gospels, use a Gospel Parallel or create your own and answer this question: What seems to be distinctive and possibly emphasized in your pericope?
2. **Locate all quotations and strong allusions within your passage**; be sure to check cross-references that are located in parallel passages (if there are any).
3. **Compare the text as quoted or strongly alluded to in the NT with the OT text**; if possible, access the Hebrew and the LXX. What changes in the text are observed? What clauses, phrases, or verses have been changed or omitted? Such differences may alert you to important themes or points of application that the NT author advances.
4. **Next, study the original context(s) of the OT passage(s) quoted or alluded to** and consider what important themes connect them to the NT passage in context, especially God's saving plan and purposes to address human problems.
5. **Consider what Jewish mode of interpretation** (*mashal*, typological, etc.) is present and whether or not a specific Jewish exegetical technique is operative, especially the Seven Rules of Hillel.
6. **Referring back to any textual differences noted in 3. above**, consider how the quotation in the NT may itself embed the author's interpretation for the audience(s).
7. **Then, identify thematically related passages.** Use Bible notes or special resources such as Nave's Topic Bible. Be selective, create a chart that lists these related passages, check them in context, and discuss their relative worth for understanding the passage, if any.
8. **Consider the discussion/interpretation of the passage in the church Fathers** and how this may shed light on your interpretation of the passage—see the Ancient Christian Commentary on Scripture Series (IVP) edited by Thomas Oden.
9. **Finally, provide a summary of what insights are gained from studying the parallel passages, quotations, allusions, and/or thematically related passages** as well as any other significant questions arising for possible focus in STEP 9: INTERPRETIVE DECISIONS.

III. TERTIARY RESEARCH

<u>Orientation</u>: At the highest levels of research, students of Scripture access primary materials in the original languages such as Hebrew, Aramaic, Classical and Koine Greek, Latin, and other pertinent research languages. TERTIARY RESEARCH involves exploring a variety of possible areas of intertextuality and "intertextural-ity" (to use Robbins's notion) including, but not limited to 1) identifying the underlying text *Vorlage* or, for the Gospels in particular, source materials; 2) investigating the inter-canonical and extra-biblical exegetical traditions as may be reflected in the Greek versions, the Targums, and other textual traditions; 3) considering the social-cultural values of literacy and performance; 4) researching the mechanisms of textual production and transmission; and 5) examining more thoroughly how and why NT authors quote, allude to, and echo the OT and other texts. Indeed, students must carefully define terms, understand underlying assumptions, and clearly explain interpretive traditions as they perform intertextual research.[28]

<u>Robbins' Analytic of "Intertexture" and Julia Kristeva</u>: Robbins has described what he calls intertexture that embraces and broadens intertextuality, which is only one form of intertexture, namely, "oral-scribal intertexture." Such "involves a text's use of any other text outside of itself, whether it is an inscription, a Greek poet, non-canonical apocalyptic material, or the Hebrew Bible. One of the ways a text configures and reconfigures is to use, either explicitly or without reference, language from other texts. There are five basic ways in which language in a text uses language that exists in another text: recitation, recontextualization, reconfiguration, narrative amplification, and thematic elaboration."[29] These five ways provide interpreters an analytic by which to assess, categorize, and understand the NT's use of other texts.

However, for Robbins intertexture entails more than one text referencing another. Thus, "[i]ntertexture is a 'text's representation of, reference to, and use of phenomena in the 'world' outside the text being interpreted.' This world includes other texts (oral-scribal intertexture), other cultures (cultural intertexture), social roles institutions, codes and relationships (social intertexture), and historical events or places (historical intertexture)."[30] What Robbins affirms is that biblical texts not only quote, allude to, or echo other biblical texts, but also non-biblical texts and media (coins, inscriptions, etc.); additionally, biblical texts refer also to values, scripts, codes and systems of a culture, social roles, institutions, relationships, and historical events.

In this, Robbins actually reestablishes something of what Julia Kristeva was describing by "intertextuality," recognizing the various cultural resonances in texts signaled by the use of words. She describes the "literary word" (using Mikhail Bakhtin's expression) "as an intersection of textual surfaces rather than a point (a fixed meaning), as a dialogue among several writings: that of

---

[28] See the helpful overview of such needs in Niall McKay, "Status Update: The Many Faces of Intertextuality in New Testament Study," *Religion & Theology* 20.1–2 (2013): 84–106.

[29] This description is from the excellent online "Dictionary of Socio-Rhetorical Terms" located at http://www.religion.emory.edu/faculty/robbins/SRI/defns/o_defns.cfm#oral-scribal accessed 8–30–2016. See also Robbins' discussion of intertexture in *Exploring*, ch. 2 and *Tapestry*, ch. 4.

[30] From http://www.religion.emory.edu/faculty/robbins/SRI/defns/i_defns.cfm#inter accessed 8–30–2016.

the writer, the address (or the character), and the contemporary or earlier cultural context."[31] For Robbins, Kristeva helped to identify the issue: "the cultural context" of words.[32] But biblical interpreters have been concerned with the underlying assumptions of Kristeva's intertextuality whereby authorial intention and fixed meanings of words in texts are replaced with ambivalence.[33] She argues, "any text is constructed as a mosaic of quotations; any text is the absorption and transformation of another."[34] This is due to the multivalency of the individual word that functions both as a mediator, "linking structural modes to cultural (historical) environment" and a regulator, "controlling mutations from diachrony to synchrony, i.e., to literary structure." Thus, "[t]he word is spatialized; through the very notion of status, it functions in three dimensions (subject-addressee-context) as a set of *dialogical*, semic elements or as a set of *ambivalent* elements." What Kristeva recognized is the profound "locatedness" of texts within their surrounding cultural context and the central role that words and combinations of words have in relation to reflecting, contesting, challenging, and subverting society, culture, and ideology.

Inner-Biblical Exegesis: Michael A. Fishbane, in his monumental book *Biblical Interpretation in Ancient Israel*, has described types of "inner-biblical exegesis" in which he distinguishes **traditum** (content of tradition) from **traditio** (the process of transmitting tradition).[35] Fishbane describes in detail types of exegesis found in Hebrew Scripture and Jewish Intertestamental texts in which *traditum* is reconfigured in *traditio* that becomes in this process the new *traditium*: scribal, legal, aggadic, and mantological. Fishbane's analytic and research provides a fertile ground for understanding Jewish exegetical traditions that connect the modes of NT's use of the OT with the exegetical practices and traditions found in the Intertestamental literature and the OT. We are reminded how important sources and inscribed traditions are.

Vorlagen and Communal-Exegetical Traditions: Generally, it would seem that the NT writers preferred the Greek LXX over the MT Hebrew scriptural text.[36] Occasionally, the NT quotations are closer to the Masoretic Text (MT). Of Paul's ninety-three OT quotations, Ellis indicates Paul follows the LXX fifty-one times (twenty-two at variance form the MT) and follows the MT only four-times (at variance from the LXX).[37] There are difficulties, however, with certainty in such a determination since 1) as Ellis affirms, Paul embeds interpretations and applications within the citations; 2) Paul combines OT texts in his citation; 3) Paul likely worked from memory; and 4) different translations and recensions of the LXX existed probably from its inception (250–100 BC). This last reality is further complicated in that later Jewish translators attempted to reclaim the

---

[31] Kristeva, *Desire in Language*, 65.

[32] Robbins, *Tapestry*, 143.

[33] Among critiques, see D. L. Meek, "Intertextuality, Inner-Biblical Exegesis, and Inner-Biblical Allusion: The Ethics of a Methodology," *Biblica* 95 (2014): 280–91, esp. 282–84.

[34] *Desire in Language*, 66; the following quotations are from the same page and *italics* are original.

[35] Michael A. Fishbane, *Biblical Interpretation in Ancient Israel* (Oxford: Clarendon, 1985).

[36] A helpful resource to find which LXX Greek words translate which Hebrew words is E. Hatch and H. A. Redpath's *Concordance to the Septuagint*.

[37] Ellis, *Paul's Use*, 12.

LXX from Christian interpretations by creating more accurate Greek recensions in the second-century as reflected in the translations of Aquila, Symmachus, and Theodotion. In the end, various factors affect the text's form but especially application. Indeed, Ellis in the conclusion to his research says,

> In many cases the Pauline rendering is intimately connected with his application of the text. These applications make use of common stock interpretations, oral and targumic traditions, and rabbinic methodology.... *Midrash pesher* as a hermeneutical method is present not only in the Gospels of Matthew and John but in the Pauline writings as well. In this method the exposition of the text determined the textual form of the quotation itself. This was variously accomplished by (1) merging pertinent verses into one strongly expressive 'prooftext', (2) adapting the grammar to the NT context and application, (3) choosing appropriate renderings from known texts or Targums, and (4) creating *ad hoc* interpretations. All these devices were designed to best express the true meaning of the text as the NT writers understood it.[38]

As a general overview for the sake of areas of research, I summarize below TEXT TYPES AND COMMUNAL-EXEGETICAL TRADITIONS that may have influenced the form of a NT quotation.

TEXT-TYPES AND COMMUNAL EXEGETICAL TRADITIONS

A. Text-Types
1. MT (Hebrew)
2. Alternative Hebrew text tradition (as indicated by the existence of Greek *Kaige* translation)
3. Targum translations and interpretive traditions (Aramaic)
4. LXX traditions—
   a. LXX—OG or Old Greek
   b. *Kaige* (first century BC, which was used for LXX revisions)
   c. Aquila (AD 130)
   d. Symmachus (AD 180)
   e. Theodotion (end of second century)
   f. Lucian of Antioch (early third century)
   g. Origen's *Hexapla*

B. Communal-Exegetical Traditions
1. *Targumim* (reflecting an early interpretive tradition)
2. Hasidim/Pharisaical Sect (see, e.g., *The Psalms of Solomon*)
3. Essene (Qumran texts)

---

[38] *Paul's Use*, 148–49 (*italics* original).

4. Priestly (e.g., *Jubilees*)
5. Apocalyptic (e.g., *4 Ezra*; *2 Baruch*)
6. Jewish Resistance (e.g., Maccabean literature, the *War Scroll* of Qumran)
7. Jesus tradition (Gospels and early church)
8. Other early Christian teaching traditions such as kerygmatic (preaching) and catena, i.e., collections of proof-texts related to Jesus being the Messiah (e.g., *Didache*)
9. Proto-Rabbinic (e.g., as may be recovered in the *Mishnah*, ca. AD 200 and later)

Example—The Use of Lev 18:5 in Gal 3:12: In a doctoral seminar of mine an OT student, Tony Chen, wrote a paper that traced the use of Lev 18:5 inter-canonically as restated at Neh 9:29 and Ezek 18:9; 20:11 and then cited in Luke 10:28 and Rom 10:5. Moreover, Chen researched how Lev 18:5 was interpreted in the extra-biblical material at Qumran. By tracking this usage, Chen uncovered an interpretive tradition that accompanied this verse: Israel had failed to obey the Law and was punished because of this failure. Thus, Paul's recitation of Lev 18:5 ("He who practices them [the laws] shall live by them") in Gal 3:15 assumes the common Jewish understanding that Israel had failed to obey the Law and had come under God's punishment. This assumed and implied Jewish interpretation of Lev 18:5 helps explain Paul's argumentative logic in Gal 3:12.[39]

EXERCISE 8–K: As an exercise of inner-biblical and possible extra-biblical exegesis, explore the use of Lev 19:18 through the NT, OT, Targums, and extrabiblical sources.

Echoes and Allusions: We are often quite eager to find and describe deeper connections in Scripture. When reviewing a book that proposed allusions in 2 Corinthians, I began to conceive possible ways how such allusions might have been intended by authors and thus also potentially received by the audience(s):

> When an interpreter perceives a scriptural allusion or cultural reference in a text, there are several possible explanations: Such allusions/references were (1) intended by the original author to be "heard" by the whole/ideal audience in such a way that, in order for the audience to understand fully the message, they must recognize the reference; (2) intended by the original author to be appreciated by a select segment of the audience, who then would understand the message more fully and would perhaps (be expected to) instruct others of its finer points; (3) intentionally placed in the text, but as a matter of authorial reflection and preparation for the communication; in other words, the reference was not intended to play a significant role in the proper understanding of the message by the receptor audience; (4)

---

[39] See the critical assessment of Paul's logic that does not understand this interpretive tradition in Mika Hietanen, "Paul's Argumentation in Galatians 3.6–14," in *Proceedings of the Fifth Conference of the International Society for the Study of Argumentation*, ed. F. H. van Eemeren et al. (Amsterdam: Sic Sac, 2003), 477–83 and Mika Hietanen, *Paul's Argumentation in Galatians: A Pragma-Dialectical Analysis* (London: Bloomsbury T&T Clark, 2007). In the abstract to the book it is stated, "Paul's argumentation is found problematic in several respects."

unconsciously placed by the author in the text due to cultural influences and general knowledge; and/or (5) the ingeniousness of the modern interpreter to hear echoes and make correlations based on verbal and contextual clues in the text.[40]

These last two possibilities should give interpreters pause and motivate them to substantiate their position that an author has intentionally and meaningfully alluded to or echoed another text.

<u>Using Hays' Validation Criteria</u>: Hays has described seven criteria (below) by which to evaluate a claim to have heard an allusion or echo.[41] Additionally, Wright in *Paul in Fresh Perspective* has utilized Hays' intertextual criteria to find "echoes of Caesar."[42] To work with such a set of criteria would benefit any probe into the socio-cultural world and its possible influence upon any ancient text. Heuristically and methodologically, such a use of "inter-textual" criteria has already been anticipated by Robbins's socio-rhetorical analytic in which Robbins discusses intertexture (discussed above). Below are Hays's criteria as re-articulated by Wright (1.–7., slightly reworded). To these I would add four more criteria (8.–11.). Altogether these eleven criteria assist in determining and/or justifying the existence of deliberate textual allusion or even echoes to other texts, historical-social-cultural artifacts (coins, inscriptions, monument, customs, etc.), and social-cultural norms, roles, or institutions as may or may not be articulated in some "textual" form:

VALIDATION CRITERIA FOR INTERTEXTURAL ALLUSIONS OR ECHOES[43]

1. **Availability**: Was the material readily available and knowable in the culture at the time?
2. **Volume**: Is the word or the syntactical pattern repeated sufficiently in the immediate context to establish an 'audible' volume? How significant is this material in the original source and in its appropriation elsewhere in the NT author's day?
3. **Recurrence**: Does the word or theme recur elsewhere in the NT corpus being studied in sufficient quantity/quality for us to be able to establish a broader base of meaning?
4. **Thematic Coherence**: Does the theme cohere well with other aspects of what the NT author is saying? How well does it sit with the rest of the train of thought of the passage and the letter?
5. **Historical Plausibility**: Could the NT author have intended this meaning, or is it anachronistic or out of context when applied to the author? Would the author's readers have understood what was being hinting at? Does the intertextuality of the wider culture, the web of allusion and echo familiar more broadly, allow, facilitate, or encourage this kind of an implicit storyline?

---

[40] Roger David Aus, *Imagery of Triumph and Rebellion in 2 Corinthians 2:14–17 and Elsewhere in the Epistle: An Example of the Combination of Greco-Roman and Judaic Traditions in the Apostle Paul*, Studies in Judaism (Lanham, MD: University Press of America, 2005).

[41] Hays, *Echoes*.

[42] Wright, *Paul: In Fresh Perspective* (Minneapolis: Fortress, 2005), 61–62.

[43] I first developed the additional criteria (8.-11.) for a conference paper, "Discerning Empires in Ephesians: Trumping the Powers by the Triumphant One Lord Jesus Messiah," presented Nov 23, 2008 in the Disputed Paulines Sessions at the annual SBL Meeting, Boston, and then expanded adding (10.) for the paper, "'The God of This Age' (2 Cor 4:4) and Paul's Empire-Resisting Gospel," presented Nov 19, 2011 in the Intertextuality in the New Testament Session presented at the Annual Meeting of SBL, San Francisco.

6. **History of Interpretation**: Have other interpreters read the text in any way like this?[44]
7. **Satisfaction**: Does this reading enable the text to speak with new coherence and clarity? Does the text, read this way, settle down and make itself at home? Is there, in Hays' word, an 'aha' of fresh understanding when we read it like this?
*8. **Appropriateness/Relevance for the needs of the original Audience(s)** (related to 4. and 7.):[45] How might these echoes or allusions have benefited the audience or addressed their needs for a continued faithful response to the discourse at hand?
*9. **Authorial Situation** (related to 5.): Is there any relationship between the author's use and reliance on these echoes and allusions and his or her historical circumstances?
*10. **Geographic Prominence** (related to 1.): Are the social-cultural *realia* to be found prominently in the region to which the NT author is writing or from which he/she is writing, such that allusions would have been meaningful to him and/or to them?
*11. **Singularity or multiplicity of Origin:** Are there alternative origins for the echoes or allusions identified that could better account for their inclusion here? Or, is one origin arguably the most likely source? Should one source necessarily preclude or exclude assigning it to one or another origin?

After gathering evidence using these criteria, we then can assess the validity of an echo/allusion.

<u>**EXERCISE 8–L**</u>: Are you able to identify and evaluate (using Hays' criteria) allusions or echoes in the following texts in Romans? What are the interpretive implications in each passage?

    Rom 2:14–16   Rom 8:33   Rom 9:6

<u>Evaluating What is Required of Audiences to Comprehend the Meaning of the Text</u>: We may consider how likely an author intended the audience to make the intertextual connection to the OT source text based upon the explicitness and elaboration provided in the NT target text itself. In the following chart, I theorize how explicitness and elaboration of the source materials (OT) in the target text (NT) may relate to how important the source text is for the meaning and how familiar with the OT source text the NT audience is expected to be. Also, we may postulate: *To the degree that the author explains and elaborates upon the textual connection, the author expects less of the audience to recall the complete original context of the source text.* At the same time, the more explicit the citation, the more likely the original context comes to mind for the audience(s).

---

[44] Wright adds an important reflection on this criterion: "Again, an aside: if the answer were always 'yes', exegetes would be out of a job, since biblical study would collapse into church history; but the fact that exegetes have often been more concerned to apply the text to their own times than to understand it within its own mean that the answer 'no' will not be particularly surprising, and certainly ought not to be taken to mean, without more ado, that something has gone wrong" (*Paul*, 61).

[45] I am indebted to Benson Goh for understanding "appropriateness" as "relevance" in terms of Relevance Theory of communication (Dan Sperber and Deirdre Wilson) and in terms of relating appropriateness/relevance to Hays' criteria of satisfaction that includes satisfaction both of the interpreter and the original audience(s).

EXPLICITNESS AND ELABORATION OF OT QUOTATIONS

	Explicitness of OT Scripture (e.g., Quotation)	**Implicitness of OT Scripture (e.g., Allusion)**
More Elaboration or Explanation	less familiar to the audience(s) more important to the meaning	more familiar to the audience(s) more important to the meaning
Less Elaboration or Explanation	less familiar to the audience(s) less important to the meaning	more familiar to the audience(s) less important to the meaning

One example to illustrate the use of this chart is Eph 2:11–22. At 2:17 Paul quotes, but does not introduce, an amplified form of Isa 57:9 that is possibly conflated with Isa 52:7.

> 17 AND HE CAME AND PREACHED PEACE TO YOU WHO WERE FAR AWAY, AND PEACE TO THOSE WHO WERE NEAR; (NASB)

Yet earlier in Eph 2:13–14, the key ideas of "far away" and "near" and "peace" from Isa 57:9 are probably alluded to, but this is debated.[46] In my analysis, much elaboration is expended to the content of Isa 57:9 spanning several verses, yet the OT source text is clearly, yet implicitly, handled since it is not introduced. We could postulate, then, that the source text is certainly important for the meaning of the target passage in Ephesians and likely more familiar to the audience. A weakness in the model is that it doesn't account for various levels of textual familiarity in the audience.

<u>Ancient Literacy: The Textual, the Oral, the Aural, the Visual, and the Dramatic:</u>[47] This chapter's focus has been on texts, but this begs the question of the influence of the spoken word (oral), the heard word (aural), the seen word (visual), and the performed word (dramatic) in relation to textuality. Greatest attention has been given to the written word, and hence to literacy. However, literacy may include the ability to read and/or to write. Also, there are levels of reading: out loud or to oneself (apparently not occurring until AD 300s). A look at the ancient Greco-Roman world reveals a complex valuation of oral, textual, and visual (re)presentation within the Mediterranean context of performance.[48] By performance, I mean the public display of spectacle ranging from the travelling orator or sophist, to the annual dramatic and choral theatrical festivals

---

[46] John Muddiman, *The Epistle to the Ephesians*, Black's New Testament Commentary (London: Continuum, 2001), 122–23. It may be that Eph 2:14 alludes to Micah 5:5; so Ben Witherington III, *The Letters to Philemon, the Colossians, and the Ephesians: A Socio-Rhetorical Commentary on the Captivity Epistles* (Grand Rapids: Eerdmans, 2007), 259.

[47] The research presented in the next pages was "extra" material not included in my essay, "The Oral, the Textual, and the Visual (or, The Good, the Bad, and the Ugly) in Jesus's and Paul's Chiastic Performance of Scripture in 2 Corinthians, Ephesians, and Mark" in an edited Volume of the International Orality Network, *forthcoming*.

[48] This three-fold valuation has been affirmed in a recent collection of essays edited by Annette Weissenrieder and Robert B. Coote, *The Interface of Orality and Writing: Speaking, Seeing, Writing in the Shaping of New Genres*, WUNT 260 (Tübingen: Mohr Siebeck, 2010).

in *many* locations, to the provincial honorific games and circuses, and to the international triumphal parades. In each, the staged visual environment, engaging oration, and performed recitation were standard fare. Thus, at all these levels of performance the oral, textual, and visual converge in meaningful ways. Helpfully, a current trend in Biblical Studies includes "Performance Criticism" as well as a recovery of the value of the visual.[49]

The oft-cited work on *Ancient Literacy* (1989) by William V. Harris estimates ancient literacy rates in regions and time periods averaging often at or less than 10% of the total population. I am concerned, first, that Harris' methodological assumptions and framework are based upon modern studies of literacy, mostly from Europe, which I would judge to be anachronistic when applied to the Mediterranean world (ch.1 et *passim*). Second, I observe a repeated argumentative pattern that entails providing data that would suggest greater literary or semi-literacy, which is then immediately followed by "But" or "However" statements with rationales that too often involve opinion or conjecture (e.g., 106–10). My concern is that in following Harris' thesis, we overstate the case *against* reading literacy in the ancient world which is different than writing literacy.

Such a concern also applies to the work of John H. Walton and D. Brent Sandy, *The Lost World of Scripture: Ancient Literary Culture and Biblical Authority*.[50] This book is really missubtitled; it should be *Ancient Oral or Hearing Culture and Biblical Authority* since the authors repeatedly argue for the predominance of hearing culture and orality in the biblical world and its implications for understanding God's revelation in Scripture.[51] In addition to their twenty-one propositions, one adage of theirs succinctly summarizes their overstated thesis: "There was no

---

[49] For example, in addition to the regular sessions of "Performance Criticism of Biblical and Other Ancient Texts" and Society for Comparative Research on Iconographic and Performative Texts" (SCRIPT) founded in 2010, there were special sessions scheduled for 2014 in "Bible Translation" on "Performance and Bible Translation"; the Greco-Roman Religions has a unit dedicated to exploring "performance contexts and purposes"; Hellenistic Judaism section has a session dedicated to "Jews on the stage – Jews and the stage: From Ezekiel the Tragedian to performance theory." See also the website "Biblical Performance Criticism: *Orality, Memory, Translation, Rhetoric, Discourse, Drama*" http://www.biblicalperformancecriticism.org/ and the video found at that site, "Orality, Print Culture and Biblical Interpretation: A video by Eugene Botha" (http://youtu.be/ulIfpF-YcoM). For biblical scholar's applications and assessments, see, e.g., Maia Kotrosits, "The Rhetoric of Intimate Spaces: Affect and Performance in the Corinthian Correspondence," *Union Seminary Quarterly Review* 62.3–4 (2010): 134–51; David Trobisch, "Performance Criticism as an Exegetical Method: A Story, Three Insights, and Two Jokes," in *The Interface of Orality and Writing: Speaking, Seeing, Writing in the Shaping of New Genres*, ed. Annette Weissenrieder and Robert B. Coote, WUNT 260 (Tübingen: Mohr Siebeck, 2010), 194–201; and Ernst R. Wendland, "Performance Criticism: Assumptions, Applications, and Assessment," *TIC Talk* 65 (2008): 1–12.

[50] John H. Walton and D. Brent Sandy, *The Lost World of Scripture: Ancient Literary Culture and Biblical Authority* (Downers Grove, Ill.: IVP Academic, 2013).

[51] Eleven of the twenty-one "propositions" (corresponding to their chapters) contain oral, orality, or hearing culture dominance, as compared to the ten referring to literary or written culture or literature, but often in a negative evaluative light: e.g., "Proposition 8: Jesus' world was predominantly non-literate and oral"; "Proposition 12: Throughout the New Testament, spoken words rather than written words were the primary focus"; "Proposition 17: The genres of the New Testament are more connected to orality than textuality"; "Proposition 18: Affirmations about the origin of Scripture confirm its fundamental oral nature."

reading public, only public reading."[52] Recent conferences and publications on orality and textuality by classical scholars describe the complexity of the data; a repeated theme is the importance of "performance" as a context to understand orality and textuality, which entails literacy.[53]

Orality influenced the production of texts; the oral and textual where constructed as and for performance. In the Greek world, the oral and textual dimensions of communication co-existed and mutually informed each other both in poetry (esp. Homer) and in the rhetorical tradition from their inception in the eighth- and fifth-centuries BC, respectively, through into the NT era and beyond. Put simply, oral metrical style and persuasive technique were conveyed in written form intended for memorization for live, visual performance. Writing down such performances allowed for broader dissemination and subsequent circulation that further facilitated careful study by later students for further emulation, often several centuries removed. This written and oral culture was embedded early in *paideia*. Homer canonized Greek culture and unified the diverse Greek world with its foundation narratives and myths. So powerful was Homer that Vergil derived from him the *Aeneid* to explain Rome's mythical foundation by relating how Anchises sailed with Odysseus and fathered Aeneas through Aphrodite/Venus. True, Vergil wrote to support the Augustan regime and its right to rule on the basis of having divine descendants (Aeneas's mother was Venus)—but the written and the performed word were powerful allies in the advancement of legitimate rule.

There is a life cycle of mimesis in representation. Indeed, all around the Greek world into the Roman period were found the annual, biannual, or quadrennial festivals with live, choreographed performances of lyric choruses and of dramatic theater that *required verbatim mastery of discourse*. For example, Pelliccia Hayden considers this in view of orality/textuality. In the Dionysia festival in Athens (beginning ca. 508 BC), there were ten competing diathryambic lyric performances requiring 500 boy choristers each; other performers were also needed. For any year for this Athenian festival, this would require some 7,000 performers out of a population of 30,000 to

---

[52] Walton and Sandy, *Lost World*, 23.

[53] E.g., Peter Keegan et al. *Written Space in the Latin West, 200 BC to AD 300* (London: Continuum, 2013); William A. Johnson and Holt N. Parker, eds., *Ancient Literacies: The Culture of Reading in Greece and Rome* (Oxford: Oxford University Press, 2009); E. Anne Mackay, ed., *Orality, Literacy, Memory in the Ancient Greek and Roman World*, Mnemosyne Supplements 298 (Leiden: Brill, 2008); Elizabeth Minchin, ed., *Orality, Literacy and Performance in the Ancient World*, Mnemosyne Supplements; Monographs on Greek and Latin Language and Literature 335 (Leiden; Boston: Brill, 2012). In addition, several monographs reassess the data from different segments and time periods; Katharine Derderian, *Leaving Words to Remember: Greek Mourning and the Advent of Literacy*, Mnemosyne, Bibliotheca Classica Batava 209 (Leiden; Boston: Brill, 2001); William A. Johnson, *Readers and Reading Culture in the High Roman Empire: A Study of Elite Communities*, Classical Culture & Society Series (Oxford: Oxford University Press, 2010); Susan Niditch, *Oral World and Written Word: Ancient Israelite Literature*, Library of Ancient Israel (Louisville: Westminster John Knox, 1996); Kevin Robb, *Literacy and Paideia in Ancient Greece* (New York: Oxford University Press, 1994); Rosalind Thomas, *Literacy and Orality in Ancient Greece*, Key Themes in Ancient History (Cambridge: Cambridge University Press, 1992); Yun Lee Too, *The Idea of the Library in the Ancient World* (Oxford: Oxford University Press, 2010); Roger D. Woodard, *Greek Writing from Knossos to Homer: A Linguistic Interpretation of the Origin of the Greek Alphabet and the Continuity of Ancient Greek Literacy* (New York: Oxford University Press, 1997).

40,000, or about 20%—this is extremely high. Hyaden concludes, "In short, we have every reason to believe that this was a society that had an experience and expectation of the verbatim repetition of precisely fixed poetic texts."[54] *The mechanism presumes a fixed, written text.* The proliferation of dramatic and choral competitions was culturally immense; so popular and prestigious were these competitions that the emperor Nero in his own newly established games, the Neronian, won the Latin oratory and verse as well as the lyre-playing contests (Seut. *Nero* 12.3).

But, what can be said of other types of performance discourse like statuary and architecture? Temples were places of spectacle and text. They could be read, as Vergil aptly indicated, when describing people gazing at the doors of the temple a Cumae: *perlegerent oculis* ("they read with their eyes"; *Aeneid* 6.34).[55] Indeed, temples were strategically constructed and located to bring more prominence to them. Let's look at one region. Between the years 35 BC to AD 60, over fifty Imperial temples and shrines have been found and identified in Asia Minor.[56] Temples honoring Augustus and *Roma* (the Roman people deified) were built in key cities in Asia Minor, and as close to Jerusalem as Caesarea Maritima by Herod the Great. Paul was housed there for two years, a location occupying the largest segment of narrative space apart from Jerusalem (Acts 23:23–26:32). A particularly fine (and unique) specimen is the imperial cult temple complex of Aphrodisias of Asia Minor, between Ephesus and Colossae, which contained eighty or more reliefs to "create visual allegory for imperial rule" constructed in the Julio-Claudian period and finished at the beginning of Nero's reign.[57] The size, composition, and representation tell the story of Rome's superiority. Each of the fifty reliefs of the nations showed them personified as women in characteristic dress in varying states of Romanization—well-dressed or with tunic falling off the shoulder and hands crossed as if bound. Under each was a designating inscribed title, ΕΘΝΟΥΣ followed by the genitive indicating the specific people group, "of the nation of the _____." Text points to image; or does the image point to the text? At this very same time and region, the apostle Paul was actively proclaiming the gospel of Christ crucified for the nations.

Rhetoric, too, reflected the textual, oral, and performative. In its earliest formal development, rhetorical technique of persuasion grew to resolve land disputes in Syracuse after the overthrow of its tyrants and the reclamation of land rights there.[58] Syracusian rhetoricians influenced the litigious Athenians, whose political reputation and career, or even life, depended on successful-

---

[54] Pelliccia Hayden, "Two Points About Rhapsodes," in *Homer, the Bible, and Beyond: Literary and Religious Canons in the Ancient World*, ed. Margalit Finkelberg and Guy G. Stroumsa; Jerusalem Studies in Religion and Culture 2 (Leiden: Brill, 2003), 97–116 at 102.

[55] Jaś Elsner, ed. *Art and Text in Roman Culture* (Cambridge: Cambridge University Press, 1996), 1.

[56] Tallied from S. R. F. Price, *Rituals and Power: The Roman Imperial Cult in Asia Minor* (Cambridge: Cambridge University Press, 1984), 249–74.

[57] See R. R. R. Smith, "The Imperial Reliefs from the Sebasteion at Aphrodisias," *JRS* 77 (1987): 88–138 at 119. He describes the complex as containing "a rare combination of buildings, sculpture, and inscriptions from a unified excavated context and providing an unrivalled picture of the physical setting of the imperial cult in a Greek city" (88).

[58] The following summary is drawn from "2.3 Written or spoken rhetoric: oratory and orality" in Long, *Ancient Rhetoric*, 31–33 et passim.

ly defending themselves in court—there were no lawyers—so men represented themselves; not uncommonly they would hire a *logographer* (lit. "a speech writer"), who would analyze the case, determine the best means to argue, and write out a speech response that then the litigant would memorize to deliver before the court or political assembly.

In this dual oral and textual climate, an important early fourth-century debate occurred between Isocrates and Alcidamus whether rhetoric should be conceived as an oral or written discipline. Alcidamus defended extemporaneous delivery, self-admittedly ironically publishing his written speech entitled, "On the Sophists" or "On the Writers of Written Discourses." At one point he argued, "[When written speeches] appear to be constructed and composed with much preparation, they fill the minds of listeners with distrust and resentment" (12).[59] A similar irony existed in the philosophical apparent disdain for "popular literacy" by Plato whose "oral" dialogical works were nevertheless written down and transmitted textually.[60] To some degree, Isocrates's view won out; philosophical works and speeches were textually published for propagandist purposes, even if not simply to "have the last word."[61]

Beginning in the third-century BC, the speeches were collected in libraries, the ten Attic orators "canonized," and subsequently studied for imitation. As rhetorical theory continued to develop and handbooks to be written, the dependence on and appeal to the Attic orators attests to the value of written speeches.[62] Something similar happens in the Latin rhetorical tradition in Cicero (ca. 60–50 BC) and Quintilian (ca. AD 80). On this topic, the classical scholar Richard L. Enos concludes: "The unity of oral and written expression was so inextricably bound in ancient discourse that its oneness was an unquestioned presumption upon which theories of rhetoric were developed."[63]

Jesus and Paul participated in this performance culture in which speakers negotiated, as Jeroen Lauwers describes, "the transfer from book reading to the performance of *paideia*."[64] *Paideia, here, means one's education. At issue is when to show one's education, when not to, and,*

---

[59] Johan Schloemann, "Entertainment and Democratic Distrust: The Audience's Attitudes towards Oral and Written Oratory in Classical Athens," in *Epea and Grammata: Oral and Written Communication in Ancient Greece*, ed. Ian Worthington and John Miles Foley, Orality and Literacy in Ancient Greece 4; Mnemosyne, bibliotheca classica Batava, Supplementum 230 (Leiden; Boston: Brill, 2002), 133–46 at 140.

[60] See Mathilde Cambron-Goulet, "The Criticism—and the Practice—of Literacy in the Ancient Philosophical Tradition," in *Orality, Literacy and Performance in the Ancient World*, ed. Elizabeth Minchin; Mnemosyne Supplements. Monographs on Greek and Latin Language and Literature 335 (Leiden; Boston: Brill, 2012), 201–26.

[61] Thomas Hubbard, "Getting the Last Word: Publication of Political Oratory as an Instrument of Historical Revisionism," in *Orality, Literacy, Memory in the Ancient Greek and Roman World*, ed. by E. Anne Mackay; Mnemosyne Supplements 298 (Leiden: Brill, 2008), 185–202.

[62] For a detailed summary, see Long, *Ancient Rhetoric*, 23–24.

[63] "Heuristic Structures of Dispositio in Oral and Written Rhetorical Composition: An Addendum to Ochs' Analysis of the Verrine Orations," *Central States Speech Journal* 35 (1984): 77–83 at 78.

[64] Jeroen Lauwers, "Reading Books, Talking Culture: The Performance of Paideia in Imperial Greek Literature," in *Orality, Literacy and Performance in the Ancient World*, ed. E. Minchin; Mnemosyne Supplements. Monographs on Greek and Latin Language and Literature 335 (Leiden; Boston: Brill, 2012), 227–44 at 228.

how to show it. Paul's physical presence was critiqued as "weak" at the same time his speech was "to be treated with scorn" (2 Cor 10:10; cf. Gal 4:14). But the need for education through written media was never in question for those entering "the public forum" (to use a metaphor of ancient political space). For example, Quintilian was commissioned by the emperor Domitian to write a rhetoric manual that he accomplished in five sections in four books. His work effectively synthesized the tradition; for students he provided reading lists, the structure of which are instructive, as explained by Amiel D. Vardi, "The reading list offered by Quintilian in the tenth book of his *Institutio Oratoria*, for instance, enumerates first Greek authors, and then Latin ones, thus reproducing the physical structure of Roman public libraries, in which Greek and Latin texts were stored in two distinct wings."[65] Indeed, Quintilian aligns with the tradition begun in the first-century BC of rhetorical theoreticians commending "reading lists in manuals of rhetoric" covering a variety of literary forms, not just oratory (poetry, historiography, and philosophy), for the purpose of mimesis and *imitatio*. Such lists followed the established practice of librarians to provide catalogues and canons of ancient authors across a broad array of literary genres.[66] But, again, such lists of written texts by librarians were constructed for the educational purpose of perfecting oratorical performance by reading for memorizing for imitation for enhanced performance.

Ancient Libraries: How common and accessible were ancient libraries? What function did they have? How might their existence relate to the topic of orality, to ancient literacy, and to reading practices? Where were libraries found? These are important questions. I should say at the outset that ancient libraries were mainly not like our own. They were integrally related to royalty, religion, and power, beginning in Egypt and exploding in the early Roman Empire. Private library collections in homes were as old as Egypt;[67] but mostly, libraries were sacred trusts located in palaces, temples, and tombs.[68] This religious dimension, however, stands out. Fayza M. Haikal concludes her survey on private library collections in Egypt that led to the establishment of the Alexandrian Library, "It is interesting to see that institutionalized research centers and libraries were often associated with religious institutions and placed under the protection of divinities or muses."[69] Not surprisingly, certain libraries gained genealogical narratives to account for their origins, authority, and even power.[70] Additionally, in his discussion of libraries, Yun Lee Too includes a

---

[65] Amiel D. Vardi, "Canons of Literary Texts at Rome," in *Homer, the Bible, and Beyond: Literary and Religious Canons in the Ancient World*, ed. Margalit Finkelberg and Guy G. Stroumsa; Jerusalem Studies in Religion and Culture 2 (Leiden: Brill, 2003), 131–52 at 132. See the extended discussion, in the same edited volume, by Hubert Cancik, "Standardization and Ranking of Texts in Greek and Roman Institutions," 117–30 at 126–28.

[66] Vardi, "Canons," 135–36.

[67] *Contra* Walton and Sandy, "Personal libraries were nearly non-existent" (*Lost World*, 21 n8).

[68] Fayza M. Haikal, "Private Collections and Temple Libraries in Ancient Egypt," in *What Happened to the Ancient Library of Alexandria?* ed. Mostafa El-Abbadi and Omnia Mounir Fathallah; Library of the Written Word 3; The Manuscript World 1 (Leiden; Boston: Brill, 2008), 39–54.

[69] Haikal, "Private Collections," 54.

[70] In his opening chapter "The Birth of *a* Library" Yun Lee Too traces one such library from Athens to the East, back to Athens, to Egypt and then to Rome (*Idea of the Library*, 19–49). He summarizes, "What will emerge from this story of textual adoption is the power of canonicity and the association of text collections with political pow-

chapter entitled, "Picture Libraries: Statues among the Books"; indeed, Too shows how text and image converge in the library and serves "as a doorway into a subjective imaginary domain."[71] We see the visual once again. Thus, although libraries were locations of focused learning—repositories for the study of both ancient and current written works, authorities, and ideas—they also reflected and participated in visual culture.

Lionel Casson in his monograph, *Libraries in the Ancient World*, describes the rise of private and public libraries.[72] We are all likely familiar with the Alexandrian library established by Ptolemy I in the third-century BC; purportedly, it had civic authority to confiscate any manuscripts from incoming vessels, to copy them, and to return the copy back to the vessels, keeping the original for the library's collection.[73] Whether apocryphal or not, the intensive library cataloguing activity exemplified at Alexandria is truly remarkable. Estimates of the number of ancient works housed there range from 100,000 to 700,000.[74] Summarizing the vastness of this collection, immediately Walton and Sandy assert, "But even with the increasing focus on written texts in the Hellenistic period, a culture of orality was still prominent."[75] However, written texts were not an increasing focus—they were an already present one.

How early and extensive was such a focus on written texts? The famous librarian at Alexandria, Callimachos of Cyrene, in the third-century BC produced a massive historical catalogue of Greek literature: "His huge work, the *pinakes*, in 120 rolls, presented a bibliography of Greek literature and a catalogue of the Alexandrian Library, organized by subject and genre, and including some biographical notes on the authors he mentions and the first line of each of their works."[76] Although we cannot know for certain the length of these rolls, 35 feet was a common length, with a maximum length of 133 feet also being recorded.[77] So, just how many records of individual titles could 120 scrolls hold?[78] If we figure four authors or works per foot on a 35 foot roll (a conservative estimate), the estimate would be around 17,000. This number is staggering to consider. What does this suggest about ancient literacy understood as the ability to "read" such that so many books would be written and come into existence and circulation? *How many ancient readers were there?*

Extensive libraries existed elsewhere, such as at Athens, Pergamum, Carthage, Ephesus (ca. AD 100) and Pompeii; others are incidentally mentioned, such as in Halicarnassus and Rhodi-

---

er. The library's passage is, as it would appear, a trajectory of power in the ancient world" (20).

[71] Too, *Idea of the Library*, 192.

[72] Casson, *Libraries*.

[73] On the historical precedent to and subsequent history of the Alexandrian library, see Mostafa El-Abbadi and Omnia Mounir Fathallah, eds., *What Happened to the Ancient Library of Alexandria?* Library of the Written Word 3; The Manuscript World 1 (Leiden; Boston: Brill, 2008).

[74] Walton and Sandy, *Lost World*, 83.

[75] Walton and Sandy, *Lost World*, 83.

[76] Goody, *Domestication of the Savage Mind*.

[77] Michael Avi-Yonah, *Ancient Scrolls: Introduction to Archaeology* (Jerusalem: Jerusalem Publishing House, 2004), 16.

[78] Ancient written works—such as in Hebrew, Greek, Latin—were split into book divisions corresponding to scroll lengths; Homer was split into 24 rolls (Avi-Yonah, *Ancient Scrolls*, 16).

apolis of Asia Minor and others.[79] Harris importantly relates, "Tens of thousands of texts were visible on the walls of Pompeii at the moment of its destruction"; yet his view that *a few hundred literate slaves or school boys* may account for these texts over a few years or decades is simply humorous.[80] Casson more optimistically surmises, "Clearly, reading and writing were not limited to an elite upper crust of the town's population. And there is no reason to think that Pompeii was exceptional; other Italian communities must have been equally literate."[81]

Indeed, evidence from Asia Minor and Egypt support broader literacy among the masses. Based on the piles of discarded papyri of literary works found at Oxyrhynchus in Egypt that date to the first few centuries, Charles Oldfather comments, "The higher education, which had practically been monopolized by Alexandria, had spread to the country."[82] For Asia Minor, Bruno Blumenfeld has shed particular light on the intellectual and literary environment since digests, compendiums, and doxographies of philosophers were in wide circulation in the rhetorical schools; Tarsus of Syria was a great center of, in particular, Stoic learning in the apostle Paul's day; Paul would have had primary and quick accessibility to these various philosophical systems should he have wanted to.[83] More generally, also quite an extensive book trade existed across the Roman world as a result of the *Pax Romana*.[84]

H. L. Pinner, exploring *The World of Books in Classical Antiquity*, concludes: "[T]he level of culture and thought in the various hellenistic lands of the Mediterranean—outside the great centres of culture—would seem to reveal no outstanding differences."[85] Several details of Pinner's review are worth summarizing (page numbers are indicated in parentheses): Egyptian papyri contain privately made copies of books (11); publishing houses developed a particular fine script for book trade (15); some books included illustrations and portraits of the author (e.g., Vergil) (16); frescos have been found in Naples of women reading books (18); book codices are known by Martial at the end of the first-century "in miniature format for traveling, for school editions and an-

---

[79] Casson, *Libraries*, 120–21. Casson soberly comments, "Our information about the existence of ancient libraries, as about so many aspects of the ancient world, derives from haphazard sources. We know of a library at Carthage only because of a writer's casual remark; we know of one at Timgad only because of the exceptionally thorough excavation of the site. It so happens that, in the miscellany of Greek and Roman writings that through hit-or-miss circumstance have come down to us, no mention occurs of libraries at, say, Marseilles or Narbonne, although there is every reason to think they existed there" (120).

[80] *Ancient Literacy*, 260.

[81] Casson, *Libraries*, 110. He also states, "by the middle of the first century A.D. literacy had reached a high level, to judge from what we find at Pompeii, that unique supplier of information about Roman daily life" (109).

[82] Charles Henry Oldfather, *The Greek Literary Texts from Greco-Roman Egypt: A Study in the History of Civilization*, University of Wisconsin Studies in the Social Sciences and History 9 (Madison: University of Wisconsin Press, 1923), 84.

[83] Bruno Blumenfeld, *The Political Paul: Justice, Democracy and Kingship in a Hellenistic Framework*, JSNTSup 210 (London: T&T Clark, 2003), esp. 19–22; see also a brief historical discussion of such doxographies being disseminated after the death of Cicero in Mark Morford, *The Roman Philosophers: From the Time of Cato the Censor to the Death of Marcus Aurelius* (London and New York: Routledge, 2002), esp. 134.

[84] See H. L. Pinner, *The World of Books in Classical Antiquity* (Leiden: A. W. Sijthoff, 1958).

[85] Pinner, *World of Books*, 27.

thologies, in short, for uses which tough is better suited than delicate papyrus." These parchment books were less expensive than papyrus and more durable (19); there was no profit in publishing, so it was done for idealistic or political reasons (26); types of works included "classics, anthologies, collections of proverbs, digests, and ... light reading matter of little value" (26).

The Function(s) of Ancient Private and Public Libraries: But how did ancient libraries function? Libraries did not primarily exist to check out books indiscriminately. The earliest librarians happily discriminated; not just anyone could access their materials.[86] Importantly, librarians were also interested in the accuracy and claim of authenticity of what they collected.[87] Concerning private libraries, from Cicero and other ancient authors we learn that friends shared access to each other's libraries; they were concerned, too, with theft. One unusually large private collection may have belonged to Philodemus (ca. 75–40 BC), an Epicurean philosopher who studied at Athens, lived in Rome, and retired at Herculaneum. A library containing some Latin but mostly Greek books of Philodemus was found at Piso's "Villa of the Papyri," the father-in-law of Julius Caesar and good friend of Philodemus. The 1,800 scrolls were kept in a room three meters square with shelved walls up to eye level; the room enjoyed immediate access to an adjacent colonnade for comfortable reading.[88] Such private library collections were often copied for populating public library holdings.[89]

In Rome the first public library planned was commissioned by Julius Caesar and entrusted to Marcus Varro, a philosopher, who had written a work, "On Libraries"; the project was taken up and finished by one of Caesar's supporters just years after his death.[90] Whereas at one time people had needed to travel to Greek cultural centers to purchase books, under the Roman Republic books gained greater and greater accessibility. Joreon Lauwers summarizes, "as a result of the construction of large public libraries by the Roman emperors and officials in the Imperial cities, books which were not in a person's home library could also be consulted if any need for that was felt."[91] By the end of the first-century AD, the Roman poet Martial described four different book makers selling his books in various sizes and editions; book dealers would employ scribes to go to a library to make a copy of a work to bring back and sell.[92] Thus, *reading literacy was widespread even if writing literacy was not.* It is particularly intriguing, too, that Paul mentions "the parchments" (τὰς μεμβράνας) in 2 Tim 4:13, likely referring to the codex book form that had only just developed in the second half of first-century AD; the earliest Christians capitalized on this new media in the production of their manuscripts;[93] such was the value of the written word.

---

[86] Casson admits, however, "At least some libraries permitted borrowing" (*Libraries*, 107).

[87] Casson recounts Domitian's repopulating of a library destroyed by fire that included sending scribes to Alexandria to check the accuracy of copies against "the trustworthy versions in Alexandria" (*Libraries*, 103).

[88] Casson, *Libraries*, 74-75. Currently, the scrolls are carbonized from the volcanic eruption of Vesuvius.

[89] Casson, *Libraries*, 102. In addition, authors would contribute their works.

[90] Casson, *Libraries*, 79–80.

[91] Lauwers, "Reading Books," 231, 80–123

[92] Casson, *Libraries*, 103–106.

[93] Comfort, *Encountering the Manuscripts*, 29–30.

TERTIARY INTERPRETIVE PROCEDURES:[94]

1. Locate all quotations and strong allusions within your passage, if any.
2. If no quotation or strong allusion to Scripture is present, then consider whether there may be a deliberate allusion or echo. Use Hays' criteria to validate or not any proposed allusion or echo.
3. If quotations or allusions are present, consider what the underlying original text (*Vorlage*) was: LXX, Hebrew, something else? What changes in the text are observed? What clauses, phrases, or verses have been changed or omitted? Such differences may alert you to important themes.
4. Next, study the original context(s) of the OT passage(s) quoted, alluded to, or echoed and consider what important themes connect them to the NT passage in context, especially God's saving plan and purposes to address human problems.
5. Consider what Jewish mode of interpretation is present (e.g., *mashal*, typological, *halakah*) and whether a specific exegetical technique may be operative (e.g., Hillel's Seven Rules).
6. Consider how the use of quoted, alluded to, or echoed material in the NT may itself embed the author's interpretation for the audience(s).
7. Survey the use of the OT passage in early and late Judaism and early Christianity, considering what communal-exegetical tradition(s) the use of Scripture may participate in.
8. Why was this scriptural material used in the NT context?
9. Consider the theological meaning and implications of the quotation, allusion, or echo.
10. Record any questions or other considerations for future research.

IV. BIBLIOGRAPHY

Primary Survey

    Gospel and Pauline Parallels

        Francis, Fred O., and J. Paul Sampley. *Pauline Parallels*. 2nd ed. Philadelphia: Fortress, 1984.

        Synopsis of the Four Gospels (Greek-English Edition of the Synopsis Quattuor Evangeliorum). Ed. Kurt Aland, 12th ed. Stuttgart: Deutsche Bibelgesellschaft, 2001.

        Throckmorton, Jr. Burton H. *Gospel Parallels: A Comparison of the Synoptic Gospels, New Revised Standard Version*. 5th rev. ed. Nashville: Thomas Nelson, 1992.

    The OT in the NT

        Archer, Gleason Leonard, Gregory Chirichigno, and Evangelical Theological Society. *Old Testament Quotations in the New Testament*. Chicago: Moody, 1983.

        Bratcher, Robert G., and United Bible Societies. Committee on Translations. *Old Testament Quotations in the New Testament*. 3rd rev. ed. Helps for Translators. London:

---

[94] These procedures can be compared with those of G. K. Beale, *Handbook on the New Testament Use of the Old Testament: Exegesis and Interpretation* (Grand Rapids: Baker Academic, 2012), 42–43.

United Bible Societies, 1987.

Evans, Craig A.. "Midrash," Pages 544–47 in *Dictionary of Jesus and the Gospels* ed. Joel B. Green, Scot McKnight, and I. Howard Marshall; 1st ed. Downers Grove, IL: InterVarsity, 1992.

Kaiser, Walter C. *The Uses of the Old Testament in the New*. Chicago: Moody Press, 1985.

Moyise, Steve. *The Old Testament in the New: An Introduction*. 2nd ed. T&T Clark Approaches to Biblical Studies. New York: Bloomsbury T&T Clark, 2015.

Scott, J. Julius. *Jewish Backgrounds of the New Testament*. Grand Rapids: Baker, 2000 [repr. of 1995]. [See particularly Scott's discussion of Jewish exegetical techniques.]

Smith, Jerome H. *The New Treasury of Scripture Knowledge: The Most Complete Listing of Cross References Available Anywhere—Every Verse, Every Theme, Every Important Word*. Nashville: Thomas Nelson, 1992.

Secondary Study

Beale, G. K. *Handbook on the New Testament Use of the Old Testament: Exegesis and Interpretation*. Grand Rapids: Baker Academic, 2012.

_____. and D. A. Carson. *Commentary on the New Testament Use of the Old Testament*. Grand Rapids: Baker Academic, 2007.

Berding, Kenneth, and Jonathan Lunde, eds. *Three Views on the New Testament Use of the Old Testament*. Grand Rapids: Zondervan, 2008.

Ellis, E. Earle. *Prophesy and Hermeneutic in Early Christianity: New Testament Essays*. Grand Rapids: Eerdmans, 1978.

_____. *Paul's Use of the Old Testament*. Grand Rapids: Baker Academic, 1981.

_____. *The Old Testament in Early Christianity: Canon and Interpretation in the Light of Modern Research*. Grand Rapids: Baker, 1991.

Evans, Craig A. *From Prophecy to Testament: The Function of the Old Testament in the New*. Peabody, MA: Hendrickson, 2004.

Hays, Richard B. *Echoes of Scripture in the Letters of Paul*. New Haven: Yale University Press, 1989.

Porter, Stanley E. *Hearing the Old Testament in the New Testament*. McMaster New Testament Studies. Grand Rapids: Eerdmans, 2006.

Tertiary Research

Hatch, Edwin, and Henry A. Redpath. *A Concordance to the Septuagint and the Other Greek Versions of the Old Testament (Including the Apocryphal Books)*. 3 Vols. Graz: Akademische Druck Verlagsanstalt, 1954; reprint. Grand Rapids: Baker, 1987.

Robbins, Vernon K. *The Tapestry of Early Christian Discourse: Rhetoric, Society, and Ideology*. London; New York: Routledge, 1996, ch. 4 [cf. idem, *Exploring the Texture of Texts*. Valley Forge, PA: Trinity Press International, 1996, ch. 2]

Ramage, Craufurd Tait. *Scripture Parallels in Ancient Classics or Bible Echoes*. Edinburgh: Adam and Charles Black, 1878.

PART IV:

MOVING TOWARDS APPROPRIATING THE WORD

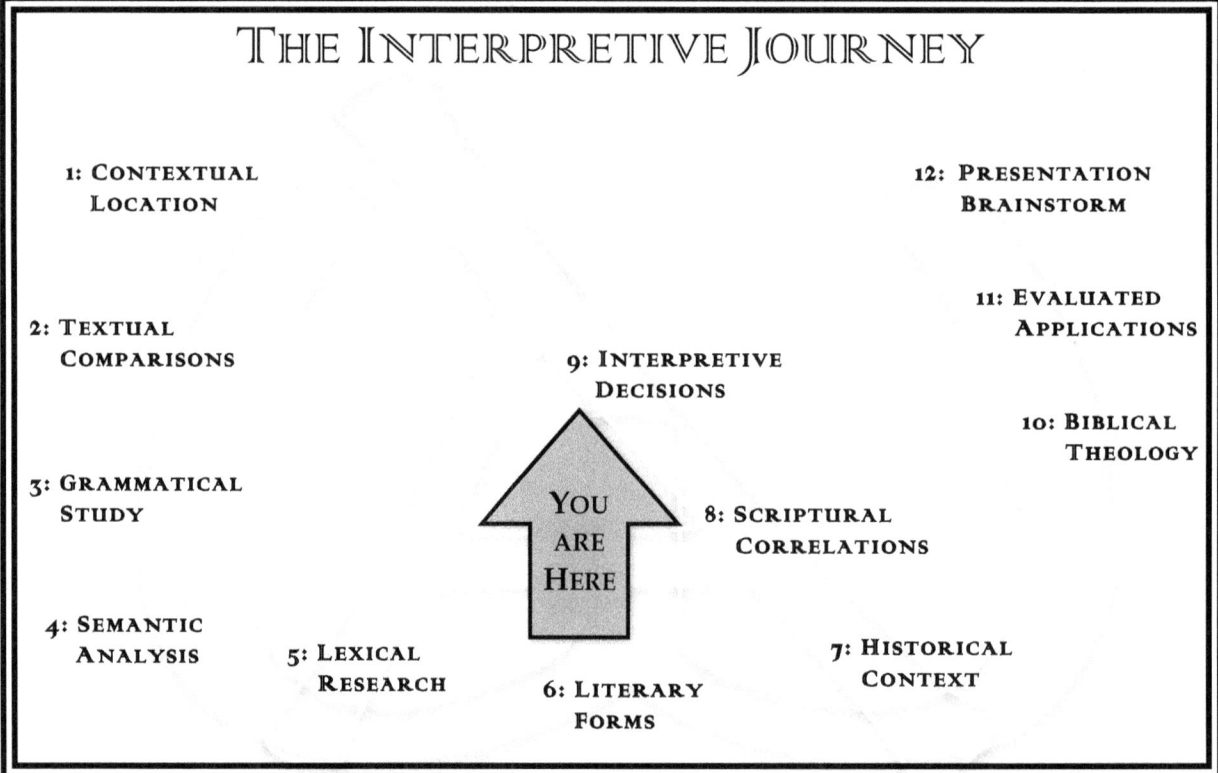

STEP 9

INTERPRETIVE DECISIONS

"If I had 60 minutes to solve a problem and my life depended on it, I'd spend 55 minutes determining the right question to ask. Once I got the right question, I could easily answer it in 5 minutes."

—Albert Einstein

Introduction: We are no Einstein, but the principle applies in our situation of attempting to interpret biblical materials. Even though there are countless books on interpreting the Bible, the actual process of *interpretation proper* is not well described even in beginning books on biblical interpretation.[1] Although these books often provide necessary "perspectives" and hermeneutical principles (genre, context, etc.), they fail to provide a step-by-step process for students to follow.

---

[1] I have been profoundly affected by my mentor David Bauer and much of the material of this chapter and the next is summarizing, adapting, and supplementing Bauer and Traina, *Inductive Bible Study*, chs. 14–16.

Essentially the process is this: Identify worthwhile questions that need answering, collect appropriate data as evidence for answering the questions, assess the data gathered, and then decide on the most likely interpretation. Principles that inform this exegetical task of interpretation include CAP (Consider All Possibilities) and MOM (Major on Majors and Minor on Minors).

I. PRIMARY SURVEY & II. SECONDARY STUDY

<u>Orientation</u>: In this chapter I have combined PRIMARY SURVEY and SECONDARY STUDY. What would differentiate them is not so much the perspective of method or the procedures, but the ability to access and evaluate relevant data. For example, performing SECONDARY STUDY, one should access and include evidence from the Greek of the NT. Before describing the "logic" of gathering and assessing evidence, one needs to understand something of what is called "the history of interpretation" and how to ask good questions that need answers. Next, one must understand the logical movement of considering types of evidence, gathering relevant evidences in an orderly fashion, drawing interpretive inferences from those stated evidences, and then weighing and deciding the best answer to the question. This ANALYTICAL INTERPRETIVE WORKFLOW is very rigorous and not always possible to perform since the evidences are so interconnected and time is limited. Thus, also PRIMARY AND SECONDARY INTERPRETIVE PROCEDURES are provided that merge sound interpretive principles and priorities with the practicality of limited time, energy, and resources.

<u>History of Interpretation</u>: There are traditions of interpretation that are rehearsed in commentaries on Scripture. This is both good and bad. More substantial commentaries will usually survey this history of interpretation and interact with it rather thoroughly. Importantly, the history of interpretation provides some parameters or even constraints on the interpretive options for a given passage. Understanding this history informs and guides our study; we join the community of interpreters. We may likely discover that there are questions and evidence that we did not discover from our own careful study. We must consider that *interpreters and commentators have invested large portions of their lives (decades even!) to ponder biblical questions, gather evidence, and then interpret the meaning of the text*. So, we would do well to consider the findings of others who have spent considerable time preparing themselves and studying to interpret Scripture well.

At the same time, only looking at the history of interpretation as found in commentaries may prevent us from properly observing what is in the text and what the text wants us to properly focus upon. Additionally, our survey of the history of interpretation may bog us down in secondary matters that too often leave *the heart of the pericope largely untouched and underappreciated*. In fact, after studying Matt 5:48 carefully in context, I was shocked at how poorly this verse was treated in major commentaries. You will be able to interpret 5:48 below.

> Interpreters and commentators have invested large portions of their lives (decades even!) to ponder biblical questions, gather evidence, and then interpret the meaning of the text.

About Interpretive Questions: Throughout this process of walking *In Step with God's Word*, you have been making observations and asking questions. It is time to select which questions you want to gather evidence to answer. Questions will typically fall within these broad areas:

1. **theological matters** of the nature of God, Christ, Holy Spirit and our relationship with God;
2. **moral**, **formative**, and **pragmatic matters** pertaining to living in the world;
3. **historical matters** concerning society, culture, and ideology; and/or
4. (apparent) **discrepancies** or **difficulties between accounts** concerning various details.

These areas may overlap. You may consult dedicated books that address "difficulties" and "hard sayings" which serious minded Bible critics and skeptics have identified (see the BIBLIOGRAPHY). However, as you consider what questions to devote time answering, remember these things:

1. What the general purport of Scripture is, namely, God's revelation of God's self to humanity, our reconciliation with him through Christ Jesus that involves moral reformation into his likeness, and the future hope of being directly in the presence of the Lord involving our glorious bodily redemption, a renewed creation, and having a place where justice dwells;
2. That Scripture comes to us from within its own cultural context and has its own integrity; we should think of *Scripture questioning us and not merely us questioning Scripture*;
3. The needs of our respective communities for whom we are interpreting Scripture; and,
4. The classical array of inductive Bible study questions that include the following:
    a. **Who, what, when where?** These ask for definitions and the clarification of referents.
    b. **How?** This asks about *manner* and *means*.
    c. **Why?** This asks for the reason or the rationale behind some action, event, or person/thing.
    d. **So what?** Considers the implications of some action, event, or person/thing.

    In this respect, understand that to answer one of these questions may logically involve answering other more essential ones. Thus, e.g., rationale questions (*Why?*) typically require you to answer questions of definition and reference (*Who? What? When? Where?*).

Additionally, characteristics of interpretive questions *should* ...

1. be based upon a **close observation** of the biblical material;
2. attempt to understand the **original message** of the author(s) for the receptor audience(s);
3. **concern some difficulty**; some questions practically answer themselves—consider carefully where clarifications are needed or whether multiple interpretations are possible;
4. be **important and relevant**—consider which questions are most important for getting at the central concerns of the passage and its appropriation today;
5. be **clear and concise** rather than vague, imprecise, and too complex or academic; and
6. be **answerable within an allotted time frame**. Some (perennial) questions are too difficult to answer adequately or to research given our limited time. We must be prudent and pragmatic in determining which question(s) to address in our formal interpretation process.

Consult Commentaries Judiciously: Commentaries will often help us see things that we would have otherwise missed; also, they helpfully make us aware of important questions and difficulties in the passage. Within the PRIMARY AND SECONDARY INTERPRETIVE PROCEDURES below, early in the process I encourage you to consult commentaries. After you have studied the pericope in such detail and have collected data and evidence, you will be in a good position to understand, engage, and evaluate commentaries. However, remember that you should not be enslaved to their interpretation; they should rather serve you. Commentaries may be problematic for several reasons: 1) they often reflect a particular theological or ideological perspective that affects their interpretation; 2) they too often focus on more academic questions and leave the heart of the passage untouched; 3) they may not treat questions arising from the text itself; 4) they may not supply good or complete evidence to support their conclusions; 5) their formatting may limit their ability to present information thoroughly or clearly; and 6) they have word limitations that prevent a more thorough treatment of the text. *So, although commentaries often present helpful information and good evidence, still it is primarily our task as interpreters to gather and evaluate all the evidence.*

Types of Evidence: Our task is to gather evidences and decide. Types of **Relevant Evidence** that bear upon answering our questions include the following representative areas. Each will be given a brief explanation. Items with an asterisk (*) are the most essential types that most interpretive questions will require for answering; these are base-line evidences for interpretation.[2]

A. ***Preliminary Word Definition**(s) considers the meaning of any key word(s) in the passage. Summarize these definitions gleaned from the standard lexicons/dictionaries.
B. ***Immediate Context** and **Broader Book Context** will provide the bulk of evidence; bring forward findings from the previous STEPS (CONTEXTUAL LOCATION, GRAMMATICAL STUDY, LEXICAL RESEARCH, etc.) to bear as statements of evidence for answering the question.
C. ***Biblical Word Usage** investigates *words outside of the NT book under study* used in the NT, OT, and LXX as may or may not relate to the interpretive question.
D. **Extra-Biblical Word Usage** investigates words found outside of Scripture; conduct research to find these words in, e.g., Josephus, Philo, philosophical writings; also you may consult the *TDNT* and other theological word books.
E. **Scriptural Testimony** gathers relevant evidence from other passages in Scripture (parallel or not) that bear upon answering the question under investigation; this necessarily involves making detailed observations on these other passages.
F. **Grammatical Inflections, Syntax, and Discourse Features** of the underlying original language (Greek, Hebrew), e.g., tense, case usage, word order, and marked constructions.
G. **Literary Form** and **Genre** were chosen because of the situation facing the audience and the author's attempt to best address it; how and when was one literary form used, or the genre? What evidence might this supply to answer an interpretive question?

---

[2] This material is a selective summary, rearrangement, and supplement of types of evidence described in Bauer and Traina, *Inductive Bible Study*, ch. 14; for further explanation and examples, you are encouraged to read this.

H. **Kinds of Terms** considers whether literal or figurative senses are present in the use of words. Much of Scripture contains metaphoric, figurative language that, although having relation to actual referents, also interprets them.[3]

I. **Disambiguation of Referent(s)** helps determine points of reference and to what a word or grammatical feature refers; e.g., do "these" in Matt 5:19–20 refer backwards or forwards?

J. **Tone** and **Atmosphere** of the passage refers to its "feeling-impact" on the audience; e.g., is Jesus or Paul expressing irritation, frustration, or anger? Or, are they encouraging and hopeful? This discernable "mood" provides evidence for how to interpret the text.

K. **Author's Viewpoint and Purpose** may sometimes be explicit in the text, or may be inferred from it; e.g., Luke 7:29–30 and John 12:36b–43 provide programmatic evaluative statements about Jesus's ministry and people's response to them. These types of generalizing or summarizing statements are not uncommon and provide important evidence.

L. **Historical-Cultural Background Information** that bears directly and indirectly on answering the question. Such material should not be anachronistic (i.e., it must be from the proper time period), but relevant for the audiences' time and place.

M. **The History of the Tradition** refers to sources and trajectories of thought in Scripture such as exegetical and theological tradition(s) that may impact answering an interpretive question; e.g., 1 John contains wording from Jesus's teaching in Matt 24 or the book of James contains many parallel teachings to the Sermon on the Mount (Matt 5–7).

N. *****The History of Interpretation** refers to the interpretation of others in commentaries, etc.

These types of evidence are representative and are not meant to be exhaustive or restrictive. Also, they move from closest to the passage and most determinative to the least determinative by ending with the history of interpretation. Why not consult the history of interpretation from the start? Well, doing so could prejudice your careful observation and unduly restrict evidence that has a bearing on answering the question. Your own careful observation and consideration of evidence may often surpass what may be found simply from reading commentaries.

<u>More than one possible Interpretation may Emerge</u>: Recognize that data can support more than one conclusion; *the evidence may indicate two or more alternative interpretations*. These interpretations may be mutually exclusive, or they may not. The alternatives may be complimentary and mutually supportive and illuminating of the passage. During the process, it may be helpful periodically and briefly to summarize data and conclusions preliminarily for the sake of clarity.

<u>Analytical Workflow of Interpretation</u>: The ANALYTICAL INTERPRETIVE WORKFLOW on the next page describes an idealized step-by-step process to arrange one's interpretative work. It moves from data stated as evidence (left column) to its interpretive inference (right column). At the same time, the evidence is prioritized from most immediate and primary in the context of the verse to more removed and secondary. *Such an analytical approach is very time consuming*; it is adapted from lecture material of Bauer and then updated in view of his book co-authored with

---

[3] Bauer and Traina (*Inductive Bible Study*, 201) cite David A. deSilva, *Perseverance in Gratitude: A Socio-Rhetorical Commentary on the Epistle "to the Hebrews"* (Grand Rapids: Eerdmans, 2000), 426.

Traina, *Inductive Bible Study*. I include it here to illustrate the rigorous possibilities of collecting evidence, drawing inferences, identifying possible conclusions, weighing evidence, and ultimately deciding on the best interpretation after selecting an important question to answer. I do not advise following this procedure for every question except in cases where time allows and need dictates.

ANALYTICAL INTERPRETIVE WORKFLOW

I. STATEMENT OF THE QUESTION

E.g., "Regarding Matt 5:19–20, what are 'these commandments' that Jesus refers to?"

II. PROVIDE VERSES UNDER INVESTIGATION WITH SEVERAL BIBLE VERSIONS

III. EXPLAIN WHY THIS QUESTION IS IMPORTANT AND INITIAL EXPECTATIONS

IV. SUMMARY OF TYPES OF EVIDENCES GATHERED

E.g., word definition, context, grammatical inflections, scriptural testimony, etc.

V. EVIDENCES GATHERED	INFERENCES MADE

(A) **Preliminary Word Definition**
o Include this type of evidence when the question involves the meaning of terms.
o Use the basic definition in an English dictionary and/or Greek or Hebrew lexicon.
(B) **Immediate and Broader Book Context**
o Begin with immediate context—the clauses and verses that immediately precede and follow the passage—then move progressively outward, to the context of the segment, then to the entire book.
1. First piece(s) of contextual evidence.
   o Cite the reference, then give a statement on the meaning of this passage as evidence.
2. Second piece(s) of contextual evidence.
   NOTE: *Don't just quote verses.*
3. Third piece(s) of contextual evidence.
   o **NOTE**: The bulk of your evidence should come from immediate context, and then the broader book context! *Often students do not spend enough time considering and stating relevant contextual evidence. Dig, Dig, Dig! Context is Everything!*
	E.g., "This evidence implies or suggests that the answer to the question is …."
	o Inferences drawn should only be possible answers to the question you are attempting to answer (located at the top of page).
	o Be sure the inference is clearly derived from the evidence; use good logic here.
	o Also, clearly explain the inference.
	
	1. → "This evidence implies that the answer to the question is…" **Interpretation A**.
	
	2. → "This evidence suggests that the answer to the question is…" **Interpretation B**.
	
	3. → "This evidence implies that the answer to the question is…" **Interpretation B**.
	"On the other hand, this evidence also suggests that the answer to the question is…" **Interpretation A**.
	   o **NOTE**: The same piece of evidence might point to two or more possible inferences, although favoring one.

STEP 9: PRIMARY SURVEY & SECONDARY STUDY 345

Summary of Context: Evidence from context generally points toward **Interpretation B** as the answer to the question, although some con evidence points toward **Interpretation A**.

(C) **Word Usage: Biblical and Extra-Biblical**
  a. New Testament Word Usage:
   1. First occurrence. Cite the NT reference **and briefly describe** the way the word is used in that passage. *Don't simply quote verses.*
   2. Second occurrence. Cite NT passage, and briefly describe the way the word is use (its meaning) in that passage.
   3. Third occurrence. Cite NT passage, and briefly describe the way the word is used (its meaning) in that passage.
  b. Old Testament Word Usage:
   1. First occurrence. Cite OT/LXX passage, **and describe** the way the word is used (its meaning) in that passage.
   2. Second occurrence. Cite OT/LXX passage, and describe the way the word is used (its meaning) in that passage.
  c. Extra-biblical Word Usage:
   1. The way the word is used within a Classical Greek context.
   2. The way the word is used within the broader in Koine Greek context.

  1. → "This implies that the answer to the question is…" **Interpretation B**.
  2. → "This implies that the answer to the question is…" **Interpretation B**.
  3. → "This implies that the answer to the question is…" **Interpretation C**.

  1. → "This implies that the answer to the question is…" **Interpretation A**.
  2. → "This implies that the answer to the question is…" **Interpretation C**.

  1. → "This implies that the answer to the question is…" **Interpretation B**.
  2. → "This implies that the answer is…" **Interpretation B**.

Summary of Word Usage: Evidence from word usage points toward **Interpretation B**, but there is some evidence supporting **Interpretation C** and less **Interpretation A**.

(D) **Scriptural Testimony**
   1. First piece of evidence from scriptural testimony (briefly state the meaning of the piece of Scriptural Testimony).
   2. Second piece of evidence from scriptural testimony (briefly state the meaning of the piece of Scriptural Testimony).

  1. → "This implies that the answer to the question is…" **Interpretation B**.
  2. → "This implies that the answer to the question is…" **Interpretation B**.

Summary of Scriptural Testimony: Evidence from scriptural testimony points toward **Interpretation B** as the answer to the question that was raised.

CONTINUE THIS PROCESS working through the other relevant types of evidences, especially considering grammatical, historical-cultural background, and the interpretation of others.

VI. CONCLUDE EVIDENCE→INFERENCE PHASE with a general summary of findings.
E.g., "Our study has shown two possible answers to the question we raised: B and C."

Interpretation A and a Brief Summary of Evidence for A	**Interpretation B** and a Brief Summary of Evidence for B	**Interpretation C** and a Brief Summary of Evidence for C

VII. DECIDE ON THE BEST INTERPRETATION

VIII. FINAL DISPLAY OF INTERPRETIVE FINDINGS

<u>Avoid Fallacious Reasoning when Making Inferences</u>: It may be assumed, but should be said here, that it is critical to avoid fallacious reasoning in this process. Many books on interpretation have discussions on interpretive fallacies. Carson has an entire book on *Exegetical Fallacies* (Baker, 2003). Bauer and Traina provide a substantive discussion of interpretive fallacies of orientation, premises, and inferences (*Inductive Bible Study*, 249–69). Orientation fallacies entail initially asking illegitimate questions and/or beginning the interpretation with an interpretation already (firmly) in mind. Premise fallacies concern improperly citing or summarizing evidence that may be incorrect, ambiguous, narrowly selective, partial, or anachronistic. Inferential fallacies (more complex) involve unstated assumptions that skew drawing appropriate inferences from evidence due to inappropriate generalization or particularization, false "either-or" logic, begging the question, attributing a false cause, appealing to authority or consensus, etc. Additionally, I have summarized "Word Study Fallacies" (pp. 184-86) in the PRIMARY SURVEY of STEP 5: LEXICAL RESEARCH.

<u>Final General Suggestions for following an ANALYTICAL INTERPRETIVE WORKFLOW</u>: As a student I found this process tiring; however, it helped me to stay focused and taught me *to connect interpretive inferences clearly to their evidential basis*. Here are some final suggestions:

1. Keep all evidence on the left side, and all inferences on the right side. Do not mix them.
2. Clearly label the evidence employed (see above, e.g., **Word Definition, Immediate Context**).
3. Deal with each type of evidence in turn. For instance, deal with **all** the evidence from immediate context before moving on to word usage. In other words, do not go back and forth between types of evidence.
4. Draw an inference from each piece of evidence; otherwise, there is no need to include it.
5. Make sure that each inference follows *directly* and *clearly* from the evidence cited.
6. Be careful to make no assertions without evidence. Also, do not here consider "applications."
7. Begin with those types of evidences that involve first-hand study of the text (context, word usage, scriptural testimony), then move to those that involve secondary sources (e.g., historical background found in Bible dictionaries, etc.). Then, consult commentaries last of all.

<u>Make a Decision</u>: Finally, after gathering the available evidence given your time and other constraints and after drawing inferences that bear upon answering the question, you are read to

make a decision on the best interpretation. Do so by weighing the evidence for each possible interpretation: Which possible answer has the ***weightiest*** and ***most evidence*** in its favor? Importantly, it is not primarily the "most" evidence, but the weightiest evidence altogether. Remember that evidence closest to the original literary and cultural setting of the verse(s) is usually the most weighty. So, after a careful weighing of the available evidence and inferences, determine which interpretation is the best and why; briefly explain which evidences are most determinative. Finally, state clearly your decision: Here are some ways to make your final presentation of findings:

        a. Listing the truths   d. Essay statements
        b. Paraphrase   e. Answer to survey questions
        c. Outlines   f. Lesson Plan

<u>Moving On</u>: After interpretation, you are not done. Ultimately you will want to integrate the answers in order to determine the meaning of whole verses, paragraphs, segments, and books as wholes. After this, you are in a prime position, first, to work on biblical theological synthesis (this is STEP 10: BIBLICAL THEOLOGY), and, second, to evaluate the truth of the passage while considering how to best appropriate Scripture (this is STEP 11: EVALUATED APPLICATIONS).

EXERCISE 9–A: Example Interpreting "these commandments" in Matt 5:19: Below is the start of an analytical interpretive workflow interpreting "these commandments" in Matt 5:19. I will first begin the interpretive workflow supplying evidences and drawing inferences. Then, starting with the greyed section, I will stop making inferences so that you may continue making your own inferences based upon the supplied "evidence." *Be sure to evaluate the provided evidence as to its clarity and relevance.* It may be unclear at times. Then, complete the analytical interpretive workflow.

I. <u>QUESTION</u>: In Matt 5:19 what are "these commandments" (TC) that Jesus mentions?

II. <u>BIBLE VERSIONS OF THE VERSE UNDER INVESTIGATION</u>:

    [NASB] 5:19 Whoever then annuls <u>one of the least of these commandments</u> [μίαν τῶν ἐντολῶν τούτων τῶν ἐλαχίστων], and teaches others *to do* the same, shall be called least in the kingdom of heaven; but whoever keeps and teaches *them*, he shall be called great in the kingdom of heaven.

    [NIV84] 5:19 Anyone who breaks <u>one of the least of these commandments</u> and teaches others to do the same will be called least in the kingdom of heaven, but whoever practices and teaches these commands will be called great in the kingdom of heaven.

    [NLT] 5:19 So if you break <u>the smallest commandment</u> and teach others to do the same, you will be the least in the Kingdom of Heaven. But anyone who obeys God's laws and teaches them will be great in the Kingdom of Heaven.

    [UBS4] 5:19 ὃς ἐὰν οὖν λύσῃ <u>μίαν τῶν ἐντολῶν τούτων τῶν ἐλαχίστων</u> καὶ διδάξῃ οὕτως τοὺς ἀνθρώπους, ἐλάχιστος κληθήσεται ἐν τῇ βασιλείᾳ τῶν οὐρανῶν· ὃς δ' ἂν ποιήσῃ καὶ διδάξῃ, οὗτος μέγας κληθήσεται ἐν τῇ βασιλείᾳ τῶν οὐρανῶν.

III. <u>WHY THIS QUESTION IS IMPORTANT AND MY INITIAL EXPECTATIONS</u>: Jesus's statements here, if referring to the OT law and its commandments, would appear to "evaluate" and "differentiate" believers today according to whether they follow the OT laws or not. This is quite problematic when viewed against Jesus's inclusion of Gentiles and the broader teaching found in the NT. For example, the apostle Paul says that Jesus "broke down [λύω] the dividing wall of hostility ... which is the law of commandments with commandments in ordinances ... to create one new humanity ... to bring peace" (Eph 2:15). Here the same verb λύω is used as is found in Matt 5:19 ["break"]. So, was Paul teaching something different than Jesus, or are these commandments that Jesus referred to something else? Are these commandments referring to the Mosaic Law, the Ten Commandments, or his teaching?

IV. <u>TYPES OF EVIDENCE USED</u>: A. word meaning, B. context, C. word usage, D. grammatical syntax and discourse features, E. scriptural testimony, and F. interpretation of others.

V. <u>EVIDENCE GATHERED AND INFERENCES DRAWN</u>:

EVIDENCE GATHERED	**INFERENCES MADE**
A. <u>Word Meaning</u>: The Greek word for commandment is *entolē* = ἐντολή. [Friberg's Analytical Lexicon] ἐντολή, ῆς, ἡ (1) of the OT law *commandment, precept, ordinance* (LU 23.56); (2) of official commands *edict, decree, order* (JN 11.57); (3) of authoritative but not official direction *order, command* (LU 15.29). [Louw-Nida] 33.330 ἐντολή, ῆς *f*; ἔνταλμα, τος *n*: (derivatives of ἐντέλλομαι 'to command,') (1) that which is authoritatively commanded - 'commandment, order.'	NOTE: I will abbreviate "these commandments" as TC below. → This implies that TC are OT law. → This implies that TC are official commands of Jesus. → This implies that TC are authoritative commands of Jesus. → This implies that these commands are authoritative commands of Jesus.

B. <u>Context</u>: Immediate (Matt 5:17–20) and Broader
  a. commandments are **plural** and modified by the demonstrative pronoun "**these**" which specifies and intensifies the commandments.
  b. The pronoun "These" may point backwards to find its referent in 5:17–18 as the Law and its *commands*.
  c. "These" may point backwards to find its referent in 5:17–18 as related to Jesus's fulfillment of the Law.
	→ This implies that TC are knowable to the audience in context.
	
	→ This implies that TC are the Law and the Prophets.
	
	→ TC are Jesus's fulfillment of the Law and Prophets that he will disclose later in the sermon.

STEP 9: PRIMARY SURVEY & SECONDARY STUDY

d. "These" may point forward to Jesus's teaching on the Law in 5:21–48 in particular (and perhaps further—see 7:12 below).	→ TC are Jesus's teaching on the Law in 5:21–48 and the rest of the Sermon.
e. TC may be "categorized" as either "least" or "greatest" and it could be argued that the Mosaic Law was so "graded" (or discussed as such by Jewish scribes)	→ This implies that TC are OT law.
f. Jesus refers to "one" of TC as opposed to many and whereas Jesus says that it is possible for one of TC to be annulled (λύω) or taught (διδάσκω); and whereas the disciples are elsewhere in Matthew involved in annulling (16:19; 18:18) and are commissioned to teach (διδάσκω) what He himself had commanded (ἐντέλλομαι—28:20), whereas Jesus himself teaches constantly (11:1; 13:54; 21:23; 22:16; 26:55; 28:20) and especially in this immediate context (5:2; 7:29 and 4:23; 9:35)…	→ This implies that TC are Jesus's teachings on a variety of subjects as the content of what the disciples are to teach to new disciples (see esp. 28:20).
g. Jesus does not expressly teach "the Law" in the Sermon on the Mount, but rather teaches a "surpassing righteousness" (5:20) that contrasts what people "hear" respecting the Law and what Jesus himself teaches about it <u>in addition to</u> other aspects of the life of righteousness (6:1, 33–34). Furthermore, Jesus discusses the fulfillment of the Law (5:17), the essential intent of the Law (7:12; 22:40) and that He expects our (righteous) "behavior" to move beyond the Law strictly speaking (19:20–21) or at least to include weightier things in the Law like "justice, mercy, and faithfulness" (23:23).	→ This implies that TC are Jesus's teaching in the sermon on the mount.
h. On the one hand, outside of the Sermon Matthew does not record Jesus teaching directly about the Law, but only in response to the questions or accusations of uncleanliness or impiety from the Jewish authorities; and then Jesus points to their failure to keep the Law (12:1–8; 15:1–14; 19:16–22; 22:36–40; 23:23). He is teaching them something about the Law that they failed to understand and live out.	→ This implies that TC are Jesus's clarifications of the Law for the purpose of living rightly and not the law itself per se.
i. On the other hand, Jesus refers to the Law and the commands (ἐντολή) throughout the Gospel of Matthew in these contexts (15:3; 19:17; 22:36–40). Also,	→ This implies that TC of Matt 5:19 are Jewish Law and commandments in the Hebrew Scriptures.

he records that Jesus "was teaching" in synagogues (4:23; 9:35; 13:35), the Jewish temple (21:23; 26:55), and the Jewish cities (11:1), which would presumably involve teaching about the Law.	
j. However, there is every reason to believe that this Sermon of the Mount is typical of Jesus's "teaching" since it begins and ends with such a referent (5:2; 7:28–29) and fits strategically within a narrative unit from 4:23 to 9:35—both of these references (nearly identical) serve to frame the narrative and indicate that the Sermon on the Mount is His "teaching."	→ This implies that TC are Jesus's teaching/command-ments in the Sermon on the Mount.
k. Jesus puts two extreme positions (annulling or keeping) in relation to TC in a parallel fashion to contrast them for rhetorical effect; yet, both types of people are apparently allowed to be "in the kingdom of heaven" (as opposed to one being "in" and one being "out"); and whereas believers in Christ will be saved, even though judged variously and such judgment is not according to the Law, but in relation to Christ…	→ This implies that TC are the Law of the OT as mentioned in 5:18.
l. On the one hand, 5:19 is the effect of the cause in 5:17–18 ("therefore"—οὖν) and it may be that 5:19 draws a conclusion directly from 5:18 specifically and its discussion of the permanency of the Law.	→ This implies that TC are the Law of the OT as mentioned in 5:18.
m. On the other hand, it may be that 5:19 is drawing a conclusion from 5:17, which is thus most prominent and specifically is focused on Jesus's fulfillment of the Law and Prophets.	→ This implies that TC are Jesus's fulfillment of the Law and the Prophets.
n. Yet, to a lesser extent, some attention is given to the Law and prophets, even if Jesus is fulfilling them.	→ So alternatively, this implies that TC are OT Law.
o. Verse 20 substantiates 5:19 by indicating the standard of righteousness that Jesus requires. This is stated by way of <u>contrast</u> with the Scribes and the Pharisees, i.e., the teachers of the Law. Also, Jesus in 5:21–48 contrasts "what people hear" with what He Himself says. What the people had heard was the teaching of the Scribes and Pharisees.	→ This implies that TC are expecting something more in terms of righteousness than what the Pharisees and Scribes have taught; therefore, "TC" are Jesus's teaching.
p. At the same time, Jesus in 5:20 speaks of the Pharisees and the Scribes who were teachers of the Law and concerned themselves with matters of the Law.	→ This implies that TC are OT law.

q. Furthermore, the contrast just mentioned is forcefully made by the repeated statements "You have heard it said…but I say to you (ἐγὼ δὲ λέγω ὑμῖν)…." (5:22, 32, 34, 39, 44; cf. 5:26). This is an emphatic expression since the "I" (ἐγώ) is repeated (unnecessarily). Also, Jesus continues this "I say to you" (λέγω ὑμῖν) often with a "truly" (which adds emphasis) in 6:2, 5, 16, 25, 29. We are prepared for this emphasis on Jesus himself as one who speaks <u>authoritatively</u> because Jesus explicitly brings the focus on Himself in 5:17 and in 5:18, 20 he uses "I say to you" (λέγω ὑμῖν).	→ This implies that TC are Jesus's authoritative teaching as seen in commandments throughout the Sermon on the Mount.
r. The contrasts that Jesus makes in 5:21–48 mainly involve the Law, particularly the Ten Commandments, in the initial statement "You have heard…" 5:21→ Exod 20:13 **No murder** 5:27→ Exod 20:27 **No adultery** 5:31→ Deut 24:1 **Divorce** 5:33→ **Oaths**? (Law?) 5:38→ Exod 21:24; Lev 24:20; Deut 19:21 **Revenge** 5:43→ Lev 19:18? **Love; hate enemy**?	→ This implies that TC in 5:19 are OT Laws, maybe even the Ten commandments.
s. However, these statements "You have heard" go outside of the Ten Commands, and at two places go beyond any specific statements in the Law (oaths; hate enemy) and apparently only refer to the oral teaching tradition of the scribes and Pharisees.	→ This implies that TC are OT Law more generally that Jesus has now clarified.
t. At the end of the main section of the Sermon on the Mount in 7:12, Jesus concludes by saying: "In everything, <u>therefore</u>, treat people the same way you want them to treat you, <u>for this is the Law and the Prophets</u>." This forms an inclusio with 5:17 (Law and Prophets) and may indicate that Jesus's fulfillment of the Law is in fact the teaching he just gave.	→ This implies that TC are Jesus's teaching in the Sermon on the Mount.
u. Jesus ends the sermon by urging someone to obey his "<u>words</u>" (Law is nowhere mentioned) and thereby to build a stable house (7:24–27). This is a generalizing statement. Thus Jesus indicates that the whole sermon has been about His words and his teaching.	→ This implies TC are Jesus's teaching and commandments in the Sermon on the Mount.

v. All the other occurrences of commandment (ἐντολή) in Matthew refer to some core moral aspect of the OT Law: the greatest commandment (Deut 6:5), the Ten commandments twice, and on two occasions Lev 19:18: 　1) Commandment of God (in the 10 Commandments) vs. Human Traditions (Matt 15:3–4); 　2) Commandments are the Ten Commands plus Lev 19:18 (Matt 19:17–19); 　3) "The great commandment of the Law" which is Deut 6:5 plus the second greatest commandment Lev 19:18 (Matt 22:36–40).	→ This implies that TC are OT moral Laws.
w. The verb form related to commandment (ἐντέλλομαι) is found in reference to authoritative commands elsewhere: Moses (19:7); the Lord (4:6 quoting Ps 91:11–12), and Jesus's commands (17:9; 28:20). Furthermore, in 28:19–20 Jesus commissions his disciples, who heard the teaching of the Sermon (5:2), to teach (διδάσκω) all that He commanded (ἐντέλλομαι). This is in the context of Jesus having "all authority" (28:18), which reminds us that his teaching on the Sermon was "with authority" (7:28–29). Jesus did not mention that the disciples should teach the Law in this commissioning, but his words.	→ This implies that TC are Jesus's teachings and commandments, some of which concern the Law.
x. The Sermon on the Mount is actually on the "mountain" (5:1). This suggests a thematic connection with Moses on Mt. Sinai and the giving of the Law there. Jesus may be giving a "renewed" Law.	→ This implies that TC are Jesus's new, authoritative commandments for the renewed people of God.
y. On the other hand, Jesus may be seen as simply restating the OT Law.	→ This implies that TC are OT law.

Summary of Evidence from Context: There appear to be two main options:
1. "These commandments" refers backwards to 5:18 and its mention of the OT Law, either as a whole, or as represented either more narrowly in the Ten Commandments (in view of 5:21–43), or more broadly as (re)stated in also the Prophets (5:17).
2. "These commandments" in 5:19 resumes 5:17 and its focus on Jesus's fulfillment of the Law and Prophets by pointing forward to Jesus's teaching in the Sermon on the Mount that ends with his appeal to build one's house on Jesus's words with no mention being made to the Law.

STEP 9: PRIMARY SURVEY & SECONDARY STUDY 353

C. <u>Word Usage</u>: (i.e., outside of Matthew) ἐντολή and ἐντέλλομαι refer to …
  a. the Law generally as *capable* of being obeyed (Luke 1:6; 23:56; Eph 6:2)
  b. the Father's command to Jesus to die for his sheep (John 10:18)
  c. God's commandments more generally (John 12:49–50; 1 Cor 7:19; Heb 7:5)
  d. Jesus's commandment to his disciples to love (John 13:34; 15:14*, 17*) or more generally (John 14:15, 21; 15:10, 12)
  e. Human commands (Mark 13:34*; John 11:57; Acts 17:15; Col 4:10; Titus 1:14)
  f. a specific commandment of the Law that causes one to stumble (Rom 7:8–13).
  g. Lev 19:18 "Love thy neighbor as thyself" that sums up the Ten commandments and any other (Rom 13:9)
  h. Paul writes the Lord's command (1 Cor 14:37)= which is what he has been writing.
  i. the Law with commandments that are abolished with Christ's crucifixion (Eph 2:15) or set aside now (Heb 7:18–19; 9:19–10:1)
  j. the "holy commandment" that Peter speaks of which concerns righteousness and comes from the Lord (2 Pet 2:21=3:2). John, too, writes about the commandments of the Lord to be followed (1 John 2:3–4, 7–8; 3:22–24; 4:21; 5:2–3; 2 John 4–6) that concern belief in Jesus and love of God and neighbor.
  k. the "commandments of God and their faith in Jesus" in Revelation that the saints are to persevere in their keeping of (12:17; 14:12).	

Summary of Word Usage:	

D. <u>Grammatical Syntax and Discourse Features</u>: a. In 5:17, there is correlative emphasis in the "not this ... but this" construction (using οὐκ ... ἀλλά) that draws attention to the "but" element, which is Jesus's fulfillment of the Law and the Prophets (see Runge, *Discourse Features*, §4.3; Long, *Koine Greek Grammar*, 83). Furthermore, the "not ... but" construction features a purpose statement of Jesus that is quite prominent because he is the protagonist and it concerns fulfillment. The focus is on Jesus and the purpose of his coming in order to fulfill. b. The use of "Therefore" (οὖν) in 5:19 after the "For" (γάρ) statement in 5:18 indicates a resumption to the previous mainline idea that is located at 5:17. (See Levinsohn, *Discourse Features*, 126–28.) So, 5:19 continues the mainline focus of 5:17 on Jesus's fulfillment. c. In 5:19 in the expression τῶν ἐντολῶν τούτων, the location of the modifier "these" (τούτων) follows "commandments" rather than precedes it, which more likely points forward than backwards according to the expectations of information flow (see Levinsohn, "A Fresh Look at Adjective-Noun Ordering in Articular Noun Phrases" presented at The International Conference of the Society of Biblical Literature, London, England, July 2011)	
E. <u>Scriptural Testimony</u>: a. Moses talks about "these (ten) commandments" ahead of time before he actually presents them. See Deut 4:1–2, 40, 44–46 and 5:1. Then the Ten Commandments are not formally presented until ch. 5. b. Deuteronomy 4:1–2 is quite interesting in this regard in the LXX (see immediately below). Notice the emphatic "I", the verb teaching (διδάσκω), the use of ἐντολή and ἐντέλλομαι, and finally the material about adding or taking away from the Law. This parallels Matt 5:17–19 and Jesus is presented as Moses-like by Matthew.	

Deuteronomy 4:1 (LXX) "Now, O Israel, listen to the statutes and the judgments which I am teaching you [ἐγὼ διδάσκω ὑμᾶς] to perform, so that you may live and go in and take possession of the land which the LORD, the God of your fathers, is giving you. 2 "<u>You shall not add to the word</u> which I am commanding you [ἐγὼ ἐντέλλομαι ὑμῖν], <u>nor take away from it</u>, that you may keep the commandments [τὰς ἐντολὰς] of the LORD your God which I command you [ἐγὼ ἐντέλλομαι ὑμῖν]."

STEP 9: PRIMARY SURVEY & SECONDARY STUDY

c. Acts 15 addresses the problem of whether Christian Gentiles should obey the Law and be circumcised. The resolution to the problem is not that they should obey the Law or any specific part of it, but rather four guidelines are provided by the Holy Spirit that likely pertain to avoiding idolatry and gross immorality for the sake of table fellowship with Jews (Acts 15:28–29).
d. Paul argues that the Christ is the end, goal, or completion of the Law (Rom 10:4).
e. Paul generally affirms that Christians and particularly Gentile Christians do not live under the Law (Galatians). The Law was to lead us to Christ. Also, the Law is summarized in the Lev 19:18 "Love your neighbor as yourself." There is a sense that Paul believes that Christians can do the Law or the essential requirements of the Law through the power of the Spirit (Rom 2:25–29; 8:1–5; Gal 5:22–23).
f. It should also be said that Paul is careful to relate his teaching to Jesus's own (e.g., 1 Cor 7). In contrast Paul does not promote a stringent adherence to the Law or even minimally to the 10 Commandments (see Rom 13:8–10; Gal 5:14, 18, 23; 6:13).
g. Paul argues in Ephesians that in Christ the Law and commandments are made null and void in order that the two ethnic groups would become one in Christ (Eph 2:13–16).
h. We as Christians are not under the Law, but under grace (Rom 6:14). We are now under the "Law of Christ" (Gal 6:2) and follow "the law of the Spirit of life in Christ Jesus" (Rom 8:2).
i. Paul's moral ethic comes from one's life being crucified with Christ (Gal 2:20) and empowered by the Holy Spirit rather than the flesh and law (Gal 5:22–23; Rom 8).

Summary of Scriptural Testimony:

F. Interpretation of Others:
a. G. Schrenk in G. Kittel, ed., *TDNT*, II.548.
"We may also refer to Mt. 5:19. Here even the smallest commandments are endorsed. They may be kept and taught. One's place in the kingdom of heaven is dependent on their fulfillment. Since the Rabbis speak of light and heavy or less and more important commandments rather than of smallest and greatest, the reference here is to the Ten Commandments as those which occupy least space in the scroll of Scripture. Once again Jesus endorses the two tables as an elementary basis. If we compare this with the antitheses which follow in Mt. 5:21ff., we shall see that the only righteousness which counts is one which does not sink below the Decalogue, but which transcends this nationally accepted Law in fulfillment of the authoritative Messianic demands of Jesus."

b. Donald Hagner, *Gospel According to Matthew 1–13*, WBC 33a (Waco, TX: Word, 1993), 108 (underlining mine):
"The key problem of this verse hinges on the meaning of the phrase τῶν ἐντολῶν τούτων τῶν ἐλαχίστων, 'the least of these commandments.' A number of scholars have concluded that the phrase refers to the teaching of Jesus as given, for example, in vv 21–48 (Banks, *JBL* 93 [1974] 239; Lohmeyer; Schweizer). But in keeping with the emphasis of the preceding verses, it is more naturally taken as a reference to the Mosaic law, and the equivalent of the "jot and tittle" of v 18 (the majority of commentators). What is in view is not the least in importance but the easiest to fulfill (cf. Montefiore, *Rabbinic Literature*). If the commandments of the OT are in view here, we must regard this statement as hyperbolic. As in the preceding verse, a literal understanding is not consistent with Jesus' own treatment of the law, nor indeed with the emphasis in v 20. What is being emphasized in this way are not the minutiae of the law that tended to captivate the Pharisees but simply a full faithfulness to the meaning of the law *as it is expounded by Jesus*. Thus, the phrase "the least of these commandments" refers to the final and full meaning of the law, but taken up and interpreted by Jesus, as for example in the material that

begins in v 21 (cf. too the description of the "great commandment" in 22:36–40 and Jesus' ability to find the heart of the law in the double love commandment; cf. Schweizer, "Matthäus 5:17–20," 402). Thus, the language of this verse, like that of the preceding verse, is familiar to the Jews, and especially to the Pharisees (a "sentence of holy law," in which human action is followed by divine action). Now, however, it has new connotations, given the larger context in which it is uttered—the fulfillment brought by Jesus. These new connotations and a fuller picture of Jesus' intention concerning the Mosaic law will emerge as we progress through the Gospel."

c. Craig Keener, *A Commentary on the Gospel of Matthew* (Grand Rapids: Eerdmans, 1999), 178–79. Jesus refers to the OT Law, but is speaking hyperbolically: "Jesus again employs hyperbolic rhetoric characteristic of sages: his words do not envision the possibility of many who would keep or break the least commandment, hence vie for the same status, nor of some who would break some commandments while breaking the others." Again, argues Keener, "Jesus' point in 5:19 is the same as the Bible teachers in his day: one cannot pick and choose among the commandments but must obey them all."

d. From the "Torahboy" accessed 1–11–2007 from the website http://www.angelfire.com/on/torahboy/fulfill.html (no longer available) Matthew 5:19="So whoever disobeys the least mitzvot (commandments) and teaches others to do so will be called the least in the Kingdom of Heaven. But, whoever obeys them and so teaches will be called great in the Kingdom of Heaven." Messiah explains to us the consequences of obeying or disobeying the Torah. Messiah's warning goes out to those individuals who think that the Torah has been canceled and who do not want to obey God's Torah. These individuals are not only disobeying God's Torah, but they are also teaching others to not obey God's Torah. Messiah says that these individuals will be called least in the Kingdom of Heaven. Disobeying Torah commands can effect one's status in the Kingdom of Heaven. The people who will be called great in the Kingdom of

> Heaven are those individuals who are obeying God's Torah and are teaching others to do the same. Those individuals who obey and teach God's Torah are often labeled "legalistic" by the others. Observing God's Torah does not make you legalistic, legalism deals primarily with HOW one observes Torah. Legalism is obeying Torah commands with the wrong intentions and the wrong motives, legalism is obeying God's commands for the purpose of earning one's own righteousness apart from faith in Messiah. Those who obey Torah will be called great and they will be blessed (Deuteronomy 28:1–14 and James 1:25)."

VI. General Summary of Findings:

VII. Decision of Meaning:

Evaluation of Evidence:

Weightiest: Amount:

VIII. Final Display of Interpretation and Summary of Findings:
(List Truths, Paraphrase the Passage, Question-Answer Format, Lesson Plan, Sermon Outline, etc.)

<u>An Alternative to the Analytical Interpretive Workflow</u>: While thinking about types of evidence and drawing inferences, we are able to follow a more manageable set of procedures for interpreting a passage. Below I provide interpretive procedures that are first listed and then given fuller explanation in the new few pages.

PRIMARY AND SECONDARY INTERPRETIVE PROCEDURES:

1. **Bring forward important questions that you have identified thus far from your careful observation and research on this passage.**
2. **Consult at least two top quality commentaries for this particular passage.**
3. **Identify main points, perennial problems, and important questions and list these.**
4. **Choose two or three questions upon which to focus your interpretive efforts.**
5. **Summarize how interpreters have interpreted those questions/problems and what evidence contributes to interpreting the passage.**
6. **Incorporate any new, additional evidence not considered by interpreters and draw inferences from such evidence as contributes to answering the question at hand.**
7. **Decide for yourself the best interpretation for each major point and interpretive problem/question.**
8. **Record any questions that may remain, especially pertaining to application today.**

1. **Bring forward important questions that you have identified thus far in your careful observation and research on this passage.** Don't undervalue your previous work of observation and interrogation (asking questions). As you walk through the interpretive journey, consider making a running list of interpretive questions. Working through a passage, often I do this mentally. It may be that you will bring forward questions that remain "alive and pressing" or have begun to "nag" you about the pericope.

2. **Consult at least two top quality commentaries for this particular passage.** What do they say are the main points of this passage? List these along with major interpretive questions or problems below. But, which commentaries should you use? I highly recommend consulting David Bauer, *An Annotated Guide to Biblical Resources for Ministry* (Wipf & Stock, 2011). Below are helpful commentary series that are accessible to laity and that require knowledge of Greek.

Commentaries accessible to lay Persons with little to no Greek	Academic Commentaries that require some knowledge of Greek
New American Commentary	*Anchor Bible Commentary*
New Beacon Bible Commentary	*Hermeneia*
Cornerstone Bible Commentary	*International Critical Commentary*
Pillar New Testament Commentaries	*New International Commentary on the NT*
Paideia Commentaries on the NT	*New International Greek Testament Commentary*
Smyth & Helwys Commentaries	*Word Biblical Commentary*
Tyndale New Testament Commentaries	*Zondervan Exegetical Commentary*

   But, there are many other good commentaries that are not a part of any series (and many more other bad ones, too). Learn to evaluate which are the better ones.

3. **Identify main points, perennial problems, and important questions and list these.** Consider crafting such using a question format that includes the specific verses involved; e.g., "1. How does Paul's statement 'were dead' in Eph 2:1 relate to 'made alive' in 2:5?" You made add your own questions to this list based upon your previous research especially if you deem these questions important enough for further investigation. Altogether this list of questions should provide an overview of the main points and interpretive questions/problems in the passage. You will need to consider which of these questions/problems are worth pursuing further. Is the question or problem merely academic? Or, does it involve an important point of interpretation and clarification for your congregation? So, this list of questions and problems will probably help guide your research by directing you to those resources treating specific verses and/or topics that may be covered in select articles, essays, and books.

4. **Choose at least two questions upon which to focus your interpretive efforts.** Prayerfully consider which questions are worth your investment of time and energy. Consider which questions may be most relevant to your ministry situation; i.e., which ones will most likely help people understand who they are in Christ and how they fulfill their God-given responsibilities?

5. **Summarize how scholars have interpreted those questions/problems and what evidence contributes to their interpretation.** Cite page numbers throughout since you may need to return to your research for some future writing project. For ease of reference, consider using the same numbers and questions as recorded in 1. and 3. above. If a commentator does not address the question/problem, indicate as much (N/A "not/addressed" or "not available").

6. **Incorporate any new, additional evidence not considered by interpreters and draw inferences from such evidence as contributes to answering the question at hand.** Commentators have limited space and often do not assemble all the relevant data that has a bearing on the interpretation of any particular question. (One exception may be Keener's four volume commentary on Acts!) Moreover, even if all the data is assembled, it may not be properly assessed to arrive at good or sound conclusions. You will need to evaluate pertinent evidence gathered from your previous exegetical work from all the previous STEPS in the interpretive journey:

Walking Inside and Around the Word	Exploring Around and Outside the Word
STEP 1: CONTEXTUAL LOCATION	STEP 5: LEXICAL RESEARCH
STEP 2: TEXTUAL COMPARISONS	STEP 6: LITERARY FORMS
STEP 3: GRAMMATICAL STUDY	STEP 7: HISTORICAL CONTEXT
STEP 4: SEMANTIC ANALYSIS	STEP 8: SCRIPTURAL CORRELATIONS

So, based upon your careful exegetical research, consider which evidences have a bearing on answering the questions you have decided to answer. State the evidence clearly and draw the appropriate inference(s). This evidence may best be included under procedure 5 above when interacting and assessing the interpretive work of others. Alternatively, it may be best to supply this evidence below in procedure 7.

7. **Decide for yourself the best interpretation for each major point and interpretive problem/question.** The basis for decision should be which interpretation has the weightiest evidence. Weigh the evidences; don't simply count the evidences. Remember that contextual evidence should carry the most weight. It is sometimes very difficult to decide between interpretive options. Another criteria that I have used are these two: 1) Which interpretation has the least problems associated with it? And, 2) Which interpretation is most sound in terms of orthodoxy and orthopraxy in terms of Jesus's teaching on holy love? After assessing the evidence given in support of one interpretation as opposed to another (or lack of evidence), you may decide to follow the ANALYTICAL INTERPRETIVE WORKFLOW presented above to resolve a very difficult question or problem. Or, you may be able to decide which interpretation is the best with the available evidence. In either case, indicate your decision clearly; if more information or evidence is needed, indicate as much. It may be that two good interpretations are equally possible and valid. As you teach or preach, consider the merits of discussing the difficulty between two interpretive options in order to help your audiences understand the reasons for each and their respective implications. People need to understand that Scripture is difficult to interpret at times.

8. **Record any questions that may remain especially pertaining to application today.**

III. TERTIARY RESEARCH

<u>Orientation</u>: At the highest levels of research, students of Scripture access primary materials in the original languages such as Hebrew, Aramaic, Semitic languages generally, Classical and Koine Greek, Latin, and, if necessary, even Syriac or Coptic. Also, they are able to access secondary studies in German and French as well as other studies written in other languages (e.g., Italian and Spanish). At this level of research we often interpret passages for the purpose of presenting scholarly research in the form of papers or published articles/essays. In what follows I will summarize the main elements of Wayne C. Booth et al., *The Craft of Research, Third Edition*, Chicago Guides to Writing, Editing, and Publishing (Chicago: The University of Chicago Press, 2008). Then, I will provide some notes prepared for my students to help them craft a scholarly paper.

<u>Main Components of Research</u>: When working with a research agenda and mounting an argument, we need to understand the essential components involved. An argument presupposes a research agenda comprised of a research topic, question/problem, and plausible answer/solution, as wells as claims, reasons, evidence, acknowledgements, responses, and a conclusion.

Research Project/Agenda = topic, question/problem, and plausible answer/solution

Argument = claim + reason + evidence + conclusion

Claim = topic + question/problem + plausible answer/solution

Reason = support for claim

Evidence = relevant supporting data + research agenda (interpreted)

Warrant = provides justification for applying evidence to support your claim; a warrant provides more generalized support for the application/suitability of supporting a claim with a specific reason and evidence

Acknowledgement = identifies scholarly views that differ from one's own and that need to be addressed

Response = addresses perceived difficulties or alternative explanations with contrary evidence

Taken together, we can visualize the argument (claim, reason, evidence, conclusion, etc.) in the following chart that summarizes the concepts of *The Craft of Research* (see pp. 113, 116).

ESSENTIAL ELEMENTS OF A RESEARCH PROJECT

Claim	Reason	Evidence	Warrant
"I claim that…	because of these reasons	based on this evidence	that is justifiably applied to the reason supporting my claim,
Acknowledgement		**Response**	**Conclusion**
although I acknowledge these alternative views, objections, and remaining questions…		and respond to them with these arguments….	So, I conclude that ….

Construction of an Argument Plan:[4] It is often helpful to build a mental model in order to sketch out a tentative plan how you will organize your argument. The basic movement will be Claim → Reason → Evidence → Conclusion while interspersing warrants (as may or may not be needed to be stated), acknowledgements and responses, and summaries as may be helpful.

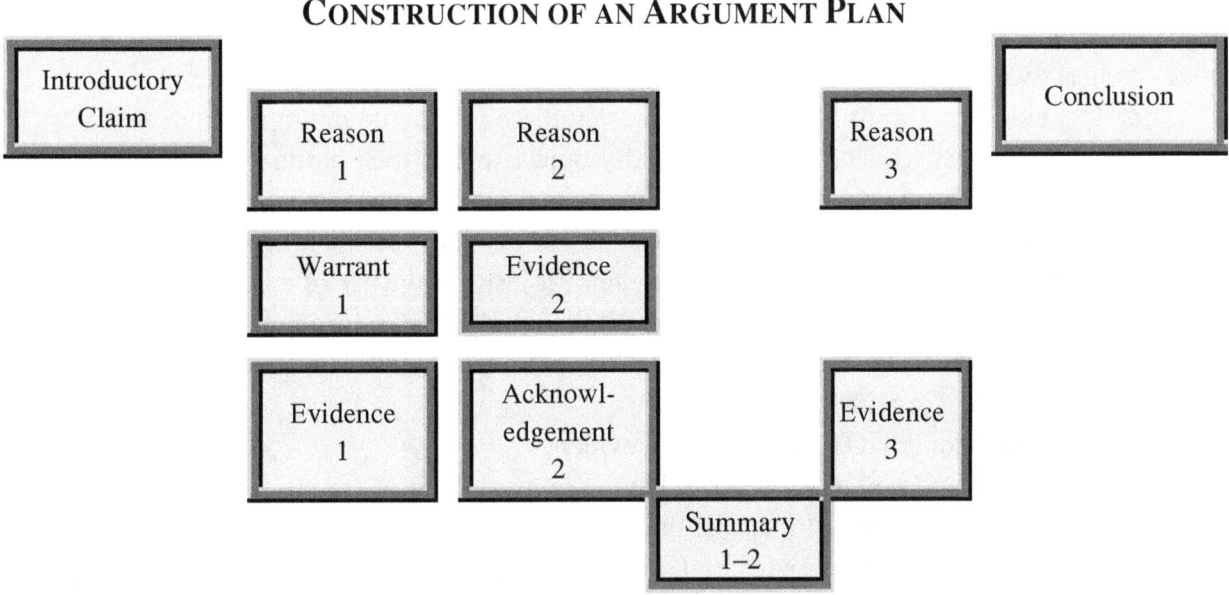

CONSTRUCTION OF AN ARGUMENT PLAN

In brief, following these guidelines may help you conceive how to develop your paper:[5]

1. **Provide a Sketch of your Working Introduction:**
   o Briefly summarize and interact with the most relevant sources (interpreters/interpretations).
   o Offer a statement of your research question.
   o If possible, provide a *"So What?"* explanation. *Clarify what is at stake.*
   o State your answer to the research question.
   o Identify key concepts that will be found throughout your research project.
2. **Plan the Body of your Paper:**
   o Sketch the background to the question/area/issue and define terms.
   o Create a page for each major section of reason/evidence.
   o Find a suitable order for the sections; these are commonly used organizational structures:
      a. Part-by-part (functional relationships, hierarchy, etc.)
      b. Chronological
      c. Short to long, simple to complex
      d. More familiar to less familiar
      e. Less contestable to more contestable
      f. More important to less important

---

[4] Cf. the diagram in Booth et al., *Craft of Research*, 131.
[5] This summarizes the discussion of Booth et al., *Craft of Research*, 179–86 with some additional thoughts.

g. Foundational understanding to prepare for what follows later for logical clarity

h. General analysis to specific applications

i. A Homeric order beginning with the stronger argument first, then the weaker one in the middle, and finally ending with a stronger argument.

3. Within Each Section consider the following:
- Highlight important concepts and terms by explaining and clarifying them.
- Indicate where to put evidence, acknowledgements, warrants, and summaries.
  a. Use evidence(s) to support reasons; present these for maximum impact and clarity.
  b. Imagine what readers would potentially object to and then outline a response. If minor enough, such acknowledgements and responses may be placed within footnotes.
  c. Decide whether it is necessary to provide an explicit statement of warrant. If there is a need to state a warrant, provide it first since it justifies the use of evidence that follows.
  d. Consider providing a summary of a detailed and complex argument unit (reasons, evidences, warrant) before moving to the next argument point.

4. Sketch a Working Conclusion:
- A conclusion should NOT introduce *new* evidence.
- A conclusion should often summarize, but not in great detail.
- A conclusion should discuss possible implications of the conclusion(s).
- A conclusion may offer consequential questions or related areas needing more investigation.

Example of Arguments, Warrants, Acknowledgements, and Responses: It may be helpful to illustrate claim, reason, evidence, warrant, and acknowledgement and response drawing upon my research on Ephesians.

Claim: Paul's Letter to the Ephesians combines Jewish/Christian theology with ancient political thought/theory to promote fidelity to Christ Jesus as supreme human political leader in counter-position to concurrent alternative claims, especially to the emperors as supreme.

Reasons with Evidence: Central and repeated topoi across Ephesians relate materially to ancient political thought, theory, and imperial propaganda such as benefactions, proclamation of the gospel, peace-making, temple building, unified head-body imagery, body growing and maturing, military triumphs with a victorious Lord, communal ethics around God and ruler as examples, acclamations of Father, Lord, Son of God, Savior, descriptions of household relationships, and military imagery of a standing army engaged in battle. For discussions of these, see my numerous articles, essays, and presentations.

Warrants justifying the application of evidence to reasons in support of the claim:
- As stated in my essay:[6] "We must not forget the rapid growth and pervasiveness of the Emperor cult in Asia Minor in the first half of the first-century;[7] between the years 35

---

[6] Fredrick J. Long, "Ephesians: Paul's Political Theology," 262–63.

[7] S. Mitchell states, "The diffusion of the cult of Augustus and of other members of his family in Asia Minor and throughout the Greek East from the beginning of the empire was rapid, indeed almost instantaneous" (*Anatolia:*

BC to AD 60, approximately fifty-two Imperial temples and shrines have been found and identified in Asia Minor.[8] Roman dominance over the Mediterranean world was pervasive for a variety of reasons.[9] Socially, politically, religiously, early Christian movements were surrounded by Emperor Worship which brought heaven and earth together.[10] The temples erected in honor of Caesar were 'often the most imposing and most frequented temple in each city.'[11] "

- o Hellenistic Kingship Theory was in circulation—the "ideal ruler" was discussed in Cicero's *Res Publica* (ca. 54–50 BC), Dio Chrysostom's four "kingship" orations (ca. AD 90). Furthermore, other interpreters have perceived Paul to be engaged precisely in such conversation in the undisputed letters (Bruno Blumenfeld) and in Ephesians in particular (Julien Smith).[12]
- o Cities in Asia Minor rivaled one another for ways to show honor to the emperors; e.g., in establishing imperial temple sites (see the work of Simon Price[13]) and in the Asian League's decision to swear in all yearly government appointments on the birthday of the "god Augustus" as shown in the "Priene" inscription found throughout Asia Minor.
- o Paul possibly wrote Ephesians after being imprisoned, exiled, and escorted away to Caesarea Maritima by 470 Roman soldiers; he then appealed to Caesar (Acts 21–26).

Land, Men, Gods in Asia Minor I [Oxford: Oxford University Press, 1993], 100; quoted and cited in Bruce W. Winter, "The Imperial Cult and the Early Christians in Pisidian Antioch (Acts XIII 13–50 and Galatians VI 11–18)" *First International Congress on Antioch in Pisidia: 2–4 Temmuz 1997, Yalvac* (ed. T. Drew-Bear et al.; Ismit: Kocaeli Press, 2000), 67. N. T. Wright is correct in his assessment, "Within this framework of imperial ideology, the emperor-cult itself was the fastest-growing religion in Paul's world, that of the Eastern Mediterranean" (*Paul in Fresh Perspective*, 64).

[8] Tallied from S. R. F. Price, *Rituals and Power*, 249–74.

[9] Price, *Rituals and Power*, is the standard work cited to this effect. But on the coordinate phenomena of Romanization, see also David Magie, *Roman Rule in Asia Minor to the End of the Third Century after Christ*, 2 vols. (Princeton: Princeton University Press, 1950) and W. M. Ramsay, *The Social Basis of Roman Power in Asia Minor* (Amsterdam: J. G. C. Anderson, 1967). Other helpful essays by Price include, "Between Man and God: Sacrifice in the Roman Imperial Cult," *JRS* 70 (1980): 28–43; "Gods and Emperors: The Greek Language of the Roman Imperial Cult," *JHS* 104 (1984): 79–95; "Noble Funeral to Divine Cult: The Consecration of Roman Emperors," in *Rituals of Royalty: Power and Ceremonial in Traditional Societies*, ed. D. Cannadine and *idem* (Cambridge: Cambridge University Press, 1987), 56–105; "The Place of Religion: Rome in the Early Empire," in *CAH* 2nd ed.; X:812–47.

[10] Wright rightly summarizes, "The gods of the Greco-Roman world were woven into the fabric of social and civic life; the newest god in the pantheon, Caesar himself, was a living example of the uniting of the divine and human spheres" (*Paul in Fresh Perspective*, 60).

[11] Burton, "Worship," 86.

[12] See especially the intriguing and well-supported thesis of Bruno Blumenfeld, *Political Paul*. He argues, "Christianity is deeply rooted in the politics of Hellenistic kingship, and analysis of the *basileia*-group fragments issues in a discussion of Hellenistic monarchy and Paul.... By grounding Pauline Christianity in Hellenistic political theory in general, and in the theory of Hellenistic monarchy in particular, this work also provides a new explanation for the success of Christianity" (13). Consider also Julien Smith, *Christ the Ideal King: Cultural Context, Rhetorical Strategy, and the Power of Divine Monarchy in Ephesians*, WUNT 313 (Tübingen: Mohr Siebeck, 2011).

[13] See cited above, Price, *Rituals and Power*.

4. **Acknowledgements** and **Responses**:

Acknowledgements	Responses

Acknowledgement #1
1. People reject Ephesians as Pauline,
  a. because of the "Gnostic" language of "filling",
  b. its accommodation to Empire (household codes),
  c. its apparent dependency on Colossians,
  d. its high ecclesiology,
  e. and generally its un-Pauline style and content.
	Response 1. It is time to reevaluate the evidence (N. T. Wright)
	  a. The filling language is sometimes "fulfilling" of OT Scripture prophetic language; also a couple of imperial inscriptions use this language of "filling"
	  b. Ephesians rather subverts empire in its use of the codes; it is missional also, vying for the gentile "nations."
	  c. This dependency is overstated; most overlap concerns epistolary and more formal features of the texts.
	  d. Ekklesia is a political term and in Ephesians it mirrors the semi-deification of human groups beside emperor and gods.
	  e. The data set is not large enough to determine this definitively; the style and content in undisputed letters varies greatly. Elsewhere, I have identified sixteen factors that can account for such variation between the Pauline Epistles.

Acknowledgement #2
2. Interpreters claim that this political background is overstated;
  a. John Barclay argues that paganism is more prominent than the emperor cult; the emperor's is but one among the multitude of deities' statues.
  b. Clinton Arnold says, e.g., no prayers were offered to the emperor.
	Response 2. I would object on the basis of what was happening "on the ground" in urban settings.
	  a. Inscriptions, parades, games, retired soldiers given citizenship by emperors, deference to Roman citizenship, inheritance steeling by emperors, social rivalry for priestly service in Imperial cult, coinage, relief aid, building projects (water, etc.), voluntary associations merging with imperial cult (see Philip A. Harland), and spontaneous praise of Emperor and his deification (even while alive) all bespeak against this rejection;
	  b. Sacrifices were made either to or for the benefit of the emperor; more poignantly, the emperor entertained constant envoys from all over the empire making requests (see, e.g., P. A. Brunt, *Roman Imperial Themes* [Oxford: OUP, 2011]) that are analogous to supplications and prayers.

Acknowledgement 3. Clinton Arnold (books on Ephesians) claims that Power language is to be accounted for on the basis of spiritual powers and magic as primary in Ephesus as per Acts account of burning magical scrolls.	**Response 3**. Arnold is himself tentative about this thesis; Also, power language is connected to Jesus's resurrection and rule over all others which is political theme and may equally or more materially relate to the belief that Roman emperors became gods at death (apotheosis) as seen on coins; imperial cult, etc.; also, "spiritual" and "heavenly" language (*epouranios*) needs to be reinterpreted in Ephesians—hence, we see human rulers and heavenly counterparts (e.g., 3:10).

We would then provide necessary summaries of the arguments before concluding.

EXERCISE 9B: What warrant exists, if any, for using ancient coins to interpret Paul's affirmation in 2 Cor 1:19a, "For Jesus Christ is the Son of God" (ὁ τοῦ θεοῦ γὰρ υἱὸς Ἰησοῦς Χριστός)?

TERTIARY PROCEDURE: STRUCTURAL NOTES FOR WRITING AN ACADEMIC PAPER

I have prepared these notes for doctoral students. I encourage them to analyze how authors organize and write articles in Biblical Studies journals such as the *Journal of Biblical Literature, New Testament Studies, Novum Testamentum*, etc.

A. OPENING: The main goals are to establish relevancy, your authority, and the research "space."
  1. **Establish the relevancy of the topic** and **identify your contribution** to the field. Some ways to accomplish both of these include the following:
     a. Explain concisely the difficulty of passage;
     b. Resolve interpretive problems through new method(s), data, or perspective(s);
     c. Correct an erroneous or problematic interpretation;
     d. Extend the insight of a method or important perspective to other passages;
     e. Exemplify a newer methodology and showcase the beneficial results; and/or
     f. Consolidate and summarize previous research that points forward to new solutions and/or some other innovation or improved perspective.
  2. **Establish your authority** in one or more of these ways:
     a. Handle original languages and ancient primary sources accurately and incisively;
     b. Show an appropriate and helpful command of the history of interpretation;
     c. Exhibit an accurate and clear taxonomy of the most important scholarly positions, issues, etc. in the most important scholarly works;
     d. Use good, confident, and descriptive writing style and avoid "weak" and uncertain words like "seems," "perhaps," "may possibly be," "feel," etc.; and/or
     e. Cite properly primary and secondary sources following the standard guidelines (e.g., *The SBL Handbook of Style*, 2nd edition).
  3. **Gain leverage to create space** into which to fit your work in one or more of these ways:
     a. Argue against alternative views or the prevailing views in the history of interpretation;
     b. Make incisive observations about the text or connections between texts;
     c. Make significant and seminal connections to the social-cultural historical background;
     d. Present evidence for making insightful appropriations of Scripture, i.e., the application of biblical texts to modern issues;
     e. Accurately and incisively deploy (new) methodology; and/or,
     f. Consider other ways to gain leverage.
  4. **Establish a clear thesis and a proper use of methodology** that arise out of a statement of a curiosity, a problem, or a lacuna in the history of interpretation.
  5. **Establish a basic outline of the paper** along with the methodology being deployed if such is needed; otherwise do so in the main body of the paper in a strategic place.

B. MAIN BODY: The main goal is to be clear, logical, and evidentiary in your argument.
  1. **Use helpful headings** according to the outline above, not too many, but representing your major argumentative movements because this helps readers track with your argument.
  2. **Consider the best "rhetorical strategy" and "logical" flow** for the presentation of material for gaining optimal persuasion.
  3. **Discuss and/or summarize methodology**; the more obscure or new is your methodology, the more it is necessary to explain or summarize it. Also briefly acknowledge any pertinent critiques of the method, if they exist, in footnotes or in the main body if serious enough.
  4. Consider whether an (extensive) **survey of the history of interpretation** is necessary; sometimes a review is quite valuable. Alternatively, you may only need to summarize representatives or work extensively with those against whom you have the largest point of disagreement and/or with whom you will be in most dialog throughout the main arguments.
  5. **Include a selective and respectful dialogue** throughout your argumentation with the most important, but also most representative, interpreters. Readers will want to know how your position compares or contrasts with, augments, or dissents from the "largest" interpretive positions or scholarly voices.
  6. **Quote people judiciously**, and only on critical points of knowledge or debate.
  7. **Properly acknowledge people with differing views**. If a position is widely held or voiced by a major scholarly figure, your acknowledgement may need to be located in the body of the paper; otherwise, you may make acknowledgements within footnotes.
  8. **Use strong style, but don't be arrogant**. Also avoid hedging your arguments by using words like "maybe," "seems," "might be," "possibly could be," etc.
  9. **Use good transitions between sections**. Such transitions add clarity and cohesiveness. They also make reading your work more pleasant.
  10. **Don't assume too much**. Often in your own thinking "connections" are obvious. However, keep your reader in mind; will they be able to follow (the logic of) your argument?
  11. **Don't assume too little**. Certain information does not need to be explained. In this regard rely on the previous work and summaries of others.
  12. **Summarize your findings** along the way, as is appropriate, in order to help readers track the progression of your argument.

C. CONCLUSION: Nothing is as more helpful than a well-crafted, incisive conclusion.
  1. **Avoid introducing new evidence** in the conclusion! If it is important enough, revise earlier portions of the paper to include such evidence there.
  2. **Short and sweet conclusions** are typically better than long and convoluted ones.
  3. **Summarize the most important and salient points**; you cannot summarize everything.
  4. **Correlate findings with contemporary trends or issues** in the academy, the church, society, and the world.
  5. **Identify any implications of your conclusions that may warrant further investigation** if this seems helpful and appropriate and space permits.

IV. BIBLIOGRAPHY

Primary Survey and Secondary Study

<u>Questions, Gathering Evidence, and Answering Questions</u>

Bauer, David R., and Robert A. Traina. *Inductive Bible Study: A Comprehensive Guide to the Practice of Hermeneutics*. Grand Rapids: Baker Academic, 2011.

Traina, Robert A. *Methodical Bible Study*. Repr. Grand Rapids: Zondervan, 2002.

Virkler, Henry A. *A Christian's Guide to Critical Thinking*. Nashville: Thomas Nelson, 1993.

——————. *Hermeneutics: Principles and Processes of Biblical Interpretation*. 1st ed. Grand Rapids: Baker, 1981.

——————. and Karelynne Ayayo. *Hermeneutics: Principles and Processes of Biblical Interpretation*. 2nd ed. Grand Rapids: Baker Academic, 2007.

<u>Researching Bible Difficulties and Hard Sayings</u>

Archer, Gleason L. *New International Encyclopedia of Bible Difficulties: Based on the NIV and the NASB*. Grand Rapids: Zondervan, 1998.

Brauch, Manfred T. *Hard Sayings of Paul*. Downers Grove, IL: InterVarsity Press, 1989.

Bruce, F. F. *Hard Sayings of Jesus*. Downers Grove, IL: InterVarsity Press, 1983.

Carroll, John T., and James R. Carroll. *Preaching the Hard Sayings of Jesus*. Peabody, MA Hendrickson, 1996.

Davids, Peter H. *More Hard Sayings of the New Testament*. Downers Grove, IL: InterVarsity Press, 1991.

Geisler, Norman L., and Thomas A. Howe. *When Critics Ask: A Popular Handbook on Bible Difficulties*. Wheaton, IL: Victor, 1992.

Kaiser, Walter C. *Hard Sayings of the Bible*. Downers Grove, IL: InterVarsity Press, 1996.

——————. *Hard Sayings of the Old Testament*. Downers Grove, IL: InterVarsity Press, 1988.

——————. *More Hard Sayings of the Old Testament*. Downers Grove, IL: InterVarsity Press, 1992.

Tertiary Research

Booth, Wayne C. et al. *The Craft of Research, Third Edition*. Chicago Guides to Writing, Editing, and Publishing. Chicago: The University of Chicago Press, 2008.

STEP 10

BIBLICAL THEOLOGY

"It is a mistake to look to the Bible to close a discussion; the Bible seeks to open one."
—William Sloane Coffin

"Theology is a very human business, a craft, and sometimes an art. In the last analysis it is always ambivalent. It can be sacred theology or diabolical theology. That depends on the hands and the hearts which further it. But which of the two it is cannot necessarily be seen by the fact that in one case it is orthodox and in the other heretical. I don't believe that God is a fussy faultfinder in dealing with theological ideas. He who provides forgiveness for a sinful life will also surely be a generous judge of theological reflections. Even an orthodox theologian can be spiritually dead, while perhaps a heretic crawls on forbidden bypaths to the sources of life."[1]
—Helmut Thielicke

---

[1] *A Little Exercise for Young Theologians*, trans. Charles L. Taylor (Grand Rapids: Eerdmans, 1962), 37.

Introduction: What is theology? We can gain a good definition of the word "theology" from its component parts: *theo-logos*. The Greek word *logos* could refer to a word or speech; it is "reasoned discourse," thoughtfully conveyed in communication, orderly and organized. The Greek word *theos* indicates the subject matter, namely, God. Thus, we may conclude that *theology is reasoned discourse about God including God's designs for all of creation*. What is meant by "biblical theology"? This is theology derived from Scripture. A presupposition of this STEP is that God lies behind, in, and through the text of Scripture as Scripture's inspiring Source and Revelation for theological thinking. Moreover, the biblical authors were inspired by God to communicate important matters in order to counter, correct, and at times condemn alternative and/or opposing claims and ideologies that are harmful for humanity and creation. Importantly, as we hear, read, and study God's Word, we are intentionally and unintentionally constructing a theology and a view of the world (i.e., a worldview) based on Scripture. Our views of God are a part of that worldview and will be either challenged, critiqued, condemned, or confirmed by our honest interpretation of Scripture. This current STEP builds fundamentally upon STEP 8: SCRIPTURAL CORRELATIONS. Foundational principles include "Major on Majors" and "Minor on Minors" (MOM), "Scripture Interprets Scripture" (SIS), the "AUthority of the NT" (AUNT), and the "Unconditional Nature of the Canon for Later Eras" (UNCLE).

> Biblical theology is vital to inform our thinking and living.

I. PRIMARY SURVEY

Orientation: For some people, the concept of theology will be entirely new; for others, it is familiar to varying degrees; for still yet others, theology may be perceived quite negatively as "dogmatic," a term once used for the discipline of theology ("dogmatic theology"). Although church teaching as dogma was formerly viewed positively, in current English usage the word *dogmatic* carries quite a negative connotation; *systems* of theological thinking may be viewed negatively as dogmatic. Yet, whether we know it or not, each of us is located within a theological tradition, especially churchgoers who belong to "ecclesial" traditions.

We might think that theology would focus solely on God; yet, theology treats a much broader array of topics where God is present within, before, and in front of "all things" in time, space, and eternity. We have much to think about how God relates to humans in the world and what will happen next! It is possible to place these categories of theology within a historical framework of God's progressive revelation as found in the Word of God, within which then we may construct biblical theology. *In fact, biblical theology—theology derived from Scripture—is vital to inform our thinking and living.* However, in addition to Scripture, other sources for theological reflection exist: *reason, tradition,* and *experience,* to which I would add *history* and *culture* (both are broader than tradition) and an *authoritative prophetic-leader* (too often problematical). Yet, Scripture is the queen of these sources; all other sources arguably should be evaluated in view of it. Those who work in other theological disciplines (such as *historical* theology or *systematic* theology) will often make appeal to Scripture.

<u>Theological Dialogue and Essential Questions</u>: With theology we enter into a responsive conversation with God through Scripture. Helmut Thielicke has succinctly stated,

> Essentially, theological method is characterized by the fact that it takes into account that God has spoken, and that now what God has spoken is to be understood and answered. But it can only be understood when I (1) recognize that what has been said is directed to me, and (2) become involved in formulating a reply. Only out of this dialogue is the theological method comprehensible (Galatians 4:9).[2]

The Word of God reveals God's Self to us in truth and calls us to respond. Reflecting on the nature of God's Word, the central questions for theological interpretation include the following:

- What can be known of God?
- What is God like?
- What does God intend for creation?
- What does God intend for humanity?
- What relationship does God have with human beings in this creation?
- What problems exist in the world? Which of these are most fundamental?
- How has God addressed these problems?
- What does the future hold for humanity and creation?
- What does God want us to be and to do now in light of the above?

Of course, under each question are many potential sub-questions. The format of presenting questions and answers is used in *catechisms* (Christian education) of mainline church denominations. On the next page is an exercise from the Heidelberg Catechism that reflects Reformed theology.

<u>Theological Topics 1</u>: To help address theological questions and speak succinctly about them, interpreters have created topical headings or categories in theology. Each topic below is built from Greek words and ends with "-logy" (from *logos*) indicating "reasoned discourse" about that subject matter. For anyone delving into theology or reading Christian theological literature more broadly, it will be helpful to become familiar with these terms. A more complete discussion with critique and benefits of "Theological Categories" is given below in SECONDARY STUDY.

MAJOR THEOLOGICAL TOPICS

CATEGORY	SUBJECT MATTER	CATEGORY	SUBJECT MATTER
theo-logy	God	*anthropo-logy*	humanity
christo-logy	Christ	*hamartia-logy*	sin and its consequences
pneumato-logy	Spirit	*soterio-logy*	salvation
angelo-logy	angels	*ecclesio-logy*	Israel and Christ's followers
demono-logy	demons	*eschato-logy*	final things and events

---

[2] *Little Exercise*, 34 (italics original).

Step 10: Primary Survey

EXERCISE 10–A: Below is Lord's Day 1 of the Heidelberg Catechism created in AD 1563.[3] The entire catechism is divided into 52 sections ("Lord's Days"); after Lord's day 1 (below), the catechism is divided into Part 1: Misery, Part 2: Deliverance, and Part 3: Gratitude. Read this opening catechism (Q&A), look up the Scripture references, and consider the final questions below.

Q&A 1

Q. What is your only comfort in life and in death?

A. That I am not my own,[1] but belong—body and soul, in life and in death—[2] to my faithful Savior, Jesus Christ.[3] He has fully paid for all my sins with his precious blood,[4] and has set me free from the tyranny of the devil.[5]

He also watches over me in such a way[6] that not a hair can fall from my head without the will of my Father in heaven;[7] in fact, all things must work together for my salvation.[8] Because I belong to him, Christ, by his Holy Spirit, assures me of eternal life[9] and makes me wholeheartedly willing and ready from now on to live for him.[10]

[1] 1 Cor 6:19–20
[2] Rom 14:7–9
[3] 1 Cor 3:23; Titus 2:14
[4] 1 Pet 1:18–19; 1 John 1:7–9; 2:2
[5] John 8:34–36; Heb 2:14–15; 1 John 3:1–11
[6] John 6:39–40; 10:27–30; 2 Thess 3:3; 1 Pet 1:5
[7] Matt 10:29–31; Luke 21:16–18
[8] Rom 8:28
[9] Rom 8:15–16; 2 Cor 1:21–22; 5:5; Eph 1:13–14
[10] Rom 8:1–17

Q&A 2

Q. What must you know to live and die in the joy of this comfort?

A. Three things:
first, how great my sin and misery are;[1]
second, how I am set free from all my sins and misery;[2]
third, how I am to thank God for such deliverance.[3]

[1] Rom 3:9–10; 1 John 1:10
[2] John 17:3; Acts 4:12; 10:43
[3] Matt 5:16; Rom 6:13; Eph 5:8–10; 2 Tim 2:15; 1 Pet 2:9–10

1. Do you agree with these affirmations? If not, where do find room for disagreement or concern?

2. What theological categories organize the whole catechism? Which categories are in Q&A 1–2?

3. In your estimation, how helpful would this method be in teaching the Faith?

4. How has your church taught you the Faith?

---

[3] As found at https://www.crcna.org/welcome/beliefs/confessions/heidelberg-catechism accessed Oct 27, 2016, slightly reformed. As explained on the website, Scripture notes were added early, but varied per edition. Those included here were approved by the 1975 Synod of the Christian Reformed Church.

Ecclesial Traditions: We can find various catechisms and each will reflect the distinctive theology and emphases of the church tradition/denomination. Churches split from one another over theological matters. Although a thorough treatment cannot be given here, these traditions summarized below will provide a basic orientation; they are given roughly in chronological order.[4] The most notable schism was between the Eastern Orthodox and Roman Catholic churches in AD 1054; before then, the universal "catholic" church struggled to find unity by holding seven Great ecumenical councils in the 4th to 8th centuries at Nicaea (twice), Constantinople (thrice), Ephesus, and Chalcedon, all locations in modern day Turkey. The next church divide after AD 1054 was during the protestant reformation in the 16th century which saw the development of the Lutheran (1517–21), Anabaptist (1525), Anglican (1534), and Reformed (1536) churches. Churches developed while articulating their distinctive theological views; for example, the Anabaptists were actively persecuted by the Lutherans and other churches. Additional churches divided over important and unimportant theological-structural differences, some of which will be noted below.

- **Orthodox Catholic**: Eastern (Greek, Russian, Romanian, etc.) and Oriental (Coptic, Ethiopian, etc.). These divisions separated with the council of Chalcedon (AD 451) over Christology. It is traditionally seated in Constantinople, modern day Istanbul, Turkey. Also, Orthodox churches deny holding to one central papacy of Roman Catholicism. Orthodox Catholic theology is rich in its Christology and spiritual formation.
- **Roman Catholicism**: Latin, Eastern, and a sizable Catholic Charismatic Renewal movement exist, all of which are typically identified with its centralized papacy. Also, Roman Catholicism is commonly known for its Mariology (veneration of Mary), veneration of the saints (including praying to them), sacramental theology (holding to seven sacraments, not just the Protestant two [baptism and communion]), and rich spiritual formation. In the 16th century the Roman Catholic stress on "works" to help secure one's salvation gave the monk Martin Luther great pause and protest to begin the Protestant Reformation.
- **Protestantism**: Lutheran, Anglican, Reformed, Anabaptist, Methodism, Baptist, Pentecostal, non- or inter-denominational evangelicalism, etc. Protestantism is quite diverse but typically is unified in its affirmations of *solo Christo* ("by Christ alone"), *sola Scriptura* ("by Scripture alone"), *sola gratia* ("by grace alone"), *sola fide* ("by faith alone"), and *soli Deo Gloria* ("glory to God alone") referring to the source, means, and purpose of salvation, while rejecting the Roman Catholic papacy, the veneration of Mary and the saints, and the extended sacraments. Indeed, much diversity attends Protestantism.
- **Other**: Mormonism, Jehovah's Witness, Unitarian, and Non-Trinitarians. Arguably, such groups are outside of orthodox Christian faith since strict adherents within these groups hold beliefs and practices that are divergent from, and sometimes quite outside of, traditional orthodox Christian teaching—e.g., holding to views of Jesus Christ at variance with Scripture.

---

[4] On these movements and distinctives, any standard treatment of Church history will suffice; see, e.g., Mark A. Noll, *Turning Points: Decisive Moments in the History of Christianity* (Grand Rapids: Baker Academic, 2012).

Each theological tradition has emphases with its own strengths and weaknesses. These theological emphases typically relate to sub-categories or areas of theology, especially soteriology (nature of salvation) and ecclesiology (the organization of the church). Why do we observe such diversity in theology? This is due in large part *because there are diverse sources for constructing theology as well as different views of interpreting Scripture.*

Theological Sources: It is widely acknowledged that a variety of sources exist from which we construct theology. A helpful way to organize these sources is the Wesleyan Quadrilateral: We can know God from Scripture, tradition, reason, and experience, with Scripture being the primary and adjudicating source. For example, when our experience comes into conflict with Scripture, we need to side with Scripture and its proper interpretation. Additional sources include the created order ("natural world"), history, culture, and authoritative-prophetic leaders. When appealed to in isolation and/or overemphasized, the use of the sources leads to detrimental extremes.

THEOLOGICAL SOURCES → TAKEN TO EXTREMES

WESLEYAN QUADRILATERAL:	**Scripture**	→ bibliolatry; irrelevancy
	(Church) Tradition	→ traditionalism; factionalism
	Reason	→ rationalism; idealism
	Experience	→ existentialism; ego/ethno-centrism
ADDITIONAL SOURCES:	**Created Order**[5]	→ naturalism; fatalism
	History	→ historicism; skepticism
	Culture[5]	→ cultural relativism
	Authoritative-Prophetic Leader	→ heresy; obscurantism

When all these legitimate sources are acknowledged together with Scripture being the foundational and governing authority, then we get a ***dynamic realism*** that is true to life and best fosters spiritual development and growth. So then, we draw upon these sources to discuss God and develop theology. I would maintain that our diverse ecclesial traditions and our divergences from orthodox Christian faith have resulted when people allowed any one of the other sources to take precedence over Scripture. Thus, we need to ground our theological thinking in Scripture.

Unity of Belief: Scripture contains normative beliefs, values, and behaviors that were later standardized in the ecclesial creeds such as the Apostles' Creed, Nicene Creed, and Athanasian Creed. However, beyond the essentials of these creeds, we Christians too often have not agreed about *particular* beliefs, values, and behaviors and have divided ourselves sometimes on quite inconsequential and trivial matters such as skin color, family lines, music style, and dress codes. To the extent that Christ's followers are not unified, the world will not recognize that God sent Jesus into the world. As Jesus said, "The glory which You have given Me I have given to them, that they

---

[5] These notions are dependent on Robert Jeffrey Hiatt, "Salvation as Healing: John Wesley's Missional Theology" (D.Miss., Asbury Theological Seminary, Wilmore, KY, 2008).

may be one, just as We are one; I in them and You in Me, that they may be perfected in unity, so that the world may know that You sent Me, and loved them, even as You have loved Me" (John 17:22–23, NASB). Christ's church would do well to follow the commonly known adage: "In essentials, unity; in non-essentials, liberty; and in all things, charity."[6]

EXERCISE 10–B: THE APOSTLES' CREED: This ancient creed of the church dates to the first few centuries AD.[7] It unifies the church universal and is often read aloud during worship services every Sunday around the world. Read this ancient creed and consider the questions that follow.

> I believe in God, the Father almighty, creator of heaven and earth.
> I believe in Jesus Christ, his only Son, our Lord, who was conceived by the Holy Spirit,
> born of the Virgin Mary, suffered under Pontius Pilate, was crucified, died, and was buried;
> he descended to the dead. On the third day he rose again; he ascended into heaven,
> he is seated at the right hand of the Father, and he will come to judge the living and the dead.
> I believe in the Holy Spirit, the holy catholic Church, the communion of saints,
> the forgiveness of sins, the resurrection of the body, and the life everlasting. Amen.

1. What are the core beliefs about God affirmed here?

2. What is the story of God's salvation? What is, has happened, is happening, and will happen?

3. What are the core aspects of human life described here?

4. What guidance does this creed provide for living day to day, if any?

Early Church Writings and Sermon Collections: The Apostolic Fathers (e.g., Ignatius, Clement of Rome, Barnabas) and subsequent church fathers of the Greek East and Latin West are an early important source of theological reflection, even if not all of their views are orthodox, e.g., Origen who knew the OT and NT extremely well and wrote numerous commentaries on the Bible as well as compiled a six column *Hexapla* of Hebrew, transliterated Hebrew, and four Greek versions (no longer extant). The early Syriac church developed collections of sermons in the sixth-century as "a distinct tool for biblical exegesis" that were organized by Scripture passage and/or by theological topic.[8] Such collections (see especially that of John Chrysostom) and similar ones today (e.g., Martin Luther, John Calvin, John Wesley) will help form and inform believers theologically through the exposition of Scripture that is reflective of their respective church tradition.

The Possibility and Necessity of (Re-)Constructing a Biblical and NT Theology: It has been a perennial question whether the recovery of a *unified* biblical theology is even possible.

---

[6] Although often attributed to John Wesley, it appears to be traceable to Rupertus Meldenius c. 1627–1628.

[7] This version (here reformatted roughly into a single paragraph) is found online from the Church of England https://www.churchofengland.org/prayer-worship/worship/texts/daily2/lordsprayercreed.aspx, accessed 10–1–2016.

[8] Philip Michael Forness, "Homilies as Tools for Exegesis: Scholarly Uses of Syriac Homiletical Collections in Late Antiquity," present at the Development of Early Christian Theology at the annual SBL Meeting, San Antonio, Texas, Nov 19, 2016.

Such a diversity of theological statements exists such that it begs the question whether any unity can be found. If so, on what basis does such unity exist? Has God intended a singular or unifying vision across Scripture? Or, has God been so revealed to allow—perhaps even to encourage—multiple "readings" of passages in our interpretations and consequent constructions of theology? Certainly, God's self-revelation in Scripture has been progressive in historical time and space; the Bible has been written by multiple authors across a variety of settings to address a multiplicity of issues. Thus, it is not surprising that the overarching themes are not always obvious and may be missed unless investigated carefully. *What unifies Scripture is its concern to urge God's people to be faithful to God in a fallen world.* By faithful, I mean the whole restoration of right relationships (righteousness) between God, humanity, and all of creation. The individual books of Scripture offer distinct contributions to theology as voices in the conversation. Yet, in addition to the human authors, there remains the Divine Author who, despite the divergent voices, may intend a greater or larger revelation and meaning through any particular passage *when placed within the larger canonical context of Scripture*. Major themes emerge across the many books that comprise Scripture. Thus, biblical theology is a synthetic enterprise that recognizes among the concert of voices *a unified chorus of God's orchestration*.

> What unifies Scripture is its concern to urge God's people to be faithful in a fallen world.

Biblical Theology Follows Biblical Interpretation: Up to this point, this book has described a rigorous process of interpretation from STEP 1: CONTEXTUAL LOCATION through STEP 9: INTERPRETIVE DECISIONS—now we have not only a unique opportunity, but also a distinct privilege and responsibility, to construct biblical theology. Because of the foundational place of Scripture for theological reflection, we are quite justified to explore the theology expressed within our pericope. At its core, the historic church has identified the central theological beliefs that are exemplified in the creeds, as briefly described above. However, because there will always be new historical discoveries, further cultural insights, and exegetical advances in our understanding of Scripture, we have a continual need to refine and update NT and biblical theology. But how do we do so? Johann Philipp Gabler provided a basic method: "(1) linguistic and historical analysis of biblical texts; (2) identification of ideas common among the biblical writers; and (3) articulation of the Bible's timeless and universal principles."[9] Important here is to identify common themes in Scripture while acknowledging that not all themes will be in common. Also, we will recognize tensions and (seeming) contradictions that reflect disparate voices in Scripture; proper evaluation of these tensions and (seeming) contradictions will occur in STEP 11: EVALUATED APPLICATIONS.

Theological Interpretation of Scripture: Within the discipline of Biblical Studies since the turn of the millennium, we have seen the re-emergence of theological interpretation. Over a period of four years, a group of leading proponents arrived at the following nine theses:[10]

---

[9] Joel B. Green, "The Bible, Theology, and Theological Interpretation," *SBL Forum*, n.p. available online: http://sbl-site.org/Article.aspx?ArticleID=308.

[10] Ellen F. Davis and Richard B. Hays, eds., *The Art of Reading Scripture* (Grand Rapids: Eerdmans, 2003).

NINE THESES OF THEOLOGICAL INTERPRETATION

(1) Scripture truthfully tells the story of God's action of creating, judging, and saving the world.
(2) Scripture is rightly understood in light of the church's rule of faith as a coherent dramatic narrative.
(3) Faithful interpretation of Scripture requires an engagement with the entire narrative: the New Testament cannot be rightly understood apart from the Old, nor can the Old be rightly understood apart from the New.
(4) Texts of Scripture do not have a single meaning limited to the intent of the original author. In accord with Jewish and Christian traditions, we affirm that Scripture has multiple complex senses given by God, the author of the whole drama.
(5) The four canonical Gospels narrate the truth about Jesus.
(6) Faithful interpretation of Scripture invites and presupposes participation in the community brought into being by God's redemptive action—the church.
(7) The saints of the church provide guidance in how to interpret and perform Scripture.
(8) Christians need to read the Bible in dialogue with diverse others outside the church.
(9) We live in the tension between the "already" and the "not yet" of the kingdom of God; consequently, Scripture calls the church to ongoing discernment, to continually fresh rereadings of the text in light of the Holy Spirit's ongoing work in the world.

Daniel Treier has helpfully concluded, "Theological interpretation of Scripture, in the end, is an essential practice in the Christian pilgrimage of seeking to know God."[11] So, let's turn to look at Christ's foundational framework and various approaches for interpreting Scripture theologically.

<u>Christ's Character of Humble Assurance</u>: For starters, I think a healthy dose of humility conjoined with a proper confidence is in order. In our attempts to understand Scripture we ought not to assume that by our own mastery we have completely comprehended it or even that we have "overstood" it; mystery will still remain. What does humility look like? Well, I think it entails earnestness in our endeavor to adequately ***reflect*** what is in the biblical text rather than to ***project*** what we might want to be there. It offers no benefit to others and us if we feign full competence and perfect completion while only mustering partial and incomplete work. Our work will be incomplete, let's face it, because of the vastness of materials and breadth of subject matter. Our work, too, will often remain quite tentative and open for reconsideration, especially in the face of new evidence that comes to our attention. And yet, we may have appropriate confidence in our conclusions if we have applied ourselves diligently in the tasks of the preceding nine interpretive STEPS; we have done our best given our time constraints, energy levels, and abilities. We are co-workers with God in this task, and *God is much*

> God is much more interested in our work than we are.

---

as quoted in Daniel J. Treier, "In the End, God: The Proper Focus of Theological Exegesis," *Princeton Theological Review* 14 (2008): 7–12 at 8.

[11] Treier, "In the End," 11.

more interested in our work than we are. At the core, we are invited into God's Story of Salvation.

The Story of God's Salvation in Four Paragraphs: God existed in eternity before time and space. In God's wisdom the universe was created along with its attendant creatures—created beings both of "natural" or "worldly" provenance and "supernatural" or "extra-worldly" provenance. We don't know all the details, yet there are additional intelligent beings beyond humans. Somehow (we don't know how), created beings rebelled against God and that rebellion was brought into the human realm. How or why God has allowed this is a matter of much debate. Moreover, we ask, Why is there so much pain and suffering in the world not only at the hands of humans to other humans, but by the forces in the created order (weather, animals) against humans and other creatures? Scripture begins to address these questions and provides remedies as well as offers a long view of God's purposes to make things right by attempting to reconcile humans—and indeed all of creation—to Himself. At the core, a fundamental problem with humans is our flawed view of God.

EXERCISE 10–C: The first theological conversation by God's creatures as recounted in Scripture is between Eve and the Serpent with Adam apparently listening on. Below is Gen 3:1–7 (NRSV).

[1] Now the serpent was more crafty than any other wild animal that the LORD God had made. He said to the woman, "Did God say, 'You shall not eat from any tree in the garden'?" [2] The woman said to the serpent, "We may eat of the fruit of the trees in the garden; [3] but God said, 'You shall not eat of the fruit of the tree that is in the middle of the garden, nor shall you touch it, or you shall die.'" [4] But the serpent said to the woman, "You will not die; [5] for God knows that when you eat of it your eyes will be opened, and you will be like God, knowing good and evil." [6] So when the woman saw that the tree was good for food, and that it was a delight to the eyes, and that the tree was to be desired to make one wise, she took of its fruit and ate; and she also gave some to her husband, who was with her, and he ate. [7] Then the eyes of both were opened, and they knew that they were naked; and they sewed fig leaves together and made loincloths for themselves.

1. What is explicitly stated or implied by the Serpent about God and His word? What is at issue?

2. What view of God does Eve apparently accept when disobeying God?

What did God set out to do after humanity's fall? God was patient, punishing, and persistent in seeking us out. With the calling of Abraham (Gen 12), God begins to reveal an expanded vision of working through Abraham's descendants to make a great nation (the Israelites) and bless all the nations of the earth (Gen 12:1–3). So, God works patiently with Abraham and his descendants, slowly revealing more about Himself until there is a political crisis of these descendants enslaved in the most powerful nation of the earth at the time, the Egyptians. God rose up a leader, Moses, educated as an Egyptian, and then directed him to lead the people out of their slavery to take possession of the land promised to Abraham. As the people leave Egypt, God punishes the Egyptians by making a mockery of their "deities"—the ten plagues show that God is supreme and there is no other. The Passover meal commemorates the exodus salvation from Egypt. So, God establishes a covenant with the people and through Moses gives them the Law—what nation did not have a law? This law established basic boundaries of right and wrong conduct, yet also distinguished them from the idolatrous nations around them. God had thus established a "beachhead" in the world. In fact, the land upon which Israel was planted was a major crossroads for the kingdoms in the ancient world, thus allowing the influence of God and His people to be experienced more broadly. And there, God allowed a temple to be built, a place for God to dwell among his people.

Well, the people of Israel continued to struggle with idolatry and rejected following after God. At one point their rebellion against God involved Israel's desiring a king to rule them; despite God's warnings, Israel took a king and eventually had many kings, most of whom led Israel astray. Prophets were raised up to confront sin, warn of punishments, and look forward to a restoration. On the one hand, God had pointed out Israel's sins and set up a sacrificial system in the Law for them to follow. On the other hand, God would need to punish His people by kicking them off the land that had been given to them. Yet, God had also revealed that a more permanent solution was coming—a purification of the heart was anticipated within a new covenantal framework (Deut 30:6; Jer 31:31–34; 32:40; Ezek 37:26; see Heb 10:16) that would feature a morally just political ruler, a Messiah, who would embody righteousness and justice. Very powerfully, the prophet Isaiah discloses important features of this Suffering Servant (Isa 40–55) who would receive God's Spirit, become a covenant for the people, and bring light to the nations (Isa 42:1–6).

As Israel was awaiting her redemption at the hand of God's appointed coming leader, the nation was ravished again and again by foreign nations (Syrians, Greeks, and Romans) to the point where the nation was fractured politically. John the Baptist appeared baptizing Israelites (an initiation rite) and pointing them to another One coming; then Jesus appears announcing that God's reign is at hand and that people should repent from their sins. This was the anticipated kingdom that Jesus was bringing. Yet, it looked differently than what people expected. Jesus did not take up arms against the foreigners (the Romans and Greeks), but cast out demons, taught love of enemies, and confronted greed and many other injustices especially as seen in the religious leaders. Jesus showed a different way to be in the world as he reached out to the poor and outcasts and did good for the glory of God. He taught the people about God's kingdom. Jesus called twelve disciples (reflecting the twelve tribes of Israel) to follow him. Before dying, Jesus issued a new Passover meal, the Last Supper, for his followers to remember him in anticipation of the future kingdom. This is the New Covenant, the new relationship God has with humanity. He revealed also that there would be a delay of final justice, but first Christ's followers (the children of Abraham by faith) would fulfill the calling of Israel to be a blessing to the nations. They are to preach the gospel to the ends of the earth. So, Jesus was crucified, died, and was buried; on the third day, he rose again, and ascended into heaven. From there, Jesus sends His Holy Spirit upon his followers to strengthen them for mission in the world. *Jesus did not save us from suffering, but through it*. And Jesus himself replaced the Temple so that his people become a holy place as God's own people—what God has always wanted (Hos 2:23; Zech 8:8; 13:9; Rev 21:7). In the end, a New Heavens and New Earth will be made. And so, Christ's followers await Jesus's coming and remain in the world empowered by the Holy Spirit to give testimony to God's saving presence in the world for all the nations.

Scope and Scale of Biblical Theology: In the narrative above (incomplete as it is), I drew upon the whole of Scripture, the Christian Canon of OT and NT. As we conceive of the scope of doing biblical theology, we can scale it outward from the passage we are interpreting. We do this by correlating key themes together. We start within the NT book itself, then expand outward to the corpus that it is within (if such exists); e.g., if our passage is in one of Paul's letters, we can consider correlating ideas across the Pauline Epistles. If it is in 2 Peter, we could do so in the Petrine letters. Then, we broaden our theological reflections to include the whole of the NT, and then expand even further to the whole of the Canon of Scripture. Obviously, the more familiar you are with Scripture, the more you are able to make informed, instructive, and incisive correlations. You will need to rely on previous interpretive work, especially STEP 8: SCRIPTURAL CORRELATIONS.

PRIMARY INTERPRETIVE PROCEDURES:

1. **Identify your theological tradition.** In a preliminary way, how might this tradition inform your theological understanding of the passage you are studying, if at all?
2. In view of your interpretive work, answer these questions if it is possible to do so:
   a. What does the passage tell us about God?
   b. What does this passage tell us about God's designs for creation?
   c. What does the passage tell us about human beings within God's creation?
   d. What does the passage tell us about the relationship between God, creation, and human beings?
3. What is the passage really driving at and pushing for? Specifically, ask the following:
   a. What does the text urge us to believe? (faith)
   b. What does the text urge us to hope for? (hope)
   c. What does the text urge us to do? (love)[12]
4. Consider what place in God's story of salvation your passage falls. How does this story of salvation illuminate and mutually inform the passage? How does your passage illuminate the story?
5. Especially in view of your work in STEP 8: SCRIPTURAL CORRELATIONS, consider how your passage contributes to a biblical theology of the particular NT book, the specific NT corpus (e.g., Johannine, Pauline, Lucan, Petrine), the NT, or the biblical Canon of Scripture.
6. If time allows and you have access to such books, investigate commentaries, biblical theological works, or sermons for specific treatments of the major themes of this passage.
7. Consolidate your theological thinking; be creative. Ask any questions that come to mind.
8. Consider specifically if anything theologically presented in this passage is *at tension* or even *in conflict* with what you understand elsewhere in Scripture. If such tensions exist, record these and consider evaluating them in STEP 11: EVALUATED APPLICATIONS.

---

[12] These three questions are from Michael J. Gorman, *Elements of Biblical Exegesis*, rev. and expanded (Peabody, MA: Hendrickson, 2009), 148.

II. SECONDARY STUDY & III. TERTIARY RESEARCH

Orientation: Biblical theology treats a broad array of topics that may be categorized. Such categories have some benefits, but also detriments. Reflecting the richness of God in relation to humanity, theology is commonly subdivided in practical, biblical, historical, and systematic areas that reflect the major sources for theological construction—Bible, church history, reason, and experience. Theological interpretation of Scripture is a renewed development in the field of Biblical Studies as is attested by the numerous recent monographs and commentaries distinctly devoted to themes or the theology of biblical books. At the secondary level of study, students of Scripture access primary materials in the original biblical languages (Hebrew, Greek, and possibly Aramaic). At a tertiary level, students may access materials in the early church in the original languages (Greek and Latin) as well as scholarly studies in German, French, etc.

Theological Categories 2: Interpreters have used topics to organize biblical theology. Each topic is typically built from a Greek word (one is from Latin: *missiology* is from *mitto* "I send") and ends with "-logy" indicating "reasoned discourse" about that the subject matter. For anyone delving into theology or reading theological literature more broadly, it will be helpful to become familiar with these terms. I have placed them within the framework of God's revelation in history.

GOD'S HISTORY OF REVELATION AND MAJOR THEOLOGICAL CATEGORIES

REVELATION IN HISTORY	TOPICS OF THEOLOGY	SUBJECT MATTER
God the Father	*theo-logy*	God
God the Son	*Christo-logy*	Christ
God the Holy Spirit	*pneumato-logy*	Spirit
Angelic Beings created	*angelo-logy*	angels
	demono-logy	demons
Creation	*proto-logy*	first things and events
	cosmo-logy	the organization of the world
Humanity created	*anthropo-logy*	humanity
Fall from God; Sin	*hamartia-logy*	sin and its consequences
God's reaching out to people	*missio-logy*	mission
Scripture	*biblio-logy*	Bible
God's saving His people	*soterio-logy*	salvation
Formation of God's people	*ecclesio-logy*	Israel and Christ's followers
Virtues of God's People	*aretology*[13]	biblical ethics and virtues
Future Events ("End Times")	*eschato-logy*	final things and events

---

[13] This category is not conventional, but I include it to allow description of biblical virtues. Aretology is from the Greek word ἀρετή "moral excellence; virtue" that was one of the four cardinal virtues in Greek culture. Otherwise, the term referred to a literary form/genre that consisted of a narrative espousing a divine figure's miraculous deeds.

At first glance, the list seems quite comprehensive; but to the extent that the categories are general, the lack of specificity may detrimentally obscure or allow one to ignore important aspects, dimensions, and details pertaining to the specific category. Moreover, sometimes it is difficult to place important biblical themes within *only* one theological category. For example, within which topic would we discuss the central notions of Covenant, Prophecy, the Kingdom of God, Christian Virtue, and Biblical Ethics? Also, how would we categorize topically God's giving of the Law to Moses for the people of God? Is this part of *soteriology* (salvation), *ecclesiology* (formation of God's people), *hamartialogy* (sin), *missiology* (outreach to others), or *angelology* (angels), etc.? Well, "Yes." It belongs to each. Let's consider the nature and function of the giving of the Law:

(1) it was given in the midst of angels (*angelology*; Deut 33:2; Acts 7:38; Gal 3:19; Heb 2:2);
(2) it helped to form and centralize God's people (*ecclesiology*);
(3) it taught the people of God about sin (*hamartialogy*) and how to avoid it (*soteriology*);
(4) and it provided a witness to God's wisdom for reaching others (*missiology*; see Deut 4:6–8).

We could also discuss the giving of the Law within other categories. So, how helpful are these topical headings, or how hurtful? Milton S. Terry in his book, *Biblical Dogmatics*, evaluates the benefits while also illustrating problems in the use of theological categories:

> A well chosen, definite terminology, such as these words of Greek origin furnish, has an unquestionable value, and a methodology which essayed to treat all Christian doctrine under the [categories] … might have much said in its favor. On the other hand, it may be affirmed that the persistent use of these terms tends to load the study of simple biblical truths with stereotyped formulas which have become obnoxious to many intelligent readers. It may also be argued that the … topics indicated are not coördinate, and some of them are not fairly entitled to a place in a system of dogmatics. Bibliology and ecclesiology should hold at most only a subordinate place in a treatise on doctrines. Hamartialogy can be logically treated under the head of anthropology, and soteriology and Christology are so closely allied that they may be brought under one caption, as is done in several of the outlines given above. Cosmology, angelology, and eschatology may also be assigned a subordinate position, so that the … topics designated by the high-sounding Greek terms named above might all be treated under three or at most four main divisions.[14]

Terry is correct to note the benefit but also the detriment of these categories. Their trite use with "stereotyped formulas" are "obnoxious" to people! At the same time, however, Terry is quite frankly wrong to diminish the importance of bibliology and ecclesiology, especially in view of our needs today. We are appreciating more and more the commonly affirmed social-communal nature of humans that squarely falls under the important topic of ecclesiology; moreover, people today question Scripture's authority and so the nature of God's Word as authoritative is quite an im-

---

[14] Milton S. Terry, *Biblical Dogmatics: An Exposition of the Principal Doctrines of the Holy Scriptures* (New York: Eaton & Mains, 1907), 42–43. Terry lists all these topics, except protology and missiology.

portant topic that falls under bibliology. Furthermore, it is problematic to place *hamartialogy* (sin) under anthropology *as if humans were created inherently sinful*. Is sin natural to humanity? Does God create humans in sin or to be sinful? Absolutely not. But Terry betrays an all too common view that humans and sin go hand-in-hand, and yet, sin is not natural to humanity; sin was introduced from another agency (the deceitful serpent). Finally, Terry over-generalizes and collapses all of the topics into three: anthropology, Christology, and Theology (doctrine of the Father).[15] Such generalization is neat and tidy, but comes at the expense of accuracy and the complexity of life.

Hardening of the Categories: At best, these topical categories help us organize and appreciate the richness of God's revelation and created cosmos. At worst, the categories isolate and estrange topics from one another, thus potentially not allowing us to see the rich complexity and awesomeness of God's being and doings and what He invites us to be and do with Him. Helpfully and, at the same time, unhelpfully, our ecclesial traditions may both illuminate as well as obscure the truth of Scripture because of the tendency to over-generalize our theological distinctives.

Orthodoxy and Orthopraxis—but also Orthopathy: Although we are familiar with orthodoxy ("right belief") and probably orthopraxis ("right practice"), within church tradition orthopathy as "right experience, disposition, and attitude" has also been affirmed among Wesleyan theologians. Henry H. Knight III explains, "Orthopathy ... does not mean everyone must experience certain feelings. It means Christians have a character which consists of holy tempers such as love for God and neighbor, faith, hope, peace, humility, and other fruit of the Spirit—what Wesley calls in one sermon the 'marks of the new birth.'"[16] *What would happen if we held right affections?*

EXERCISES 10–D: Given these portions of Scripture, reply to the questions further below.

Luke 15:1–10 (NRSV) [1] Now all the tax collectors and sinners were coming near to listen to him. [2] And the Pharisees and the scribes were grumbling and saying, "This fellow welcomes sinners and eats with them." [3] So he told them this parable: [4] "Which one of you, having a hundred sheep and losing one of them, does not leave the ninety-nine in the wilderness and go after the one that is lost until he finds it? [5] When he has found it, he lays it on his shoulders and rejoices. [6] And when he comes home, he calls together his friends and neighbors, saying to them, 'Rejoice with me, for I have found my sheep that was lost.' [7] Just so, I tell you, there will be more joy in heaven over one sinner who repents than over ninety-nine righteous persons who need no repentance. [8] "Or what woman having ten silver coins, if she loses one of them, does not light a lamp, sweep the house, and search carefully until she finds it? [9] When she has found it, she calls together her friends and neighbors, saying, 'Rejoice with me, for I have found the coin that I had lost.' [10] Just so, I tell you, there is joy in the presence of the angels of God over one sinner who repents."

James 4:1–10 (NRSV) [1] Those conflicts and disputes among you, where do they come from? Do they not come from your cravings that are at war within you? [2] You want something and do not

---

[15] As per Terry's first, second, and third parts of his book.

[16] "Wesley's 'Orthopathy'" at http://www.catalystresources.org/consider-wesley-21/ accessed 7-20-2017. I am grateful to Robert A. Barlow for bringing orthopathy to my attention.

have it; so you commit murder. And you covet something and cannot obtain it; so you engage in disputes and conflicts. You do not have, because you do not ask. ³ You ask and do not receive, because you ask wrongly, in order to spend what you get on your pleasures. ⁴ Adulterers! Do you not know that friendship with the world is enmity with God? Therefore whoever wishes to be a friend of the world becomes an enemy of God. ⁵ Or do you suppose that it is for nothing that the scripture says, "God yearns jealously for the spirit that he has made to dwell in us"? ⁶ But he gives all the more grace; therefore it says, "God opposes the proud, but gives grace to the humble." ⁷ Submit yourselves therefore to God. Resist the devil, and he will flee from you. ⁸ Draw near to God, and he will draw near to you. Cleanse your hands, you sinners, and purify your hearts, you double-minded. ⁹ Lament and mourn and weep. Let your laughter be turned into mourning and your joy into dejection. ¹⁰ Humble yourselves before the Lord, and he will exalt you.

1. Which major theological categories are arguably present? Identify and specify verse references.
2. How does the recognition of each theological category illuminate the passage and vice versa?
3. How does the passage inform orthodoxy, orthopraxy, and especially orthopathy?

Branches of Theology: The discipline of theological study has been sub-divided into branches or areas according to the primary source used: natural, philosophical, historical, biblical, systematic (dogmatic), and practical (pastoral). Even within these branches, there may be a particular restriction (e.g., in biblical to OT or NT) or a specific focus (e.g., in historical to a particular ecclesial tradition like Orthodox, Lutheran, Reformed, or Wesleyan). Also, it should be said that these areas overlap. Below is a brief description of each branch of theology.

(1) **Natural Theology** considers the cosmos as a whole and constructs theology on the basis of empirical evidence apart from any external claim to authority such as Scripture or a church tradition. Natural theology relies on experience, the natural-created order, and reason.

(2) **Historical Theology** considers distinctive theological traditions (Jewish, early church, Gnostic, Catholic, Cappadocian, Orthodox, Lutheran, etc.) and progressive developments in theological understanding within those traditions as a basis for articulating theology in conversation with other theologies.

(3) **Philosophical Theology** typically works within historical theological traditions to explore implications and interrelationships of theological notions on a philosophical basis.

(4) **Practical Theology** attempts to explicate and relate biblical-theological truths in light of the contemporaneous life and ministry of the church that is consonant with the created order.

(5) **Biblical Theology** attempts to enumerate theology from Scriptural materials on the basis of individual books, corpora, testaments (OT or NT), and/or the canon as a whole. According to George Eldon Ladd, "Biblical theology is primarily a descriptive discipline. It is not initially concerned with the final meaning of the teachings of the Bible or their relevance for today. This is the task of systematic theology. Biblical theology has the task of expounding the theology found in the Bible in its own historical setting, and its own terms, categories, and thought forms. It is the obvious *intent* of the Bible to tell a story about God and his acts

in history for humanity's salvation."[17] Theological interpretation (see further below) is concerned with addressing how biblical theology impacts our world today.

(6) **Systematic Theology** attempts to synthesize theological truths from various sources into a clear presentation or system of thought in light of the broad spectrum of human knowledge. This last point is especially important: all human knowledge and understanding is brought together with theological knowledge. There is less concern to align with a particular church tradition and more of an attempt to interact creatively with modern ideas and philosophy to address systematically and comprehensively virtually all matters of human life within the purview of God, particularly as revealed in Scripture. See, e.g., Wolfhart Pannenberg's three volume *Systematic Theology* or Emil Brunner's three volume *Dogmatics*. Of these branches, systematic and practical theologies are more synthetic by integrating the other theological sources.

INTERRELATION OF THE MAJOR BRANCHES OF THEOLOGY

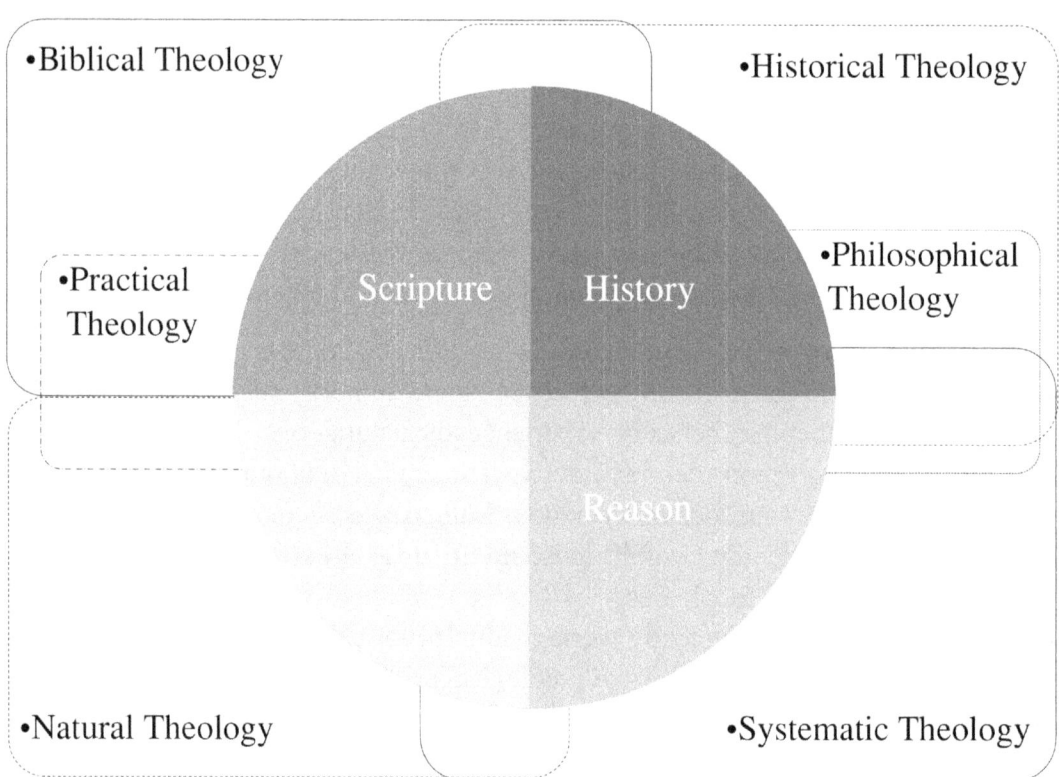

Interrelation of Theological Branches, yet Scripture is Foundational: The diagram above attempts to describe the relationship between the major branches of theology, although it does so imperfectly. Why? Because apart from natural theology, *Scripture is commonly acknowledged as the wellspring for all other theologies when properly received as God's self-revelation*. These other theologies are founded upon Scripture even as they extend and apply the truth of scriptural the-

---

[17] *A Theology of the New Testament*, rev. ed. (Grand Rapids: Eerdmans, 1993), 20.

ology in historical, ecclesial, philosophical, systematic, and practical ways. Brian S. Rosner summarizes well the foundational place of biblical theology:

> Biblical theology is principally concerned with the overall theological message of the whole Bible. It seeks to understand the parts in relation to the whole and, to achieve this, it must work with the mutual interaction of the literary, historical, and theological dimensions of the various corpora, and with the inter-relationships of these within the whole canon of Scripture. Only in this way do we take proper account of the fact that God has spoken to us in Scripture.[18]

History of and Method for Biblical Theology: As can be seen in the bibliography, much scholarly attention has been given to biblical theology. Because of this, there has been significant debate about appropriate methods for doing biblical theology. Gerhard Hasel has provided an excellent survey of the history of NT theology through 1970s, and I will summarize here the major approaches that he discusses and his critiques of them.[19]

- **Thematic Approach** whereby one tracks a theme or themes through the NT. The criticisms to such an approach are its selective nature (e.g., On what basis is one theme chosen over another?), proneness to congeniality (i.e., choosing passages that align with one's starting point), and neglect of minority voices across the NT and the Bible as a whole.
- **Existentialist Approach** whereby the ancient message of Jesus and about Jesus is brought into our contemporary settings through a "translation" process of removing pre-scientific understandings of miracles, etc. and favoring the church's proclamation of Christ in contrast to the historical Jesus. Among the problems with such a view are the separation of the historical Jesus from the proclaimed Christ and the problematical "Western" historical assumptions (closed causes and effects within history, anti-supernaturalism, etc.) such that historical inquiry is often opposed to faith.
- **Historical Approach** whereby the early Christian movement is understood against the religio-historical environment of the first-century. Important questions for this approach is to what extent one is justified only to use NT documents as a closed canon and whether or not to consider the early church fathers and "alternative Christianities" as evidenced in extra-biblical documents of the second- and third-centuries for theological construction.
- **Salvation History Approach** whereby one working historically nevertheless acknowledges the important role of God's revelation within history and that the NT culminates this revelation with Jesus's salvific coming. This approach remains historically descriptive.

Hasel concludes his book (ch. 5) by proposing six guidelines for constructing a NT theology: 1) it is a historical-theological discipline; 2) it is focused on the NT itself; 3) it centers on Jesus's mes-

---

[18] B. S. Rosner, "Biblical Theology," ed. T. Desmond Alexander and Brian S. Rosner, *New Dictionary of Biblical Theology* (Downers Grove, IL: InterVarsity, 2000), 3.

[19] *New Testament Theology: Basic Issues in the Current Debate* (Grand Rapids: Eerdmans, 1978), ch.2.

sage; 4) it acknowledges distinct voices of individual books and corpora (Johannine, Pauline, etc.); 5) while most finally attending to major themes across the whole NT to construct a NT theology; and 6) it understands that NT theology belongs integrally to the OT in Biblical Theology.

Principles of Theological Exegesis: Michael Gorman has articulated eight principles beginning with these first two: "Theological exegesis ... is biblical interpretation that takes place in an ecclesial context [church community] and is grounded in certain fundamental theological principles, especially (1) the principle of divine self-revelation and address and (2) the principle of the unity and catholicity, or universality, of the church."[20] Within principle (1), Gorman stresses the incarnational nature of Scripture, that is, that it is both of divine origin and of human creation. In principle (2), he affirms that just as the church is universal, so also "all Scripture is written for all God's people in all ages and places."[21] To these are added other principles:

(1) **Incarnational Principle**: Scripture is both of Divine and Human origin.
(2) **Universal Principle**: As the church is universal/catholic, so Scripture is for all people.
(3) **Ecclesial Principle**: The church is the proper location of the interpretation of Scripture.
(4) **Canonical Principle**: Scripture must be read within its canonical context.
(5) **Coherence Principle**: Despite diversity within, Scripture is unified in telling one story.
(6) **Charismatic Principle**: God's Spirit encourages and empowers theological interpretation.
(7) **Transformative Principle**: Theological interpretation cooperates with Scripture to transform God's people for performing and embodying Scripture.
(8) **Constructive Principle**: Theological interpretation assists the church in articulating its beliefs, values, convictions, and life-giving practices.

Missional Hermeneutics: We should add to this list the view that God is in the business of seeking and saving the lost (Luke 19:10). God desires all people to be saved (1 Tim 2:4). To read Scripture properly, we would do well to pay attention to how the *biblical materials may be synthesized around God's mission to bless all people in the gospel of Christ*. An important voice in this perspective is Brian D. Russell who sets forth a reading of Scripture from the perspective of God's mission in the world in his book *(re)Aligning with God: Reading Scripture for Church and World* (Eugene, Or: Cascade, 2015).

> Biblical materials may be synthesized around God's mission to bless all people in the gospel of Christ.

EXERCISE 10–E: Coherence Principle in Theological Performance: My final assignment for biblical theological students is synthetic based on the coherence principle. Students are asked to construct a biblical theology by selecting one portion of Scripture and correlating it with others.

1. What biblical passage would you choose to connect to others to construct a biblical theology?
2. Briefly sketch the main theological connections and relationships. Be creative.

---

[20] Gorman, *Biblical Exegesis*, 147.
[21] *Ibid.*, 150.

Scriptural Quotation Approach: Another approach to consider was articulated many decades ago and exemplified by E. Earle Ellis. He has understood the profound relationship of the NT's use of the OT in the theology of the early church. At places in his book, *Paul's Use of the Old Testament* (Grand Rapids: Baker, 1957), Ellis describes theological themes organized according to Paul's use of Scripture.

RÉSUMÉ OF THEOLOGICAL THEMES FROM PAUL'S QUOTATION OF SCRIPTURE[22]

Faith and Works	*Jew and Gentiles*	*Ethics*	*Wisdom*	*Eschatology*
Rom 1:17; 4:3, 6–7, 17–18; 10:4–6; Gal 3:6, 8–13, 16; 4:22–24	Rom 9:7, 9, 12–13, 15, 17, 25–29, 33; 10:16, 18–21; 11:3–4, 8–10, 26–27; 15:9–11, 21; Gal 3:8	Rom 12:19; 13:8; 14:11; 15:3; 1 Cor 6:16; 9:9; 10:7, 26; 2 Cor 6:16–18; 8:15; 9:9; Gal 5:14, 31; 6:2–3	Rom 11:24–25; 1 Cor 1:19, 31; 2:9, 16; 3:19–20	1 Cor 15:27, 45, 54–55

You could rightly think that these theological themes are important enough to warrant explicit connection to or support from the OT. However, we could multiply the references if strong allusions are included in the tally. For example, Eph 2:17–18 speaks to the unity of Jew and Gentile alluding to Isa 57:19 (also echoed in Rom 10:14). Indeed, Ellis rightly concludes, "the subjects on which the apostle dwells read like an outline of biblical theology" before providing this "index":

INDEX OF THEOLOGICAL TOPICS FROM PAUL'S QUOTATION OF SCRIPTURE[23]

1. The Fall of Man and its Effects (Rom 5:12ff)
2. The Universality of Sin (Rom 3:10ff)
3. The Coming of Christ and the Gospel (Rom 1:2; Gal 3:8, 14)
4. The Obedience and Sufferings of Christ (Rom 15:3)
5. The Resurrection of Christ (1 Cor 15:1ff)
6. The Lordship and Dominion of Christ (1 Cor 15:25, 27)
7. The Sovereignty of God (Rom 9:15, 17, 20)
8. Divine Election (Rom 9:7, 10ff; 11:4–5)
9. The Rejection of Israel and Calling of the Gentiles (Rom 9:25ff; 10:16ff)
10. The Universality of the Gospel (Rom 10:18)
11. The Forgiveness of Sin (Rom 4:6; 9:33; 10:11ff)
12. Justification by Faith (Rom 1:17; 4:1ff; 10:5ff)
13. Baptism and the Lord's Supper (1 Cor 10:1ff)
14. The Gifts of the Spirit (Eph 4:8)

---

[22] *Paul's Use*, 125.
[23] *Ibid.*, 116.

> 15. Christian Conduct (Rom 12:19; 13:9; 1 Cor 9:9)
> 16. The Persecution of Christians (Rom 8:36)
> 17. The Final Salvation of the Jews (Rom 11:26)
> 18. The Parousia of Christ (2 Thess 1:8–10)
> 19. The Final Judgment (Rom 14:11)
> 20. The Final Overthrow of Death (1 Cor 15:54ff)

EXERCISE 10–F: Evaluate Ellis' index of theological topics above by looking up the verses and double-checking the use of the OT in context.

a. Do Ellis' topical descriptions adequately reflect Paul's use of Scripture? Are there any of Ellis' topics that may possibly reflect theological and categorical presupposition(s) on his part?

b. Often you will find more related themes in context—what might Ellis have underrepresented?

c. Finally, if time permits, reconstruct the index. If you are in substantial agreement with Ellis, then identify, analyze, and topicalize any ***strong allusions*** to the OT in Paul's writings; how do Paul's strong allusions align with Ellis' index?

Concerning the temple theme in relation to the nations/gentiles, Ellis argues about Paul, "There is, then, an interrelated 'complex' of ideas covering such important Pauline themes as the 'seed' of David, the true Israel, the temple of God, the body of Christ, and the calling of the Gentiles. It is a pattern which lies in the substructure of NT theology, and, in its nucleus, it has its origins in the sayings of the Lord."[24] Ellis also describes important scriptural themes of the two covenants and Exodus typology.[25]

Following Ellis's lead (who follows C. H. Dodd), we may extend this to understand how Jesus was the source of the early church's exposition of Scripture.[26] Which Scripture texts did Jesus himself quote, refer to, allude to, and thus interpret? (Recall CHAPTER ALPHA.) Such verses may provide a framework from which to construct a biblical theology. Of particular interest is Jesus's own self-referencing use of Scripture to affirm his identity when asked if he was the Messiah. He replied, "I am and you will see the Son of Man sitting at the right hand of Power and coming with the clouds of heaven" (Mark 14:62//Matt 26:64//Luke 22:69–70), which combines Ps 110:1 and Dan 7:13. Taking this a step further, we may consider God the Father's affirmation of Jesus at his baptism and transfiguration: "You are my beloved Son with whom I am well-pleased" (e.g., Matt 3:17; 17:5; Mark 1:11; Luke 9:35; 2 Pet 1:17) as powerfully combining Gen 22 ("beloved"), Ps 2 ("my son"), and Isa 42:1 ("well-pleased," which is quoted in Matt 12:18).

Relatedly, Richard Bauckham proposes understanding the early church's Christology by reference to the use of OT texts that refer to YHWH God as Lord but now applied to Jesus as

---

[24] *Ibid.*, 92
[25] *Ibid.*, 130–31.
[26] *Ibid.*, 113.

Lord.[27] Also, Ben Witherington is producing a three-volume work that describes how the three most commonly cited OT books (Deuteronomy, Psalms, and Isaiah) are interpreted and used in the NT. Much exciting work remains to be done to synthesize biblical materials into vital theology.

SECONDARY AND TERTIARY INTERPRETIVE PROCEDURES:

The following procedures incorporate some elements of the PRIMARY INTERPRETIVE PROCEDURES.

1. **Identify your theological tradition. In a preliminary way, how might this inform your theological understanding of the passage?**
2. **In view of your interpretive work, answer these questions if it is possible to do so:**
    a. **What does the passage tell us about God?**
    b. **What does this passage tell us about God's designs for creation?**
    c. **What does the passage tell us about human beings within God's creation?**
    d. **What does the passage tell us about the relationship between God, creation, and human beings?**
3. **What is the passage really driving at and pushing for? Specifically, ask the following:**
    a. **What does the text urge us to believe? (faith)**
    b. **What does the text urge us to hope for? (hope)**
    c. **What does the text urge us to do? (love)**[28]
4. **Consider how this passage is located within God's biblical, covenantal story. Where is it within salvation history? Where is it in view of God's mission?**
5. **Based on systematic and biblical theological categories such as Christology, Pneumatology, eschatology, ecclesiology, ethics, etc., consider what contributions your passage makes to these areas.**
6. **Especially in view of your STEP 8: SCRIPTURAL CORRELATION work, consider how your passage contributes to a biblical theology of the particular NT book, the specific NT corpus (e.g., Johannine, Pauline, Lucan, Petrine), the NT, or the biblical Canon of Scripture.**
7. **Investigate commentaries, biblical theological works, or sermons for specific treatments of the major themes of this passage.**
8. **Consolidate your theological thinking; be creative. Ask any questions that may arise.**
9. **Consider specifically if anything theologically presented in this passage is *at tension* or even *in conflict* with what you understand elsewhere in Scripture. If present, these items may be evaluated further in STEP 11: EVALUATED APPLICATIONS.**

---

[27] See Bauckham, "Paul's Christology of Divine Identity," pages 182–232 in *Jesus and the God of Israel: God Crucified and Other Studies on the New Testament's Christology of Divine Identity* (Grand Rapids: Eerdmans, 2008).

[28] These three questions are from Gorman, *Biblical Exegesis*, 148.

IV. Bibliography

Primary Survey

Church History

Gonzalez, Justo. *The Story of Christianity*. 2 vols. 2nd ed. San Francisco: HarperOne, 2010.

Shelly, Bruce. *Church History in Plain Language*. 4th ed. Nashville: Thomas Nelson, 2012.

Walls, Andrew F. *The Missionary Movement in Christian History: Studies in the Transmission of Faith*. Maryknoll, NY: Orbis, 1996.

Sermon Collections: There are many, but these are recommended (thanks to Stacy R. Minger):

Early Church: John Chrysostom, Ambrose of Milan, Augustine, The Cappadocian Fathers (Basil the Great, Gregory of Nyssa, and Gregory of Nazianzus), and Gregory the Great.

Reformation Preachers: Martin Luther, John Calvin, Jonathan Edwards, and John Wesley for whom many collections are available, but see especially Kenneth J. Collins and Jason E. Vickers. *The Sermons of John Wesley: A Collection for the Christian Journey*. Nashville: Abingdon, 2013.

More Recent Preachers: Karl Barth, Dietrich Bonhoeffer, Luke Powery, Elizabeth Achtemeier, Fleming Rutledge, and Ellen F. Davis.

Scripture and Theology

Bartholomew, Craig G. and Michael W. Goheen, *The Drama of Scripture*. Grand Rapids: Baker Academic, 2004.

_____. *The True Story of the Whole World: Finding Your Place In the Biblical Drama*. Grand Rapids: Faith Alive Christian Resources, 2009.

Carson, D. A. is editor of the New Studies in Biblical Theology Series with multiple volumes. See also Carson's many books treating NT exegesis and theology.

Gladding, Sean. *The Story of God, the Story of Us*. Downers Grove, IL: InterVarsity, 2010.

McLaren, Brian D. *The Story We Find Ourselves In: Further Adventures of a New Kind of Christian*. San Francisco: Jossey Bass, 2003

Green, Joel B. *Reading Scripture as Wesleyans*. Nashville: Abingdon, 2010.

Hart, Trevor. *Faith Thinking: The Dynamics of Christian Theology*. Downers Grove, IL: InterVarsity, 1995.

Jones, Scott J. *John Wesley's Conception & Use of Scripture*. Nashville: Kingswood, 1995.

Marshall, I. Howard. *Beyond the Bible: Moving from Scripture to Theology*. Grand Rapids: Baker, 2004.

O'Keefe, John J., and R. R. Reno. *Sanctified Vision: An Introduction to Early Christian Interpretation of the Bible*. Baltimore: The Johns Hopkins University Press, 2005.

Perrin, Nicholas et al. eds. *Jesus, Paul, and the People of God: A Theological Dialogue with N. T. Wright*. Downers Grove, IL: IVP Academic, 2011.

Richter, Sandra. *The Epic of Eden: A Christian Entry into the Old Testament*. Downers Grove, IL: InterVarsity Press, 2008.

Vanhoozer, Kevin J., et al. eds. *Theological Interpretation of the New Testament: A Book-by-Book Survey*. Grand Rapids: Baker Academic, 2008.

Seamands, Stephen A. *Give Them Christ: Preaching His Incarnation, Crucifixion, Resurrection, Ascension and Return*. Downers Grove, IL: InterVarsity Press, 2012.

Young, Frances. *Virtuoso Theology: The Bible and Interpretation*. Eugene, OR: Wipf & Stock, 2002.

Wright, N. T. *Justification: God's Plan & Paul's Vision*. Downers Grove, IL: IVP Academic, 2009.

_____. *Surprised by Hope: Rethinking Heaven, the Resurrection, and the Mission of the Church*. New York: HarperOne, 2008. [See also Wright's many other books.]

Theological Interpretation

Adam, A. K. M., et al. *Reading Scripture with the Church: Toward a Hermeneutic for Theological Interpretation*. Grand Rapids: Baker, 2006.

Bartholomew, Craig G., et al. eds. *Out of Egypt: Biblical Theology and Biblical Interpretation*. Scripture and Hermeneutics Series 5. Grand Rapids: Zondervan, 2004.

Billings, J. Todd. *The Word of God for the People of God: An Entryway to the Theological Interpretation of Scripture*. Grand Rapids: Eerdmans, 2010.

Bryan, Christopher. *And God Spoke: The Authority of the Bible for the Church Today*. Cambridge: Cowley, 2002.

Callen, Barry L., and Richard P. Thompson, eds. *Reading the Bible in Wesleyan Ways: Some Constructive Proposals*. Kansas City, MS: Beacon Hill, 2004.

Fowl, Stephen, ed. *The Theological Interpretation of Scripture: Classic and Contemporary Readings*. Blackwell Readings in Modern Theology. Cambridge, MA: Blackwell, 1997.

Fowl, Stephen E. *Engaging Scripture: A Model for Theological Interpretation*. Cambridge, MA: Blackwell, 1998.

Treier, Daniel J. *Introducing Theological Interpretation of Scripture: Recovering a Christian Practice*. Grand Rapids: Baker Academic, 2008.

Vanhoozer, Kevin J., ed., *Dictionary for Theological Interpretation of the Bible*. Grand Rapids: Baker Academic, 2005.

Vanhoozer, Kevin J., et al. eds. *Theological Interpretation of the New Testament: A Book-by-Book Survey*. Grand Rapids: Baker Academic, 2008.

Watson, Francis. *The Fourfold Gospel: A Theological Reading of the New Testament Portraits of Jesus*. Grand Rapids: Baker Academic, 2016.

Secondary Study and Tertiary Research

Biblical Theology

Alexander, T. Desmond, et al. *New Dictionary of Biblical Theology: Exploring the Unity & Diversity of Scripture*. Downers Grove, IL: InterVarsity Press, 2000.

Balla, Peter. *Challenges to New Testament Theology: An Attempt to Justify the Enterprise*. Tübingen: Mohr Siebeck, 1997.

Barr, James. *The Concept of Biblical Theology: An Old Testament Perspective*. Minneapolis: Fortress, 1999.

Bray, Gerald L. *God Is Love: A Biblical and Systematic Theology*. Wheaton, IL: Crossway, 2012.

Childs, Brevard. *Biblical Theology of the Old and New Testaments: Theological Reflection on the Christian Bible*. Minneapolis: Fortress, 1993.

Feldmeier, Reinhard, and Hermann Spieckermann. *God of the Living: A Biblical Theology*. Translated by Mark E. Biddle. Waco, TX: Baylor University Press, 2011.

Grindheim, Sigurd. *Introducing Biblical Theology*. London: T&T Clark, 2013

Hafemann, Scott J. ed. *Biblical Theology: Retrospect and Prospect*. Downers Grove, IL: InterVarsity Press, 2002.

Kaiser, Walter C., Jr. *The Promise-Plan of God: A Biblical Theology of the Old and New Testaments*. Grand Rapids: Zondervan, 2008.

Klink, Edward W., and Darian R. Lockett. *Understanding Biblical Theology: A Comparison of Theory and Practice*. Grand Rapids: Zondervan, 2012.

Kraftchick, Steven J. et al. *Biblical Theology: Problems and Perspectives*. Nashville: Abingdon, 1995.

Stuhlmacher, Peter. *How to Do Biblical Theology*. Allison Park, PA: Pickwick, 1995.

NT Theology

Beale, G. K. *The Temple and the Church's Mission: A Biblical Theology of the Dwelling Place of God*. New Studies in Biblical Theology 17. Downers Grove, IL: InterVarsity Press, 2004.

_____. *A New Testament Biblical Theology: The Unfolding of the Old Testament in the New*. Grand Rapids: Baker, 2011.

Caird, G. B. *New Testament Theology*. Completed and edited by L. D. Hurst. Oxford: Clarendon, 1994.

Dunn, James D. G. *New Testament Theology: An Introduction*. Library of Biblical Theology. Nashville: Abingdon, 2009.

Dunn, James D. G., editor of the New Testament Theology Series. 21 vols. Cambridge: Cambridge University Press, 1991–2003.

Esler, Philip F. *New Testament Theology: Communion and Community*. Minneapolis: Fortress, 2005.

Guthrie, Donald. *New Testament Theology*. Leicester, England, and Downers Grove, IL: InterVarsity Press, 1981.

Hatina, Thomas. *New Testament Theology and Its Quest for Relevance: Ancient Texts and Modern Readers*. New York: Bloomsbury T&T Clark, 2013.

Hasel, Gerhard. *New Testament Theology: Basic Issues in the Current Debate*. Grand Rapids: Eerdmans, 1978

Isaak, Jon M. *New Testament Theology: Extending the Table*. Eugene, OR: Wipf and Stock, 2011.

Jeremias, Joachim. *New Testament Theology: The Proclamation of Jesus*. Trans. John Bowden. New York: Charles Scribner's Sons, 1971.

Kümmel, Werner Georg. *The Theology of the New Testament According to Its Major Witnesses: Jesus–Paul–John*. Trans. John E. Steely. Nashville: Abingdon, 1973.

Ladd, George Eldon. *A Theology of the New Testament*. Rev. ed. Grand Rapids: Eerdmans, 1993.

Marshall, I. Howard. *New Testament Theology: Many Witnesses, One Gospel*. Downers Grove, IL: InterVarsity Press, 2004.

Matera, Frank J. *New Testament Theology: Exploring Diversity and Unity*. Louisville: Westminster John Knox, 2007.

Morris, Leon. *New Testament Theology*. Grand Rapids: Zondervan, 1986.

Neill, Stephen. *Jesus Through Many Eyes: Introduction to the Theology of the New Testament*. Minneapolis: Fortress, 1976.

Richardson, Alan. *An Introduction to the Theology of the New Testament*. New York: Harper & Row, 1958.

Schnelle, Udo. *Theology of the New Testament*. Translated by M. Eugene Boring. Grand Rapids: Baker, 2009.

Schreiner, Thomas R. *New Testament Theology: Magnifying God in Christ*. Grand Rapids: Baker, 2008.

_____. *The King in His Beauty: A Biblical Theology of the Old and New Testaments*. Grand Rapids: Baker, 2013.

Strecker, Georg. *Theology of the New Testament*. Louisville: Westminster John Knox, 2000.

Thielman, Frank. *Theology of the New Testament: A Canonical and Synthetic Approach*. Grand Rapids: Zondervan, 2005.

Via, Dan O. *What is New Testament Theology?* Minneapolis: Fortress, 2002.

Witherington III, Ben. *The Indelible Image: The Theological and Ethical Thought World of the New Testament*. 2 vols. Downers Grove, IL: IVP Academic, 2009. [See also his other books treating NT theology.]

Wright, N. T. *Jesus and the Victory of God*. Christian Origins and the Question of God 2. Minneapolis: Fortress, 1996.

_____. *Paul and the Faithfulness of God*. Christian Origins and the Question of God 4, Parts 1 and 2. Minneapolis: Fortress, 2013.

_____. *The Climax of the Covenant: Christ and the Law in Pauline Theology*. Minneapolis: Fortress, 1992.

_____. *The New Testament and the People of God*. Christian Origins and the Question of God 1. Minneapolis: Fortress, 1992.

_____. *The Resurrection of the Son of God*. Christian Origins and the Question of God 3. Minneapolis: Fortress, 2003.

Theological Interpretation

Bockmuehl, Markus and Alan J. Torrance, eds. *Scripture's Doctrine and Theology's Bible: How the New Testament Shapes Christian Dogmatics*. Grand Rapids: Baker Academic, 2008.

Green, Joel B., and Max Turner, eds. *Between Two Horizons: Spanning New Testament Studies and Systematic Theology*. Grand Rapids: Eerdmans, 2000.

Spinks, D. Christopher. *The Bible and the Crisis of Meaning: Debates on the Theological Interpretation of Scripture*. London: T&T Clark, 2007.

Treier, Daniel J. "Biblical Theology and/or Theological Interpretation of Scripture? Defining the Relationship," *Scottish Journal of Theology* 61:1 (2008): 16–31.

Watson, Francis. *Text, Church, and World: Biblical Interpretation in Theological Perspective*. Grand Rapids: Eerdmans, 1994.

Systematic and Biblical Theology

Brunner, Emil. *Dogmatics*. Translated by Olive Wyon. 3 vols. Philadelphia: Westminster Press, 1949–1962.

Green, Joel B. and Max Turner, eds. *Between Two Horizons: Spanning New Testament Studies and Systematic Theology*. Grand Rapids: Eerdmans, 1999.

Pannenberg, Wolfhart. *An Introduction to Systematic Theology*. Grand Rapids: Eerdmans, 1991.

_____. *Jesus, God and Man*. Translated by Lewis L. Wilkins and Duane A. Priebe. Philadelphia: Westminster, 1968.

_____. *Systematic Theology*. Translated by Geoffrey W. Bromiley. 3 vols. Grand Rapids: Eerdmans, 1991.

Watson, Francis. *Text and Truth: Redefining Biblical Theology*. Grand Rapids: Eerdmans, 2009.

STEP 11
EVALUATED APPLICATIONS

"The Bible is a book that has been read more and examined less
than any book that ever existed."
—Thomas Paine

"No man ever believes that the Bible means what it says:
He is always convinced that it says what he means."
—George Bernard Shaw

"The Holy Book of the living God suffers more
from its exponents today than from its opponents."
—Leonard Ravenhill

"The applicatory step is that for which all else exists. It represents the final purpose of Bible study."
—Robert A. Traina, *Methodical Bible Study*, 217

Introduction: The quotations on the previous page reflect the complexity of handling Scripture and applying it (or not) in our lives here and now.[1] Much is at stake for this topic. The great NT scholar I. Howard Marshall has aptly stated that we should attempt to interpret the Bible (especially its appropriation today) learning from Scripture itself.[2] In this STEP, I will only provide some basic parameters and establish some best practices as much as possible in view of Scripture itself. I also offer this caveat: This STEP assumes the previous STEPS. It contains difficult but rich material. Texts have meaning in the original context, and from this meaning a derived significance today. In the preceding ten STEPS, we have attempted to hear and attend to what was meant by the NT authors who addressed their respective audiences. As has been said, a text can't mean what it never meant. Yet, a text may have distinct significance in various contemporary settings, and so have multiple applications. Thus, our appropriation of Scripture today through various applications in our respective contexts logically comes after our interpretative work. Furthermore, in the previous STEP 10: BIBLICAL THEOLOGY we learned that theology provides an essential framework for discerning what is most important in Scripture. In STEP 11: EVALUATED APPLICATIONS we consider foundational principles of evaluating what we should apply and how we should appropriate Scripture in our lives within our respective communities. The processes of evaluation, application, and appropriation involve the most intimate and nuclear family members of interpretive principles: "Major on Majors" and "Minor on Minors" (MOM) and "Priority on Praxis" (POP), "Scripture interprets Scripture" (SIS), and "Be reaching out" (BRO).

I. PRIMARY SURVEY

Orientation: Moving from the Bible to our communities is paramount. Within Scripture we have both transcultural truth and situation-bound truths. Richard B. Hays maintains, "It is impossible to distinguish 'timeless truth' from 'culturally conditioned elements' in the New Testament."[3] We might want to mine for raw nuggets of pure truth, but these truths are embedded in human cultural expressions. Similarly, Gordon D. Fee and Douglas Stuart have succinctly summarized, "Interpretation of the Bible is demanded by the 'tension' that exists between its *eternal relevance* and its *historical particularity*."[4] Scripture has "eternal relevance" for living here and now while at the same time reflecting past time "historical particularity." It's difficult to separate these two aspects. Yet, it is better to envision a "continuum of particularity or transcendence" between transcendent applicability (eternal relevance) and historical particularity.[5]

---

[1] These popular quotations are from among the many at http://www.tentmaker.org/Quotes/biblequotes.htm accessed Sept 26, 2016. I have not checked their accuracy, and yet this does not alter their relevance to the discussion.

[2] *Beyond the Bible: Moving from Scripture to Theology* (Grand Rapids: Baker, 2004), 32, 48.

[3] *The Moral Vision of the New Testament: Community, Cross, New Creation: A Contemporary Introduction to New Testament Ethics* (San Francisco: HarperSanFrancisco, 1996), 300.

[4] Gordon D. Fee and Douglas Stuart, *How to Read the Bible for All Its Worth: A Guide to Understanding the Bible*, 3rd ed. (Grand Rapids: Zondervan, 2003), 21, emphasis original.

[5] So Bauer and Traina, *Inductive Bible Study*, 294.

STEP 11: PRIMARY SURVEY

CONTINUUM OF PARTICULARITY AND TRANSCENDENCE

historical particularity ———— *transcendent applicability*

On the one hand, if some value, attitude, command, or promise in the biblical text has transcendent applicability, it will bear upon our present circumstances. On the other hand, if some value, attitude, command, or promise has historical particularity, *it may not be readily applicable*.

EXERCISE 11–A: In view of the CONTINUUM OF PARTICULARITY AND TRANSCENDENCE, consider these commands from 1 Thess 5:16–27 (skipping 5:24; HCSB) and answer the questions below.

> ¹⁶ Rejoice always!
> ¹⁷ Pray constantly.
> ¹⁸ Give thanks in everything, for this is God's will for you in Christ Jesus.
> ¹⁹ Don't stifle the Spirit.
> ²⁰ Don't despise prophecies,
> ²¹ but test all things. Hold on to what is good.
> ²² Stay away from every kind of evil.
> ²³ Now may the God of peace Himself sanctify you completely….
> ²⁵ Brothers, pray for us also.
> ²⁶ Greet all the brothers with a holy kiss.
> ²⁷ I charge you by the Lord that this letter be read to all the brothers.

1. Which commands show a degree of historical particularity? How was this determination made?
2. For commands with historical particularity, are you able to discern some underlying principle that allows them to have transcendent applicability today? On what basis can you decide this?

These commands occur at the end of Paul's letter where he concludes with more generalized and broadly applicable commands. But even among these, we discern some specificity, from which nevertheless we may discern undergirding principles that may apply today. On the matter of the "holy kiss," see EXERCISE 11–C below.

<u>Scale of Abstraction and Easy of Applicability</u>: William J. Webb explores transcultural analysis setting forth principles of evaluation; see the brief discussion in TERTIARY RESEARCH.[6] One basis of evaluation is whether the biblical idea or command has cultural components that are not completely analogous to our setting. Thus, Webb discusses how commands may be given in varying degrees of abstraction (one extreme) or concreteness (the other extreme). For example, the command to "love your neighbor" is rather abstract as is, whereas the command in Lev 19:10 "Leave the corners of your fields unharvested" for people to come and glean for free is rather concrete. Between these commands we could place the command "Care for the poor." Webb explains: "[H]ow high one climbs on the ladder of abstraction to form a principle depends upon the

---

[6] William J. Webb, *Slaves, Women & Homosexuals: Exploring the Hermeneutics of Cultural Analysis* (Downers Grove, IL: IVP Academic, 2001), 209–11.

similarities and the differences between the ancient and modern worlds. Differences push one up the ladder [i.e., to abstraction]; similarities push one down [i.e., to concreteness]."[7]

EXERCISE 11–B: Consider these verses from Eph 5:15–18 (NASB) as you answer the following questions given the findings from previously completed interpretive work.

[15] Therefore be careful how you walk, not as unwise men but as wise, [16] making the most of your time, because the days are evil. [17] So then do not be foolish, but understand what the will of the Lord is. [18] And do not get drunk with wine, for that is dissipation, but be filled with the Spirit...

1. Having done your interpretive work in STEP 5: LEXICAL RESEARCH on the word "will" ($\vartheta\acute{\epsilon}\lambda\eta\mu\alpha$), you find that in Ephesians God's will is to adopt people into the divine family (1:5) and to have Christ sum up all things in God's economy for the salvation of all (1:9–14). Also, when researching STEP 8: SCRIPTURAL CORRELATIONS, you realize that the clause "making the most of your time" is found in Col 4:5–6: "Conduct yourselves with wisdom toward outsiders, making the most of the opportunity. [6] Let your speech always be with grace, as though seasoned with salt, so that you will know how you should respond to each person." Therefore, in light of this evidence, what truths can be discerned in Eph 5:15–17?
2. Turning to 5:18a, what is the truth of this verse? Is it transcultural or situation bound?
3. One application would be not to get drunk with wine. But, what about getting drunk with bourbon or Kentucky Bourbon Ale? Are people in Kentucky allowed to get drunk in other ways?
4. Finally, you remember from STEP 7: HISTORICAL CONTEXT that "getting drunk with wine" was a major form of entertainment in the ancient world. Also, in STEP 5: LEXICAL RESEARCH you learned that "dissipation" means "a waste of time." In view of the entertainment culture and wasting of time, how do these additional considerations inspire other areas of application?

The fact that Scripture contains historically specific commands as well as transcendent ones requires the people of God to *evaluate*, *apply*, and *appropriate* those passages that we have interpreted. We continue our discussion by defining these three terms.

Evaluation *refers to the assessment of something to determine its value or contribution to a process*. This statement by Traina is profoundly true:

> Contrary to common belief and practice, a Scriptural unit is not ready to apply as soon as its meaning has been discovered. Interpretation needs to be followed by a process of assessment whereby the relevance and worth of a passage are ascertained before its employment can have a valid foundation.... For the haphazard employment of Scriptural statements without their prior evaluation may lead to spiritual disaster. On the other hand, if proper appraisal occurs, then valid application is well on its way.[8]

---

[7] *Slaves, Women & Homosexuals*, 54.
[8] *Methodical Bible Study*, 203.

We must learn to evaluate which is defined as follows: "1. to determine or fix the value of; 2. to determine the significance, worth, or condition of, usually by careful appraisal and study."[9] Traina summarizes nicely: "To evaluate is to assess the worth of something, to appraise its excellence, relevance, and usefulness."[10]

<u>Evaluation Involves Three Movements</u>: First, we begin by recognizing that we are particular members of a society, culture, sub-culture, and group (like a church) and that our group carries along with it certain assumptions, presuppositions, and "baggage" that affect how we view the verses we are seeking to apply. We may have difficulty seeing clearly what is really there. So, we begin evaluation with a sober assessment of ourselves in our respective communities.

Second, evaluation involves our careful consideration of what truths are found within the pericope and whether they are **transcendent/transcultural truths** (i.e., ready to appropriate and apply to other times and places including our own) or **situation-bound truths** (i.e., so closely bound to the original historical situation that they are not directly applicable to other times and places including our own). Indeed, our interpretation of the passage may reveal considerable agreement or coherence among biblical passages or considerable tension and even contradiction between different parts of the Bible. Bauer and Traina delineate four facets to such biblical analysis of evaluation: 1) the legitimacy of making applications today, 2) the scope of applicability, 3) the force of application, and 4) the degree of concession needed in application, For example, "pray constantly" is required for believers (so, it has limited scope), even though it would be good for unbelievers also to pray. In terms of force, "pray constantly" is important, but this is not the basis of one's salvation. Moreover, some degree of concession is allowable since we grow in our ability to pray constantly—we can learn to remain open and listen to God throughout the day; prayer is indeed a two-way conversation.[11] Also, some commands relate to the core of the faith and have tremendous force (e.g., "Repent, for the Kingdom of God has arrived!" Matt 4:17) while others are significantly qualified by the original circumstances and have greatly reduced applicability. For example, Jesus said: "And whatever city or village you enter, inquire who is worthy in it, and stay at his house until you leave" (Matt 10:11). But this command was for his disciples in the context of Judea during Jesus's ministry. We would need to evaluate how legitimate this is for application today—its scope, force, and any concessions.

Third, we must evaluate our present situation to understand what similarities and differences exist in relation to the passage. In the case of Matt 10:11 above, our travels are much different then in Mediterranean peasant cultures where people noticed strangers and it was expected to show hospitality to them. Also, to jump from house to house would appear suspect like some freeloading charlatan wanting only food and shelter. For Jesus and his disciples, such a family that welcomed them signaled where to begin proclaiming the good news which was also expected of

---

[9] Definition from http://www.merriam-webster.com/dictionary/evaluate accessed 10–1–2016.

[10] *Methodical Bible Study*, 204.

[11] Such constancy in prayer is described in Brother Lawrence and Frank Charles Laubach, *Practicing His Presence* (Beaumont, TX: SeedSowers, 1973).

guests who reported relevant "news" and political happenings. However, if one were to consider underlying principles for application today, when entering a town missionaries should perceive 1) where people are receptive to strangers; and 2) where one may be welcomed to share political-philosophical ideas. For example, when arriving in the cities, the apostle Paul would visit Jewish synagogues (or places of prayer as at Philippi as seen in Acts 16:13–14) and preach the gospel there. Similarly, in Athens Paul went to the Areopagus (Mars Hill) that was an open venue for presenting new ideas. Thus, evaluation occurs first with oneself, then with the passage of Scripture under investigation in relation to other passages, and finally, with the circumstances addressed in the passage in view of our present circumstances to find points of comparison and contrast.

EXERCISE 11–C: Paul issues a command in 1 Cor 16:20b: "Greet one another with a holy kiss." Below are important findings from your interpretation work from the previous STEPS:

- You discover that Paul repeats this command in 1 Thess 5:26, 2 Cor 13:12, and Rom 16:16 and the command is found in 1 Pet 5:14.
- You discover that such kissing was lips to lips.
- In your interpretation you discover that kissing in the Mediterranean world was common practice when family members greeted one another.
- The early Christian practice of kissing of one another across social classes, ethnicities, and genders radically communicated the truth of the inclusive new family of God.
- The adjective "holy" was added probably to disallow any sexual motive/impurity in the kiss.
- In the first centuries after Christ, the early church was accused of sexual immorality and eventually limited the holy kisses according to gender (men kissing men and women kissing women).

As you evaluate this command, you recognize that it occurs at the end of these letters and seemingly provided an important command for normative Christian practice.

1. What settings in your life would a holy kiss be appropriate as commanded, if at all?

2. To the best of your ability to determine, what is the underlying principle in the original text?

3. What would be analogous practices of greeting in your contexts that would be appropriate?

4. Do you think other believers might have different feelings and even practices about this? Why?

Application *refers to the various ways Scripture may be put into practice.* Since what is addressed in Scripture may be speaking multidimensionally and simultaneously to values, relationships, behaviors, thinking, etc., we may postulate *theoretically* a good number of possible ways to embody the particular passage of Scripture. It has been said that *a biblical passage has one meaning/interpretation, but multiple applications in various life-settings*. Indeed, the primary role of the Holy Spirit in each person's life is to prompt, encourage, and empower holy living. In response, we can prayerfully consider places of application. Consider the following diagram and these areas.

- o Our **worldview** fundamentally will inform, shape, and foster our core **values** and what we care about;
- o Our **thought-life** and **thinking** direct our life trajectories; honoring God or not; "reality-based" or not; love-based or not;
- o **Attitudes**, **desires**, and **affections** are deep seated aspects of who we are and who we are becoming; do these align with Jesus and God's Kingdom or not;
- o **Behavior** and **conduct** outwardly manifest all the above in private and in public and bear upon core relationships with ourselves, our families, other believers, our neighbors or not; our witness to all people or not; our caring for creation or not.

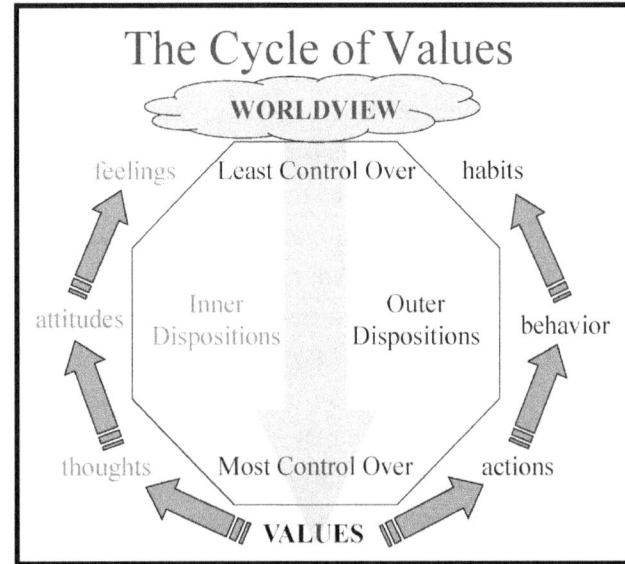

Common dangers in application include 1) thinking too narrowly of one specific situation; 2) focusing on only one application area; and, 3) being self-referential and imposing one's own specific application(s) to everyone else. We must remember that the role of the Holy Spirit is *to convict people where a change of mind and heart is needed (i.e., repentance)*. Sermons too often focus either on "correct (theological) thinking" or on "(specific) proper actions." However, people are more complex than this and Scripture addresses more than these two areas. Indeed, at issue is our worldview that entails stories of ultimate reality, ultimate questions and their answers, cultural symbols by which to communicate these stories and answers, and finally "a way-of-being-in-the-world" that would involve values, attitudes, actions, etc.[12] Our worldviews need serious overhauling which will affect our values, attitudes, behaviors, habits, and feelings, all of which can be influenced (or not) by the Holy Spirit. Most essentially, our view of the world should have a vision for God's Kingdom as embodied in Jesus and empowered by the Holy Spirit in our lives.

<u>Initial Suggestions for Application</u>: Once you have carefully completed evaluations, you may be justified to consider specific points of application and real-life scenarios and examples.

1. Be specific; think of specific scenarios and situations that have some significant correspondence to the biblical passage.
2. It is often helpful to bring in illustrations or real life scenarios similar to the biblical text and/or that illustrate your application points and their favorable consequences. Conversely, negative examples may be helpful to consider in view of their harmful consequences.
3. One method that I have used on occasion is to consider what might *prevent* people from applying the scriptural passage in specific ways: fears, behavior patterns, lack of accountability, negative media saturation, competing values, discouraging relationships, health, etc.

---

[12] Wright, *People of God*, 123–24. Worldviews entail stories, questions/answers, symbols, and praxis/conduct.

Appropriation *refers to the personal and communal embodiment of the truth of Scripture*, which is something that this book cannot accomplish for you. How you appropriate Scripture is a matter of prayerful conviction and empowered obedience through the guidance of the Holy Spirit and self-surrender in trust to God's provision. It is a yearning to imitate God in Christ by the help of the Holy Spirit within the community of faith as a witness to the world. The role of the Holy Spirit is primary here in leading us to conviction and/or affirmation in our stance towards obeying the truth of Scripture. Appropriation is individual, but it will always have communal impact since we live in relationship to one another. *Appropriation will always foster Christ-likeness, and should be measured in terms of holy love for God, neighbor, and self.* In the end, I believe that *scriptural study without application and appropriation is like a person without a soul; unless we actually embody and appropriate Scripture in increasing measure, our study of it is no good.* If we don't study and submit to Scripture, our awareness of possible applications will be myopic, and therefore our appropriations will be selectively convenient and even circular—we come to Scripture self-determined in the kinds of appropriation we will submit to. Such appropriation is haphazard and detrimental to discipleship. Incomplete and selective appropriation of Scripture leads to factionalism and sectarian thinking; it polarizes individuals around "teaching" camps that claim scriptural support while ignoring the more central truth, message, and story of Scripture.

Motivation for Appropriation: C. S. Lewis in his *Letters to Malcolm chiefly on Prayer* very aptly described an underlying concern to live faithfully to God rather than to succumb to sinful living: "The only way in which I can make real to myself ... the heinousness of sin is to remember that every sin is the distortion of an energy breathed into us—an energy which, if not thus distorted, would have blossomed into one of those holy acts whereof 'God did it' and 'I did it' are both true descriptions. We poison the wine as He decants it into us; murder a melody He would play with us as the instrument.... Hence all sin, whatever else it is, is sacrilege."[13]

Orthodoxy, Orthopathy, and Orthopraxy: People are caught in the balance between right thinking about God (orthodoxy), right disposition and attitude (orthopathy), and right living (orthopraxy). Between these three, people are often more interested in orthodoxy than the other two. Why? Doctrines stand outside of and apart from us and provide a focus and orientation apart from ourselves; doctrines and God become "objectified"—*unless* we dare to see ourselves within God's story, to which the doctrines themselves give testimony. *It is easier "to believe" correctly than "to live" correctly;* it is easier to give mental assent to truths than to walk differently in the world. To know is not necessarily to be and to do, although knowing precedes being and doing.

> It is easier "to believe" correctly than "to live" correctly.

Let me provide an example. I was asked once to evaluate and provide critical feedback for a denominational doctrinal statement on holiness. In the statement I was quite surprised to find no description of how Scripture teaches people to grow in holiness (Eph 4:20–24; Rom 12:1–2, etc.), nor a description of how love is the goal of holiness (Matt 5:48; Eph 5:1–2; 1 Pet 1:22, etc.). In-

---

[13] C. S. Lewis, *Letters to Malcolm: Chiefly on Prayer* (New York: Harcourt, Brace & World, 1964), 69.

stead, the doctrinal statement was attempting to adjudicate between two very contentious views of *when holiness was attained*—whether it is a process or instantaneous. In my view the doctrinal statement failed terribly to address both the *goal* of holiness (i.e., love) and the means and practical steps of growth towards holy love that are described in Scripture. In trying to address the theoretical "when," the statement missed the mark of holiness altogether and majored on a minor rather than majoring on majors. Especially because holiness is such a commonly misunderstood, frightening, and foreign idea to people, it is paramount to describe it well and fully. So then, *what should we "major on" to rightly evaluate and appropriate Scripture today?*

<u>Beware of the Pendulum Swinging Extremes</u>: Actually, when it comes to application and appropriation, two extremes typically face us. One extreme takes all of Scripture at face value as literally as we possibly can; if there is a command, then we must obey it exactly as stated. The problem with this is that what we think is "face value" is not "face value" for someone else. Moreover, there are tensions in Scripture that may appear quite contradictory. When this happens, *we tend to read Scripture how best suites our Christian sub-culture thus perpetuating our own versions of Christianity*. We pick and choose texts to take seriously and apply woodenly. Such a literalistic extreme, which indeed comes from a very high view of Scripture, often serves to protect us from the other extreme of skepticism that "explains away the text" and often reflects a low view of Scripture. In this latter view, everything in Scripture is culture-bound and hence liable to be discounted and explained away; Scripture is antiquated and needs to be updated. Both extremes—literalism and skepticism—are often in reaction to each other. However, a third way exists that is much more reasonable, requires more work, is "humanizing" in the best sense of the word, and walks in step with the overall message of God's Word.

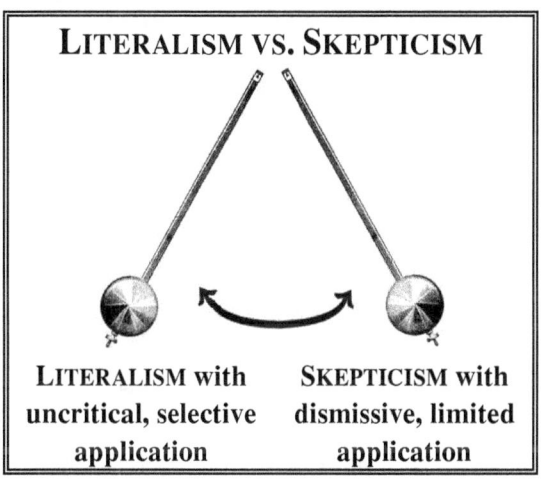

LITERALISM VS. SKEPTICISM

LITERALISM with uncritical, selective application

SKEPTICISM with dismissive, limited application

<u>Bringing Forward Unresolved Interpretive Problems</u>: While walking through the STEPS of interpreting God's Word, you have had opportunities to observe the text carefully, to understand it on its own terms, to ask questions, and to seek evidence to interpret these questions. Even after this rigorous process—or perhaps because of it—you have compared your passage and what it communicates with other biblical materials, and some difficulties may remain. Gorman very helpfully describes several different options when we face challenging material within our scriptural study. He asks, will you...

- ❖ ignore the text?
- ❖ challenge the text?
- ❖ look for a means of reconciliation?
- ❖ review and revise your exegesis?
- ❖ alter your beliefs and/or behavior?
- ❖ consult with others?[14]

---

[14] *Biblical Exegesis*, 163.

What you choose will likely depend on how important the passage is, who is speaking (e.g., Jesus, or Paul), what it may be commanding, and how challenging it might be for you to take it to heart and live differently.

Our Faithful Posture of Obedience to God: The most important attribute that interpreters of God's Word have is their willingness to obey. As a university student, I remember hearing a statement by Os Guinness in one of his talks, "Honest questions need answers; emotionally-based questions answers need." There are real and important questions that people need to have resolved about Scripture, the nature of God, and Jesus. However, there are some questions raised that are motivated by emotional needs that may excuse us from knowing the truth and taking responsibility according to the truth. Our affections and disposition will influence our willingness and ability to obey God and His Word. A former colleague of mine admitted to me that, while he was flagrantly disobedient to the Word of God, his view of Scripture was lessened correspondingly with his disobedience. Unfortunately, we each share a propensity to point the finger at others rather than at ourselves as attested by Helmut Thielicke,

> The man who studies theology, and especially he who studies dogmatics, might watch carefully whether he increasingly does not think in the third rather than in the second person. You know what I mean by that. This transition from one to the other level of thought, from a personal relationship with God to a merely technical reference, usually is exactly synchronized with the moment that I no longer can read the word of Holy Scripture as a word to me, but only as the object of exegetical endeavors. This is the first step towards the worst and most widespread ministers' disease. For the minster frequently can hardly expound a text as a letter which has been written to him, but he reads the text under the impulse of the question, How would it be used in a sermon?[15]

It is important as we evaluate Scripture that we are prayerfully open to self-evaluation and the discernment of the Spirit probing our hearts.

Principlizing Bridge and Connecting to God's Story: J. Scott Duvall and J. Daniel Hays have attempted to represent the movement from the biblical world to our world over a wide gaping river representing Culture, Language, Time, Covenant, and Situation that must be traversed by the "Principlizing Bridge."[16] In this view, the process of interpretation will involve crossing this river and coming back again with principles from Scripture for living today.

---

[15] Thielicke, *Little Exercise*, 34.

[16] Duvall and Hays, *Grasping God's Word*, 39–50. The diagram is based upon theirs, but the images are quite different and represent different habitations—homes, temples, cathedrals, huts, villages, cities—to reflect the diversity of human culture. The village scene in the center is of Extremadura, Spain. The bridge and modern city of Wiesbaden, Germany (upper right) are adapted from Frank Koester, *Modern City Planning and Maintenance* (New York: McBride, Nast and Company, 1914), 58 and 101; the "Marine View Terrace" in San Francisco (bottom right) is slightly adapted from J. S. Cahill, "Architectural Creations of Mr. Henry C. Smith, A.I.A.," *The Architect and Engineer of California* 44.1 (1916): 40. The sacrificial scene to the god Asclepius (bottom center) is slightly adapted from Victor Duruy, *History of Greece, and of the Greek People: From the Earliest Times to the Roman Conquest*,

THE PRINCIPLIZING BRIDGE[17]

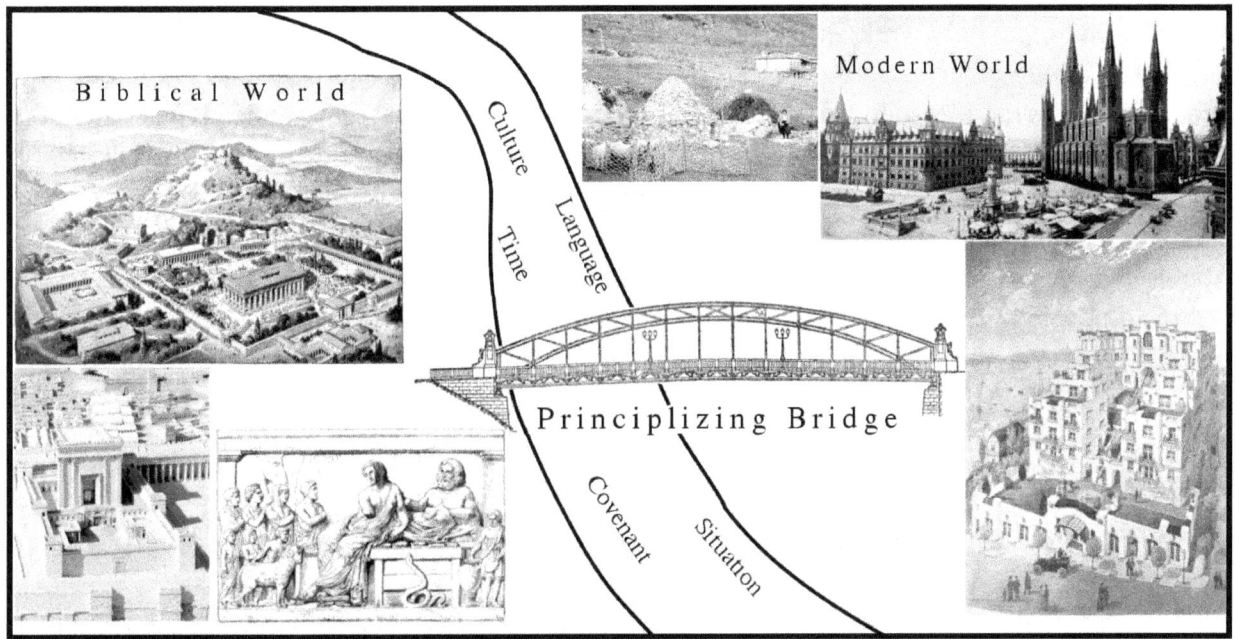

The questions Duvall and Hays provide to guide students in the process are as follow:[18]

1. What did the text mean to the biblical audience?
2. What are the differences between the biblical audience and us?
3. What is the theological principle(s) in the text?
4. How should individual Christians today apply the theological principle(s) in their lives?

One problem with these questions is that *Scripture consists of more than principles*; it tells a story.

EXERCISE 11–D: Interpreters have proposed a variety of themes as central in Scripture including these: the Covenants of God, the Kingdom of God, the People of God, the Temple of God, the Stewardship of Creation, and the Love of God (God's love for us and our love of God).

1. What do you think is the overall message of Scripture?

2. How does this message relate to your understanding of the purposes of God in the world?

---

trans. M. M. Ripley, vol.1.2 (Boston: Estes and Lauriat, 1890), 417. In the bottom left is a model of Herod's Temple in Jerusalem. In the upper left is a reconstructed city of Olympia in Greece, slightly adapted from William Carey Morey, *Outlines of Greek History: With a Survey of Ancient Oriental Nations* (New York: American Book Company, 1903), 152. These images are in the public domain.

[17] In Duvall and Hays's diagram, the modern world shows three paths emerging from the bridge, thus reflecting many applicational possibilities.

[18] Duvall and Hays, *Grasping God's Word*, 214.

At the core of Scripture is the story of restored relationships: The Word of God explains the story of God's mission in the world to redeem humanity and place it within proper relationship to Himself and all of creation. People in the first-century were not unlike people today—we long to belong to something bigger than ourselves, to the Divine. At the center of this story is the one God who sent a suffering Messiah who died on the cross and was raised from the dead, placed Him at His right hand, and bestows His own Spirit upon believers who is working among us in the world now. So, while it is helpful to understand that interpretive "gaps" exist; that we need to cross from the biblical world to our present on; and that we may at times benefit by identifying principles, this should not come at the expense of recognizing the broader story and goal of God to redeem and restore all people to Himself and each other within the created order.

Rules, Principles, Paradigms, and Symbolic World: R. Hays advocates for a more expansive approach by identifying several "modes" communicated in the biblical materials. He summarizes these "modes" as follows:

- ***Rules***: direct commandments or prohibitions of specific behaviors
- ***Principles***: general frameworks of moral consideration by which particular decisions about action are to be governed
- ***Paradigms***: stories or summary accounts of characters who model exemplary conduct (or negative paradigms: characters who model reprehensible conduct)
- A ***Symbolic World*** that creates the perceptual categories through which we interpret reality

In Hays's view, the Symbolic World—that which we can nearly equate with a view of the world or worldview—consists of the human condition and the character of God. He adds, "[t]he presence of all these modes of discourse within the New Testament suggests that all of them are potentially legitimate modes of discourse for our own normative reflection."[19] So, we will do well then, when evaluating our biblical materials, to consider the presence of rules, principles, paradigms, and the worldview as expressed in fundamental symbols.

Major Types of NT Discourse—Narrative and Behavioral: Before we evaluate our passage, it would be helpful to understand that the NT contains two main types of writing: Showing (narrative) and telling (behavioral). The difference between the two is that whereas narratives are stories that depict good and bad characters (as well as some "in-progress" ones) for the purpose of following the good and avoiding the bad (i.e., Hays's "paradigms"), behavioral texts directly tell us what to do using arguments and exhortations. The Gospels and Acts are examples of the narrative type; they are primarily "descriptive" and not necessarily "prescriptive" in telling us what to do. For example, the Book of Acts contains some very weighty "summary" statements of what the first believers did (2:42–47; 4:32–35); the question is, however, whether such summaries are immediately prescriptive for us or primarily descriptive and still in need of evaluation before our appropriation today. Importantly, too, there are teaching sections in the Gospels (e.g., Matt 5–7, 10, 13, 18, 23–25) that are behavioral. NT letters are behavioral discourse that attempt to change the audiences'

---

[19] Hays, *Moral Vision*, 209.

views and actions more directly through argumentative reasoning peppered with commands and prohibitions (i.e., Hays's "rules"). Even so, these commands may address specific scenarios that are not quite analogous today. Furthermore, inside NT letters we can find narrative material, e.g., the accounting of Paul's calling in Gal 1:11–2:21; see also, e.g., 2 Cor 1-2, 7.

<u>Commands, Prohibitions, Promises, and Warnings</u>: When the NT authors issue commands or give prohibitions (negative commands), we listen. When promises or warnings are given, we believe them. The problem is that these commands and promises were issued within specific contexts and may entail conditions, which if not met, invalidate the promise. Certainly, we should take all such promises and commands with utmost earnestness, but we also need to properly understand them and their application in context. Not uncommonly, we may misunderstand a proverb for a promise: "Raise up a child in the way s/he should go, and s/he will not depart from it" (Prov 22:6). This is not a promise, but a proverb; many a parent has gnashed their teeth on this verse (I've met them). We should certainly work and pray for this, but children still make choices for themselves.

EXERCISE 11–E: Below are instructions that Jesus gave to the twelve apostles when he sends them out to preach the gospel in the surrounding area (Matt 10:5–42 NRSV). Consider the following:

1. In the space provided to the right, identify any commands, prohibitions, promises, and warnings.
2. Which of these contain culturally specific language that would prevent them from having immediate application today?
3. Of these commands identified in 2., can you discern any undergirding principles or paradigms?
4. What view of the world or symbolic world is conveyed within these instructions?
5. Finally, is there any sense that Jesus's mission for the twelve apostles is like or unlike the church's mission today? If so, how might these similarities or differences affect how we evaluate and apply these commands, prohibitions, promises, and warnings today? If time allows, consult Marshall, *Beyond the Bible*, 68 and his surrounding discussion.

⁵These twelve Jesus sent out with the following instructions:
"Go nowhere among the Gentiles, and enter no town of the Samaritans,
⁶but go rather to the lost sheep of the house of Israel.
⁷As you go, proclaim the good news, 'The kingdom of heaven has come near.'
⁸Cure the sick, raise the dead, cleanse the lepers, cast out demons.
You received without payment; give without payment.
⁹Take no gold, or silver, or copper in your belts, ¹⁰no bag for your journey,
or two tunics, or sandals, or a staff; for laborers deserve their food.
¹¹Whatever town or village you enter, find out who in it is worthy,
and stay there until you leave. ¹²As you enter the house, greet it.
¹³If the house is worthy, let your peace come upon it;
but if it is not worthy, let your peace return to you.
¹⁴If anyone
will not welcome you or listen to your words,
shake off the dust from your feet as you leave that house or town.
¹⁵Truly I tell you, it will be more tolerable for the land of Sodom

and Gomorrah on the day of judgment than for that town.
^{16} "See, I am sending you out like sheep into the midst of wolves;
   so be wise as serpents and innocent as doves. ^{17} Beware of them,
   for they will hand you over to councils and flog you in their synagogues;
     ^{18} and you will be dragged before governors and kings because of me,
   as a testimony to them and the Gentiles.
^{19} When they hand you over, do not worry about how you are to speak
   or what you are to say; for what you are to say will be given to you at that time;
     ^{20} for it is not you who speak, but the Spirit of your Father speaking through you.
^{21} Brother will betray brother to death, and a father his child, and children will rise
   against parents and have them put to death; ^{22} and you will be hated by all because of my name.
   But the one who endures to the end will be saved.
^{23} When they persecute you in one town, flee to the next; for truly I tell you,
   you will not have gone through all the towns of Israel before the Son of Man comes.
^{24} "A disciple is not above the teacher, nor a slave above the master;
     ^{25} it is enough for the disciple to be like the teacher, and the slave like the master.
   If they have called the master of the house Beelzebul,
   how much more will they malign those of his household!
^{26} "So have no fear of them; for nothing is covered up that will not be uncovered,
   and nothing secret that will not become known. ^{27} What I say to you in the dark,
   tell in the light; and what you hear whispered, proclaim from the housetops.
^{28} Do not fear those who kill the body but cannot kill the soul;
   rather fear him who can destroy both soul and body in hell.
^{29} Are not two sparrows sold for a penny? Yet not one of them will fall to the ground
   apart from your Father. ^{30} And even the hairs of your head are all counted.
^{31} So do not be afraid; you are of more value than many sparrows.
^{32} "Everyone therefore who acknowledges me before others,
   I also will acknowledge before my Father in heaven;
     ^{33} but whoever denies me before others, I also will deny before my Father in heaven.
^{34} "Do not think that I have come to bring peace to the earth; I have not come to bring peace, but a sword.
^{35} For I have come to set a man against his father, and a daughter against her mother,
   and a daughter-in-law against her mother-in-law;
   ^{36} and one's foes will be members of one's own household.
^{37} Whoever loves father or mother more than me is not worthy of me;
   and whoever loves son or daughter more than me is not worthy of me;
     ^{38} and whoever does not take up the cross and follow me is not worthy of me.
^{39} Those who find their life will lose it, and those who lose their life for my sake will find it.
^{40} "Whoever welcomes you welcomes me, and whoever welcomes me welcomes the one who sent me.
^{41} Whoever welcomes a prophet in the name of a prophet will receive a prophet's reward;
   and whoever welcomes a righteous person in the name of a righteous person
   will receive the reward of the righteous;
     ^{42} and whoever gives even a cup of cold water to one of these little ones
   in the name of a disciple—truly I tell you, none of these will lose their reward."

Focal Lenses: As we consider moving from the ancient biblical text to our communities today, from its meaning to our appropriation, it is optimal if we wear the right kind of lenses to see the "focal images" of the big picture that God paints across Scripture. R. Hays explains: "[O]ne might think of such images as root metaphors embedded in the New Testament texts; they encapsulate the crucial elements of the narrative and serve to focus our attention on the common ground shared by the various [biblical] witnesses."[20] For Hays, the focal images of Scripture are Community, the Cross, and the New Creation; the criteria he uses to establish these are 1) its *distribution* across the *entire* NT, 2) its relative *lack of tension* (hence, *agreement*) with significant ethical and moral teachings of the NT, and 3) its highlighting *central* ethical concerns of the biblical materials.[21] I would expand these lenses to the seven depicted and discussed below on the basis of Scripture's testimony of God's presence before, amidst, and for the benefit of all of creation.

SEVEN FOCAL LENSES OF SCRIPTURE

1. *Creation*
2. *Called Community*
3. *Covenants*
4. *Christ*
5. *Cross*
6. *Commissioned Community*
7. *New Creation*

Focal Lens #1—Creation with God's Kingly Authority: Ultimate power is associated with God's ability to create. Human rulers also create kingdoms with monuments and infrastructure that support and promote their rule. Kings leave monuments and inscriptions heralding their accomplishments and acclaiming their heroic saving deeds. All such attempts to rule and create really mimic God's creation and rule. God's monument for all to see, however, is creation itself (Rom 1:20). Specifically, humans bear God's "image"—the Hebrew word referred to small idol monuments of some deity. What this implies, then, is that we humans reflect God's reign as our King and true God. We are under God's rule. Specifically, God's purposes are what humans should attend to. Thus, as we hold to creation as a focal theme, we aspire to align with God's plan in creation—for humans to be stewards of creation ruling over it with justice, purity, and goodness.

Focal Lens #2—Called Community of God's People—All are Invited: The genius in God's self-revelation in Scripture is *meeting fallen humanity right where we are*. God revealed himself to specific people to begin a history of redemption; and he called them to go where he directed them. What is amazing about God's revelation as YHWH and further through his Son Jesus and the Spirit is God's incarnational nature—that is, God meets us where we are in different languages, different societies, different locations, and different cultures. To help communicate the invitation to join God's people, *Scripture comes to us both as a friend and as a foreigner, a familiar face and a stranger*. The purpose and calling of God's people has always involved reaching out to others, to be a light to the nations (Gen 12:3; 22:18; 26:4; 28:14; Isa 42:1–6; Acts 3:25; Gal 3:8, etc.). Scrip-

---

[20] Hays, *Moral Vision*, 194.
[21] Hays, *Moral Vision*, 195, emphasis added.

ture does not set up "one culture" while eradicating all others; nor does Scripture establish rules microscopically treating every aspect of human life that become immediately applicable for every person in every culture around the globe. Most essentially, Scripture testifies to God's *reaching out and meeting us in our respective locations* in order to foster as much as possible restored relationships with Himself, with ourselves, with others, and with all of creation.

> Scripture comes to us both as a friend and as a foreigner, a familiar face and a stranger.

Indeed, Scripture is most essentially concerned about holy, restored, loving, and authentic relationships of God with humans, a human with him- or herself, humans with humans, and humans with the rest of the created order. These relationships are certainly interrelated and mutually impact each other, and yet it is helpful to have them distinctly identified as Scripture itself often does. Among believers, disagreements exist about what is the true identity and nature of God, of humans, and of the rest of the created order. Then too, we will debate about what is in need of restoration, what is meant by "holy" and "love," and what constitutes true and authentic relationships. Nevertheless, as we ponder *how* to evaluate Scripture and *how* to appropriate it for our respective communities today, we should allow these core relationships to guide our work. Furthermore, as God's people we invite all people to join in the good work that He has called us to do.

Focal Lens #3—Covenants, Old and New: Another focal lens is that of "covenants," and specifically, the Old Mosaic Covenant and the New Covenant in Christ. The word covenant or testament is an agreement between two parties. However, in biblical use the two parties are not equals—One is Supreme and the other is human. In fact, the particular form of the Old Covenant as seen especially written in Exodus and re-written a second time in Deuteronomy ("second law") is the ancient Near-Eastern suzerain treaty form between the suzerain and its subjected vassal kingdom. The covenant of God, then, reflects how God rules and establishes rules for his people how they should live, what they should care about, and what they should expect. Importantly, the Old Covenant is now fulfilled in the New Covenant of Christ. There are vast differences of some content of the daily activities and expectations—e.g., the sacrificial system is effectively and entirely replaced by Christ. Christ takes central place. However, the Old Covenant and the OT reveal God's will to God's people in their specific contexts; the OT is the Word of God even though we approach it now through the NT revelation of Jesus Christ: We learn much about God, God's purposes, creation, the nature of humanity, and how God wants us to live within creation. As we evaluate NT passages, we must consider whether the topic, question, or issue is addressed in the OT, how it is addressed, and what implications this might have for our appropriation today.

Focal Lens #4—Christ and God's Self-Revelation: Jesus is the pinnacle of God's self-revelation within human history. Thus, the NT's testimony about Jesus sets the bar for evaluating Scripture. As Traina has said, "The Scriptures themselves indicate that the ultimate standard for determining which truths are universal is Jesus Christ, who, as the Incarnate Son of God, embodies that which is of timeless and supreme value."[22] Unfortunately, however, *Jesus did not speak to*

---

[22] *Methodical Bible Study*, 206.

every aspect of human life. Yet, in his life, ministry, suffering death, resurrection, and ascension Jesus left his followers important teachings and perspectives by which to live in order to fulfill God's mission until He returns in the fullness of God's kingdom.

EXERCISE 11-F: Concerning the question of the permissibility of divorce under the Mosaic Law, what sources of authority and what focal lenses are present in Matt 19:3–8?

> [19:3] Then some Pharisees came to him [Jesus] in order to test him. They asked, "Is it lawful to divorce a wife for any cause?"[19:4] He answered, "Have you not read that from the beginning the Creator ***made them male and female***,[19:5] and said, '***For this reason a man will leave his father and mother and will be united with his wife, and the two will become one flesh***'?[19:6] So they are no longer two, but one flesh. Therefore what God has joined together, let no one separate." [19:7] They said to him, "Why then did Moses command us *to give **a certificate of dismissal** and to divorce* her?" [19:8] Jesus said to them, "Moses permitted you to divorce your wives because of your hard hearts, but from the beginning it was not this way. (NET, emphasis original)

Jesus's Impact: It is relatively clear that Jesus's life, teaching, death, resurrection, ascension, expectant coming, and the future ages continued to impact the early church as seen in their writings. For example, Paul acknowledged the influence of Jesus's teaching on normative Christian living as he addressed the Corinthian believers on marriage in 1 Cor 7:10–13, 15–16 (NASB):

> [10] But to the married I give instructions, not I, but the Lord, that the wife should not leave her husband [11] (but if she does leave, she must remain unmarried, or else be reconciled to her husband), and that the husband should not divorce his wife. [12] But to the rest I say, not the Lord, that if any brother has a wife who is an unbeliever, and she consents to live with him, he must not divorce her. [13] And a woman who has an unbelieving husband, and he consents to live with her, she must not send her husband away.... [15] Yet if the unbelieving one leaves, let him leave; the brother or the sister is not under bondage in such *cases,* but God has called us to peace. [16] For how do you know, O wife, whether you will save your husband? Or how do you know, O husband, whether you will save your wife?

Notice how Paul differentiated between instructions from the Lord in 7:10 ("not I, but the Lord") and his own instructions in 7:12 ("I say, not the Lord"). What Paul means by this is that the Lord Jesus addressed the matter of marriage and divorce in his earthly teaching (see Matt 5:31–32; 19:3–9; Mark 10:2–12; Luke 16:18); however, Jesus did not address the situation of someone becoming a believer after already being married to an unbeliever, and then the unbeliever wanting to leave.

Moving Beyond Jesus? Jesus sadly could not address every circumstance facing humanity. His life and teaching are "underdeveloped." Marshall contextualizes Jesus's teaching ministry with four considerations: 1) it was given "in the dawn of the kingdom of God" before his death and resurrection; 2) it was elementary for the first followers who even then struggled to understand it; 3) it was given within the setting of first-century Judaism and was mainly addressed to Jews; and, 4) it used language conventions (imagery, analogies, etc.) suitable to that time. Hence, Marshall concludes that Jesus lived in between the Old and New Covenants such that his teaching "now has to be translated for the new situation (afterward)" ***and*** that Jesus's teaching was "undeveloped."[23] I would prefer to call it "underdeveloped." Certain things he didn't have to say *because he assumed them from the clear moral teaching in Hebrew Scripture*. Moreover, the apostles proclaimed Jesus as Lord to new audiences in different cultures thus developing Jesus's teaching tradition informed by the Spirit to combat opposing ones (1 Tim 4:1). They wrote biblical texts for various new contexts extending the truth of Jesus which were recognized eventually as canonical Scripture.[24]

EXERCISE 11–G: While travelling and listening to a radio program once, a host was discussing Jesus and homosexual behavior with an expert guest. The guest indicated that Jesus never taught against homosexuality and rather promoted love; so we ought to be like Jesus on this matter.

1. How would you evaluate the claims of the guest?
2. Consider what Jesus taught about matters of magic, bestiality (sex with animals), and abortion. If Jesus did not teach against or condemn these practices, does this mean that Jesus accepts these behaviors?
3. What guiding resource did Jesus assume as true when it came to matters of sexual expression in marriage? See particularly Matt 19:3–6.

Focal Lens #5—The Cross and being Co-Crucified to the World: The cross in Jesus's life was both a reality and a metaphor for dying to this world because of its rejection of God; Jesus also called his followers to come after him and take up their crosses (Matt 10:38; 16:24//Mark 8:34//Luke 9:23). In fact, Jesus stated that refusing to bear one's cross disbarred someone from being his follower (Luke 14:27). *Bearing one's cross is a counter-cultural expression that aligns with what Scripture generally calls God's people to represent*. Time does not allow me to discuss the full theme of the cross in the NT as it is explicitly and implicitly found. However, the cross for disciples of Jesus means identifying with and following Jesus and dying to sin. For example, the apostle Paul confessed, "I am co-crucified with Christ and I no longer live, but Christ lives in me" (Gal 2:20). This statement is part of his thesis statement in Galatians where Paul sought to win the Galatian Christ-followers to adopt the right way of living (see 5:24; 6:14). However, this statement is no isolated example since Christ, the cross, and our identification in death with Him are elaborated elsewhere (Rom 6:6; 1 Cor 1:18; 2 Cor 4:7–12). Peter, too, associated Christ's death on the cross with our death to sin: "He himself bore our sins in his body on the cross in order that we would die to sin and live to righteousness" (1 Pet 2:24). So, as we evaluate scriptural passages as followers of Christ, we consider how God in the passage is calling us to take up our crosses and follow after Jesus.

> Bearing one's cross is a counter-cultural expression that aligns with what Scripture generally calls God's people to represent.

---

[23] Summarizing and quoting partially from Marshall, *Beyond the Bible*, 63–64.

[24] Summarizing Marshall, *Beyond the Bible*, 50–54.

Focal Lens #6—The Commission of God's People: At Pentecost in the bestowing of the Holy Spirit, God's people received the ability to speak in languages found across the Mediterranean basin. Babel is undone, although language distinctions remain. At the core God is asking His people to be and do in the world as He has been/is being and has done/is doing in the world. God seeks after people, relentlessly and patiently so. Scripture has been given to God's people within this context to help prepare them to fulfill this calling in the world. Gorman has depicted the CONTEXTS OF THEOLOGICAL EXEGESIS. To aid our reading of text, Gorman proposes the following questions:

o How does this text call us to *imagine and envision the world*?
o What does this text call us to *unlearn and then learn afresh*?
o What *powers* that could deceive, seduce, and harm the world or the church does this text *unveil and challenge*—or call us to unveil and challenge?
o How does this text call us as God's people to be both *different from and involved in the world*?[25]

As we evaluate a scriptural passage, we should consider how it speaks to the mission of God's people.

Focal Lens #7—The New Creation (Restoration) as the Goal of God's Purposes: Jesus embodied the Kingdom of God and ushered in the beginning of the new creation (Matt 19:28). God's purposes for humanity are most fully disclosed in Jesus. Throughout the NT we get glimpses of what Jesus gave us as "new": new selves (2 Cor 5:17; Eph 4:24; Col 3:10), new communities (Gal 6:15–16), a new unified humanity (Eph 2:10, 15), and eventually a new heavens and earth, "a place where justice dwells" (2 Pet 2:13; Rev 21–22). Indeed, Peter and Paul each make reference to "grace" that will be given to the followers of Christ in the ages to come (Eph 2:7; 1 Pet 1:13; 3:7; 5:10). Moreover, we are awaiting the resurrection of our bodies that at present experience death, and yet, we trust that we will be raised to new life (Rom 8:18–25). Consequently, we live differently in the world now and we prepare ourselves for that future moment when we will see Jesus face-to-face in the presence of God (John 17:24; 2 Cor 3:18; 1 John 3:2). So, given the scope and scale of God's redemptive and restorative purposes, for any given biblical passage we must discern what God is saying then and now for his people to know, to believe, to do, to live, and to hope in preparation for the future restoration of creation in the final form of the New Creation.

---

[25] Image (recreated) and questions are from his *Biblical Exegesis*, 157–58 (italics original).

Appeal to the OT: In the process of evaluation, you will need to consider whether the rules, principles, paradigms, or (notions of) the symbolic world that are present within the passage are found elsewhere in Scripture. For example, it may be that the OT Law will be a source for the rule or principle. Therefore, it is necessary to properly understand the role and place of the Law of Moses in God's revelation. Below are "Dos" and "Don'ts" set forth by Gordon D. Fee and Douglas Stuart that should guide your evaluation of OT Law as a source for NT evaluation.

HOW TO BEST INTERPRET THE OT LAW: SOME "DOS" AND "DON'TS"[26]

1. Do see the OT law as God's fully inspired Word *for* you.
   Don't see the OT law as God's direct command *to* you.
2. Do see the OT law as the basis for the Old Covenant, and therefore for Israel's history. Don't see the OT law as binding on Christians in the New Covenant except where specifically renewed.
3. Do see God's justice, love, and high standards revealed in the OT law.
   Don't forget to see that God's mercy is made equal to the severity of the standards.
4. Do see the OT law as a paradigm—providing examples for the full range of expected behavior.
   Don't see the OT law as complete. It is not technically comprehensive.
5. Do remember that the *essence* of the Law (10 Commandments and the two chief laws—love God and love your neighbor) is repeated in the prophets and renewed in the NT.
   Don't expect the OT law to be cited frequently by the prophets or the NT.
6. Do see the OT law as a generous gift to Israel, bringing much blessing when obeyed. Don't see the OT law as a grouping of arbitrary, annoying regulations limiting people's freedom.

Be Attentive to the Holy Spirit in this Process:[27] The Spirit is better than the Law even though "the Law is holy, and the commandment is holy and righteous and good" (Rom 7:12). Why is this? Because we cannot write enough law codes to address all the complexities of human life. However, if we have God's infinite Spirit, we have someone who will aide our living in our respective contexts. Additionally, the Holy Spirit will be urging us to focus on, receive, and appropriate the most pertinent aspects of God's Word for the salvific purposes of Christ-like formation, doing good to all, and bringing light to all people.

The Important Principle of Analogy: Although human cultures have different localized practices, something is still common between them; they are analogous in some ways (e.g., the importance of "law"). Behind such laws and common practices are matters of ultimate purpose and values of the heart. Therefore, the principle of analogy is critical for thoughtful and penetrating evaluation-application. John H. Hayes and Carl R. Holladay suggest a set of questions for pastors to use to discern what are analogous practices between the biblical text and current settings:

---

[26] *How to Read the Bible for All Its Worth*, 180 (abbreviations added)

[27] On this topic in great depth, see the monumental work of Craig S. Keener, *Spirit Hermeneutics*.

What situation in the contemporary world and the immediate congregation is analogous to the situation addressed in the text? How are the participants in the modern situation analogous to those—the speaker, the audience, ancient Israel, the early church—in the original situation? What form and content should be given in and to the sermon in order for it to serve an analogous function in the modern situation as the text in its situation? How can the total context of 'what it meant' inform and enlighten 'what it means'?[28]

<u>Guidelines for Consulting Biblical Passages for Evaluated Applications</u>: By now you may be overwhelmed with information pertinent to evaluation and application. However, there is much more to consider. So, I offer you these final guidelines.

- ○ ***Understand where you are in God's Word***, e.g., which covenant is operative and where in God's progressive revelation the passage occurs.
- ○ ***Retain the integrity of each passage***, e.g., rather than stringing together passages to support this or that view on a matter, we must respect the integrity of each passage of Scripture in its own context. Let the clearest and most relevant passages be most valued.
- ○ ***Understand how the genre and literary forms of each passage affect the evaluation***.
- ○ ***Discern the tone and atmosphere of the passage*** whether there is sarcasm, irony, cynicism, hyperbole, parody, joking, understatement, or allegorical presentation. Consider how the presence of these affects the evaluative contribution of the specific passage.
- ○ ***Respect the incompleteness or partial nature of each passage***; i.e., other passages will not typically exhaust a topic nor address it in a way that exactly corresponds to your passage.
- ○ ***Remember the principle of love***; e.g., St. Augustine has said, "Whoever, then, thinks that he understands the Holy Scriptures, or any part of them, but puts such an interpretation upon them as does not tend to build up this twofold love of God and our neighbor, does not yet understand them as he ought" (*On Christian Doctrine* I.40).
- ○ ***Avoid the following practices and approaches***: using a "monkey-see-monkey-do" approach to appropriation uncritically following others, interpreting and applying passages through allegorizing them, decontextualizing passages, being selective in your evaluation by neglecting other important voices in Scripture (like Jesus), overly moralizing historical narratives by drawing out inappropriate applications for people today, personalizing passages, falsely appropriating the text by reading back into the passage from our contemporary setting, and wrongly combining passages to support this or that application point when the passages are not truly addressing the same thing nor are truly analogous.[29]
- ○ ***Consider that tensions or "contradictions" will provide an opportunity to clarify ideas.***
- ○ ***Finally, understand the need for some degree of tentativeness of evaluation*** because relevant new information may be discovered and brought to light that may significantly qualify or even correct your interpretation, evaluation, and possible applications.

---

[28] *Biblical Exegesis: A Beginner's Handbook,* rev. ed. (Atlanta: John Knox, 1987), 152.

[29] These are among other ideas from Fee and Stuart, *Read the Bible*, 103–5.

PRIMARY INTERPRETIVE PROCEDURES:

1. **First, evaluate yourself.** To what church tradition do you belong? Have you been working with presuppositions or assumptions that the text has brought into question? Is your interpretation of the passage "honest and humble" or "agenda-driven"? Has there been personal or cultural "baggage" that has arisen while you have worked on this text? Are you able to acknowledge this and set it aside in order to rightly think about the meaning, application, and individual and communal appropriation of the text?

2. **What is the mode of your discourse—narrative or behavioral? How does this inform your evaluative work?**
   a. If narrative, who are the positive examples as **paradigms** for people to follow? What values, attitudes, beliefs, and actions are depicted as **principles** that may be considered exemplary for others to imitate? List these. Conversely, who are the negative examples? What values, attitudes, beliefs, and actions are depicted that should be avoided? List these.
   b. If behavioral, what commands or prohibitions as **rules** are present? In the course of argumentation, what values, attitudes, beliefs, and actions are present that the author expects the audience(s) to adopt and follow? List these.
   c. Regardless of discourse type, what is being communicated about God and humans in the **symbolic world**? What other significant information is communicated?

3. **Next, with the whole passage in view treating each verse or sets of verses, identify and state as succinctly as possible the rules, principles, paradigms, or (notions of) the symbolic world.** *Try to keep the statements accurate to the particulars of the passage without simply restating the verse.* Specifically, consider these questions to help identify these:
   a. What ethical and communal demands are specified in the passage?
   b. What does the passage reveal about the nature of God?
   c. What does the passage reveal about the nature of human beings?
   d. What does the passage reveal about the relationship between God and human beings?[30]
   e. What does the passage reveal about creation and our relationship to it?

4. **Locate where the rules, principles, paradigms, or (notions of) the symbolic world identified in 3. above may be found elsewhere conveyed in the same book, the same author, the Gospels (esp. Jesus), the rest of the NT, and finally also the OT. Time constraints will often limit your ability to check thoroughly each possible location.**
   a. *How consistently are the items described?*
   b. *How is each item clarified, qualified, or contested?* By what author or voice? In this order:
      i. Jesus.
      ii. The NT author or corpus; or elsewhere in the NT.

---

[30] The middle three classic questions are those employed in the *Disciple Bible Study* curriculum by Cokesbury.

iii. The OT. Consider where this occurs in God's story and how this affects evaluation.
iv. When evaluating these, let the most relevant and clearest passages have more weight.

5. **Evaluate whether the values, attitudes, beliefs, and actions identified are culture/situation-bound or if they have transcendent applicability. Even if they are cultural/situation-bound, consider whether an underlying principle exists that may have relevance today.**
   Before attempting to apply/appropriate the passage in your setting, you must evaluate whether the principles in the text are transcendent or situation-bound. *If they are culture/situation-bound, then their application to your social-cultural setting is probably not direct;* in this case you will need to consider what was the underlying principle that "governed" the situational appropriation for the original audience(s) in the initial/original context of communication. Also you must consider whether the truth stated is *complete or incomplete* due to the constraint of the initial situation. In either case, it may be possible to restate the truth so as to be transcultural. Here are fundamental questions to consider:

   a. *Most fundamentally,* does Jesus speak to this issue at all either directly or indirectly? Does he accept the truth as binding? Or, does he qualify it in some way?

   b. Where else in Scripture is this principle addressed *directly* in the OT or the NT?
      i. If it relates to a theme in the OT, does the principle pertain to particular circumstances under the Mosaic covenant?
      ii. Are these circumstances replicated or renewed in whole or in part under Christ's new covenant? If in part, what does this suggest about applying/appropriating the passage today?

   c. Are there other passages that may *indirectly* speak to the principle at hand? How similar or different are these other passages that may affect their application/appropriation today?

   d. After you have identified these other passages (from a., b. and c.), consider these questions:
      i. How directly or clearly is this principle addressed?
      ii. Do these other scriptural passages agree about the principle or do they differ?
      iii. If they are not in agreement, how does the one Scriptural passage qualify or possibly restate (or negate) the other? Which passage should have precedence over the other? Why?
      iv. Consider whether the principle is "updated" under the New Covenant as indicated in the teaching of Jesus, the apostles, or the authors of the NT.

   e. **Finally**, decide whether each rule, principle, paradigm, and notion of the symbolic world identified is universal (transcultural) or culture bound. If it is culture bound, consider whether the principle can be stated more generally to give it transcultural application; often it can be in light of the whole of Scripture.

6. **Honestly acknowledge what ambiguities remain. How might these ambiguities provide a space for God to allow us to grow as free(d) human agents following Christ and guided by the Holy Spirit?**

7. **Analyze your contemporary situation.** Reflect on and describe your current social-cultural situations as unpleasant as this may be—your living environment, your community, and society vis-à-vis these transcultural rules, principles, etc. *Begin to consider especially what scenarios or relationships are similar to yours and thus may help you to bridge the gap between the biblical text and your life and community.*

8. **For each transcendent value, attitude, belief, and action consider areas of application that cover the many facets of human relationships and existence.** How does the transcultural principle speak to you and your community to change or affirm your current living? Here are some suggested areas to consider.

   a. Our basic relationships include:
      i. God as Father, Son, and Holy Spirit
      ii. oneself
      iii. one's family
      iv. one's family of believers
      v. one's neighbors generally (including those that might be an "enemy" towards us)
      vi. one's civic environment (church, workplace, town, county, state, country, etc.)
      vii. the created order.

   b. One's life may be understood as consisting of a ***worldview*** with a set of ***values*** that affects our ***thinking*** and ***actions*** that in turn influence our ***attitudes***, ***behaviors***, ***habits***, and ***feelings***.

   c. In terms of a church setting, think of ***vision***, ***mission statement***, and ***policies***.

   d. Scripture constantly addresses the issue of an accurate esteem/knowledge of God, self, others, and creation in terms of motivation, purpose, and outcomes that should correspond to right values, thinking, and behavior in relation to God, self, neighbor (including "enemies"), and creation. Applications may be general at times and specific at other times.

   e. Finally, it may be helpful to consider and list what *current attitudes/values might prevent you from living out the transcultural scriptural rules, principles, paradigms, and notions of the symbolic world that have been discovered.* Performing this exercise may help us realize what changes need to take place in our hearts before we are in a position to be obedient.

9. **Consider what in the passage is most essentially in need of proclamation and appropriation today concerning God, humans, creation, and (each of) their interrelationships.**

10. **Finally, prayerfully consider areas for you to appropriate the truth of Scripture.** Pray over your work giving thanks to God for abilities to interpret Scripture. This is truly a gift that also comes with responsibility. James 3:1 says, "Let not many *of you* become teachers, my brethren, knowing that as such we will incur a stricter judgment" (NASB). Choose one or two truths (values, attitudes, beliefs, actions) that speak to your own individual situation and describe as openly as possible how the Holy Spirit may be leading you to live differently. Use discretion if sharing such information publically or if it may become public knowledge.

II. SECONDARY STUDY

Orientation—Merging Horizons: Peter Cotterell and Max Turner maintain, "It is difficult to argue with [Hans-Georg] Gadamer's pragmatic assertion that any text must necessarily relate to two horizons: the horizon of the original event of bringing the text into existence, and the horizon of the reader of the text. It is out of this recognition of two horizons that the distinction between meaning and significance arises."[31] Cotterell and Turner continue by quoting E. D. Hirsch on the meaning of "significance" as "textual meaning as related to some context, indeed any context beyond itself."[32] Truly, the work of STEP 11: EVALUATED APPLICATIONS is to understand the significance and impact of God's Word in our respective contexts today. In SECONDARY STUDY, we extend the discussion thus far through relating our work to biblical ethics and going into more depth in our understanding and analysis. Also, additional appropriate exercises will be provided.

Biblical Theology and Biblical Ethics: Our discussion of BIBLICAL THEOLOGY in STEP 10 entails the area of biblical ethics that could have been treated there. However, I thought it would be most valuable to provide the discussion here. I particularly appreciate the summary of T. B. Maston who locates appropriately biblical ethics within the history of God's revelation in the OT and the NT that culminates with Jesus. Maston's instructive conclusions summarize succinctly core concerns of Scripture as God's Word and lay a foundation for its evaluation for appropriation.

PRINCIPLES OF BIBLICAL ETHICS[33]

1. *Ethics has a very important place in both the OT and the NT.*
2. *Biblical Ethics has been neglected in a great deal of Bible study.*
3. *God is as central in the ethics of the Bible as He is in its theology.*
4. *The dominant ethical appeal in the Bible is for the people of God to be like Him.*
5. *Religion and ethics are thoroughly integrated in the Bible.*
6. *Theology and ethics belong together.*
7. *A rather remarkable unity exists in the midst of diversity in the ethical content of the Bible as a whole.*
8. *The developmental nature of the unity within the OT is climaxed in the ministry and messages of the great eighth-century prophets.*
9. *The movement/progress in Scripture is particularly clear when moving from the OT to the NT.*
10. The fact that God's revelation of His will is climaxed in Christ means that *the OT should be interpreted and particularly evaluated in the light of the fuller revelation in the NT.*
11. While the climax of biblical ethics is reached in the life and teachings of Jesus, *there is a sense in которой the biblical ethic attains its most significant stage in the post-resurrection pe-*

---

[31] *Linguistics & Biblical Interpretation* (Downers Grove, IL: InterVarsity Press, 1989), 53.

[32] Hirsch, *The Aims of Interpretation* (Chicago: The University of Chicago Press, 1976), 3.

[33] This material is slightly adapted (*italics* original) from T. B. Maston, *Biblical Ethics: A Guide to the Ethical Message of the Scriptures from Genesis Through Revelation* (Macon, GA: Mercer University Press, 1982), 281–88.

> *riod.* This is particularly true of the emphasis that daily Christian living is a natural outgrowth of a vital, life-changing union with the resurrected Christ.
> 12. Another way of stating what we have been saying is to suggest that *the ethical teachings of the Bible are not on a plain, but are part of a path.*
> 13. *The biblical perspective concerning history is an important factor and really an integral phase of biblical ethics.* There is clearly evident in the Bible a theology of history.
> 14. *Eschatology,* which represents a particular aspect or view of history, *is rather closely related to ethics in the Bible....* The eschatological has a prominent place in the teachings of the prophets and in the ministry and message of Jesus.
> 15. *The biblical ethic is so deep and broad,* as is true of the Christian life in general, *that it cannot be described adequately by the use of any one term....* Many terms may be used and still the depths of the biblical ethic will not be fully fathomed [such as] "a covenant ethic," "a *koinonia* ethic," "a love ethic," "a will of God ethic," "a kingdom of God ethic," "an eschatological ethic," "a perfectionistic ethic," "a disciples' ethic," "a Holy Spirit ethic,"... "a holiness ethic," ... and "an ethic of the cross" which in a sense is the central unifying symbol of the divine revelation and of the Christian life.
> 16. *Much of the biblical ethic is just as relevant today as it was in the days in which the books of the Bible were written.*
> 17. *My conviction that the Bible is authoritative has been strengthened* as this study has progressed.
> 18. *There is a very sense in which the authority is Christ's* since He is the climax of the revelation of God.

<u>Unified Body of Believers and Individual Members</u>: As we consider how to conceptualize specific points of application today, it is critical to understand how interconnected we are, each one to one another. The interconnection of believers to one another and their right relationship is often indicated in the NT texts through the strategic use of pronouns and special grammatical constructions denoting distributive benefits and relationships. For example, the reciprocal pronoun ἀλλήλων *one another* conveys the mutuality of believers as a core value to form and maintain proper healthy relationships with one another. Consider, too, Paul's statements in Rom 12:4–5:

> 12:4 καθάπερ γὰρ ἐν ἑνὶ σώματι πολλὰ μέλη ἔχομεν, τὰ δὲ μέλη πάντα οὐ τὴν αὐτὴν ἔχει πρᾶξιν,
>   4 *For just indeed as we are many members in one body, moreover all the members do not have the same function,*
>
> 12:5 οὕτως οἱ πολλοὶ ἓν σῶμά ἐσμεν ἐν Χριστῷ, τὸ δὲ καθ' εἷς ἀλλήλων μέλη.
>   5 *thus we, who are many, are one body in Christ, but individually members one of another.*

Notice the unity of the one body and simultaneously the diversity of individual members who nevertheless belong to one another. Such descriptions are found at 1 Cor 12:12–14 and Eph 4:4, 16.

EXERCISE 11–H: Below in Eph 5:21–24 are Paul's statements about believers in relationship to one another as an outflow of being filled with the Holy Spirit (5:18).

Eph 5:21–24 [21] being subject to one another in reverence to Christ, [22] wives in relation to their own husbands as to the Lord, [23] because a husband is head of the wife just as also Christ is head of the church assembly, Himself being savior of the body. [24] Yet, as the church assembly subjects itself to Christ, thus also the wives to their husbands in every respect.

1. From these verses, describe each distinctive relationship and the integrity/boundary of the persons in these relationships as stated explicitly or implied.

2. How significant is it that 5:22–24 is framed by 5:21 and 5:18?

3. Is there any sense of hierarchy in these verses? If so, how is this qualified?

4. Of these relationships, which is most foundational? On what basis do you determine this?

Types of Discourse and Different Modes of Appropriation: Texts have different purposes and their aims are implied in their form and orientation. Robert E. Longacre, followed by Robert A. Dooley and Stephen H. Levinsohn, described the main types of literature according to characteristics of their being agent-oriented, having a temporal sequence, and/or projecting into the future.[34] Of these eight, the NT contains five of them: (some) prophecy, (much) narrative, (much) behavioral, (some) encomium/censure, and (little) procedural. The dark-greyed ones do not apply.

MAIN TYPES OF BIBLICAL DISCOURSE

		AGENT ORIENTATION			PROJECTED OR ANTICIPATED
		+	−		
TEMPORAL SEQUENCE	+	Prophecy (promise, warning)	Procedural (how to do it)	+	
		Narrative (story)	Past Procedural (how it was done)	−	
	−	Exhortation (behavioral)	Projected Budget	+	
		Encomium/Censure (behavioral)	Scientific Paper	−	

I would argue furthermore that each different type of discourse would place certain constraints on its audiences for types and ranges of suitable applications and appropriations. Let me explain.

---

[34] The following chart merges the charts of Dooley and Levinsohn, *Analyzing Discourse: A Manual of Basic Concepts* (Dallas: SIL International, 2001), 4 and Longacre, *The Grammar of Discourse*, 2nd ed. (New York: Plenum, 1996), 10, from which comes Dooley & Levinsohn's chart. Longacre believes letters may have many of these features.

- **Prophecy** directs the audience to remain faithful to God and to adhere to what God expects of his people (such as justice, goodness, and mercy) when facing pressing and distressing situations in view of future positive or negative consequences.
- **Narratives** describe events and the actions of "good" characters, "bad" characters," and "in-progress" characters (e.g., the disciples) while expecting the audience to discern the difference between them and to follow what is good and honorable as displayed in the good responses and actions of the good or in-progress characters and to avoid what is bad and dishonorable as displayed in the bad responses and actions of the bad and in-progress characters. It is important to understand the difference between "description" (showing) and "prescription" (telling what to do) since the latter is more typical of exhortation.
- **Exhortations** will often attempt to persuade and dissuade the audience in view of their specific situation to adopt a certain course of action and to adhere to core values. Not uncommonly, good behaviors (virtues) will be contrasted with bad ones (vices), and these may be placed within the context of future positive and negative consequences.
- **Encomium** and **censure** praise or vilify, respectively, the life/actions of persons for the purpose of promoting or demoting such actions/behaviors in the minds and hearts of the audience.
- **Procedural** passages delineate a proper course of action given any typical or perhaps extenuating circumstances.

Although considering the general type of discourse provides an initial framework, more careful attention to specific literary forms and original settings (as can be known) will be required.

<u>**EXERCISE 11–I**</u>: Given the selection of NT passages below, follow these steps.

1. Choose one passage and identify the primary type of discourse.

2. Decide what the passage wanted the audiences to do, avoid, value, and believe.

3. Consider what may be present that would indicate a specific setting is being addressed.

4. Briefly evaluate *what* is urged to be done, avoided, valued, and believed against the whole of Scripture. Which of these appear to be transcultural and which more culture-bound? Is there anything among these that is in tension with Scripture?

5. Reflect on possible areas of application for what should be done, avoided, valued, and/or believed.

6. Prayerfully consider one way you should appropriate the significance of the passage today.

Rev 2:8–11	Luke 12:41–48	Gal 1:11–24	Matt 13:24–30	Phil 4:8–9
Rom 15:7–13	Matt 4:18–22	1 Tim 5:3–16	2 Thess 3:1–5	Rev 18:1–3

STEP 11: SECONDARY STUDY

SECONDARY INTERPRETIVE PROCEDURES: Follow the PRIMARY INTERPRETIVE PROCEDURES. Below I will describe the workflow outlined in the PRIMARY PROCEDURES while working through Eph 5:7–14. Remember that such work presupposes previous interpretive work; so first, below are given important contextual considerations and the main ideas of this passage.

a. In 5:1–5 believers are commanded to imitate God in Christ; also believers should not be sexually immoral, greedy, or impure, nor engage in obscene, silly, and vulgar speech.
b. Believers should be careful not to participate with sinners (5:7–8a, 11a, 12) so as to forfeit God's inheritance (5:5) and experience God's wrath that comes upon the disobedient (5:6).
c. As children of Light (an important metaphor in the symbolic world), believers should shine as light by their goodness, righteousness, and truthfulness as is pleasing to the Lord (5:8b–10)
d. Christians expose/refute the sinfulness of people by bringing them into the Light (5:11b, 13).
e. The ultimate purpose of items a.–d. above is to introduce people into Christ's light, i.e., their conversion to Christ where He shines on them (5:14).

Ephesians 5:7-14 (NASB) ⁷Therefore do not be partakers with them; ⁸for you were formerly darkness, but now you are Light in the Lord; walk as children of Light ⁹(for the fruit of the Light consists in all goodness and righteousness and truth), ¹⁰trying to learn what is pleasing to the Lord. ¹¹Do not participate in the unfruitful deeds of darkness, but instead even expose them; ¹²for it is disgraceful even to speak of the things which are done by them in secret. ¹³But all things become visible when they are exposed by the light, for everything that becomes visible is light. ¹⁴For this reason it says, "Awake, sleeper, And arise from the dead, And Christ will shine on you."

1. Evaluate Yourself: Assumptions, Presuppositions, Baggage, Confession:

I am assuming that this passage is about being appropriately different in the world because of one's relationship with God in Christ, different in a good way, a way that shines for the benefit of others leading to their conversion in Christ. Do I have enough of a real concern for evangelism? I get sad when I judge myself not to have enough courage at times—to speak up. I find myself wanting to, and I do, but sometimes I wonder how effective I am. I also wonder how full of light I am—is it bright enough? Is Christ's light sufficiently shining through me? Am I holding it back—is it a trickle rather than a full beam? I feel secluded within my narrow world of teaching/church/family/neighborhood—a holy huddle. How many non-Christian or pre-Christian people do I know ... really know, as a friend? When shopping I think about sharing Christ (in the better moments), well, at least being kind saying, "The Lord bless you!" In other settings (like church meetings), I take the prophetic dimension of exposing/refuting seriously, but I struggle how "best" to express myself. How much should one expose/refute by way of word or by way of deeds or action? How does the Holy Spirit guide me in such moments? Do I need to listen more?

2. What is the mode of the discourse? How does this inform your evaluative work? It is behavioral, so I am expecting rules and principles couched within a symbolic world of expression.

3. **With the whole passage in view treating each verse or sets of verses, identify and state as succinctly as possible the rules, principles, paradigms, or (notions of) the symbolic world.**

   Eph 5:7 Therefore do not be partakers with them; **8a** for you were formerly darkness, ... **11a** Do not participate in the unfruitful deeds of darkness, ... **12** for it is disgraceful even to speak of the things which are done by them in secret.

   Rule 1: Believers should not participate with sinners and sinful actions.
   Rule 2: Believers should not participate with dark deeds because such are not fruitful.
   Principle 1: Humans generally like partnership even if it means being "companions in crime."
   Principle 2: Humans hide from their sin.
   Principle 3: Believers were once in darkness.
   Principle 4: It is shameful to discuss sinful acts done in secret.
   Symbolic World: Light is good and darkness is bad. Believers are called to be Light.

4. **Locations of the rules, principles, paradigms, and notions of symbolic world in Scripture:**

   Rules 1 & 2 are similar enough to be treated together.

   Ephesians: In the immediate context vice lists describe darkness (5:3–6) as things to be avoided generally. These appear to be transcultural.

   In Paul: In 1 Cor 5–6 Paul urges believers to be morally upright and distinct from sinful believers (see esp. 5:9–10; 6:9). He clarifies, however, that we cannot NOT associate with immoral people of this world, "for then you would have to go out of the world" (5:10).

   1 Peter: Calls believers to be holy, to abstain from sinfulness, and to do good deeds for others to see (2:11–12); believers should also be separate from sinful people (4:1–7).

   Jesus: In the Beatitudes Jesus encouraged being recognizable and standing for righteousness (and being persecuted) (Matt 5:10–16); Jesus, however, ministered among and was friends with "sinners" (Luke 15:1 and *passim*) and was criticized for this (Luke 5:30; 7:35; 15:1–2); Jesus indicated that he came "to call the sinners to repentance" (Luke 5:32).

   In OT: The OT calls God's people to be separate from the surrounding sinful nations. This is the meaning of "Be holy for I am Holy" (Lev 11:44–45; 19:2; 20:7; also in 1 Pet 1:15–16). Psalm 1 illustrates maintaining a distinction of someone delighting in God's Law in contrast to someone associating with sinners, scoffers, and mockers, and their consequences.

   Principles 1–3 and **Symbolic World** are acknowledged in Scripture and also human experience. On hiding in sin, see Isa 29:15; 47:10; on being the light of the world and doing good for people to see and glorify God, see Matt 5:14–16; cf. Phil 2:15.

   Principle 4 if referring to slander/gossip, is condemned in Prov 11:13; 20:19 and Rom 1:29–30. If referring to handling sin privately, Jesus encouraged such if confronting sin (Matt 18:15).

5. **Final Evaluation:** Essentially, the rules, principles, and notions of the symbolic world appear to have transcultural applicability, but we should acknowledge some ambiguity and tensions.

6. Acknowledge Ambiguities and Tensions that may remain:

Ambiguity: Paul has just discussed sexual immorality, greed, and vulgar speech that may be idolatrous and the most common kinds of sin. What kinds of sin does Paul have in mind in 5:7–14? Would abuse of power be included? (Cf. Jesus's call to humility and service.) Also, Principle 4 involves some ambiguity whether the shame 1) increases in the perpetrator (and this does not help them), 2) attaches to those discussing the sin because it allows them some participation in it, or 3) is understood generally in society as shameful. Also, I could imagine that cultures have different protocols for how to handle sinful perpetrators. Such practices should be evaluated in light of the breadth of Scripture, especially God-in-Christ's desire for mercy and love and holiness.

Tensions: Paul admits that we cannot remove ourselves from interacting with sinful people in the world (1 Cor 5:11). Indeed, Jesus ate and drank with sinners. Did Jesus distinguish between proud sinners and humble sinners? Or, are we not expected to be like Jesus in this regard? This seems unlikely. So, this tension causes me some pause about too readily labeling people as sinners and staying away from them—Jesus interacted with "sinners."

7. Analysis of Our Contemporary Situation:

In terms of **friendships**, it is important to maintain good friendships and family relationships, but it is difficult to discuss matters of sinful actions that others accept. We often condone sins by not addressing sin with friends and family.

In terms of the **church relationships**, the "world" is in the church; but the church is to witness to the world. BUT, there is also a "holy huddle" mentality in Christian circles.

In terms of **social trends**, once "socially" condemnable sins required people to go to places outside the home (brothel, bar, adult book stores, etc.) to participate in them. NOW, our vices have become very personalized, "private," available online, and enter easily into our homes and minds. Moreover, societal stigmas are lessened regarding sin; sinful lifestyles of various kinds are tolerated or even celebrated; celebrities are on display.

8. Areas of Applications, considering worldview, examples, thinking, vision, attitude, instruction, values, actions, home, community, consequences, mission, policies, etc.

Worldview: Are we convinced that God will disinherit people due to their identification with sinful actions? Address how we conceive of ultimate judgment and the consequences of sin.

Example: Keep looking to Jesus as an example of properly relating to all people, especially those who are actively engaged in the deeds of darkness and are thus estranged by such sin.

Community: Examine all interpersonal relationships—are some encouraging sinful behaviors?

Attitudes: Rather than having a stringent "in-group" and "out-group" mentality, we should encourage a mission mentality and view unbelievers as "prebelievers" recognizing that our best chance of reaching them is by being good ourselves and not participating in sinful actions.

Actions: Join a small group to encourage proper behavior and be accountable not to sin, etc.

Value: Being the Light for the sake of others knowing that there are negative consequences for us if we remain in the darkness.

9. Consider what in the passage is most essentially in need of proclamation and appropriation today concerning God, humans, creation, and (each of) their interrelationships.

The "metaphors we live by" (see the book of that name by George Lakoff) influence our thinking and living. Believers are light in the world. This is for the benefit of all around us. While we pull away from the darkness and its fruitless deeds, we should not hide our light nor shine it in people's faces. Rather, Christ shines through us and awakens people revealing himself to them.

10. Individual Appropriation:

1. I am considering prayerfully whether there may be "culturally acceptable" sin in my life;
2. If so, I will confess this and come into the Light (i.e., repent of this sin). I want to shine brightly and humbly for Christ.
3. I will continue to seek understanding how the Holy Spirit convicts me to be holy and how to be prepared for the mission of exposing/refuting sin for the benefit of those around me.

<u>Exercise 11–J</u>: Given the two remaining portions of Eph 5 provided below, select one and work through the PRIMARY INTERPRETIVE PROCEDURES as illustrated above for 5:7–8a, 11a, 12.

Eph 5:8b-10 (NASB) but now you are Light in the Lord; walk as children of Light ^{9}(for the fruit of the Light consists in all goodness and righteousness and truth), ^{10}trying to learn what is pleasing to the Lord.

Eph 5:11b, 13–14 (NASB) but instead even expose them;… ^{13}But all things become visible when they are exposed by the light, for everything that becomes visible is light. ^{14}For this reason it says, "Awake, sleeper, And arise from the dead, And Christ will shine on you."

III. TERTIARY RESEARCH

<u>Orientation</u>: The work of evaluation and application is difficult if not even quite contentious. Thus far, I have attempted to sketch out best practices for people in the church and those engaged in pastoral and teaching ministries. For TERTIARY RESEARCH we consider the hermeneutics of evaluation and/or pursue the interpretation of various passages concerning important, perennial topics and questions. So, I offer additional complex exercises in what follows.

<u>EXERCISE 11–K</u>: In Matt 5:22 Jesus condemned anger, calling someone "raca" (Aramaic for empty-head), and calling someone a "fool" (μωρός in Greek). It would seem that Jesus condemns calling someone a derogatory name. Yet, we can find NT examples from John the Baptist, Jesus, Paul, and James who call people various names; see, respectively, Luke 3:7, Matt 23:27, 2 Cor 11:13, and Jas 4:4). How do we interpret and evaluate Matt 5:22?

STEP 11: TERTIARY RESEARCH

EXERCISE 11–L: Read the following books treating the area of evaluation and application and identify key issues of dispute that need clarity if not resolution.

Hays, Richard B. *The Moral Vision of the New Testament: Community, Cross, New Creation: A Contemporary Introduction to NT Ethics*. San Francisco: HarperSanFrancisco, 1996.
Marshall, I. Howard. *Beyond the Bible: Moving from Scripture to Theology*. Grand Rapids: Baker, 2004, including the response essays by Kevin J. Vanhoozer and Stanley E. Porter.
William J. Webb, *Slaves, Women & Homosexuals: Exploring the Hermeneutics of Cultural Analysis*. Downers Grove, IL: IVP Academic, 2001.

EXERCISE 11–M: Read Wayne Grudem, *Evangelical Feminism?: A New Path to Liberalism?* (Wheaton, IL: Crossway, 2006), esp. chs.4–6 as well as the books and articles of those he critiques who advocate "trajectory hermeneutics" such as William Webb and David L. Thompson. To what extent, if at all, is Grudem accurate and correct in his critique? Why or why not? Does Grudem have legitimate concerns? What are the fault lines dividing these devout interpreters of Scripture?

EXERCISE 11–N: Drawing on the evaluative process of Webb (perhaps adjusted based upon critiques), apply his "hermeneutics of cultural analysis" to one of these topics (or a comparable one) in order to assess and articulate its relevant applicability today in your setting:

1. Sabbath Observance
2. War/Killing
3. Tithing: Is 10% required still or is something else the standard?
4. Divorce and Remarriage
5. Creationism: What are believers expected to believe?
6. Historicism of Gen 1–11, or of Adam and Eve, or Flood, etc.
7. OT Land and Temple Fulfillment; should we expect a Temple in the future as God's plan?
8. Church Organization; e.g., elder board, or overseer(s), or charismatic gifting?
9. Spiritual Gifts Today in terms of which ones and when and how they should be used

Suggestions for writing a research paper:

a. Provide a basic "typology of positions" on the issue (what Webb does in ch.1).
b. Connected to this, indicate the critical biblical passages involved.
c. Discuss your hermeneutical approach using Webb's, a modification of Webb's, or an alternative hermeneutic to Webb's; provide a justification for your chosen hermeneutical approach.
d. Perform your cultural analysis of the passages according to Webb's criteria or their equivalent if you think they should be modified.
e. Acknowledge any weak points in your analysis and indicate what degree of confidence you place in your analysis using a confidence scale (certainly, very probably, probably, possibly...).
f. Suggest ways in which your conclusions might best be put into practice in the various venues where it would be prudent to do so.

IV. BIBLIOGRAPHY

Primary Survey

Application

The *NIV Application Commentary* series and the *New Beacon Bible Commentary*

Cultural Analysis and Contextualization

Flemming, Dean. *Contextualization in the New Testament: Patterns for Theology and Mission*. Downers Grove, IL: InterVarsity, 2005.

Vanhoozer, Kevin J., et al. eds. *Everyday Theology: How to Read Cultural Texts and Interpret Trends*. Grand Rapids: Baker, 2007.

Hermeneutics of Evaluation and Application

Traina, Robert A. *Methodical Bible Study: A New Approach to Hermeneutics*. Wilmore, KY: Robert A. Traina, Asbury Theological Seminary, 1952. Repr., Grand Rapids: Zondervan, 2002, Ch. 3 "Evaluation and Application."

Vanhoozer, Kevin J., and Craig L. Blomberg. *Is There a Meaning in This Text?: The Bible, the Reader, and the Morality of Literary Knowledge*. Grand Rapids: Zondervan, 2009.

Virkler, Henry A. and Karelynne Ayayo, *Hermeneutics: Principles and Processes of Biblical Interpretation*. 2nd ed. Grand Rapids: Baker Academic, 2007, Ch.8 "Applying the Biblical Message: A Proposal for the Transcultural Problem."

Missions and Discipleship

Wright, Christopher. *The Mission of God*. Downers Grove, IL: InterVarsity, 2006.

Wright, N. T. *Following Jesus: Biblical Reflections on Discipleship*. Grand Rapids: Eerdmans, 1995.

Secondary Study and Tertiary Research

Application

The *Word Biblical Commentary* series includes a section ("Explanation") that attempts to bridge the gap from past meaning to present significance.

Hermeneutics of Evaluation and Application

Bauer, David R. and Robert A. Traina, *Inductive Bible Study: A Comprehensive Guide to the Practice of Hermeneutics*. Grand Rapids: Baker Academic, 2011, Part 4 "Evaluating and Appropriating."

Hays, Richard B. *The Moral Vision of the New Testament: Community, Cross, New Creation: A Contemporary Introduction to New Testament Ethics*. San Francisco: HarperSanFrancisco, 1996.

Marshall, I. Howard. *Beyond the Bible: Moving from Scripture to Theology*. Grand Rapids: Baker, 2004.

Webb, William J. *Slaves, Women & Homosexuals: Exploring the Hermeneutics of Cultural Analysis*. Downers Grove, IL: IVP Academic, 2001.

STEP 12

PRESENTATION BRAINSTORM

"Stories make us more alive, more human, more courageous, more loving."
—Madeleine L'Engle

"If history were taught in the form of stories, it would never be forgotten."
—Rudyard Kipling

Introduction: Stories and illustrations paint pictures. The need to communicate the truth of Scripture effectively will often require a careful consideration of how best to "package" the truth of the passage that you have been interpreting. To help persons see the import of the good news of Scripture, it is important to coordinate your communication with what was discovered in the passage in the previous interpretive STEPS. In this STEP 12: PRESENTATION BRAINSTORM we discuss the what, why, and how of creating and offering stories, analogies, and illustrations as well as provide a process for doing so based upon your interpretation of a biblical passage. In this STEP there is no gradation of primary, secondary, or tertiary levels of study.

PERSPECTIVES ON STORIES, ANALOGIES, AND ILLUSTRATIONS

Defining Terms: Stories, analogies, and illustrations are vehicles and tools to enhance communication and its comprehension. I will generally treat these interchangeably, although we may discern important distinctions. **Stories** relate how people (or agents) act or experience the world through a series of events to overcome some question, problem, or deficiency. **Illustrations** are depictions (scenarios, pictures, examples) to help clarify and illuminate the essential truth of something. **Analogies** are comparisons of two seemingly different things in order to clarify and illuminate one of them. Illustrations often work by analogy, but usually involve more closely related items. For example, Jesus *illustrates* the truth of the kingdom of God by holding a child while talking to the disciples (Matt 18:2–4). In doing so, Jesus was actually showing that children are valuable and also that to be in the kingdom one must be like a child by being trusting, receiving God's blessing, remaining in Jesus's presence, etc. To give another example, Jesus uses an *analogy* when a foreign woman begged him to help her: "And he answered and said, 'It is not good to take the children's bread and throw it to the dogs'" (Matt 15:26). Jesus compares the woman implicitly with the dogs in the story (!); these are seemingly different things. He wasn't directly calling her a dog but was speaking analogically while also reflecting how Jews sometimes referred to non-Jews. We might wonder why Jesus spoke this way, but he did. But in response, she gained the upper hand by extending the analogy further: "But she said, 'Yes, Lord; but even the dogs feed on the crumbs that fall from their masters' table'" (15:27). Recall, too, the prophet Nathan's confrontation of King David after his affair with Bathsheba and the murder of her husband Uriah; it was enacted using a parable, an analogous story depicting an injustice done by a rich man to a poor man regarding a beloved ewe lamb (2 Sam 12:1–7). Well-conceived and constructed stories, analogies, and illustrations are impactful.

The Theology of Communication: In STEP 10: BIBLICAL THEOLOGY we discussed one important outcome of biblical interpretation: the construction of theology. In this STEP 12: PRESENTATION BRAINSTORM we are considering an initial movement of articulating the truth of Scripture for teaching and preaching in various settings—church, work, home, or anywhere. Hayes and Holladay are correct to note that biblical theology envisions broader audiences in various locations whereas preaching and teaching have more "occasional" settings and distinctive audiences and "life settings"; it is "more concrete and more specific."[1] Hayes and Holladay have considered the complex move from ancient text to modern sermon. In the church setting, "The preacher, like the professional theologian, stands at the end of a long process of interpretation, and is responsible for recognizing the multiple dimensions of the biblical text, such as its historical and literary dimensions. Similarly, the preacher does well to acknowledge the diversity of theological outlook reflected within the biblical writings."[2] In their view, three questions help to describe the task and the problems: "How does one translate the form and content of the original text into another form and content? How does one assess both the ancient and modern contexts in order to see analogies and patterns of relationships? How can one be responsible to both the text and its context or the sermon and its context?"[3] Bridging text and sermon may be achieved by stories and illustrations.

The final presentation of one's exposition of the biblical text implicitly carries with it a mode of interpretation and a theology. Put another way, the crafting of a sermon or a teaching lesson conveys and communicates one's exegesis of the passage (good or bad) and one's theology (biblically based or not). Thus, Hayes and Holladay helpfully remind us of this fact:

> When the Bible is read and appropriated through artistic creativity, whether it is in the form of music, painting, drama, or any of the other forms of artistic expression, exegesis is also carried out, even if it appears to be implicit. Handel's *Messiah* presupposes an exegesis of various portions of the Bible, as does MacLeish's *JB*, and in both cases the biblical text has been read and exegeted prior to the artistic production which has resulted from such interpretation.[4]

Thus, however we decide to "package" our teaching or preaching, such artistic representation will convey our interpretation and theology.

<u>Jesus is the Master of Communication</u>: Jesus is a prime model of communicating his understanding of Scripture and God the Father through stories, parables, and illustrations from everyday life. His parables are remarkable and most memorable. True, he was working with people whose hearts were hard and so the use of such analogies and illustrations were his best avenue to reach them (Matt 13:13–15). In this regard, *it is not a good thing that pastors must rely so heavily on illustrations to keep people's attention*; yet, to help people understand the truth of Scripture, illustrations are quite appropriate. And, the more "down to earth" and connected to our lived-in experiences the better. These common and mundane matters help to convey important spiritual truths. Read again the chart of TEACHING FORMS OF JESUS in STEP 6 (pp. 225-26). We could add to this that Jesus was aware of contemporary events and he helped people understand them; e.g., the Galileans whom Pilate killed; and those killed when the tower of Siloam fell (Luke 13:1–5). Similarly, we should consider contemporary events as possible sources of reflection and illustration—newspapers, headlines, etc. We should be careful, however, what we may implicitly affirm.

---

[1] *Biblical Exegesis: A Beginner's Handbook,* rev. ed. (Atlanta: John Knox, 1987), 149–50
[2] *Biblical Exegesis*, 150
[3] *Biblical Exegesis*, 150–51.
[4] *Biblical Exegesis*, 155.

Paul's Illustrations from Domains of Life: The Apostle Paul also communicated with a variety of analogies and metaphors from financial, military, household, agricultural, and urban life:[5]

LIFE DOMAINS AS METAPHORS IN THE PAULINE EPISTLES

- **Military Triumph and Religious Procession**: "God leads us in *triumphal procession* … and manifests a *fragrant aroma*" (2 Cor 2:14–16; 4:7, 10; cf. 1 Cor 4:9; Eph 4:8; Col 2:15)
- **City Design**: "the *judgment seat* of Christ" (2 Cor 5:10)
- **Imperial Warfare**: "that you wage *the good fight/warfare*" (1 Tim 1:18; cf. 2 Cor 10:4; Eph 6:13–19; 2 Tim 2:3; 3:6)
- **Classical Architecture and Temple Construction**: "The *firm foundation* of God stands having this seal" (2 Tim 2:19; cf. 1 Cor 3:9, 10, 16, 17; Eph 2:20–22; Col 2:7; 1 Tim 3:13, 15; 2 Tim 2:19)
- **Ancient Agriculture**: "The *laboring farmer* must be the first to partake of the fruits" (2 Tim 2:6; cf. Rom 5:5; 11:17; 1 Cor 3:9; 9:10–11; Gal 6:8; 1 Tim 4:10; 5:17–18; 6:10; Titus 1:13; 3:14)
- **Athletic Training**: "*Nourished* on the words of faith … *discipline* yourself for godliness" (1 Tim 4:6–8)
- **Athletic Contests**: "And if also a man *competes in the games*, he is not crowned unless he *competed* lawfully" (2 Tim 2:5; cf. 1 Cor 9:25; Eph 6:12; 1 Tim 6:12; 2 Tim 4:7)
- **Household Management**: The list of credentials for overseers/deacons in the Pastorals.[6]
- **Roman Law**: "That being justified we might be made *heirs* according to the hope of eternal life" (Titus 3:7; cf. Rom 8:17, 24 and *passim*); "So also we when we were children were held in bondage under the elemental principles of the world, that we might receive the *adoption* of sons" (Gal 4:3; cf. Rom 8:14, 21; Eph 1:5); "But I say that so long as the heir is a child he is not different from a *bondservant* [δοῦλος] being lord of all" (Gal 4:1; cf. Rom 3:25; 6:19; 1 Cor 7:21, 22; Phil 2:7, 8)
- **Medical Science**: "If any man teaches a different doctrine and doesn't consent to *sound words*" (1 Tim 6:3; cf. Titus 1:9, 13; 2:1; 2 Tim 2:17; 3:17; 4:3)
- **Seafaring Life**: "*were shipwrecked* concerning the faith" (1 Tim 1:19; cf. 6:19)
- **Commercial Life**: "Supposing godliness is a means of *gain*" (1 Tim 6:5; cf. 2 Tim 1:12, 14)
- **Hunting Game**: "the *snare* of the devil" (1 Tim 3:7; cf. 6:9; 2 Tim 2:26)

By referring to common life experiences and settings, Paul was speaking the language of his audiences. The best way to recognize such pictorial-metaphoric language is by accessing the original language of the NT, namely, Greek.

---

[5] This list expands that found in A. E. Humphreys, *The Epistles to Timothy and Titus with Introduction and Notes* (Cambridge: Cambridge University Press, 1895), 262–63 and the summary of Humprheys by Howard Tillman Kuist, *The Pedagogy of St. Paul* (New York: George H. Doran Company, 1925), 102.

[6] See Edwin Hatch, *The Organization of the Early Christian Churches. Eight Lectures Delivered Before the University of Oxford, in the Year 1880, on the Foundation of the Late Rev. John Bampton* (3rd ed.; London: Longmans, Green, and Co., 1918).

EXERCISE 12–A: Studying 1 Tim 4:6–10, you see that Paul moves from nourishing, to bodily discipline/exercise, to striving/competition. What life-domain does Paul evoke? What does Paul "map" onto these earthly actions? How might you update his analogy for your audiences today?

"Picturing" the Text by Working with the Original Languages: From your word study work in STEP 5: LEXICAL RESEARCH, you may have discovered figurative use of language or a "domain" or setting of life that is native to the wording of the passage. This is one important value of accessing the underlying biblical languages. David Hansen has affirmed this value when saying,

> Greek and Hebrew look like piles of seaweed to me, but I open the text in the original language and try to work through it with the help of the English. I don't think I can make a better English translation. I don't expect to overturn scholarly exegesis with my word studies. Reading the text in its original languages accomplishes two vital things. Looking at the text in its original tongue is another way to fiddle with it. It is a way of spending unhurried, inefficient time with the text. It forces me to slow down and listen more intently. It's a way of chewing on it. This slow work with the text produces the second benefit of original language study: pictures. Ancient Hebrew and Koine Greek are rich in pictures and metaphors. The pictures underlying the words (especially the theological terms) freshen theology and deliver natural images for preaching.[7]

EXERCISE 12–B: Consider what domains of life are evoked explicitly and implicitly in Mark's versions of Jesus's feeding of the 5,000 (Mark 6:33–44). The Greek words that may help you consider this have been provided; also consult Keener's *IVP Background Commentary* (1st or 2nd edition) on Mark 6:40 and 6:42–44 for possible domains evoked as well as Ben Witherington III, *The Gospel of Mark: A Socio-Rhetorical Commentary* (Grand Rapids: Eerdmans, 2001), 219–20.

[34] When Jesus went ashore, he saw a large crowd and felt compassion for them because they were like sheep without a shepherd; and he began to teach them many things....[39] And he commanded them all to sit down group by group [συμπόσια συμπόσια] on the green grass. [40] They sat group by group [πρασιαὶ πρασιαί] in hundreds [ἑκατὸν] and fifties [πεντήκοντα]....[42] They all ate and were satisfied, [43] and they picked up twelve full baskets [κόφινος] of the broken pieces and also of the fish. [44] There were 5,000 men who ate the loaves.

Human Scale, Imagination, and Simulation: One value of stories and illustrations is that notions, values, and behaviors may gain "human scale" in the imaginations of the audiences; i.e., they see how truth is embodied. Such internalization is important as people listen and begin possibly even to picture themselves doing, saying, believing, or valuing what Scripture encourages of God's people. In fact, such simulation is powerfully effective to help people begin to embody actions. In sports training, athletes gain much benefit simulating in the mind's eye the perfect swing.

---

[7] David Hansen, *The Art of Pastoring: Ministry Without All the Answers* (Downers Grove, IL: InterVarsity, 2012), 103–4.

God's Mission and Speaking Human: Russell has explained the opportunity for God's people to adopt a missional hermeneutic towards Scripture and communication:

> We must learn the art and craft of reading the Bible simultaneously for both the world and for the church. We need to help persons who have grown up inside the church to recapture the missional vibrancy and confidence of the apostolic church of the first four centuries by reintroducing them to the biblical story. We must likewise introduce the life-challenging message of Scripture to those on the *outside* of the church. Scripture is for both *insiders* and *outsiders* because God desires to bring healing, hope, restoration, and wholeness to all people. We thus must learn to speak human.[8]

How do we speak human? Russell explains: "We want to connect the Gospel with the [current] context so that the person we're speaking with actually hears what we think we're trying to say."[9] Thus, we must move from the truth that is in Scripture, then in us, and then to the world around us.

Therapeutic Metaphors (Stories): Bill Dillon and Pat Walt call a well-crafted story a "therapeutic metaphor."[10] Stories and illustrations have a way of disarming people and warming them up to become receptive to what you are communicating. Dillon and Walt provide the following guidelines to create a therapeutic story; remember too that practice will improve your storytelling.

1. Ask yourself, **"What is the situation or problem?"**
2. **Create an analogy to the situation**. "What is this situation like?" Analogy connects something you don't know about to something you do know about. It does this by paying attention to 'function', not 'form'. What are the functional attributes of what you don't know about, and where in your experience do you understand those functions?
3. **Visualize the answer**. Come up with a picture that would answer the question, "What is this situation like?"
4. **Use the picture as a reference point** for making up your metaphor in the story.
5. **Select an outcome and visualize a picture of that**.
6. **Run the storyline from the reference picture to the outcome picture**.
7. **Tell the story**, dwelling on details for the experiences that you want to elicit.

Priestly, Prophetic, and Advisory Communicative Roles: It may be helpful for communicators of Scripture (whether preachers, teachers, or witnesses) to understand their potential roles as priest, prophet, and sage, using the categories of Hayes and Holladay.[11] As **priest**, the communicator of God's Word stands as representative between God's Word and the people to convey the constitutive reality of God for God's people, that is, to reflect what is sacred, what is the people's

---

[8] Brian D. Russell, *(re)Aligning with God*, xiii.

[9] Russell "How to Speak Human Part 1" at https://www.youtube.com/watch?v=s5ifwRyazFg (11–22–2016).

[10] This material is slightly adapted from the Global Change Seminary – "It's your Move!" website Segment #5 "The Role of Humanity – the Role of Metaphor" accessed 1–27–2107 at http://www.global-change-seminar.org/raps/rap_5b.htm.

[11] *Biblical Exegesis*, 151. I am adjusting and elaborating on their categories and descriptions.

identity before God, and what is celebrated ritually. As **prophet**, the communicator confronts society, culture, and community and calls God's people to take action, embody, and reconstitute what is communicated principally in Scripture. As **sage**, the communicator advises the community by offering instruction, correction, wisdom, and insight from God's Word that informs their living in community; such illumination may spur reformation within God's people. So, as communicators we must consider how best to convey the truth(s) of the passage; we should consider whether the scriptural passage may be calling us to take a stance as priest, prophet, or sage. Accordingly, such a stance will affect what stories and illustrations should be selected and how best to communicate the message of the passage.

Importance of Locations or "Space" and Critical Space Theory: Increasingly, we are becoming aware of how spatially oriented and interconnected we are as human beings. One theorist of critical-space, Edward W. Soja, has described three types of spaces:[12] **Firstspace** refers to the actual physical space or what is present in the existing space—it is observable and "perceived"; **secondspace** refers to how the space is configured for use, how it is "conceived"; **thirdspace** is the actual use of the space, how it is "lived-in." Importantly, thirdspace is an open space where humans struggle to occupy and reconfigure the first-space in view of their own second-space conceptions for an envisioned lived-in thirdspace. Thus in actual practice, people struggle to occupy and (re-)configure space based upon their ideology and theological commitments. We must all

> Conceptions of space and place are important for our lives and imaginations.

negotiate firstspaces (physical environs) and secondspaces (conceptions of these environs) as we occupy our lived-in thirdspaces. Although disagreements of definitions and applications of critical space theory exist, what is important here in STEP 12: PRESENTATION BRAINSTORM is that *conceptions of space and place are important for our lives and imaginations and are often contested.* Within the field of Biblical Studies, a growing number of studies investigate critical space.[13]

The NT documents repeatedly give testimony to how important space is. For example, Jesus probably envisioned himself as a sacred place in which forgiveness of sins could be offered; he forgave sins outside of the temple system (e.g., Mark 2:9–12). Indeed, he understood himself to be a temple-space, "a stone that the builders rejected" (Mark 12:10 quoting Ps 118:22).[14] To give but another example, Jesus made a tumultuous journey across the Sea of Galilee while calming a storm by rebuking the wind before arriving in the country of Gedarenes; he was immediately met by a demoniac possessed of "Legion" and he cast them out into a herd of swine that ran down into the sea and perished; then Jesus was asked to leave by the swineherds after commanding the restored

---

[12] *Thirdspace: Journeys to Los Angeles and Other Real-and-Imagined Places* (Cambridge, MA: Blackwell, 1996); he developed the ideas of Henri Lefebvre, *The Production of Space* (Cambridge, MA: Blackwell, 1991).

[13] See, e.g., the works of these editors and the volume itself by Jon L. Berquist and Claudia V. Camp, eds., *Constructions of Space I: Theory, Geography, and Narrative*, T&T Clark Library of Biblical Studies 481 (New York: T&T Clark International, 2007). I am fortunate to have a number of doctoral students who are working in this field of research including Jon Ensor, Andrew Coutras, and Stephen Knisley.

[14] See, e.g., the compelling book by Nicholas Perrin, *Jesus the Temple* (Grand Rapids: Baker, 2011).

man to return to his people and report what the Lord did for him (Mark 4:35–5:20). From the perspective of critical space theory, a terrifying and uncontrollable firstspace (the sea), a dangerous secondspace (the demoniac), and a contested lived in thirdspace (the Gentile region) are transformed by Jesus into safe, saved, and clean spaces respectively through his infusion of thirdspace activity of miracle, restoration, and proclamation as seen embodied in the restored man.

EXERCISE 12–C: Jesus strategically took his disciples to Caesarea Philippi to ask them who he was (Matt 16:13–20). Why did he take them there? Consider the following questions.

1. Describe the firstspace of Caesarea Philippi; what significant geographic features were present?
2. Consider the secondspace and thirdspace of Caesarea Philippi; what can we know about how this city and its main geographic features were conceived and lived in?
3. Given Jesus's teaching at this location on the nature of his followers as a church assembly, how was Jesus helping his disciples envision their mission in these contested spaces?
4. Finally, how helpful would it be to illustrate the truth of Matt 16:12–20 by showing pictures of the physical cult sites (many are available online) and explaining that Jesus's teaching was contesting these in actual third (lived-in) space?

Connecting to People's Mind-Space: Using an appropriate story, analogy, or illustration will activate people's lived-in experiences and more readily allow your points to find a home in the conception of the audience. You can find many excellent websites to search for a suitable story, illustration, or analogy. At "Topnotch Quotes" is found this excellent description of their power:

> Analogies and stories are one of the most powerful speech strategies available to a technical presenter. An analogy or story anchors a complex technical idea to a concept or idea that an audience already understands. When you use an analogy, you are using the audience's prior knowledge and understandings to explain your technical concept. This is a much deeper form of learning because it is anchored to something that was already in their brain. As a result, the retention of concepts explained with analogies can be much higher because the listener's brain already has a place to file that information, instead of having to create an entirely new file from scratch.[15]

It is important to be discerning, however, in the stories and illustrations that we choose to use.

EXERCISE 12–D: Online are images of the cityscape of ancient Roman Corinth (see one on the next page). Read 2 Cor 5 from the perspective of Roman Corinth as if walking into town. Imagine what you would see moving from the outside of the city, through its various types of buildings, and then to the center of its seat of administrative power located in the center at the agora (hint: see 5:10). Tents of various kinds may have been seen; next temples and shrines featuring statues naked gods and goddesses. Consider how Paul may have been helping believers at Corinth to reconfigure

---

[15] Accessed 1-27-2017 at http://topnotchquotes.com/?page_id=1146#.WIuA4ZJhc0o.

their understanding of space and ultimate power: What is truly sacred? Who occupies the true governing authority over matters of judgment? In this light, consider how you might help audiences understand this important message in 2 Cor 5. What illustrations and analogies could you use from your own life experience?

The Agora and Environs of Roman Corinth[16]

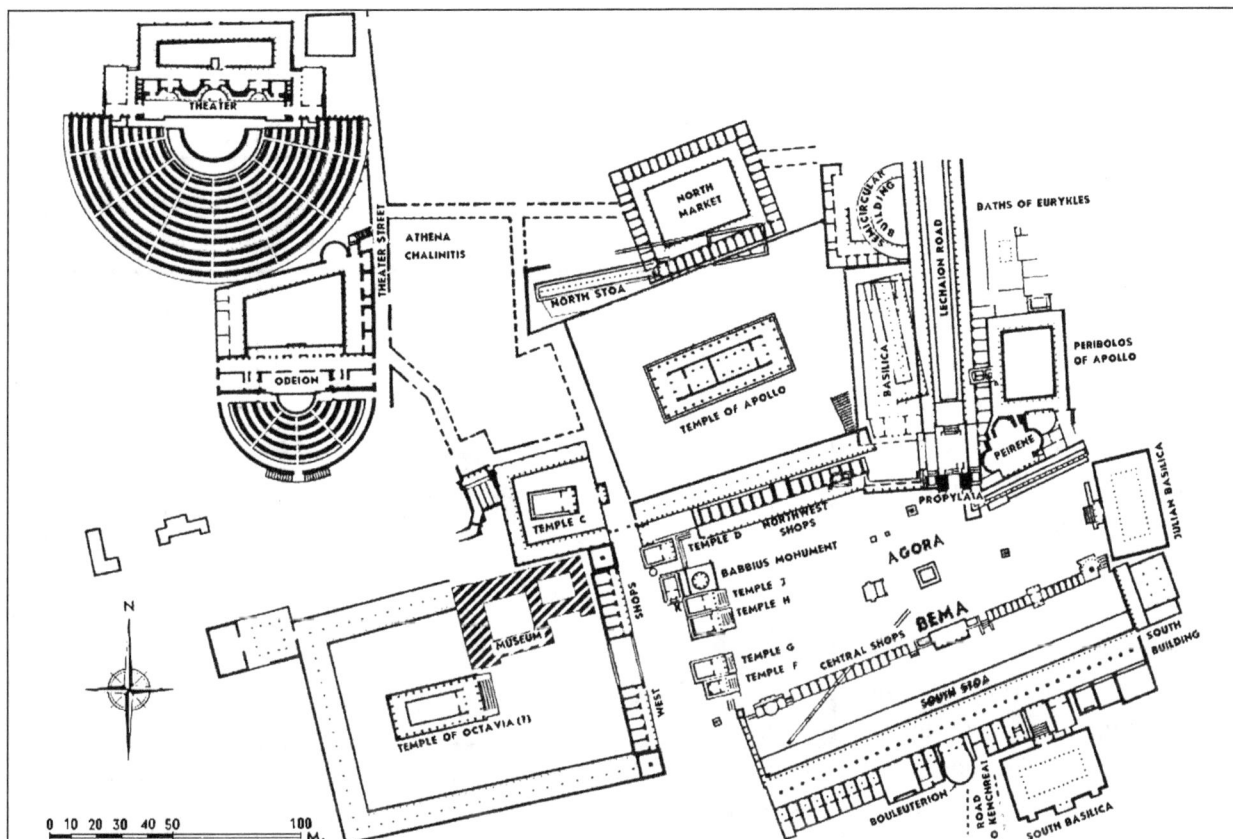

Using Infographics: Increasingly, graphic design has become important for teaching, preaching, and worship. Images tell a story; when such images include a few well-placed and incisive words, they become even more impactful. However, infographics take time to create; not many of us have the skills or can afford the time to do so. For this book I have spent countless hours searching for copyright free images, getting permissions to use images, or creating them. Fortunately, online resources exist.[17] Also, Logos Bible Software offers many colorful infographic resources;[18] Steve Runge has created "Animated High Definition Commentaries."[19] For example,

---

[16] Image adapted from Nicos Papahatzis, *Ancient Corinth* (Athens: Εκδοτικη Αθηνων, 2005).

[17] e.g., www.bible-infographics.com/

[18] *Logos Bible Software Infographics* (Bellingham, WA: Lexham, 2009) and Shiloh Hubbard et al. with Logos Bible Software and KarBel Media. *Faithlife Study Bible Infographics* (Bellingham, WA: Logos Bible Software, 2012).

[19] Steven E. Runge, *Animated High Definition Commentary: Philippians* (Bellingham, WA: Lexham, 2016).

Runge shows the significance of making explicit mention of and thus highlighting the Imperial guards ("the whole Praetorium") in Phil 1:13–14 with the infographic at right. Paul could have just said that he preached the gospel to all people, yet he explicitly mentions this special group. Why? This allowed the Philippians to understand Paul's courage and benefit in being imprisoned despite what people might otherwise think. Below, too, Runge is able to depict Paul's repeated admonition to "rejoice in the Lord" with an image showing the rejoicing as an umbrella safeguarding a person from rain depicted as words of fear, worry, doubt, discouragement, etc.[20] This infographic creatively maps to a commonly understood metaphor in American culture that BAD CIRCUMSTANCES ARE LIKE A RAINY DAY. Thus, the infographic creatively communicates the import of Paul's message for the Philippians with a metaphor that also American people (perhaps even most Westerners) would understand; it reflects effective and thoughtful repackaging of the biblical message for optimal reception.

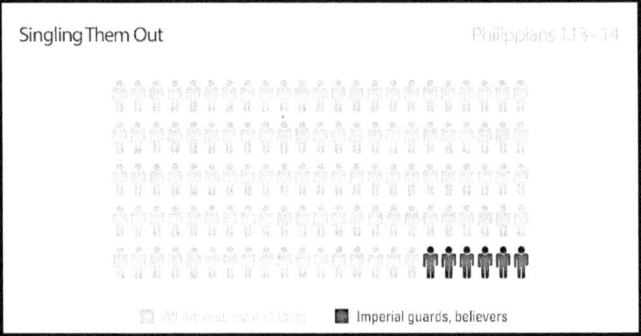

Yet, we may also offer the following two questions as critique: First, does Paul have just any human circumstances in mind (suffering or pain in general) or particular hardships associated with proclaiming the gospel and being imprisoned for such? Second, how transportable is the umbrella/rain metaphor to other cultural settings? For example, could a missionary in Sudan, Peru, or Papua New Guinea use such an infographic where the metaphor may not work, rain may be viewed positively, and/or umbrellas do not exist? Remember CIE.

<u>Offensive Stories, Fake Stories, and Political Correctness</u>: We should be careful not to offend unnecessarily in our selection and use of stories and illustrations. How will people hear them who are from different backgrounds and have experienced specific hardships? Also, it is off-putting to use stories or relate accounts that are quite inaccurate or even false. Every now and then I hear such stories related with passion in a sermon only to have someone lean over and say, "That never happened! The story is not true. I've heard it before and checked it out." So, we must be discerning and double-check the accuracy of "incredible" stories. Finally, it may be that we some-

---

[20] Both examples have been changed to grayscale and are used by permission from Runge, *Philippians*, s.v.

times need to use stories that push the envelop so to speak, that provoke people to deeper thought by relating hard or difficult situations. This takes great discernment! Jesus at times spoke parables that contained quite negative elements and used them to convey certain aspects of the Kingdom of God: like yeast (Matt 13:13), family disruptions (Luke 15:11–32), beatings and slayings (Luke 19:11–27 and Mark 12:1–12), and wastefulness (Luke 16:1–9). Finally, consider the following statement that warns against using "pacified" and politically correct stories.

> [T]he infinite values, lessons, and significance of stories and storytelling of all sorts represent much deeper human interest than should be controlled by the arbitrary application of 'political correctness' in everything that what we read and share. Otherwise ninety-nine percent the world's fairy tales would be outlawed and banned, and nearly all books (especially the Holy Bible), newspapers, films and every other media would not exist.[21]

Thus, it may be helpful here to consider some Do's and Don'ts when using stories and analogies:

DOS AND DON'TS WHEN USING STORIES AND ANALOGIES

1. Do carefully consider appropriate stories and analogies for your teaching and preaching;
   Don't do this at the expense of careful interpretation of the passage.
2. Do provide stories and analogies in your teaching/preaching for the most important point(s);
   Don't overwhelm the content of your message with stories.
3. Do practice telling stories and consider how best to convey an illustration;
   Don't worry so much about performance but let the urgency of the message compel you.
4. Do consider asking people (like a special committee) to help find relevant stories;
   Don't promise to use all of the stories they may help you to find.
5. Do provide passage-specific and application-specific stories;
   Don't too narrowly focus on one passage-specific application at the expense of others.
6. Do provide age- and audience-appropriate stories and analogies;
   Don't under- or overestimate the ability of people to understand your illustrations.
7. Do use sophisticated and carefully conceived analogies and illustrations;
   Don't use overly-complicated and convoluted analogies and illustrations.
8. Do research the truthfulness of "actual" events or stories and cite sources as necessary;
   Don't be off-putting by relating a false story; acknowledge any mistakes when made.
9. Do provide provocative stories that prompt people to think more deeply about a topic;
   Don't unnecessarily offend people with your stories.

EXERCISE 12–E: What have been the most effective stories, analogies, and illustrations that you can remember from a sermon or lecture? What made them effective? Conversely, what have been the most ineffective or troublesome stories, illustrations, or examples? Why was this so?

---

[21] Accessed 1–27–2017 at http://www.businessballs.com/stories.htm (original bolding removed). See also the further comments on this topic on this page.

Sensory-Aesthetic Texture: Throughout *In Step with God's Word*, I have referred to Robbins who has sought to describe a rich "textural" interpretive environment by which students of Scripture may make acute observations of the text using the metaphor of "textures." The metaphor affirms that texts are like rich tapestries that may be viewed from different vantage points; we may choose to study this or that pattern, this or that color, or this or that texture. The beauty is in the whole and is never entirely appreciated if viewed simply from one perspective. But too often in Biblical Studies, we simply focus on one thing. So, Robbins attempts to rectify this by offering his textural approach. He describes "sensory-aesthetic texture" as a feature of inner texture and provides the following concise description in the online *Dictionary of Socio-Rhetorical Terms*:

> **sensory-aesthetic texture**: resides prominently in the interaction among the senses (sight, sound, touch, smell, taste), motor activities (walking, reaching, grasping, etc.), and subjective modes (emotion, intuition, imagination, thought, reason, humor, etc.) the text evokes or embodies. This texture is comprised of three body zones: emotion fused thought, self-expressive speech, and purposeful action.[22]

Essentially, we may observe biblical authors drawing our attention to the thoughts, speech, and actions of human agents. When they do so, *they communicate something about the embodiment of values, principles, virtues/vices, etc*. From the perspective of preparing to communicate the truth of our passage, such bodily descriptions are "low hanging fruit" inviting us to brainstorm and conceive of ways that we can communicate the rules, principles, paradigms, and notions of the symbolic world to our audiences in analogous ways.

On Homiletical Texture and BIG IDEAS: William Frank Brosend II has proposed the existence of a "homiletical texture" of biblical materials adding to Robbins's metaphor and analytical approach.[23] Brosend explains that homiletical texture compliments the biblical passage by attending to 1) the inner texture of the text considering rhetorical structure, argumentation, and topics; and 2) the intertexture (i.e., how one text draws on other texts or ancient artifacts) and sociocultural texture: "what does this text, the texts to which it interrelates, and the sociocultural world from which and to which it was written reveal about how it might best be preached?"[24] What this means is that any given passage will direct its audiences to the BIG IDEAS that are rooted in human experience and metaphor. These BIG IDEAS may gain our attention in sensory-aesthetic texture, which then helps us to consider analogous stories, illustrations, and examples which we communicate to our audiences. In particular, we may discover ancient artifacts in our research that will help convey the truth of Scripture. So, attention to a text's sensory aesthetic texture and its connection to the ancient world (i.e., its *realia*) will assist us to find and use appropriate and powerful stories, illustrations, and artifacts to communicate its BIG IDEAS while also conveying the value of the full human person (mind, body, soul, emotions) and our human experiences (senses).

---

[22] Accessed 1–30–2017 at http://www.religion.emory.edu/faculty/robbins/SRI/defns/s_defns.cfm#sensory.

[23] *James and Jude* (Cambridge: Cambridge University Press, 2004), 9; he is self-consciously doing so.

[24] Ibid., 9

STEP 12: PRESENTATION BRAINSTORM

<u>Example from Ephesians 5:7–14</u>: Let me now provide an example using Eph 5:7–14 from STEP 11: EVALUATED APPLICATIONS. The chart helps to facilitate text-specific brainstorming. I begin by bringing forward the scriptural text itself since I don't ever want to lose sight of it. Then a column contains the rules, principles, and any applications that I think are worth illustrating. Next, we have a column to identify the BIG IDEAS and sensory aesthetic dimensions of the text. The last column is for brainstorming; include here any scriptural stories (cite verses), adages, illustrations, analogies, news report, film scene, poem, book portion, theological ideas, etc.

Firstly, Eph 5:7–14 presents a <u>prophetic call</u> for believers to be Light. **Secondly**, the purpose of this call is to help believers understand that they are to occupy this *important and universally acknowledged "positive" and "honest" social-public space.*			
Scripture Text	**Rules, Principles, etc.**	**BIG IDEAS & Sensory Aesthetics**	**Brainstorms**
Eph 5:7 Therefore do not be partakers with them;	**Rule 1:** Believers should not participate with sinners and sinful actions. **Principle 1:** Humans generally like partnership, even "companions in crime."	PEER PRESSURE COMMUNITY & PARTNERSHIP purposive action TOGETHERNESS	-"birds of like-feather…" -mob mentalities (an extreme example) -Going along with groups cliques (common example) -"holy huddle" (pros and cons) -The Trinity (ultimate partnership)
8a for you were formerly darkness, …**11a** Do not participate in the unfruitful deeds of darkness, …	**Rule 2:** Believers should not participate with dark deeds because such are not fruitful. **Principle 2:** Humans hide from their sin. **Principle 3:** Believers were once in darkness. **Symbolic World:** Light is good and darkness is bad. Believers are called to be Light.	purposive actions PRODUCTIVITY fruitfulness SHAME/GUILT CHANGE LIGHT VS. DARK LIGHT (sight implied)	-change is good; but change from what to what? -If plants that don't produce, we wonder what went wrong. -We like productivity; our work life depends on this; should we expect God to be different in this regard? -heroes transformed -Movie images of dark vs. light (StarWars, etc.) -Why are we sometimes fascinated with darkness??? -Light is energy; it spreads and helps plants grow.
12 for it is disgraceful even to speak of the things which are done by them in secret.	**Principle 4:** It is shameful to discuss sinful acts done in secret.	PUBLIC SHAME speech & action secretive actions	-the gossip story -Paul discussed earlier words that gives grace to those who hear them (4:29). -hide-n-seek play; this is real

PRESENTATION BRAINSTORM PROCEDURES:

1. **Consider whether the scriptural passage calls you to function primarily in a *priestly*, *prophetic*, or *advisory* role. What implications does this have for how you as priest, prophet, or sage "package" your teaching or preaching?**
2. **Determine what physical or ideological spaces are contested and/or (re)claimed.**
3. Next, creating a chart (if this is helpful for you), **bring forward a) the biblical verses, b) your transcultural rules, principles, paradigms, and notions of the symbolic world, and c) the most important applications from STEP 11: EVALUATED APPLICATIONS.**
4. Then, **consider how the scriptural text and its principles connect with our world in terms of BIG IDEAS and/or the presence of any explicit or implicit sensory-aesthetic descriptions.**
   a. What BIG IDEAS are present that may evoke certain images in our minds?
   b. Which of the five senses are appealed to in the verse? Auditory (hearing), Olfactory (smell), Visual (sight), Gustatory (taste), Sensory (touch). In other words, what sensory-aesthetic texture (using Robbins' expression) is present?
5. **Freely brainstorm about what could help communicate the truths of the passage. Consider the following areas:**
   a. some artifact or social-cultural information from the biblical world discovered in your work
   b. known or common stories; personal stories are alright to use, but be careful relating your life "successes" and "failures" as these will become wearisome for people to hear repeatedly
   c. analogies or illustrations to help explain an important aspect of the rule, principle, etc.
   d. the nature of the world, i.e., "how things are" in the created order
   e. situations that we often find ourselves in that would convey the biblical truths
   f. news reports and popular magazines; keep up to date with news and film
   g. great classic literature (Dickens, Dostoevsky, etc.) and plays (Shakespeare, Sophocles, etc.)
   h. films and TV series
6. **Consider forming a small group** with whom you walk through the Interpretive Journey in step with God's Word or with whom you share your interpretive work and **then solicit their input for finding the most poignant and impactful stories, etc.** Many well-known preachers have people helping them find suitable illustrations and analogies.
7. **If needed, consult resources devoted to offering stories and illustrations for speakers.**
   a. Sermon illustration guides are arranged topically. I have used on occasion Paul Lee Tan's *Encyclopedia of 7700 Illustrations: Signs of the Times* (Rockville, MD: Assurance, 1979).
   b. Also, there are many places on the internet that specialize in this sort of thing related even to specific biblical passages, e.g., http://www.sermoncentral.com/.
   c. Finally, be sure to check the validity and truthfulness of "real life" stories and illustrations. Also, you need to consider whether the stories and illustrations are consonant with your interpretation and evaluation of the biblical passage and truly helpful to clarify and enhance the message of the scriptural passage and its impact.

PART V:

EMBODYING AND AWAITING THE WORD

The Interpretive Journey

You Are Here

1: Contextual Location

2: Textual Comparisons

3: Grammatical Study

4: Semantic Analysis

5: Lexical Research

6: Literary Forms

7: Historical Context

8: Scriptural Correlations

9: Interpretive Decisions

10: Biblical Theology

11: Evaluated Applications

12: Presentation Brainstorm

Chapter Omega
A Postlude on Embodiment and an Eschatology for the Future

"The wisdom of what a person says is in direct proportion to his progress in learning the Holy Scriptures—and I am not speaking of intensive reading or memorization, but real understanding and careful investigation of their meaning. Some people read them but neglect them; by their reading they profit in knowledge, by their neglect they forfeit understanding."

"So anyone who thinks that he has understood the divine Scriptures or any part of them, but cannot by his understanding build up this double love of God and neighbor, has not yet succeeded in understanding them."

—Augustine of Hippo, *On Christian Doctrine*

"And if I have prophecy, and know all mysteries and all knowledge, and if I have all faith so that I can remove mountains, but do not have love, I am nothing.... Love never ends. But if there are prophecies, they will be set aside; if there are tongues, they will cease; if there is knowledge, it will be set aside. For we know in part, and we prophesy in part, but when what is perfect comes, the partial will be set aside."

—The Apostle Paul, 1 Cor 13:2, 8–10

Embodiment: Saint Augustine understood that obeying the Scriptures leads to spiritual growth.[1] It is not enough to know; one must understand and embody the Scriptures. Augustine rightly understood this to entail love of God and neighbor. Indeed, this focal point of Scripture is affirmed across the NT—to love God and to your neighbor as yourself, which sums up the OT

---

[1] Edward L. Smither, *Augustine as Mentor: A Model for Preparing Spiritual Leaders* (Nashville, TN: B&H, 2009), 228. Smither provides the following references in support: *Sermon* 82.12.15; 227.1; *Letter* 36.1.1; *Expositions in Psalms* 69.6; *Tractates on the First Letter of John* 3.1; *On Instructing Beginners* 7.11; cf. Possidius, *Life of Augustine* 19.3–4; *On Teaching Christianity* 4.6.9; 4.53.

Law (Matt 19:19; Mark 12:31; Luke 10:27; Rom 13:9; Gal 5:14; Jas 2:8). This is the new commandment of Jesus: to love one another (John 13:34; 15:12, 17; 1 John 2:7–8; 3:11, 23; 2 John 5). This love remains even beyond knowledge. The Apostle Paul taught also that knowledge would pass away when the "perfect" or maturity/completeness comes. When is this? What is this perfectness/maturity that Paul speaks off? Whatever we interpret this to mean (the Lord's coming or the coming of our moral maturity), this entails love because love endures forever.

<u>The NT's Eschatological Framework</u>: The NT's message is set within an eschatological framework. Not surprisingly, Jesus himself supplied this framework. That is, Jesus envisioned certain events as "certain" to occur in the future. It is therefore paramount to have these in mind as we study and embody the message of the NT. These envisioned events include the following: 1) his coming death, resurrection, and ascension (Mark 8:31; 9:31; 10:33–34); 2) the tragic fall of Jerusalem (Mark 13//Matt 24//Luke 21; see esp. Luke 19:41–44); 3) the ongoing missionary work of his disciples empowered by the Spirit (Matt 10; 28:18–20; Luke 24:46–49; Acts 1:8); 4) the spread of God's Kingdom like yeast in the dough, like wheat sown in the field, and like fish ready for the net (Matt 13); and 5) his coming return ($\pi\alpha\rho o u\sigma i\alpha$) in the fullness of the Kingdom (Mark 13:32; Matt 24:36–39). Of his coming Jesus forewarned that no one would know when it would occur and so he commanded his disciples to be alert (Matt 24:42) and to be doing what the Master expects them to do (24:45–51). Following this, Jesus provided the parables of the ten Virgins and the Sheep and Goats (Matt 25). These two parables remind us of the danger of complacency and the real possibility of not simply missing out on the honor of serving the needy and finding Jesus there (Matt 25:34–39) and the joy of helping find lost sheep (see Luke 15:5–7, 9–10, 20–24), but also missing out on everlasting life and experiencing instead everlasting punishment (Matt 25:46).

<u>New Heavens and New Earth</u>: What we long for is something better in this life even as we attempt to help people and improve life-circumstances now. The prophet Isaiah envisioned new heavens and a new earth (Isa 66). In God's work in Jesus, we have the hope and promise of new heavens and a new earth, a place "where justice dwells" (2 Pet 3:13). It is no accident that the Book of Revelation concludes with a vision of the new heavens and new earth descending from heaven (20:1–22:5) before issuing final exhortations (22:10–21). Indeed, it is in light of this promise that Peter urged believers to live differently in the world as we await the Lord's return:

> [14] Therefore, beloved, expecting these things [New Heavens and a New Earth], be diligent to be found by Him in peace, spotless and blameless, [15] and consider the patience of our Lord to be salvation, just as also our beloved brother Paul according to the wisdom given him wrote to you, [16] as also in all his letters, speaking in them concerning these things, among which there are some things hard to understand that the untaught and unstable distort, as also the rest of the Scriptures, to their own destruction. (2 Pet 3:14–16)

Here we most notice that the Scriptures may be misinterpreted to the detriment of people, and perhaps especially the eschatological passages concerning our promised future. And so we strive both to be faithful in our interpretation and obedient in our embodiment as we await Christ's return and the New Heavens and New Earth. Remember, *knowledge will pass away but love endures forever*.

Author Index
(Modern & Ancient)

Aarts, Joris 291
Achtemeier, Elizabeth 292
Achtemeier, Paul J. 232n23, 288
Adam, A. K. M. 393
Aland, Barbara 78n5, 83n11, 100, 102-3
Aland, Kurt 78n5, 100, 103, 334
Alexander, T. Desmond 387n18, 393
Alexander the Great 255, 262, 268
Alfoldi, Andreas 202n45
Ambrose (of Milan) 92, 392
Ambrosiaster 92, 94
Archer, Gleason L. 334, 369
Aristophanes 80, 197
Aristotle 56, 80, 153, 236, 243-44, 246, 261
Arndt, W. F. 214
Arnold, Clinton E. 266, 289, 366
Arthur, Kay 27, 61n13, 69, 71
Augustine xiii, 53n3, 84, 92, 226-27, 244, 392, 417, 447
Augustus (emperor) 88, 196, 208-10, 257, 277-78, 286n72, 291-92, 328, 362n7, 365
Aune, David Edward 240, 252, 273, 275n41, 291
Aus, Roger Davis 323n49
Avi-Yonah, Michael 331n77-78
Awabdy, Mark A. 19n10, 295n3
Ayayo, Karelynne 72, 252, 369, 430
Bailey, Daniel P. 233n27
Bailey, James L. 252
Bailey, Kenneth E. 240
Bakewell, Geoffrey W. 219
Balch, David L. 60n9, 290
Balla, Peter 293
Balz, Horst 199
Banks, Robert J. 289, 356
Barlow, Robert A. 384n16
Barnabas 376
Barr, James 394
Barrett, C. K. 289

Barrett, David P. 80n9, 103
Barry, John D. 79n7
Barth, Karl 392
Barth, Markus 83, 194n26
Bartholomew, Craig G. 392-93
Barton, John 217, 275
Basil the Great 92, 392
Bauckham, Richard 317, 390, 391n29
Bauer, David R. v, 3n1, 31n18, 32-33, 34n24, 40n28, 44, 61, 61n12.n14, 68n21, 69, 70n23, 71n23, 72, 103, 152n2, 214, 339n1, 342n2, 343, 343n3, 346, 360, 369, 398n5, 401, 430
Bauer, Walter 214
Baur, F. C. 56n7
BDAG 29n16, 123, 183, 185, 188, 191, 193, 195n33, 199, 200, 214, 280, 285
Beale, G. K. 334, 335, 394
Beasley-Murray, George R. 30n17
Beckwith, Roger T. 56n6, 72
Bell, Albert A. 270n25, 289
Berquist, Jon L. 437n13
Best, Ernest 205, 283-84
Bhabha, Homi K. 242n43
Billings, J. Todd 393
Black, David Alan 65n18, 84n16, 103, 126n19, 147, 252, 273n33,
Blasi, Anthony J. 292
Blass, F. 148
Blomberg, Craig L. 227, 237, 252, 430
Bloomquist, Gregory L. 238n37, 277n42
Blumenfeld, Bruno 332, 365
Bockmuehl, Markus 396
Bonhoeffer, Dietrich 392
Booth, Wayne C. 362, 363n4-5, 369
Boring, M. Eugene 290, 395
Botha, Eugene 326n49
Bratcher, Robert G. 334
Brauch, Manfred T. 369
Braun, Herbert 276
Bray, Gerald L. 394
Bright, Steve 300-301

Bromiley, G. W. 288, 290, 396
Brosend II, William Frank 442
Brother Lawrence 401n11
Broughton, Thomas R. S. 210n71
Brown, Colin 199, 288
Brown, Raymond E. 288
Bruce, F. F. 71, 369
Bruehler, Bart B. 242
Brunner, Emil 386, 396
Brunt, P. A. 366
Bryan, Christopher 393
Bullinger, E. W. 108n4, 147, 237n32-33
Bultmann, Rudolf Karl 230
Burridge, Richard A. 230
Buttrick, G. A. 288
Byatt, Anthony. 289
Caird, G. B. 394
Callen, Barry L. 393
Callimachos of Cyrene 331
Calvin, John 376, 392
Cambron-Goulet, Mathilde 329n60
Camp, Claudia V. 437n13
Campbell, Constantine R. 148
Cancik, Hubert 330n65
Cannadine, D. 365n9
Carroll, James R. 369
Carroll, John T. 369
Carson, D. A. 148, 184, 218, 260, 288, 335, 346, 392
Carter, Warren 197n35, 262
Childs, Brevard 394
Chirichigno, Gregory 334
Cicero (politician/philosopher) 153, 196, 232, 236n29, 244, 329, 332n83, 333, 365
Claudius (emperor) 203n48, 208, 210, 256
Clement of Alexandria 79, 84, 99
Clement of Rome 255, 376
Coffin, William Sloane 370
Collins, Kenneth J. 392
Comfort, Philip Wesley 80n9, 84n16, 93-94, 103, 333n93
Cooper, Craig R. 219n9
Coote, Robert B. 325n48, 326n49
Cosby, Michael R. 233n28

Coutras, Andrew 437
Craigmiles, Shawn x
Crawford, Michael 291
Croy, N. Clayton 147
Curtius Rufus 194
Cuss, Dominique 208n61
Dana, Harvey E. 120n10
Danker, Frederick W. 200-201, 203, 214
Davids, Peter H. 289, 369
Davis, Ellen F. 392, 377n10
Debrunner, A. 148
Deissmann, G. Adolf 185, 200, 202, 208, 247
Delitzsch, Franz 299
Delobel, Joël 83
DeMaris, Richard E. 292
DePriest, Roger G. 237n36
Derderian, Katharine 327n53
deSilva, David A. 270, 288-89, 343n3
Didymus (church father) 92
Dillon, Bill 436
Dio Chrysostom (orator) 195n32, 365
Diogenes Laertius 276
Dockery, David S. 252, 273n33
Dodd, C. H. 390
Dongell, Joseph R. 153n5
Dooley, Robert A. 423
Draisma, Sipke 299n6
Dunn, James D. G. 194n28, 394
Duvall, J. Scott 31n18, 32, 71, 155, 252, 406-7
Edlin, Jim 18n8
Edwards, Jonathan 392
Ehrman, Bart D. 81n10, 102, 104
Einstein, Albert 238, 339,
El-Abbadi, Mostafa 330n68, 331n73
Elliott, John H. 269n21, 274n34-37, 292
Elliot, Rich 85n17, 104
Ellis, E. Earle 312, 315, 320-21, 335, 389-90
Elsner, Jaś 328n55
Enos, Richard L. 329
Ensor, Jon 437

Epictetus 276
Erasmus 73, 87
Esler, Philip F. 292, 294
Eusebius (ch. father) 57, 79, 92, 99
Evans, Craig A. 288-89, 315n25, 316n26, 335
Fanning, Buist M. 149
Fathallah, Omnia Mounir 330n68, 331n73
Fauconnier, Gilles 153n6
Fee, Gordon D. 71-72, 90, 92, 147, 155, 172, 191n15, 252, 398, 416, 417n29
Feldmeier, Reinhard 394
Ferguson, Everett 289
Finkelberg, Margalit 328n54, 330n65
Fishbane, Michael A. 320
Fishwick, Duncan 209, 210n72
Flemming, Dean 430
Foley, John Miles 329n59
Forness, Philip Michael 376n8
Fowl, Stephen 393
Francis, Fred O. 334
Freedman, D. Noel 288, 290
Fresch, Christopher J. 121-22, 123
Friedland, Elise A. 292
Friedrich, G. 290
Fuentes, Carlos 293
Fuller, Daniel P. 69, 176n1, 182, 187n14, 191n16
Gadamer, Hans-Georg 421
Geden, H. K. 213
Geertz, Clifford 272n30, 273n31
Geisler, Norman L. 369
Georgi, Dieter 101n32, 239
Giffin, Ryan x
Gingrich, F. W. 214
Gladding, Sean 392
Goh, Benson x, 20, 324n45
Goheen, Michael W. 392
Gonzalez, Justo 392
Goodrick, Edward W. 180, 181n7, 213
Goody, Jack 219, 331n76
Gorgias (rhetorician) 244-45
Gorman, Michael J. 381n12, 388, 391n28, 405, 415

Gowler, David B. 277n42
Grant, Michael 202n45, 291
Green, Gene L. 106n1, 193-94, 213n74
Green, Joel B. 252, 275n38, 288, 335, 377n9, 392, 396
Greenlee, J. Harold 79n6, 83, 85n18, 99, 103
Gregory of Nazianzus 392
Gregory of Nyssa 392
Gregory the Great 392
Grindheim, Sigurd 394
Groening, Matt 150
Grudem, Wayne 429
Grundmann, Walter 276
Guinness, Os 406
Gupta, Nijay K. 194
Gurevitch, Michael 215n2
Guthrie, Donald 288, 394
Guthrie, George H. 155, 172
Hadrian (emperor)
Hafemann, Scott J. 394
Hagner, Donald 356
Haikal, Fayza M. 330
Halcomb, T Michael W. 18n6, 69, 72
Hansen, David 435
Hanson, K. C. 104
Harland, Philip A. 366
Harris, Murray J. 93-94
Harris, William V. 314n22, 326, 332
Harrison, James R. 277n43, 286n73
Hart, Trevor 392
Hartley, John 215
Harvey, John D. 237
Hasel, Gerhard 387, 394
Hatch, Edwin 190, 320n36, 335, 434n6
Hatina, Thomas 394
Hawthorne, G. 289
Hayden, Pelliccia 327, 328n54
Hayes, John H. 416, 432-33, 436
Hays, J. Daniel 31n18, 32, 71, 252, 406-7
Hays, Richard B. 198, 212, 299n6, 311, 323-24, 334-35, 377n10, 398, 408-9, 411, 429-30
Headley, Anthony J. 220

Heiser, Michael S. 263
Hesiod 197
Hiatt, Robert Jeffrey 375n5
Hietanen, Mika 322n39
Hillel (Rabbi) 315-16, 318, 334
Hills, Julian v, 101n32, 239
Hippolytus 79, 92
Hiramatsu, Kei x
Hirsch, E. D. 421
Hoehner, Harold W. 197n36, 204, 283-84, 286
Holladay, Carl R. 416, 432-33, 436
Hollenbach, Barbara 153n4
Hollington, Sophy 117n8
Holmes, Michael W. 89-90, 102-3
Holum, Kenneth G. 210n72
Homer 56, 80, 186, 198, 200, 212, 327-28, 330n65, 331n78
Honoré, A. M. 296n4
Horrell, David G. 292
Horsley, G. H. R. 196n33
Horsley, Richard A. 264
Hort, F. J. A. 74, 90, 104, 126, 181
Howard, W. F. 148
Howe, Thomas A. 369
Hubbard, Moyer V. 270n25, 289
Hubbard, Shiloh 439n18
Hubbard, Thomas 329n61
Hull Jr., Robert F. 83, 103
Humphreys, Colin J. 257,
Humphreys, A. E. 434n5
Hurtado, Larry W. 12n3, 13
Ignatius 255, 376
Irenaeus 79
Isaac, Jon M. 395
Iverson, Kelly R. 60n11
Jeal, Roy 242n44
Jeffers, James S. 289
Jensen, Irving Lester 69, 72
Jeremias, Joachim 395
Jesus Christ Chapter Alpha *et passim*. See under Subject Index
John Chrysostom 92, 199, 376, 392
Johnson, Luke Timothy 106, 107n3, 288
Johnson, William A. 327n53
Jones, H. S. 214

Jones, Scott J. 392
Jülicher, Adolf 226
Julius Caesar 196, 208-9, 333
Justin Martyr 79, 255
Kaiser, Walter C. Jr. 155, 172, 335, 369, 394
Kee, Howard Clark 269, 291
Keegan, Peter 327n53
Keener, Craig S. 29n15, 230, 258, 266, 289-90, 357, 361, 416, 435
Keil, Carl Friedrich 299
Kennedy, George A. 239n39, 243, 246n47
Kipling, Rudyard 431
Kittel, Gerhard 199, 267, 290, 356
Klauck, Hans-Josef 233n27, 246, 290
Klink, Edward W. 394
Knight III, Henry H. 384
Knisley, Stephen 437
Koester, Helmut 290-91
Kohlenberger, John R. 180-81, 213
Kotrosits, Maia 326n49
Kraftchick, Steven J. 394
Kreitzer, L. Joseph 203n48, 291
Kristeva, Julia 299n6, 319-20
Kuist, Howard Tillman 434n5
Kümmel, Werner Georg 291, 395
L&N 182, 184, 189, 199, 214, 297n5
Ladd, George Eldon 253, 385, 395
Laubach, Frank Charles 401n11
Lauwers, Jeroen 329, 333
Lawrence, Paul 288
L'Engle, Madeleine 431
Lee, John A. L. 193
Lee, Michelle V. 195n29
Lefebvre, Henri 242n43, 437n12
Levinsohn, Stephen H. 121-23, 125n17, 137, 139-40, 142-44, 146, 149, 354, 423
Levy, Mark R. 215n2
Lewis, C. S. 404
Liddell, H. G. 214
Lightfoot, John 290
Lincoln, Andrew T. 194n28, 283n50
Livingstone, Sophia 215
Lockett, Darian R. 394

Lohmeyer, E. 356
Long, Fredrick J. 123, 130n25, 144n36, 147-48, 151n1, 153n3.7, 155n9-10, 194n23, 208n60, 249n53, 277n43, 286n73, 295n3, 328n58, 329n62, 354, 364n6
Longacre, Robert E. 423
Loriot, James 153n4
Louw, Johannes P. 149, 155, 172, 182, 184, 189, 214, 348
LSJ 177, 183, 188, 191, 196, 199, 200, 203, 208n61, 214, 225
Luther, Martin 374, 376, 392
Mackay, E. Anne 327n53, 329n61
Magie, David 365n9
Maier, Harry O. 203n48, 292
Malina, Bruce J. 270, 290
Manders, Erika 291
Mantey, Julius R. 120n10
Marshall, I. Howard 213, 257, 335, 392, 395, 398, 409, 413-14, 429-30
Martin, Dale 195n32
Martin, Ralph P. 288-89
Maston, T. B. 421
Matera, Frank J. 395
Mattingly, Harold 202, 291
McCormick, Michael 202
McDonald, Lee Martin 55n4, 71-72
McKay, Niall 319n28
McKinney, Lawrence E. 203n48
McKnight, Scot 395
McLaren, Brian D. 26n14, 27, 392
McRay, John R. 53n2
Meek, D. L. 320n33
Meeks, Wayne A. 290
Mellor, Ronald 209, 286n72
Metzger, Bruce M. 5, 55, 72, 92-94, 99, 102-4
Meyer, Ben F. 259
Milligan, George 200
Minchin, Elizabeth 327n53, 329n60
Minger, Stacy R. 392
Mitchell, L. C. 232n22
Mitchell, Margaret M. 195n32, 232n26

Mitchell, S. 364n7
Montefiore, C. G. 356
Morford, Mark 332n83
Morris, Leon 395
Morrison, Craig E. 121n14, 149
Moule, C. F. D. 148
Moulton, H. K. 213
Moulton, J. H. 148, 200
Moulton, W. F. 213
Moyise, Steve 335
Muddiman, John 88, 325n46
Mulholland, Jr., H. Robert 273-74
Murphy, James J. 244
Nave, Orville J. 308-9, 318
Neill, Stephen 395
Nero (emperor) 195-96, 208, 256
Nestle, E. 5, 60, 83, 97, 103
Neufeld, Dietmar 292
Nida, Eugene A. 36, 179, 180n4, 182, 184, 189, 214, 216, 348
Niditch, Susan 327n53
Nock, A. D. 205, 208, 210n69, 283,
Noll, Mark A. 374n4
Nostradamus 300-301
O'Brien, Peter T. 204, 284
O'Keefe, John J. 392
O'Sullivan, Tim 215n1
Oakley, Todd 43
Oden, Thomas 315, 315
Ogden, Daniel 261n15
Oldfather, Charles Henry 332
Omanson, Roger L. 5, 93-94, 103
Origen 79, 86, 92, 99, 321, 376
Oropeza, B. J. 242n44
Osborne, Grant R. 34n24
Oster, Richard E. 203n48, 291
Ovid 196
Paine, Thomas 397
Pannenberg, Wolfhart 386, 396
Papahatzis, Nicos 439n16
Parasuraman, Raja 44n30
Parker, David C. 84n15, 97, 104
Parker, Holt N. 327n53
Patzia, Arthur G. 55n4-5, 71
Paul, A. 238n37
Penner, Todd C. 107n3
Perrin, Nicholas 392, 437n14

Phillips, Doug x
Philodemus (rhetorician) 333
Pierpont, William G. 90, 103
Pilch, John J. 270, 290, 292
Pindar 197
Pinner, H. L. 332
Pitts, A. W. 103, 194n25, 208n60
Pliny 255
Plato 56, 80, 195n32, 244, 246, 329
Plutarch 194, 261
Pompey 255
Porter, C. 216n5
Porter, Stanley E. 56n7, 78n4, 85n18, 103, 106n1, 121n13, 128n23, 130n25, 131, 145, 149, 182n10, 194n25, 208n60, 288, 335, 429
Poster, Carol 231n22, 247n49
Powell, Mark Allan 288
Powery, Luke 392
Price, S. R. F. 328n56, 365
Quintilian (rhetorician) 108n4, 236, 244, 329-30
Racinet, M. A. 271n28
Ralph, Margaret Nutting 252
Ramage, Craufurd Tait 335
Ramsay, W. M. 257n3, 365n9
Randi, James 301
Rasmussen, Carl 288
Ravenhill, Leonard 397
Read-Heimerdinger, Jenny 142-44
Redpath, H. A. 190, 320n36, 335
Reed, David 79n7
Reinach, Salomon 292
Reno, R. R. 392
Richards, E. Randolph 56n7
Richardson, Alan 395
Richter, Sandra 263, 392
Rickard, Lindsay x
Rickard, Nathan x
Robb, Kevin 327n53
Robbins, Vernon K. v, 3n1, 63, 177n2, 194n24, 242-44, 251-52, 275, 277n42, 278n46, 319-20, 323, 335, 442, 444
Robinson, Maurice A. 90, 103
Rohrbaugh, Richard L. 269-70, 275n39, 290, 292

Rosner, Brian S. 387
Royse, James R. 86n19
Runge, Steven E. 121, 123, 142, 148, 354, 439-40
Rupertus Meldenius 376n6
Rushdie, Salman 293
Russell, Brian D. 263, 388, 436
Rutledge, Fleming 392
Ryken, Leland 252
Sakenfeld, K. D. 289
Sampley, J. Paul 195n28.30, 282-85, 290, 334
Sandy, D. Brent 326, 327n52, 330n67, 331
Scaife, A. Ross v
Schaps, David M. 291
Schellenberg, Ryan S. 232n24
Schlier, Heinrich 194n27-28
Schloemann, Johan 329n59
Schlossberg, Edwin 105
Schnackenburg, Rudolf 205, 283-84
Schneider, Gerhard 119
Schnelle, Udo 395
Schreiner, Thomas R. 63, 395
Schrenk, G. 356
Schürer, Emil 291
Schweizer, Edward 194n28, 356-57
Scott, J. Julius 335
Scott, R. 214
Seal, David 314n23
Seamands, Stephen 393
Seneca (philosopher) 195, 232
Seneca the Elder 244
Shaw, George Bernard 397
Shelly, Bruce 392
Sherk, Robert K. 208n62, 210n70
Smith, Craig A. 237-38
Smith, Jerome H. 308n14, 335
Smith, Joseph 127n20
Smith, Julien 365
Smith, Mahlon H. 210n72
Smith, Robert E. 149
Smith, R. R. R. 328n67
Smither, Edward L. 448n1
Soja, Edward W. 242n43, 437
Song, Changwon 231n21
Southerland, Kevin x

Author Index

Sperber, Dan 106n1, 194, 324n45
Spicq, Ceslas 200, 203, 209
Spieckermann, Hermann 394
Spinks, D. Christopher 396
Stambaugh, J. E. 290
Stegemann, Ekkehard 291
Stegemenn, Wolfgang 291
Stein, Robert H. 53n3, 227n15, 252
Steinbeck, John 175-76
Stewart, Eric C. 292
Stewart, Robert B. 102
Stirewalt, M. Luther 246n48, 247
Stockhausen, Carol Kern v
Strabo 246
Stroumsa, Guy G. 328n54, 330n65
Stowers, Stanley Kent 230n21
Strecker, Georg 395
Strecker, Ivo 238
Strong, James 180-81, 183, 186, 188, 213-14
Stuart, Douglas K. 71, 252, 398, 416, 417n29
Stuhlmacher, Peter 394
Swanson, James 183, 186, 214, 308n13
Sydenham, Edward A. 202, 291
Tagg, Caroline 106n2
Talbert, Charles H. 194n28, 240n40, 283n49-50, 284
Tan, Paul Lee 444
Tatian (church father) 297
Taylor, Richard A. 121n14, 149
Terry, Milton S. 383-84
Tertullian 79
Thatcher, Tom 216n5
Thayer, Joseph Henry 186, 188, 199, 214
Theissen, Gerd 291
Theon (Aelius) 244-46, 313
Thielicke, Helmut 370, 372, 406
Thielman, Frank 204, 284-85, 395
Thiselton, Anthony C. 60n10, 195n32
Thomas, Rosalind 327n53
Thompson, David L. 61n12, 69, 72, 429
Thompson, Richard P. 393

Thorsteinsson, Runar M. 231n21
Throckmorton, Jr. Burton H. 334
Thucydides v, 80, 155
Tiberius (emperor) 210, 258, 277-78
Tischendorf, Constantin 78, 104
Titus (emperor) 208
Todorov, Tzvetan 216
Too, Yun Lee 327n53, 330-31, 330n70
Torrance, Alan J. 396
Torrey, R. A. 308n14
Traina, Robert A. 3n1, 31n18, 32-33, 34n24, 35n25, 40n28, 44, 61, 61n12.n14, 69, 70n23, 71n23, 72, 147, 221n13, 339n1, 342n2, 343n3, 344, 346, 369, 397, 398n5, 400- 401, 412, 430
Trajan (Emperor) 208, 255
Tregelles, Samuel Prideaux 90, 104
Treier, Daniel J. 378, 393, 396
Trimm, James 316n26
Trobisch, David 56n7, 326n49
Turner, Mark 153n6
Turner, Max 396, 421
Turner, Nigel 148
van Eemeren, F. H. 322n39
Van Meter, David 291
Vander Broek, Lyle D. 240, 252
Vanhoozer, Kevin J. 393, 429-30
Vardi, Amiel D. 330
Vergil/Virgil 196, 313, 327-28, 332
Vespasian (emperor) 208
Via, Dan O. 395
Vickers, Jason E. 392
Virkler, Henry A. 72, 252, 369, 420
Von Thaden, Jr., Robert H. 242
Votaw, Clyde W. 136n27
Wachtel, Klaus 103
Wald, Oletta 69, 72
Wallace, Daniel B. 83, 102, 119-20, 128-29, 143, 148
Walls, Andrew F. 392
Walt, Pat 436
Walton, John H. 268, 326, 327n52, 330n67, 331
Ward-Perkins, J. B. 292
Watson, Duane F. 194n24, 313n21

Watson, Francis 393, 396
Webb, William J. 399, 429-30
Wegner, Paul D. 102
Weissenrieder, Annette 325n48, 326n49
Welborn, Laurence L. 277n43, 286n73
Wendland, Ernst R. 65, 137, 326n49
Wendland, Paul 208n61
Wengst, Klaus 264
Wenham, John 53n3
Wenkel, David H. 292
Wesley, John 220, 375n5, 376, 384, 392
Westcott, B. F. 74, 90, 104, 126, 181
Westfall, Cynthia Long 121
Whately, Richard 73
White, John L. 247
White, Leland J. 274n34
White, Wilbert Webster 44, 61n12
Wigram, George V. 185n5, 213
Wilson, Deirdre 106n1, 194, 324n45
Winter, Bruce W. 270n27, 275, 365n7
Wiseman, B. 238n37
Wisse, Jakob 236
Witherington III, Ben 33, 90, 92, 232n26, 266, 289-90, 325n46, 391, 395, 435
Wittgenstein, Ludwig 150
Wood, D. R. W. 289
Woodard, Roger D. 327n53
Worthington, Ian 329n59
Wright, Christopher 430
Wright, N. T. 20n11, 34n24, 259-60, 323, 324n44, 365n7.10, 366, 392-93, 395, 403n12, 430
Xenophon (historian) 233
Young, Frances 393
Young, Richard A. 148
Zanker, Paul 292
Zerwick, Maximilian 127n20
Zodhiates, Spiros 186, 188-89, 214

Subject Index

A

abutted(-ing) · 115, 170-171, 280
Accordance · 101, 103, 181, 213
accusative · 118, 135, 143, 167
acknowledge(-ing) · 45, 65, 377, 387-388, 409
acknowledgement(s) · 40, 223, 362-364, 366, 368
adjectival(-ly) · 109, 111, 115, 118, 133, 141, 145, 158-159, 167, 280
adjective(s) · 109-111, 115-116, 132-135, 157, 159, 167, 169, 284, 402
adjuncts · 126
admonish(-es,-ing) · 247, 261, 314
admonition(s) · 261
adopt(-ed,-ing) · 121, 144, 236, 257, 259-260, 275, 400, 414, 418, 424, 436
adoption · 190, 330, 434
adulterers · 385
adultery · 95, 270, 302, 350
adverb(s) · 109, 111, 113, 115-119, 122, 125-126, 136, 138, 141, 157-159, 167
adverbial(-ly) · 109, 111, 115, 123, 133-136, 141, 149, 158-159, 164, 167
adversative · 120-123
aesthetic(s) · 238, 442-443
affixes(-d) · 189, 197, 211
Aktionsart · 128-129
Alexandria · 99, 244, 246, 313, 330-333, 449
Alexandrian · 86, 97, 99, 330-331
allegorical · 26, 225-227, 247, 314, 417
allegorically · 197, 211, 226
allegorize(-ing) · 226, 417
allegory(-ies) · 129, 239, 314, 328
alludes(-ing) · 19, 21-23, 225, 248, 308-309, 312, 318, 323, 325, 334, 389
allusion(s) · 15, 22, 43, 65, 92, 294, 300, 305-309, 311-312, 318, 320, 322-325, 334, 389-390
alternation · 69-70, 152, 172, 237, 239
Anabaptist(s) · 374
anachronism · 260, 275
anachronistic · 185, 323, 326, 343, 346
analogous(-ly) · 14, 88, 236, 306, 308, 314, 366, 399, 402, 409, 416-417, 432, 442
analogy(-ies) · 43, 88, 194, 218, 225, 243, 254, 283, 286, 314, 316, 414, 416, 432-436, 438-439, 441, 443-444
anaphoric · 144
anarthrous · 136, 142-144
angel(s) · 10, 22, 77, 227-228, 270, 372, 382-384
angelology · 383
antecedent · 108, 115, 118, 127, 205, 283
anthropological · 272
anthropology · 269, 383-384
anti-supernatural(-ism) · 275, 387
antonyms · 184, 187-192, 198, 212, 214
aorist · 127-132, 134, 136-138, 170
Aphrodisias · 328
Aphrodite · 327
apocalypse · 52, 54, 63, 67, 217, 229, 241, 273
apocalyptic · 71, 177, 239, 242-243, 251-252, 319, 322
apocrypha · 58, 206, 255
apocryphal · 190, 255, 331, 335
apologetic(-ally) · 35-36, 39, 247
apology(-ies) · 153, 200, 232, 240, 244
apophthegm · 239
apostle(s) · 24, 30, 56-57, 110-111, 203, 210, 220, 226-227, 233, 246, 250, 255, 290, 294, 305-306, 317, 323, 328, 332, 348, 375-376, 389, 402, 409, 414, 419, 434, 447-448
apostolic · 57, 183, 376, 436
apostolicity · 57
apotheosis · 366
apparatus,-i · 65, 84, 90, 92, 100, 103-104, 126, 311
applicable(–ility) · 144, 204, 283, 398-399, 401, 412, 419, 426, 429
application(s) · 4, 41-43, 45, 65-67, 72, 125-126, 147, 181, 183, 187, 192, 208, 253, 259-260, 266, 273, 309, 314-315, 318, 320-321, 326, 346-347, 359, 361-362, 364, 367, 377, 381, 391, 397-398, 400-405, 409, 417-424, 427-430, 437, 441, 443-444
applicational · 407
applicatory · 397
apposition · 111, 114-115, 118, 145, 171
appositional(-ly) · 115, 118, 145, 159, 167-168, 172, 285
appropriated · 311, 433
appropriating · 3-4, 260, 417, 419
appropriation(s) · 3, 20, 31, 42-43, 65-66, 208, 267, 274, 323, 341, 367, 398, 404-405, 408, 411-412, 417-421, 423, 428
Arabic · 79, 95
Aramaic · 37, 53, 77, 198, 212, 272, 305, 319, 321, 362, 382, 428
archaeological · 254, 272-273, 287
archeological · 199, 264-265, 271, 277, 291
archeology · 202, 210, 264, 331
architecture · 272, 277, 287, 292, 328, 434
aretology · 382
arthrous · 142-144
article(s) · 20, 34, 72, 103, 105, 117, 125, 127, 133, 136, 139, 142-147, 149, 159, 167, 199, 203, 213, 229, 232, 241, 257, 261, 267-270, 272, 286, 289, 300, 360, 362, 364, 367, 377, 429
articular · 136, 142-144, 149, 354
artifact(s) · 42, 200, 207, 210-211, 264, 266, 272, 287, 323, 442, 444
artificial proofs · 245
artistic · 433
ascension · 9-10, 23-24, 29, 393, 413, 448
Asclepius · 205, 208, 283, 406
Asia Minor · 88, 196, 201, 208-210, 256, 276, 281, 283, 286, 328, 332, 364-365
Asian League · 208, 365
aspect(ual) · 110, 128-130, 132, 145, 148-149
assumption(s) · 26-27, 53-54, 69, 151, 184, 216, 230, 275, 319-320, 326, 346, 387, 401, 418, 425
asyndeton · 121, 124-125, 139-140, 145, 147, 170
Athens, Athenian(s) · 219, 244, 246, 327-331, 333, 402, 439
athletes · 435
athletic(s) · 254, 281, 313
atlas(es) · 257, 288
attributive(-ly) · 138, 145, 167
AUNT(AUthority of the NT) · 41, 176, 371
authorial · 38-40, 198, 238, 320, 322, 324
authorship · 50, 71, 231
autographs · 34, 78, 97

B

Babylon · 254
Babylonian · 303, 308
background(s) · 56, 68, 72, 130-131, 152, 193-195, 200, 203, 205, 228, 247, 266-269, 272-273, 283-284, 288-290, 297, 335, 343, 345-346, 363, 366-367, 435, 440
backgrounded · 131
beatitude(s) · 62, 221-223, 426
beautician · 284
beautified · 284
beautiful · 270, 284-285
beauty · 183, 284, 442
beginning-middle-closing · 63-64
behavior(s) · 107, 189, 221, 261, 348, 375, 402-403, 405, 408, 414, 416, 420, 424, 427, 435
behavioral · 59, 408, 418, 423, 425
beloved (Beloved · 12-14, 235, 296-297, 390, 432, 448
benediction · 234, 239
benefaction(s) · 183, 364
benefactor(s) · 196, 201, 203, 275
beneficiary · 114, 126, 171-172, 188
Berakah · 239
Bethlehem · 257, 302
BibleWorks · 101, 103-104, 181, 189, 213
bibliolatry · 375
bibliology · 383
biographer · 230
biographical · 52, 219-220, 239, 331
biography(-ies) · 52, 55, 63, 67, 197, 217, 229-230, 241
brainstorm(-s,-ing) · 218, 442-444
BRO (Be reaching Out) · 41, 398
Byzantine · 87, 90, 99, 103, 182
Byzantium · 200, 202

C

Caesar · 80, 88, 172, 195-196, 203, 208-209, 256, 258, 278, 282-283, 323, 333, 365, 451
Caesarea Maritima · 210, 256, 328, 365
Caesarea Philippi · 438

Subject Index

Caesar-Roma · 286
Caesar-savior · 209, 286
canon(s) · 38, 40-41, 50-51, 53, 55-57, 71-72, 176-177, 187, 192, 225, 262, 328, 330, 335, 371, 381, 385, 387, 391
canonical(-ly) · 35, 38-39, 52, 58, 294, 377-378, 388, 395, 414
canonicity · 330
canonization · 38
canonize(-d) · 254, 327, 329
CAP (Consider All Possibilities) · 40-41, 151, 182, 340
catechism(s) · 372-374
catholic · 52-54, 89-90, 99-100, 374, 376, 385, 388
catholicism · 374
catholicity · 388
causation · 61, 68-69, 152-154, 223
causative · 221
cause · 164-165, 171
cause-effect · 51, 243
chiasm · 19-20, 69-70, 152, 172, 204, 220, 237-240, 249-250, 280, 283, 285-286
chiasmic · 238
chiastic(-ally) · 19, 205, 221, 237-238, 240, 249, 278, 280-283, 286, 325
chreia · 33, 239, 245, 313
Christ · 8, 10, 20-25, 28, 30, 34-35, 39, 41, 43, 64, 67, 77, 81, 88, 91, 108-109, 111-112, 131, 139, 143-144, 163-165, 169-172, 177-178, 188, 193-195, 197, 204-205, 207, 209, 219-220, 227, 231, 235, 245-246, 248-250, 256-257, 261, 264, 266, 268, 276-280, 282-286, 291, 296-297, 304, 312, 314, 317-318, 328, 341, 348, 353, 355, 360, 364-365, 367, 372-376, 378, 380, 382, 387-390, 393, 395, 399-400, 402, 404, 411-412, 414-415, 419, 421-423, 425, 428, 434, 448, 451
Christ-followers · 27, 414
Christian(s) · 6, 19, 24-25, 27, 49-51, 57, 60, 63, 79, 83, 86, 95, 148, 177, 183, 187, 192-194, 198, 205, 208, 212-214, 220, 230, 242-243, 247, 249, 255, 259, 264, 268, 270, 273, 275-276, 283, 288, 290, 292, 300, 305, 314-315, 317-318, 321-322, 333, 335, 355, 364-365, 369, 372-376, 378, 381, 383-384, 387, 389, 392-396, 402, 405, 407, 413, 416-417, 421, 425, 427, 434, 447
Christianities · 387
Christianity · 99, 196, 202-203, 205, 208, 252, 264, 270, 273, 283, 289-292, 334-335, 365, 374, 392, 405, 447
Christ-like(ness) · 404, 416
Christocentric · 11
Christological · 304
Christology · 317, 374, 383-384, 390-391
chronological · 113, 219-220, 257, 374
chronology · 113, 217, 254, 256
church(es) · 9, 22, 24, 26, 28, 30-31, 37, 39-40, 51-53, 55-57, 72, 74, 77, 79, 81-83, 86-88, 92, 95-96, 99, 125, 182, 191, 193-195, 197, 199, 204-205, 209-210, 213, 226-227, 235, 239, 256, 261, 263, 271, 276-278, 280, 282-286, 289, 297, 304, 311, 315, 318, 322, 324, 368, 371-378, 382, 384-390, 392-394, 396, 401-402, 409, 413, 415, 418, 420, 423, 425, 427-429, 433-434, 436, 438, 450, 453
CIE (Context is Everything) · 41-42, 50, 65, 176-177, 182, 316, 440
circularity · 262
circumcise, see also uncircumcision · 12, 25
circumcised · 15, 25, 355
circumcision, see also uncircumcision · 249, 266, 316
circumstantial · 133-134, 145, 169
citizen(s) · 195, 246, 248, 250
citizenship · 248-249, 266, 366
classical · 56, 80, 155, 183, 191, 193-194, 200, 203, 219, 245, 261, 264, 272, 284, 291, 313, 319, 327, 329, 332, 341, 345, 362, 434
Classics · 155, 335
clausal · 65, 113
clause(s) · 50, 111, 115, 118, 135, 145, 149, 159
climactic · 221, 223, 295, 299
climactically · 152
climax · 61-62, 69, 152, 234, 269, 303, 395, 421
climaxed · 421
co-crucified · 414
co-crucifixion · 170
co-deified · 88
codex,codices · 56, 78, 83-84, 104, 333
co-divine · 88
cohere(s) · 217, 221, 242, 323
coherence · 238, 323-324, 388, 401
coherence-based · 100
coherent · 123, 217, 301, 378
cohesiveness · 70, 368
coin(s) · 193, 202-203, 207, 210-211, 272, 277-278, 291-292, 319, 323, 366-367, 384
coinage · 88, 197, 202-203, 211, 291, 366
communal · 26, 28-29, 232, 364, 404, 418
community(-ies) · 9, 28, 32, 37, 39-41, 43, 66, 72, 232, 262, 270, 274-275, 289, 298, 304, 312, 314, 327, 332, 341, 394, 398, 401, 411-412, 415, 427, 429-430
commutatio · 237
comparative · 37, 145, 221, 232, 326
comparison · 57, 61-62, 66, 69, 75, 78, 80, 89-90, 94, 103, 113, 124, 132, 152-154, 164-165, 221, 230, 239, 280, 283, 298, 306-307, 313-314, 334, 394, 402
comparison(s) · 154, 225, 432
compassion · 14-15, 39, 59, 302, 435
compassionately · 39
complement(s) · 93, 156-158, 164, 169, 238
complementary · 135
component(s) · 50, 111-112, 141, 150, 156, 183, 185, 362, 371, 399
componential · 179-180
compound(s) · 112, 170, 189-191
compounded(-ing) · 145, 188, 191
concordance(s) · 180-183, 186, 190-191, 213, 308, 320, 335
condition(s) · 30, 133, 249, 401, 408-409
conditional · 40, 120, 124, 134, 136, 141, 145
conjecture(-d) · 8, 59, 92-93, 326
conjunction(s) · 29, 35, 64, 70, 109, 112-113, 115-121, 124-125, 136, 138-140, 145-146, 151, 156, 158-159, 162, 164, 166-167, 169, 201, 240-241, 248
conjunctive · 159, 167
connections · 74, 113-114, 165, 193, 272, 311, 322, 367-368, 388
connective(s) · 113, 139, 147
connector(s) · 122, 124, 240
connotation(s) · 280, 286, 356, 371
Constantinople (Byzantium, Istanbul) · 99, 200, 202, 264-265, 271, 374
constituent(s) · 105, 114-119, 138-139, 141, 144, 147, 151
constrain(-s,-ed,-ing) · 36, 64, 66, 122-123, 193, 197, 216, 261
constraint(s) · 43, 50, 57, 65-67, 70, 120-125, 130, 139, 145, 179, 231, 240, 261, 340, 346, 378, 418-419, 423
context(s) · 3-4, 6, 13, 17, 19, 21, 26, 29, 33, 36, 40, 42, 45, 49-50, 53-55, 59, 61-63, 65-68, 70, 86, 102, 105-106, 116, 120-123, 125, 127-129, 131, 133, 136, 143-144, 150, 153, 156, 171-172, 176-180, 182, 185-187, 191-194, 196, 198-199, 203-204, 208-209, 212, 216, 218-219, 221, 225, 228-229, 231, 233, 240, 248, 253-254, 259, 261-262, 266-268, 272, 278, 283-284, 287-288, 290, 297, 299-301, 304, 306, 309, 311-312, 314, 316, 318, 320-321, 323-328, 334, 339-346, 348, 350, 352, 356, 361, 365, 377, 388, 390, 398, 400-402, 409, 412, 414-417, 419, 421, 424, 426, 433, 436
contextual(-ly) · 4, 14, 27-28, 40, 42, 45, 49-51, 55, 61, 63, 65-67, 85, 92, 106, 114, 129, 131, 134, 139, 151, 182, 191, 193, 197-198, 212, 220, 229, 241, 261-262, 272, 310-311, 323, 342, 344, 361, 377, 425
contextualization · 430
contextualize · 54, 298
contrast(s) · 69, 113, 123, 152, 154, 162, 164-165, 237, 314, 348, 350, 368
contrasted(-ing) · 116, 122, 171, 187, 192, 198, 212, 221, 285, 424
contrastive · 120, 123, 171, 221-222, 237-238
conversion · 425
converts · 57, 203, 208
coordinating · 112, 119-122, 124-125, 139-140, 156, 166-167, 169, 240
Corinth · 277, 438-439
Corinthian(s) · 7, 31, 52, 54, 56, 60, 66, 93, 139, 148-149, 153, 168, 185, 195, 224, 231-232, 237, 240, 242, 255-256, 275, 290, 322-323, 325-326, 413

correlate(-d,-ing) · 32, 153, 233, 254, 264, 298, 308, 315, 381, 388
correlation(s) · 153, 238, 248, 273, 308, 323, 381, 391
correlative · 126-127, 145, 222, 354
cosmology · 383
cosmos · 51, 195, 242, 286, 384-385
council(s) · 53, 57, 256, 281, 374, 409
counter-cultural · 414
covenant(s) · 13-15, 55, 63, 67, 217, 220, 229, 241, 249, 263, 266, 268, 299, 310, 316, 379-380, 383, 390, 395, 406-407, 411-412, 414, 416-417, 419, 421
covenantal · 36, 301, 311, 380, 391
creation · 3, 26, 28, 32, 34, 36, 43, 78, 81, 187, 192, 216, 254, 293, 341, 371-372, 377, 381-382, 388, 391, 398, 403, 407-408, 411-412, 415, 418, 420, 428-430
creationism · 429
Creator · 243, 376, 413
creed(s) · 375-377
creedal · 242, 251
Critical Space Theory · 437
critical-realism · 34, 259
critical-space · 437
cross(-es) · 9, 23, 97, 218, 228, 250, 306, 308, 311, 335, 398, 408-409, 411, 414, 421, 429-430
cruciality · 68, 152
crucifixion · 69, 152, 170, 262, 353, 393
crucify(-ied) · 22, 55, 91, 170, 245, 317, 328, 355, 376, 380, 391
cult(s) · 88, 177, 195-196, 208-210, 286, 328, 364-366, 438
cultic(-ally) · 239, 249-250
cultic-religious · 244
cultural(-ly) · 26, 42, 66, 125, 194, 200, 215, 230, 240, 243, 254, 259, 261, 267, 269, 272-277, 282, 292, 319, 322, 328, 333, 341, 347, 365, 375, 377, 398-399, 403, 409, 418-419, 428-430, 440
culture(s) · 3, 28, 32, 51, 59, 77, 178, 194, 198, 211-212, 215, 217, 219, 238, 251, 253, 261, 267, 270-272, 277, 285, 287, 289, 291, 319-320, 323, 326-332, 341, 371, 375, 382, 400-401, 406, 411, 414, 416, 419, 427, 437, 440

culture-bound · 43, 66, 405, 424

D

database(s) (see also PHI, TLG, etc.) · 5, 80, 96, 100-101, 104, 165, 189, 200-201, 203, 207, 211, 281, 286, 289
Davidic · 268, 294, 300-301
decorum · 261, 270
dedication · 88, 210
deductive · 248
deification · 366
deified · 88, 172, 209, 286, 328
deities · 202, 366, 379
deity · 88, 233, 411
deliberate · 323, 334
deliberation · 136-137
deliberative · 129, 136, 244-245
demoniac · 208, 437
demonology · 372, 382
demons · 31, 372, 380, 382, 409
demos · 88, 281
denarius,-i · 227, 277-278
deutero-canonical · 53
diachrony · 320
Diadochi · 255
diagram(s) · 28, 101, 139, 157-158, 160, 163, 166-167, 170, 172, 179, 236, 259-260, 363, 386, 402, 406-407
diagrammed · 167-168, 172
diagramming · 151, 155-156, 159, 161, 163, 166-167, 249
diathyrambic · 327
diatribe · 125, 230-231
differentiate(-s,-ed,-ing) · 16, 62, 84, 110, 130, 164, 223, 237, 285, 340, 348, 413
disambiguating · 141
disambiguation · 193, 213, 343
disciple(s) · 10-12, 16-17, 19, 29-30, 68, 107, 111, 134, 152, 223, 230, 244, 314, 348, 350, 353, 380, 401, 409, 414, 418, 421, 424, 432, 438, 448
discipleship · 39, 404, 430
discontinuity · 141
discontinuous · 158, 171-172
dispositio · 329
disposition · 31-32, 183, 222, 234, 239, 384, 404, 406
dispositional · 233, 245
Disputed-Paulines · 102
dittography · 84, 101
divine(-ly) · 3, 28, 34, 57, 83, 88, 128, 138, 164, 183, 185, 195, 208-209, 250, 258, 278, 299, 306, 317, 327, 356, 365, 377, 382, 388-389, 391, 400, 408, 421, 447
divinities · 88, 330
divinity · 196, 209
divisio · 245
division · 59, 84, 185, 243
divisional · 64
divisions · 57, 59, 63, 67, 71, 331, 374, 383
divorce(-ing) · 66-67, 304, 413
doctrinal · 57, 85, 234, 248, 404
doctrine(s) · 31, 34, 53, 383-384, 396, 404, 417, 434, 447
doxographies · 332
doxology · 85, 234
drama · 326, 378, 392, 433

E

ecclesial · 35, 37, 39-41, 51, 57, 242, 371, 374-375, 384-385, 387-388
ecclesiological · 88
ecclesiology · 366, 375, 383, 391
echo(-es) · 12, 198, 212, 299, 311-312, 319, 322-324, 334-335
echoed · 323, 334, 389
education · 33, 198, 212, 232-233, 236, 245-246, 250-251, 273, 313-314, 329, 332, 372
Egypt · 86, 201-203, 247, 255, 258, 302, 304, 330, 332, 379, 393
Egyptian(s) · 79, 201, 276, 332, 379
ekklesia · 204-205, 209-210, 244, 279, 282-283, 286, 366
ekphrasis · 239
elaborate(-s,-ed,-ing) · 64, 154-155, 187, 192, 198, 212, 234, 248, 285, 324, 414, 436
elaboration · 172, 223, 237-238, 245, 248, 319, 324-325
elaborative · 127, 141, 145, 217
ellipsis · 145
elliptical · 169
embodiment · 42, 209, 404, 442, 447-448
embody(-ies,-ed,-ing) · 14, 36, 40, 81, 202, 208, 222-223, 269, 380, 388, 402-404, 412, 415, 435, 437-438, 442, 447-448
emotion(s) · 442
emotional · 125, 170, 234, 236, 406
emotionalize · 31
emotionally-based · 406
empathy · 45, 236
emperor(s) · 88, 195-196, 205, 209-210, 243, 255-256, 270, 277, 282-283, 286, 328, 330, 333, 364-366, 449-450, 452-453

emperor-cult · 365
emphases · 374-375
emphasis · 12, 17, 26, 73, 88, 113, 123, 126, 128, 139, 141-145, 147-148, 182, 194-195, 208, 229, 238, 273, 285-287, 350, 354, 356, 398, 411, 413, 421
emphasize(-s,-ed,-ing) · 67, 119, 122, 131, 134, 143, 164, 170, 172, 250, 268, 278, 285-286, 309, 318, 356
emphatic · 105, 113, 120, 122, 124, 126-127, 136, 145-147, 170-172, 204, 211, 284-286, 350, 354
empire(s) · 51, 59, 194-195, 197, 201-203, 208-210, 230, 242-243, 246, 255, 276, 291-292, 308, 323, 327, 330, 364-366
encomium · 313, 423-424
encyclopedia(s) · 53, 85, 104, 288, 369, 444
enthymemes · 245
environment (cognitive) · 106, 179, 186, 193, 207, 211, 245, 282, 320, 332, 387, 420, 442
Ephesus · 204, 209, 246, 264, 273, 283, 286, 328, 331, 366, 374
epicheireme · 239, 245
epideictic · 244-245
epigraphic(-al) · 201, 203
epigraphy · 200-201, 281
epilogue · 234
epistemological · 34, 38, 258
epistemology · 34, 215
epistle(s) · 60, 63, 83, 88, 93, 195, 231-232, 246-247, 269, 298, 323, 325, 343
epistolary · 129, 231, 233-235, 239, 246, 366
epistolography · 231, 246
eschatological · 234, 314, 421, 448
eschatology · 178, 383, 389, 391, 421, 447
Essene · 321
ethic(-al) · 232, 234, 236, 355, 395, 411, 418, 421
ethics · 320, 364, 382-383, 389, 391, 398, 421, 429-430
ethnic(-ities) · 355, 402
ethno-centrism · 375
ethos · 236, 245
etymological · 185, 197, 211
etymology · 185, 197, 211
evaluate(-s,-ed,-ing) · 3, 5, 37, 42-43, 66, 81, 87, 191, 203, 218, 225, 238, 275, 323-324, 340, 342, 347-348, 360-361, 371, 381, 383, 390-391, 398, 400-

402, 404, 406, 408-409, 412, 414-415, 418-419, 421, 424-425, 427-428, 430
evaluation(s) · 3, 99, 124, 232, 358, 377, 398-403, 408, 416-417, 419, 421, 426, 428-430, 444
evaluation-application · 416
evaluative · 326, 343, 417-418, 425, 429
evangelical · 26, 35, 237, 334, 429
evangelicalism · 374
evangelism · 26, 425
evangelist(s) · 9, 317
evangelistic(-ically) · 39, 41
evangelize · 39
evidence(s) · 4, 32, 40, 43, 53-55, 57, 61, 66, 69, 85-86, 90, 92-94, 96-97, 125, 182, 185-186, 197, 204, 210, 218, 231, 257-258, 262, 269, 275, 284, 287, 300, 315, 324, 332, 340-348, 352, 358-364, 366-369, 378, 385, 400, 405
evidenced · 96, 247, 286, 387
evidential(-ly) · 246, 275, 346
evidentiary · 368
exception(s) · 107, 124, 131, 133, 141, 145, 182, 234, 261, 361
exceptive · 141
exclamation(s) · 65, 109
exclamatory · 137
exegesis · 26, 40, 63, 72, 83, 85, 101, 117, 121, 138-139, 147-149, 155, 191, 233, 272, 274-275, 316, 320, 322, 334-335, 376, 378, 381, 388, 391-392, 405, 415, 417, 433, 435-436
exegete(s) · 83, 324
exegeted · 433
exegetical(-ly) · 3-5, 25, 33, 40, 42, 63, 101, 108, 119, 126-127, 133, 137, 147-148, 155, 184, 195, 197, 199, 211, 218, 248, 251, 254, 260, 312, 317-321, 326, 334-335, 340, 343, 346, 360-361, 377, 406
exhort(s) · 97, 234, 239, 247
exhortation(s) · 64, 137, 140, 154-155, 227, 239, 408, 423-424, 448
exhortative · 123, 154
exile · 254
explanatory · 76, 85, 120
explicate · 134, 385
explication · 283
explicatures · 106
explicit · 15, 72, 106, 123, 129, 153, 167, 172, 178, 223, 228, 232, 274, 280, 282, 285, 294,

302, 306, 309, 311, 316, 324, 343, 364, 389, 440, 444
explicitness · 324
extra-biblical · 179, 319, 322, 342, 345, 387

F

faith · 13, 23, 31, 34, 45, 57, 91, 107-109, 131, 140, 169, 171-172, 178, 180, 235, 264, 310, 312, 353, 356, 373-375, 378, 380-381, 384, 387, 389, 391-392, 401, 404, 434, 447
faith-based · 34
faithful · 27-28, 32, 34, 41, 43, 57, 65, 324, 373, 377-378, 406, 424, 448
faithfully · 12, 56-57, 404
faithfulness · 39, 171, 222, 301, 348, 356
fallacious · 346
fallacy(-ies) · 184-186, 197, 199, 211, 218, 260, 346
Father · 9, 12-15, 22, 28, 30-31, 33, 77, 116, 153-154, 180, 196, 227-228, 235, 248, 250, 300, 302-303, 353, 364, 373, 376, 382, 384, 390, 409, 420, 433
fellowship · 27-28, 34, 250, 270, 355
figurative · 107-108, 183, 239, 343, 435
firstspace(s) (Critical Space Theory) · 437, 242-243
focal · 170, 283, 411-415, 447
focus · 4, 15-16, 19, 23, 26, 37-38, 41, 64, 69, 81, 114, 121, 125, 130, 140, 152, 172, 179, 189-191, 204, 206, 250, 261, 282, 294, 299, 318, 325-326, 331, 340, 342, 350, 352, 354, 359-360, 371, 378, 385, 403-404, 411, 416, 441-442
foreground(-s,-ed) · 130-131
forgive(n) · 76, 227
forgiveness · 12, 34, 45, 197, 310, 370, 376, 389, 437
frame(s) · 131, 141, 215, 240, 243, 295, 341, 348
framed · 423
framework(s) · 15, 19, 57, 64, 121, 133, 141, 164, 217-218, 254, 260-261, 263, 287, 304, 326, 332, 365, 371, 378, 380, 382, 390, 398, 408, 424, 448
frontal · 203, 216
fronted · 140, 145
frontground(-ed) · 130-131

fronting · 141
fulfill(-s,-ed,-ing) · 11, 14-16, 25, 55, 76, 155, 296, 301-305, 308, 314, 350, 354, 356, 360, 366, 380, 412-413, 415
fulfillment · 16, 25, 299-300, 302, 304-305, 348, 350, 352, 354, 356, 429
fundamentalism · 35
future · 30-31, 109-110, 127-129, 131, 136-137, 164-165, 202, 207, 215, 262, 267, 334, 341, 360, 372, 380, 382, 413, 415, 423-424, 429, 447-448

G

Galilee · 258, 295-296, 437
genealogical · 100, 143, 219-220, 330
genealogy(-ies) · 239, 294, 303
generalization · 61, 68, 152, 346, 384
generalize(-s,-d,-ing) · 25, 55, 64-66, 216, 221, 238, 343, 350, 362, 399
genitival · 167
genitive · 118, 134, 136, 141, 145, 167, 169, 171, 328
genre(s) · 37-38, 50, 54-55, 63, 67, 71, 215-218, 229-230, 232, 241-242, 252, 254, 257, 269, 325-326, 330-331, 339, 342, 382, 417
Gentile(s) · 17, 24-25, 57, 83, 134, 180, 188, 203, 205, 207-208, 210, 220, 230, 246, 248-250, 266, 283, 311-312, 348, 355, 389-390, 409, 438
geographic(-ic,-ically) · 57, 87-88, 99, 101, 113, 219-220, 247, 276, 438
geography · 257
geo-political · 21
gift(s) · 24, 30-31, 37, 134, 138, 183, 224, 261, 281, 317, 416, 420
gifted(-ing) · 185, 429
Gnostic · 57, 195, 205, 283, 366, 385
Gnosticism · 284
Gnostic-redeemer · 194
goddess(-es) · 88, 183, 209, 232, 286, 438
God-fearers · 298
gods · 88, 177, 183, 196, 209, 271, 276, 282, 285, 365-366, 438
gospel(s) · 6, 10-11, 13-20, 22, 24, 29-30, 33, 39, 43, 45, 50, 52-57,

67, 69, 74, 77, 79-80, 82-83, 86-87, 89, 95, 97, 99, 102, 106-107, 143-144, 152, 184, 186, 191-192, 197, 206, 216-217, 224, 226-228, 230, 232, 235, 245, 250, 255-256, 263, 270, 273-274, 277, 285, 287-288, 290, 294-298, 302, 309, 312, 318-319, 321-323, 328, 334-335, 348, 356, 364, 378, 380, 388-389, 393, 395, 402, 408-409, 418, 435-436, 440
grace · 22, 64, 77, 89-90, 109, 131, 137-138, 155, 183, 207, 234-235, 315, 317, 355, 374, 385, 400, 415, 443
graceful · 232
gracious · 183
GRAMMA (GRAMmatical Mode of Analysis) · 41, 105, 151
grammar(s) · 34, 50, 95, 102, 105-106, 108, 117, 126, 147, 153, 161, 172, 313, 321
grammarians · 128-129, 133
grammatical(-ly) · 3-5, 40-42, 45, 60-61, 64, 66, 70, 85-86, 97, 100, 105, 110, 112, 115, 118, 123, 129, 145, 150-151, 153, 187, 191, 198, 212, 219, 240, 243, 278, 285, 342-345, 348, 354, 361, 422
GRAMPS (GRAMmatical Procedure of Study) · 41, 105, 151
graphic(s) · 167, 296, 439
graphically · 71, 79
Greco-Roman · 56, 183, 185, 193-194, 198-199, 201-203, 207, 212-213, 230-233, 239, 244-246, 250, 252, 257, 266, 270-271, 275, 289-290, 313-314, 323, 325-326, 332, 365
Greece · 208, 219, 255, 327, 329, 406
gustatory · 61
gynaikonomos(-io) · 261

H

Haggadah · 314, 320
haplography · 101
hardships · 440
harmonization(s) · 85, 297
harmonize(-ed,-ing) · 85-87, 95, 228, 297
head(s) · 22, 106, 178, 194, 197, 204-205, 234, 270-271, 276-277, 279-280, 283, 285, 300, 316, 373, 383, 409, 423

head-body · 194-195, 205, 283, 286, 364
head-coverings · 271
headship · 194-195
heal · 17, 110
healed · 16-17, 32, 110-111, 243
healing · 15, 110, 240, 316, 436
Hebraica · 290
Hebrew · 8, 11-15, 26, 37, 41, 51, 53, 55-56, 77, 84, 110, 121, 149, 166, 175-176, 180-181, 190, 193-194, 198, 206, 212, 225, 227, 248, 255, 262, 272, 284, 305, 313-314, 318-321, 331, 334, 342, 344, 348, 362, 376, 382, 411, 414, 435
hell · 409
Hellenistic · 121, 193-194, 196, 202, 205, 208, 261, 290-291, 326, 331-332, 365
Hellenization · 255, 316
Herculaneum · 333
hermeneutic(s) · 3, 26, 29, 31, 72, 252, 304, 316, 335, 369, 388, 393, 399, 416, 428-430, 436
hermeneutical(-ly) · 34, 38, 69, 72, 201, 262, 315, 321, 339, 429
Hermogenes · 244, 246, 313
Herod · 144, 210, 256-258, 328, 407
Herodians · 107
Hillel · 304-305, 315-316, 318, 334, 451
historiae · 194
historian(s) · 155, 216-217, 233, 257-258, 453
historic · 130-131, 145, 304, 377
historical · 3-4, 34-35, 37-42, 45, 52-53, 56-57, 61, 66, 71, 127, 129-130, 148, 151, 172, 179, 186, 197, 200, 202, 204, 209, 211, 217, 228, 230-231, 238, 242, 253-255, 257-263, 267, 269, 272, 274-275, 278, 286-289, 291-292, 297, 300, 313, 319-320, 323-324, 329, 331-332, 341, 346, 361, 367, 371, 377, 382, 385, 387, 398-401, 417, 433
historical(-ly) · 3, 34-35, 37-40, 42, 52-53, 56-57, 71, 87, 90, 127, 129, 151, 185-186, 193, 197, 200, 202, 209, 211, 217, 230, 238, 242, 253-255, 257-263, 267, 269, 272, 274, 278, 286-287, 297, 300, 313, 319-320, 324, 331-332, 341, 346, 367, 371, 377, 382, 385, 387, 398-401, 417, 433

historical-critical · 68, 274
historical-cultural · 343
historical-social-cultural · 65, 272, 323
historical-theological · 387
historicism · 375, 429
historicity · 57, 257
historiographic(-al) · 230, 258
historiography · 54, 217, 330
hodayah · 239
Holy Spirit (see also Spirit) · 10, 14, 20, 22, 24, 28-33, 37, 77, 146, 187, 192, 199, 231, 296-297, 306, 310, 341, 355, 373, 376, 378, 380, 382, 402-404, 415-416, 419-421, 423, 425, 428
homiletical · 376, 442
homily(-ies) · 220, 244, 376
homoeoteleuton · 84-85, 101
homoioarchton · 84
homosexual(s) · 399-400, 414, 429-430
homosexuality · 414
honor · 19, 243, 269-271, 274-275, 277, 280-282, 289, 303-304, 365, 448
honorable · 244, 424
honored · 209, 280-282
honorific · 200, 244, 326
honoring · 328, 403
honors · 281
honor-shame · 270
hortatory · 123, 136, 234
house · 19, 71, 80, 93, 103, 289, 303, 331
household(s) · 26, 188, 194, 209, 239, 243, 248, 250, 276, 286, 305, 364, 366, 409, 434
humble · 378, 385, 418, 427
humbly · 260, 428
humility · 45, 378, 384, 427
humor(-ous) · 332, 442
husband(s) · 59, 125, 144, 204-205, 261, 276, 279-280, 282-283, 285, 379, 413, 423, 432
hyperbole · 34, 108, 225, 239, 314, 417

I

ideological(-ly) · 36, 39, 41, 51, 66, 213, 215, 238, 250-251, 275-277, 283, 286, 342, 444
ideology(-ies) · 39, 64, 202, 238, 263, 278, 283, 286-287, 296, 320, 335, 341, 365, 371, 437
idol(s) · 298, 411
idolatry(-ous) · 298, 311, 314, 355, 380, 427
illocutionary · 149
illustration(s) · 43, 69, 195, 225, 289, 332, 403, 432-444
imperatival · 97
imperative(s) · 97, 132, 137-138, 267
imperfect · 130
imperfective · 127-128, 130-131
imperial · 88, 171-172, 194, 201-203, 208-209, 242-243, 247, 251, 264, 271, 281, 286, 291-292, 328-329, 333, 364-366, 434, 440
imperial cult · 88, 328, 366
imperial-political · 249
implicatures · 106
inartificial proofs · 245
incarnated · 42, 65, 82
incarnation · 205, 393
incarnational · 34, 95, 144, 388, 411
inclusio · 55, 70, 172, 237, 247, 324, 348, 350
induction · 243
inductive · 3, 34, 40, 50, 61, 71, 341
inerrant(-cy) · 34-35, 39
infallible · 33
infinitive(s) · 97, 109, 111, 119, 132, 135-138, 159, 167
inflection(s) · 293, 344
infographic(s) · 439
inscription(s) · 84, 193, 196-197, 199-203, 207-208, 211, 244, 264-266, 272, 277-278, 281, 286, 319, 323, 328, 365-366, 411
inscriptional · 200-201, 211, 219, 281, 283, 286-287
interjections · 115, 118, 159, 167
interlocutor · 230-231
interrogation · 61, 69, 152, 359
interrogative · 108
Intertestamental · 212, 254-255, 320
intertextual · 248, 319, 323-324
intertextuality · 198, 212, 294, 299, 319, 323
intertextural · 319, 323
intertexture · 3, 319, 323, 442
ironic(-ally) · 247, 329
irony · 107, 329, 417
Israel · 13-14, 18, 22, 24, 220, 249, 255, 263, 266, 283-285, 294, 299, 304, 306, 311, 313-314, 320, 322, 327, 354, 372, 380, 382, 389-391, 409, 416-417
Israelite(s) · 311, 327, 379-380

J

Jerusalem · 11-12, 15, 17, 19-21, 55, 58, 157, 192, 210, 227, 246, 255-256, 260, 262-263, 294-295, 298, 310, 313, 328, 330-331, 407, 448
Jesus · 8-27, 29-31, 34, 36, 39, 41, 49, 55-58, 69, 77, 81, 83, 91, 95, 106-111, 116, 119, 131, 134, 139, 143-144, 152, 155, 157, 162-165, 169, 172, 177-178, 187, 192, 194-195, 197, 202, 208, 210, 216, 220, 222-223, 225-228, 230, 235, 237, 243, 248-250, 252, 255-264, 266, 268, 270, 273, 275-276, 278, 288, 291, 294-297, 299, 302-308, 310-312, 314-317, 322-323, 325-326, 329, 335, 341, 343-344, 347-348, 350, 352-356, 361, 364, 366-367, 369, 373-376, 378, 380, 387, 390-393, 395-396, 399, 401, 403, 406, 409, 411-415, 417-419, 421, 426-428, 430, 432-433, 435, 437-438, 441, 448, 451
Jew(s) · 8, 11, 15, 25-26, 49, 55, 57, 77, 83, 107, 143, 176, 178, 203, 207, 212, 216, 219, 226, 230, 246, 248, 250-251, 255-256, 264-266, 268, 270, 276, 278, 283, 291, 294, 298, 304-306, 310-316, 318, 320, 322, 326, 334-335, 348, 355-356, 364, 378, 385, 389, 402, 413, 432
Jewish · 8, 11, 15, 26, 49, 55, 57, 107, 143, 176, 207, 212, 216, 219, 226, 250-251, 255-256, 264-265, 268, 270, 276, 278, 283, 291, 294, 304-306, 310, 312-316, 318, 320, 322, 334-335, 348, 364, 378, 385, 402
John the Baptist · 15-16, 69, 152, 256, 263, 380, 428
Judaic · 323
Judaism · 56, 72, 202, 317, 323, 326, 334, 413
Judea(n) · 210, 255, 258, 262, 276, 295, 401
Judiazers · 25
Juno · 210
Jupiter · 196, 210
Jupiter-Zeus (See Zeus) · 208
justice · 230, 332
justification · 24-25, 34, 300, 362, 389, 393, 429

SUBJECT INDEX

justified(-ing) · 9, 109, 131, 182, 312, 323, 364, 377, 387, 403, 434

K

kerygma · 248
kerygmatic · 239, 248-249, 322
Kethubim · 51-53
king(s) · 7, 13-14, 24, 36, 51, 53, 58-59, 68, 74, 152, 197, 209, 227, 243, 254-255, 257, 268, 294, 299-301, 303, 308, 311, 365, 380, 395, 409, 411, 432
Kingdom of God · 17, 194, 260, 307-308, 378, 383, 401, 407, 413, 415, 421, 432, 441
kingdom(s) · 15, 17-18, 21-22, 36, 43, 62, 119, 180, 194, 222-223, 242-243, 254, 260, 294, 299-300, 307-308, 310, 347-348, 356, 378, 380, 383, 401, 403, 407, 409, 411-413, 415, 421, 432, 441, 448
kingly · 243, 411
kingship · 268, 294, 332, 365
Koine Greek · 108, 114, 121, 123-125, 127, 130, 137, 141, 145, 147-148, 155, 272, 319, 345, 354, 362, 435

L

Latin · 15, 73, 79, 84, 99, 104, 110, 172, 198, 200-201, 203, 207, 212, 257, 272, 283, 300, 313, 319, 327-331, 333, 362, 374, 376, 382
Law · 11-12, 15-16, 25-26, 51, 53, 55, 68, 109, 151, 169, 217, 227, 266, 294, 301, 306, 322, 348, 350, 352-356, 380, 383, 395, 413, 416, 426, 434, 448
law(s) · 50-51, 61, 68, 76-77, 151, 170, 188, 196-197, 218, 222, 239, 248-250, 310, 312-314, 322, 347-348, 350, 355-356, 379, 412, 416
lawful · 231, 413
lawfully · 434
lawgiver · 197
lawless · 76, 310
lectionary(-ies) · 49, 79, 84
lexeme · 145
lexical(-ly) · 3-4, 42, 45, 60-61, 74, 82, 96, 116-117, 129, 145, 154-155, 172, 175-176, 179, 182-183, 188-189, 191, 193-194, 199-201, 211, 213, 240, 272, 278, 283, 308, 342, 346, 361, 400, 435
lexico-grammatical · 200
lexicographers · 199
lexicography · 50, 121, 149, 185, 193
lexicon(s) · 29, 126, 180, 182-186, 188-189, 191, 193, 199-200, 211, 213-214, 342, 344, 348
librarian(s) · 330-331, 333
library(-ies) · 44, 56, 201, 252, 267, 272, 288, 290, 314, 327, 329-333, 394, 437
linguist(s) · 36, 106, 121, 153, 219, 246
linguistic(s) · 43, 61, 65, 105-106, 121, 126, 139, 147-149, 153, 182, 200-201, 208, 327, 377, 421
literacy · 219, 251, 312, 314, 319, 325-327, 329-333
literalistic · 300, 405
literarily · 38, 50
liturgical · 83, 85
logographer · 329
Logos · 101, 103, 132, 142, 148, 165, 181, 183-184, 189-190, 213-214, 236, 308, 439
lord(s) · 8, 15, 17-18, 20-23, 39, 77, 85, 95, 106-108, 111, 131, 137, 163-165, 178, 192, 194, 196, 205, 231, 235, 243, 250, 255-257, 261, 266, 269, 277, 279-280, 283, 295, 299-300, 305, 310, 317, 323, 341, 350, 353, 364, 373, 376, 379, 385, 389-390, 399-400, 413-414, 423, 425, 428, 432, 438, 440, 448
love · 12, 21-22, 28, 31-32, 34, 39, 41, 45, 60, 65, 108, 116, 119, 140, 172, 178, 204, 222, 224-225, 227, 235, 279-282, 284, 306, 353, 356, 361, 380-381, 384, 391, 399, 404, 407, 412, 414, 416-417, 421, 427, 447-448
lovely · 15
loves(-ed,-ing) · 22, 32, 43, 116, 159-160, 162, 171-172, 197, 279-280, 306, 376, 409, 412, 431
Lutheran(s) · 374, 385

M

martyr · 56, 79, 239, 255, 451
martyrdom · 57
martyred · 256
mashal · 225, 314, 318, 334
Masoretic · 8, 320
maxim(s) · 239, 278, 313
Mediterranean · 42, 88, 177, 193, 210, 217, 239-240, 244, 249, 254, 261, 264, 306, 312-314, 325-326, 332, 365, 401-402, 415
megillah · 313
memory · 230, 245, 271, 315, 320, 326-327, 329
Messiah · 11, 14, 16, 18-21, 36, 155, 196, 205-206, 248-250, 268, 276, 283, 299-301, 304-305, 322-323, 356, 380, 390, 408, 433
Messiahship · 20
messianic · 13, 15, 206, 268, 299, 304, 356
metacomment(s) · 5, 145
metaphor(s) · 3, 29, 63, 107, 154-155, 195, 205, 229, 238-239, 252, 254, 280, 283-286, 289, 330, 411, 414, 425, 428, 434-436, 440, 442
metaphoric(-ally) · 178, 194, 217, 225, 343
metathesis · 84
midrash(-ic) · 239-240, 248-249, 312-316, 321, 335
millennialism · 270
millennium · 87, 268, 377
Mishnah · 313, 322
missiology · 382-383
mission(s) · 200, 393-394, 430, 436
missional(-ly) · 35, 39, 43, 263, 366, 375, 388, 436
missional-evangelical · 35, 39
missional-evangelistic · 39
missionary(-ies) · 9, 256, 261, 402, 440, 448
missions · 430
mitigation(-ing) · 137
MOM (Major on Majors) · 41, 176, 340, 371, 398
monument(s) · 201-202, 247, 323, 411
monumental · 236, 320, 416
Mormonism · 374
Mosaic · 15, 348, 356, 412-413, 419
mosaic(s) · 84, 193, 210, 272, 277, 287, 320
Moses · 11, 24-25, 51, 55, 94, 228, 254, 263, 301, 306, 311, 316, 350, 354, 379, 383, 413, 416
Muslims · 95
mysteries · 282, 447
mysterious · 13, 20
mystery · 91-92, 95, 182, 274, 378
mystery-gods · 208
myth(s) · 209, 327
mythical · 300, 327
mythology · 313

N

narratio · 239, 245
narration · 234
narrative(s) · 15, 20, 54, 56, 63, 65, 67, 69, 114, 122-123, 127, 130-131, 133, 137-138, 142, 145, 148-149, 152, 215, 217, 224-225, 229, 236, 239, 241, 258-260, 270, 289, 294-295, 297, 301, 313-314, 319, 327-328, 330, 348, 378, 381-382, 408, 411, 417-418, 423-424, 437
Nazarene · 302, 305
Nazareth · 34, 57, 296, 305
Nazarite · 305, 316
nominative(s) · 94, 126-127, 145, 156
non-Greek · 138
non-Indicative(s) · 127, 132, 138, 148
non-Jews(-ish) · 178, 208, 432
non-literary · 247
non-literate · 326
Non-Trinitarians · 374
noun(s) · 49, 94, 108-111, 114-115, 118, 126, 133, 135, 140, 142-143, 149, 157, 159, 167, 177, 183, 188-189, 286, 305, 354
numismatic · 202-203, 287, 291
numismatic(s) · 203, 277-278, 291

O

olfactory · 61
Olympus, Olympia · 407
optative(s) · 132, 137
oral · 232, 236-237, 325-327, 329
oral-aural · 61
orality · 251, 314, 326-328, 331
oral-literary · 237
orally · 60
oral-scribal · 319
oration(s) · 244, 326, 329, 365
orator(s) · 325, 329, 450
oratoria · 236, 330
oratorical · 236, 330
oratory · 328-330
orthodox · 57, 81, 370, 374-376
Orthodox (churches) · 374, 385
orthodoxy · 361, 384-385, 404
orthopathy · 384-385, 404
orthopraxis · 384
orthopraxy · 361, 385, 404

ostraca · 79, 84
Oxyrhynchus · 202, 247, 332

P

pagan(s) · 88, 125, 298
paganism · 366
pantheon · 365
papyrological · 201, 287
papyrus(-i) · 74, 78-80, 82-83, 86, 90, 97, 99, 104, 193, 197, 201, 211, 246-247, 272, 332
parable(s) · 13-17, 71, 114, 218, 225-229, 239, 252, 260, 302-303, 307-308, 311, 314, 384, 432-433, 441, 448
parades · 326, 366
paradigm(s) · 274, 408-409, 416, 418-420, 426, 442, 444
paradosis · 208
paradox(es) · 238-239
paragraph(s) · 50, 60, 63-65, 67-68, 70-71, 81, 112, 114, 119, 121, 126, 150-151, 153, 177, 196, 235, 240, 246, 347, 376, 379
paragraphing · 125
paraphrase · 313, 347, 359
paraphrasing · 180
parenesis · 239-240
parenetic · 234, 247
parody(-ies) · 107, 240, 417
parousia · 389
participle(s) · 109, 111, 132-135, 138, 141, 145, 159, 167, 169
particle(s) · 119, 121, 136, 138
particularization · 61, 68, 152, 346
particularizes(-ed,-ing) · 68, 152, 221-222, 316
partitio · 239
partition(s) · 234, 236
partitioned · 53, 60
Passover · 12, 15, 379-380
pathos · 236, 245
patron(s) · 210, 275
patronage · 270, 275, 289
patron-client · 270, 275
Pauline(s) · 50, 52, 54, 56-57, 63, 79, 99, 184, 186, 191, 201, 206, 224, 230-231, 234, 237, 245, 247, 255, 270, 321, 323, 334, 365-366, 381, 388, 390-391, 395, 434
peace · 15, 64, 131, 196, 208, 222, 227, 234-235, 248-250, 263-264, 266, 287, 300, 305, 325, 348, 384, 399, 409, 413, 448
peacemaker(s) · 39, 62, 222-223
peace-making · 223, 364
pedagogue · 106, 121

pedagogy · 434
Pentateuch · 51, 312
Pentecost · 29, 415
Pentecostal · 374
People of God · 34, 259, 276, 350, 383, 392-393, 395, 400, 403, 407, 421
perfect · 128-132, 138, 170
perfective · 110, 127-131, 170
performance · 43, 60, 63, 233, 236, 314, 319, 325-329, 441
Pergamum · 210, 244, 255, 264, 331
periphrastic · 134-135, 138, 145
peristaseis · 239
peroration(n) · 234, 239, 245
Perseus · 200
personification(s) · 88, 202, 209, 286
personified · 88, 286, 328
Pesher · 314
Peshitta · 79
Pharisee(s) · 16, 76, 107, 227, 255, 350, 356, 384, 413
Philippi · 402
philological · 60, 101, 193, 197
philologist · 185, 202
philology · 193, 202
philosopher(s) · 177, 195, 197, 208, 211, 246, 258, 332-333, 449, 452
philosophical · 28, 51, 230, 232, 244, 247, 258, 329, 332, 342, 385, 387
philosophies · 36
philosophy · 246, 313, 330, 386
phrasal · 113, 126
phrase(s) · 18, 30, 50, 60, 65, 68, 107, 109, 111-113, 115, 117-119, 123, 126, 138, 140-141, 143, 149, 151-152, 157, 159, 166-167, 169, 171-172, 178-179, 183-184, 191, 194, 204, 267, 272, 282-284, 286, 289, 300, 310-311, 316, 318, 334, 354, 356
pictorial-metaphoric · 434
picture(s) · 82, 121, 210, 263, 271, 285, 299, 328, 331, 356, 411, 432, 435-436, 438
picturing · 203, 292, 435
Pilate · 144, 210, 258, 376, 433
pinakes · 331
plot · 114
pluperfect(-ive) · 109, 128-131, 138
Pneumatology · 391
poet · 319, 333
poetic · 65, 247, 328
poetry · 53-54, 63, 67, 71, 217, 229,

241, 313, 327, 330
politic · 178, 283
political(-ly) · 41, 88, 177, 194-195, 197, 202, 209, 243-244, 247-248, 250-251, 257, 263, 269, 276, 283, 286, 298, 328-330, 332-333, 364-366, 379-380, 402, 440-441
political-civic · 248
political-philosophical · 402
political-religious · 258
politicians · 65
politics · 177, 194, 219, 273, 365
POP (Priority on Praxis) · 41, 398
positivism · 258
post-nuclear · 133-134
potency · 137, 145
pragmatic(s) · 105-106, 108, 121, 123, 125-126, 130-131, 142, 144-149, 193-194, 213, 341, 421
pragmatically · 142
praise(-s,-ed,-ing) · 153-154, 196, 208, 244, 247, 275, 281, 303, 366, 424
praiseworthy · 196
praxis · 41, 259, 398, 403
pray(-s,-ed,-ing) · 14, 22, 39, 136, 146, 235, 270, 399, 401, 409, 420
prayer(s) · 12, 19, 59, 76, 85, 137, 233-235, 239, 255, 266, 287, 303, 366, 401-402, 404
prayerful(-ly) · 9, 32, 39, 59, 360, 402, 404, 406, 420, 424, 428
praying · 53, 296-297, 374
precreation · 243, 251
prefix(-es) · 188-189
preposed · 140, 145
preposition(s) · 109, 112, 119, 135, 145, 157, 183, 188-189
prepositional · 109, 111, 113, 115, 117-118, 123, 126, 138, 141, 157, 159, 166-167, 169, 171-172, 189
presupposition(s) · 39-40, 254, 260, 274, 371, 390, 401, 418, 425
presuppositional · 38
pre-understanding · 31, 176
Priene · 208, 365
priest(s) · 19, 21, 23, 144, 227, 243, 266, 270, 278, 436, 444
priesthood(s) · 227, 258, 281, 286
priestly · 242-243, 251, 294, 322, 366, 436, 444
probatio · 234, 239, 245
proem, proemium · 234, 239
progymnasmata · 239, 244-246, 251, 313

prohibition(s) · 408-409, 418
prologue(s) · 216
prominence · 5, 121, 130-131, 140-142, 144-149, 167, 204, 268, 285, 287, 306, 324, 328
prominent · 131, 151, 204, 280, 282, 285-286, 298, 331, 350, 354, 366, 421
promise(-s,-ed) · 10, 12, 22, 29, 218, 220, 249, 266, 310, 312, 379, 399, 409, 423, 441, 448
pronominal · 145, 280
pronoun(s) · 108-109, 111, 115-116, 118, 126-127, 136, 138, 140-141, 145, 159, 167, 170-172, 222, 285-286, 348, 422
proof-texting · 26
propaganda · 202, 247, 364
prophecy(-ies) · 14, 16, 31, 53-54, 57, 63, 67, 125, 217, 229, 241, 252, 270, 285, 295, 299-302, 304-306, 335, 383, 399, 423-424, 447
prophesy(-ing,-ied) · 81, 125, 155, 335, 447
prophet · 24
prophet(s) · 13, 15, 17-18, 51, 53, 55-56, 62, 85, 185, 222-223, 243, 250, 263, 294-295, 299, 305-306, 311, 317, 350, 380, 409, 416, 421, 432, 436, 444, 448
prophetic(-ally) · 13, 15, 19-20, 53-54, 71, 217, 239, 242-243, 251, 304, 314, 366, 371, 425, 436, 443-444
prosopopoieia · 245
protasis · 141, 145
Protestant(-ism) · 26, 53, 286, 374
prothesis · 234, 239
provenance · 71, 195, 262, 379
proverb(-s,-ial) · 71, 218, 225, 239, 314, 333, 409
Proverbs · 52-55, 217-218, 252, 254
Psalmists · 16
Psalter, Psalm(s) · 11, 52-55, 217, 254, 294, 312, 314, 321, 391, 447
Pseudepigrapha · 206
pseudepigraphal · 207
punctuate(d) · 60, 89, 126, 222
punctuation · 7-8, 65, 89, 98, 125

Q

Quadrilateral · 375
Qumran · 26, 255, 304, 314, 321-322

SUBJECT INDEX

R

Rabbi(-s,-inic) · 107, 176, 315, 321, 356, 451
ratiocinatio · 239
rationale(s) · 13, 68, 121, 152, 326, 341
rationalism · 375
realia · 42, 272-273, 287, 324, 442
reconcile(-s,-d) · 40, 121, 163-165, 223, 250, 269, 316, 379, 413
reconciliation · 39, 45, 111, 163-165, 195, 204, 223, 232, 283, 341, 405
recontextualization · 319
redaction · 296-297
Reformation · 53, 374, 392
Reformed · 372-374, 385
refutatio · 239, 245
refutation · 234
regula fidei · 57
relativism · 258-259, 375
relevance · 6, 190, 195, 211-212, 285, 306, 324, 347, 385, 398, 400-401, 419
Relevance Theory · 106, 193, 324
religio-historical · 387
religion(s) · 64, 82, 202, 258, 273-275, 290-291, 319, 326, 328, 330, 365, 421, 442
reoccurrence · 62, 218, 221, 223
reoccurring · 61
repent(-s,-ing) · 15, 39, 146, 228, 380, 384, 401, 428
repentance · 12, 28, 170, 263, 384, 403, 426
repetition(s) · 61, 64, 68, 137, 145, 152, 171-172, 211, 239-240, 328
result · 113, 134, 136
resultative · 110, 131, 170, 221-222
resultative-stative · 127, 131
resumption · 122-123, 140, 354
resumptive · 140
resurrected · 11-12, 421
resurrection · 9-12, 14, 17, 23-25, 29, 69, 143-144, 152, 164-165, 194, 227, 243, 248, 255-256, 258, 263, 316, 366, 376, 389, 393, 396, 413, 415, 448
rhetoric · 43, 61, 64, 153, 177, 194-195, 200-201, 231-232, 237-240, 242-246, 250-251, 278, 313, 326, 328-330, 335, 356
rhetorical(-ly) · 19, 33, 50, 52, 70, 106, 153, 172, 199-200, 225, 231-236, 238-239, 242, 244-248, 251, 275, 313, 327-330, 332, 348, 365, 368, 442

rhetorician · 108, 236, 328, 450, 452
rhetorolect · 3, 242, 249-251
righteous · 56, 109, 112, 167, 269, 282, 303, 312, 348, 384, 409, 416
righteousness · 13, 62, 89-90, 169, 180, 222-223, 243, 274, 296, 300, 312, 348, 350, 353, 356, 377, 380, 414, 425-426, 428
Roma (divinization of the Roman People) · 88, 209-210, 283, 286, 328
Romanization · 365
Romans · 6, 52, 54, 56, 59, 83, 97, 121, 149, 168-169, 209, 224, 230, 247, 256, 276-277, 290, 294, 324, 380

S

Sabbath · 69, 152, 237, 298, 316, 429
Sadducees · 107, 255, 303
sage(s) · 176, 230, 356, 436, 444
salvation · 14-16, 26, 32, 34, 108, 131, 162, 165, 178, 204-208, 210, 220, 223, 239, 304-306, 315, 372-376, 379, 381-383, 386-387, 389, 391, 400-401, 448
salvific · 34, 207, 220, 286, 301, 387, 416
Samaria · 143, 210, 295
Samaritan(s) · 134, 225-227, 409
sanctification · 34, 59
sanctify(-ied,-ing) · 32, 35, 39, 279-280, 392, 399
sanctuary, see temple · 23
sarcasm · 417
savior(s) · 193, 196, 204-210, 279-280, 282-286, 364, 373, 423
schema(s) · 193-194, 196-197, 211, 213, 237
scholia · 197
scriptural(-ly) · 4, 13-15, 21, 26-27, 29, 31-32, 34-35, 37, 39-40, 42-43, 45, 49, 56, 61, 65, 84, 92, 164, 177, 180, 198, 212, 244, 248-249, 251, 253, 260, 293-294, 302-304, 307-309, 311, 314, 320, 322, 334, 342, 344-346, 348, 354-355, 361, 371, 381, 385-386, 389-391, 400, 403-405, 414-415, 419-420, 437, 443-444
Scripture(s) · 3, 8-15, 17, 19-21, 23-45, 49-50, 53-56, 61, 65, 68-69, 71-72, 79, 95, 139, 151,
166, 198-199, 212-213, 219, 225-226, 237, 248, 253, 255, 258, 260, 262-263, 266-267, 269, 272, 276, 294, 297-299, 302-306, 308, 311-312, 314-315, 318-320, 322, 325-326, 334-335, 340-343, 347-348, 356, 361-362, 366-367, 371-379, 381-393, 396, 398, 400, 402-408, 411-412, 414-417, 419-421, 424, 426-427, 429-430, 432-433, 435-436, 442-443, 447-448
sculpture · 292, 328
sebasteion · 328
sebastoi · 281
secondspace (Critical Space Theory) · 242-243, 437-438
segment · 69-71, 122, 322, 328, 344, 436
segmentation · 65, 93, 125
self-adulation · 245
semantic(-ally) · 3-4, 42, 45, 50, 60-62, 68-71, 112-113, 120-121, 126, 130, 135, 138, 150-153, 155-157, 159-161, 163-166, 168, 170, 172, 179, 182-183, 188-191, 201, 203, 214, 218, 221-223, 225, 228, 238, 249, 278, 280, 297, 361
semiotic(s) · 43, 179, 299
sermon(s) · 16, 26, 52, 55, 62-63, 67, 217, 222, 229, 241, 274, 343, 348, 350, 352, 359, 376, 381, 384, 391-392, 403, 406, 417, 433, 440-441, 444, 447
sex · 36, 414
sexual(-ly) · 59, 83, 270, 402, 414, 425, 427
SIS (Scripture Interprets Scripture) · 41, 294, 371, 398
skepticism · 258-259, 375, 405
skeptics · 341
social(-ly) · 16, 39, 42, 66, 83, 176, 178, 186, 188, 194, 196-198, 203, 211, 219, 230, 238-239, 243, 249-251, 254, 261, 267, 269-270, 272-277, 280-281, 285-286, 290-292, 319, 332, 365-366, 402, 427
social-communal · 102, 383
social-cultural · 3, 66-67, 178-180, 207-209, 216, 225, 228, 253, 266, 305, 319, 323-324, 367, 419-420, 444
social-cultural-political · 208
social-cultural-political-religious · 200
social-elite · 211

social-historical · 273, 278, 287
social-political · 177, 204, 208
social-public · 443
social-religious · 88, 286
social-religious-political · 41, 250
social-scientific(-ally) · 272, 274, 287
societal · 260, 427
societal-cultural · 216
socio-cultural · 228, 267, 323, 442
socio-historical · 274
sociological · 269, 273-275, 287, 292
sociology · 269
socio-political · 178, 281
socio-rhetorical · 3, 242, 266, 323
software (Bible, etc.) · 165, 181, 189-190, 200, 272
soter (see also savior) · 207-208, 283
soteria · 208
soteriology · 375, 383
space(s) · 3, 20, 35, 66, 143, 146, 157, 159-160, 164, 166-167, 178, 210-211, 218, 235, 242-244, 249-251, 271, 327-328, 330, 356, 361, 367-368, 371, 377, 379, 409, 419, 437-439, 443-444
Spaces · 242-243, 326
spatial · 3
spatial(-ly) · 39, 437
spatiality · 242
spatialized · 320
Spirit (Holy) · 13-14, 28-33, 37, 39, 41, 67, 81, 91, 185, 199, 222, 224, 248, 250, 266, 296, 312, 355, 372, 380, 382, 384, 388-389, 399-400, 403-404, 406, 408-409, 411, 414, 416, 448
spirit(s) · 10, 30-31, 40, 62, 119, 185, 208, 222-223, 231, 235, 385
spiritual(-ly) · 26, 31-33, 51, 183, 204, 223, 227, 263, 283-284, 366, 370, 374-375, 400, 429, 433, 447
spirituality · 31, 57
spiritualization · 26
stasis · 245-246
statue(s), statuary · 88, 207, 209, 271-272, 277, 292, 328, 331, 366, 438
stewards,-ship · 28, 407, 411
Stoic(s) · 194-195, 332
story(-ies) · 3, 43, 55, 63, 67, 75, 81, 83, 95, 103, 114, 126, 138, 215, 217, 225-226, 229, 239-241, 257, 259-260, 263, 293-294,

304, 309, 311, 314, 326, 328, 330, 376, 378, 381, 385, 388, 391-392, 403-404, 406-408, 419, 423, 431-433, 435-444
story-creating · 259
story-laden · 259
storyline · 131, 251, 323, 436
storytelling · 259-260, 436, 441
stylus · 78
suasoriae · 244
sub-culture(s) · 271, 401, 405
subordinate(-ing) · 108-109, 112, 115-121, 124, 135-136, 139-141, 146, 155, 157, 159-160, 162-163, 166-167, 170, 227, 383
substantiate(-d,-s) · 164, 223, 323, 350
suffix · 123
symbol(s) · 83, 179, 259, 273-274, 403, 408, 421
symbolic · 269, 274, 408-409, 416, 418-420, 425-426, 442-444
symbolize(-ed,-ing) · 209-210
synagogue(s) · 14, 55, 88, 144, 244, 298, 313-314, 348, 402, 409
synonyms (-ous) · 60, 184, 187-192, 198, 212, 214
Synoptic(s) · 50, 52-54, 57, 80, 102, 192, 244-245, 270, 275, 290, 294-297, 334
syntactical · 60, 187, 238, 323
syntax · 40, 60, 117, 119, 147-148, 161, 172, 300, 342, 348, 354

T

tabernacle · 23
Talmud · 290
TaNaK · 51, 53, 55-56
Targum(s), targumim · 305, 319, 321-322
temple(s) · 19-20, 55-56, 69, 152, 178, 188, 192, 209-210, 231, 242-243, 248, 250, 254-256, 262-266, 272, 286-287, 294-295, 300, 304, 310, 328, 330, 348, 364-365, 380, 390, 394, 407, 429, 434, 437
text-critical · 5, 88, 93, 95-97, 101-103
text-critics · 86
text-linguistic(s) · 137, 155
text-type(s) · 86-87
textural · 442
texture(s) · 3, 63, 277, 335, 442, 444
theologian(s) · 257, 298, 370, 384, 433

theological(-ly) · 34-37, 39-40, 43-44, 50, 60-61, 69, 76, 80-81, 95, 100, 102, 149, 153, 176, 178-180, 186, 189, 191, 193, 195, 199-200, 211, 214, 219-220, 232, 237, 247, 259, 267, 288, 290, 311, 334, 341-343, 347, 370-379, 381-396, 403, 407, 415, 430, 433, 435, 437, 443
theology · 4, 34, 42-43, 45, 50, 53, 81, 86, 155, 194-195, 199, 208, 263, 286, 288, 296-297, 319, 347, 364, 370-372, 374-377, 381-382, 384-396, 398, 406, 421, 429-430, 432-433, 435
thirdspace (Critical Space Theory) · 242-243, 437-438
TLG · 200, 207
topos, topoi · 153, 242, 245, 251, 275-277, 364
Torah · 51, 53, 82, 313, 356
transcultural · 43, 66, 398-401, 419-420, 424, 426, 430, 444
transition(s) · 30, 64, 67, 70, 141, 234, 269, 368, 406
transitional · 64, 70, 133, 219, 221, 231
translating · 262
translation · 3, 6-8, 12, 15, 18, 59, 62, 64, 66, 73-76, 82, 89, 95-96, 117, 119, 125, 139, 160, 165-166, 177, 184, 193, 224, 231, 246, 270, 284, 305, 307, 321, 387, 435
translation(s) · 58, 76, 78, 93, 103, 122, 124, 137, 139, 149, 307, 326, 334
translational · 120
translations · 3, 5, 9, 12, 42, 59-60, 65-66, 73-74, 77-78, 81-83, 95-96, 98-99, 126, 134, 182, 195, 254, 263, 315, 320-321
translator(s · 93, 95, 320
translator(s) · 5, 65, 93, 103, 214, 334
transposed · 98
transposition · 84, 97, 237
Trinity · 63, 205, 277, 290, 335, 443
TRISMEGISTOS · 202
typological(-ly) · 14, 306, 318, 334
typology · 304, 306, 390, 429

U

uncial(s) · 78-79, 85, 100
uncircumcision, see also circumcision · 249, 266

UNCLE(Unconditional Nature of the Canon for Later Eras) · 41, 176, 371
Unitarian · 374

V

variant(s) · 5, 34, 65, 80-83, 85-88, 90-98, 100-103, 142, 144, 315
versification · 57, 59, 64, 70
vice(s) · 220-221, 239, 385, 424, 426-427, 442
virtue(s) · 56, 202, 222, 239, 261, 281, 382-383, 424, 442
visual · 61, 165, 237, 325, 327-328, 331, 444
visualization · 243
visualize(-es, -ed) · 51, 117, 132, 207, 362, 436
visualize(-s,-ed) · 436
visually · 308
vituperative · 244, 247
vocation(al) · 13-14, 155, 239
vocative · 118, 124, 145, 167
voice · 13, 39, 59, 110, 127-128, 162, 164-165, 231, 296, 302, 310, 316, 388, 418

W

wa-homer · 164, 316
war, warfare · 155, 196, 210, 255, 310, 322, 384, 429, 434
warrant, to warrant · 190-191, 245, 251, 275, 287, 362-364, 367-368, 389
Wesleyan(s) · 18, 220, 375, 384-385, 392-393
wife,wives · 60, 66, 125, 144, 204-205, 218, 261, 270-271, 276, 279-280, 282-284, 304, 413, 423
wisdom · 19, 33, 52-54, 63, 67, 91-93, 177, 197, 217, 229, 239, 241-243, 251, 255, 312, 379, 383, 389, 400, 437, 447-448
witness(-es,-ed,-ing) · 10, 12, 21, 23, 30, 59, 77, 79, 82-85, 87-88, 90, 93-94, 96-103, 169, 297, 303, 374, 383, 395, 403-404, 411, 427, 436
woman,women · 59, 95, 108-109, 111, 261, 270, 273, 379, 384, 399-400, 413, 429-430, 432
worldview · 51, 177, 259-260, 263, 371, 403, 408, 420, 427

Z

Zeus · 195, 208

Chart, Diagram, & Illustration Index

Note: Headings are in **bold**. All items in the LIST OF CHARTS, DIAGRAMS, AND ILLUSTRATIONS (xi-xiv) are below and put into CAPS.

Abbreviations
  BIBLES (COMMON ENGLISH TRANSLATIONS) · 58
  BIBLICAL BOOK ABBREVIATIONS · 7, 59
  COMMON ABBREVIATIONS · 8, 59
Application, see STEP 11: EVALUATED APPLICATIONS
  CYCLE OF VALUES · 403
  PARTICULARITY AND TRANSCENDENCE · 399
  THE PRINCIPLIZING BRIDGE · 407
Bibles (English)
  COMPARISON OF FOOTNOTES OF SELECT MODERN ENGLISH TRANSLATIONS · 307
Canon
  CANON FORMATION (HISTORICAL FACTORS) · 56
  CANONICAL ORDER · 52
  HEBREW BIBLE OR *TANAK* · 51
  PROTESTANT OLD TESTAMENT 39 BOOKS · 53
Chiasm
  CHIASM OF EPHESIANS 2:11–22 · 249
  CHIASTIC STRUCTURE OF EPH 5:22–24 · 205
  OBJECTIVE CRITERIA TO EVALUATE CHIASMS · 238
  STRUCTURAL DEPICTION OF EPH 5:22–27 · 279
Chronology
  INTERTESTAMENTAL DATES 255
  NT DATES (WITH *BIBLICAL SOURCES*) 255
  OT DATES (WITH *BIBLICAL SOURCES*) 254
  POST-NEW TESTAMENT DATES (WITH *SOURCES*) · 255
CLAUSAL CONNECTIONS (TYPES OF) · 113. See also Conjunctions and Connectors.
Conjunctions
  "SEMANTICS" OF CONJUNCTIONS · 120
  PROCESSING CONSTRAINTS OF COORDINATING CONNECTORS · 122
  PROCESSING CONSTRAINTS OF SUBORDINATING CONNECTORS · 124
Constituent Marking
  IN ENGLISH · 115
  IN GREEK · 118

CONTEXT (LEVELS OF) · 50, 176
CORINTH (ROMAN), AGORA AND ENVIRONS OF · 439
Diagramming, see esp. STEP 3: GRAMMATICAL STUDY and STEP 4: SEMANTIC ANALYSIS
Education
  MEDITERRANEAN EDUCATIONAL SYSTEMS · 313
English Grammar
  CLAUSAL CONNECTIONS (TYPES OF) · 113
  CONSTITUENT MARKING · 115
  MODIFIERS (TYPES OF) · 159
  PARTS OF SPEECH · 108
  PHRASAL MODIFYING RELATIONS · 126
  VERBS IMPORTANT CHARACTERISTICS · 110
Ethics (Biblical) PRINCIPLES OF BIBLICAL ETHICS · 421
Evaluation, see STEP 11: EVALUATED APPLICATIONS
Genres, see STEP 6: LITERARY FORMS
  MAIN TYPES OF BIBLICAL DISCOURSE · 423
  MAJOR BIBLICAL GENRES · 217
Greek Grammar, see esp. STEPS 3 and 4
  CONSTITUENT MARKING · 118
  EMPHATIC AND PRAGMATIC CONSTRUCTIONS · 145
  FREQUENCY OF VERB TENSES AND MOODS · 132
  "HOPE" IN GREEK STUDY · 117
  PRONOUNS · 127
  TYPES OF GREEK MODIFIERS · 167
  VERBAL ASPECT & *AKTIONSART* "CATEGORIES" · 129
  VERBAL ASPECT & PRAGMATICS IN NARRATIVE · 130
  WORD ORDER VARIATIONS AND PROMINENCE · 141
Historical-Criticism, see STEP 7: HISTORICAL CONTEXT
  CRITICAL-LITERARY APPROACH TO THE BIBLE · 27
  CRITICAL-REALISM AND HISTORICAL INQUIRY · 259
  LITERALISM VS. SKEPTICISM · 405
Imperial Cult (see emperor's name in Author Index)
  ARTIFACTS OF THE EMPEROR AND ROMA CULT · 210
INFOGRAPHICS FOR PHILIPPIANS · 440
Inscriptions
  WARNING INSCRIPTION AT THE JEWISH TEMPLE · 265
  SEARCH RESULTS FROM THE PHI DATABASE · 281
  TWO INSCRIPTIONS WITH ἔνδοξος "GLORIOUS" · 281
Interpretation, see STEP 9: INTERPRETIVE DECISIONS
  ANALYTICAL INTERPRETIVE WORKFLOW · 344
  CONSTRUCTION OF ARGUMENT PLAN · 363
  ESSENTIAL ELEMENTS OF RESEARCH · 362
  HOW TO STUDY THE BIBLE (W. W. WHITE) · 44
  INTERPRETATION OF MATT 5:19 · 347
  INTERPRETIVE JOURNEY · 4, 45
  INTERPRETIVE PRINCIPLES (FAMILY OF) · 41

Intertestamental Period
    INTERTESTAMENTAL DATES · 255
Intertextuality, see STEP 8: SCRIPTURAL CORRELATIONS
    THE SEVEN RULES OF HILLEL · 316
    TEXT-TYPES AND COMMUNAL EXEGETICAL TRADITIONS · 321
    VALIDATION CRITERIA FOR INTERTEXTUAL ALLUSIONS OR ECHOES · 323
    EXPLICITNESS & ELABORATION OF OT QUOTATIONS · 325
Law (OT)
    HOW TO BEST INTERPRET THE OT LAW · 416
Letter (ancient), or Epistle
    GRECO-ROMAN *DOCUMENTARY* LETTER FORMS · 233
    PAULINE EPISTOLARY AND RHETORICAL FORMS · 234
Lexicons
    BDAG · 29n16, 123, 183, 185, 188, 191, 193, 195n33, 199, 200, 214, 280, 285
    L&N · 182, 184, 189, 199, 214, 297n5
    LSJ · 177, 183, 188, 191, 196, 199, 200, 203, 208n61, 214, 225
    Spicq · 200, 203, 209
    Strong's · 180-81, 183, 186, 188, 213-14
    Swanson's · 183, 186, 214
    TDNT · 194n26-27, 196n34, 199, 276, 342, 356
    Thayer's · 186, 188, 199, 214
    Zodhiates (Spiros) · 186, 188-89, 214
Lists
    CATALOG OF NT LISTS · 224
    FEATURES OF BIBLICAL LISTS · 220
LITERARY FORM, see esp. STEP 6: LITERARY FORMS
    CATALOG OF NT LISTS · 224
    FEATURES OF BIBLICAL LISTS · 220
    IDENTIFYING LITERARY FORMS · 240
    TEACHING FORMS OF JESUS · 225
    TYPES OF LITERARY FORMS IN THE NT · 239
MAJOR SEMANTIC RELATIONSHIPS · 68, 152
    SUPPORTING SEMANTIC RELATIONSHIPS · 69, 152
Metaphor
    LIFE DOMAINS AS METAPHORS IN PAUL · 434
Modifiers
    TYPES OF MODIFIERS · 159
    TYPES OF GREEK MODIFIERS · 167
Narratives
    BASIC OBSERVATIONS FOR · 114
New Testament (NT)
    CANON FORMATION (HISTORICAL FACTORS) · 56
    CANONICAL ORDER · 52
    IMPORTANT NT DATES (WITH *BIBLICAL SOURCES*) · 255
    MORE-DETAILED NT CHRONOLOGY · 256
Numismatics
    DENARIUS COIN MINTED UNDER TIBERIUS · 277
Parables
    AUGUSTINE'S ALLEGORICAL INTERPRETATION OF GOOD SAMARITAN PARABLE · 227
    COMMON PARABLES STRUCTURES (BLOMBERG) · 227
PARTS OF SPEECH · 108
Phrases
    PHRASAL MODIFYING RELATIONS · 126
    PHRASAL MEANINGS (TYPES OF) · 113
Prophecy
    A "PROPHECY" OF NOSTRADAMUS · 300
Observation
    OBSERVATIONS/QUESTIONS FOR EPH 5:22–33 · 280
Old Testament (OT)
    HEBREW BIBLE OR *TANAK* 51
    IMPORTANT OT DATES (WITH *BIBLICAL SOURCES*) · 254
    IN THE BOOK OF ACTS 24
    HOW TO BEST INTERPRET THE OT LAW · 416
    MAJOR TYPES OF THE NT'S USE OF THE OT · 306
    PROTESTANT OLD TESTAMENT 39 BOOKS · 53
    QUOTATION AND CITATION IN MATTHEW · 302
Rhetoric, Ancient Greco-Roman
    PAULINE EPISTOLARY AND RHETORICAL FORMS · 234
    MODES OF PERSUASION · 236
    "ARENAS" OF ANCIENT RHETORICAL INVENTION · 244
    "AREAS" FOR INVESTIGATING NT RHETORIC · 245
Rhetorolects
    BLENDED SPACES & LOCATIONS IN EARLY CHRISTIAN RHETOROLECTS · 243
    SOCIAL, CULTURAL, AND IDEOLOGICAL TOPOI IN EPH 2:10 · 276
Roma
    ARTIFACTS OF THE EMPEROR AND ROMA CULT · 210
Semantic Diagramming and Analysis
    ZONES (OF SEMANTIC DIAGRAMMING) · 156–159
    TYPES OF MODIFIERS 159
    SEMANTIC ANALYSIS OF ROM 5:10–11 · 164
    TYPES OF GREEK MODIFIERS 167
    TYPES OF MODIFIERS AND ZONES · 168
Septuagint (LXX)
    LXX USAGE GRAPHIC FOR Περιπατέω · 190
Gospels (Synoptic)
    RELATIONSHIP BETWEEN SYNOPTIC GOSPELS · 295

CHART, DIAGRAM, & ILLUSTRATION INDEX

Textual-criticism, see STEP 2: TEXTUAL COMPARISONS
    CLASSICAL TEXTS COMPARED TO THE NT · 80
    COMMONLY CONFUSED UNCIAL LETTERS · 85
    CHURCH FATHER QUOTATIONS OF THE NT · 79
    EXTANT MANUSCRIPTS OF THE NT · 79
    "EXTRA" VERSES IN ENGLISH VERSIONS · 75
    IMAGE OF PAPYRUS 52 (P^{52}) · 82, 97
    MANUSCRIPTS BY TEXT-TYPE LOCATION · 99
    "MISSING" VERSES IN THE NIV · 76
    NA^{27} & UBS^4 VARIANTS IN 1 COR 2:1–5 · 91, 92
    NA^{27} VARIANTS IN ROM 12:1–2 · 98
    PALEOGRAPHY OF NT MANUSCRIPTS · 78
    SIGLA OF GNT CRITICAL EDITIONS · 98
    TEXTUAL DISTRIBUTION THROUGH LOCALES · 87
    TEXTUAL VARIANTS IN 2 COR 3:9 IN TEXTUAL · 94

Stories, see STEP 12: PRESENTATION BRAINSTORM
    STORIES AND ANALOGIES, DOS AND DON'TS · 441

Theological Interpretation, see STEP 10: BIBLICAL THEOLOGY
    BRANCHES OF THEOLOGY · 386
    CONTEXTS OF THEOLOGICAL EXEGESIS · 415
    GOD'S REVELATION/THEOLOGICAL CATEGORIES · 382
    MAJOR THEOLOGICAL TOPICS · 372
    NINE THESES OF THEOLOGICAL INTERPRETATION · 378
    SEVEN FOCAL LENSES OF SCRIPTURE · 411
    THEOLOGICAL SOURCES → TO EXTREMES · 375
    THEOLOGICAL THEMES FROM PAUL'S QUOTATION OF SCRIPTURE · 389
    THEOLOGICAL TOPICS FROM PAUL'S QUOTATION OF SCRIPTURE · 389

Verbs
    IMPORTANT CHARACTERISTICS IN ENGLISH ·110
    VERBAL ASPECT & PRAGMATICS IN NARRATIVE ·130
    VERBAL ASPECT AND *AKTIONSART* "CATEGORIES" ·129
    FREQUENCY OF VERB TENSES AND MOODS ·132

Women in the NT
    WOMEN'S HEAD COVERINGS · 271

WORD OF GOD PERMEATING GOD'S PEOPLE · 28

Word Study, see esp. STEP 5: LEXICAL RESEARCH
    CONTEXT (LEVELS OF) · 50, 176
    GREEK SYNONYMS OF "BODY" IN THE NT · 184
    LXX USAGE GRAPHIC FOR Περιπατέω · 190
    ΣΩΤΗΡ AND CLOSE COGNATES · 207
    ΣΩΤΗΡ AND CLOSE COGNATES IN THE NT · 206

SCRIPTURE INDEX & ANCIENT TEXTS AND ARTIFACTS

NOTE: This index is organized by the name of the scriptural book (placed in bold) beginning with numbers (e.g., **1 Corinthians**) and then alphabetized. Any specific references are placed below the book name. The underlined Scripture reference(s) are part of a special or extended discussion on one or more of the pages given. The **CAPPED AND BOLDED SCRIPTURE REFERENCE(S)** are found in a Chart, Diagram, or Illustration on one or more pages given. The Scripture reference(s) marked with an asterisk (*) are a part of an EXERCISE on one or more pages given. *Italicized book names and references* (no bold) are from the OT Pseudepigrapha or the OT Apocrypha.

1

1–2 Chronicles · *294*
  1 Chr 21:5 · *316*
  1 Chr 27:1 · *316*
1–2 Corinthians · *54, 56*
1 Corinthians · *7, 31, 60, 139, 149, 185, 195, 224, 231, 240, 256*
  1 Cor 1:12–13 · *224*
  1 Cor 1:18 · *206, 414*
  1 Cor 1:19 · *389*
  1 Cor 1:20 · *224*
  1 Cor 1:21 · *206*
  1 Cor 1:22–24 · *224*
  1 Cor 1:26–29 · *224*
  1 Cor 1:30 · *224*
  1 Cor 1:31 · *389*
  1 Cor 2:1* · *31, 81, 90-92, 95, 182, 232*
  <u>1 Cor 2:1–4</u> · *90, 232*
  1 COR 2:1–5 · *91-92*
  1 Cor 2:3 · *224*
  1 Cor 2:9 · *389*
  1 Cor 2:10 · *185*
  1 Cor 2:10–11 · *31*
  1 Cor 2:16 · *389*
  1 Cor 3:6 · *224*
  1 Cor 3:9 · *434*
  1 Cor 3:10 · *434*
  1 Cor 3:11–16 · *224*
  1 Cor 3:15 · *206*
  1 Cor 3:16 · *434*
  1 Cor 3:17 · *434*
  1 Cor 3:19–20 · *389*
  1 Cor 3:21–23 · *224*
  1 Cor 3:23* · *373*
  1 Cor 4:7–13 · *224*
  1 Cor 4:9 · *434*
  1 Cor 5–6 · *426*
  1 Cor 5:5 · *185, 206*
  1 Cor 5:9–10 · *426*
  1 Cor 5:9–13 · *224*
  1 Cor 5:10 · *426*
  1 Cor 5:11 · *427*
  1 Cor 6:7* · *128*
  1 Cor 6:9 · *426*
  1 Cor 6:9–11 · *224*
  1 Cor 6:12a · *125*
  1 Cor 6:12–13 · *312*
  1 Cor 6:12–20* · *231*
  1 Cor 6:13a · *125*
  1 Cor 6:16 · *389*
  1 Cor 6:18b · *125*
  1 Cor 6:19–20* · *373*
  1 Cor 6:20 · *86*
  1 Cor 7* · *66-67, 353, 355, 413, 434*
  1 Cor 7:1* · *66-67, 353, 413*
  1 Cor 7:10 · *67, 413*
  1 Cor 7:10–13 · *413*
  1 Cor 7:12 · *67, 413*
  1 Cor 7:15–16 · *413*
  1 Cor 7:16 · *206*
  1 Cor 7:19 · *353*
  1 Cor 7:21 · *434*
  1 Cor 7:22 · *434*
  1 Cor 7:25 · *67*
  1 Cor 7:40 · *67*
  1 Cor 8:12 · *113*
  1 Cor 8:9 · *113*
  1 Cor 9:9* · *315, 389*
  1 Cor 9:10–11 · *434*
  1 Cor 9:11–12 · *316*
  1 Cor 9:22 · *206*
  1 Cor 9:25 · *434*
  1 Cor 10 · *70, 113, 304, 311, 314, 389*
  1 Cor 10:1–3 · *389*
  1 Cor 10:1–6 · *311*
  1 Cor 10:5 · *113*
  1 Cor 10:6 · *304, 311*
  1 Cor 10:7 · *311, 389*
  1 Cor 10:11 · *304*
  1 Cor 10:12 · *113*
  1 Cor 10:26 · *389*
  1 Cor 10:33 · *206*
  1 Cor 10:33–11:2 · *70*
  1 Cor 11 · *60*
  1 Cor 11:1 · *19-20, 60, 195, 270, 295, 302, 305, 348*
  1 Cor 11:10b* · *270*
  1 Cor 11:1–2 · *64*
  1 Cor 11:1–16 · *195*
  1 Cor 11:15b* · *270*
  1 Cor 11:2–16* · *270*
  1 Cor 11:4–6* · *270*
  1 Cor 12–14 · *30, 70, 224*
  1 Cor 12–14* · *30, 70*
  1 Cor 12 · *30, 70, 195, 422*
  1 Cor 12:4 · *185*
  1 Cor 12:8 · *185*
  1 Cor 12:11 · *185*
  1 Cor 12:12–14 · *422*
  1 Cor 12:13 · *185*
  1 Cor 12:22 · *316*
  1 Cor 13:2 · *447*
  1 Cor 13:8–10 · *447*
  1 Cor 13:13 · *45*
  1 Cor 14:1–5 · *69, 152*
  1 Cor 14:12 · *31*
  1 Cor 14:16 · *113*
  1 Cor 14:21 · *126, 306*
  1 Cor 14:22–25* · *125*
  1 Cor 14:25 · *81, 126*
  1 Cor 14:32 · *185*
  1 Cor 14:34–35 · *261*
  1 Cor 14:37 · *353*
  1 Cor 15:1–3 · *389*
  1 Cor 15:1–8 · *10*
  1 Cor 15:1–11 · *224*
  1 Cor 15:2 · *206*
  1 Cor 15:6 · *113*
  1 Cor 15:8 · *113*
  1 Cor 15:23–25 · *22*
  1 Cor 15:25 · *22, 389*
  1 Cor 15:27 · *389*
  1 Cor 15:35–44 · *224*
  1 Cor 15:45 · *389*
  1 Cor 15:54–55 · *389*
  1 Cor 15:54–56 · *389*
  1 Cor 16:19–24 · *64*
  1 Cor 16:20b* · *402*
1 Enoch 10:2 · *207*
1 Enoch 14:2 · *207*
1–3 John · *7, 52, 58*
1 John · *30-31, 55, 77, 81, 84-86, 95, 155, 206, 217, 224, 241, 343, 353, 373, 415, 448*
  1 John 1:1 · *224*
  1 John 1:7–9* · *373*
  1 John 1:10* · *373*
  1 John 2:2* · *373*
  1 John 2:3–4 · *353*
  1 John 2:7–8 · *353, 448*
  1 John 2:8–10 · *155*
  1 John 2:12–14 · *224*
  1 John 2:16 · *224*
  1 John 2:18* · *241*
  1 John 2:23 · *84, 86*
  1 John 2:27 · *31*
  1 John 3:1–11* · *373*

1 John 3:2 · *415*
1 John 3:11 · *448*
1 John 3:22–24 · *353*
1 John 3:23 · *448*
1 John 4:1–6 · *31*
1 John 4:6 · *30*
1 John 4:14 · *206*
1 John 4:21 · *353*
1 John 5:2–3 · *353*
1 John 5:6 · *30*
1 John 5:7 · *77, 81, 85*
1 John 5:7–8* · *81, 85, 224*
1 John 5:8 · *95*
1 Kgdms 10:19 (LXX) · *205*
1 Kings · *254*
  1 Kgs 1–11 · *254*
  1 Kgs 10:1–3 · *314*
  1 Kgs 11:41 · *255*
  1 Kgs 12–25 · *254*
  1 Kgs 14:19 · *255*
  1 Kgs 14:29 · *255*
1–2 Peter · *54*
1 Peter · *60, 137, 224, 256, 426*
  1 Pet 1:2 · *224*
  1 Pet 1:5* · *206, 373*
  1 Pet 1:9 · *206*
  1 Pet 1:10 · *206*
  1 Pet 1:13 · *415*
  1 Pet 1:15–16 · *426*
  1 Pet 1:18–19* · *373*
  1 Pet 1:22 · *404*
  1 Pet 2 · *32, 241, 304, 373, 414*
  1 Pet 2:1–3 · *32, 224*
  1 Pet 2:2 · *206*
  1 Pet 2:6–10* · *241*
  1 Pet 2:9 · *224*
  1 Pet 2:9–10* · *373*
  1 Pet 2:11–12 · *426*
  1 Pet 2:17 · *224*
  1 Pet 2:24 · *414*
  1 Pet 3:1–7 · *261*
  1 Pet 3:3 · *224*
  1 Pet 3:7 · *415*
  1 Pet 3:8–12 · *224*
  1 Pet 3:10–12 · *21*
  1 Pet 3:18–4:6 · *10*
  1 Pet 3:18–22 · *10*
  1 Pet 3:21 · *206*
  1 Pet 3:22 · *224*
  1 Pet 4:1–4 · *224*
  1 Pet 4:1–7 · *426*
  1 Pet 4:6 · *10*
  1 Pet 4:15 · *224*
  1 Pet 4:18 · *206*
  1 Pet 5:1–3 · *224*
  1 Pet 5:10 · *224, 415*
  1 Pet 5:14* · *402*
1 Samuel · *54, 217*
  1 Sam 1:11 · *316*
1–2 Thessalonians · *54, 224*
1 Thessalonians · *54, 139, 149, 224*
  1 Thess 1:3 · *224*
  1 Thess 1:9 · *298*
  1 Thess 2:3–12 · *298*
  1 Thess 2:7 · *84*
  1 Thess 2:16 · *206*
  1 Thess 3 · *298*
  1 Thess 4:3–4* · *179*
  1 Thess 4:7 · *195*
  1 Thess 4:8 · *123*
  1 Thess 4:16–17 · *224*
  1 Thess 5:4–11* · *108*
  1 Thess 5:5 · *155*
  1 Thess 5:8 · *206*
  1 Thess 5:8–11 · *178*
  1 Thess 5:9 · *206*
  1 Thess 5:14 · *224*
  1 Thess 5:15–22 · *224*
  1 Thess 5:16–27* · *399*
  1 Thess 5:23 · *224*
  1 Thess 5:26* · *402*
  1 Thess 5:27 · *56, 247*
1–2 Timothy · *54*
1 Timothy · *84, 139-140, 149, 224, 256*
  1 Tim 1:1 · *206-207*
  1 Tim 1:3 · *140*
  1 Tim 1:3–4 · *140*
  1 Tim 1:3–11 · *139*
  1 Tim 1:3–2:10 · *139*
  1 Tim 1:5 · *140*
  1 Tim 1:8 · *140*
  1 Tim 1:8–11 · *224*
  1 Tim 1:9 · *139-140*
  1 Tim 1:10 · *139-140*
  1 Tim 1:12 · *139-140*
  1 Tim 1:12–17 · *139-140*
  1 Tim 1:13 · *224*
  1 Tim 1:13b · *139-140*
  1 Tim 1:14 · *140*
  1 Tim 1:15 · *139-140, 206*
  1 Tim 1:16 · *139-140*
  1 Tim 1:17 · *140, 224*
  1 Tim 1:18 · *140, 434*
  1 Tim 1:18–19 · *140*
  1 Tim 1:18–2:10 · *140*
  1 Tim 1:19 · *434*
  1 Tim 1:19b–20 · *140*
  1 Tim 2:1 · *32, 59, 113, 125, 140, 144, 224, 261*
  1 Tim 2:1–7 · *32, 261*
  1 Tim 2:1–8 · *59*
  1 Tim 2:1–15 · *59*
  1 Tim 2:3 · *206-207*
  1 Tim 2:3–4 · *140*
  1 Tim 2:4 · *206, 261, 388*
  1 Tim 2:5–7 · *140*
  1 Tim 2:7 · *224*
  1 Tim 2:8 · *140*
  1 Tim 2:9 · *140*
  1 Tim 2:9–10 · *224*
  1 Tim 2:9–15 · *59*
  <u>1 Tim 2:11</u> · *125, 261*
  1 Tim 2:11–15 · *125, 144*
  1 Tim 2:15 · *144, 206, 224*
  1 Tim 3:1 · *93*
  1 Tim 3:1–15 · *224*
  1 Tim 3:7 · *434*
  1 Tim 3:13 · *434*
  1 Tim 3:15 · *93, 434*
  1 Tim 3:16 · *84, 224*
  1 Tim 4:1 · *30-31, 207, 414, 434*
  1 Tim 4:6–8 · *434*
  1 Tim 4:6–10* · *435*
  1 Tim 4:10 · *206-207, 434*
  1 Tim 4:12–13 · *224*
  1 Tim 4:16 · *206*
  1 Tim 5:3–16* · *424*
  1 Tim 5:9–10 · *224*
  1 Tim 5:13–14 · *224*
  1 Tim 5:17–18 · *434*
  1 Tim 6:3 · *434*
  1 Tim 6:3–5 · *224*
  1 Tim 6:5 · *434*
  1 Tim 6:9 · *434*
  1 Tim 6:10 · *434*
  1 Tim 6:11 · *224*
  1 Tim 6:12 · *434*
  1 Tim 6:19 · *434*
1–2 Samuel · *254*
1–2 Maccabees · *53*
1–4 Maccabees · *322*
  1 Macc 4:30 · *206*
  3 Macc 6:29 · *206*
  3 Macc 6:32 · *206*
  3 Macc 7:16 · *206*

2

2 Baruch · *322*
2 Chronicles · *52-53, 254, 294*
  2 Chr 9:1–12 · *314*
  2 Chr 10–36 · *254*
  2 Chr 16:11 · *255*
  2 Chr 20:34 · *255*
  2 Chr 24:20–21 · *56*
  2 Chr 25:26 · *255*
  2 Chr 27:7 · *255*
  2 Chr 32:32 · *255*
  2 Chr 36 · *254*
2 Corinthians · *7, 52, 93, 148, 153, 224, 232, 237, 240, 256, 290, 322-323, 325*
  2 Cor 1–2 · *409*
  2 Cor 1:1 · *111, 113, 232, 247, 367*
  2 Cor 1:4* · *128*
  2 Cor 1:6 · *206*
  2 Cor 1:8–16* · *241*
  2 Cor 1:11 · *113*
  2 Cor 1:19a* · *367*
  2 Cor 1:21–22* · *373*
  2 Cor 2:14–15* · *226*
  2 Cor 2:14–16 · *434*
  2 Cor 2:14–17 · *323*
  2 Cor 2:15 · *206*
  2 Cor 3:7–8* · *226*
  2 Cor 3:7–9 · *316*
  2 Cor 3:9 · *93-94*
  2 Cor 3:9* · *226*
  2 Cor 3:11 · *316*
  2 Cor 3:18 · *415*
  2 Cor 4:4 · *277, 323*
  2 Cor 4:6 · *31, 155*
  2 Cor 4:7 · *434*
  2 Cor 4:7–12 · *224, 414*
  2 Cor 4:10 · *434*
  2 Cor 5* · *232, 415, 434, 438*
  2 Cor 5:5* · *373*
  2 Cor 5:10* · *232, 415, 434, 438*
  2 Cor 5:11 · *232*
  2 Cor 5:17 · *415*
  2 Cor 6:1* · *315*
  2 Cor 6:2 · *206*
  2 Cor 6:2* · *315*
  2 Cor 6:1–2* · *226*
  2 Cor 6:1–13 · *224*
  2 Cor 6:11 · *168*

2 Cor 6:14 · *155*
2 Cor 6:14–18* · *226*
2 Cor 6:15 · *113*
2 Cor 6:16–18 · *389*
2 Cor 7 · *409*
2 Cor 7:2–16 · *240*
2 Cor 7:8 · *240*
2 Cor 7:10 · *206*
2 Cor 7:12 · *135*
2 Cor 8–9 · *275*
2 Cor 8:11 · *135*
2 Cor 8:15 · *389*
2 Cor 9:6 · *240*
2 Cor 9:6–8* · *241*
2 Cor 9:7 · *240*
2 Cor 9:8 · *90, 240*
2 Cor 9:8–9 · *89*
2 Cor 9:9 · *89, 389*
2 Cor 9:9–10 · *90*
2 Cor 9:10 · *89*
2 Cor 9:12–15 · *275*
2 Cor 10:1 · *92*
2 Cor 10:4 · *434*
2 Cor 10:10 · *56, 232, 330*
2 Cor 11:2–3* · *226*
2 Cor 11:4 · *224*
2 Cor 11:13* · *428*
2 Cor 11:16–12:10 · *240*
2 Cor 11:25–33 · *224*
2 Cor 12:10b* · *226*
2 Cor 12:19–21 · *224*
2 Cor 12:5 · *122*
2 Cor 12:7 · *240*
2 Cor 12:9 · *240*
2 Cor 13:11 · *224*
2 Cor 13:12* · *402*
2 Cor 13:14 · *224*
2 Esd 19:27 · *205*
2 John · *353, 373, 448*
  2 John 3 · *224*
  2 John 4–6 · *353*
  2 John 5 · *448*
2 Kings · *51, 53, 254*
  2 Kgs 1:18 · *255*
  2 Kgs 8:23 · *255*
  2 Kgs 17 · *254*
  2 Kgs 24–25 · *254*
2 Peter · *52, 70, 224, 256, 294, 381*
  2 Pet 1:1 · *206*
  2 Peter 1:2–11 · *224*
  2 Pet 1:11 · *206*
  2 Pet 1:17 · *12, 390*

2 Pet 1:17–18 · *12*
2 Peter 2 · *224*
2 Pet 2:13 · *415*
2 Pet 2:20 · *206*
2 Pet 2:21 · *353*
2 Pet 3:2 · *206, 353*
2 Peter 3:3–4 · *224*
2 Peter 3:10 · *224*
2 Pet 3:13 · *448*
2 Pet 3:14–16 · *448*
2 Pet 3:15 · *56, 206*
2 Pet 3:15–16 · *56*
2 Pet 3:18 · *206*
2 Samuel · *51, 53*
  2 Sam 1:18 · *255*
  2 Sam 7:14* · *317*
  2 Sam 11 · *68, 152*
  2 Sam 12:1–7 · *432*
  2 Sam 24:9 · *316*
2 Thessalonians · *52, 54, 224, 256*
  2 Thess 1:8–10 · *389*
  2 Thess 2:10 · *206*
  2 Thess 2:1–2 · *224*
  2 Thess 2:2 · *247*
  2 Thess 2:13 · *206*
  2 Thess 3:1–5* · *424*
  2 Thess 3:3* · *373*
  2 Thess 3:6–12 · *224*
2 Timothy · *52, 224, 256*
  2 Tim 1:9 · *206*
  2 Tim 1:10 · *206-207*
  2 Tim 1:12 · *434*
  2 Tim 1:14 · *434*
  2 Tim 2:1–7 · *224*
  2 Tim 2:3 · *434*
  2 Tim 2:5 · *434*
  2 Tim 2:6 · *434*
  2 Tim 2:10 · *206*
  2 Tim 2:11–13 · *224*
  2 Tim 2:14 · *195*
  2 Tim 2:15* · *373*
  2 Tim 2:17 · *434*
  2 Tim 2:19 · *434*
  2 Tim 2:22 · *224*
  2 Tim 2:26 · *434*
  2 Tim 3:1–9 · *224*
  2 Tim 3:6 · *434*
  2 Tim 3:10–11 · *224*
  2 Tim 3:15 · *206*
  2 Tim 3:16 · *224*
  2 Tim 3:17 · *434*
  2 Tim 4:1–5 · *224*

2 Tim 4:3 · *434*
2 Tim 4:7 · *224, 434*
2 Tim 4:13 · *333*
2 Tim 4:15* · *128*
2 Tim 4:18 · *206*

3

3 John · *54*
  3 John 10 · *224*

4

4 Ezra · *322*

A

Acts · *7, 10, 18, 21-22, 24, 30-31, 33, 52, 55, 58, 68, 76-77, 79, 81, 90, 97, 99, 113, 142-144, 146, 152, 155, 192, 203, 206, 210, 216-217, 224, 245-246, 255-257, 266, 273, 276, 290, 297-298, 306, 310, 316, 328, 353, 355, 361, 365-366, 373, 383, 402, 408, 411, 448*
  Acts 1 · *10, 68, 76-77, 113, 142-143, 152, 192, 203, 224, 255-256, 273, 276, 297-298, 353, 355, 402, 448*
  Acts 1–2 · *255*
  Acts 1:1–8 · *10*
  Acts 1:2 · *297*
  Acts 1:5 · *297*
  Acts 1:8 · *68, 143, 152, 224, 297, 448*
  Acts 1:9–11 · *10*
  Acts 1:16 · *25, 297*
  Acts 1:20 · *24*
  Acts 1:24 · *297*
  Acts 2:1–12 · *224*
  Acts 2:4 · *297*
  Acts 2:17–21 · *21, 24, 224*
  Acts 2:21 · *206*
  Acts 2:25 · *316*
  Acts 2:25–28 · *24*
  Acts 2:33 · *297*
  Acts 2:33–36 · *22*
  Acts 2:34 · *316*
  Acts 2:34–35 · *24*
  Acts 2:38 · *297*
  Acts 2:40 · *206*
  Acts 2:42–47 · *224, 408*

Acts 2:47 · *206*
Acts 3:18 · *25*
Acts 3:21 · *25*
Acts 3:22–23 · *24*
Acts 3:24 · *24-25*
Acts 3:25 · *24-25, 411*
Acts 4:8 · *297*
Acts 4:9 · *206*
Acts 4:11 · *24*
Acts 4:12 · *206*
Acts 4:12* · *373*
Acts 4:25 · *297*
Acts 4:31 · *297*
Acts 4:32–35 · *408*
Acts 5:3 · *297*
Acts 5:31 · *206*
Acts 5:32 · *297*
Acts 6:1–6 · *224*
Acts 6:5 · *297*
Acts 6:6 · *297*
Acts 6:13 · *25*
Acts 7 · *18, 24, 58, 143, 256, 306, 310, 383*
Acts 7:3 · *24*
Acts 7:7 · *24*
Acts 7:8 · *143*
Acts 7:25 · *206*
Acts 7:27–28 · *24*
Acts 7:32 · *24*
Acts 7:34 · *24*
Acts 7:37 · *24*
Acts 7:38 · *383*
Acts 7:40 · *24*
Acts 7:42–43 · *24*
Acts 7:48–50 · *24*
Acts 7:51 · *297*
Acts 7:55 · *297*
Acts 7:56 · *18, 58*
Acts 8:1 · *143*
Acts 8:5 · *143*
Acts 8:9 · *143*
Acts 8:14 · *143*
Acts 8:15 · *297*
Acts 8:17 · *297*
Acts 8:18–24 · *146*
Acts 8:19 · *297*
Acts 8:29–40 · *30*
Acts 8:32–35 · *24*
Acts 8:37 · *76-77*
Acts 9 · *144, 246, 255-256*
Acts 9–28 · *255*
Acts 9:2 · *144*
Acts 9:3 · *144*

Acts 9:11 · *297*
Acts 9:17 · *297*
Acts 9:30 · *246*
Acts 9:31 · *143, 297*
Acts 9:40 · *297*
Acts 10:9 · *297*
Acts 10:30 · *297*
Acts 10:38 · *297*
Acts 10:43 · *25*
Acts 10:43* · *373*
Acts 10:44–45 · *297*
Acts 10:47 · *297*
Acts 11:5 · *297*
Acts 11:14 · *206*
Acts 11:15–16 · *297*
Acts 11:24 · *297*
Acts 11:25–30 · *256*
Acts 11:26–28:31 · *99*
Acts 11:29–30 · *298*
Acts 12:1–2 · *256*
Acts 12:12 · *297*
Acts 13–28 · *142*
Acts 13:2 · *297*
Acts 13:2–14:28 · *256*
Acts 13:3 · *297*
Acts 13:4 · *297*
Acts 13:9 · *297*
Acts 13:13–50 · *365*
Acts 13:23 · *206*
Acts 13:26 · *206*
Acts 13:33 · *24*
Acts 13:34 · *24*
Acts 13:35 · *24*
Acts 13:39 · *25*
Acts 13:41 · *24*
Acts 13:47 · *24, 206*
Acts 13:52 · *297*
Acts 14:9 · *206*
Acts 14:23 · *297*
Acts 15 · *76-77, 256, 298, 355*
Acts 15:1 · *206*
Acts 15:3 · *143*
Acts 15:8 · *297*
Acts 15:11 · *206*
Acts 15:15 · *25*
Acts 15:15–18 · *25*
Acts 15:28 · *297*
Acts 15:28–29 · *355*
Acts 15:34 · *76-77*
Acts 15:40–18:23 · *256*
Acts 16:6 · *297*
Acts 16:13–14 · *402*

Acts 16:16 · *113*
Acts 16:17 · *206*
Acts 16:25 · *297*
Acts 16:30 · *206*
Acts 16:31 · *206*
Acts 17:1–9 · *298*
Acts 17:2–3 · *25*
Acts 17:4 · *298*
Acts 17:11 · *25*
Acts 17:15 · *353*
Acts 17:24 · *192*
Acts 17:28 · *276*
Acts 17:34 · *224*
Acts 18:9 · *92*
Acts 18:12–17 · *256*
Acts 18:13 · *25*
Acts 18:23–21:16 · *256*
Acts 18:24 · *25*
Acts 18:28 · *25*
Acts 19:2 · *297*
Acts 19:6 · *297*
Acts 19:23–27 · *273*
Acts 19:23–41 · *203*
Acts 20:23 · *30-31, 297*
Acts 20:28 · *297*
Acts 20:36 · *297*
Acts 21–26 · *365*
Acts 21:5 · *297*
Acts 21:11 · *30-31, 297*
Acts 21:17–26:32 · *256*
Acts 21:21 · *25*
Acts 21:24 · *25*
Acts 21:27–29* · *266*
Acts 21:28 · *25*
Acts 21:39 · *246*
Acts 22:3 · *25, 246*
Acts 23:5 · *25*
Acts 22:12 · *25*
Acts 22:17 · *297*
Acts 23:23 · *210*
Acts 23:23–26:32 · *328*
Acts 24:6 · *25*
Acts 24:6–8* · *81*
Acts 24:7 · *76-77*
Acts 24:14 · *25*
Acts 25:8 · *25*
Acts 25:8–12 · *210*
Acts 25:21 · *210*
Acts 26:18 · *31*
Acts 26:22 · *25*
Acts 26:23 · *155*
Acts 26:27 · *25*
Acts 26:32 · *210*

Acts 27–28 · *256*
Acts 27:20 · *206*
Acts 27:24 · *210*
Acts 27:31 · *206*
Acts 27:34 · *206*
Acts 28:8 · *297*
Acts 28:19 · *210*
Acts 28:23 · *25*
Acts 28:25 · *297*
Acts 28:25–27 · *25*
Acts 28:26–27 · *21, 224*
Acts 28:28 · *206*
Acts 28:29 · *76-77*
Additions to Esther · *255*
Amos · *7, 13, 24-25, 51, 53, 58, 254, 303-304*
Amos 5:20 · *303-304*
Amos 5:25–27 · *24*
Amos 7:1–9:1 · *13*
Amos 8:9 · *303-304*
Amos 9:11–12 · *25*

B

Baruch · *53, 255*
Bar 4:22 · *206*
Bel and the Dragon · *255*

C

Colossians · *52, 54, 59, 194, 203, 224, 240, 256, 283-284, 292, 294, 325, 366*
Col 1:9–12 · *32, 224*
Col 1:13–20 · *224*
Col 1:27 · *85, 274*
Col 2:2 · *85, 274*
Col 2:7 · *434*
Col 2:15 · *434*
Col 2:17 · *185, 194*
Col 2:20 · *274*
Col 2:20–23 · *224*
Col 3:1 · *22-23, 261, 415*
Col 3:1–4 · *23*
Col 3:5–17 · *224*
Col 3:10 · *415*
Col 3:18 · *261*
Col 3:18–4:1 · *224*
Col 4:5–6* · *400*
Col 4:10 · *353*
Col 4:16 · *56, 247*

D

Daniel · *18, 20, 23, 51-54, 217, 254-255*
Dan 4:12 · *302, 308*
Dan 7–12 · *54, 217*
Dan 7 · *18-21, 23, 303, 390*
Dan 7:13 · *18-21, 23, 303, 390*
Dan 7:13b · *303*
Dan 7:13–14 · *18-19*
Dan 7:14 · *19, 23*
Dan 9:27 · *303*
Dan 11:31 · *303*
Dan 12:11 · *303*
Dan 12:3a · *303*
Deuteronomy · *51, 53, 55, 217, 254, 294, 354, 356, 391, 412*
Deut 4:1 · *354*
Deut 4:1–2 · *354*
Deut 4:1–10 · *177*
Deut 4:6–8 · *383*
Deut 4:27–31 · *306*
Deut 4:36 · *316*
Deut 4:40 · *354*
Deut 4:44–46 · *354*
Deut 5:1 · *354*
Deut 5:16a · *303-304*
Deut 5:17 · *302-303*
Deut 5:17–20 · *303*
Deut 5:18 · *302*
Deut 6–8 · *14*
Deut 6:5 · *303, 350*
Deut 6:13 · *302*
Deut 6:16 · *302*
Deut 7:6 · *311*
Deut 8:3b · *302*
Deut 14:2 · *311*
Deut 18:15 · *24*
Deut 18:18 · *24*
Deut 18:19 · *24*
Deut 19:15b · *303*
Deut 19:21 · *302, 350*
Deut 23:21 · *302*
Deut 23:23 · *302*
Deut 24:1 · *302-304, 350*
Deut 24:3 · *302, 304*
Deut 25:4* · *315*
Deut 25:5 · *303*
Deut 28:1–14 · *356*
Deut 28:13 · *194*
Deut 28:36 · *306*

Deut 28:44 · *194*
Deut 28:49 · *306*
Deut 28:52 · *306*
Deut 29–30 · *306*
Deut 30:4 · *303*
Deut 30:6 · *380*
Deut 32:15 · *205*
Deut 32:43* · *317*
Deut 33:2 · *383*

E

Ecclesiastes · *36, 52-53, 55, 254*
Ecclesiasticus · *53, 255*
Ephesians · *52, 54, 70, 83, 88, 178, 193-194, 197, 201, 203-205, 208-209, 224, 237, 240, 248-249, 256, 281-286, 292, 294, 323, 325, 355, 364-366, 400, 425-426, 443*
Eph 1–3 · *83*
Eph 1:4 · *60, 285, 311*
Eph 1:4–5 · *60*
Eph 1:5 · *434*
Eph 1:5* · *400*
Eph 1:9–14* · *400*
Eph 1:13 · *199, 206, 373*
Eph 1:13–14* · *373*
Eph 1:14 · *311*
Eph 1:17–21 · *31*
Eph 1:18–23 · *22*
Eph 1:18a · *135*
Eph 1:19–21 · *248*
Eph 1:20 · *22*
Eph 1:20–23 · *194*
Eph 1:22 · *194*
Eph 1:22–23 · *204, 284*
Eph 2:1 · *32, 170, 177, 188, 195, 197, 220, 229, 241, 247, 250, 266, 276, 325, 348, 353, 355, 360, 389, 415*
Eph 2:1–10 · *204, 208, 284*
Eph 2:2 · *208*
Eph 2:2–3 · *178*
Eph 2:4–7 · *22*
Eph 2:5 · *204, 208, 284, 360*
Eph 2:5, 8 · *206*
Eph 2:6 · *22*
Eph 2:7 · *415*
Eph 2:10 · *32, 177, 195, 197, 204, 208, 276, 284, 415*
Eph 2:11–12* · *250*
Eph 2:11–13 · *248*
Eph 2:11–16 · *248*
Eph 2:11–20 · *178*
Eph 2:11–22 · *208, 220, 229, 241, 247, 249, 283, 325*
Eph 2:12 · *220*
Eph 2:13–14 · *197, 325*
Eph 2:13–16 · *355*
Eph 2:14 · *325*
Eph 2:14–18 · *204, 284*
Eph 2:14a · *248*
Eph 2:14b–16 · *248*
Eph 2:15 · *348, 353, 415*
Eph 2:17 · *248, 325*
Eph 2:17–18 · *170, 248, 389*
Eph 2:17–18* · *170, 389*
Eph 2:17–22 · *248*
Eph 2:18–22 · *220*
Eph 2:19–22 · *170, 188, 248*
Eph 2:19–22* · *170, 188*
Eph 2:20 · *171*
Eph 2:20–22 · *434*
Eph 3:10 · *366*
Eph 3:16–19 · *31*
Eph 3:21 · *88*
Eph 4:1–3 · *224*
Eph 4:1–16 · *249*
Eph 4:4 · *422*
Eph 4:4–5 · *224*
Eph 4:4–6 · *283*
Eph 4:8 · *10, 389, 434*
Eph 4:8–9 · *10*
Eph 4:11 · *9*
Eph 4:11–16 · *178*
Eph 4:13 · *197, 283*
Eph 4:15–16 · *204, 284*
Eph 4:16 · *422*
Eph 4:17 · *137*
Eph 4:17–19 · *224*
Eph 4:20–24 · *197, 224, 404*
Eph 4:23 · *31-32*
Eph 4:24 · *415*
Eph 4:25–32 · *224*
Eph 4:29 · *425, 443*
Eph 4:30 · *32*
Eph 4:31 · *219-220*
Eph 4:31* · *219-220*
Eph 4:7–11* · *317*
Eph 4:7–16 · *283*
Eph 5* · *32, 69, 146, 152, 155, 172, 204-206, 210, 261, 278-280, 282, 373, 400, 404, 423, 425-426, 428, 443*
Eph 5:1–2 · *69, 152, 172, 224, 404*
Eph 5:1–5 · *425*
Eph 5:1–6* · *146*
Eph 5:2 · *204, 284*
Eph 5:3–6 · *426*
Eph 5:3–9 · *224*
Eph 5:5 · *425, 428*
Eph 5:6 · *425, 428*
Eph 5:7 · *425-426, 443*
Eph 5:7–14 · *425, 427, 443*
Eph 5:7–8a* · *425, 428*
Eph 5:8 · *155, 373, 428*
Eph 5:8a · *425, 443*
Eph 5:8–10* · *373*
Eph 5:8b–10 · *425, 428*
Eph 5:8b–10* · *428*
Eph 5:11a* · *425, 428, 443*
Eph 5:11b* · *425, 428*
Eph 5:12 · *425, 428, 443*
Eph 5:12* · *425, 428*
Eph 5:13 · *425, 428*
Eph 5:13–14* · *428*
Eph 5:14 · *425, 428*
Eph 5:15–17* · *400*
Eph 5:15–18* · *400*
Eph 5:15–22 · *224*
Eph 5:17–22 · *32*
Eph 5:18* · *423*
Eph 5:18a* · *400*
Eph 5:21* · *423*
Eph 5:21–24* · *423*
Eph 5:21–33 · *195, 261, 282*
Eph 5:22—27 · *279*
Eph 5:22–24 · *204-205, 280*
Eph 5:22–24* · *423*
Eph 5:22–27 · *278, 280*
Eph 5:22–33 · *278, 280, 282*
Eph 5:23 · *204, 206, 210, 280, 282, 284-285*
Eph 5:23–24 · *210, 240, 282, 286*
Eph 5:23c · *240*
Eph 5:25 · *280*
Eph 5:25–27 · *280*
Eph 5:26 · *280, 284-285*
Eph 5:27 · *204, 282, 284-285*
Eph 5:28–30 · *280*
Eph 5:31–33 · *280*
Eph 5:33 · *204, 284*
Eph 6:2 · *64, 353*
Eph 6:10–20 · *199, 287*
Eph 6:12 · *434*
Eph 6:13–19 · *434*
Eph 6:17 · *206*
Eph 6:23–24 · *64*
Esther · *52-53, 55, 217, 254*
Exodus · *51, 53, 55, 217, 254, 257-258, 294, 316, 390, 412*
Exod 2:14 · *24*
Exod 3:5 · *24*
Exod 3:6 · *24, 303*
Exod 3:7 · *24*
Exod 3:8 · *24*
Exod 3:10 · *24*
Exod 3:15 · *303*
Exod 3:16 · *303*
Exod 4:22–23 · *302, 304*
Exod 19:5–6 · *311*
Exod 19:16 · *303*
Exod 20:12a · *303-304*
Exod 20:13 · *302-303, 350*
Exod 20:13–16 · *303*
Exod 20:14 · *302*
Exod 19:20 · *316*
Exod 20:22 · *316*
Exod 20:27 · *350*
Exod 21:17 · *303-304*
Exod 21:24 · *302, 350*
Exod 22:28 · *25*
Exod 24:8 · *316*
Exod 25:22 · *316*
Exod 32:1 · *24*
Exod 32:6 · *311*
Ezekiel · *13, 18, 51, 53, 254, 308, 326*
Ezek 1:1–2:10 · *13*
Ezek 2:1 · *18*
Ezek 2:3 · *18*
Ezek 2:6 · *18*
Ezek 2:8 · *18*
Ezek 16:8–14 · *284-285*
Ezek 16:10–14 · *284*
Ezek 17:23 · *302, 307-308*
Ezek 18:9 · *322*
Ezek 20:11 · *322*
Ezek 31:6 · *302, 308*
Ezek 32:7 · *303-304*
Ezek 34:11–16 · *311*
Ezek 34:23 · *311*

Ezek 37:26 · *380*
Ezra · *7, 26, 53-54, 58, 254*

G

Galatians · *52, 54, 56, 224, 256, 290, 294, 298, 322, 355, 365, 372, 414*
Gal 1:2 · *247*
Gal 1:11–2:21 · *409*
Gal 1:11–24 · *424*
Gal 1:13–14 · *224*
Gal 1:15–16 · *294*
Gal 1:15–2:14 · *224*
Gal 1:15–21 · *256*
Gal 1:18–19 · *256*
Gal 2 · *82, 113, 170, 298, 355, 414*
Gal 2:18 · *170*
Gal 2:19 · *170*
Gal 2:20 · *82, 170, 355, 414*
Gal 2:21 · *113*
Gal 3 · *312*
Gal 3:1 · *109, 245, 322, 383*
Gal 3:6 · *389*
Gal 3:6–14* · *312*
Gal 3:8 · *389, 411*
Gal 3:8–13 · *389*
Gal 3:11–12 · *109*
Gal 3:12 · *322*
Gal 3:14 · *389*
Gal 3:15 · *322*
Gal 3:16 · *389*
Gal 3:19 · *383*
Gal 3:28 · *224*
Gal 4:1 · *330, 434*
Gal 4:3 · *434*
Gal 4:9 · *372*
Gal 4:10 · *224*
Gal 4:14 · *330*
Gal 4:21–31 · *314*
Gal 4:22–24 · *389*
Gal 4:26 · *21, 155*
Gal 5:1 · *195*
Gal 5:1–21 · *355, 389, 448*
Gal 5:13 · *195*
Gal 5:16–18 · *222*
Gal 5:18 · *355*
Gal 5:19–21 · *222*
Gal 5:19–23 · *224*
Gal 5:21–22* · *222*
Gal 5:22 · *222*
Gal 5:22–23 · *355*

Gal 5:23 · *355*
Gal 5:23b · *222*
Gal 5:24 · *414*
Gal 5:25 · *222*
Gal 5:26 · *224*
Gal 5:31 · *389*
Gal 6:2 · *355*
Gal 6:2–3 · *389*
Gal 6:8 · *434*
Gal 6:9–10 · *32*
Gal 6:11–18 · *365*
Gal 6:13 · *355*
Gal 6:14 · *414*
Gal 6:15–16 · *415*
Gal 6:18 · *64*
Genesis · *12, 51, 53, 56, 254, 421*
Gen 1–11* · *429*
Gen 1:27 · *303, 316*
Gen 2:7 · *316*
Gen 2:21–23 · *316*
Gen 2:24 · *303*
Gen 3:1–7* · *379*
Gen 4:7 · *176*
Gen 5:1 · *255*
Gen 5:2 · *303*
Gen 12 · *24, 379, 411*
Gen 12:1 · *24, 379*
Gen 12:1–3 · *379*
Gen 12:3 · *411*
Gen 15:13–14 · *24*
Gen 22 · *12-13, 24, 302, 390*
Gen 22:2 · *12-13, 302*
Gen 22:12 · *13*
Gen 22:16 · *13*
Gen 22:18 · *24, 411*
Gen 26:4 · *411*
Gen 28:14 · *411*

H

Habakkuk · *51, 53, 254, 314*
Hab 1:5 · *24*
Hab 3:18 · *205*
Haggai · *51, 53, 254*
Hebrews · *52, 54-55, 83, 155, 217, 224, 256, 309-310, 317, 343*
Heb 1:2 · *56*
Heb 1:2–4 · *224*
Heb 1:3 · *10, 22-23*
Heb 1:5* · *317*
Heb 1:5–14 · *224*

Heb 1:5–14* · *317*
Heb 1:6* · *317*
Heb 1:7* · *317*
Heb 1:8–9* · *317*
Heb 1:10–12* · *317*
Heb 1:13 · *22, 317*
Heb 1:13* · *22, 317*
Heb 1:14 · *206*
Heb 2:2 · *317, 383*
Heb 2:2–3* · *317*
Heb 2:3 · *206*
Heb 2:3–4 · *224*
Heb 2:4 · *30*
Heb 2:6–8 · *224*
Heb 2:10 · *206*
Heb 2:14–15* · *373*
Heb 3:7–19 · *314*
Heb 5:6 · *22*
Heb 5:7 · *206*
Heb 5:9 · *206*
Heb 5:10 · *22*
Heb 5:12–14 · *32*
Heb 6:1–2 · *224*
Heb 6:20 · *22, 113*
Heb 6:4 · *31*
Heb 6:4–6 · *224*
Heb 6:9 · *206*
Heb 7:3 · *22*
Heb 7:5 · *353*
Heb 7:17 · *22*
Heb 7:18–19 · *353*
Heb 7:21 · *22*
Heb 7:25 · *206*
Heb 7:26 · *224*
Heb 8:1 · *22*
Heb 8:1–2 · *23*
Heb 8:8–12 · *21, 310*
Heb 8:10–11 · *224*
Heb 9:2 · *224*
Heb 9:11–22 · *316*
Heb 9:13–14* · *317*
Heb 9:19–10:1 · *353*
Heb 9:20 · *316*
Heb 9:28 · *206*
Heb 10 · *23, 310, 317, 380*
Heb 10:11–12 · *23*
Heb 10:12 · *22*
Heb 10:13 · *22*
Heb 10:15–18 · *310*
Heb 10:16 · *380*
Heb 10:19–25 · *224*
Heb 10:28–29* · *317*
Heb 10:29 · *224*

Heb 11 · *224, 310*
Heb 11:7 · *206*
Heb 12* · *21, 23, 123, 155, 203, 309-310, 317*
Heb 12–13* · *309*
Heb 12:1 · *23, 123*
Heb 12:2 · *22*
Heb 12:9* · *317*
Heb 12:18–24 · *224*
Heb 12:22 · *21, 155*
Heb 12:23* · *203*
Heb 12:25* · *317*
Heb 12:26–29 · *310*
Heb 12:29* · *309*
Heb 13 · *224*
Hosea · *51, 53, 254, 304*
Hos 2:23 · *380*
Hos 6:6 · *302*
Hos 11:1 · *304*
Hos 11:1a · *302*

I

Isaiah · *12-17, 19, 30, 51, 53-54, 85, 217, 248, 254-255, 268, 294-295, 299-301, 304, 306, 312, 314, 380, 391, 448*
Isa 2:5 · *155*
Isa 4:2 · *305*
Isa 5 · *15, 19, 24, 76, 155, 248, 268, 302-303, 311, 325, 389*
Isa 5:1–2 · *303, 311*
Isa 5:1–7 · *311, 314*
Isa 5:20 · *155*
Isa 6:1–13 · *13*
Isa 6:9–10 · *21, 25, 302*
Isa 7 · *299, 301-302*
Isa 7–9 · *301*
Isa 7:14 · *299-300, 302*
Isa 7:15–25 · *299*
Isa 8–9 · *299*
Isa 8:8 · *299*
Isa 8:10 · *299, 302*
Isa 8:14 · *75*
Isa 8:15 · *75*
Isa 8:18 · *299*
Isa 8:19 · *301*
Isa 9:1–2 · *302*
Isa 9:2 · *155*
Isa 9:2–6 · *155*
Isa 9:6–7 · *300, 302*
Isa 11:1 · *302, 305*
Isa 11:10 · *302, 305*

Isa 11:10b · *302*
Isa 12:2 · *205*
Isa 13:10 · *303-304*
Isa 17:10 · *205*
Isa 17:8 · *196*
Isa 19:3 · *301*
Isa 24:23 · *303-304*
Isa 27:13 · *303*
Isa 28:11–12 · *306*
Isa 29:4 · *301*
Isa 29:13 · *303*
Isa 29:15 · *426*
Isa 35:5–6a · *302*
Isa 40–55 · *380*
Isa 40:3 · *15, 294-295, 302*
Isa 40:11 · *311*
Isa 40:12–31 · *254*
Isa 42 · *12-14, 302, 380, 390, 411*
Isa 42:1 · *12-14, 302, 380, 390, 411*
Isa 42:1–3 · *12*
Isa 42:1–4 · *302*
Isa 42:1–6 · *380, 411*
Isa 42:6 · *13-14, 155, 411*
Isa 44:25 · *301*
Isa 45:1 · *254*
Isa 45:21 · *205*
Isa 47:9 · *301*
Isa 47:10 · *426*
Isa 47:12–13 · *301*
Isa 49:6 · *24, 155*
Isa 49:8* · *315*
Isa 52:7 · *325*
Isa 52:13–53:12 · *268*
Isa 53:4a · *302*
Isa 53:7–8 · *24*
Isa 53:12 · *76*
Isa 55:3 · *24*
Isa 56:7 · *15, 19, 303*
Isa 56:7a · *303*
Isa 57:9 · *325*
Isa 57:19 · *248, 389*
Isa 59:20–60:3 · *155*
Isa 61 · *15, 314*
Isa 61:1 · *302*
Isa 62:11 · *205-206, 303*
Isa 66 · *24, 76, 448*
Isa 66:1–2 · *24*
Isa 66:24 · *76*

J

James · *52, 54, 58-59, 65, 73, 224, 256, 269, 300, 343, 356, 384, 420, 428, 442*
Jas 1:11 · *224*
Jas 1:19 · *224*
Jas 1:21 · *206*
Jas 1:25 · *356*
Jas 2:1–4 · *224*
Jas 2:8 · 21 · *448*
Jas 2:14 · *206*
Jas 2:14–16 · *224*
Jas 3:1 · *420*
Jas 3:7–8 · *224*
Jas 3:9–10* · *269*
Jas 3:15–18 · *224*
Jas 4:1–10* · *384*
Jas 4:1–5:10 · *70*
Jas 4:4* · *428*
Jas 4:7–10 · *224*
Jas 4:12 · *206*
Jas 4:15 · *135*
Jas 5:1–6* · *269*
Jas 5:12 · *224*
Jas 5:15 · *206*
Jas 5:20 · *206*
Jdt 9:11 · 206
Jeremiah · *51, 53-54, 217, 254, 294, 306*
Jer 1:5 · *294*
Jer 3:1 · *302*
Jer 6:16b · *302*
Jer 7 · *19, 303*
Jer 7:11 · *19, 303*
Jer 7:11a · *303*
Jer 19:10–11 · *306*
Jer 19:1–4 · *306*
Jer 23:5 · *305*
Jer 31:15 · *302*
Jer 31:31–34 · *21, 310, 316, 380*
Jer 31:33–34 · *310*
Jer 32:6–10 · *306*
Jer 32:6–9 · *303*
Jer 32:40 · *380*
Jer 33:15 · *305*
Job · *7, 52-54, 58, 217, 254*
Joel · *7, 21, 24, 51, 53, 58, 254, 303-304, 317*
Joel 2:10 · *303-304*
Joel 2:28–32 · *21, 24*
Joel 2:32 · *317*
Joel 3:15 · *303-304*
John · *7, 10, 15, 17-18, 21-23, 29-32, 52, 54, 56, 58, 72, 75-77, 82-84, 88-89, 95, 97, 99, 112-113, 115-118, 133, 143, 145, 155, 159-162, 176, 179, 184, 192, 197, 206, 216, 220, 224-226, 247, 255-256, 258, 263, 294, 296-298, 311, 316, 321, 343, 353, 373, 376, 415, 448*
John 1:4–9 · *155*
John 1:33 · *297*
John 1:51 · *18, 58*
John 2:1–12 · *295*
John 2:13–25 · *294*
John 2:21 · *192*
John 3:13 · *18*
John 3:14 · *18*
John 3:15 · *119*
John 3:16 · *115-118, 159-161*
John 3:16* · *115-118, 159-161*
John 3:16–17* · *161*
John 3:17 · *159, 162, 206*
John 3:32–35 · *30*
John 4:1–2 · *295*
John 4:4 · *143*
John 4:4–42 · *295*
John 4:5 · *143*
John 4:7 · *143*
John 4:22 · *206*
John 4:42 · *206*
John 4:43–54 · *295*
John 5:1 · *294*
John 5:4 · *76-77*
John 5:27 · *18*
John 5:34 · *206*
John 6 · *295*
John 6:26–27* · *226*
John 6:35 · *225*
John 6:35* · *226*
John 6:39–40* · *373*
John 6:53 · *18*
John 6:62 · *18*
John 7:2–14 · *294*
John 7:16–18 · *30*
John 7:16–19* · *226*
John 7:23 · *316*
John 7:37–38* · *226*
John 7:53–8:11 · *75-77, 95*
John 8:12 · *155*
John 8:26–29 · *30*
John 8:28 · *18*
John 8:34–36* · *373*
John 8:42 · *225*
John 8:42–43 · *30*
John 8:58 · *113*
John 9:3–5* · *226*
John 9:5 · *155*
John 9:35 · *18*
John 10:1–21 · *311*
John 10:9 · *206*
John 10:18 · *353*
John 10:24–36 · *316*
John 10:27–30* · *373*
John 10:34–36* · *226*
John 11:3 · *113, 263*
John 11:12 · *206*
John 11:25–26* · *226*
John 11:35 · *263*
John 11:55–12:19 · *294*
John 11:57 · *348, 353*
John 11:9–10* · *226*
John 12:23 · *18*
John 12:27 · *206*
John 12:34 · *18, 22-23*
John 12:35–36 · *155*
John 12:36b–43 · *343*
John 12:39–41 · *21*
John 12:45 · *133*
John 12:47 · *206*
John 12:47–50 · *30*
John 12:49–50 · *353*
John 13–17 · *29*
John 13:14 · *84*
John 13:31 · *18, 58*
John 13:31–35 · *145*
John 13:34 · *353, 448*
John 14:15 · *353*
John 14:16 · *297*
John 14:17 · *30*
John 14:21 · *353*
John 14:26 · *29-30, 297*
John 14:26a · *29*
John 15:10 · *353*
John 15:12 · *353, 448*
John 15:14 · *353*
John 15:17 · *353, 448*
John 15:18–20 · *316*
John 15:26 · *30*
John 16:5–11 · *224*
John 16:8–9 · *32*
John 16:13 · *29*
John 16:26 · *297*

John 17:3* · *179*
John 17:9 · *297*
John 17:20 · *297*
John 17:22–23 · *376*
John 17:24 · *415*
John 18:4 · *30*
John 18:20 · *224*
John 19:20 · *224*
John 20:4–5 · *75*
John 20:14–18 · *10*
John 20:19–29 · *10*
John 20:22 · *297*
John 20:27 · *224*
John 20:31 · *56*
John 21 · *10, 29, 56*
John 21:15–17 · *224*
John 21:24–25 · *29*

Jonah · *7, 51, 53, 55, 58, 254, 302, 314*
Jonah 1:17 · *302*

Joshua · *51, 53, 254*
Jubilees · *322*

Jude · *7, 52, 54-55, 58, 70, 93, 206, 217, 224, 256, 294, 442*
Jude 2 · *224*
Jude 3 · *206*
Jude 5 · *206*
Jude 5–16 · *224*
Jude 19 · *224*
Jude 20–21 · *224*
Jude 22–23 · *224*
Jude 23 · *206*
Jude 25 · *206, 224*

Judges · *51, 53, 254*
Judg 3:9 · *205*
Judg 3:15 · *205*
Judg 12:3 · *205*
Judg 13:5 · *302, 305, 316*
Judg 13:5–7 · *302, 305*

Judith · *53, 255*

L

Lamentations · *52-53, 254*
Leviticus · *51, 53, 68, 152, 254, 316*
Lev 1:1 · *316*
Lev 11:44–45 · *426*
Lev 18:5 · *322*
Lev 19:10 · *399*
Lev 19:12a · *302*
Lev 19:18 · *21, 302-303, 322, 350, 353, 355*
Lev 19:18b · *302-303*
Lev 19:2 · *426*
Lev 20:6 · *301*
Lev 20:7 · *426*
Lev 20:9 · *303-304*
Lev 24:20 · *302, 350*
Lev 26:33 · *306*

Luke–Acts · *50, 53, 184, 186, 191, 297*
Luke · *7, 9-13, 15-18, 21-24, 26, 51-58, 65, 68, 74-75, 77, 80, 85-86, 95, 99, 113, 133, 135, 139, 143-144, 152, 155, 202-203, 206, 216, 224-228, 235, 255, 257-258, 263, 278, 280, 295-298, 307-308, 314, 316, 322, 343, 353, 373, 384, 388, 390, 413-414, 424, 426, 428, 433, 441, 448*
Luke 1–3 · *144*
Luke 1:6 · *353*
Luke 1:1–3 · *56*
Luke 1:1–4 · *68, 152*
Luke 1:10 · *297*
Luke 1:15 · *297*
Luke 1:33 · *19, 23*
Luke 1:35 · *297*
Luke 1:41 · *297*
Luke 1:46–55 · *15*
Luke 1:47 · *206*
Luke 1:50 · *12, 15*
Luke 1:67 · *297*
Luke 1:69 · *206*
Luke 1:71 · *206*
Luke 1:77 · *206*
Luke 2:2 · *12, 15, 135, 206, 257*
Luke 2:11 · *206*
Luke 2:20 · *206*
Luke 2:21–23 · *12*
Luke 2:21–24 · *15*
Luke 2:25–26 · *297*
Luke 2:27b · *135*
Luke 2:32 · *155*
Luke 2:39 · *12, 15*
Luke 2:41–42 · *12*
Luke 2:41–43 · *15*
Luke 2:46–47 · *26*
Luke 3:1–2* · *224, 258*
Luke 3:6 · *206*
Luke 3:7* · *133, 428*
Luke 3:7–18 · *224*
Luke 3:7–9 · *263*
Luke 3:8 · *17*
Luke 3:9 · *263*
Luke 3:16 · *297*
Luke 3:21 · *297*
Luke 3:21–22* · *296*
Luke 3:22 · *12, 297*
Luke 4:1 · *144, 297*
Luke 4:4 · *144*
Luke 4:8 · *144*
Luke 4:12 · *144*
Luke 4:14 · *144*
Luke 4:16–21 · *16, 225*
Luke 4:18 · *13, 16, 314*
Luke 4:18–21 · *314*
Luke 4:21 · *15*
Luke 5:16 · *297*
Luke 5:24 · *18*
Luke 5:30 · *426*
Luke 5:32 · *426*
Luke 6:1–6 · *314*
Luke 6:5 · *18*
Luke 6:9 · *206*
Luke 6:12 · *297*
Luke 6:20 · *16*
Luke 6:20–22 · *16*
Luke 6:20–26 · *224*
Luke 6:20–49 · *139*
Luke 6:22 · *18, 58*
Luke 6:24 · *16*
Luke 6:28 · *297*
Luke 6:32* · *226*
Luke 6:39 · *16*
Luke 7:17–23 · *16*
Luke 7:21–22 · *16*
Luke 7:22 · *16*
Luke 7:25 · *280*
Luke 7:27 · *16*
Luke 7:29–30 · *343*
Luke 7:31–32* · *226*
Luke 7:34 · *18*
Luke 7:35 · *426*
Luke 7:36–50 · *65*
Luke 7:50 · *206*
Luke 8:8 · *75*
Luke 8:10 · *21*
Luke 8:12 · *206*
Luke 8:18 · *225*
Luke 8:20 · *75*
Luke 8:36 · *206*
Luke 8:48 · *206*
Luke 8:50 · *206*
Luke 9 · *12, 144, 295, 390, 414*
Luke 9:18 · *297*
Luke 9:22 · *18, 298*
Luke 9:23 · *414*
Luke 9:23* · *226*
Luke 9:24 · *206*
Luke 9:26 · *18*
Luke 9:28 · *144*
Luke 9:28–29 · *297*
Luke 9:31* · *295*
Luke 9:35 · *12, 390*
Luke 9:44 · *18*
Luke 9:51* · *295*
Luke 9:53* · *295*
Luke 9:56 · *18*
Luke 9:58 · *18*
Luke 10:21 · *297*
Luke 10:27 · *21, 448*
Luke 10:28 · *322*
Luke 10:30–37 · *225-227*
Luke 11:1–2 · *297*
Luke 11:13 · *297, 316*
Luke 11:15 · *75*
Luke 11:19* · *226*
Luke 11:29–32 · *314*
Luke 11:30 · *18*
Luke 12:10 · *18, 297*
Luke 12:12 · *297*
Luke 12:13–15 · *225*
Luke 12:16–21 · *16*
Luke 12:24 · *316*
Luke 12:28 · *316*
Luke 12:40 · *18*
Luke 12:41–48* · *424*
Luke 12:8 · *18*
Luke 13:1–5 · *433*
Luke 13:17 · *280*
Luke 13:18 · *307*
Luke 13:18–19 · *307*
Luke 13:19 · *307-308*
Luke 13:19b · *308*
Luke 13:20 · *307*
Luke 13:22–25* · *295*
Luke 13:23 · *206*
Luke 13:33–35* · *295*
Luke 14:12–14 · *16*
Luke 14:21 · *16*
Luke 14:27 · *9, 414*
Luke 14:35 · *75*
Luke 15:1 · *227, 384, 426, 441*
Luke 15:1–2 · *426*
Luke 15:1–10* · *384*
Luke 15:11–32 · *227, 441*

Luke 15:5–7 · *448*
Luke 15:9–10 · *448*
Luke 15:20–24 · *448*
Luke 15:23–30 · *298*
Luke 15:29 · *348*
Luke 16:16 · *51*
Luke 16:18 · *413*
Luke 16:1–9 · *441*
Luke 16:19–26 · *16*
Luke 16:19–31* · *228*
Luke 16:20 · *16*
Luke 16:22 · *16*
Luke 16:25 · *113*
Luke 17:6 · *307*
Luke 17:11 · *143*
Luke 17:11* · *295*
Luke 17:19 · *206*
Luke 17:22 · *18*
Luke 17:24 · *18*
Luke 17:26 · *18*
Luke 17:30 · *18*
Luke 17:36 · *75, 77*
Luke 18:1 · *297*
Luke 18:8 · *18*
Luke 18:9–14 · *227*
Luke 18:10–11 · *297*
Luke 18:18–20 · *86*
Luke 18:19 · *85*
Luke 18:22 · *16*
Luke 18:26 · *206*
Luke 18:31 · *18*
Luke 18:31* · *295*
Luke 18:31–33 · *17*
Luke 18:35 · *16*
Luke 18:42 · *206*
Luke 19:8 · *16*
Luke 19:9 · *206*
Luke 19:10 · *18, 75, 206, 388*
Luke 19:11* · *295*
Luke 19:11–27 · *441*
Luke 19:28* · *295*
Luke 19:41 · *263, 448*
Luke 19:41–44 · *17, 263, 448*
Luke 19:41–45* · *295*
Luke 20:3–4 · *225*
Luke 20:13 · *13*
Luke 20:20–26 · *202*
Luke 20:23–35* · *278*
Luke 20:41–44* · *226*
Luke 20:42–43 · *22*
Luke 20:47 · *75, 297*

Luke 21 · *17, 19, 23, 255, 373, 448*
Luke 21:3 · *16*
Luke 21:10–28 · *224*
Luke 21:16–18* · *373*
Luke 21:20–24 · *263*
Luke 21:23 · *17, 263*
Luke 21:27 · *18, 23*
Luke 21:36 · *18*
Luke 22 · *139*
Luke 22:5 · *298*
Luke 22:20 · *74-75*
Luke 22:22 · *18*
Luke 22:25* · *203*
Luke 22:37 · *75*
Luke 22:39 · *21*
Luke 22:40–41 · *297*
Luke 22:43 · *75, 77*
Luke 22:43–44 · *77*
Luke 22:44 · *75, 77, 297*
Luke 22:46 · *297*
Luke 22:48 · *18*
Luke 22:69 · *18, 22, 390*
Luke 22:69–70 · *390*
Luke 23:1–4 · *224*
Luke 23:2* · *278*
Luke 23:17 · *75, 77*
Luke 23:25–35 · *298*
Luke 23:35 · *206*
Luke 23:37 · *206*
Luke 23:39 · *206*
Luke 23:56 · *348, 353*
Luke 24:1–12 · *10*
Luke 24:7 · *18*
Luke 24:12 · *74-75*
Luke 24:13–35 · *10*
Luke 24:15 · *144*
Luke 24:25 · *55*
Luke 24:32 · *11*
Luke 24:33–34 · *11*
Luke 24:35 · *11*
Luke 24:36–49 · *10*
Luke 24:40 · *74-75*
Luke 24:44 · *11-12, 52, 55*
Luke 24:44–49 · *12, 224*
Luke 24:45–49a · *11*
Luke 24:46 · *56, 448*
Luke 24:46–49 · *448*
Luke 24:50–53 · *10*
Luke 24:53 · *85*
Luke 28:21 · *298*

M

Malachi · *51, 53-54, 85, 217, 254, 295, 306*
Mal 3:1 · *15-16, 294-295, 302*
Mal 3:1a · *295, 302*
Mal 3:1b · *295*
Mal 4:5–6 · *303*
Mark · *7, 9, 12-13, 15, 18-23, 26, 52-54, 58, 60, 69-70, 75-77, 80, 83-86, 95, 99, 106-107, 113, 118, 143-144, 152, 184, 202, 206, 224-227, 235, 237, 255-256, 260, 266, 290, 294-298, 306-307, 311, 314, 325, 353, 390, 413-414, 435, 437, 441, 448*
Mark 1:2 · *15, 26, 85-86, 294-295, 306*
Mark 1:2–3 · *15, 85, 294-295, 306*
Mark 1:8 · *297*
Mark 1:9 · *143, 296*
Mark 1:9–11* · *296*
Mark 1:10 · *69, 152*
Mark 1:11 · *12, 390*
Mark 1:15 · *15*
Mark 1:35 · *297*
Mark 2:9–12* · *437*
Mark 2:10 · *18*
Mark 2:27 · *69, 152, 226, 237*
Mark 2:27* · *226*
Mark 2:28 · *18*
Mark 3:4 · *206*
Mark 3:13–19 · *224*
Mark 3:22 · *75*
Mark 3:29 · *297*
Mark 4:9 · *75*
Mark 4:12 · *21*
Mark 4:23 · *75*
Mark 4:26–29 · *227*
Mark 4:26–29* · *226*
Mark 4:30–32 · *307-308*
Mark 4:30–33 · *225*
Mark 4:35–5:20 · *438*
Mark 5:23 · *206*
Mark 5:25–27 · *224*
Mark 5:25–34 · *224*
Mark 5:28 · *206*
Mark 5:31–16:20 · *99*
Mark 5:33 · *224*

Mark 5:34 · *206*
Mark 6:4 · *13*
Mark 6:7–32 · *69, 152*
Mark 6:14–29 · *256*
Mark 6:15 · *13*
Mark 6:29 · *85*
Mark 6:33–44* · *435*
Mark 6:40* · *435*
Mark 6:42–44* · *435*
Mark 6:46 · *297*
Mark 6:56 · *206*
Mark 7:16 · *75-76*
Mark 7:21–22 · *224*
Mark 8:28 · *13*
Mark 8:30–34 · *224*
Mark 8:31 · *12, 18*
Mark 8:34 · *414*
Mark 8:35 · *206*
Mark 8:38 · *18*
Mark 9:7 · *12*
Mark 9:9 · *18, 58*
Mark 9:12 · *18*
Mark 9:17 · *107*
Mark 9:29 · *75*
Mark 9:30 · *18*
Mark 9:31 · *18, 224*
Mark 9:35 · *225*
Mark 9:35–37 · *225*
Mark 9:44 · *75-76*
Mark 9:46 · *75-76*
Mark 9:48 · *75*
Mark 9:50 · *225*
Mark 10:2–12 · *413*
Mark 10:17–19 · *86*
Mark 10:17–31 · *107*
Mark 10:18 · *85*
Mark 10:25* · *260*
Mark 10:26 · *206*
Mark 10:33 · *18*
Mark 10:33–34 · *18, 224*
Mark 10:45 · *18*
Mark 10:52 · *206*
Mark 11–12 · *20*
Mark 11:12–14 · *19*
Mark 11:15a · *19*
Mark 11:15b–16 · *19*
Mark 11:16–18* · *266*
Mark 11:17 · *19-20, 295*
Mark 11:17d · *19, 295*
Mark 11:18 · *19-20*
Mark 11:19 · *19*
Mark 11:20–25 · *19*
Mark 11:24–25 · *297*

Mark 11:26 · *75-76*
Mark 12:1 · *20*
Mark 12:1–10* · *226*
Mark 12:1–12 · *311, 314, 441*
Mark 12:10 · *437*
Mark 12:11–12 · *20*
Mark 12:13–17 · *202*
Mark 12:14 · *107*
Mark 12:19 · *107*
Mark 12:24 · *74-75*
Mark 12:24–26 · *20*
Mark 12:27 · *84*
Mark 12:29–31 · *20*
Mark 12:31 · *21, 448*
Mark 12:32 · *107*
Mark 12:33 · *21*
Mark 12:34 · *19-20*
Mark 12:35 · *20-21*
Mark 12:35–37 · *20*
Mark 12:36 · *22, 297*
Mark 12:40 · *75, 297*
Mark 13 · *19, 23, 255, 353, 448*
Mark 13:11 · *297*
Mark 13:13 · *206*
Mark 13:18 · *297*
Mark 13:20 · *206*
Mark 13:26 · *18, 23*
Mark 13:32 · *448*
Mark 13:34 · *353*
Mark 14:21 · *18*
Mark 14:24 · *75*
Mark 14:25 · *113*
Mark 14:32 · *297*
Mark 14:35 · *297*
Mark 14:38–39 · *297*
Mark 14:41 · *18*
Mark 14:43 · *113*
Mark 14:61–62 · *20-21*
Mark 14:61–64 · *21*
Mark 14:62 · *18, 22-23, 390*
Mark 14:65 · *84*
Mark 15 · *23, 60, 75-76, 144*
Mark 15:1 · *144*
Mark 15:2 · *144*
Mark 15:4 · *144*
Mark 15:5 · *144*
Mark 15:6 · *75*
Mark 15:9 · *144*
Mark 15:12 · *144*
Mark 15:14 · *144*
Mark 15:15 · *144*

Mark 15:28 · *75-76*
Mark 15:30 · *206*
Mark 15:31 · *206*
Mark 15:34 · *23*
Mark 15:38 · *69, 152*
Mark 15:39 · *60*
Mark 16:1–8 · *9*
Mark 16:8 · *206*
Mark 16:9 · *75, 77, 86, 95*
Mark 16:9–20 · *75, 77, 95*
Mark 16:16 · *206*
Mark 16:19 · *22*
Matthew · *12, 15-16, 52-54, 58, 77, 80, 86, 99, 106-107, 143, 255-256, 274, 290, 295, 297, 302-305, 321, 348, 350, 353-354, 356*
Matt 1–13 · *356*
Matt 1:1–17* · *70*
Matt 1:16 · *143*
Matt 1:18 · *143, 297*
Matt 1:20 · *297*
Matt 1:21 · *206*
Matt 1:22–23 · *299, 302, 304*
Matt 2:5–6 · *302, 304*
Matt 2:11 · *134*
Matt 2:15 · *302, 304*
Matt 2:17–18 · *302*
Matt 2:23 · *302, 305*
Matt 3:2 · *15, 307*
Matt 3:3 · *302*
Matt 3:11 · *297*
Matt 3:13 · *69, 152, 296*
Matt 3:13–17* · *296*
Matt 3:17 · *12, 302, 390*
Matt 4:4 · *302*
Matt 4:6 · *302, 350*
Matt 4:7 · *302*
Matt 4:10 · *302*
Matt 4:10* · *226*
Matt 4:1–11* · *304*
Matt 4:15–16 · *302*
Matt 4:16 · *155*
Matt 4:17 · *15, 224, 401*
Matt 4:17–22 · *224*
Matt 4:18–22* · *424*
Matt 4:23 · *348*
Matt 5–7 · *70, 224, 343, 408*
Matt 5:1 · *350*
Matt 5:1b · *134*
Matt 5:2 · *348, 350*
Matt 5:3 · *222-223*

Matt 5:3* · *32, 62, 119, 221-222, 304, 413*
Matt 5:3–9 · *223*
Matt 5:3–10 · *223*
Matt 5:3–12 · *62, 222*
Matt 5:3–12* · *62, 222*
Matt 5:3–16 · *32*
Matt 5:7* · *128*
Matt 5:9 · *223*
Matt 5:10 · *222-223*
Matt 5:10–12 · *223*
Matt 5:10–16 · *426*
Matt 5:11 · *223*
Matt 5:11–12 · *223*
Matt 5:12 · *223*
Matt 5:13 · *154*
Matt 5:13–16* · *153-154*
Matt 5:14 · *155*
Matt 5:14–15 · *154*
Matt 5:14–16 · *426*
Matt 5:16 · *154-155*
Matt 5:16* · *373*
Matt 5:17 · *16, 51, 302, 314, 348, 350, 352, 354*
Matt 5:17–18 · *348*
Matt 5:17–19 · *354*
Matt 5:17–20 · *348, 356*
Matt 5:17–48 · *314*
Matt 5:18 · *348, 350, 352, 354, 356*
Matt 5:19 · *123, 343-344, 347-348, 350, 352, 354, 356*
Matt 5:19* · *123, 343-344, 347-348*
Matt 5:19–20 · *343-344*
Matt 5:20 · *348, 350, 356*
Matt 5:21 · *302, 350*
Matt 5:21–23 · *356*
Matt 5:21–43 · *352*
Matt 5:21–48 · *348, 350, 356*
Matt 5:22 · *350*
Matt 5:22* · *428*
Matt 5:26 · *350*
Matt 5:27 · *302, 350*
Matt 5:29* · *226*
Matt 5:31 · *302, 304, 350, 413*
Matt 5:31–32 · *413*
Matt 5:32 · *350*
Matt 5:33 · *302, 350*
Matt 5:34 · *350*
Matt 5:38 · *302, 350*

Matt 5:39 · *350*
Matt 5:43 · *21, 302, 350*
Matt 5:44 · *76, 297, 350*
Matt 5:48 · *340, 404*
Matt 6:1 · *348*
Matt 6:2 · *350*
Matt 6:5 · *350*
Matt 6:5–7 · *297*
Matt 6:9 · *297*
Matt 6:13 · *85*
Matt 6:15 · *75*
Matt 6:16 · *350*
Matt 6:21 · *225*
Matt 6:25 · *350*
Matt 6:25–34* · *180*
Matt 6:26 · *316*
Matt 6:29 · *310, 350*
Matt 6:30 · *316*
Matt 6:33–34 · *348*
Matt 7:3–5 · *225*
Matt 7:11 · *316*
Matt 7:12 · *16, 51, 348, 350*
Matt 7:23 · *302*
Matt 7:24–27 · *350*
Matt 7:28–29 · *348, 350*
Matt 7:29 · *348*
Matt 8:2 · *107*
Matt 8:6 · *107*
Matt 8:8 · *107*
Matt 8:16–17* · *298*
Matt 8:17 · *302*
Matt 8:19 · *107*
Matt 8:20 · *18*
Matt 8:25 · *107, 206*
Matt 9:6 · *18*
Matt 9:13 · *302*
Matt 9:21 · *206*
Matt 9:22 · *206*
Matt 9:28 · *107*
Matt 9:34 · *74-75*
Matt 9:35 · *348*
Matt 10 · *408*
Matt 10:5 · *134, 409*
Matt 10:5–42 · *409*
Matt 10:11 · *401*
Matt 10:21–22 · *305*
Matt 10:22 · *135, 206*
Matt 10:23 · *18*
Matt 10:25 · *316*
Matt 10:29–31* · *373*
Matt 10:35 · *305-306*
Matt 10:35–36 · *302, 305*
Matt 10:38 · *9, 414*

Matt 11:1 · *348*
Matt 11:10 · *302*
Matt 11:13 · *51*
Matt 11:19 · *18*
Matt 11:21 · *58*
Matt 11:29 · *302*
Matt 11:5 · *302*
Matt 12:1–8* · *298, 348*
Matt 12:6 · *55*
Matt 12:7 · *302*
Matt 12:8 · *18*
Matt 12:12 · *316*
Matt 12:15–21 · *13*
Matt 12:17–21 · *302, 305*
Matt 12:18 · *12, 390*
Matt 12:18–21 · *12*
Matt 12:32 · *18, 113, 297*
Matt 12:38 · *107*
Matt 12:40 · *18, 302*
Matt 12:41 · *55*
Matt 12:42 · *55*
Matt 12:47 · *75*
Matt 13 · *16-17, 21, 75, 81, 224-227, 241, 307-308, 408, 424, 433, 441, 448*
Matt 13:3–9 · *225*
Matt 13:9 · *75*
Matt 13:10 · *17*
Matt 13:10–17 · *16*
Matt 13:13* · *81, 433, 441*
Matt 13:13–15 · *433*
Matt 13:14 · *16, 21*
Matt 13:14–15 · *16, 21, 302*
Matt 13:15* · *81*
Matt 13:16 · *17*
Matt 13:18–23 · *226*
Matt 13:24 · *241, 307, 424*
Matt 13:24–30* · *241, 424*
Matt 13:31 · *307*
Matt 13:31–32 · *308*
Matt 13:31–33 · *307*
Matt 13:32 · *302, 307*
Matt 13:35 · *16, 302, 348*
Matt 13:36–43 · *226*
Matt 13:37 · *18*
Matt 13:41 · *18*
Matt 13:43 · *75, 303*
Matt 13:44–46 · *227*
Matt 13:49–50 · *226*
Matt 13:54 · *348*
Matt 14 · *144*
Matt 14:1 · *144*
Matt 14:3 · *144*

Matt 14:23 · *297*
Matt 14:28 · *107*
Matt 14:30 · *206*
Matt 14:6a · *144*
Matt 14:6b · *144*
Matt 15:1–14 · *348*
Matt 15:3 · *348*
Matt 15:3–4 · *350*
Matt 15:4 · *303-304*
Matt 15:7–9 · *303*
Matt 15:19 · *224*
Matt 15:22 · *107*
Matt 15:25 · *107*
Matt 15:26 · *432*
Matt 15:27 · *107, 432*
Matt 15:28 · *145*
Matt 16:12–20* · *438*
Matt 16:13 · *18*
Matt 16:13–20* · *438*
Matt 16:13–21* · *298*
Matt 16:19 · *348*
Matt 16:22 · *107*
Matt 16:24 · *9, 414*
Matt 16:25 · *206*
Matt 16:25* · *226*
Matt 16:27 · *18, 303-304*
Matt 16:28 · *18*
Matt 17:4 · *107*
Matt 17:5 · *12, 390*
Matt 17:9 · *18, 58, 350*
Matt 17:10–11 · *303*
Matt 17:12 · *18*
Matt 17:15 · *107, 302*
Matt 17:20* · *226*
Matt 17:21 · *75-76*
Matt 17:22 · *18*
Matt 17:24 · *107*
Matt 18 · *408*
Matt 18:2–4 · *432*
Matt 18:11 · *18, 75-76*
Matt 18:15 · *426*
Matt 18:16 · *303*
Matt 18:18 · *348*
Matt 18:21 · *107*
Matt 18:21–35 · *227*
Matt 18:35 · *75*
Matt 19:3–6* · *414*
Matt 19:3–8* · *413*
Matt 19:3–9 · *413*
Matt 19:4–5 · *303*
Matt 19:7 · *303, 350*
Matt 19:13 · *297*
Matt 19:16 · *107*

Matt 19:16–18 · *86*
Matt 19:16–22 · *348*
Matt 19:17 · *85, 348, 350*
Matt 19:17–19 · *350*
Matt 19:18–19 · *303*
Matt 19:19 · *21, 448*
Matt 19:20–21 · *348*
Matt 19:22 · *135*
Matt 19:25 · *206*
Matt 19:28 · *18, 415*
Matt 20:18 · *18*
Matt 20:30 · *107*
Matt 21:4–5 · *303*
Matt 21:9 · *303*
Matt 21:13 · *303*
Matt 21:16 · *303*
Matt 21:23 · *348*
Matt 21:28–31* · *226*
Matt 21:33 · *303*
Matt 21:42 · *303*
Matt 21:44 · *75*
Matt 22:15–22 · *202*
Matt 22:16 · *107, 348*
Matt 22:19–21* · *226*
Matt 22:24 · *107, 303*
Matt 22:31–32 · *303*
Matt 22:36 · *107*
Matt 22:36–40 · *348, 350, 356*
Matt 22:37 · *303*
Matt 22:39 · *303*
Matt 22:40 · *51, 348*
Matt 22:41–46 · *268*
Matt 22:43–44 · *303*
Matt 22:44 · *22*
Matt 23–25 · *224, 408*
Matt 23:14 · *75-76, 95*
Matt 23:23 · *348*
Matt 23:27* · *428*
Matt 23:34–35 · *55*
Matt 23:35 · *52*
Matt 23:39 · *303*
Matt 24 · *19, 23, 75, 255, 304, 343, 448*
Matt 24:13 · *206*
Matt 24:15 · *303*
Matt 24:20 · *297*
Matt 24:22 · *206*
Matt 24:27 · *18*
Matt 24:29 · *303*
Matt 24:29–30 · *304*
Matt 24:30 · *18, 23, 303*
Matt 24:31 · *303*

Matt 24:36–39 · *448*
Matt 24:37 · *18*
Matt 24:39 · *18*
Matt 24:40 · *75*
Matt 24:42 · *448*
Matt 24:44 · *18*
Matt 24:45–51 · *448*
Matt 25 · *448*
Matt 25:31 · *18*
Matt 25:34–39 · *448*
Matt 25:46 · *448*
Matt 26:2 · *18*
Matt 26:22 · *107*
Matt 26:24 · *18, 302-303*
Matt 26:25 · *107*
Matt 26:29 · *75*
Matt 26:31 · *303*
Matt 26:36 · *297*
Matt 26:39 · *297*
Matt 26:41–42 · *297*
Matt 26:44 · *297*
Matt 26:45 · *18*
Matt 26:49 · *107*
Matt 26:54–56 · *302-303*
Matt 26:55 · *348*
Matt 26:64 · *18, 22-23, 303, 390*
Matt 27:9 · *306*
Matt 27:9–10 · *303*
Matt 27:15 · *75*
Matt 27:40 · *206*
Matt 27:42 · *206*
Matt 27:43 · *303*
Matt 27:46 · *23, 303*
Matt 27:49 · *206*
Matt 28:9 · *143*
Matt 28:10 · *143*
Matt 28:1–15 · *9*
Matt 28:16 · *143*
Matt 28:16–20 · *9*
Matt 28:18 · *9, 19, 21, 23, 68, 143, 152, 350*
Matt 28:18–20 · *9, 21, 68, 152, 224*
Matt 28:19 · *297*
Matt 28:19–20 · *350*
Matt 28:20 · *348, 350*
Micah · *51, 53, 205, 254, 302, 304-306, 325*
Micah 5:2 · *302*
Micah 5:5 · *325*
Micah 7:6 · *302, 305-306*
Micah 7:6–7 · *305*

N

Micah 7:7 · *205*
Micah 7:9 · *306*
Micah 7:18 · *306*

Nahum · *51, 53, 254, 314*
Nehemiah · *26, 53-54, 217, 254*
  Neh 8 · *26*
  Neh 8:2–3 · *26*
  Neh 8:4–5 · *26*
  Neh 8:6 · *26*
  Neh 8:7–8 · *26*
  Neh 8:9 · *26*
  Neh 8:10 · *26*
  Neh 8:13 · *26*
  Neh 9:29 · *322*
  Neh 9:6* · *317*
Numbers · *51, 53, 254*
  Num 7:89 · *316*
  Num 21:14 · *255*
  Num 30:2 · *302*

O

Obadiah · *51, 53, 254*
Odes Sol. 2:15 · 206
Odes Sol. 4:18 · 206
Odes Sol. 9:47 · 206

P

Philippians · *52, 54, 59, 206, 224, 256, 439-440*
  Phil 1:13–14 · *440*
  Phil 1:16 · *316*
  Phil 1:19 · *206*
  Phil 1:28 · *206*
  Phil 2:1–2 · *224*
  Phil 2:7 · *434*
  Phil 2:8 · *434*
  Phil 2:12 · *206, 316*
  Phil 2:15 · *426*
  Phil 3:1–16 · *224*
  Phil 3:20 · *206*
  Phil 4:8–9* · *424*
  Phil 4:20–23 · *64*
Philemon · *52, 54, 70, 201, 224, 235, 242, 247, 256, 325*
  Phlm 1–2 · *224*
  Phlm 22–23 · *224*
Proverbs · *52-55, 217-218, 254*

Prov 11:13 · *426*
Prov 20:19 · *426*
Prov 22:6 · *409*
Prov 24:12 · *303-304*
Psalms · *11, 52-55, 217, 254, 294, 312, 314, 321, 391*
  Ps 02 · *12-13, 23-24, 205, 302-304, 317, 390*
  Ps 2:7 · *12-13, 24, 302, 317*
  Ps 2:7* · *12-13, 24, 302, 317*
  Ps 2:8 · *13*
  Ps 6:8a · *302*
  Ps 8:2 · *303*
  Ps 8:3 · *303*
  Ps 16:10 · *24*
  Ps 16:8–11 · *24, 316*
  Ps 22:1 · *23, 303*
  Ps 22:24 · *23*
  Ps 22:8 · *303*
  Ps 23:5 · *205*
  Ps 24:5 · *205*
  Ps 26:1 · *205*
  Ps 26:9 · *205*
  Ps 28:4 · *303-304*
  Ps 34:12–16 · *21*
  Ps 45:6–7* · *317*
  Ps 61:3 · *205*
  Ps 61:7 · *205*
  Ps 62:12 · *303-304*
  Ps 64:6 · *205*
  Ps 69:25 · *24*
  Ps 78:2 · *16, 302*
  Ps 78:9 · *205*
  Ps 91:11–12 · *302, 350*
  Ps 94:1 · *205*
  Ps 95:7–11 · *314*
  Ps 97:7* · *317*
  Ps 102:25–27* · *317*
  Ps 103:17 · *15*
  Ps 103:31 · *196*
  Ps 104 · *254*
  Ps 104:4* · *317*
  Ps 104:12 · *302, 308*
  Ps 109:8 · *24*
  Ps 110:1* · *18, 20-22, 24, 303, 316-317, 390*
  Ps 110:1a · *303*
  Ps 110:4 · *22*
  Ps 112:9 · *89*
  Ps 118:22 · *24, 303, 437*
  Ps 118:22–23 · *303*
  Ps 118:26 · *303*
  Ps 118:26a · *303*

Ps 136 · *254*
Ps 151 · *255*
Pss. Sol. 3:6 · 206
Pss. Sol. 8:33 · 206
Pss. Sol. 16:4 · 206
Pss. Sol. 17:3 · 206

R

Revelation · *19, 23, 30, 52, 54, 79, 99, 184, 192, 217, 223-224, 255-256, 273, 290, 353, 371, 382, 421, 448*
  Rev 1:4–6 · *224*
  Rev 1:4–6* · *241*
  Rev 1:7 · *19, 23*
  Rev 1:8 · *224*
  Rev 1:8–3:22* · *70*
  Rev 1:9 · *224*
  Rev 1:9–20 · *19*
  Rev 1:11 · *224*
  Rev 1:12–16 · *224*
  Rev 1:13 · *19, 23*
  Rev 1:19 · *224*
  Rev 2–3 · *224*
  Rev 2:7 · *75*
  Rev 2:8–11* · *424*
  Rev 2:11 · *75*
  Rev 2:17 · *75*
  Rev 2:29 · *75*
  Rev 3:6 · *75*
  Rev 3:12 · *21*
  Rev 3:13 · *75*
  Rev 3:22 · *75*
  Rev 4:5–7 · *224*
  Rev 4:9 · *224*
  Rev 4:11 · *224*
  Rev 05 · *10, 19*
  Rev 5:11–13 · *224*
  Rev 5:12 · *19*
  Rev 5:5–6 · *10*
  Rev 5:6–7 · *19*
  Rev 7:10 · *206*
  Rev 9:1–12* · *241*
  Rev 9:21 · *224*
  Rev 10:11 · *19, 23*
  Rev 11:11 · *113*
  Rev 11:15 · *19, 23*
  Rev 12:10 · *206*
  Rev 12:17 · *353*
  Rev 13:9 · *75*
  Rev 14:12 · *353*
  Rev 14:14 · *19, 23*

Rev 18:1–3* · *424*
Rev 19:1 · *206*
Rev 19:6 · *19, 23*
Rev 19:8* · *179*
Rev 20:1–22:5 · *448*
Rev 21:2 · *21*
Rev 21:7 · *380*
Rev 21:8 · *224*
Rev 21:9–10 · *155*
Rev 21:10 · *21*
Rev 21:22 · *192*
Rev 21–22 · *415*
Rev 22:10–21 · *448*
Rev 22:15 · *224*
Romans · *6, 52, 54, 56, 59, 83, 97, 121, 149, 168-169, 209, 224, 230, 247, 256, 276-277, 290, 294, 324, 380*
  Rom 1 · *6, 97, 224, 230, 277*
  Rom 1:2 · *113, 312, 389, 411, 426*
  Rom 1:5 · *203*
  Rom 1:11 · *113*
  Rom 1:13 · *203*
  Rom 1:16 · *68, 152, 206*
  Rom 1:17 · *389*
  Rom 1:20 · *312, 411*
  Rom 1:20–32 · *312*
  Rom 1:21 · *113*
  Rom 1:21–22 · *113*
  Rom 1:25 · *113*
  Rom 1:27 · *113*
  Rom 1:28 · *113*
  Rom 1:29–30 · *426*
  Rom 1:29–31 · *224*
  Rom 2:8 · *113*
  Rom 2:14–16* · *324*
  Rom 2:17–19 · *113*
  Rom 2:19 · *113*
  Rom 2:25–29 · *355*
  Rom 3:1–19 · *170*
  Rom 3:2 · *125*
  Rom 3:9–10* · *373*
  Rom 3:9–20 · *224, 316*
  Rom 3:9b · *125*
  Rom 3:10–12 · *389*
  Rom 3:21–23 · *168*
  Rom 3:25 · *434*
  Rom 3:27 · *125*
  Rom 3:29 · *125*
  Rom 4:3 · *389*
  Rom 4:6 · *113, 389*
  Rom 4:6–7 · *389*

Rom 4:16 · *113*
Rom 4:17–18 · *389*
Rom 5:1 · *84, 111, 113, 131, 163-165, 389*
Rom 5:1–2* · *131*
Rom 5:2 · *109, 113*
Rom 5:3–5 · *224*
Rom 5:5 · *434*
Rom 5:6–7 · *112*
Rom 5:6–7* · *112*
Rom 5:7 · *109*
Rom 5:8–10 · *131*
Rom 5:8–9 · *316*
Rom 5:9 · *206*
Rom 5:10 · *206, 316*
Rom 5:10* · *163-165*
Rom 5:10–11* · *163-165*
Rom 5:11* · *111, 163*
Rom 5:12–14 · *389*
Rom 5:14 · *113*
Rom 5:15 · *113, 316*
Rom 5:17 · *316*
Rom 5:18 · *113*
Rom 5:21 · *113*
Rom 6 · *121*
Rom 6:1–2 · *125*
Rom 6:6 · *414*
Rom 6:13* · *373*
Rom 6:14 · *355*
Rom 6:15–16 · *125*
Rom 6:19 · *434*
Rom 7:8–13 · *353*
Rom 7:12 · *224, 416*
Rom 8 · *22, 324, 355, 373, 389, 415, 434*
Rom 8:1–5 · *355*
Rom 8:1–17* · *373*
Rom 8:2 · *355, 373*
Rom 8:15–16* · *373*
Rom 8:17 · *434*
Rom 8:18–25 · *415*
Rom 8:21 · *434*
Rom 8:24 · *206, 434*
Rom 8:28* · *373*
Rom 8:28–30 · *224*
Rom 8:31–39 · *224*
Rom 8:33* · *324*
Rom 8:34 · *22*
Rom 8:36 · *389*
Rom 9–11 · *7, 70, 312*
Rom 9:3–5 · *224*
Rom 9:6* · *324*
Rom 9:7 · *389*
Rom 9:9 · *389*
Rom 9:10–12 · *389*
Rom 9:12–13 · *389*
Rom 9:15 · *389*
Rom 9:16 · *113*
Rom 9:17 · *389*
Rom 9:20 · *389*
Rom 9:21 · *312*
Rom 9:25 · *113, 389*
Rom 9:25–27 · *389*
Rom 9:25–29 · *389*
Rom 9:25–9 · *312*
Rom 9:27 · *206*
Rom 9:33 · *389*
Rom 10:1 · *206*
Rom 10:4 · *355*
Rom 10:4–6 · *389*
Rom 10:5 · *322*
Rom 10:5–7 · *389*
Rom 10:9 · *206*
Rom 10:10 · *206*
Rom 10:11–13 · *389*
Rom 10:13 · *206, 317*
Rom 10:14 · *389*
Rom 10:16 · *389*
Rom 10:16–18 · *389*
Rom 10:18 · *389*
Rom 10:18–21 · *389*
Rom 11:1 · *224*
Rom 11:3–4 · *389*
Rom 11:4–5 · *389*
Rom 11:8 · *21*
Rom 11:8–10 · *389*
Rom 11:11 · *206*
Rom 11:12 · *316*
Rom 11:13 · *203*
Rom 11:14 · *206*
Rom 11:17 · *434*
Rom 11:24 · *316*
Rom 11:24–25 · *389*
Rom 11:26 · *206, 389*
Rom 11:26–27 · *389*
Rom 11:30–31 · *113*
Rom 12:1 · *6, 97*
Rom 12:1–2 · *32, 97-98, 224, 404*
Rom 12:1–8 · *6, 97*
Rom 12:2 · *6, 97*
Rom 12:3–8 · *224*
Rom 12:4–5 · *422*
Rom 12:6 · *138*
Rom 12:9–21 · *224*
Rom 12:9–21* · *241*
Rom 12:19 · *21, 389*
Rom 13:8 · *389*
Rom 13:8–10 · *355*
Rom 13:9 · *21, 224, 353, 389, 448*
Rom 13:11 · *206*
Rom 13:12 · *155*
Rom 13:13 · *224*
Rom 14:1–3 · *389*
Rom 14:7–9* · *373*
Rom 14:11 · *389*
Rom 15:3 · *389*
Rom 15:7–13* · *424*
Rom 15:8–13 · *224*
Rom 15:8–19 · *203*
Rom 15:9–11 · *389*
Rom 15:12 · *302*
Rom 15:21 · *389*
Rom 16 · *224*
Rom 16:16* · *402*
Rom 16:20–27 · *64*
Rom 16:24 · *76-77*
Ruth · *7, 52-53, 55, 58, 217, 254*

S

Sirach · *312*
  Sir 35:19 · *304*
  Sir 39:14 · *196*
  Sir 51:1 · *206*
Song of Songs · *52-53*
Susanna · *255*

T

The Letter of Jeremiah · *255*
The Prayer of Azariah · *255*
The Prayer of Manasseh · *255*
Titus · *7, 32, 52, 54, 58, 206-208, 224, 256, 353, 373, 434*
  Titus 1:3 · *206-207*
  Titus 1:4 · *206-207*
  Titus 1:5–16 · *224*
  Titus 1:9 · *434*
  Titus 1:13 · *434*
  Titus 1:14 · *353*
  Titus 2:1 · *434*
  Titus 2:1–10 · *224*
  Titus 2:10 · *206-207*
  Titus 2:11 · *32, 206*
  Titus 2:11–14 · *32*
  Titus 2:12 · *224*
  Titus 2:13 · *206-207*
  Titus 2:14* · *373*
  Titus 2:15 · *224*
  Titus 3:1–3 · *224*
  Titus 3:4 · *206-207*
  Titus 3:5 · *32, 206*
  Titus 3:6 · *206-207*
  Titus 3:7 · *434*
  Titus 3:14 · *434*
Tobit · *53, 255*

W

Wisdom of Sirach · *255*
  Wis 16:7 · *206*
Wisdom of Solomon · *255*

Z

Zechariah · *51, 53, 56, 254, 306*
  Zech 3:8 · *305*
  Zech 6:12 · *305*
  Zech 8:8 · *380*
  Zech 9:9 · *303*
  Zech 9:14 · *303*
  Zech 11:12–13 · *303*
  Zech 12:10 · *303*
  Zech 13:7b · *303*
  Zech 13:9 · *380*
Zephaniah · *51, 53, 254*
  Zeph 1:15 · *303-304*

OTHER ANCIENT TEXTS

Antisthenes, *Ajax* · 244
Aphthonius, *Progymnasmata* · 244
Augustine, *Expositions in Psalms* 69.6 · 447
Augustine, *Letter* 36.1.1 · 447
Augustine, *On Christian Doctrine* · 447
Augustine, *On Christian Doctrine* I.40 · 417
Augustine, *On Instructing Beginners* 7.11 · 447
Augustine, *On Teaching Christianity* 4.6.9 · 447
Augustine, *Sermon* 82.12.15 · 447
Augustine, *Tractates on the First Letter of John* 3:1 · 447
Callimachos of Cyrene, *Pinakes* · 331
Cicero, *Res Publica* (*Rep.*) VI.26.29 · 197
Cicero, *Res Publica* VI.24.26 · 197
Ciceros, *Letters* · 232
Curtius Rufus, *Historiae Alexandri Magni Macedonensis* 10.9.1 · 194
Demetrius, *On Style* 224–26 · 232
Demetrius, *On Style* 228 · 232
Didache · 322
Dio Chrysostom, *Kingship Orations* · 365
Dio Chrysostom, *Orations* (*Or.*) 1.32; 3.104–7; 17.19; 34.23 · 195
Gorgias, *Helen* · 244
Hermogenes, *Progymnasmata* · 244
John Chrysostom, *Homily on 2 Cor* 3:7 · 199
Josephus, *Jewish Antiquities* (*AJ*) 17.2.4 · 257
Josephus, *Jewish Antiquities* (*Ant.*) 15.293, 339; 16.13 · 210
Josephus, *The Jewish War* (*War*) 1.80 · 210
LXX (Aquila's recension) · 321
LXX (Kaige recension) · 321
LXX (Lucian's recension) · 321
LXX (Symmachus's recension) · 321
LXX (Theodotion's recension) · 321
Mishnah · 322
Origen, *Hexapla* · 321
Ovid, *Metamorphoses* 14.805–9 · 196
Ovid, *Metamorphoses* 15.745–59 · 196
Ovid, *Metamorphoses* 15.758–59 · 196
Ovid, *Metamorphoses* 15.838 · 196
Ovid, *Metamorphoses* 15.850 · 196
Philo, *De Praem. et Poen.* 114 · 194
Philo, *De Praem. et Poen.* 125 · 194
Plato, *Pheadrus*, *Gorgias*, *Apology* · 244
Plato, *Republic* (*Rep.*) 1.352E-54 · 195
Plato, *Republic* (*Rep.*) 5.470C-D and 2.370A-B · 195
Plutarch, *Advice to Bride and Groom*, 32 · 261
Plutarch, *Galba* 4.3 · 194
Possidius, *Life of Augustine* 19.3–4 · 447
Quintilian, *Institutio Oratoria* · 236, 330
Quintilian, *Institutio Oratoria* (*Inst.*) 9.3.85 · 237
Qumran texts · 321
Qumran, *War Scroll* · 322
Rhetorica Ad Alexandrum · 244
Rhetorica ad Herennium (*Rhet. Her.*) 2.19.28 · 248
Rhetorica ad Herennium 4.39 · 237
Seneca the Elder, *Suasoriae et Controversiae* · 244
Seneca, *Letters* · 232
Suetonius, *Nero* 12.3 · 328
Suetonius, *Augustus* 52 · 209
Strabo, *Geography*, 14.5.13 · 246
Tacitus, *Annals* (*Ann.*) 1.12.12 · 194
Tacitus, *Annals* (*Ann.*) 4.37.4 · 210
Theon, *Progymnasmata* · 244–245
Thucydides, *The Peloponnesian War* VI.53–61 · 155
Virgil, *Aeneid* 6.34 · 328
Virgil, *Eclogues* 4.46–54 · 196
Xenophon, *Cyropaedia* 4.5.27–33 · 233

INSCRIPTIONS (For the abbreviations, see the PHI Inscriptional Database)

CIG 3991 · 196
TAM V,2 1098 · 196
Tralles 32 · 196

ARTIFACTS AND COINS

BMC.48 (RIC.30) · 277
RIC 1 Claudius 120 · 210
Istanbul Archeological Museum Inv. 2196 T · 265
Istanbul Archeological Museum Inv. 5466 T · 271
Kunsthistorisches Museum in Vienna (IXa 59) · 210

NOTES

NOTES

NOTES